THE JERUSALEM ANTHOLOGY

 A Literary Guid

THE JERUSALEM ANTHOLOGY

 A Literary Guide

JPS Jerusalem Collection
Deluxe Edition

REUVEN HAMMER

 THE JEWISH PUBLICATION SOCIETY
Philadelphia • Jerusalem
5756   1995

Library of Congress Cataloging-in-Publication Data

The Jerusalem anthology : a literary guide / [compiled by] Reuven
    Hammer. — 1st ed.
        p.   cm.
    "JPS Jerusalem collection deluxe ed."
    Includes bibliographical references and index.
    ISBN 0–8276–0551–X
    1. Jerusalem—Literary collections.   2. Jerusalem in the Bible.
3. Jerusalem in rabbinical literature.   4. Jerusalem in Judaism.
5. Jewish literature.   6. Jerusalem—History—Sources.   I. Hammer,
Reuven.
PN6071.J38J45   1995
808'.032569442—dc20   95–17222
                                                              CIP

Designed by Elizabeth Anne O'Donnell
Typeset by University Graphics

Cover Illustration: *Solomon's Temple,* serigraph by David Sharir, Old City
of Jaffa, Israel. Copyright © and courtesy of Pucker Gallery, Boston.

FOR RAḤEL, MY LIFE'S COMPANION

You are beautiful, my darling, as Tirzah,   יָפָה אַתְּ רַעְיָתִי כְּתִרְצָה

Comely as Jerusalem   נָאוָה כִּירוּשָׁלָ͏ִם

SONG OF SONGS 6:4

Publication of this volume was made possible
by a generous grant from

Geraldine and Harold Cramer

in honor of their parents

Esther and Charles Hassuk
and
Blanche and A. Harry Cramer ז״ל

ꙮ Contents

THE SIXTH GATE
Jerusalem in the Literature of the Turkish and Mandatory Periods   215

THE SEVENTH GATE
Jerusalem in Modern Nonfiction 291

THE EIGHTH GATE
Jerusalem in Modern Fiction   359

THE NINTH GATE
Jerusalem in Modern Poetry   401

THE TENTH GATE
Jerusalem in Jewish Folklore   445

✑ Illustrations

ॐ Color Plates

Ketubah (marriage contract), Venice, 1759.

Jerusalem as the Center of the World; from *Travels According to the Bible*, 1581.

Fireworks over Jerusalem; May 21, 1992.

View of Jerusalem; Keller-Reutlinger, Paul-Wilhelm (?), 19th century.

The Temple Mount, 1937; Ludwig Blum (1891–1974).

The Walls of Jerusalem; Abel Pann, 1918.

Jerusalem Landscape, 1947; Ludwig Blum (1891–1974).

View of Jerusalem and Holy Sites; 19th-century woodcut.

Jerusalem, 1948; Mordecai Levanon (1901–1968).

✏ Chronological Table

B.C.E.	3000	Earliest settlement of Jerusalem.
	2000–1800	Abraham visits Salem. Binding of Isaac on Mount Moriah.
	ca. 1200	Joshua's conquest of the Land.
	ca. 996	David captures Jerusalem.
	ca. 960	Solomon builds First Temple.
	701	Hezekiah's tunnel built. Sennacherib's invasion. Siege fails.
	586	Babylonians capture Jerusalem, destroy First Temple. Exile to Babylonia.
	520	Returnees from Babylonia build Second Temple and restore the city wall; Persians rule.
	333	Alexander the Great conquers the Land.
	164	Maccabean revolt.
	c.20	Herod rebuilds the Second Temple.
C.E.	70	Jewish War (66–73); Jerusalem, Second Temple destroyed.
	131	Aelia Capitolina founded by Hadrian.
	135	Bar Kokhba Revolt.
	326	Constantine legalizes Christianity (313) and builds Church of Holy Sepulchre. Byzantine period (326–614).
	640	Muslim Conquest.
	691	Dome of the Rock built.
	1099	Crusaders capture Jerusalem; Latin Kingdom of Jerusalem.
	1187	Saladin captures Jerusalem; second Muslim period.
	1212	City walls rebuilt but torn down seven years later.
	1247–1517	Mamelukes rule.
	1514	Ottoman Turk conquest.
	1537	Suliman rebuilds walls.
	1860	First settlement outside walls; New City begins.
	1917	British conquest.

1948   Establishment of State of Israel. Arab Legion occupies Old City, destroys part of Jewish Quarter. Jerusalem divided between Jordan and Israel.

1967   Six Day War; Jerusalem reunited under Israeli rule.

1968   Jewish Quarter rebuilding begins.

ꙮ Foreword

For any city to celebrate its three-thousandth anniversary is an unusual and significant event, but for a city to celebrate three thousand years as the capital of the same people who first founded it is surely unique. In 1996 Jerusalem, the political capital of Israel and the unquestioned heart of the people of Israel, will commemorate three thousand years since King David made what was then a village into his capital. In order to unify all the tribes of Israel, he selected a site that did not belong to one particular tribe but to the entire people. He brought the Ark of the Covenant, the religious symbol of the Jewish nation, to an obscure threshing floor at the top of the slope on which the village was built and thus defined the site as both the royal and the religious center of power for Israel.

Since then, Jerusalem, in spite of many changes in control and changes in name over the centuries, has remained the City of David. There have been periods when Jews were not permitted to live in Jerusalem, though modern research indicates that such times were fewer than was previously thought, but there was never a moment when Jerusalem did not live within the Jews—as individuals and as a people.

Jewish independent rule over Jerusalem ceased in the year 70 C.E. and was not restored until 1948, and fully in 1967. We are the privileged generation of Jews who have seen with our own eyes the return to Zion. We are those spoken of by the psalmist: "When the Lord restored our exiles to Zion, it was like a dream" (Pss. 126:1). Unfortunately, life in a modern and complex city like Jerusalem is not always so dreamlike. The dream becomes a daily reality with which we must cope; that reality is frequently fraught with difficulty and even tragedy. As Mayor of Jerusalem for twenty-eight years, my work involved not only building Jerusalem physically, so that it would realize its potential of being a "crown of beauty" as well as a practical and livable place, but also finding paths of coexistence between Jews and Arabs and between Jews and Jews. This was particularly challenging, as Jerusalem is made up of so many diverse groups.

Yet Jerusalem must be the center for all Jews; tolerance must reign amongst us, and Jews and Arabs must live together in peace. For a united Jerusalem to exist and flourish, we have to forge mutual respect and a willingness to understand and accommodate each other.

It has been a privilege to serve Jerusalem and its people for many decades and to be the first Jewish Mayor of modern united Jerusalem. I prefer to think of myself and my work here not in terms of Herod, who for all his building cared more for himself than for the city, but as the heir of Nehemiah. It was Nehemiah who, at the end of the first exile, came back to Jerusalem in order to seek its "good" and energetically put the people to work. "Half my servants did work and half held lances and shields, bows and armor" (Neh. 4:10). His task, like ours, was not easy, but he succeeded in laying the foundations for the new Jerusalem which existed until the end of the Second Temple period.

We too have returned to Zion from exile. We too face enemies and problems, but we have dedicated ourselves to building and to creating a renewed Jerusalem that will be worthy of its past and able to endure into the future. May Jerusalem's next millennium be remembered as Jerusalem's true age of gold, a time of harmony and peace.

—Teddy Kollek

ꙮ Author's Preface

Compiling an anthology about a subject that has been under discussion for thousands of years in a variety of world cultures—as Jerusalem has—is a challenge of the first order. Before even beginning the work, it was necessary to determine the parameters that would be dealt with. One volume, no matter how large, could never encompass all the possibilities. Since this work is being compiled in honor of a specific celebration, the trimillennium of David's entry into Jerusalem, it was decided that only Jewish writings on the subject would be included. Wonderful and fascinating things have been written about Jerusalem through the ages by non-Jews, for many of whom Jerusalem has a sacred status, but this book will be confined to writings by Jews as an expression of their experiences or their feelings about Jerusalem. Thus the book really deals with Jerusalem in Jewish consciousness.

Another basic decision was to use original material rather than things written "about. . . ." There are extremely fine essays and books that tell about the history of Jerusalem and that describe Jerusalem during various periods of its history. There are also excellent essays in various languages that describe Jerusalem in the literature of certain eras. Some of these essays, which I read in order to discover the whereabouts of original sources, are listed in the bibliography. However, with the exception of some introductory material to set the scene and some concluding material to summarize it, the pieces here are material written at the time by people who were present at the events they describe. Thus, accounts of the Six Day War are by people who fought in it or witnessed it as civilians, and not by those who later wrote books about it. These latter will also be found in the bibliography. These pieces are reproduced as originally written, with their peculiarities of spelling and transliteration; thus, there are inconsistencies from piece to piece. Another decision was to avoid political polemics as much as possible In the section that discusses the future of Jerusalem, some political ideas are presented, but this is certainly not the main focus of this work.

These decisions having been made, the problems of what to include remained daunting. Building upon what I knew and spending untold hours in the libraries of Jerusalem, I uncovered layer after layer, book after book, and article after article. If it is true, as the sages said, that "one good deed leads to another," it is equally true that one good book leads to another. And so I went from clue to clue, from article to article, from generation to generation. As an organizing principle, I decided to build on historical-cultural eras and to include the outstanding literature of each era in connection with Jerusalem. In addition, other material—including a tour, music, Jerusalem Day services, and children's stories—has been added to make the book useful. Since the book is in English, it was necessary either to find material already translated into English (or, in more modern times, written in English) or to have it translated. It was simply not possible to translate into English everything I wished to include, but there are many selections of prose and poetry that appear here in English for the first time. In this connection, I am indebted to those who either made their superb translations available to me, such as David Simcha Segal and Gabriel Levine, or who undertook it especially for me, such as Aura Hammer. Some selections, including all of the rabbinic sayings, were translated by myself. Another problem was the availability of rights. There is nothing in this volume that I did not wish to include, but some things that I wanted to publish were simply not available. At all times the problem of space was acute. Even in the biblical selections, there was more material than could be included. Therefore, there are undoubtedly things missing that were worthy of inclusion, but in the end difficult and subjective decisions had to be made. There is enough worthy material left over for several other Jerusalem anthologies to be compiled from different perspectives.

It will be immediately obvious that a disproportionate amount of space has been devoted to works of the last hundred years. The reasons are equally obvious. The amount of such material available is enormous, varied, and of great interest. More people write and publish now than ever before. Furthermore, the variety of approaches is in itself of interest. This is our time and the events concerning Jerusalem that have occurred in it are unequaled for the last nineteen hundred years. They deserve our attention.

There are at least two ways to read any anthology, including this. One is to find the specific piece or topic that interests you. The other is to read it cover to cover. I would like to suggest, however, for those who have the leisure, a cover-to-cover reading (skipping here or there something that really does not interest you) because in that way you will experience the continuity of Jerusalem, building layer upon layer of meaning and history, much as the city itself is built of layers of actual building material. Nothing is left behind. It recurs and transforms itself. The last items are much better understood if one has read the first ones and those inbetween. The effect is definitely cumulative. Nothing has been lost or forgotten. It is as if each layer were transparent and they all reflect themselves in the upper ones. The individual sections too, when read as a whole, tell the story of an era. Even the section on modern poetry has been designed so that, when read sequentially, it paints a cumulative portrait of the Jerusalem of today.

I am deeply indebted to the libraries of Jerusalem and the librarians of Jerusalem, without whom this book would never have been put together. Yad Ben Zvi is an absolute treasure-house of Jerusalem-related literature, and its librarians made everything easily accessible to me. The National Library at the Hebrew University was equally indispensable. I am extremely grateful to the library of Hebrew Union College in Jerusalem for the use of its fine facilities, and to the Schocken Institute for access to some rare volumes. I am also very grateful to those in charge of the collections of photographs and graphics at the Central Zionist Archives, the National and University Library,

Jerusalem, the Israel Museum, the department of photography of the Israeli Government Press Office and the Museum of Photography at Tel-Hai Industrial Park for the extensive help given me and for making their vast collections readily available. I am especially indebted to the Central Zionist Archives, the Government Press Office, Mr. William P. Wolfe, and the Museum of Photography for their generosity in granting the use of their photographs.

In an enterprise such as this, it is necessary to turn to innumerable publishers, writers, and translators for permission to use their works. I am especially thankful to those who, either for personal reasons or because of their love of Jerusalem, went out of their way to be helpful and graciously to permit the use of their works. My appreciation is also extended to Dr. Ellen Frankel, Editor-in-Chief of the Jewish Publication Society, who originally broached this idea and helped in its realization and to my wife, Raḥel, without whom this book or any of my books would not have been possible. In the case of this work, that is so in a special way because her desire to live in Jerusalem preceded mine and inspired our decision to make Jerusalem our home. Living in Jerusalem since 1973, after having visited it many times starting in 1955, has been our privilege. We came to Jerusalem on the 9th of Av 5733, exactly twenty-one years ago today, remembering the tradition that on Tisha B'Av the destruction took place and on Tisha B'Av the messiah would be born. We felt that our aliya was a beginning of redemption. It is a decision we have never regretted. In a small way, this volume is the repayment of our debt to Jerusalem and voices our prayer that there may always be peace in Jerusalem and tranquillity in all her palaces.

—Reuven Hammer
Jerusalem, 9th of Av 5754

ꙮ Sources and Acknowledgments

PROLOGUE

THE FIRST GATE
Jerusalem in Biblical Literature

THE SECOND GATE
Jerusalem in Second Temple Literature

The First Book of Maccabees, ed. and trans. by Sidney Tedesche, Dropsie College Edition published by Harper and Bros., New York, 1950.

The Second Book of Maccabees, R. H. Charles, *The Apocrypha and Pseudepigrapha*, Vol. 1, Oxford 1913.

"Noncanonical Psalms from Qumran," Eileen M. Schuller, *Harvard Semitic Studies 28*, Atlanta 1986, by permission of Harvard Semitic Studies.

"Apostrophe to Zion," from *The Psalm Scrolls of Qumran Cave 11* by J A Sanders (1965), © Oxford University Press 1965, by permission of Oxford University Press.

"The Writings of Philo," from Loeb Classical Library, *Philo* Volumes V, VII, and X, translated by F. H. Colson, Cambridge Mass.: Harvard University Press, 1962, reprinted by permission of Harvard University Press and the Loeb Classical Library.

"The Writings of Josephus Flavius," from *The Life and Works of Flavius Josephus*, translated by Willian Whiston, The John C. Winston Co.

THE THIRD GATE
Jerusalem in Rabbinic Literature

Translations by Reuven Hammer.

THE FOURTH GATE
Jerusalem in the Literature of the Geonic Period

"Redemption," Saadia Gaon, from *Saadia Gaon, The Book of Beliefs and Opinions*, translated by Samuel Rosenblatt, New Haven, Conn.: Yale University Press, 1948. Reprinted by permission of Yale University Press.

"Jerusalem Rebuilt," from The Book of Zerubabel, and "Heavenly Jerusalem" from *Midrashei Geula* (Hebrew), ed. Judah Even-Shemuel. Translated by Reuven Hammer.

"The Prayer for Jerusalem," from *Siddur Rav Saadia Gaon* (Hebrew), ed. S. Assaf-I. Davidson-I. Joel, Jerusalem, 1963. Translated by Reuven Hammer.

"The Jews Return to Jerusalem," from *Texts and Studies in Jewish History* (Hebrew), Simha Assaf, Mosad HaRav Kuk, 1946. Translated by Reuven Hammer.

"No Jerusalem," from *Mahzor for Yom Kippur* (Hebrew), ed. Daniel Goldsmidt, Keren Yerushalyim, Jerusalem 1970. Translated by Reuven Hammer.

"Prayer for Jerusalem: Burial Kaddish" translated by Reuven Hammer.

THE FIFTH GATE
Jerusalem in Writings of the Middle Ages

"Jacob HaCohen," "Rabbi Samuel ben Samson," "Isaac Chelo," "Meshullam ben R. Menahem," "Obadia Da Bertinora," from *Jewish Travelers*, Elkan Nathan Adler, George Routledge and Sons LTD, London, 1930.

"Rabbi Benjamin of Tudela," from *The Itinerary of Benjamin of Tudela*, Marcus Nathan Adler, London 1907.

"Rabbi Moses ben Nahman, Letter to His Son," from *Sefer Yerushalayim*, (Hebrew), Talmi, translated by Reuven Hammer; "Biblical Commentary" from *Studies in Judaism, First Series*, Solomon Schechter, Jewish Publication Society, Philadelphia, 1896.

"Elijah of Ferrara, Letter to His Sons," "An Unknown Writer," "Rabbi Isaiah Hurwitz," from *Letters of Jews through the Ages*, ed. F. Kobler Frazn, Ararat Publishing Society, London, 1952.

"Rabbi Eshtori HaParhi," "Prayer at the Wall," translated by Reuven Hammer.

"Rabbi Moses ben Israel Naphtali Porges Praeger," from *Roads to Zion*, Kurt Wilhelm; Trans. I. M. Lask, Schocken Books, New York, 1948.

"Zion and Jerusalem," "The Destruction of the Temple," "The Foundation Stone," from *The Wisdom of the Zohar*, Fischel Lachover and Isaiah Tishby, translated by David Goldstein, Oxford University Press, Littman Library, Oxford 1989. Reprinted by permission of Oxford University Press and the Litman Library. University Press, Oxford 1989.

"Dove in the Rock," "The Temple Above," "For Her Sake," "A Supernal City," "Two Kings," "The Dry Place," from *The Zohar*, translated by Harry Sperling and Maurice Simon, Soncino Press, London, 1933. London.

"Customs Relating to Jerusalem," translated by Reuven Hammer

"Joy of the Whole World," Yose ben Yose, translated by Zalman Dimitrovsky, from *Zion in Jewish Literature*, ed. Abraham Halkin, the Theodor Herzl Foundation Inc., New York 1961. Reprinted by permission of Theodor Herzl Foundation.

"The Lights of Zion," Yannai, Hebrew text in *Piyyute Yannai*, Schocken, Berlin, 1938. Translated by Reuven Hammer.

"I Remember," Ammitai ben Shephatiah. Hebrew text in *Sefer Yerushalayim* (Hebrew) Ephraim and Menachem Talmi, Tel Aviv, no year. Translated by Reuven Hammer.

"My Heart Seethes," Shmuel Hanagid. Translated by David Simha Segal. Printed by permission of David Simha Segal.

"Beloved Hasten," Meshullam ben Kolonymous, from *Selected Religious Poems*. Translated by Israel Zangwill.

"Hoshana," "A Voice Proclaims," "Come My Beloved," Solomon Halevi Alkabetz, "Cry, O Zion." Translated by Reuven Hammer.

"Earth's Beauty," "The Poet Replies to One Who Would Dissuade Him from Removing to the Land of Israel," Judah Halevi, translated by David Simha Segal. Printed by permission of David Simha Segal.

"My Heart's in the East," "Solomon's Pavilions," "Ode to Sion," Judah Halevi. Translated by Gabriel Levin. Printed by permission of Gabriel Levin.

"Lament for Zion," Hebrew text in *The Penguin Book of Hebrew Verse*, ed. T. Carmi, Penguin Press. Translated by Reuven Hammer.

"Shalom to the City Shalem," Judah Alharizi, Hebrew text in *Anthologia Hebraica* (Hebrew), ed. H. Brody, Leipzig, 1922. Translated by Reuven Hammer.

"Jerusalem: Chapter 28 of the Book of Tahkemoni," Judah Alharizi, from *The Book of Tahkemoni*. Translated by David Simha Segal. This text is part of an ongoing project which is to be published by the Littmen Library of Jewish Civilization as: Judah al-Harizi, *The Book of Takhemoni*, translated from the Hebrew by David Segal, with annotations and an introduction (ISBN 1-874774-03-X) and is reprinted with their permission. This translation does not necessarily reproduce the exact form of words that will appear in the books's final published version.

"In the Gates of Jerusalem," Rabbi Moshe ben Nahman. Hebrew text in *Sefer Yerushalayim*, Ephraim and Menachem Talmi, Tel Aviv, no year. Translated by Reuven Hammer.

"Awake, Awake!" Rabbi Moshe ben Nahman, from *The Western Wall*, M. M. Kasher, translated by Charles Wengov, Judaica Press, New York. Reprinted by permission of Judaica Press.

THE SIXTH GATE
Jerusalem in the Literature of the Turkish and Mandatory Periods

"Seek Ye the Peace of Jerusalem," Gedaliah of Siemiatycze, from *Roads To Zion*, Kurt Wilhelm, trans. I.M.Lask, Schocken Books, New York, 1948.

"Water Drawing Festival," Rabbi Yehoseph Schwarz, from *Tracks to the Promised Land*, ed. Nahman Ran, Terra Sancta Arts Ltd., Tel Aviv 1987. Reprinted by permission of Terra Sancta Arts Ltd.

"Life in Jerusalem," Avraham Yaari, from *The Goodly Heritage*, Avraham Yaari, Youth and Hechalutz Department of the Zionist Organization, Jerusalem, 1958. Reprinted by permission of Youth and Hechalutz.

"A Revelation at the Wall," Israel Meir Sofer, from *The Western Wall*, ed. Meir Ben Dov, Ministry of Defence, Tel Aviv, 1983.

"Sir Moses Purchases a Piece of Land," Dr. L. Loewe, from *The Diaries of Sir Moses and Lady Montefiore*, ed. Dr. Louis Loewe, Belford-Clark Co., Chicago, 1890.

"A Narrative of a Forty Day's Sojourn in the Holy Land," Sir Moses Montefiore, from *A Narrative of a 40 Days' Sojourn in the Holy Land*, Sir Moses Montefiore, Wertheimer, Lea and Co., London, 1875.

"To Jerusalem," Lugwig A. Frankl, "The Wall Is Ours," Mordecai ben Hillel Ha-Kohen, "Land of Delight," A. S. Hirschberg, "Sound the Shofar!," Moshe Segal, from *The Western Wall*, ed. Meir Ben Dov, Ministry of Defence, Tel Aviv, 1983.

"Coming to Jerusalem," Eliezer Ben Yehudah, from *Sefer Yerushalayim* (Hebrew), Ephraim and Menachem Talmi, Tel Aviv, no year. Translated by Reuven Hammer.

"At the End of Days," "The Third Temple," Menahem Usishkin, from *HaKotel Hamaaravi* (Hebrew), S. Ben Zion. Translated by Reuven Hammer.

"Truth from the Land of Israel," from *Kol Kitvei Ahad Haam* (Hebrew), Ahad Haam, Dvir, Tel Aviv, 1956. Translated by Reuven Hammer.

"My Memoirs," Yosef Yoel Rivlin, from *Liyushalayim* (Hebrew), ed. Gedalya Alkoshi, et al, Agudat HaSofrim B'Yisrael, Yachdav, 5728. Translated by Reuven Hammer.

"Raise a Banner to Zion," Saul Tschernichovsky, from *Shirim*, Schocken Tel Aviv, 1951. Translated by Reuven Hammer.

"In Palestine," Theodore Herzl, from *The Diaries of Theodore Herzl*, ed. Marvin Lowenthal, Dial Press, New York, 1956. Reprinted by permission of Doubleday, a division of Doubleday, Dell Publishing Group, Inc.

"At the Western Wall," Shneur Dov Har HaZahav, "Zion My Pure One," M. Dolitzki, from *Kinor David* (Hebrew), A. M. Luntz, Jerusalem 5663. Translated by Reuven Hammer.

"Jerusalem Rebuilt," Boris Schatz, from *Yerushalayim Benuyah* (Hebrew). Translated by Reuven Hammer.

"The Western Wall," A. M. Lunz, from *HaKotel HaMaaravi* (Hebrew), Jerusalem 1911. Translated by Reuven Hammer

"How the Glorious Day of Deliverance Came to Jerusalem," Hemda Ben Yehuda, from *Jerusalem: Its Redemption and Future*, Christian Herald, New York, 1918.

"Memoirs," Yitzhak Shiryon, from *Yerushalayim 1917/18* (Hebrew), Koresh Publishers, Jerusalem, 1993. Translated by Reuven Hammer.

"The Renaissance of the Jewish Soul," Chaim Weizmann, from *The Jewish Anthology*, ed. Edmond Fleg, Harcourt, Brace and Co., New York 1925. Translated by Maurice Samuels. Reprinted by permission of Behrman House, Inc.

"Pogrom in Jerusalem," "Foundations," "A Visit to Jerusalem," Chaim Weizmann, from *Trial and Error*, Chaim Weizmann, Jewish Publication Society, Philadelphia 1949. Reprinted by permission of the Jewish Publication Society.

"My Life," Golda Meir, from *My Life*, Golda Meir, George Weidenfeld and Nicolson Lmt., London, 1975. Reprinted by permission of George Weidenfeld and Nicolson.

"A Jerusalem Diary," Simon Greenberg. Unpublished writing of Simon Greenberg. Used by permission of his estate.

"To S. Z. Schocken after the 1929 Riots," S. Y. Agnon, from *Me-Atzmi el Atzmi* (Hebrew), Schocken, Jerusalem, 1976, which appeared in *The Jerusalem Quarterly* 9, Fall 1978. Reprinted by permission of Schocken Publishers, Tel Aviv.

"Jerusalem, God's Veiled Bride," Else Lasker-Schueler, from *Retrievements: A Jerusalem Anthology*, Dennis Silk. Reprinted by permission of the translators, Dennis Silk and Yehudah Amichai.

"The Love of Jerusalem," HaRav Avraham Yitzhak HaCohen Kuk, from *Jerusalem, Holy City and Temple* (Hebrew), ed. Y. Gliss, Mosad HaRav Kuk, Jerusalem, 1977. Translated by Reuven Hammer.

THE SEVENTH GATE
Jerusalem in Modern Nonfiction

"Jerusalem, the Eternal Capital," David Ben-Gurion, from *The Story of Jerusalem*, ed. Dr. Beno Rothenberg, translated by M. Kohansky and Ben-Ami Sharfstein, Am Oved Publishers, Tel Aviv, 1967. Reprinted by permission of Merkaz Moreshet Ben-Gurion, Midreshet Sde Boker.

"Jerusalem Is Called Liberty," Walter Lever, from *Jerusalem Is Called Liberty*, Walter Lever, Massada Press, Inc., Jerusalem, 1951. Reprinted by permission of Massada Press Ltd.

"The Faithful City," Dov Joseph, from *The Faithful City*, Dov Joseph, Simon and Schuster, New York, 1960. Copyright © 1960 by Dov Joseph. Copyright renewed © 1988 by Dov Joseph. Reprinted by permission of Simon and Schuster, Inc.

"The Siege of Jerusalem," Pauline Rose, from *The Seige of Jerusalem*, Pauline Rose, Patmos Publishers, London, no year.

"Going into Captivity," Aharon Liron, from *The Old City of Jerusalem in Siege and Battle* (Hebrew), Aharon Liron, Ministry of Defence Publications Department, Tel Aviv 1957. Translated by Reuven Hammer.

"Jerusalem Embattled," Harry Levin, from *Jerusalem Embattled*, Harry Levin, Victor Gollancz, London, 1958. All our attempts at tracing the copyright holder of *Jerusalem Embattled* were unsuccessful.

"The First Yom HaAtzmaut," Yona Cohen, from *Jerusalem Under Siege* (Hebrew), Yona Cohen, Milo Publishers, 1976. Translated by Reuven Hammer.

"A Generation's Dream Is Realized," Uzi Narkiss, from *The Liberation of Jerusalem*, Uzi Narkiss, Vallentine Mitchell and Co. Ltd, London, 1983. Reprinted by permission of Vallentine Mitchell and Co. Ltd, London.

"Redeeming the Vow," Rabbi Shlomo Goren, from *Jerusalem Eternal*, ed. Azriel Eisenberg, Board of Jewish Education, New York, 1971.

"Window on Mount Zion," Pauline Rose, from *Window on Mount Zion*, Pauline Rose, W. H. Allen, London, 1973.

"Like a Psalm of Praise" "Tonight We're Making History, A Discussion" "Strange City," Amos Oz, translated by Dvora A. Susman and Edna Berlyn, "Jerusalem of My Childhood," Muki Tzur, from *The Seventh Day*, Andre Deutsch Ltd, London, 1970. English version © Henry Near, 1970. Reprinted by permission of Henry Near.

"Fear and Trembling," Moshe Amirav, "Kissing History," Abraham Duvdevani, from *The Lions' Gate* (Hebrew) as printed in *The Western Wall*, ed. Meir Ben Dov, Ministry of Defence, Tel Aviv, 1983.

"At the Western Wall," Elie Wiesel, from *Hadassah Magazine*, July, 1967. Reprinted by permission of *Hadassah Magazine* and Elie Wiesel.

"City of Dreams," Rinna Samuel, from *Hadassah Magazine*, September, 1967. Reprinted by permission of *Hadassah Magazine* and Rinna Samuel.

"Jerusalem—A Charismatic City," Abraham Joshua Heschel, from *Israel: An Echo of Eternity*, Abraham Joshua Heschel, Farrar, Straus and Giroux, New York, 1967. Reprinted by permission of Mrs. A. J. Heschel.

"Next Year in Jerusalem!" Anatoly Shcharansky, from *Passover Haggadah: The Feast of Freedom*, Rabbinical Assembly, 1982.

THE EIGHTH GATE
Jerusalem in Modern Fiction

"City of Many Days," Shulamith Hareven, from *City of Many Days*, © 1993 by Shulamith Hareven, translated by Hillel Halkin and the author. Published by Mercury House, San Francisco, CA, and reprinted by permission.

"Tehila: The Praise of Jerusalem," S. Y. Agnon, from "Tehila," translated by Walter Lever. Reprinted by permission of Youth and Hehalutz Department of the Zionist Organization, Jerusalem.

"The Debt of Blood," Elisha Porat, from *Kametz Alef* by Elisha Porat, translated by Dalia Bilu, 1982. Printed by permission of Elisha Porat.

"In the Heart of the Seas," S. Y. Agnon, from *In the Heart of the Seas*, S. Y. Agnon, Schocken Books, New York, 1947. Copyright © Schocken Books, published by Pantheon Books, a division of Random House, Inc. and reprinted by permission.

"Jerusalem Plays Hide and Seek," Ariella Deem, from *Jerusalem Plays Hide and Seek*, translated by Nelly Segal, Jewish Publication Society, Philadelphia, 1987. Reprinted by permission of the Jewish Publication Society.

"Father's Notebook," Chaim Brandwein, from *In the Courtyards of Jerusalem*, Chaim Brandwein, translated by Hillel Halkin, Jewish Publication Society, Philadelphia, 1967. Reprinted by permission of the Jewish Publication Society.

"A Journey through the Land of Israel," Pinchas Sadeh, translated by Hillel Halkin, from *The Tri-Quarterly Review* 39, Spring 1977. Reprinted by permission of Hillel Halkin.

THE NINTH GATE
Jerusalem in Modern Poetry

"From Jerusalem: A First Poem," "Jerusalem Moon," "To Jerusalem Yes," Gabriel Preil, from *Sunset Possibilities and Other Poems*, Gabriel Preil, translated by Robert Friend, Jewish Publication Society, Philadelphia 1985. Reprinted by permission of the Jewish Publication Society.

"The First Day," "Leaving Jerusalem," Marcia Falk, from *This Year in Jerusalem*, Marcia Falk, State Street Press, 1986, copyright © 1986 by Marcia Falk. Reprinted by permission of Marcia Falk.

"In the Jerusalem Hills," Leah Goldberg, from *Mukdam U'meuhar* (Hebrew), Sifriat HaPoalim, 5719. Translated by Aura Hammer. Printed by permission of Sifriat HaPoalim. © All rights for the original Hebrew version are reserved by Sifriat HaPoalim.

"Heavenly Jerusalem, Jerusalem of the Earth," Leah Goldberg, from *Selected Poems*, Leah Goldberg, translated by Robert Friend, Menard/Panjandrum, 1976. Reprinted by permission of ACUM.

"At Your Feet, Jerusalem," Uri Zvi Greenberg; "Jerusalem," David Rokeah; "Passover in Jerusalem," Avigdor HaMeiri, from *Modern Hebrew Poetry*, ed. and translated by Ruth Finer Mintz, University of California Press, Berkeley and Los Angeles, 1966. Reprinted by permission of the University of California Press and Ruth Finer Mintz.

"On Nevi'im Street" (The Street of the Prophets), Yehoash Biber. Translated by Aura Hammer.

"Longing (i)," "Jerusalem Poems iii," Ruth Finer Mintz, from *Jerusalem Poems, Love Songs*, Ruth Finer Mintz, Massada Press 1976. Reprinted by permission of Ruth Finer Mintz.

"On Ben Peleh: Jerusalem," Shin Shalom, from *On Ben Peleh*, Shin Shalom, translated by Victor E. Reichert and Moses Zalesky, Youth and HeHalutz Department, Zionist Organization, Jerusalem, 1963. Reprinted by permission of Youth and HeHalutz Department.

"Holy Grandmothers in Jerusalem," Esther Raab, translated by Abraham Biran, from *Anthology of Modern Hebrew Poetry*, vol I, selected by S. Y. Penueli and A. Ukhamani. English © The Institute for the Translation of Hebrew Literature. Reprinted by permission of The Institute for the Translation of Hebrew Literature.

"Religious Quarter," A. C. Jacobs. Reprinted from *Retrievements*, ed. Dennis Silk, Keter Press, Jerusalem, 1968. Efforts to trace the copyright owner, Mr. Jacobs, have not succeeded.

"Building Partner," "Lesson in Geology," Elisha Porat, translated by Riva Rubin. Printed by permission of Elisha Porat.

"To My City Jerusalem, 1967," Amir Gilboa, translated by Shirley Kaufman with Shlomit Rimmon, from *Tri Quarterly Review*, 39, Northwestern University, Evanston, Ill. Reprinted by permission of ACUM. © All rights for the original Hebrew are reserved by the author.

"Homage to Jerusalem; Jerusalem 1967," Yehuda Amichai, translated by Harold Schimmel, reprinted by permission of Harold Schimmel, Yehuda Amichai and ACUM. © All rights for the original Hebrew are reserved by the author.

"Jerusalem, 1968," David Rokeah, translated by Alan Brownjohn, from *Jerusalem: Most Fair of Cities*, Armon Press, 1977. Reprinted by permission of ACUM. © All rights for the original Hebrew are reserved by the author.

"Jerusalem," Else Lasker-Schueler, translated by Audru Durchslag and Jeanette Litman-Demeestere, from *Hebrew Ballads and Other Poems*, Jewish Publication Society, Philadelphia, 1980. Reprinted by permission of the Jewish Publication Society.

"Autumn in Jerusalem," Oded Peled, translated by Aura Hammer, from a series of Jerusalem poems (unpublished). Printed by permission of Oded Peled and Aura Hammer.

"A View of Jerusalem," T. Carmi, from *Selected Poems*, T. Carmi and Dan Pagis, Abelard-Schuman. Reprinted by permission of ACUM. © All rights for the original Hebrew are reserved by the author.

"City of Wound," Haim Guri, from *Flowers of Fire* (Hebrew), Tarshish Publishers, 1964. Translated by Aura Hammer. Printed by permission of ACUM and Aura Hammer. © All rights for the original Hebrew are reserved by the author.

"I Stood in Jerusalem," Zelda, translated by Zvi Jagendorf, from *Tri-Quarterly Review*, 39, Spring 1977, Northwestern University, Evanston, Ill. 1977. Reprinted by permission of Zvi Jagendorf.

"House Dog," Uri Zvi Greenberg, from *In the Midst of the World and Time* (Hebrew), Hakibbutz Hameuchad, 1929. Translated by Aura Hammer. Published by permission of ACUM and Aura Hammer. © All rights for the original Hebrew version are reserved by the estate of the author.

"Jerusalem," Moshe HaNa-ami, from *Lamerchav*, January 4, 1963. Translated by Aura Hammer. Printed by permission of Aura Hammer and ACUM. © All rights for the original Hebrew are reserved by the author.

"Suddenly the Sun Lets the Peaks Go and Leaps," Benzion Ben Shalom, from *Israel Argosy* 8, ed. Isaac Halevy-Levin, Thomas Yoseloff, Inc., New York, 1962. Reprinted by permission of Youth and Hechalutz Department of the World Zionist Organization.

"The Warm Stone on the Hill of Jerusalem," Ayin Tur-Malka, from *Ken Shel Zardim* (Hebrew) Kerem Press. Translated by Aura Hammer. Printed by permission of Aura

Hammer, Ayin Tur-Malka and ACUM. © All rights for the original Hebrew are reserved by the author.

"Jerusalem's Walls," Israel Efrat, from *How Deep It Is Planted* (Hebrew), Devir, 1966, translated by Aura Hammer. Printed by permission of Aura Hammer.

"Abu-Tor," David Rokeah, from *Keno shel Yam* (Hebrew), Arbeh Publishers, 5723. Translated by Aura Hammer. Printed by permission of ACUM and Aura Hammer. © All rights to the original Hebrew are reserved by the author.

"Evening in Jerusalem," "Your Bliss and Calm," Yehuda Karni, from *An Anthology of Modern Hebrew Poetry*, ed. and translated by Abraham Birman, Abelard-Schuman, London, 1968. Efforts to trace the copyright holder have been unsuccessful.

"Siege," David Rokeach, from *An Anthology of Modern Hebrew Poetry*, ed. Abraham Birman, translated by D. Saraph, Abelard-Schuman, London, 1968.

"I Don't Know if Mount Zion," Abba Kovner, translated by Warren Bargad and Stanley F. Chyet, from *Israeli Poetry*, ed. Warren Bargad and Stanley F. Chyet, Indiana University Press, Bloomington, Ind., 1986. Reprinted by permission of Indiana University Press and ACUM. © All rights to the original Hebrew are reserved by the author.

"Moriah," Levi Ben Amitai, from *Vilirushalayim* (Hebrew), ed. by G. Alkoshi, Yahdav Press, Jerusalem. Translated by Reuven Hammer. Printed by permission of ACUM. All rights for the original Hebrew are reserved by the author.

"City of David," Zerubavel Gilad, from *Hakichali* (Hebrew), HaKibbutz HaMeuchad, 5738. Translated by Aura Hammer. Printed by permission of Aura Hammer.

"Jerusalem," Yaakov Fichman, from *An Anthology of Modern Hebrew Poetry*, selected by S. Y. Penueli and A. Ukhmani, vol. 1, Institute for the Translation of Hebrew Literature and Israel University Press. Translated by Robert Friend. English © The Institute for the Translation of Hebrew Literature. Reprinted by permission of the Institute for the Translation of Hebrew Literature and ACUM. © All rights to the original Hebrew are reserved by the author.

"Penalty Kick," Ronny Someck, from *Panther* (Hebrew), Zemorah Bitan. Translated by Aura Hammer. Reprinted by permission of ACUM and Aura Hammer. © All rights for the original Hebrew version are reserved by the author.

"Old Age," "Retirement," Elisha Porat. Translated by Aura Hammer. Printed by permission of Elisha Porat and Aura Hammer.

"Jerusalem: Ladders of Love," Gabriel Preil, from *The Literary Review*, Winter 1983, vol. 26 number 2, Fairleigh Dickinson University, Madison, N.J. Efforts to locate the copyright holder have been unsuccessful.

"From the Streets of Jerusalem," Abba Kovner, from *Tatzpiot* (Hebrew), Sifriat HaPoalim, 1977. Translated by Aura Hammer. Reprinted by permission of ACUM and Aura Hammer. © All rights for the original Hebrew are reserved by the author.

"Tourists," Yehuda Amichai, from *Great Tranquility*, Yehuda Amichai. Translated by Glenda Abramson and Tidor Parfitt. Copyright © 1983 by Yehuda Amichai. Reprinted by permission of HarperCollins Publishers, Inc.

THE TENTH GATE
Jerusalem in Jewish Folklore

"Jerusalem of Gold," Shalom M. Paul. This article is a slightly abridged version of the article *Jerusalem of Gold—A Song and an Ancient Crown* which appeared in *Biblical Archaeology Review* 3 (1977). Reprinted by permission of *Biblical Archaeology Review* and Shalom Paul.

"King David's Tomb in Jerusalem," from *Folktales of Israel*, edited by Dov Noy with the assistance of Dan Ben Amos, University of Chicago Press, 1963. Reprinted by permission of the University of Chicago Press.

"Asmodeus and the Shamir," "Alexander Enters Jerusalem," "The Pasha's Lance." from *The Classic Tales*, by Ellen Frankel. Reprinted by permission of Jason Aronson.

"Seven Hundred Years of Sanctity," Meir Ben Dov, from *HaAretz*, July 22, 1988. Translated by Reuven Hammer. Printed by permission of Meir Ben Dov.

"Jerusalem Recipes," Danby Meital. Printed by permission of Danby Meital.

THE ELEVENTH GATE
Archaeology of the Old City

"Walking the Old City: A Jerusalem Tour," Herbert Alexander, from *Condé Nast Traveler* magazine, March 1993. Reprinted courtesy *Condé Nast Traveler*. Copyright © 1993 by The Condé Nast Publications, Inc.

"Twenty-five Years of Excavations in Jerusalem, 1967–1992," Hillel Geva, from *Ancient Jerusalem Revealed*, ed. Hillel Geva, Israel Exploration Society, Jerusalem, 1994. Reprinted by permission of the Israel Exploration Society.

THE TWELFTH GATE
Jerusalem in Children's Literature

"The Two Brothers," Chaya M. Burstein, from *A Kid's Catalogue of Israel*, Chaya M. Burstein, Jewish Publication Society, Philadelphia, 1988. Reprinted with permission of the Jewish Publication Society.

"Two Doves," Levin Kipnis, reprinted from *Kav HaOfek* (Hebrew), Duby Tal and Moni Haramati, Ministry of Defence, 1990. Translated by Reuven Hammer.

"A Private War Diary," Galila Ron-Feder-Amit, from *A Private War Diary* (Hebrew), Galila Ron-Feder-Amit, Adam Publishers, Tel Aviv, 1992. Translated by Reuven Hammer.

"K'tonton Goes Up to Jerusalem," Sadie Rose Weilerstein, from *The Best of K'tonton*, Sadie Rose Weilerstein, The Jewish Publication Society, Philadelphia, 1980. Reprinted by permission of the Jewish Publication Society.

THE THIRTEENTH GATE
Jerusalem Day Services

"The Order of Service for Jerusalem Day," Israeli Chief Rabbinate. "A Suggested Order Of Readings For Jerusalem Day," Reuven Hammer.

THE FOURTEENTH GATE
Jerusalem in Song

Y'rushalayim Shel Zahav courtesy of Chappel Music Company, Hal Leonard and ACUM, Tel Aviv, Israel. All other songs courtesy of ACUM, Tel Aviv, Israel. Music notations and graphics courtesy of Tara Publications, Cedarhurst, NY.

Y'rushalayim Shel Zahav

L'man'an Tsiyon

Uri Tsiyon

Hakotel

Od Yishama

Ki Mitsiyon

Sisu et Y'rushalayim

Y'rushalayim (Meal pisgat har hatsofim)

Lach Y'rushalayim

Tsiyon Tamati

THE FIFTEENTH GATE
Jerusalem: Toward the Future

"Jerusalem," Avraham B. Yehoshua, from *The Jerusalem Quarterly*, Spring 1981. Reprinted by permission of A. B. Yehoshua.

"Jerusalem—Today and Tomorrow," Teddy Kollek, from *Jerusalem: Problems and Prospects*, ed. Joel Kramer, Praeger Publishers, New York, 1980. Reprinted by permission of Teddy Kollek.

"Jerusalem: The Torn City," Meron Benvenisti, from *The Torn City*, Meron Benvenisti. Reprinted by permission of Meron Benvenisti.

EPILOGUE

"Jerusalem, Holy City," R. J. Zvi Werblowsky, from *Jerusalem 5000 Years of History*, Les Dossiers d'Archeologie, March 1992, Paris. Reprinted by permission of Les Dossiers d'Archeologie and R. J. Zvi Werblowsky.

"Jerusalem the Irreplaceable," André Neher, from *Jerusalem: Most Fair of Cities*, Armon, 1977, taken from "Dans tes portes Jerusalem," Albin Michel, Paris. Translated by Lida Schechtman. Reprinted by permission of Dr. Rina Neher.

"Pray for the Well-Being of Jerusalem," S. Y. Agnon, from *Meatzmi L'Atzmi* (Hebrew), Schocken Press, Tel Aviv. Translated by Reuven Hammer. Printed by permission of Schocken Press.

THE JERUSALEM ANTHOLOGY

∾ A Literary Guide

Jerusalem. The Tomb of David on Mount Zion, 1880. Photograph by La Maison Bonfils (The Museum of Photography at Tel-Hai Industrial Park; with permission)

⊘⫸ Introduction

Jerusalem in Jewish Consciousness

Reuven Hammer

For three thousand years Jerusalem has held a unique place in the mind and heart of the people Israel. Other cities played a role in the history of Israel centuries before Jerusalem did. Abraham lived in Beersheba. The first purchase of land in Canaan by a Hebrew was in Hebron. Jacob's sacred site was Beth El (which some later traditions identified with Jerusalem!). The Ark of the Covenant dwelt in Shilo before Jerusalem was conquered. The first capital of David's kingdom was the ancient city of Hebron. Yet, ultimately, none of these cities assumed the importance, the centrality, the sacredness, which was bestowed upon Jerusalem.

It would not be an exaggeration to say that no city in the history of the nations has been as important a part of the consciousness of a people for as long and continuous a period of time as has Jerusalem. For three thousand years it has been the capital of the kingdom of the people of Israel, whatever name and form that people assumed. Even when there was no kingdom, during the seventy years of the first exile and the nearly nineteen hundred years of the second exile, Jerusalem was the capital of the stateless people called the Jews. The eternal pledge made by the exiled levitical singers—"If I forget you, O Jerusalem, let my right hand wither . . ." (Pss. 137:5)—became the watchword of Jews from that moment to this. The symbolism of having it recited at the conclusion of each wedding ceremony—fulfilling the verse, "Let my tongue stick to my palate if I cease to think of you, if I do not keep Jerusalem in memory *even at my happiest hour*" (Pss. 137:6)—is a powerful expression of the desire to pass this pledge from generation to generation. Even when they could not live in Jerusalem, could not set foot in it, Jews faced Jerusalem in devotion three times daily and prayed for its restoration not only during those three prayers but after every meal. Twice a year, at the conclusion of the two most impressive moments of the Jewish year, Yom Kippur and the Passover Seder, all participants pledge, "Next year in Jerusalem!" If modern leaders of the Zionist movement contemplated the possibility of a Jewish state devoid of Jerusalem or of an Israel with its capital elsewhere, they soon discovered that this was an impossibility and that the defense of Jerusalem and the proclamation of Jerusalem as Israel's capital were essential to Israel's existence.

There were ancient cities such as Babylon that were centers of civilization when Jerusalem was little more than a small village. They have long ceased to exist. Athens, which comes closer to playing a central role in the life of a people than any other of the world's cities, was nevertheless only one of the important cities of the various Greek states. Rome was the capital of a mighty empire and was indeed the metropolis of its time, but it also became a parasite, "the inveterate sponger" (Lewis Mumford, *The City in History* [New York: Harcourt, Brace and World, 1961], p. 228.) a condition that led to its eventual destruction. Furthermore, Rome assumed its role long after Jerusalem had become the "city of the great King" (Pss. 48:3) and later changed completely to become the spiritual center of a mighty faith rather than the capital of an empire. Jerusalem's three thousand continuous years of centrality to Judaism and the Jewish people remains unique.

There is no doubt that, although the original reasons for David's choice of Jerusalem were political and geographic, the driving force that created this eternal Jerusalem in the Jewish consciousness was religious. As Lewis Mumford wrote, "The first germ of the city, then, is in the ceremonial meeting place that serves as the goal for pilgrimage: a site to which family or clan groups are drawn back, at seasonal intervals, because it concentrates . . . certain 'spiritual' or supernatural powers, powers of higher potency and greater duration, of wider cosmic significance, than the ordinary processes of life." (ibid, p. 10). It was the identification of Jerusalem with the earthly dwelling place of the Presence of God (the *Shekhina*) that ultimately rendered it unique. Jerusalem was chosen as "the place" where God would dwell and thus became the pilgrim site for Jews throughout the ages. The trip to Jerusalem at the Festivals during the period of the Second Temple attracted Jews from the entire Mediterranean basin and assumed gigantic, even legendary, proportions.

The designation of Mount Zion (the Temple Mount, not the hill called Mount Zion today) in Jerusalem as "the mountain of the Lord . . . His holy place" (Pss. 24:3) was the culmination of a long process by which the tradition of the appearance of God upon Mount Sinai—"the mountain of God" (Exod. 3:1)—was transferred to Mount Zion. It is the presence of God that creates sanctity. There is no place that has sanctity built into it. Holiness is the quality of God, as we see from the words that Isaiah ascribes to the angels when he sees the Lord: "Holy, holy, holy! The Lord of Hosts! His presence fills all the earth!" (Isa. 6:3). Mount Sinai was holy because of God's appearance upon it, but when the Israelites left the wilderness, they took the mountain with them by erecting the Sanctuary containing the Ark of the Covenant, which served as a portable Sinai. There, too, the presence of God would appear to them: "When Moses had finished the work, the cloud covered the Tent of Meeting, and the Presence of the Lord filled the Tabernacle" (Exod. 40:33–34). By placing the Ark, the central feature of the Tabernacle, upon the mountain in Jerusalem (see 2 Sam. 6:12–19), David laid the foundation for the sanctity of that mountain and the holiness of Jerusalem. The erection of a permanent building by Solomon—"I have now built for You a stately House, a place where You may dwell forever" (1 Kings 8:13)—a revolutionary step in the faith of Israel, signaled the permanence of the Presence of God on the holy mountain. In this way, the Mountain of God, Sinai, merged with Mount Zion and became the holy mountain. Centuries later, this process was capped when the almost mythical Mount Moriah of the binding of Isaac—named by Abraham "Adonai-yireh, whence the present saying,

'On the mount of the Lord there is vision' " (Gen. 22:14)—was identified with Mount Zion as well: "Then Solomon began to build the House of the Lord in Jerusalem on Mount Moriah . . ." (2 Chron. 3:1). As the midrash put it so succinctly, "The foundations of Jerusalem exist because of the merit of two holy mountains: Mount Sinai and Mount Moriah" (Yalkut Shimoni Pss. 836).

Thus the sanctity of the Temple created an aura and eventually a legal status of sanctity for the entire city (J. A. Seelingman, "Jerusalem in Jewish-Hellenistic Thought" [12th Archaeological Convention, 1957] p. 194). But sanctity in Judaism is not divorced from worldly matters. Jerusalem was never to be turned into a "spiritual center" with no political reality. It had to play this dual role at all times.

If the presence of the Temple rendered Jerusalem holy, the presence of the king, also chosen by God, rendered it politically central. Again, Mumford: "In the urban implosion, the king stands at the center: he is the polar magnet that draws to the heart of the city and brings under the control of the palace and the temple all the new forces of civilization. Sometimes the king founded new cities; sometimes he transformed old country towns that had long been a-building, placing them under the authority of his governors; in either case his rule made a decisive change in their form and contents" (ibid, p. 35).

As early as the times of the prophets, a third, universal and eschatological, meaning was attached to Jerusalem. The same prophets who saw Jerusalem as all too real a city, an urban gathering of sinners, comparable to Sodom and Gomorrah, doomed to destruction unless redeemed by repentance, also saw it as the eventual site of the redemption. They had the unique vision of Jerusalem as the center of the hope of humankind:

The Mount of the Lord's House
Shall stand firm above the mountains
And tower above the hills;
And all the nations
Shall gaze upon it with joy.
And the many peoples shall go and shall say:
"Come,
Let us go up to the Mount of the Lord,
To the House of the God of Jacob;
That He may instruct us in His ways.
And that we may walk in His paths."
For instruction shall come forth from Zion,

The word of the Lord from Jerusalem.

Thus He will judge among the nations

And arbitrate for the many peoples,

And they shall beat their swords into plowshares

And their spears into pruning hooks:

Nations shall not take up

Sword against nation;

They shall never again know war. (Isa. 2:2–4)

This is a prophecy that still causes us to stand in awe of its magnificent vision.

Without for a moment losing its reality as an actual city central to a real nation living a this-worldly existence, the writings of the prophets turned Jerusalem into a symbol of messianic perfection. Lurking behind the Jerusalem of tailors and shoemakers, of sages, priests, and kings, is that mystic vision of a Jerusalem to which all nations will come to acknowledge the One God and from which instruction will issue to transform the world into a place of justice and peace.

A shadow of this vision was the eternal hope of Jews that the condition of destruction would eventually be reversed and that a rebuilt Jerusalem would welcome back her children as a mother embraces a long-lost child. "As a mother comforts her son, so will I comfort you and you shall find comfort in Jerusalem" (Isa. 66:13).

Jerusalem's centrality to Judaism and the Jewish people, then, ultimately stands on three pillars: its identification as the sacred place chosen by God; its political centrality as the capital and dwelling of the chosen king; its place in the prophetic and later rabbinic and mystic visions of the messianic era.

Even though the religious, mystical significance grew with the centuries, and certainly distance and exile tended to emphasize the other-worldly Jerusalem, the real Jerusalem never ceased to exist in Jewish consciousness:

> Said the Holy One, "I will not enter heavenly Jerusalem until I enter earthly Jerusalem" (Taanit 5a).

In the Middle Ages, the sacred poetry would mourn for Jerusalem and praise it in mystic terms, but the travelers would write of the real city—its problems of housing, food, and simply making a living.

In modern times, the attitudes became more varied. There was a time when, for the Zionist pioneers bent upon establishing a new political entity and in revolt against the traditions of the European-Jewish past, Jerusalem was in danger of becoming a symbol of the old ways they wanted to leave behind, whereas Tel Aviv, Rehovot, or Degania would be seen as the new image of the new Jew. In the long run, however, Jerusalem was irreplaceable, and the echoes of its sanctity created a special aura that could be reinterpreted but not replaced. Thus Boris Schatz, Usishkin, and Ahad HaAm all have visions of the future Jerusalem, which becomes a universal center for the greatest hopes and aspirations of Israel and all humankind. Chaim Weizmann cannot envision the great center of learning, the Hebrew University, anywhere else but on Mount Scopus. The efforts made during the War for Independence to keep control of the Old City and, above all, the events of the Six Day War testify to the unique place held by Jerusalem in the minds of the vast majority of Israelis and Jews, religious or secular.

In the minds of secular thinkers today Jerusalem is no less central. For some this may be a result of its long history. It is so interwoven with every event in Judaism, with thought and writings, with hopes and dreams, that it cannot be forgotten or dispensed with. And even the secular will suddenly find that there is a spiritual, almost a mystical meaning, which cannot so easily be dismissed. A. B. Yehoshua cannot write about Jerusalem without recalling the prophets who walked there, the deep connection of the Jewish people to it, and the "wonderful spiritual power poured out over this city," all the while struggling with the difficulties which Jerusalem presents in real terms today.

Although there is no lack of superstition in the attitudes of some toward Jerusalem and its most sacred site, the Wall, there is no doubt that in that one blinding moment of miraculous revelation in 1967 when the city of Jerusalem was "built up, a city knit together" (Pss. 122:3), the secular and the religious alike experienced some higher meaning than mere stones can convey. And if that moment cannot be sustained—as even the Israelites at the Sea were unable to sustain *that* supreme moment—it nevertheless became a transforming event for those who experienced it.

❧

Jerusalem is a city in which ancient writings have new meanings, in which one can walk the streets and read the words of the prophets, the psalmists, the rabbis, the philosophers, the mystics, the medievals, the poets, the travelers, and the moderns, the warriors, the theologians, and the statesmen on the sites where they were written or to which they refer, and find meaning in them. Somehow this city that was "knit together" also binds together the entire past of Jewry with its future and with the entire people of Israel wherever they may be.

It is the aim of this book to bind together somehow the three thousand years of Jewish Jerusalem and to create a feeling of unity—or at least of continuity—in the Jewish consciousness of Jerusalem. For, in fact, Jerusalem, both vertically through its history and horizontally in its present reality, can hardly be termed a unity. Each period of history has its own flavor and uniqueness. The Jerusalem of David, the Jerusalem of Ezra, the Jerusalem of Herod, the Jerusalem of the Romans, of the Byzantines, of the Mamelukes, of the Crusaders, of the Turks, the Jerusalem of the last century, and the Jerusalem of today are very different cities. And while the Jerusalem of today may share one civil administration, the life of Meah Shearim and that of secular neighborhoods, the Jerusalem of the *shuk* and that of Talbiah, of the Katamonim and Rehavia, of the Bucharian sector, French Hill and Talpiot Mizrah, to say nothing of Jewish versus Arab

Jerusalem, seem anything but united. Yet they are at least intertwined. And in the Jewish consciousness—which is the basic concern of this volume—there is a binding together that connects the earliest writings of the Bible with the works of our own day. It is not the history of Jerusalem as such that concerns us, not its politics or geography, but the way in which the Jewish consciousness has perceived Jerusalem, has been created by it, and has in turn created a Jerusalem that includes streets and alleys but goes beyond that into feelings, values, beliefs, and prophetic hopes.

PROLOGUE

Aerial view of the Temple Mount and the remains uncovered in the Ophel area south of it; looking west (Ancient Jerusalem Revealed. Israel Exploration Society; with permission)

৩৩ History, Faith, and Beauty

Joshua Prawer

Joshua Prawer was Professor of Mediaeval History at the Hebrew University in Jerusalem.

Few panoramas are more beautiful, few views more impressive, than that of Jerusalem seen from the Mount of Olives. In the early hours, when the dew of the night still sparkles on the domes, minarets, and the flat roofs of the city, when the transparent fog lifts its lace from the walls and the sun's rays strike the reddish stone of Jerusalem, the worldly tourist and the pious pilgrim behold one of the greatest wonders of the world: the Holy City.

Few can look at it dispassionately. The viewer, be he Jew, Moslem, or Christian, brings with him the remembered tales of his childhood, the teaching of his adult years, the collective memory of his race or religion: all impinge on the wondrous picture laid out before him. Each adds a dimension of things experienced and lived—once upon a time: Jewish Priests moving on the Temple Esplanade, Roman legions garrisoned in the Fortress of Antonia, Jesus bearing the Cross, Mohammed reining in his steed Burak to pray in the Sacred Enclosure.

Traditions, history, creeds—their number is legion—were created in the city and drew their vital forces from it. Since David bought a threshing floor from the Jebusite Araunah on Mount Moriah and established there the abode of King and God, no generation has felt free to bypass this place. Israelite, Crusader, Briton and Israeli established here the Capital of the State, although politics, economy and strategy might have turned the choice to other places. Jew, Byzantine, Arab and Turk marked it as a center of their religious practice.

One looks again at the city—and the inner town encompassed in the girdle of its Osmanli walls begins to expand. Here at the corner of the Temple area, just below the silvery dome of the Mosque of el-Aksa, the caressing eye moves with the slope to the ancient sources of the Valley of Kidron. The sunrays strike pebble and stone below the green mantle of the slope. One just looks and murmurs: here it all began. Here on this slope was the City of David founded some three thousand years ago.

So little geography, so much history! David's city was an elongated strip of land, laboriously climbing from the Pool of Siloam in the Kidron Valley to the Temple Esplanade; barely nine hundred yards of parched soil precariously clinging to a narrow backbone of a steep hill no more than two hundred yards wide. Walls which protected the old Jebusite settlement were strengthened by David and later enlarged to include the Hill of Moriah with the Royal Palace and the Temple of Solomon. The Spring of Gihon in the north and the Source of Rogel in the south assured water for man and beast and the orchards of the surroundings. A marvellous tunnel was cut in the rock by the architects of King Hezekiah to bring water from outside the city into the Pool of Siloam (then inside the walls), making it self-sufficient in times of war. Just above the old Jebusite settlement and the City of David was the Holy of Holies of the first great monotheistic religion, which gave birth to its two mighty descendants that did not always willingly acknowledge their parentage, but eagerly accepted its teachings. Here was the First Temple of a religion which needed neither painting nor sculpture to represent the Unrepresentable.

⟐

Temple, palace, fortress—Jerusalem became the capital of the Kingdom and as such it remained for the next five hundred years.

When mighty Babylon destroyed the Temple, sacked the city and led its inhabitants into captivity, the nation preserved in song and prophecy the image of the erstwhile glory of its capital. Those who returned from the Rivers of Babylon three generations later held it their holy duty to reconstruct the ancient capital and build the Second Temple. Thus was ushered in the most glorious period in Jerusalem's history.

The city slowly regained and surpassed its former position. Its fortifications and those around the Temple area were strengthened and then the city densely populated. Newer suburbs were encompassed by new ramparts joined to the ancient walls.

The capture of the city by Antiochus Epiphanes and the profanation of the Temple were not more than a short-lived, though tragic, episode. The Hasmonean revolt liberated the city, purified the Temple and re-established the Divine cult of the independent State. Jerusalem again became the anchor of the people. Here was the heart of a state and of a nation, whose sons, far as they might be, turned and turn their faces day after day to the Temple, acknowledging its great place in their lives, acknowledging their identity as individuals and as a nation. Thus were forged the indestructible links which endured two thousand years of exile and preserved a nation proud of its heritage, even when it lost the outer trappings of statehood.

Hellenistic culture, the most pervading in the world, had by then long reached the Holy Land. The deep valley, the Tyropoeon, which divided the hills in the west from the Temple Esplanade and its prolongation of the City of David, was spanned by bridges, thus connecting the old historic city with the new aristocratic quarters, the so-called "Antioch in Jerusalem." Another quarter stretched far to the north, and a new line of walls encompassed the old and new. In the middle, between old and new, the Hasmoneans built their palace-fortress, the "Hakra." Slowly, the older parts of the city, the Lower City and the City of David, lost their importance; the new Upper City in the west became the centre. With Herod, the city already foreshadowed the pattern of the future. The city fortifications in the west, based on the three great towers, became the city's Citadel, which was to serve Byzantines, Arabs, Crusaders, and Turks. To the south of the Citadel, Herod built his palace. After a thousand years of evolution, the city was at the peak of its earthly magnificence.

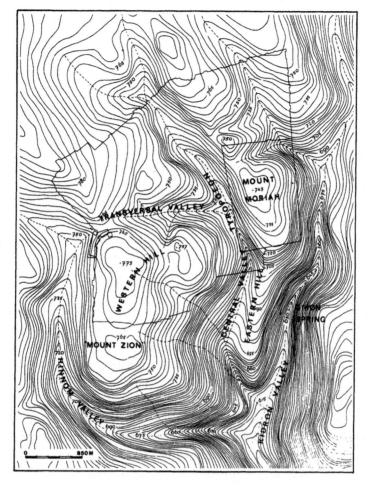

Topographical map of ancient Jerusalem (Ancient Jerusalem Revealed. *Israel Exploration Society; with permission*)

Then, with Titus, it all collapsed. His legions burned the Temple and sacked the city.

A triumphal arch was erected in the Forum of Rome. Jews were led into captivity, bearing the seven-branched candelabrum from the Temple, thus announcing the exile of a nation. Money struck by the Emperor bore the haughty inscription: "Judaea Capta." For the first but not the last time, the founders and heirs of the city were barred from it by an imperial decree.

But the nation was not destroyed. Two generations later a charismatic leader, Bar-Kokhba, raised the banner of revolt, fighting for Faith and State and the liberation of the nation. But neither faith nor justice could withstand the iron fist of Imperial Rome. The city fell, and the conqueror decided to erect a monument to his victory. A new city was built on the site, marked by a ploughshare: Aelia Capitolina, perpetuating the name of Aelius Hadrianus, proclaimed the victory of the Deities of the Capitoline Hill of Rome over the Invisible God of Jerusalem.

◇

But the Romans did not reckon sufficiently with the indestructibility of faith and spirit. Judaism would survive without a Temple and the Jew without a state. His invisible God was everywhere. His permanence was the permanence of the Nation. Two thousand years this nation would wait for salvation, straining its ears to hear the approaching steps of the Messiah. Generation after generation would feel that the time had come, and Messianic movements would convulse the communities dispersed in the four corners of the earth.

Persecuted by pagan, Christian, and Moslem, the Jew created for himself another reality, sealed in the innermost recesses of his soul, a reality which would withstand the pressing walls of darkness around him. Jerusalem—the living city—mingles with Jerusalem the Heavenly, as Heaven bounds the horizon over the sacred mountains of Judea. This Jerusalem grew in stature, blending memories and expectations; it became a city of gold and silver and of sapphires and rubies, of precious stones and of luxurious spices—a city and Temple which would one day be lowered in clouds from Heaven and float down onto Mount Moriah, proclaiming to all nations: Come ye and let us go up to the mountain of the Lord.

For others, a Saviour had already come. A generation before Titus, Jesus was crucified. A seemingly dangerous rebel against the Eagles of Rome, he appeared to others as the Innocent Lamb offering himself in expiation of the sins of mankind. Barely distinguishable from the community in which they arose, a group of disciples, threatened with destruction at the hands of Titus, had fled the city, taking with them a belief in the oneness of God, the universality of His call, the moral code of their ancestors and their Holy Scriptures, in addition to the Good Tidings that mankind was already saved through God's Incarnation and His Crucifixion. They also took with them the image of Jerusalem, "Hierosolyma," the Holy Solyma, no longer a city of reality, but a symbol of the City of God, Heavenly Jerusalem.

Thus Jew and Christian, one in the Diaspora, the other in the communities of converts which sprang up all around the Mediterranean, bore the torch of a monotheistic religion to a pagan world, spreading the name of Jerusalem, the half-ruined city of Judea, to the remotest corners of the world. One prayed turning to Jerusalem, invoking its holy name in every prayer and closing the most solemn annual Atonement liturgy with: "Next year in Jerusalem." The other turned in prayer to the rising sun in the east, building altars in a hundred thousand churches all over the world. From fog-covered Ireland to the steppes of Central Asia, from frozen Greenland to the sundrenched Sahara, millions repeated the name of Jerusalem and Zion mingled with the burning supplication: "Let Thy Kingdom Come."

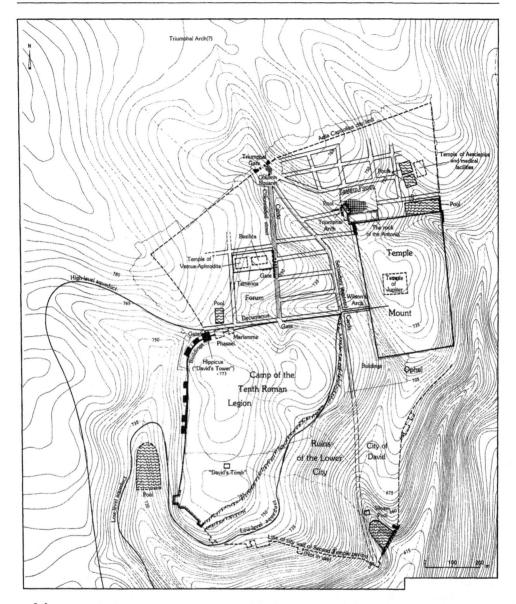

Map of Jerusalem during the Roman period (Ancient Jerusalem Revealed. *Israel Exploration Society; with permission*)

And yet the Heavenly Jerusalem could not and did not cut off its links with the one below. Once the Roman Empire became Christian, and the once-persecuted religion proclaimed the official faith of the Empire, a mighty wave of pilgrims turned to the East, to approach and behold, to touch and pray before the stones which had witnessed the earthly presence of the Saviour. Sanctuary and chapel, church and oratory rose where tradition pointed. Soon a mantle of white marble and of columns resplendent in form and colour, adorned the city, and Christian, Byzantine Jerusalem replaced Aelia Capitolina, rejoicing in its ascendancy and proclaiming its victory in a hundred crosses over domes and towers. Christianity, successor and "heir in spirit" to Ancient Israel, inherited sanctuaries commemorating the sites of the "Old Testament." Many a church was built over a Jewish abode and monument. The debt to the living descendants of Israel was not acknowledged. They were barred from residing in the city. It was on the perimeter that Jews gathered. A new Jewish liturgy was created, the liturgy of the Mourners of Zion, the liturgy of those who contemplated the city from the Mount of Olives, who saw churches built on the Temple Mount and the Byzantine Governor ensconced where the Jewish kings had dwelt. The Jew could enter to pray at the ruins of his Temple, but he was not allowed to settle.

Frustration and persecution caused the Jews and Samaritans, then hostile to one another, to join the invading Persian armies. The invasion was soon repelled; Heraclius the Emperor entered Jerusalem through the Golden Gate bringing back the True Cross. The triumph was short-lived. A new prophet was moving in the Hejaz, from Mecca to Medina, inaugurating a new era in the annals of mankind. All that happened before was relegated to the realm of the "Jahiliya," the Age of Obscurantism. Mohammed was proclaiming the Unity and the Oneness of Allah. A generation later the swift steeds of Arabia were neighing at the gates of Alexandria and Antioch.

Jerusalem capitulated. Its Byzantine garrison left, and the Christian Patriarch representing the city was granted an "Aman," a treaty of peace for its inhabitants and their property. At the deathbed of Byzantine Jerusalem, the Patriarch did not deem anything more urgent than an assurance from the Moslem conquerors that no Jew would be allowed to settle in the city.

For the new conqueror the city was still "Ilya," the Roman "Aelia," but the Semitic element quickly overcame the foreign heritage. Soon the city became known in Arabic as "Bet al-Makdas," the ancient Hebrew "Bet-Hamikdash," the House of the Temple, or "al-Kuds," the Holy, for short, and still its Arabic name today. Hesitantly at first, more consciously later, Jerusalem entered its first Moslem period. By then it had run half of its recorded history.

The conqueror felt and acknowledged his debt to the other monotheistic religions. He saw himself as their ultimate heir, successor, and fulfiller. Judaism, among other things, left to him the legacy of Jerusalem. Mohammed, on his marvellous horse, flew during the Great Night from Mecca to Jerusalem and prayed at the Outermost Mosque (el-Aksa).

Thus the Temple Esplanade became the Haram esh-Sherif, the Noble Sanctuary. The Church of the Holy Sepulchre and some other churches were preserved, but the new conqueror proceeded to impress his own seal on the city. Many a church was transformed into a mosque, its altar removed and a new oratory added: the "mihrab," the niche turned to Mecca. But the conqueror wanted new buildings, his own glories, to compete with the Christian shrines, to excel in beauty and surpass in height. The Temple area saw Byzantine architects employing the richest materials available, building the Dome of the Great Mosque, the Kubbat al-Sakhra, over the Holy Rock of the Jewish Temple.

The place of Jerusalem in Islam was finally decided when a political upheaval in the Hejaz gave the Moslems of the north an opportunity to compete with the southern Holy Places. Jerusalem was proclaimed the third Holy Place of Islam and the Haram esh-Sherif a legitimate aim of the "Hajj," of the holy pilgrimage, incumbent at least once in a lifetime on every true Believer.

For four hundred years Islam ruled in Jerusalem. The population of the city, to a large degree still Christian, saw its churches decaying, repairs dependent on the goodwill of the new rulers; any new building was entirely prohibited. The Jewish community circumvented the prohibition and infiltrated the city. They settled near the Western Wall beneath the Mosque of el-Aksa, later in the northeastern quarter of the city, between the Damascus Gate and the Gate of Jehosaphat. Christian and Jew alike were tolerated, but long periods of relative peace were succeeded by outbursts of fanaticism and persecution. Churches and synagogues were destroyed. Christians and Jews were forced to wear distinguishing signs and prohibited from riding the noble animal, the horse, which was reserved for Moslems only. And yet both communities survived. By the middle of the eleventh century the city was divided into a Christian Quarter, near the Holy Sepulchre, a Jewish Quarter to its East, and the large Moslem Quarter around the Temple area. A pattern of coexistence, not yet on a basis of equality, but for the mediaeval world one of toleration, was coming into being.

The city, together with the southern part of the country, often changed its rulers. At times it was ruled by the Caliphate of Baghdad, at others by Egypt and finally by the Seljuk Turks, who expelled the Egyptians. All this had little or no influence on the city. Garrisons changed in the Citadel (the "Tower of David"); the communities prayed for whomever happened to be in power but took little part in politics.

The city slumbered placidly on, outside the mainstream of events, when its name brought about one of the greatest revolutions in history: the Crusades. It was in the name of Jerusalem and the Holy Sepulchre that Europe mobilized its lusty and war-loving forces and poured them into the East. In a Europe where the peasant or burgher hardly knew the name of his neighbouring district, there was one name known to all. This name was Jerusalem, proclaimed in every prayer, recalled on every feast day, calling its name to the illiterate from frescoes, sculptures, and stained glass. The seed sown a thousand years earlier in Jerusalem was bearing unexpected fruit—a movement of conquest and colonisation in the name of the liberation of Jerusalem and of the Holy Sepulchre from the Moslem yoke. Pent-up religious feelings, lusts for spoils and war, a Messianic tension which perceived the trumpets of the approaching Day of Judgment, all pushed Europe to the East.

The city was taken by storm in the mid-summer of 1099, with a monstrous massacre of its population. Moslem and Jew were slaughtered in the greatest carnage the city had experienced since its destruction by the Roman legions of Titus. In this welter of blood, a new state was created: The Latin Kingdom of Jerusalem. No name could have been more appropriate. Not only was its capital Jerusalem, but its *raison d'être*, its whole meaning, was based on that unique name: Jerusalem.

Down went the crescents from the domes, down came the minarets. European Christianity hoisted its cross-spangled banners over the battlements, erected gilded crosses over what had been mosques. The new Church of the Holy Sepulchre, encompassing what remained of the ancient Byzantine basilica and a romanesque cathedral, was planted anew in the Christian Quarter; the Great Mosque became the Temple of the Lord; the el-Aksa became the "Temple of Solomon." The seals of the Kings of Jerusalem and their coins bore the effigies of the three monumental buildings: Tower of David, Holy Sepulchre, and the Temple of the Lord—all adorned with Latin crosses and flying banners.

Jews and Moslems alike were barred from living in the city. The former Moslem ruler now met the persecuted Jew on a clandestine pilgrimage to pray and to bewail the hallowed stones of the ancient sanctuaries.

For two hundred years the name of Jerusalem resounded in every castle, church, and monastery throughout mediaeval Christendom. And Jerusalem itself saw an entirely new population settled inside its walls: Europeans who felt that here was the root of their faith and Jerusalem their lawful heritage. French replaced Arabic, the Latin liturgy was ousting the Greek. From Scotland to Russia and from Norway to Spain and Italy, Jerusalem was on everybody's lips. Geographical maps, which had just come again into being, would mark Jerusalem as the Navel of the world and around it, bowing to it, Asia, Africa, and Europe.

The Kingdom thrived for a hundred years—and then was captured by Saladin, leaving in its wake names like Godfrey de Bouillon, Baldwin, and Richard Coeur de Lion. For a short time it became Christian again, adding its title to that of the King of Germany and Emperor of the Holy Roman Empire, only to fall again to the power of the Mamelukes of Egypt.

Between Crescent and Cross, the Jews found a foothold in the city. Suffering with every convulsion in the tortuous history of the country, they had their own view of the evolution of history. Their sufferings were an assurance of approaching salvation, and the wars of the mighty a hastening of the Day of Judgment. The lost cause of the Crusades, despite the inhuman efforts and sacrifices, was a clear sign that the Land of Israel could not and would not suffer any foreign domination. Its wastes and ruins, the great Nahmanides taught, were the work of Providence, to prevent anybody from settling the heritage of God and His Chosen People. It was thus amidst ruins caused by Moslem, Mongol, and Tartar invasions that a Jewish community settled in Jerusalem in the mid-thirteenth century, a settlement which existed uninterruptedly for seven centuries, until 1948. European persecutions would result in waves of migration, atrocities would strengthen the belief that the day of Judgement was nearing. Squabbles with the local Christians and Moslems would result in outbreaks of fanaticism; but on the whole, the population of the city was ruled by the iron hand of the Mamelukes and later the Ottoman Turks, and settled down to the difficult task of peaceful living.

The three great quarters of the city as we know them today were established at the end of the Middle Ages. Each community lived in its own quarter, ruled by its spiritual leaders according to its religious precepts. The official power, arbitrary and exploiting, was placated by the gain of income from pilgrims, ransom from the inhabitants and the bribery which had become a calculated expense of those who wanted to live in the city. Times of peace often bring neglect; and so it happened that at the end of the Middle Ages, the city's walls and fortifications were crumbling and a good many of its most beautiful monuments were lying in the dust. Ended was the great Mameluke effort of the fourteenth century to embellish the city with new buildings, often using parts of Crusader churches, like the Gothic rosaces, which look strange over fountains and "sebils" (drinking places). The water supply of the city, also restored in the same period, was suffering from neglect.

The Ottoman Turks, who had put an end to the existence of the Byzantine Empire and firmly established themselves on the Bosphorus, were marking time for a general onslaught on the chivalrous but inefficient Mameluke regime on the Nile. Egypt was incorporated in the great Ottoman empire, and Jerusalem came into the fold of the new Turkish State. Its population was spared the horrors of war. Neither city not citizen was deeply affected by the transition from one Moslem power to another.

Suleiman the Magnificent decided to restore the city, and a new girdle of walls was thrown around it. The old Herodian walls with their giant rectangular stones, which bore the weights of Byzantine, Arab, Crusader, and Mameluke layers of restoration, were now topped by Turkish additions. Inscriptions spaced between the towers along the three miles of walls proclaimed the magnificence of the Sultan, the ruler of Turks, Arabs, and Persians. Lovely stone—carved knobs, ornamental crenellations over gates, and decorative battlements over ramparts—made the city appear more Oriental than ever. Mosques were restored and redecorated, institutes of study and theology established, water supplies restored.

The new zeal did not last more than a generation. Jerusalem fell back into slumber, awakened from time to time by the strife of contending pashas, fights for central power at Istambul, and later the intervention of European powers into the affairs of the "Sick Man of Europe." Archaeological research and biblical studies of foreign institutes were begun. In all this bustle, the ancient Jewish community led its existence as well as it could. The expulsion of the Jews from Spain and Portugal resulted in a wave of immigrants to Safad and Jerusalem. The newcomers brought with them their native Spanish language, thus adding a Romance language to the Yiddish and Arabic spoken by earlier generations. Centers of study of the Torah and Talmud were enriched by the study of the Kabbala, and sacred mysticism held to have the power to speed the coming of the tarrying Messiah. Messianic movements of a Shabbetai Zvi or of the hassidim occasionally convulsed the community.

At the mercy of the Turkish pasha and despoiled by Beduins and revenue-thirsty of-ficials, Christians and Jews endured the misery in the city for no other reason than for the place it had in their hearts. What could have been stranger than the proclamation of Napoleon to the Jews of Asia and Africa, during his Egyptian and Palestinian cam-paign, inviting them to come and settle Jerusalem!

European interventions moved from protests and declarations at Istambul to estab-lishing facts in Jerusalem. Consulates were opened, a missionary movement of Catholics, Greek-Orthodox, and Protestants, supported by the governments and private associa-tions, was converging on the city.

The other name of Jerusalem, Zion, was in the meantime heard in Europe. Zionism, with its declared aim of a Jewish return to the ancestral homeland, expressed in polit-ical terms the centuries-long, innermost desires of a nation. The Jewish community, which had made its first steps outside the hampering walls, in the mid-nineteenth century, laying foundation to new quarters, had grown steadily since the turn of the century. The new quarters still resembled the Old City's narrow streets, enclosed mar-kets and squares, the pathetic trees thriving on flagstones and blank house walls facing the outside; half-living, half-fortress areas proved the determination to strike roots again in the Holy City.

The great upheaval of World War I saw General Edward Allenby reading a procla-mation on the steps of the Citadel, a proclamation which was translated into the city's seven languages. Six hundred years after the Crusaders, a European power was again rul-ing the city, this time as a Mandatory of international agreements, with the declared aim of the restoration of a Jewish Homeland in the Holy Land.

After a short period—and what are thirty years in the three-thousand-year history of the city?—Jerusalem was evacuated by the British, and the vicissitudes of war divided it between Jordanian and Israeli. The modern Israeli capital spread south and westward, its Knesset, University and museum adding a contemporary contrast. But the Holy Places, contrary to every agreement and promise, were closed to Jews and Israeli Moslems, and, except during Christmas and Easter, to Israeli Christians.

The anomaly could not last for long and the Jordanians brought about its end by shelling the New City on the fateful Fifth of June, 1967. The next day Israeli troops broke through their lines, suffering heavy losses because of a decision not to shell the areas around the Holy Places. The new and the historical city were free the day after that. The city walls are no longer an obstacle and a barrier, but a historical monument to be admired, one of the most famous in the world.

ᒪᑐ

A city of a hundred mosques, synagogues, and churches, a city where the bearded Eastern priest rubs shoulders with the bearded rabbi, the white-clad "Haji" wearing the sign of pilgrimage on his fez beckons to the tourist, and the sunburned Israeli says "Shalom" to the Latin monk. They all belong to Jerusalem, they all live freely in it.

You look again at the city walls where they enclose the Temple Area. The stones speak to you. Each layer records a phrase of history. The connoisseur may anywhere else wrinkle his nose at the mixture of styles; here he sees them blending, as the patina of ages and slanting rays of the sun mellow one into the other. And so it is with the spirit of humility, which here finds a common denominator between creeds and nations.

☙ Jerusalem: A Tapestry in Time

Samuel Heilman

Samuel Heilman is a professor of sociology at Queens College of the City University of New York.

Jerusalem: it is not one, but many. It is a place in which people actually live; it is a place which lives in them. It is a figment of the imagination, an idea. It is visible, open to discovery; it is unseen, hidden to all but insiders. It is constructed of mortar and stone and inhabited by flesh and bone; it is formed of spirit and faith and filled by belief and memory. It is the Omphalos Mundi—Navel of the World; it is a centuries-old but recently rebuilt city of Judean Hills, situated on the western edge of an arid wilderness.

Jerusalem is also called the city of peace; but throughout all memory, it has been a focal point of conflict. And so what is significant to some may be irrelevant to others. One people's shrine becomes another's ruin. The center for one group is the periphery for another. What one inhabitant wishes to save, another would destroy. What one would uncover, another would bury. One's dream and hope is another's nightmare and curse.

There are those who look upon the city as layers of history, a site to be archeologically uncovered, a place where one epoch is built upon another: the ancient Jebusite city lies beneath the City of David, which in turn merges into houses from the Second Temple and Hasmonean periods, built hundreds of years later. Then, with the Roman conquest of the city and the final exile of the Judeans, Jerusalem—or Aelia Capitolina, as the conquerors now called the place—went through two millennia of incarnations: Byzantine, Persian, Moslem, Umayyad or Syrian, Abbasid or Baghdadi, Fatimid, Crusader, Mameluke or Egyptian, Ottoman, and British. After 1948, the city—a vulnerable border town—was divided for nineteen years by an armistice between the Israelis and the Jordanians. And in 1967, after the armistice was broken, it became at last the united capital of the modern state of Israel.

To those who dig, tracing the lines of history in the dirt and reconstructing it from the shards thus uncovered is what gives this city its ultimate meaning. Only in the journey toward the deepest layers, through other people's memories, down to the bedrock, does Jerusalem reveal itself and its attachments.

But everyone digs to the level of his interest and concern. For the Jews, only relics from the ancient period—a short spell in the days of the Patriarchs and then from David in 1200 B.C.E. to the destruction of the Second Temple in the year 70 C.E.—and the period of the Return to Zion, beginning under the Ottomans, growing under the British and blooming after the Israeli War of Independence, are important. All else remains a rime of exile.

Yet despite that long exile, to many Jews the memories and attachments of Jerusalem are visible, comprehensible, and undeniable. This is our land, say many of them, the land of our forebears. Here is our history and here is our future. We have never forgotten thee, O Jerusalem, and now that we are returned, we shall never leave.

And why? Because over the course of nearly two and a half millennia, Jerusalem remained the spiritual center of the universe, the crown of Jewish glory and apex of all hope. Distance from it was measured not in space but by intensity of yearning to be there. Six hundred and fifty-six times the city is mentioned in Scripture, and scores more in liturgy. On the summit of Mount Moriah, atop the *Even Sh'tiyyah*, or Foundation Stone, the Patriarch Abraham bound his son Isaac to be offered up to God, and upon that same stone, many believe, Jacob—the father of the children of Israel—rested his head during his prophetic dream. In Jerusalem, Kind David set up his capital, Zion, and on Moriah his son Solomon built the Holy Temple—God's resting place and, for the children of Israel, the holiest spot on earth. From Jerusalem and Zion, many have come to believe, began the Jewish exile, and here, the faithful say, upon arrival of the Messiah, bringing with him the resurrected dead, the final redemption will come. "The Lord loves the gates of Zion more than all the dwellings of Jacob," sang the Psalmist. "And the people blessed all those who were willing to dwell in Jerusalem," proclaimed the prophet Nehemiah.

Even in the face of that prophecy, some Jews ironically prefer a Jerusalem whose image in formed by the patterns of life that emerged in Eastern Europe, in the ghettoes of Sanz or Mattersdorf, Ger or Belz. If God happened to have placed His Holy Temple atop Moriah, they have only to close their eyes when they pray at its remaining stones, and thus be transported back to the Jerusalem of their Eastern European dreams, awaiting the days of the Messiah when those dreams will come true.

But Jerusalem is not important only to the faithful Jews. Others, for whom religion is but a relic or at best a part of national consciousness and folk life, hear more clearly the distant voice of Nehemiah and look upon the city as the soul of their homeland, the starting point of national history, the ground in which are planted the seeds of a growing national consciousness.

Many Jews who live the Zionist dream—call them Israelis—see Jerusalem in this way. For these people, beneath what *their* prophet Theodor Herzl called in his diaries "the musty deposits of two thousand years of inhumanity, intolerance and uncleanliness," lie the nuggets of collective memory in which are embedded all the hopes of an exiled people for national revival in the land of its origins, the Promised Land. To retrieve and re-collect them and thereby overcome the estrangement of exile, Jerusalem must—these Jews believe—be penetrated, explored, plumbed and protected. As the Bible would have a man know a woman, so must the people of Israel know this Jerusalem: in body and spirit.

Since the days of its conquest by King David, no other nation has made Jerusalem its capital, the heart of its nation. To Jerusalem Nehemiah and Ezra returned to renew the days of old. Here Solomon's Temple which the Babylonians had destroyed was rebuilt. In Jerusalem began the short-lived revolt of Bar Kochba against the occupying

Roman legions. From here, some believe, began the Diaspora, that most unnatural condition of the Jews; and here, some trust, the Return to Zion, the naturalization of the Jews, will at last be completed.

Although overlooked during the Zionist settlement process, in the days when Tel Aviv grew miraculously out of sand dunes and the swamps of the Hula Valley were drained while the fields of Degania were plowed, the return to Jerusalem remained the ends of hope. The last word of "Ha-Tik'vah," the song that would become the national anthem of the new Jewish State of Israel, was and remains "Jerusalem."

𝒷

And so in the end, Jerusalem must be understood as a tapestry in time. Woven into its present is an unforgettable past, and intertwined with both is an idealized future. Normally, the sequence of time imposed by everyday life cannot be reversed or reordered; but in Jerusalem normal time can be rearranged. It is therefore not surprising that people who wander within its borders often find the present least accessible or engaging, while they make their ways easily into the past or gain sudden access to some messianic timescape yet to come. Sometimes they can even grab hold of the ephemeral moment outside the flow of time as we know it—an interval which, although hardly more than a promise or hope, is clung to with the greatest fervor by those who are touched by it. So those who spend time in the city sooner or later find themselves somehow leaping back and forth from the ancient days to distant prophecies, occasionally getting caught up in the spaces in between.

THE FIRST GATE

Jerusalem in Biblical Literature

Entrance to the Old City, Jaffa Gate, 1925
(Central Zionist Archives; with permission)

THE TORAH AND HISTORICAL BOOKS

Considering its great importance in later historical and prophetic books, the entrance of Jerusalem upon the Jewish literary scene in the Torah, the most sacred part of Scripture, is modest indeed. It does not even appear by the name by which we know it, but is assumed to be referred to by the name Salem in the story of Abraham's victory in a war to liberate his nephew Lot. At that time:

> And Melchizedek, king of Salem, brought out bread and wine; he was a priest of God Most High. He blessed him, saying,
> "Blessed be Abram of God Most High,
> Creator of heaven and earth.
> And blessed be God Most High,
> Who has delivered your foes into your hand."
> (GEN. 14:18–20)

Although Jewish tradition has long identified Mount Moriah upon which Abraham is prepared to offer his son Isaac (Gen. 22:2,14) as the site of the Temple—that is, the acropolis of Jerusalem—this specific identification is found only in 2 Chronicles 3:1:

> Then Solomon began to build the House of the Lord in Jerusalem on Mount Moriah, where [the Lord] had appeared to his father David, at the place which David had designated, at the threshing floor of Ornan the Jebusite.

Since Chronicles is a late book, dating from the Second Temple period, and since both the parallel story in the earlier book of Kings (1 Kings 6:1) and the story of David's purchase of the threshing floor (2 Sam. 24:18–25) do not mention this identification, scholars tend to regard it as a late invention. In any case, Jewish tradition made this identification between the two so that the verse explaining the meaning of Moriah:

> And Abraham named that site Adonai-yireh [that is, the Lord will see], whence the present saying, "On the mount of the Lord there is vision."
> (GEN. 22:14)

was understood as explaining the sacredness of the particular mountain upon which the Temple was built.

Similarly, while Jewish tradition has always assumed that the many references in the book of Deuteronomy to "the site [or place] that the Lord shall choose" (see for example 14:25, 16:2, 16:15) indicated Jerusalem, the name of the city does not appear there. This is understandable since the book purports to report the words of Moses before he could have known of Jerusalem. However, in view of the fact that Deuteronomy 16:16, in commanding males to appear before the Lord three times a year in the place the Lord shall choose, uses language which seems to echo deliberately the explanation of Mount Moriah in Genesis 22:14, it may well be that by the time Deuteronomy was promulgated in the seventh century B.C.E. the identification between Moriah and the Temple mount was already assumed. That Jerusalem had any place in the consciousness of Israel during the pre-conquest era is doubtful indeed.

It is only when we come to the historical narratives referring to the conquest of the Land found in the Early Prophets that Jerusalem is called by name and explicitly enters the stage of Israelite history. The first specific mention of Jerusalem by name is found in Joshua 10:1–5:

> When King Adoni-zedek of Jerusalem learned that Joshua had captured Ai and proscribed it, treating Ai and its king as he had treated Jericho and its king, and that, moreover, the people of Gibeon had come to terms with Israel and remained among them, he was very frightened. . . . So King Adoni-zedek of Jerusalem sent this message to King Hoham of Hebron, King Piram of Jarmuth, King Japhia of Lachish, and King Debir of Eglon: "Come up and help me defeat Gibeon; for it has come to terms with Joshua and the Israelites."

Their attack against the Gibeonites was countered by Joshua in his famous victory when the sun stood still in Gibeon. The king of Jerusalem, along with the others, was captured and put to death. There is no mention, however, of a capture of Jerusalem.

If this is indeed the same city as Salem mentioned above, the kings there must have had the word *zedek* as part of their royal nomenclature. It has also been suggested that the first part of the name of the city may have been like that of Ur-Kasdim, possibly from the Sumerian *uru*, meaning "city." This was Ur-Shalem—that is, Yerushalem, eventually Yerushalayim. Another suggestion is that it derives from the words *yarah*—"is found"—and *Shulmanu*—the name of a West Semitic deity. The popular etymology of "ir-shalom"—the city of peace—would then be no more than a midrashic invention of noble intention and poetic meaning.

Jerusalem appears next in the description of the borders of the tribe of Judah, which also mentions some of the major features of the city:

> Then the boundary ascended into the Valley of Ben-hinnom, along the southern flank of the Jebusites—that is, Jerusalem. The boundary then ran up to the top of the hill which flanks the Valley of Hinnom on the west, at the northern end of the Valley of Rephaim. (JOSH. 15:8)

Yet another name for Jerusalem is given when it is numbered among the towns of the tribe of Benjamin:

> Zela, Eleph, and Jebus—that is Jerusalem . . . (JOSH. 18:28)

The first Israelite conquest of the city came when the tribe of Judah captured it after the death of Joshua:

> The Judites attacked Jerusalem and captured it; they put it to the sword and set the city on fire. (JUDG. 1:8)

For whatever reason, the tribe of Judah does not seem to have retained it, for in the same chapter, it is described as being within the borders of Benjamin, who also does not dislodge its Cannanite inhabitants:

> The Benjaminites did not dispossess the Jebusite inhabitants of Jerusalem; so the Jebusites have dwelt with the Benjaminites in Jerusalem to this day. (JUDG. 1:21)

That it actually remained in Jebusite hands is clear from yet another incidental reference as part of the story of the concubine in Gibeah:

> He set out and traveled as far as the vicinity of Jebus—that is, Jerusalem; he had with him a pair of laden donkeys, and his concubine was with him. Since they were close to Jebus, and the day was very far spent, the attendant said to his master, "Let us turn aside to this town of the Jebusites and spend the night in it." But his master said to him, "We will not turn aside to a town of aliens who are not of Israel, but will continue to Gibeah." (JUDG. 19:10–12)

It remained for David to capture this city which had been so inconsequential and peripheral to Israel and make it the capital of the kingdom:

> The king and his men set out for Jerusalem against the Jebusites who inhabited the region. David was told, "You will never get in here! Even the blind and the lame will turn you back." ... But David captured the stronghold of Zion; it is now the City of David. ... David occupied the stronghold and renamed it the City of David; David also fortified the surrounding area, from the Millo inward. (2 SAM. 5:6–7, 9)

David had reigned in Hebron seven years and six months. His reasons for moving from Hebron to Jerusalem are not explained. It is generally assumed that a city which had not previously been occupied by one of the tribes, one which was on the border between two tribes, could more easily be accepted by all the tribes as their capital. Eventually, it was the amalgam of David, the chosen king, with Jerusalem, "the place I shall choose," which created the overwhelming importance and indeed centrality of Jerusalem in Jewish consciousness and history. Because it is the city of David, if for no other reason, it came to occupy the position it has today and has had for the last three thousand years.

David's building program to transform the city began at once:

> King Hiram of Tyre sent envoys to David with cedar logs, carpenters, and stonemasons; and they built a palace for David. (2 SAM. 5:11)

From that time on, the history of Israel and the history of Jerusalem become synonymous. All the major events of the rest of the book of Samuel—as well as of the two books of Kings, Ezra, and Nehemiah—take place in Jerusalem.

Evidently, David's plan was to create in Jerusalem not only the political capital of the kingdom, but the religious capital, as well. His first attempt at it, however, ended in disaster:

> They loaded the Ark of God onto a new cart and conveyed it from the house of Abinadab, which was on the hill; and Abinadab's sons, Uzza and Ahio, guided the new cart. . . . But when they came to the threshing floor of Nacon, Uzzah reached out for the Ark of God and grasped it, for the oxen had stumbled. The Lord was incensed at Uzzah. And God struck him down on the spot for his indiscretion, and he died there beside the Ark of God. David was distressed because the Lord had inflicted a breach upon Uzzah; and that place was named Perez-uzzah [that is, "the Breach of Uzzah"] as it is still called.
>
> David was afraid of the Lord that day; he said, "How can I let the Ark of the Lord come to me?" So David would not bring the Ark to his place in the City of David. . . . *(2 Sam. 6:3–10)*

Three months later, the second attempt was more successful:

> Thereupon David went and brought up the Ark of God from the house of Obed-edom to the City of David, amid rejoicing. . . . Thus David and all the House of Israel brought up the Ark of the Lord with shouts and with blasts of the horn. . . . They brought in the Ark of the Lord and set it up in its place inside the tent which David had pitched for it, and David sacrificed burnt offerings and offerings of well-being before the Lord. *(2 Sam. 6:12–18)*

Nevertheless, David was not permitted to construct a building, as opposed to a tent, to house the Ark. The desert tradition of a tent was still understood to be authoritative (2 Sam. 7:4–7). The building of the Temple was left for Solomon:

> And so I propose to build a house for the name of the Lord my God, as the Lord promised my father David, saying, "Your son, whom I will set on your throne in your place, shall build the house for My name." *(1 Kings 5:19)*

Solomon was an ambitious builder. He was not content with what David had built but built his own palace and the walls around Jerusalem:

> He married Pharoah's daughter and brought her to the City of David [to live there] until he had finished building his palace, and the House of the Lord, and the walls around Jerusalem. *(1 Kings 3:1)*

With wood supplied by Hiram of Lebanon, with "huge blocks of choice stone," with the forced labor of 30,000 men as well as "70,000 porters and 80,000 quarriers" (1 Kings 5:29–31) the house was built:

> In the fourth year, in the month of Ziv, the foundations of the House were laid; and in the eleventh year, in the month of Bul—that is, the eighth

---

← *City of David* (Ancient Jerusalem Revealed. *Israel Exploration Society; with permission*)

month—the House was completed according to all its details and all its speci-
fications. It took him seven years to build it. . . .

Then Solomon convoked the elders of Israel—all the heads of the tribes
and the ancestral chieftains of the Israelites—before King Solomon in Jerusalem, to bring up the Ark of the Covenant of the Lord from the City of David,
that is, Zion. *(1 KINGS 6:37–38; 8:1)*

The great ceremony of the dedication and Solomon's monumental prayer made it clear
that although the house could never contain God, nevertheless this was no mere sanctuary, but the special place in which prayers would be heard and toward which God's
attention would be given. If God would not dwell there, He assured them that "My
name shall abide there" (1 Kings 8:29). The difference may have been theologically important, but was too subtle to make an impact on the people. Furthermore, Solomon
received the Lord's assurance that:

I consecrate this House which you have built and I set My name there forever. My eyes and My heart shall ever be there. *(1 KINGS 9:3)*

The connection between David and Jerusalem is often stressed in verses such as 1 Kings
11:32:

But one tribe shall remain his—for the sake of My servant David and for the
sake of Jerusalem, the city that I have chosen out of all the tribes of Israel.

Thus the chosen House of David, the chosen City of David, and the chosen House of
the Lord all combined to give Jerusalem a unique status. It became the very heart and
soul of the people of Israel. When the book of Deuteronomy was found and accepted
as the word of God in the year 622 B.C.E., the place of Jerusalem became even more important in that those laws forbade sacrifice anywhere else. Males were required to come
and bring their offerings before the Lord only in Jerusalem. The Passover lamb could
be offered nowhere else. All other sanctuaries were destroyed. The impact of those laws
was enormous. It is ironic that Jerusalem attained its full status and importance only
thirty-two years before it was destroyed in 586 B.C.E. This pattern was to be echoed
when Herod's Temple was completed only a few years before its destruction in 70 C.E.

David's conquest and fortification of Jerusalem did not make it safe from attack. The
first such attack took place in 927 B.C.E. during the reign of Rehoboam, son of Solomon:

In the fifth year of King Rehoboam, King Shishak of Egypt marched against
Jerusalem and carried off the treasures of the House of the Lord and the treasures of the royal palace. *(1 KINGS 14:25–26)*

Another attack was made during the reign of King Joash (837–798 B.C.E.):

At that time, King Hazael of Aram came up and attacked Gath and captured
it; and Hazael proceeded to march on Jerusalem. Thereupon King Joash of
Judah took all the objects that had been consecrated by his fathers, King
Jehoshaphat, Jehoram, and Ahaziah of Judah, and by himself, and all the gold

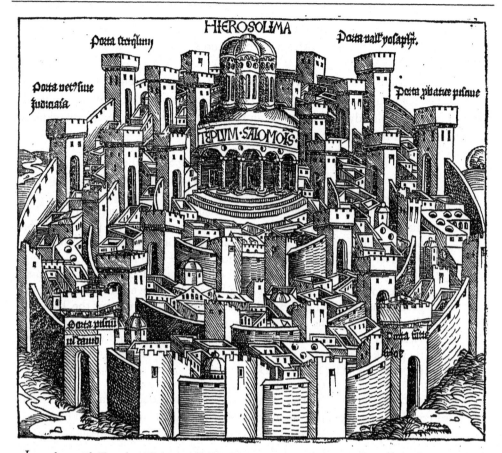

Jerusalem with Temple of Solomon, Liber Chronicorum, *Nurenberg, 1493 (Collection of the National and University Library, Jerusalem; with permission)*

that there was in the treasuries of the Temple of the Lord and in the royal palace, and he sent them to King Hazael of Aram, who then turned back from his march on Jerusalem. *(2 KINGS 12:18–19)*

Jerusalem was also attacked by its rival kingdom of Israel, which had split off in 933 B.C.E. during the reign of Solomon's son Rehoboam. Many years later, the city was plundered by King Jehoash of Israel (800–785 B.C.E.):

He marched on Jerusalem, and he made a breach of four hundred cubits in the wall of Jerusalem, from the Ephraim Gate to the Corner Gate. *(2 KINGS 14:13)*

Yet another attack came in 735 B.C.E. when Pekah, King of Israel, confederated with King Rezin of Aram to attack King Ahaz in Jerusalem, "but could not overcome [him]."

(2 Kings 16:5). Ahaz saved himself, however, by sending the treasures of Jerusalem to King Tiglath-pileser of Assyria, who in turn captured Damascus and put Rezin to death (2 Kings 16:9).

The most serious attack, however, came in 701 during the reign of King Hezekiah. In a foretaste of what was to come, Sennacherib of Assyria attacked. The northern kingdom of Israel had already been captured and its ten tribes sent into exile. Hezekiah was anxious to avoid the same fate:

> In the fourteenth year of King Hezekiah, King Sennacherib of Assyria marched against all the fortified towns of Judah and seized them. King Hezekiah sent this message to the king of Assyria at Lachish: "I have done wrong; withdraw from me; and I shall bear whatever you impose on me." So the king of Assyria imposed upon King Hezekiah of Judah a payment of three hundred talents of silver and thirty talents of gold. Hezekiah gave him all the silver that was on hand in the House of the Lord and in the treasuries of the palace. At that time Hezekiah cut down the doors and the doorposts of the Temple of the Lord, which King Hezekiah had overlaid [with gold], and gave them to the king of Assyria. But the king of Assyria sent the Tartan, the Rabsaris, and the Rabshakeh from Lachish with a large force to King Hezekiah in Jerusalem. They marched up to Jerusalem; and when they arrived, they took up a position near the conduit of the Upper Pool, by the road of the Fuller's Field. *(2 KINGS 18:13–17)*

A demand of capitulation was made which ironically included the fact that obviously the Lord could not be depended upon to defend Jerusalem, since "He is the very one whose shrines and altars Hezekiah did away with, telling Judah and Jerusalem, 'You must worship only at this altar in Jerusalem' " (2 Kings 18:22).

Hezekiah was frightened by the demand of capitulation. The prophet Isaiah, however, assured him that God was not about to abandon the city He had chosen:

He shall not enter this city:

He shall not shoot an arrow at it,

Or advance upon it with a shield,

Or pile up a siege mound against it.

He shall go back

By the way he came;

He shall not enter this city

          —declares the Lord.

I will protect and save this city for My sake,

And for the sake of My servant David.

        (2 KINGS 19:32–34)

That night the Assyrian camp was smitten by a plague, and the Assyrians were forced to retreat.

Isaiah's assurance of victory was based upon his belief in Jerusalem's special status as the city of God:

Fair Maiden Zion despises you,

She mocks at you;

Fair Jerusalem shakes

Her head at you.

Whom have your blasphemed and reviled?

Against whom made loud your voice

And haughtily raised your eyes?

Against the Holy One of Israel!

(2 KINGS 19:21–22)

David is the creator of Jerusalem, Solomon its builder, and Isaiah its prophet. It is he who personifies the city, raising it to almost mythological proportions, and proclaims its sanctity.

On the historical plane, it was Hezekiah who further improved the city. His main achievement was "how he made the pool and the conduit and brought the water into the city" (2 Kings 20:20).

The same Isaiah who assured Hezekiah that the city would be safe during his reign also predicted, however, the eventual destruction of Jerusalem by the Babylonians:

> A time is coming when everything in your palace which your ancestors have stored up to this day will be carried off to Babylon: nothing will remain behind, said the Lord. (2 KINGS 20:17)

The reason for this prophecy becomes clear during the reign of Hezekiah's son Manasseh (693–638 B.C.E.) who

> . . . rebuilt the shrines that his father Hezekiah had destroyed; he erected altars for Baal and made a sacred post, as King Ahab of Israel had done. He bowed down to all the host of heaven and worshiped them, and he built altars for them in the House of the Lord, of which the Lord had said, "I will establish My name in Jerusalem." He built altars for all the host of heaven in the two courts of the House of the Lord. He consigned his son to the fire; he practiced soothsaying and divination, and consulted ghosts and familiar spirits; he did much that was displeasing to the Lord, to vex Him. The scupltured image of Asherah that he made he placed in the House concerning which the Lord had said to David and to his son Solomon, "In this House and in Jerusalem, which I chose out of all the tribes of Israel, I will establish My name forever. . . ."

The Silwan tunnel cut by Hezekiah. September 1967 (Israel Government Press Office; with permission)

"Assuredly, thus said the Lord, the God of Israel: I am going to bring such a disaster on Jerusalem and Judah that both ears of everyone who hears it will tingle. I will apply to Jerusalem the measuring line of Samaria and the weights of the House of Ahab; I will wipe Jerusalem clean as one wipes a dish and turns it upside down. . . ."

Moreover, Manasseh put so many innocent persons to death that he filled Jerusalem [with blood] from end to end. . . . *(2 KINGS 21:3–7, 12–13, 16)*

It was during the reign of Manasseh's son, the pious Josiah (638–609 B.C.E.), that Jerusalem reached it peak. In Josiah's work of restoring the Temple, which had fallen into disrepair, a book was discovered which scholars today identify with Deuteronomy. It predicted disaster, but it also made demands that were new in regard to the centralization of the cult. As a result, Josiah carried out a sweeping religious reform in Jerusalem and throughout the country:

> Then the king ordered the high priest Hilkiah, the priests of the second rank, and the guards of the threshold to bring out of the Temple of the Lord all the objects for Baal and Asherah and all the host of heaven. He burned them outside Jerusalem in the fields of Kidron, and he removed the ashes to Bethel. . . . He also defiled Topheth, which is in the Valley of Ben-hinnom, so that no one might consign his son or daughter to the fire of Molech. He did away with the horses that the kings of Judah had dedicated to the sun at the entrance of the House of the Lord, near the chamber of the eunuch Nathan-melech, which was in the precincts. He burned the chariots of the sun. And the king tore down the altars made by the kings of Judah on the roof by the upper chamber of Ahaz, and the altars made by Manasseh in the two courts of the House of the Lord. He removed them quickly from there and scattered their rubble in the Kidron Valley. . . . *(2 KINGS 23:4–7; 10–12)*

He commanded that the Passover be observed according to the new regulations:

> Only in the eighteenth year of King Josiah was such a passover sacrifice offered in that manner to the Lord in Jerusalem. *(2 KINGS 23:23)*

After the death of Josiah in a vain stand against Pharoah Neco, Jerusalem's independence was at an end. The kings who followed became vassals of Nebuchadnezzar. The beginning of the destruction occurred when Jehoiachin rebelled in 597 B.C.E.:

> At that time the troops of King Nebuchadnezzar of Babylon marched against Jerusalem, and the city came under siege. King Nebuchadnezzar of Babylon advanced against the city while his troops were besieging it. Thereupon King Jehoiachin of Judah, along with his mother, and his courtiers, commanders, and officers, surrendered to the king of Babylon. The king of Babylon took him captive in the eighth year of his reign. He carried off from Jerusalem all the treasures of the House of the Lord and the treasures of the royal palace; he stripped off all the golden decorations in the Temple of the Lord—which King Solomon of Israel had made—as the Lord had warned. He exiled all of Jerusalem: all the commanders and all the warriors—ten thousand exiles—as well as all the craftsmen and smiths; only the poorest people in the land were left. *(2 KINGS 24:10–14)*

When his successor, Zedekiah, also rebelled, the final siege began:

> On the tenth day of the tenth month, Nebuchadnezzar moved against Jerusalem with his whole army. He besieged it; and they built towers against it all around. The city continued in a state of siege until the eleventh year of King Zedekiah. By the ninth day [of the fourth month] the famine had become acute in the city; there was no food left for the common people.

Then [the wall of] the city was breached. All the soldiers [left the city] by night through the gate between the double walls, which is near the king's garden—the Chaldeans were all around the city; and [the king] set out for the Arabah. But the Chaldean troops pursued the king, and they overtook him in the steppes of Jericho as his entire force left him and scattered. They captured the king and brought him before the king of Babylon at Riblah; and they put him on trial. They slaughtered Zedekiah's sons before his eyes; then Zedekiah's eyes were put out. He was chained in bronze fetters and he was brought to Babylon.

On the seventh day of the fifth month—that was the nineteenth year of King Nebuchadnezzar of Babylon—Nebuzaradan, the chief of the guards, an officer of the king of Babylon, came to Jerusalem. He burned the House of the Lord, the king's palace, and all the houses of Jerusalem; he burned down the house of every notable person. The entire Chaldean force that was with the chief of the guard tore down the walls of Jerusalem on every side. The remnants of the people that was left in the city, the defectors who had gone over to the king of Babylon—and the remnant of the population—were taken into exile by Nebuzaradan, the chief of the guards. But some of the poorest in the land were left by the chief of the guards, to be vinedressers and field hands.

The Chaldeans broke up the bronze columns of the House of the Lord, the stands, and the bronze tank that was in the House of the Lord; and they carried the bronze away to Babylon. They also took all the pails, scrapers, snuffers, ladles, and all the other bronze vessels used in the service. The chief of the guards took whatever was of gold and whatever was of silver: fire pans and sprinkling bowls. The two columns, the one tank, and the stands which Solomon provided for the House of the Lord—all these objects contained bronze beyond weighing. The one column was eighteen cubits high. It had a bronze capital above it; the height of the capital was three cubits, and there was a meshwork [decorated] with pomegranates about the capital, all made of bronze. And the like was true of the other column with its meshwork. *(2 KINGS 25:1–17)*

Thus was the Jerusalem of the First Temple period destroyed in 586 B.C.E.

The Biblical historical account of Jerusalem continues some seventy years later when Cyrus of Persia, now the ruler of Babylonia, issues a decree permitting a return to Jerusalem:

In the first year of King Cyrus of Persia, when the word of the Lord spoken by Jeremiah was fulfilled, the Lord roused the spirit of King Cyrus of Persia to issue a proclamation throughout his realm by word of mouth and in writing as follows:

"Thus said King Cyrus of Persia: The Lord God of Heaven has given me all the kingdoms of the earth and has charged me with building Him a house in Jerusalem, which is in Judah. Anyone of you of all His people—may his God be with him, and let him go up to Jerusalem that is in Judah and build the House of the Lord God of Israel, the God that is in Jerusalem; and all who

The Broad Wall, built at the end of the First Temple period, uncovered in the Jewish Quarter; looking northeast (Ancient Jerusalem Revealed. Israel Exploration Society; with permission)

stay behind, wherever he may be living, let the people of his place assist him with silver, gold, goods, and livestock, beside the freewill offering to the House of God that is in Jerusalem." *(EZRA 1:1–3)*

Those who returned commenced the work of re-establishing Jerusalem and its institutions:

When the seventh month arrived—the Israelites being settled in their towns —the entire people assembled as one man in Jerusalem. Then Jeshua son of Jozadak and his brother priests, and Zerubbabel son of Shealtiel and his brothers set to and built the altar of the God of Israel to offer burnt offerings upon

it as is written in the Teaching of Moses, the man of God. They set up the altar on its site because they were in fear of the peoples of the land, and they
offered burnt offerings on it to the Lord, burnt offerings each morning and
evening. Then they celebrated the festival of Tabernacles as is written. . . .
From the first day of the seventh month they began to make burnt offerings
to the Lord, though the foundation of the Temple of the Lord had not been
laid. . . .

When the builders had laid the foundation of the Temple of the Lord,
priests in their vestments with trumpets, and Levites sons of Asaph with cymbals were stationed to give praise to the Lord, as King David of Israel had ordained. They sang songs extolling and praising the Lord, "For He is good, His
steadfast love for Israel is eternal." All the people raised a great shout extolling the Lord because the foundation of the House of the Lord had been
laid. Many of the priests and Levites and the chiefs of the clans, the old men
who had seen the first house, wept loudly at the sight of the founding of this
house. Many others shouted joyously at the top of their voices. The people
could not distinguish the shouts of joy from the people's weeping, for the people raised a great shout, the sound of which could be heard from afar. (EZRA
3:1–4, 6, 10–13)

After much tribulation, the house was finally finished—

. . . on the third of the month of Adar in the sixth year of the reign of King
Darius. The Israelites, the priests, and the Levites, and all the other exiles celebrated the dedication of the House of God with joy. (EZRA 6:15–16)

The condition of the city itself, however, remained poor:

The narrative of Nehemiah son of Hacaliah:
In the month of Kislev of the twentieth year, when I was in the fortress of
Shushan, Hanani, one of my brothers, together with some men of Judah, ar-
rived, and I asked them about the Jews, the remnant who had survived the
captivity, and about Jerusalem. They replied, "The survivors who have sur-
vived the captivity there in the province are in dire trouble and disgrace;
Jerusalem's wall is full of breaches, and its gates have been destroyed by fire."
(NEH. 1:1–3)

Nehemiah, the king's cupbearer, appealed to Artaxerxes:

I answered the king, "May the king live forever! How should I not look bad
when the city of the graveyard of my ancestors lies in ruins, and its gates have
been consumed by fire?" The king said to me, "What is your request?" With a
prayer to the God of Heaven, I answered the king, "If it please the king, and
if your servant has found favor with you, send me to Judah, to the city of my
ancestors' graves, to rebuild it." (NEH.2:3–5)

Receiving permission, he left for Jerusalem:

I arrived in Jerusalem. After I was there three days I got up at night, I and a
few men with me, and telling no one what my God had put into my mind

to do for Jerusalem, and taking no other beast than the one on which I was riding, I went out by the Valley Gate, at night, toward the Jackals' Spring and the Dung Gate; and I surveyed the walls of Jerusalem that were breached and its gates, consumed by fire. I proceeded to the Fountain Gate and to the King's Pool, where there was no room for the beast under me to continue. So I went up the wadi by night, surveying the wall, and, entering again by the Valley Gate, I returned. The prefects knew nothing of where I had gone or what I had done, since I had not yet divulged it to the Jews—the priests, the nobles, the prefects, or the rest of the officials.

Then I said to them, "You see the bad state we are in—Jerusalem lying in ruins and its gates destroyed by fire. Come, let us rebuild the wall of Jerusalem and suffer no more disgrace." (NEH. 2:11–17)

Against active opposition from the Samaritans, the rebuilding of the walls began:

And they all conspired together to come and fight against Jerusalem and to throw it into confusion. Because of them we prayed to our God, and set up a watch over them day and night. . . .

From that day on, half my servants did work and half held lances and shields, bows and armor. And the officers stood behind the whole house of Judah who were rebuilding the wall. The basket-carriers were burdened, doing work with one hand while the other held a weapon. As for the builders, each had his sword girded at his side as he was building. The trumpeter stood beside me. I said to the nobles, the prefects, and the rest of the people, "There is much work and it is spread out; we are scattered over the wall, far from one another. When you hear a trumpet call, gather yourselves to me at that place; our God will fight for us!" And so we worked on, while half were holding lances, from the break of day until the stars appeared.

I further said to the people at that time, "Let every man with his servant lodge in Jerusalem, that we may use the night to stand guard and the day to work." Nor did I, my brothers, my servants, or the guards following me ever take off our clothes, [or] each his weapon, even at the water. . . .

When the wall was rebuilt and I had set up the doors, tasks were assigned to the gatekeepers, the singers, and the Levites. I put Hanani my brother and Hananiah, the captain of the fortress, in charge of Jerusalem, for he was a more trustworthy and God-fearing man than most. I said to them, "The gates of Jerusalem are not to be opened until the heat of the day, and before you leave your posts let the doors be closed and barred. And assign the inhabitants of Jerusalem to watches, each man to his watch, and each in front of his own house."

The city was broad and large, the people in it were few, and houses were not yet built. (NEH. 4:2–3, 10–17; 7:1–4)

The feelings of the time may best be gauged by the praise lauded upon those who chose to live there:

The officers of the people settled in Jerusalem; the rest of the people cast lots for one out of ten to come and settle in the holy city of Jerusalem, and the

other nine-tenths to stay in the towns. The people gave their blessing to all
the men who willingly settled in Jerusalem. *(NEH. 11:1–2)*

Beyond this point, the historical books of the Bible offer us no information about
Jerusalem in the days of the Second Temple.

THE PROPHETS

The sacredness of Jerusalem is taken for granted by the prophets. As a result, it is both
held to a high standard of morality, and therefore denounced for its failings, and lauded
as the sacred city of God. As the major city of the kingdom of Judah and as its religious
center, Jerusalem was often singled out for denunciation by the prophets because of the
lack of morality of its leaders and many of its inhabitants. The eighth-century prophet
Micah saw how the doctrine of God's dwelling in Jerusalem led to false assumptions
concerning the city's status and indestructibility:

Because of this I will lament and wail;

I will go stripped and naked!

I will lament as sadly as the jackals,

As mournfully as the ostriches.

For her wound in incurable,

It has reached Judah,

It has spread to the gate of my people, to Jerusalem.

(MICAH 1:8–9)

Disaster from the Lord descended

Upon the gate of Jerusalem.

Hitch the steeds to the chariot,

Inhabitant of Lachish!

It is the beginning

Of Fair Zion's guilt;

Israel's transgressions

Can be traced to you!

(MICAH 1:12–13)

Hear this, you rulers of the House of Jacob,

You chiefs of the House of Israel,

Who detest justice
And make crooked all that is straight,
Who build Zion with crime,
Jerusalem with iniquity!
Her rulers judge for gifts,
Her priests give rulings for a fee,
And her prophets divine for pay;
Yet they rely upon the Lord, saying,
"The Lord is in our midst;
No calamity shall overtake us."
Assuredly, because of you
Zion shall be plowed as a field,
And Jerusalem shall become heaps of ruins,
And the Temple Mount
A shrine in the woods.

(MICAH 3:9–12)

His contemporary, First Isaiah, spoke in a similar condemnatory vein, going so far as to compare Jerusalem with the cities that had come to represent total degredation:

Fair Zion is left
Like a booth in a vineyard,
Like a hut in a cucumber field,
Like a city beleaguered.
Had not the Lord of Hosts
Left us some survivors,
We should be like Sodom,
Another Gomorrah.

Hear the words of the Lord,
You chieftains of Sodom;
Give ear to our God's instruction,
You folk of Gomorrah!
"What need have I of all your sacrifices?"
Says the Lord.

I am sated with burnt offerings of rams,
And suet of fatlings,
And blood of bulls;
And I have no delight
In lambs and he-goats.
That you come to appear before Me—
Who asked that of you?
Trample My courts no more;
Bringing oblations is futile,
Incense is offensive to Me.
New moon and sabbath,
Proclaiming of solemnities,
Assemblies with iniquity,
I cannot abide.
Your new moons and fixed seasons
Fill Me with loathing;
They are become a burden to Me,
I cannot endure them.

(ISA. 1:8–14)

Alas, she has become a harlot,
The faithful city
That was filled with justice,
Where righteousness dwelt—
But now murderers.
Your silver has turned to dross;
Your wine is cut with water.
Your rulers are rogues
And cronies of thieves,
Every one avid for presents
And greedy for gifts;
They do not judge the case of the orphan,
And the widow's cause never reaches them.

(ISA. 1:21–23)

Ah, Jerusalem has stumbled,
And Judah has fallen,
Because by word and deed
They insult the Lord,
Defying His majestic glance.
Their partiality in judgment accuses them;
They avow their sins like Sodom,
They do not conceal them.
Woe to them! For ill
Have they served themselves.

(ISA. 3:8–9)

The Lord said:
"Because the daughters of Zion
Are so vain
And walk with heads thrown back,
With roving eyes,
And with mincing gait,
Making a tinkling with their feet"—
My Lord will bare the pates
Of the daughters of Zion,
The Lord will uncover their heads.

(ISA. 3:16–17)

Using his poetic name for Jerusalem—Ariel, the lion of God—Isaiah predicts terrible war against the city:

"Ah, Ariel, Ariel,
City where David camped!
Add year to year,
Let festivals come in their cycles!
And I will harass Ariel,
And there shall be sorrow and sighing.
She shall be to Me like Ariel,
And I will camp against you round about;

I will lay siege to you with a mound,

And I will set up siegeworks against you.

And you shall speak from lower then the ground,

Your speech shall be humbler than the sod;

Your speech shall sound like a ghost's from the ground,

Your voice shall chirp from the sod.

And like fine dust shall be

The multitude of your strangers;

And like flying chaff,

The multitude of tyrants."

And suddenly, in an instant,

She shall be remembered of the Lord of Hosts

With roaring, and shaking, and deafening noise,

Storm, and tempest, and blaze of consuming fire.

Then, like a dream, a vision of the night,

Shall be the multitude of nations

That war upon Ariel,

And all her besiegers, and the siegeworks against her,

And those who harass her.

Like one who is hungry

And dreams he is eating,

But wakes to find himself empty;

And like one who is thirsty

And dreams he is drinking,

But wakes to find himself faint

And utterly parched—

So shall be all the multitude of nations

That war upon Mount Zion.

(ISA. 29:1–8)

Jeremiah, who began to prophecy in 625 B.C.E., some eighty years after Isaiah had begun his work, similarly denounced the wickedness of the city and called for repentance:

For thus said the Lord to the men of Judah and to Jerusalem:

Break up the untilled ground,
And do not sow among the thorns.
Open your hearts to the Lord,
Remove the thickening about your hearts—
O men of Judah and inhabitants of Jerusalem—
Lest My wrath break forth like fire,
And burn, with none to quench it,
Because of your wicked acts.

Proclaim in Judah,
Announce in Jerusalem,
And say:
"Blow the horn in the land!"
Shout aloud and say:
"Assemble, and let us go
Into the fortified cities!"
Set up a signpost: To Zion.
Take refuge, do not delay!
For I bring evil from the north,
And great disaster.

                              (JER. 4:3–6)

Roam the streets of Jerusalem,
Search its squares,
Look about and take note:
You will not find a man,
There is none who acts justly,
Who seeks integrity—
That I should pardon her.

              (JER. 5:1–2)

Why is this people—Jerusalem—rebellious
With a persistent rebellion?
They cling to deceit,
They refuse to return.
I have listened and heard:

They do not speak honestly.
No one regrets his wickedness
And says, "What have I done!"
They all persist in their wayward course
Like a steed dashing forward in the fray.

(JER. 8:5–6)

This shall be your lot,
Your measured portion from Me

—declares the Lord.

Because you forgot Me
And trusted in falsehood,
I in turn will lift your skirts over your face
And your shame shall be seen.
I behold your adulteries,
Your lustful neighing,
Your unbridled depravity, your vile acts
On the hills of the countryside.
Woe to you, O Jerusalem,
Who will not be clean!
How much longer shall it be?

(JER. 13:25–27)

But what I see in the prophets of Jerusalem
Is something horrifying:
Adultery and false dealing.
They encourage evildoers,
So that no one turns back from his wickedness.
To me they are all like Sodom
And [all] its inhabitants like Gomorrah.

(JER. 23:14–15)

Unlike Isaiah, Jeremiah has no message of immediate salvation. Where Isaiah had predicted that a siege against Jerusalem would not succeed, Jeremiah proclaims its coming destruction. Only a complete change of heart could possibly avert disaster.

Flee for refuge, O people of Benjamin,

Out of the midst of Jerusalem!

Blow the horn in Tekoa,

Set up a signal at Beth-haccherem!

For evil is appearing from the north,

And great disaster.

Fair Zion, the lovely and delicate,

I will destroy.

(JER. 6:1–2)

Even the Temple of the Lord, Jerusalem's glory, is to Jeremiah nothing more than a den of thieves. Standing at the very site, he delivers a scathing oration:

> Hear the word of the Lord, all you of Judah who enter these gates to worship the Lord!
>
> Thus said the Lord of Hosts, the God of Israel: Mend your ways and your actions, and I will let you dwell in this place. Don't put your trust in illusions and say, "The Temple of the Lord, the Temple of the Lord, the Temple of the Lord are these [buildings]." . . . Will you steal and murder and commit adultery and swear falsely, and sacrifice to Baal, and follow other gods who you have not experienced, and then come and stand before Me in this House which bears My name and say, "We are safe?"—[Safe] to do all these abhorrent things! Do you consider this House, which bears My name, to be a den of thieves? As for Me, I have been watching—declares the Lord.
>
> Just go to My place at Shiloh, where I had established My name formerly, and see what I did to it because of the wickedness of My people Israel. And now, because you do all these things—declares the Lord—and though I spoke to you persistently, you would not listen; and though I called to you, you would not respond—therefore I will do to the House which bears My name, on which you rely, and to the place which I gave you and your fathers just what I did to Shiloh. And I will cast you out of My presence as I cast out your brothers, the whole brood of Ephraim.
>
> As for you, do not pray for this people, do not raise a cry of prayer on their behalf, do not plead with Me; for I will not listen to you. Don't you see what they are doing in the towns of Judah and in the streets of Jerusalem? The children gather sticks, the fathers build the fire, and the mothers knead dough, to make cakes for the Queen of Heaven, and they pour out libations to other gods, to vex Me. . . . They have set up their abominations in the House which is called by My name, and they have defiled it. And they have built the shrines of Topheth in the Valley of Ben-hinnom to burn their sons and daughters in fire—which I never commanded, which never came to My mind.
>
> Assuredly, a time is coming—declares the Lord—when men shall no longer speak of Topheth or the Valley of Ben-hinnom, but of the Valley of Slaugh-

ter; and they shall bury in Topheth until no room is left. The carcasses of this people shall be food for the birds of the sky and the beasts of the earth, with none to frighten them off. And I will silence in the towns of Judah and the streets of Jerusalem the sound of mirth and gladness, the voice of bridegroom and bride. For the whole land shall fall to ruin. (JER. 7:2–4, 9–18, 30–34)

Ezekiel, who was with the exiles in Babylonia even before the destruction of Jerusalem in 586 B.C.E., also prophesied the ruin of Jerusalem, albeit in a very different style:

Thus said the Lord God: I set this Jerusalem in the midst of nations, with countries round about her. But she rebelled against My rules and My laws, acting more wickedly than the nations and the countries round about her; she rejected My rules and disobeyed My laws. Assuredly, thus said the Lord God: Because you have outdone the nations that are round about you—you have not obeyed My laws nor followed My rules, nor have you observed the rules of the nations round about you—assuredly, thus said the Lord God: I, in turn, am going to deal with you, and I will execute judgments in your midst in the sight of the nations. On account of all your abominations, I will do among you what I have never done, and the like of which I will never do again. (EZEK. 5:5–9)

In one of his mystic visions, Ezekiel sees God calling to "men in charge of the city," divine creatures charged with the destruction of Jerusalem, and instructing one of them to mark those few who will be spared in the coming destruction:

And the Lord said to him, "Pass through the city, through Jerusalem, and put a mark on the foreheads of the men who moan and groan because of all the abominations that are committed in it." To the others He said in my hearing, "Follow him through the city and strike; sow no pity or compassion. Kill off graybeard, youth and maiden, women and children; but do not touch any person who bears the mark. Begin here at My Sanctuary." So they began with the elders who were in front of the House. And He said to them, "Defile the House and fill the courts with the slain. Then go forth." So they went forth and began to kill in the city. When they were out killing, and I remained alone, I flung myself on my face and cried out, "Ah, Lord God! Are you going to annihilate all that is left of Israel, pouring out Your fury upon Jerusalem?" He answered me, "The iniquity of the Houses of Judah and Israel is very very great, the land is full of crime and the city is full of corruption. For they say, 'The Lord has forsaken the land, and the Lord does not see.' I, in turn, will show no pity or compassion; I will give them their deserts." (EZEK. 9:4–11)

Assuredly, thus said the Lord God: Like the wood of the grapevine among the trees of the forest, which I have designated to be fuel for fire, so will I treat the inhabitants of Jerusalem. I will set My face against them; they escaped from fire, but fire shall consume them. When I set my face against them, you shall know that I am the Lord. I will make the land a desolation, because they committed trespass—declares the Lord God. (EZEK. 15:6–8)

The word of the Lord came to me: Further, O mortal, arraign, arraign the city of bloodshed; declare to her all her abhorrent deeds! Say: Thus said the Lord God: O city in whose midst blood is shed, so that your hour is approaching; within which fetishes are made, so that you have become unclean! You stand guilty of the blood you have shed, defiled by the fetishes you have made. You have brought on your day; you have reached your year. Therefore I will make you the mockery of the nations and the scorn of all the lands. Both the near and the far shall scorn you, O besmirched of name, O laden with iniquity! *(Ezek. 22:1–5)*

His extensive and elaborate parable of Jerusalem as an unfaithful woman, which occupies the entire sixteenth chapter, is perhaps the most devastating of all the prophetic denunciations:

The word of the Lord came to me: O mortal, proclaim Jerusalem's abominations to her, and say: Thus said the Lord God to Jerusalem: By origin and birth you are from the land of the Canaanites—your father was an Amorite and your mother a Hittite. As for your birth, when you were born your navel cord was not cut, and you were not bathed in water to smooth you; you were not rubbed with salt, nor were you swaddled. No one pitied you enough to do any one of these things for you out of compassion for you; on the day you were born, you were left lying, rejected, in the open field. When I passed by you and saw you wallowing in your blood, I said to you: "Live in spite of your blood." Yea, I said to you, "Live in spite of your blood." I let you grow like the plants of the field; and you continued to grow until you attained to womanhood, until your breasts became firm and your hair sprouted.

You were still naked and bare when I passed by you [again] and saw that your time for love had arrived. So I spread My robe over you and covered your nakedness, and I entered into a covenant with you by oath—declares the Lord God; thus you became Mine. I bathed you in water, and washed the blood off you and anointed you with oil. I clothed you with embroidered garments, and gave you sandals of *taḥash*-leather to wear, and wound fine linen about your head, and dressed you in silks. I decked you out in finery and put bracelets on your arms and a chain around your neck. I put a ring in your nose, and earrings in your ears, and a splendid crown on your head. You adorned yourself with gold and silver, and your apparel was of fine linen, silk, and embroidery. Your food was choice flour, honey, and oil. You grew more and more beautiful, and became fit for royalty. Your beauty won you fame among the nations, for it was perfected through the splendor which I set upon you—declares the Lord God.

But confident in your beauty and fame, you played the harlot: you lavished your favors on every passerby; they were his. . . .

I will inflict upon you the punishment of women who commit adultery and murder, and I will direct bloody and impassioned fury against you. I will deliver you into their hands, and they shall tear down your eminence and level your mounds; and they shall strip you of your clothing and take away your dazzling jewels, leaving you naked and bare. Then they shall assemble a mob against you to pelt you with stones and pierce you with their swords. They shall put your houses to the flames and execute punishment upon you in the sight of many women; thus I will put a stop to your harlotry, and you shall pay no more fees. When I have satisfied My fury upon you and My rage has departed from you, then I will be tranquil; I will be angry no more. (EZEK. 16:1–15, 38–42)

See also Ezekiel 23.

These same prophets forsee a wonderful future for Jerusalem after it has been punished:

In the days to come,
The Mount of the Lord's House shall stand
Firm above the mountains;
And it shall tower above the hills.
The peoples shall gaze upon it with joy,
And many nations shall go and shall say:
"Come,
Let us go up to the Mount of the Lord,
To the House of the God of Jacob;
That He may instruct us in His ways,
And that we may walk in His paths."
For instruction shall come forth from Zion,
The word of the Lord from Jerusalem.
Thus He will judge among the many peoples,
And arbitrate for the multitude of nations,
However distant;
And they shall beat their swords into plowshares
And their spears into pruning hooks.
Nations shall not take up
Sword against nation;
They shall never again know war;
But every man shall sit
Under his grapevine or fig tree
With no one to disturb him.
For it was the Lord of Hosts who spoke.

(MICAH 4:1–4)

This prophecy is also found in First Isaiah, 2:2–4, who above all abounds in pictures of the glorious future of Jerusalem:

"I will restore your magistrates as of old,

And your counselors as of yore.

After that you shall be called

City of Righteousness, Faithful city."

Zion shall be saved by justice,

Her repentant ones, by righteousness.

(ISA. 1:26–27)

O mount of Fair Zion!

O hill of Jerusalem!

Lo! The Sovereign Lord of Hosts

Will hew off the tree-crowns with an ax:

The tall ones shall be felled,

The lofty ones cut down:

The thickets of the forest shall be hacked away with iron,

And the Lebanon trees shall fall in their majesty.

But a shoot shall grow out of the stump of Jesse,

A twig shall sprout from his stock.

The spirit of the Lord shall alight upon him:

A spirit of wisdom and insight,

A spirit of counsel and valor,

A spirit of devotion and reverence for the Lord.

(ISA. 10:32–11:2)

The Lord is exalted,

He dwells on high!

[Of old] He filled Zion

With justice and righteousness.

Faithfulness to Your charge was [her] wealth,

Wisdom and devotion [her] triumph,

Reverence for the Lord—that was her treasure.

(ISA. 33:5–6)

When you gaze upon Zion, our city of assembly,

Your eyes shall behold Jerusalem

As a secure homestead,

A tent not to be transported,

Whose pegs shall never be pulled up,

And none of whose ropes shall break.

For there the Lord in His greatness shall be for us

Like a region of rivers, of broad streams,

Where no floating vessels can sail

And no mighty craft can travel—

Their ropes are slack,

They cannot steady the sockets of their masts,

They cannot spread a sail.

For the Lord shall be our ruler, The Lord shall be our prince,

The Lord shall be our king:

He shall deliver us.

Then shall indeed much spoil be divided,

Even the lame shall seize booty.

And none who lives there shall say, "I am sick";

It shall be inhabited by folk whose sin has been forgiven.

(ISA. 33:20–24)

And a highway shall appear there,

Which shall be called the Sacred Way.

No one unclean shall pass along it,

But it shall be for them.

No traveler, not even fools, shall go astray.

No lion shall be there,

No ferocious beast shall set foot on it—

These shall not be found there.

But the redeemed shall walk it;

And the ransomed of the Lord shall return,

And come with shouting to Zion,

Crowned with joy everlasting.

They shall attain joy and gladness,
While sorrow and sighing flee.

(ISA. 35:8–10)

It was Isaiah too who assured King Hezekiah that the king of Assyria would not succeed in invading Jerusalem:

For a remnant shall come forth from Jerusalem,
Survivors from Mount Zion.
The zeal of the Lord of Hosts
Shall bring this to pass.

Assuredly, thus said the Lord concerning the king of Assyria:
He shall not enter this city;
He shall not shoot an arrow at it,
Or advance upon it with a shield,
Or pile up a siege mound against it.
He shall go back
By the way he came,
He shall not enter this city

—declares the Lord;

I will protect and save this city for My sake
And for the sake of My servant David.

(ISA. 37:32–35)

Jeremiah and Ezekiel also forsaw an eventual restoration. Even those who had denounced so completely believed that after the destruction there would be an everlasting rebuilding:

For the day is coming when watchmen
Shall proclaim on the heights of Ephraim:
Come, let us go up to Zion,
To the Lord our God! . . .
For the Lord will ransom Jacob,
Redeem him from one too strong for him.
They shall come and shout on the heights of Zion,

Radiant over the bounty of the Lord—

Over new grain and wine and oil,

And over sheep and cattle.

They shall fare like a watered garden,

They shall never languish again.

Then shall maidens dance gaily,

Young men and old alike.

I will turn their mourning to joy,

I will comfort them and cheer them in their grief.

I will give the priests their fill of fatness,

And my people shall enjoy My full bounty

—declares the Lord.

(JER. 31:6, 12–14)

> But now, assuredly, thus said the Lord, the God of Israel, concerning this city of which you say, "It is being delivered into the hands of the king of Babylon through the sword, through famine, and through pestilence": See, I will gather them from all the lands to which I have banished them in My anger and wrath, and in great rage; and I will bring them back to this place and let them dwell secure. . . . Thus said the Lord: Again there shall be heard in this place, which you say is ruined, without man or beast—in the towns of Judah and the streets of Jerusalem that are desolate, without man, without inhabitants, without beast—the sound of mirth and gladness, the voice of bridegroom and bride, the voice of those who cry, "Give thanks to the Lord of Hosts, for the Lord is good, for His kindness is everlasting!" as they bring thanksgiving offerings to the House of the Lord. . . . (JER. 32:36–37; 33:10–11)

So, too, Ezekiel:

> Truly, thus said the Lord God: I will deal with you as you have dealt, for you have spurned the pact and violated the covenant. Nevertheless, I will remember the covevant I made with you in the days of your youth, and I will establish it with you as an everlasting covenant. You shall remember your ways and feel ashamed, when you receive your older sisters and your younger sisters, and I give them to you as daughters, though they are not of your covenant. I will establish My covenant with you, and you shall know I am the Lord. Thus you shall remember and feel shame, and you shall be too abashed to open your mouth again, when I have forgiven you for all that you did—declares the Lord God. (EZEK. 16:59–63)

The prophet who wrote most extensively and exclusively in praise of Jerusalem was the anonymous prophet whose work is found in the book of Isaiah, beginning with chapter

40. Commonly referred to as Second Isaiah, he lived in the Babylonian exile and mourned the state of destruction:

Your holy cities have become a desert:
Zion has become a desert,
Jerusalem a desolation.
Our holy Temple, our pride,
Where our fathers praised You,
Has been consumed by fire:
And all that was dear to us is ruined.

> (ISA. 64:9–10)

and foresaw the coming restoration:

Comfort, oh comfort My people,
Says your God.
Speak tenderly to Jerusalem,
And declare to her
That her term of service of over,
That her iniquity is expiated;
For she has received at the hand of the Lord
Double for all her sins.

> (ISA. 40:1–2)

Ascend a lofty mountain,
O herald of joy to Zion;
Raise your voice with power,
O herald of joy to Jerusalem—
Raise it, have no fear;
Announce to the cities of Judah:
Behold your God!

> (ISA. 40:9)

But confirm the word of My servant
And fulfill the prediction of My messengers.
It is I who say of Jerusalem, "It shall be inhabited,"

And of the towns of Judah, "They shall be rebuilt;
And I will restore their ruined places."
[I], who said to the deep, "Be dry;
I will dry up your floods,"
Am the same who says of Cyrus, "He is My shepherd;
He shall fulfill all My purposes!
He shall say of Jerusalem, 'She shall be rebuilt,'
And to the Temple: 'You shall be founded again.' "

(ISA. 44:26–28)

Zion says,
"The Lord has forsaken me.
My Lord has forgotten me."
Can a woman forget her baby,
Or disown the child of her womb?
Though she might forget,
I never could forget you.
See, I have engraved you
On the palms of My hands,
Your walls are ever before Me.
Swiftly your children are coming;
Those who ravaged and ruined you shall leave you.
Look up all around you and see:
They are all assembled, are come to you!
As I live

—declared the Lord —

You shall don them all like jewels,
Deck yourself with them like a bride.
As for your ruins and desolate places
And your land laid waste—
You shall soon be crowded with settlers,
While destroyers stay far from you.
The children you thought you had lost
Shall yet say in your hearing,

"This place is too crowded for me;
Make room for me to settle."

(ISA. 49:14–20)

Truly the Lord has comforted Zion,
Comforted all her ruins;
He has made her wilderness like Eden,
Her desert like the Garden of the Lord.
Gladness and joy shall abide there,
Thanksgiving and the sound of music.

(ISA. 51:3)

So let the ransomed of the Lord return,
And come with shouting to Zion,
Crowned with joy everlasting.
Let them attain joy and gladness,
While sorrow and sighing flee.

(ISA. 51:11)

I, who planted the skies and made firm the earth,
Have said to Zion: You are My people!
Rouse, rouse yourself!
Arise, O Jerusalem,
You who from the Lord's hand
Have drunk the cup of His wrath,
You who have drained to the dregs
The bowl, the cup of reeling!

(ISA. 51:16–17)

Awake, awake, O Zion!
Clothe yourself in splendor;
Put on your robes of majesty,
Jerusalem, holy city!
For the uncircumcised and the unclean
Shall never enter you again.
Arise, shake off the dust,
Sit [on your throne], Jerusalem!

Loose the bonds from your neck,

O captive one, Fair Zion!

(ISA. 52:1–2)

How welcome on the mountain

Are the footsteps of the herald

Announcing happiness,

Heralding good fortune,

Announcing victory,

Telling Zion, "Your God is King!"

Hark!

Your watchmen raise their voices,

As one they shout for joy;

For every eye shall behold

The Lord's return to Zion.

Raise a shout together,

O ruins of Jerusalem!

For the Lord will comfort His people,

Will redeem Jerusalem.

The Lord will bare His holy arm

In the sight of all the nations,

And the very ends of the earth shall see

The victory of our God.

(ISA. 52:7–10)

Unhappy, storm-tossed one, uncomforted!

I will lay carbuncles as your building stones

And make your foundations of sapphires.

I will make your battlements of rubies,

Your gates of precious stones,

The whole encircling wall of gems.

And all your children shall be disciples of the Lord,

And great shall be the happiness of your children.

You shall be established through righteousness.

You shall be safe from oppression,

And shall have no fear;

From ruin, and it shall not come near you.

(ISA. 54:11–14)

Arise, shine, for your light has dawned;

The Presence of the Lord has shone upon you!

Behold! Darkness shall cover the earth,

And thick clouds the peoples;

But upon you the Lord will shine,

And His Presence be seen over you.

And nations shall walk by your light;

Kings, by your shining radiance.

Raise your eyes and look about:

They have all gathered and come to you.

Your sons shall be brought from afar,

Your daughters like babes on shoulders.

As you behold, you will glow;

Your heart will throb and thrill—

For the wealth of the sea shall pass on to you,

The riches of nations shall flow to you. . . .

(ISA. 60:1–5)

Aliens shall rebuild your walls,

Their kings shall wait upon you—

For in anger I struck you down,

But in favor I take you back.

Your gates shall always stay open—

Day and night they shall never be shut—

To let in the wealth of the nations,

With their kings in procession.

For the nation or the kingdom

That does not serve you shall perish;

Such nations shall be destroyed.

The majesty of Lebanon shall come to you—

Cypress and pine and box—

To adorn the site of My Sanctuary,
To glorify the place where My feet rest.

Bowing before you, shall come
The children of those who tormented you;
Prostrate at the soles of your feet
Shall be all those who reviled you;
And you shall be called
"City of the Lord,
Zion of the Holy One of Israel."
Whereas you have been forsaken,
Rejected, with none passing through,
I will make you a pride everlasting,
A joy for age after age.
You shall suck the milk of the nations,
Suckle at royal breasts.
And you shall know
That I the Lord am your Savior,
I, The Mighty One of Jacob, am your redeemer.
Instead of copper I will bring gold,
Instead of iron I will bring silver;
Instead of wood, copper;
And instead of stone, iron.
And I will appoint Well-being as your government,
Prosperity as your officials.
The cry "Violence!"
Shall no more be heard in your land,
Nor "Wrack and ruin!"
Within your borders.
And you shall name your walls "Victory"
And your gates "Renown."

(ISA. 60:10–18)

For the sake of Zion I will not be silent,
For the sake of Jerusalem I will not be still,

Till her victory emerge resplendent

And her triumph like a flaming torch.

Nations shall see your victory,

And every king your majesty;

And you shall be called by a new name

Which the Lord Himself shall bestow.

You shall be a glorious crown

In the hand of the Lord,

And a royal diadem

In the palm of your God.

Nevermore shall you be called "Forsaken,"

Nor shall your land be called "Desolate";

But you shall be called "I delight in her,"

And your land "Espoused."

For the Lord takes delight in you,

And your land shall be espoused.

As a youth espouses a maiden

Your sons shall espouse you;

And as a bridegroom rejoices over his bride,

So will your God rejoice over you.

Upon your walls, O Jerusalem,

I have set watchmen,

Who shall never be silent

By day or by night.

O you, the Lord's remembrancers,

Take no rest

And give no rest to Him,

Until He establish Jerusalem

And make her renowned on earth.

(ISA. 62:1–7)

For behold! I am creating

A new heaven and a new earth;

The former things shall not be remembered,

They shall never come to mind.

Be glad, then, and rejoice forever

In what I am creating.

For I shall create Jerusalem as a joy,

And her people as a delight;

And I will rejoice in Jerusalem

And delight in her people.

Never again shall be heard there

The sounds of weeping and wailing.

No more shall there be an infant or a graybeard

Who does not live out his days.

He who dies at a hundred years

Shall be reckoned a youth,

And he who fails to reach a hundred

Shall be reckoned accursed.

They shall build houses and dwell in them,

They shall plant vineyards and enjoy their fruit.

(ISA. 65:17–21)

Who ever heard the like?

Who ever witnessed such events?

Can a land pass through travail

In a single day?

Or is a nation born

All at once?

Yet Zion travailed

And at once bore her children!

Shall I who bring on labor not bring about birth?

—says the Lord.

Shall I who cause birth shut the womb?

—said your God.

Rejoice with Jerusalem and be glad for her,

All you who love her!

Join in her jubilation,

All you who mourned over her—

That you may suck from her breast

Consolation to the full,

That you may draw from her bosom

Glory to your delight.

For thus said the Lord:

I will extend to her

Prosperity like a stream,

The wealth of nations

Like a wadi in flood;

And you shall drink of it.

You shall be carried on shoulders

And dandled upon knees.

As a mother comforts her son

So I will comfort you;

You shall find comfort in Jerusalem.

(ISA. 66:8–13)

The post-exilic prophet Zechariah was concerned largely with the return of the exiles and the rebuilding of Jerusalem:

> Then the angel who talked with me said to me: "Proclaim! Thus said the Lord of Hosts: I am very jealous for Jerusalem—for Zion—and I am very angry with those nations that are at ease; for I was only angry a little, but they overdid the punishment. Assuredly, thus said the Lord: I graciously return to Jerusalem. My House shall be built in her—declares the Lord of Hosts—the measuring line is being applied to Jerusalem. Proclaim further: Thus said the Lord of Hosts: My towns shall yet overflow with bounty. For the Lord will again comfort Zion; He will choose Jerusalem again." (ZECH. 1:14–17)

> I looked up, and I saw a man holding a measuring line. "Where are you going?" I asked. "To measure Jerusalem," he replied, "to see how long and wide it is to be." But the angel who talked with me came forward, and another angel came forward to meet him. The former said to him, "Run to that young man and tell him:
> "Jerusalem shall be peopled as a city without walls, so many shall be the men and cattle it contains. And I Myself—declares the Lord—will be a wall of fire around it, and I will be a glory inside it.
> "Away, away! Flee from the land of the north—says the Lord—though I swept you [there] like the four winds of heaven—declares the Lord."

Away, escape, O Zion, you who dwell in Fair Babylon! For thus said the Lord of Hosts—He who sent me after glory—concerning the nations that have taken you as spoil: "Whoever touches you touches the pupil of his own eye. For I will lift My hand against them, and they shall be spoil for those they enslaved."—Then you shall know that I was sent by the Lord of Hosts.

Shout for joy, Fair Zion! For lo, I come; and I will dwell in your midst—declares the Lord. In that day many nations will attach themselves to the Lord and become His people, and He will dwell in your midst. Then you will know that I was sent to you by the Lord of Hosts.

The Lord will take Judah to Himself as His portion in the Holy Land, and He will choose Jerusalem once more.

Be silent, all flesh, before the Lord!

For He is roused from His holy habitation.

(ZECH. 2:5–17)

Thus said the Lord of Hosts: I am very jealous for Zion, I am fiercely jealous for her. Thus said the Lord: I have returned to Zion, and I will dwell in Jerusalem. Jerusalem will be called the City of Faithfulness, and the mount of the Lord of Hosts the Holy Mount.

Thus said the Lord of Hosts: There shall yet be old men and women in the squares of Jerusalem, each with staff in hand because of their great age. And the squares of the city shall be crowded with boys and girls playing in the squares. Thus said the Lord of Hosts: Though it will seem impossible to the remnant of this people in those days, shall it also be impossible to Me?—declares the Lord of Hosts. Thus said the Lord of Hosts: I will rescue My people from the lands of the east and from the lands of the west, and will bring them home to dwell in Jerusalem. They shall be My people, and I will be their God—in truth and sincerity. *(ZECH. 8:2–8)*

Rejoice greatly, Fair Zion;

Raise a shout, Fair Jerusalem!

Lo, your king is coming to you.

He is victorious, triumphant,

Yet humble, riding on an ass,

On a donkey foaled by a she-ass.

He shall banish chariots from Ephraim

And horses from Jerusalem;

The warrior's bow shall be banished.

He shall call on the nations to surrender,

And his rule shall extend from sea to sea

And from ocean to land's end.

(ZECH. 9:9–10)

Zechariah's vision is apocalyptic, with the eventual triumph coming after much tribulation and resulting in Jerusalem's becoming the pilgrim site for the entire world:

Lo, a day of the Lord is coming when your spoil shall be divided in your very midst! For I will gather all the nations to Jerusalem for war: the city shall be captured, the houses plundered, and the women violated; and a part of the city shall go into exile. But the rest of the population shall not be uprooted from the city.

Then the Lord will come forth and make war on those nations as He is wont to make war on a day of battle. On that day, He will set His feet on the Mount of Olives, near Jerusalem on the east; and the Mount of Olives shall split across from east to west, and one part of the Mount shall shift to the north and the other to the south, [forming] a huge gorge. And the Valley in the Hills shall be stopped up, for the Valley of the Hills shall reach only to Azal; it shall be stopped up as it was stopped up as a result of the earthquake in the days of King Uzziah of Judah.—And the Lord my God, with all the holy beings, will come to you.

In that day, there shall be neither sunlight nor cold moonlight, but there shall be a continuous day—only the Lord knows when—of neither day nor night, and there shall be light at eventide.

In that day, fresh water shall flow from Jerusalem, part of it to the Eastern Sea and part to the Western Sea, throughout the summer and winter.

And the Lord shall be king over all the earth; in that day there shall be one Lord with one name.

Then the whole country shall become like the Arabah, from Geba to Rimmon south of Jerusalem. The latter, however, shall perch high up where it is, and shall be inhabited from the Gate of Benjamin to the site of the Old Gate, down to the Corner Gate, and from the Tower of Hananel to the king's winepresses. Never again shall destruction be decreed, and Jerusalem shall dwell secure.

As for those people that warred against Jerusalem, the Lord will smite them with this plague: their flesh shall rot away while they stand on their feet. . . .

All who survive of all those nations that came up against Jerusalem shall make a pilgrimage year by year to bow low to the King Lord of Hosts and to observe the Feast of Booths. Any of the earth's communities that does not make the pilgrimage to Jerusalem to bow low to the King Lord of Hosts shall receive no rain. . . .

In that day, even the bells on the horses shall be inscribed "Holy to the Lord." The metal pots in the House of the Lord shall be like the basins before the altar; indeed, every metal pot in Jerusalem and in Judah shall be holy to the Lord of Hosts. And all those who sacrifice shall come and take of these to boil [their sacrificial meat] in; in that day there shall be no more traders in the House of the Lord of Hosts. (ZECH. 14:1–12, 16–17, 20–21)

THE WRITINGS

Two books in the third section of the Bible, the Writings, contain poetic material concerning Jerusalem: Psalms and Lamentations.

Jerusalem and its wonders are frequently the subject of the psalms. The most well known is Psalm 48:

The Lord is great and much acclaimed
  in the city of our God,
  His holy mountain—
  fair-crested, joy of all the earth,
  Mount Zion, summit of Zaphon,
  city of the great king.
Through its citadels, God has made Himself known as a haven,
See, the kings joined forces;
  they advanced together.
At the mere sight of it they were stunned,
  they were terrified, they panicked;
  they were seized there with a trembling,
  like a woman in the throes of labor,
  as the Tarshish fleet was wrecked
  in an easterly gale.
The like of what we heard we have now witnessed
  in the city of the Lord of Hosts,
  in the city of our God—
  may God preserve it forever!   *Selah.*

In Your temple, God,
  we meditate upon Your faithful care.
The praise of You, God, like Your name,
  reaches to the ends of the earth;
  Your right hand is filled with beneficence.
Let Mount Zion rejoice!
Let the towns of Judah exult,
  because of Your judgments.

Walk around Zion,
  circle it;
  count its towers,
  take note of its ramparts;

go through its citadels,

that you may recount it to a future age.

For God—He is our God forever;

He will lead us evermore.

Psalm 87 celebrates the connection of God and Zion:

The Lord loves the gates of Zion,

His foundation on the holy mountains,

more than all the dwellings of Jacob.

Glorious things are spoken of you,

O city of God.   *Selah.*

I mention Rahab and Babylonia among those who acknowledge Me;

Philistia, and Tyre, and Cush—each was born there.

Indeed, it shall be said of Zion,

"Every man was born there."

He, the Most High, will preserve it.

The Lord will inscribe in the register of peoples

that each was born there.   *Selah.*

Singers and dancers alike [will say]:

"All my roots are in You."

Psalm 122 speaks specifically about the Temple and the city which contains it, Jerusalem. This is one of the psalms recited by pilgrims as they ascended the Temple Mount:

I rejoiced when they said to me,

"We are going to the house of the Lord."

Our feet stood inside your gates, O Jerusalem,

Jerusalem built up, a city knit together,

to which tribes would make pilgrimage,

the tribes of the Lord,

—as was enjoined upon Israel—

to praise the name of the Lord.

There the thrones of judgment stood,

thrones of the house of David.

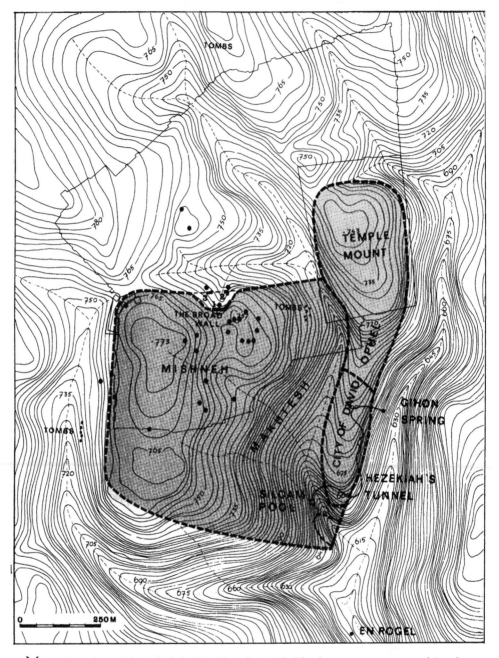

*M*ap *of Jerusalem at the end of the First Temple period. The dots represent excavated Israelite sites (Ancient Jerusalem Revealed.* Israel Exploration Society; *with permission)*

Pray for the well-being of Jerusalem:

    "May those who love you be at peace.

May there be well-being within your ramparts,

    peace in your citadels."

For the sake of my kin and friends,

    I pray for your well-being;

    for the sake of the house of the Lord our God,

    I seek your good.

Other psalms intended for pilgrims contain similar references:

Those who trust in the Lord

    are like Mount Zion

    that cannot be moved,

    enduring forever.

Jerusalem, hills enfold it,

    and the Lord enfolds His people

    now and forever.

                (Pss. 125:1–2)

May the Lord bless you from Zion;

    may you share the prosperity of Jerusalem

    all the days of your life,

    and live to see your children's children.

May all be well with Israel!

                (Pss. 128:5–6)

For the Lord has chosen Zion;

    He has desired it for His seat.

"This is my resting-place for all time;

    here I will dwell, for I desire it.

I will amply bless its store of food,

    give its needy their fill of bread.

I will clothe its priests in victory,

    its loyal ones shall sing for joy.

There I will make a horn sprout for David;

I have prepared a lamp for My anointed one.
I will clothe his enemies in disgrace,
    while on him his crown shall sparkle."
                        (PSS. 132:13–18)

You will surely arise and take pity on Zion,
    For it is time to be gracious to her;
    the appointed time has come.
Your servants take delight in its stones,
    and cherish its dust.
The nations will fear the name of the Lord,
    all the kings of the earth, Your glory.
For the Lord has built Zion;
    He has appeared in all His glory.
He has turned to the prayer of the destitute
    and has not spurned their prayer.
May this be written down for a coming generation,
    that people yet to be created may praise the Lord.
For He looks down from His holy height;
    the Lord beholds the earth from heaven
    to hear the groans of the prisoner,
    to release those condemned to death;
    that the fame of the Lord may be recounted in Zion,
    His praises in Jerusalem,
    when the nations gather together,
    the kingdoms, to serve the Lord.
                        (PSS. 102:14–23)

Some of the Jerusalem psalms reflect specific historic events:

By the waters of Babylon,
    there we sat,
    sat and wept,
    as we thought of Zion.
There on the poplars

we hung up our lyres,

    for our captors asked us there for songs,

    our tormentors, for amusement,

    "Sing us one of the songs of Zion."

How can we sing a song of the Lord

    on alien soil?

If I forget you, O Jerusalem,

    let my right hand wither;

    let my tongue stick to my palate

    if I cease to think of you,

    if I do not keep Jerusalem in memory

    even at my happiest hour.

Remember, O Lord, against the Edomites

    the day of Jerusalem's fall;

    how they cried, "Strip her, strip her

    to her very foundations!"

Fair Babylon, you predator,

    a blessing on him who repays you in kind

    what you have inflicted on us;

    a blessing on him who seizes your babies

    and dashes them against the rocks!

                      (Pss. 137)

When the Lord restores the fortunes of Zion

    —we see it as in a dream—

    our mouths shall be filled with laughter,

    our tongues, with songs of joy.

Then shall they say among the nations,

    "The Lord has done great things for them!"

The Lord will do great things for us

    and we shall rejoice.

Restore our fortunes, O Lord,

    like watercourses in the Negeb.

They who sow in tears

shall reap with songs of joy.

Though he goes along weeping,

    carrying the seed-bag,

    he shall come back with songs of joy,

    carrying his sheaves.

(Pss. 126)

Hallelujah.

It is good to chant hymns to our God;

    it is pleasant to sing glorious praise.

The Lord rebuilds Jerusalem;

    He gathers in the exiles of Israel.

He heals their broken hearts,

    and binds up their wounds. . . .

O Jerusalem, glorify the Lord;

    praise your God, O Zion!

For He made the bars of your gates strong,

    and blessed your children within you.

He endows your realm with well-being,

    and satisfies you with choice wheat.

(Pss. 147:1–3, 12–14)

The Book of Lamentations contains several chapters that are descriptions of Jerusalem at the time of the destruction:

Alas!

Lonely sits the city

Once great with people!

She that was great among nations

Is become like a widow;

The princess among states

Is become a thrall.

Bitterly she weeps in the night,

Her cheek wet with tears.

There is none to comfort her

Of all her friends.
All her allies have betrayed her;
They have become her foes.

Judah has gone into exile
Because of misery and harsh oppression;
When she settled among the nations,
She found no rest;
All her pursuers overtook her
In the narrow places.

Zion's roads are in mourning,
Empty of festival pilgrims;
All her gates are deserted.
Her priests sigh,
Her maidens are unhappy—
She is utterly disconsolate!

Her enemies are now the masters,
Her foes are at ease,
Because the Lord has afflicted her
For her many transgressions;
Her infants have gone into captivity
Before the enemy.

Gone from Fair Zion are all
That were her glory;
Her leaders were like stags
That found no pasture;
They could only walk feebly
Before the pursuer.

All the precious things she had
In the days of old
Jerusalem recalled
In her days of woe and sorrow,
When her people fell by enemy hands
With none to help her;

When enemies looked on and gloated
Over her downfall.
Jerusalem has greatly sinned,
Therefore she is become a mockery.
All who admired her despise her,
For they have seen her disgraced;
And she can only sigh
And shrink back.
Her uncleanness clings to her skirts.
She gave no thought to her future;
She has sunk appallingly,
With none to comfort her.—
See, O Lord, my misery;
How the enemy jeers!
The foe has laid hands
On everything dear to her.
She has seen her Sanctuary
Invaded by nations
Which You have denied admission
Into Your community.
All her inhabitants sigh
As they search for bread;
They have bartered their treasures for food,
To keep themselves alive.—
See, O Lord, and behold,
How abject I have become!

Zion spreads out her hands,
She has no one to comfort her;
The Lord has summoned against Jacob
His enemies all about him;
Jerusalem has become among them
A thing unclean.

(LAM. 1:1–11, 17)

What can I take as witness or liken
To you, O Fair Jerusalem?
What can I match with you to console you,
O Fair Maiden Zion?
For your ruin is vast as the sea:
Who can heal you?
Your seers prophesied to you
Delusion and folly,
They did not expose your iniquity
So as to restore your fortunes,
But prophesied to you oracles
Of delusion and deception.
All who pass your way
Clap their hands at you;
They hiss and wag their head
At Fair Jerusalem:
"Is this the city that was called
Perfect in Beauty,
Joy of All the Earth?"
All your enemies
Jeer at you;
They hiss and gnash their teeth,
And cry: "We've ruined her!
Ah, this is the day we hoped for;
We have lived to see it!"

(LAM. 2:13–16)

The Lord vented all His fury,
Poured out His blazing wrath;
He kindled a fire in Zion
Which consumed its foundations.
The kings of the earth did not believe,
Nor any of the inhabitants of the world,
That foe or adversary could enter

The gates of Jerusalem.

It was for the sins of her prophets,

The iniquities of her priests,

Who had shed in her midst

The blood of the just. . . .

Rejoice and exult, Fair Edom,

Who dwell in the land of Uz!

To you, too, the cup shall pass,

You shall get drunk and expose your nakedness.

Your iniquity, Fair Zion, is expiated;

He will exile you no longer.

Your iniquity, Fair Edom, he will note;

He will uncover your sins.

(LAM. 4:11–13, 21–22)

They have ravished women in Zion,

Maidens in the towns of Judah.

Princes have been hanged by them;

No respect has been shown to elders.

Young men must carry millstones,

And youths stagger under loads of wood.

The old men are gone from the gate,

The young men from their music.

Gone is the joy of our hearts;

Our dancing is turned into mourning.

The crown has fallen from our head;

Woe to us that we have sinned!

Because of this our hearts are sick,

Because of these our eyes are dimmed:

Because of Mount Zion, which lies desolate;

Jackals prowl over it.

But You, O Lord, are enthroned forever,

Your throne endures through the ages.

Why have You forgotten us utterly,

Forsaken us for all time?

Take us back, O Lord, to Yourself,

And let us come back;

Renew our days as of old!

For truly, You have rejected us,

Bitterly raged against us.

(LAM. 5:11–22)

In printed texts and when Lamentations is chanted on Tisha b'Av, the commemoration of Jerusalem's destruction, the words "Take us back, O Lord, to Yourself,/And let us come back;/Renew our days of old!" are repeated at the end. In this way, the reading concludes not with despair but on a note of hope.

THE SECOND GATE

Jerusalem in Second Temple Literature

The Citadel of David, late 1960s

During the period of the Second Temple, from the return from the Babylonian Exile in the fifth century B.C.E. *until the first century* C.E., *the writing of books in Biblical style continued. Apocalyptic writing also continued in the century following the destruction. These books were not accepted into the canon of Jewish scripture and were preserved in Greek translations by the Church. In addition there were other sacred works composed by the members of the Dead Sea sect which were totally unknown until the discovery of these scrolls in the 1940s. Other important works from this time are the philosophical writings of the Jewish philosopher from Alexandria, Philo, writing in the first century* B.C.E., *and the historical books by Josephus Flavius in the first century* C.E.

ꙮ The Book of Tobit

The Book of Tobit found in the Apocrypha is a tale of the pious Tobit, who was exiled to Assyria and who endangered his life in order to fulfill the precepts of Judaism concerning burial. Thought to have been written in the second century B.C.E. *prior to the Maccabean revolt, it contains this hymn predicting the restoration of Jerusalem.*

I shall exalt my God,

And my soul exalt the King of Heaven,

And shall rejoice in His majesty.

Let all men speak and give thanks to Him in Jerusalem.

O Jerusalem, holy city! He will chastise you for the deeds of your sons,

But will again have mercy on the sons of righteousness.

Give thanks to the Lord with goodness,

And bless the Everlasting King!

That your tabernacle may be builded in you again with joy,

And that He may make glad in you all that are captives

And love in you all that are miserable; for all generations of eternity.

A bright light shall shine unto all ends of the earth;

Many nations shall come to you from afar,

And the inhabitants of the utmost ends of the earth unto your holy name,

Bearing gifts in their hands unto the King of Heaven.

Generations of generations shall utter praises in you,

And to the name of the elect one, for generations to eternity.

Cursed shall be all they that shall speak an evil word;

Cursed shall be all they that demolish you

And throw down your walls;

And all they that overthrow your towers.

And set fire your habitations.

But blessed shall be forever those that revere you.

Then go, and be exceeding glad for the sons of the righteous,

For they shall all be gathered together

And bless the everlasting Lord.

Blessed shall they be that shall rejoice for your peace.

And blessed be all men that shall sorrow for you

For all your afflictions;

Because in you they shall rejoice and shall see your joy forever.

O my soul, bless the Lord, the great King!

For Jerusalem will be built as His house for all ages.

Happy shall I be if the remnant of my seed come to see your glory

And give thanks to the King of Heaven!

And the gates of Jerusalem shall be builded with sapphire and emerald

And all your walls with precious stone.

The towers of Jerusalem shall be builded with gold,

And their battlements with pure gold.

The streets of Jerusalem shall be paved

With carbuncle and stone of Ophir.

And the gates of Jerusalem shall utter hymns of Exultation,

And all her dwellings shall say, "Hallelujah."

Blessed is the God of Israel,

And the blessed shall bless the Name

That is holy forever and ever.

(TOBIT 13:9–18)

✑ The Letter of Aristeas

There is disagreement about the dating of this work, written in Greek, probably in Alexandria. Many conjecture that it stems from the time of Antiochus Epiphanes, about 170 B.C.E., and was a defense of Judaism. Aristeas, a Jew in the court of Ptolemy II (285–246 B.C.E.) is sent to Jerusalem to bring scholars to translate the Bible into Greek. In a letter written to his brother, he describes his journey to Jerusalem. If it was indeed written in the second century B.C.E., it provides us with a rare description of the Second Temple and Jerusalem prior to its complete rebuilding by Herod. However, the lavishness of the description itself, as well as some of the details, which seem imaginary, have led scholars to believe that the description was written after the destruction of Herod's Temple and was based upon memories of that magnificent structure and not of the simple building constructed by the returnees from Babylon.

When we reached the region we beheld the city situated in the center of all Judaea upon a mountain which rises to a lofty height. Upon its crest stood the Temple in all its splendor; and there were three encompassing walls, above seventy cubits in height and of a breadth and length in keeping with the structure of the edifice. The whole was built with a lavishness and sumptuousness beyond all precedent. From the construction of the doorway and its fastenings to the doorposts and the solidity of the lintel it was obvious that no expense had been spared. The style of the curtain corresponded in every respect to the door; especially when the fabric was kept in unceasing motion by the current of wind beneath, since, the current being from below, the curtain bulged out from the bottom to its highest extent, the spectacle was highly agreeable and hard to tear oneself from. The altar was built in keeping with the size of the place and of the offerings consumed upon it by fire, and the ascent was on a similar scale. The ascent was gradual, from a proper regard for decency, and the ministering priests were swathed in "coats of fine linen" reaching to the ankles. The edifice looks toward the east, and its back to the west. The entire floor is paved with stones and sloped downward to the appropriate places, to admit of flushing with water in order to wash away the blood of the sacrifices; for many myriads of beasts are offered on the days of the festivals. The water supply is inexhaustible, for an abundant natural spring pours forth within the Temple area, and there are furthermore marvelous underground reservoirs passing description, to a distance of five stades, as was pointed out, round the foundations of the Temple; of these each had innumerable pipes, so that the various channels converged at the several reservoirs. The floors and sides of these reservoirs, they explained, were overlaid with lead, and above them a great mass of plaster was laid, everything being made secure. There are numerous outlets, they said, at the foot of the altar, invisible to all except those engaged in the ministration, so that the vast accumulation of sacrificial blood is cleansed away in the twinkling of an eye. I am myself convinced of the system of reservoirs, and I shall show how my belief was confirmed. They took me more than four

Herodian construction of large ashlars at the southern wall of the Temple Mount (Ancient Jerusalem Revealed. Israel Exploration Society; with permission)

stades out of the city, and at a certain place bade me bend over and listen to the rushing noise of the meeting of the waters. Thus the size of the cisterns was made evident to me, as I have described them.

In its exhibition of strength and in its orderly and silent performance the ministration of the priests could in no way be surpassed. . . . Complete silence prevails, so that one might suppose that not a person was present in the place, though those performing the service amount to some seven hundred—besides the great multitude of persons bringing sacrifices to be offered—but everything is done with reverence and in a manner worthy of the great divinity. . . .

To obtain a thorough knowledge of everything we ascended the citadel of the city which lies hard by and looked about. It is situated on a very lofty spot and is fortified with a number of towers which are built of large blocks of stone right up to the very top, as a protection, so we were informed, for the precincts of the Temple, so that in case of any attack or revolution or enemy invasion no one could make his way into the walls which encompass the Temple. On the towers of the citadel are set artillery and various other engines of war, and their lofty eminence commands the aforesaid walls. The towers are guarded, furthermore, by the most loyal of men, who have given demonstrative proof of devotion to their country. These men had orders not to quit the citadel, except on festivals, and then only by turns, nor did they permit anyone to enter. Very scrupulous care was exercised even when they received an order from their leader to admit any visitors as sightseers, as happened in our case, for though we were unarmed and only two, they would barely admit us to study the arrangements for the sacrifices. They said they were pledged to such conduct by oaths: they had all sworn, and of necessity and religious scruple they fulfilled the stipulation of their oath, that though they were five hundred they would not admit more than five persons at the same time; for the citadel was the whole defense of the Temple, and he that founded it had thus secured its protection.

The extent of the city is moderate, its compass being about forty stades, as far as one may conjecture. In the position of its towers and of the thoroughfares, some of which appear above and some below, with the cross-streets cutting through them, it has the familiar aspects of a theater, for, the city being built upon a mountain, its parts rise one above another, and there are stairs to the thoroughfares. Some persons make their way at the higher level and some underneath, and they are careful to keep apart as they go, so that those in a state of purification may touch nothing improper. . . .

☯ Jubilees

Jubilees, written in Hebrew in the late second century B.C.E., was preserved only in Greek even though it greatly influenced many Jewish works. Much of it consists of the words of an angel, speaking to Moses on Mount Sinai, who recapitulates much of the Bible, giving specific dates to events and elaborating on the Biblical narrative.

And He said to the angel of the presence, "Write for Moses from the first creation until My sanctuary is built in their midst forever and ever. And the Lord will appear in the sight of all. And everyone will know that I am the God of Israel and the father of all the children of Jacob and king upon Mount Zion forever and ever. And Zion and Jerusalem will be holy."

And the angel of the presence, who went before the camp of Israel, took the tablets of the division of years from the time of creation of the law and testimony according to their weeks [of years], according to the jubilees, year by year throughout the full number of jubilees, from [the day of creation until] the day of the new creation when the heaven and earth and all of their creatures shall be renewed according to the powers of heaven and according to the whole nature of earth, until the sanctuary of the Lord is created in Jerusalem upon Mount Zion. And all of the lights will be renewed for healing and peace and blessing for all the elect of Israel and in order that it might be thus from that day and unto all the days of the earth. (JUB. 1:27–29)

ഈ The First Book of Maccabees

Written in Hebrew, this book recounts in straight narrative the history of the struggle between the Syrian Greeks and the Jews, eventually under the leadership of the Maccabees, between 175 and 135 B.C.E. Because the book was not included in the canon, the Hebrew was lost, and the text was preserved only in Greek.

After smiting Egypt, in the one hundred and forty-third year [168 B.C.E.], Antiochus turned back, went up against Israel, and entered Jerusalem with a great army. He entered the Temple in his arrogance, and took the golden altar, the lamp for the light and all its equipment, the table of the show-bread, the cups, the bowls and the golden censers, the curtain, the crowns; and the golden adornment on the front of the sanctuary he stripped off entirely. He seized the silver, the gold, and the precious vessels; he also took the hidden treasures which he found. Taking them all, he carried them away to his own country. He massacred people and spoke most arrogantly.

And great was the sadness in Israel, everywhere;

Both rulers and elders groaned;

Maidens and young men languished,

The beauty of the women was altered.

Every bridegroom took up lamentation,

And she that sat in a bridal-chamber mourned.

Shaken was the earth over those who dwelt therein,

And the whole house of Jacob was clothed with shame.

After two years, the king sent the officer of the Mysians to the cities of Judah, and entered Jerusalem with a strong force. He spoke peaceful words to them craftily, and they trusted him. Then he fell suddenly upon the city, and dealt it a great blow, destroying many people of Israel. He despoiled the city, burnt it with fire, razed its houses and its surrounding walls. They led the women and children captive, and took possession of the cattle. They fortified the city of David with a high and strong wall with mighty towers, and it became their citadel. They put sinful people therein, men who were transgressors against the Torah; and they entrenched themselves in it. They stored up arms and provisions, and after collecting together the spoils of Jerusalem, they laid them up there. They became a great menace, for it served them as an ambuscade against the sanctuary, an evil adversary against Israel continually.

They shed innocent blood around the altar,

And polluted the sanctuary.

Because of them the inhabitants of Jerusalem fled,

She became a dwelling place of foreigners,

And foreign she became to her own brood,

And her children forsook her.

Her sanctuary was laid waste like a wilderness,

Her feasts were turned into sadness,

Her sabbaths into a reproach,

Her honor into contempt.

As great as had been her glory,

By so much was her dishonor increased.

And her high renown was turned into sadness.

(1 MAC. 1:20–40)

On the twenty-fifth day of Kislev in the one hundred and forty-sixth year [168 B.C.E.], he erected an abomination of desolation upon the altar, and in the surrounding cities of Judah they erected altars. They burned incense also at the doors of the houses and in the streets. The books of the Torah which they found, they tore into pieces and burned. Wherever a book of the covenant was found in anyone's possession, or if anyone respected the Torah, the decree of the king imposed the sentence of death upon him. Month after month they dealt brutally with every Israelite who was found in the cities. On the twenty-fifth of the month they offered sacrifices upon the altar which was set on the altar of burnt-offering. *(1 MAC. 1:54–59)*

✎

At that time Mattathias, son of John, son of Simeon, a priest of the family of Joarib, moved away from Jerusalem and settled in Modin. . . . When he saw the blasphemous things that were taking place in Judah and Jerusalem, he said:

"Wretched am I, why was I born to behold,

The dissolution of my people and the destruction of the holy city,

To sit idly by while it is given into the hands of its enemies,

The sanctuary into the hand of foreigners?

Her people have become as a man without honor,

Her glorious treasures captured, taken away;

Her infants have been killed in her streets,

Her young men, by the sword of the enemy.

What nation has not shared,

And what kingdom has not seized her spoil?

All her adornment has been taken away.

Instead of a free woman, she has become a slave.

Yea, behold, our sanctuary and our beauty,

And our glory have been laid waste!

The heathen have profaned them.

Why then should life continue for us?"

(1 MAC. 2:1–13)

Judah and his brothers said, "Now that our enemies are crushed, let us go up to purify and dedicate the sanctuary."

The entire army gathered together and went up to Mount Zion. They saw the sanctuary desolated and the altar profaned, the gates burned up, the weeds growing in the courts as in a forest or as on one of the mountains, and the priests' chambers torn down. They tore their garments and made great lamentation, and put ashes on their heads, and fell on their faces on the ground, blew solemn blasts upon the trumpets, and cried out to Heaven. Judah appointed certain men to fight against the garrison in the citadel, until he could cleanse the sanctuary. He selected priests without blemish, whose delight was in the Torah, and they purified the sanctuary, carrying out the stones that had defiled it into an unclean place. They took counsel as to what they should do about the altar of burnt offering, which had been defiled. A good plan occurred to them, namely, to tear it down, lest it become a reproach to them, because the heathen had defiled it. So they pulled down the altar, and put away the stones in the Temple Mount, in a suitable place, until a prophet should come to decide what to do with them. They took whole stones, according to the Torah, and constructed a new altar like the former one. They built the sanctuary and the interior of the Temple, and hallowed the courts, and made new holy vessels, and brought the candlestick, the altar of incense, and the table into the Temple. They burned incense on the altar, and lit the lights on the candlestick so that they would shed light in the Temple. They put loaves of bread upon the table, hung up the curtains, and finished all the work which they had undertaken to do.

On the twenty-fifth day of the ninth month, that is the month of Kislev, in the one hundred and forty-ninth year [165 B.C.E.], they arose early and offered sacrifice according to the Torah upon the new altar of burnt offering which they had made. At the same time and on the same day on which the heathen had profaned it, on that very day it was consecrated with songs and harps and lutes and cymbals. All the people fell on their faces and prostrated themselves, and uttered praises to Heaven who had caused them to prosper. They celebrated the dedication of the altar for eight days, brought

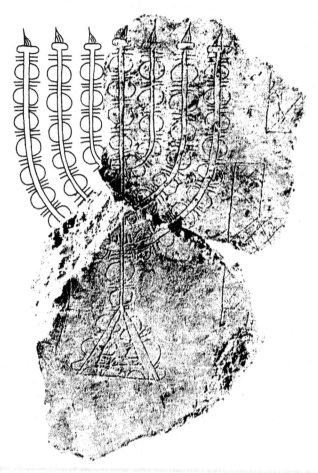

A menorah and other objects incised on a plastered wall in the Jewish Quarter during the Herodian period (Ancient Jerusalem Revealed. Israel Exploration Society; with permission)

burnt offerings with joy, and offered a sacrifice of deliverance and praise. They also adorned the front of the Temple with golden crowns and small shields, and rededicated the gates and the priests' chambers, and fitted then with doors. Thus there was great joy among the people, and the reproach caused by the heathen was removed. Judah and his brothers and the entire congregation of Israel decreed that the days of dedication of the altar should be kept with gladness and joy at their due season, year after year, for eight days from the twenty-fifth of the month of Kislev. At that time they built high walls and strong towers around Mount Zion, so that the heathen could never again come and destroy them, as they had done before. (*1 MAC. 4:36–60*)

ᶜᵂ The Second Book of Maccabees

Like First Maccabees, this book recounts the story of the events of the second century
B.C.E. *Second Maccabees, however, was written in Greek by a Hellenized Jew and was*
intended for the Greek-speaking Jews of Egypt. It is more rhetorical than First
Maccabees.

Now about this time Antiochus made his second inroad into Egypt. And it so befell
that throughout all the city of Jerusalem for almost forty days horsemen were seen charg-
ing in mid-air, wearing robes inwrought with gold, armed with lances, and arrayed in
troops: swords flashing, squadrons of horse in array, assaults and charges repeated from
one side and another, shields shaken, spears massed together, darts hurtling to and fro,
the sheen of golden trappings, and corselets of all kinds. Which made all men pray that
the apparition might betoken good.

Now a false rumour got abroad that Antiochus had died. Whereupon Jason took not
less than a thousand men, and made a sudden attack on the city; the troops stationed
on the walls were routed, and, as the city was now practically captured, Menelaus took
refuge in the citadel, while Jason proceeded to slaughter his fellow-citizens without
mercy, reckless of the fact that to get any advantage over kinfolk is the worst kind of
disadvantage, and imagining to himself that he was winning trophies from foes and not
from fellow-countrymen. He failed to secure the place of power, however; and in the
end he reaped only shame from his conspiracy, and had to pass over again as a fugitive
into the country of the Ammonites. . . . Now when tidings of what had happened
reached the king, he thought Judaea was in revolt. He therefore started from Egypt in
a fury, stormed the city, and commanded his soldiers to cut down without mercy any
one they met, and to slay those who sheltered in their houses. So there was a massacre
of young and old, an extermination of boys, women, and children, a slaughter of vir-
gins and innocents. In the short space of three days eighty thousand were destroyed,
forty thousand of them in close combat, and as many again were sold into slavery. Not
content with this, he dared to enter the most holy temple on earth, under the guidance
of Menelaus, who proved himself a traitor both to the laws and to his country; he laid
polluted hands on the sacred vessels, and swept off with his profane hands what other
kings had dedicated to enhance the glory and honour of the Place. Uplifted in spirit,
Antiochus did not consider that it was on account of the sins of those who dwelt in
the city that the Sovereign Lord was provoked to anger for a little while; hence His in-
difference to the Place. Had they not been involved in so many sins, this fellow would
have fared like Heliodorus, who was sent by King Seleucus to pry into the treasury—
he would have been scourged as soon as he pressed forward, and turned back from his
presumption. But the Lord did not choose the nation for the sake of the Place; He chose
the Place for the sake of the nation. And so the Place, after partaking in the calamities

that befell the nation, shared afterwards in its prosperity; forsaken in the wrath of the Almighty, it was restored again in full glory when the great Sovereign became reconciled.

Antiochus, then, carried off from the temple eighteen hundred talents and hurried away to Antioch, thinking in his arrogance to make the land navigable and the sea passable by foot—so uplifted was he in heart. *(2 MAC. 5:1–21)*

✺

Shortly after this the king sent an old Athenian to compel the Jews to depart from the laws of their fathers, and to cease living by the laws of God; further, the sanctuary in Jerusalem was to be polluted and called after Zeus Olympius, while the sanctuary at Gerizim was also to be called after Zeus Xenius, in keeping with the hospitable character of the inhabitants. Now this proved a sore and altogether crushing visitation of evil. For the heathen filled the temple with riot and revelling, dallying with harlots and lying with women inside the sacred precincts, besides bringing in what was forbidden, the altar was filled with abominable sacrifices which the law prohibited. And a man could neither keep the sabbath, nor celebrate the feasts of the fathers, nor so much as confess himself to be a Jew. On the king's birthday every month [one day each month was designated the King's birthday and so celebrated—ed.] they were taken—bitter was the necessity—to share in the sacrifice, and when the festival of the Dionysia came round they were compelled to wear ivy wreaths for the procession in honour of Dionysus. *(2 MAC. 6:1–8)*

✺

Now Maccabaeus and his followers, under the leadership of the Lord, recaptured the temple and the city, and pulled down the altars erected by the aliens in the marketplace, as well as the sacred inclosures. After cleansing the sanctuary, they erected another altar of sacrifice, and striking fire out of flints they offered sacrifices after a lapse of two years, with incense, lamps, and the presentation of the shew-bread. This done, they fell prostrate before the Lord with entreaties that they might never again incur such disasters, but that, if ever they should sin, he would chasten them with forbearance, instead of handing them over to blasphemous and barbarous pagans. Now it so happened that the cleansing of the sanctuary took place on the very day on which it had been profaned by aliens, on the twenty-fifth day of the same month, which is Chislev. And they celebrated it for eight days with gladness like a feast of tabernacles, remembering how, not long before, during the feast of tabernacles they had been wandering like wild beasts in the mountains and the caves. So, bearing wands wreathed with leaves and fair boughs and palms, they offered hymns of praise to him who had prospered the cleansing of his own place, and also passed a public order and decree that all the Jewish nation should keep these . . . days every year. *(2 MAC. 10:1–8)*

⟁ The Psalms of Solomon

This collection of psalms is ascribed to Solomon with no historical or literary justification. They are thought to have been compiled in the first century B.C.E. They were first published in the seventeenth century from a Greek manuscript. The historical references may refer to events in the time of Pompey (63 B.C.E.).

God is a righteous judge and he will not be impressed by appearances.
For the gentiles insulted Jerusalem, trampling [her] down;

  he dragged her beauty down from the throne of glory.
She put on sackcloth instead of beautiful clothes,

  a rope around her head instead of a crown.
She took off the wreath of glory which God had put on her;

  in dishonor her beauty was thrown to the ground.

And I saw and implored in the Lord's presence and said,

  "Let it be enough, Lord, to make your hand heavy on Jerusalem by bringing
  gentiles [upon her]."
For they ridiculed [her] and did not refrain in anger and vicious rage,

  and they will be finished unless you, Lord, censure them in your anger.
For they have not done it in zeal, but in emotional passion

  to pour out their anger against us in plunder.

                             (PSS. OF SOLOMON 2:19–24)

Sound in Zion the signal trumpet of the sanctuary;

  announce in Jerusalem the voice of one bringing good news,

  for God has been merciful to Israel in watching over them.
Stand on a high place, Jerusalem, and look at your children,

  from the east and west assembled together by the Lord.
From the north they come in the joy of their God;

  from distant islands God has assembled them.
He flattened high mountains into level ground for them;

  the hills fled at their coming.
The forests shaded them as they passed by;

  God made every fragrant tree to grow for them.
So that Israel might proceed under the supervision of the glory of their God.

Jerusalem, put on [the] clothes of your glory,

    prepare the robe of your holiness,

    for God has spoken well of Israel forevermore.

May the Lord do what he has spoken about Israel and Jerusalem;

    may the Lord lift up Israel in the name of his glory.

May the mercy of the Lord be upon Israel forevermore.

                        (PSS. OF SOLOMON 11:1–9)

✢ Noncanonical Psalms from Qumran

Among the many nonbiblical works found in the Dead Sea Scrolls were various psalms which feature the city of Jerusalem. The dates of these psalms are unknown, but obviously precede the destruction of the Temple in 70 C.E.

Jerusalem [is the city] the Lord [chose],
From everlasting to (everlasting). . . .
[For the name] of the Lord is invoked upon it,
[And His glory] is seen upon Jerusalem [and] Zion.
Who can utter the name of the Lord,
And who can proclaim all [His] praise?
The Lord remembered him with His favor,
and visited him,
that He might show him the prosperity of His chosen ones
to make him rejoice [in the joy of His people.]

4Q380

APOSTROPHE TO ZION

I remember thee for blessing, O Zion:
with all my might have I loved thee.
May thy memory be blessed forever!
Great is thy hope, O Zion;
that peace and thy longed-for salvation will come.
Generation after generation will dwell in thee
and generations of saints will be thy splendor:
Those who yearn for the day of thy salvation
that they may rejoice in the greatness of thy glory.
On the abundance of thy glory they are nourished
and in thy splendid squares will they toddle.
The merits of thy prophets wilt thou remember,
and in the deeds of thy pious ones wilt thou glory.
Purge violence from thy midst:

falsehood and iniquity will be cut off from thee.

Thy sons will rejoice in thy midst

and thy precious ones will be united with thee.

How they have hoped for thy salvation,

thy pure one have mourned for thee.

Hope for thee does not perish, O Zion,

nor is hope in thee forgotten.

Who has ever perished [in] righteousness,

or who has ever survived in his iniquity?

Man is tested according to his way:

every man is requited according to his deeds;

all about are thine enemies cut off, O Zion,

and all thy foes have been scattered.

Praise of thee is pleasing, O Zion,

cherished through all the world.

Many times do I remember thee for blessing;

with all my heart I bless thee.

Mayest thou attain unto everlasting righteousness,

and blessings of the honorable mayst thou receive.

Accept a vision bespoken of thee,

and dreams of prophets sought for thee.

Be exalted, and spread wide, O Zion;

praise the Most High, thy saviour;

let my soul be glad to thy glory.

11QPs

⤜ Second Baruch

Sometimes known as the Apocalypse of Baruch, this book claims to be the work of Jeremiah's scribe, Baruch. It is thought to have been written after the destruction of the Second Temple, sometime toward the end of the first century C.E. or the beginning of the second. Many of the ideas found in it are also found in the midrashic writings that originated at a similar period.

And the Lord said to me:

This city will be delivered up for a time,

And the people will be chastened for a time,

And the world will not be forgotten.

Or do you think that this is the city of which I said: On the palms of my hands I have carved you? (Isa. 49:16) It is not this building that is in your midst now; it is that which will be revealed, with me, that was already prepared from the moment that I decided to create Paradise. And I showed it to Adam before he sinned. But when he transgressed the commandment, it was taken away from him—as also Paradise. After these things I showed it to my servant Abraham in the night between the portions of the victims. And again I showed it also to Moses on Mount Sinai when I showed him the likeness of the tabernacle and all its vessels. Behold, now it is preserved with me—as also Paradise. (2 BAR. 4:1–6)

⤜

And behold, suddenly a strong spirit lifted me and carried me above the wall of Jerusalem. And I saw, and behold, there were standing four angels at the four corners of the city, each of them with a burning torch in his hands. And another angel came down from heaven and said to them, "Hold your torches and do not light them before I say it to you. Because I was sent first to speak a word to the earth and then to deposit in it what the Lord, the Most High, has commanded me." And I saw that he descended in the Holy of Holies and that he took from there the veil, the holy ephod, the mercy seat, the two tables, the holy raiment of the priests, the altar of incense, the forty-eight precious stones with which the priests were clothed, and all the holy vessels of the tabernacle. And he said to the earth with a loud voice:

Earth, earth, earth, hear the word of the mighty God,

and receive the things which I commit to you,

and guard them until the last times,

so that you may restore them when you are ordered,

so that strangers may not get possession of them.

For the time has arrived when Jerusalem will also be delivered up for a time,

until the moment that it will be said that it will be restored forever.

And the earth opened its mouth and swallowed them up.

After these things I heard this angel saying to the angels who held the torches:

> Now destroy the walls and overthrow them to their foundations so that the enemies do not boast and say, "We have overthrown the wall of Zion and we have burnt down the place of the mighty God." (2 BAR. 6:3–7:1)

Blessed is he who was not born,

or he who was born and died.

But we, the living, woe to us,

because we have seen the afflictions of Zion,

and that which has befallen Jerusalem. . . .

You, farmers, sow not again.

And you, O earth, who do you give the fruit of your harvest?

Keep within you the sweetness of your sustenance.

And you, vine, why do you still give your wine?

For an offering will not be given again from you in Zion,

and the first fruits will not again be offered.

And you, heaven, keep your dew within you,

and do not open the treasuries of rain.

And you, sun, keep the light of your rays within you.

And you, moon, extinguish the multitude of your light.

For why should the light rise again,

where the light of Zion is darkened?

(2 BAR. 10:6–12)

Do you think that there is no mourning among the angels before the Mighty One, that Zion is delivered up in this way? Behold, the nations rejoice in their hearts, and the multitudes are before their idols and say, "She who has trodden others down for such a long time has been trodden down; and she who has subjugated has been subjugated." Do you think that the Most High rejoices in these things or that his name has been glorified? (2 BAR. 67:2–4)

☙ Fourth Baruch

Although this book has come down to us only in Christian versions, it is based upon a Jewish work written after the destruction of the Temple in 70 C.E. It purports to describe the way in which Jeremiah hides the vessels of the Temple, the destruction of the First Temple, and the way in which eventually Jeremiah returns with the exiles to worship in the rebuilt Temple at the behest of Baruch, who writes to him.

But when the hour of night arrived, as the Lord had said to Jeremiah, they went together onto the walls of the city, Jeremiah and Baruch. And behold, there was a sound of trumpets, and angels came out of heaven holding torches in their hands, and they stood on the walls of the city. And when Jeremiah and Baruch saw them, they wept, saying, "Now we know that the word is true." And Jeremiah pleaded with the angels, saying, "I implore you not to destroy the city just yet, until I have a word with the Lord." And the Lord spoke to the angels saying, "Don't destroy the city until I speak to my chosen one, Jeremiah." Then Jeremiah spoke, saying, "Please Lord, let me speak before you." And the Lord said, "Speak, my chosen one, Jeremiah." And Jeremiah said, "Behold, Lord, we know now that you are delivering the city into the hands of its enemies, and they will carry the people off into Babylon. What do you want me to do with the holy vessels of the [Temple] service?" And the Lord said to him, "Take them and deliver them to the earth, saying, 'Hear, earth, the voice of him who created you. . . . Guard the vessels of the [Temple] service unto the coming of the beloved one.' "

. . . Jeremiah and Baruch went into the sanctuary and, gathering up the vessels of the [Temple] service, they delivered them to the earth, just as the Lord had instructed them. And immediately the earth swallowed them up. (4 BAR. *3:1–11, 18–19*)

And when it was morning, behold the host of the Chaldeans surrounded the city. And the great angel trumpeted, saying, "Come into the city, host of the Chaldeans; for behold the gate has been opened for you. Therefore, let the king come in with his multitude and take all the people captive." But Jeremiah, taking the keys of the Temple, went outside of the city and, facing the sun, he tossed them, saying, "I say to you, sun, take the keys of the Temple of God and keep them until the day in which the Lord will question you about them. Because we were not found worthy of keeping them, for we were false stewards." (4 BAR. *4:1–5*)

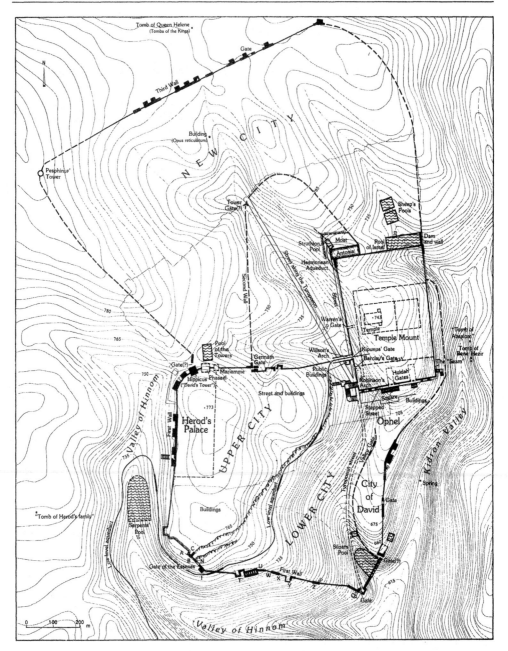

Map of Jerusalem at the end of the Second Temple period (Ancient Jerusalem Revealed. Israel Exploration Society; with permission)

☼ The Writings of Philo

Philo Judaeus, also known as Philo of Alexandria, lived from ca. 20 B.C.E. to 50 C.E. A member of an aristocratic Jewish family, he was well acquainted with the great works of classical antiquity and wrote in a rich and classical Greek. We know little of his life, however, and less of his background in Jewish knowledge. He did make a trip to Jerusalem and extensively philosophized upon its place in Judaism.

THE EMBASSY TO GAIUS

Philo recounts his mission to Rome to protest the erection of statues to the emperor in synagogues and then in the Temple.

We had travelled from Rome to Puteoli following Gaius, who had come down to the sea side and was spending some time round the bay passing from one to another of the numerous and expensively furnished country houses which he owned. While we were anxiously considering the statement of our case, there came to us one with a troubled look in his bloodshot eyes and gasping convulsively. He drew us a little way apart since there were some people standing near and said, "Have you heard the new tidings?" and when he was going to report it he was brought up short, as a flood of tears streamed from his eyes. He began again and the second time stopped short and so too a third time. When we saw this we were all in a flutter and bade him tell us the matter which he said had brought him there. "For," we said, "you have not come just to have your weeping witnessed. If the facts are worth tears do not be the only one to feel sorrow." He managed with difficulty while sobbing and breathing spasmodically to say, "Our temple is lost, Gaius has ordered a colossal statue to be set up within the inner sanctuary dedicated to himself under the name of Zeus." *(XXIX 185–188)*

[Agrippa] took a tablet and wrote to him [Gaius] as follows:

> . . . All men, my emperor, have planted in them a passionate love of their native land and a high esteem for their own laws; and on this there is no need to instruct you, who love your native city as ardently as you honour your own customs. . . . I as you know am by birth a Jew, and my native city is Jerusalem in which is situated the sacred shrine of the most high God. . . . As for the holy city, I must say what befits me to say. While she, as I have said, is my native city she is also the mother city not of one country Judaea but of most of the others in virtue of the colonies sent out at divers times to the neighbouring lands Egypt, Phoenicia, the part of Syria called the Hollow and the rest as well and the lands lying far apart, Pamphylia, Cilicia, most of Asia up

to Bithynia and the corners of Pontus, similarly also into Europe, Thessaly, Boeotia, Macedonia, Aetolia, Attica, Argos, Corinth and most of the best parts of Peloponnese. And not only are the mainlands full of Jewish colonies but also the most highly esteemed of the islands Euboea, Cyprus, Crete. I say nothing of the countries beyond the Euphrates, for except for a small part they all, Babylon and of the other satrapies those where the land within their confines is highly fertile, have Jewish inhabitants. So that if my own home-city is granted a share of your goodwill the benefit extends not to one city but to myriads of the others situated in every region of the inhabited world. . . . It was in Jerusalem, my emperor, that your much-prayed-for succession was first announced, and from the holy city the rumour travelled to the mainlands on both sides, and for that reason it deserves to hold the premier place in your esteem. . . . I come finally to my supplication for the temple. This temple, my Lord Gaius, has never from the first admitted any figure wrought by men's hands, because it is the sanctuary of the true God. For the works of painters and modellers are representations of gods perceived by sense but to paint or mould a likeness of the invisible was held by our ancestors to be against their religion. Your grandfather Agrippa visited and paid honour to the temple, and so did Augustus by the letters in which he ordered the first fruits to be sent from every quarter and by instituting the perpetual sacrifice. Your great-grand-mother too. . . . Thus no one, Greek or non-Greek, no satrap, no king, no mortal enemy, no faction, no war, no storming or sacking of the city, nor any existing thing ever brought about so great a violation of the temple as the set-ting up in it of an image or statue or any hand-wrought object for worship. . . .

Your maternal grandfather M. Agrippa, being in Judaea when Herod my grandfather was king of the country, saw fit to come up from the coast to the capital situated in the centre of the land. But when he surveyed the temple and the rich array of the priests and the worship paid by the native popula-tion he was filled with wonder thinking that he had seen something to be profoundly reverenced, something greater than words could describe. His dis-course to those of his friends who were there with him consisted of nothing else but praise of the sanctuary and all that pertained to it. Thus throughout the days which he spent in the city out of courtesy to Herod he resorted to the precinct, delighting himself with the spectacle both of the ornate structure and of the sacrifices and the ritual observed in the services and the majestic aspect of the high priest when arrayed in the sacred vestments and conducting the holy rites. . . .

Now they say [the statue] is to be in the inmost part of the temple in the special sanctuary itself, into which the Grand Priest enters once a year only on the Fast as it is called, to offer incense and to pray according to ancestral practice for a full supply of blessings and prosperity and peace for all mankind. And if any priest, to say nothing of other Jews, and not merely one of the lowest priests but of those who are ranked directly below the chief, goes in ei-ther by himself or with the High Priest, and further even if the High Priest enters on two days of the year or thrice or four times on the same day death without appeal is his doom. So greatly careful was the law-giver to guard the inmost sanctuary, the one and only place which he wished to keep preserved untrodden and untouched. How many deaths think you would those who have been trained to holiness in these matters willingly endure if they should see the statue imported thither? I believe that they would slaughter their whole families, women and children alike, and finally immolate themselves upon the corpses of their kin. . . .

But what of your grandfather, the best of the emperors that ever were to this day, he who first received the title of Augustus for his virtue and good fortune, who disseminated peace everywhere over sea and land to the ends of the world? Did he not, hearing by report the story of the temple and that it had no work of man's hands, a visible effigy of an invisible being, erected in it, marvel and pay it honour? . . . He gave orders for a continuation of whole burnt offerings every day to the Most High God to be charged to his own purse. . . . Under such an instructor in piety your great-grandmother Julia Augusta adorned the temple with golden vials and libation bowls and a multitude of other sumptuous offerings.

Gaius received the letter and, as he read it, its every sentiment filled him with resentment at the ill-success of his project, yet at the same time he began to bend under the claims for justice coupled with supplication . . . and he ordered letters to be sent to Publius Petronius, governor of Syria, that he should forbear to take further steps to violate the tradition of the temple of the Jews. (XXXVI 276–XLI 333)

On Dreams

Now the city of God is called in the Hebrew Jerusalem and its name when translated is "vision of peace." Therefore do not seek for the city of the Existent among the regions of the earth, since it is not wrought of wood or stone, but in a soul, in which there is no warring, whose sight is keen, which has set before it as its aim to live in contemplation and peace. For what grander or holier house could we find for God in the whole range of existence than the vision-seeking mind, the mind which is eager to see all things and never even in its dreams has a wish for faction or turmoil? I hear once more the voice of the invisible spirit, the familiar secret tenant saying, "Friend, it would seem that there is a matter great and precious of which thou knowest nothing, and this I will ungrudgingly shew thee, for many other well-timed lessons have I given thee. Know then, good friend, that God alone is the real veritable peace, free from all illusion, but the whole substance of things created only to perish is one constant war. For God is a being of free-will; the world of things is Fatality. Whosoever then has the strength to forsake war and Fatality, creation and perishing, and cross over to the camp of the uncreated, of the imperishable, of free-will, of peace, may justly be called the dwelling-place and city of God." (II 250–253)

THE SPECIAL LAWS

The highest, and in the truest sense the holy, temple of God is, as we must believe, the whole universe, having for its sanctuary the most sacred part of all existence, even heaven, for its votive ornaments the stars, for its priests the angels who are servitors to His powers, unbodied souls, not compounds or rational and irrational nature, as we are, but with the irrational eliminated, all mind through and through, pure intelligences, in the likeness of the monad. There is also the temple made by hands; for it was right that no check should be given to the forwardness of those who pay their tribute to piety and desire by means of sacrifices either to give thanks for the blessings that befall them or to ask for pardon and forgiveness for their sins. But he provided that there should not be temples built either in many places or many in the same place, for he judged that since God is one, there should be also only one temple. Further, he does not consent to those who wish to perform the rites in their houses, but bids them rise up from the ends of the earth and come to this temple. In this way he also applies the severest test to their dispositions. For one who is not going to sacrifice in a religious spirit would never bring himself to leave his country and friends and kinsfolk and sojourn in a strange land, but clearly it must be the stronger attraction of piety which leads him to endure separation from his most familiar and dearest friends who form as it were a single whole with himself.

And we have the surest proof of this in what actually happens. Countless multitudes from countless cities come, some over land, others over sea, from east and west and north and south at every feast. They take the temple for their port as a general haven and safe refuge from the bustle and great turmoil of life, and they seek to find calm weather, and, released from the cares whose yoke has been heavy upon them from their earliest years, to enjoy a brief breathing-space in scenes of genial cheerfulness. Thus filled with comfortable hopes they devote the leisure, as is their bounden duty, to holiness and honouring of God. Friendships are formed between those who hitherto knew not each other, and the sacrifices and libations are the occasion of reciprocity of feeling and constitute the surest pledge that all are of one mind.

This temple is enclosed by an outermost wall of very great length and breadth, which gains additional solidity by four porticos so adorned as to present a very costly appearance. Each of them is twofold, and the stone and timber used as its materials and supplied in abundance, combined with the skill of experienced craftsmen and the care bestowed upon it by the master-builders, have produced a very perfect piece of work. The inner walls are smaller and in a severer style of architecture. Right in the very middle stands the sanctuary itself with a beauty baffling description, to judge from what is exposed to view. For all inside is unseen except by the High Priest alone, and indeed he, though charged with the duty of entering once a year, gets no view of anything. For he takes with him a brazier full of lighted coals and incense, and the great quantity of the vapour which this naturally gives forth covers everything around it, beclouds the eyesight and prevents it from being able to penetrate to any distance. The huge size and height of the sanctuary make it in spite of its comparatively low situation as prominent an object as any of the highest mountains. In fact, so vast are the buildings that they are seen conspicuously and strike the eye with admiration, especially in the case of foreign visitors, who compare them with the architecture of their own public edifices and are amazed both at their beauty and magnificence.

But there is no grove within the walled area by order of the law, for many reasons. First, because the temple which is truly holy does not seek to provide pleasure and hours of easy enjoyment but the austerity of religion; secondly, because the means used to promote the verdure of trees, being the excrements of men and irrational animals, cannot be brought in there without profanity; thirdly, because the plants of the wild kind of vegetation are of no use, but only, as the poets say, "a burden to the soil," while those of the cultivated variety which produce fruits of the same quality will distract the weak-minded from the solemnity of the sacred rites. Furthermore, overgrown places and dense thickets are the resort of malefactors, who use their obscurity for their own safety and as an ambush whence they can suddenly attack whomsoever they wish. Broad spaces and openness and absence of restriction on every side, where there is nothing to hinder the sight, are most suitable to a temple, to enable those who enter and spend their time there to have an accurate view. (I, XII 66–XIII 75)

ஒ The Writings of Josephus Flavius

Josephus was a military commander who participated in the Great Revolt against the Romans as commander of Galilee (66 C.E.) but surrendered to the Romans in 67 C.E. under suspicious circumstances. A prisoner of the Romans, he managed to ingratiate himself with them and became a favorite of Roman rulers and a citizen of Rome, where he settled. He became the historian of the war and also recounted all of Jewish history for the Roman world.

ANTIQUITIES OF THE JEWS

And now Herod, in the eighteenth year of his reign . . . undertook a very great work, that is, to build of himself the temple of God, and make it larger in compass, and to raise it to a most magnificent altitude, as esteeming it to be the most glorious of all his actions, as it really was, to bring it to perfection; and that this would be sufficient for an everlasting memorial of him; but as he knew the multitude were not ready nor willing to assist him in so vast a design, he thought to prepare them first by making a speech to them, and then set about the work itself; so he called them together, and spake thus to them: ". . . Our fathers, indeed, when they were returned from Babylon, built this temple to God Almighty, yet does it want sixty cubits of its largeness in altitude; for so much did that first temple which Solomon built exceed this temple; nor let anyone condemn our fathers for their negligence or want of piety herein, for it was not their fault that the temple was no higher; for they were Cyrus, and Darius the son of Hystaspes, who determined the measures for its rebuilding; and it hath been by reason of the subjection of those fathers of ours to them and to their posterity, and after them to the Macedonians, that they had not the opportunity to follow the original model of this pious edifice, nor could raise it to its ancient altitude; but since I am now, by God's will, your governor, and I have had peace a long time, and have gained great riches and large revenues, and, what is the principal thing of all, I am at amity with and well regarded by the Romans, who, if I may say so, are the rulers of the whole world, I will do my endeavour to correct that imperfection, which hath arisen from the necessity of our affairs, and the slavery we have been under formerly, and to make a thankful return, after the most pious manner, to God, for what blessings I have received from him, by giving me this kingdom, and that by rendering his temple as complete as I am able."

And this was the speech which Herod made to them; but still this speech affrighted many of the people, as being unexpected by them; and because it seemed incredible, it did not encourage them, but put a damp upon them, for they were afraid that he would pull down the whole edifice, and not be able to bring his intentions to perfection for its rebuilding; and this danger appeared to them to be very great, and the vastness of the undertaking to be such as could hardly be accomplished. But while they were in this disposition, the king encouraged them, and told them he would not pull down their temple till all things were gotten ready for building it up entirely again. And as he promised them this beforehand, so he did not break his word with them, but got ready a thousand wagons, that were to bring stones for the building, and chose out ten thousand of the most skillful workmen, and bought a thousand sacerdotal garments for as many of the priests, and had some of them taught the arts of stone-cutters, and others of carpenters, and then began to build; but this not till every thing was well prepared for the work.

So Herod took away the old foundations, and laid others, and erected the temple upon them, being in length a hundred cubits, and in height twenty additional cubits, which, upon the sinking of their foundations, fell down; and this part it was that we resolved to raise again in the days of Nero. Now the temple was built of stones that were white and strong, and each of their length was twenty-five cubits, their height was eight, and their breadth about twelve; and the whole structure, as also the structure of the royal cloister, was on each side much lower, but the middle was much higher, till they were visible to those that dwelt in the country for a great many furlongs, but chiefly to such as lived over against them, and those that approached to them. The temple had doors also at the entrance, and lintels over them, of the same height as the temple itself. They were adorned with embroidered veils, with their flowers of purple, and pillars interwoven; and over these, but under the crown-work, was spread out a golden vine, with its branches hanging down from a great height, the largeness and fine workmanship of which was a surprising sight to the spectators, to see what vast materials there were, and with what great skill the workmanship was done. He also encompassed the entire temple with very large cloisters, contriving them to be in a due proportion thereto; and he laid out larger sums of money upon them than had been done before him, till it seemed that no one else had so greatly adorned the temple as he had done. There was a large wall to both the cloisters, which wall was itself the most prodigious work that was ever heard of by man. The hill was a rocky ascent that declined by degrees toward the east parts of the city, till it came to an elevated level. This hill it was which Solomon, who was the first of our kings, by Divine revelation, encompassed with a wall; it was of excellent workmanship upwards, and round the top of it. He also built a wall below, beginning at the bottom, which was encompassed by a deep valley; and at the south side he laid rocks together, and bound them one to another with lead, and included some of the inner parts, till it proceeded to a great height, and till both the largeness of the square edifice and its altitude were immense, and till the vastness of the stones in the front were plainly visible on the outside, yet so that the inward parts were fastened together with iron, and preserved the joints immovable for all future times. When this work was done in this manner, and joined together as part of the hill itself to the very top of it, he wrought it all into one outward surface, and filled up the hollow places which were about the wall, and made it a level on the external upper surface, and a smooth level also. This hill was walled all around, and in compass four furlongs each angle containing in length a furlong: but within this wall, and on the very top of all, there ran another wall of stone also, having, on the east quarter, a double cloister, of the same length with the wall; in the midst of which was the temple itself. This cloister looked to the gates of the temple; and it had been adorned by many kings in former times; and round about the entire temple were fixed the spoils taken from barbarous nations; all these had been dedicated to the temple by Herod, with the addition of those he had taken from the Arabians.

Now on the north side was built a citadel, whose walls were square, and strong, and of extraordinary firmness. This citadel was built by the kings of the Asamonean race, who were also high priests before Herod, and they called it the Tower, in which were reposited the vestments of the high priest, which the high priest only put on at the time when he was to offer sacrifice. . . .

Now in the western quarters of the enclosure of the temple there were four gates; the first led to the king's palace, and went to a passage over the intermediate valley; two more led to the suburbs of the city; and the last led to the other city, where the road descended down into the valley by a great number of steps, and thence up again by the ascent; for the city lay over against the temple in the manner of a theatre, and was encompassed with a deep valley along the entire south quarter; but the fourth front of the temple, which was southward, had indeed itself gates in its middle, as also had the royal cloisters, with three walks, which reached in length from the east valley unto that on the west, for it was impossible it should reach any farther: and this cloister deserves to be mentioned better than any other under the sun; for while the valley was very deep, and its bottom could not be seen, if you looked from above into the depth, this further vastly high elevation of the cloister stood upon that height, insomuch that if any one looked down from the top of the battlements, or down both those altitudes, he would be giddy, while his sight could not reach to such an immense depth. This cloister had pillars that stood in four rows one over against the other all along. . . . the roofs were adorned with deep sculptures in wood, representing many sorts of figures. The middle was much higher than the rest, and the wall of the front was adorned with beams, resting upon pillars, that were interwoven into it, and that front was all of polished stone, insomuch that its fineness, to such as had not seen it, was incredible, and to such as had seen it, was greatly amazing. Thus was the first enclosure. In the midst of which, and not far from it, was the second, to be gone up to by a few steps: this was encompassed by a stone wall for a partition, with an inscription, which forbade any foreigner to go in under pain of death. Now this inner enclosure had on its southern and northern quarters three gates [equally] distant one from another; but on the east quarter, toward the sun-rising, there was one large gate, through which such as were pure came in, together with their wives; but the temple further inward in that gate was not allowed to the women; but still more inward was there a third [court of the] temple, whereinto it was not lawful for any but the priests alone to enter. The temple itself was within this; and before that temple was the altar, upon which we offer our sacrifices and burnt-offerings to God. Into none of these did king Herod enter, for he was forbidden, because he was not a priest. However, he took good care of the cloisters and the outer enclosures, and these he built in eight years.

But the temple itself was built by the priests in a year and six months; upon which all the people were full of joy; and presently they returned thanks, in the first place, to God; and in the next place, for the alacrity the king had showed. They feasted and celebrated this rebuilding of the temple: and for the king, he sacrificed three hundred oxen to God, as did the rest every one according to his ability; the number of which sacrifices is not possible to set down, for it cannot be that we should truly relate it; for at the same time with this celebration for the work about the temple fell also the day of the king's inauguration, which he kept of an old custom as a festival, and it now coincided with the other, which coincidence of them both made the festival most illustrious. . . .

It is also reported that during the time that the temple was building, it did not rain in the day time, but that the showers fell in the nights, so that the work was not hindered. (BOOK XV, CHAP. XI, 1–7)

WARS OF THE JEWS

THE FAMINE UNDER THE SIEGE OF TITUS

The famine was too hard for all other passions, and it is destructive to nothing so much as to modesty; for what was otherwise worthy of reverence was in this case despised; insomuch that children pulled the very morsel that their fathers were eating out of their mouths, and what was still more to be pitied, so did the mothers do as to their infants; and when those that were most dear were perishing under their hands, they were not ashamed to take from them the very last drops that might preserve their lives: and while they ate after this manner, yet were they not concealed in so doing; but the seditious every where came upon them immediately, and snatched away from them what they had gotten from others; for when they saw any house shut up, this was to them a signal that the people within had gotten some food; whereupon they broke open the doors, and ran in, and took pieces of what they were eating almost up out of their very throats, and this by force: the old men who held their food fast, were beaten; and if the women hid what they had within their hands, their hair was torn for so doing; nor was there any commiseration shown either to the aged or to the infants, but they lifted up children from the ground as they hung upon the morsels they had gotten, and shook them down upon the floor. . . .

And now did Titus consult with his commanders what was to be done. Those that were of the warmest tempers thought he should bring the whole army against the city and storm the wall; for that hitherto no more than a part of their army had fought with the Jews; but that in case the entire army was to come at once, they would not be able to sustain their attacks, but would be overwhelmed by their darts. But of those that were for a more cautious management, some were for raising their banks again; and others advised to let the banks alone, but to lie still before the city, to guard against the coming out of Jews, and against their carrying provisions into the city, and so to leave the enemy to the famine, and this without direct fighting with them; for that despair was not to be conquered, especially as to those who are desirous to die by the sword, while a more terrible misery than that is reserved for them. However, Titus did not think it fit for so great an army to lie entirely idle, and that yet it was in vain to fight with those that would be destroyed one by another; he also showed them how impracticable it was to cast up any more banks, for want of materials, and to guard against the Jews coming out still more impracticable; and also, that to encompass the whole city round with his army was not very easy, by reason of its magnitude, and the difficulty of the situation, and on other accounts dangerous, upon the sallies the Jews might make out of the city. For although they might guard the known passages out of the place, yet would they, when they found themselves under the greatest distress, contrive secret passages out, as being well acquainted with all such places; and if any provisions were carried in by stealth, the siege would thereby be longer delayed. He also owned that he was afraid that the length of time thus to be spent would diminish the glory of his success; for though it be true that length of time will perfect every thing, yet that to do what we do in a little time is still necessary to the gaining reputation. That therefore his opinion was, that if they aimed at quickness joined with security, they must build a wall about the whole city; which was, he thought the only way to prevent the Jews from coming out any way, and that then they would either entirely surrender it up to him, or be still the more easily conquered when the famine had further weakened them. . . . Titus began the wall from the camp of the Assyrians, where his own camp was pitched, and drew it down to the lower parts of Cenopolis; thence it went along the valley of Cedron, to the Mount of Olives; it then bent towards the south, and encompassed the mountain as far as the rock called Peristereon, and that other hill which lies next to it, and is over the valley which reaches to Siloam; whence it bended again to the west, and went down to the valley of the Fountain, beyond which it went up again at the monument of Ananus the high priest, and encompassing the mountain where Pompey had formerly pitched his camp, it returned back to the north side of the city, and was carried on as far as a certain village called "The House of the Erebinthi"; after which it encompassed Herod's monument, and there, on the east, was joined to Titus' own camp, where it began. . . .

So all hope of escaping was now cut off from the Jews, together with their liberty of going out of the city. Then did the famine widen its progress, and devoured the people by whole houses and families; the upper rooms were full of women and children that were dying of famine, and the lanes of the city were full of the dead bodies of the aged; the children also and the young men wandered about the market-places like shadows, all swelled with the famine, and fell down dead, wheresoever their misery seized them. As for burying them, those that were sick themselves were not able to do it; and those that were hearty and well were deterred from doing it by the great multitude of those dead bodies, and by the uncertainty there was how soon they should die themselves; for many died as they were burying others, and many went to their coffins before that fatal hour was come. Nor were there any lamentations made under these calamities, nor were heard any mournful complaints; but the famine confounded all natural passions; for those who were just going to die looked upon those they were gone to rest before them with dry eyes and open mouths. A deep silence also, and a kind of deadly night, had seized upon the city. . . . (BOOK V, CHAP. X, 3; CHAP. XII, 1–3)

THE DESTRUCTION OF THE TEMPLE AND THE CITY

And now two of the legions had completed their banks on the eighth day of the month Lous [Ab]. Whereupon Titus gave orders that the battering rams should be brought, and set over against the western edifice of the inner temple; for before these were brought, the firmest of all the other engines had battered the wall for six days together without ceasing, without making any impression upon it; but the vast largeness and strong connexion of the stones were superior to that engine, and to the other battering rams also. Other Romans did indeed undermine the foundations of the northern gate, and after a world of pains removed the outermost stones, yet was the gate still upheld by the inner stones, and stood still unhurt; till the workmen, despairing of all such attempts by engines and crows, brought their ladders to the cloisters. Now the Jews did not interrupt them in so doing; but when they were gotten up, they fell upon them and fought with them; some of them they thrust down, and threw them backwards headlong; others of them they met and slew; they also beat many of those that went down the ladders again, and slew them with their swords before they could bring their shields to protect them; nay, some of the ladders they threw down from above when they were full of armed men; a great slaughter was made of the Jews also at the same time, while those that bore the ensigns fought hard for them, as deeming it a terrible thing, and what would tend to their great shame, if they permitted them to be stolen away. Yet did the Jews at length get possession of these engines, and destroyed those that had gone up the ladders, while the rest were so intimidated by what those suffered who were slain, that they retired; although none of the Romans died without having done good service before his death. Of the seditious, those that had fought bravely in the former battles did the like now, as besides them did Eleazar, the brother's son of Simon the tyrant. But when Titus perceived that his endeavours to spare a foreign temple were turned to the damage of his soldiers, and made them be killed, he gave order to set the gates on fire. . . .

And now the soldiers had already put fire to the gates, and the silver that was over them quickly carried the flames to the wood that was within it, whence it spread itself all on the sudden, and caught hold on the cloisters. Upon the Jews seeing this fire all about them, their spirits sunk together with their bodies, and they were under such astonishment, that not one of them made any haste, either to defend himself or to quench the fire, but they stood as mute spectators of it only. However, they did not so grieve at the loss of what was now burning, as to grow wiser thereby for the time to come; but as though the holy house itself had been on fire already, they whetted their passions against the Romans. This fire prevailed during that day and the next also; for the soldiers were not able to burn all the cloisters that were round about together at one time, but only by pieces. . . .

So Titus retired into the tower of the Antonia, and resolved to storm the temple the next day, early in the morning, with his whole army, and to encamp round about the holy house. But as for that house, God had, for certain, long ago doomed it to the fire; and now that fatal day was come, according to the revolution of ages; it was the tenth day of the month Lous [Ab], upon which it was formerly burnt by the king of Babylon; although these flames took their rise from the Jews themselves and were occasioned by them; for upon Titus retiring, the seditious lay still for a little while, and then attacked the Romans again, when those that guarded the holy house fought with those that quenched the fire that was burning in the inner [court of the] temple; but these Romans put the Jews to flight, and proceeded as far as the holy house itself. At which time one of the soldiers, without staying for any orders, and without any concern or dread upon him at so great an undertaking, and being hurried on by a certain divine fury, snatched somewhat out of the materials that were on fire, and being lifted up by another soldier, he set fire to a golden window, through which there was a passage to the rooms that were round about the holy house, on the north side of it. As the flames went upward, the Jews made a great clamour, such as so mighty an affliction required, and ran together to prevent it; and now they spared not their lives any longer, nor suffered any thing to restrain their force, since that holy house was perishing, for whose sake it was that they kept such a guard about it.

And now a certain person came running to Titus, and told him of this fire, as he was resting himself in his tent after the last battle; whereupon he rose up in great haste, and, as he was, ran to the holy house, in order to have a stop put to the fire; after him followed all his commanders, and after them followed the several legions, in great astonishment; so there was a great clamour and tumult raised, as was natural upon the disorderly motion of so great an army. Then did Caesar, both by calling to the soldiers that were fighting, with a loud voice, and by giving a signal to them with his right hand, order them to quench the fire. But they did not hear what he said, though he spake so loud, having their ears already dinned by a greater noise another way; nor did they attend to the signal he made with his hand neither, as still some of them were distracted with fighting, and others with passion. But as for the legions that came running thither, neither any persuasions nor any threatenings could restrain their violence, but each one's own passions was his commander at this time; and as they were crowding into the temple together, many of them were trampled on by one another, while a great number fell among the ruins of the cloisters, which were still hot and smoking, and were

The Temple Mount and the monumental stairway at the Ophel along its southern wall; looking north (Ancient Jerusalem Revealed. *Israel Exploration Society; with permission*)

destroyed in the same miserable way with those whom they had conquered; and when they were come near the holy house, they made as if they did not so much as hear Caesar's orders to the contrary; but they encouraged those that were before them to set it on fire. As for the seditious, they were in too great distress already to afford their assistance; they were every where slain, and every where beaten; and as for a great part of the people, they were weak and without arms, and had their throats cut wherever they were caught. Now round about the altar lay dead bodies heaped one upon another, as at the steps going up to it ran a great quantity of their blood, whither also the dead bodies that were slain above [on the altar] fell down.

And now, since Caesar was no way able to restrain the enthusiastic fury of the soldiers, and the fire proceeded on more and more, he went into the holy place of the temple, with his commanders, and saw it, with what was in it, which he found to be far superior to what the relations of foreigners contained, and not inferior to what we ourselves boasted of and believed about it. But as the flame had not as yet reached to its inward parts, but was still consuming the rooms that were about the holy house, and Titus supposing what the fact was, that the house itself might yet be saved, he came in haste and endeavoured to persuade the soldiers to quench the fire, and gave order to Liberalius the centurion, and one of those spearmen that were about him, to beat the soldiers that were refractory with their staves, and to restrain them; yet were their passions too hard for the regards they had for Caesar, and the dread they had of him who forbade them, as was their hatred of the Jews, and a certain vehement inclination to fight them, too hard for them also. Moreover the hope of plunder induced many to go on, as having this opinion, that all the places within were full of money, and as seeing that all round about it was made of gold. And besides, one of those that went into the place prevented Caesar, when he ran so hastily out to restrain the soldiers, and threw the fire upon the hinges of the gate, in the dark; whereby the flame burst out from within the holy house itself immediately, when the commanders returned and Caesar with them, and when nobody any longer forbade those that were without to set fire to it. And thus was the holy house burnt down, without Caesar's approbation. . . .

While the holy house was on fire, everything was plundered that came to hand, and ten thousand of those that were caught were slain; nor was there a commiseration of any age, or any reverence of gravity, but children, and old men, and profane persons, and priests were all slain in the same manner. . . . The flame also was carried a long way, and made an echo, together with the groans of those that were slain; and because this hill was high, and the works at the temple were very great, one would have thought the whole city had been on fire. Nor can one imagine any thing either greater or more terrible than this noise; for there was at once a shout of the Roman legions, who were marching all together, and a sad clamour of the seditious, who were now surrounded with fire and sword . . . one would have thought that the hill itself, on which the temple stood, was seething hot, as full of fire on every part of it, that the blood was larger in quantity than the fire, and those that were slain more in number than those that slew them; for the ground did no where appear visible, for the dead bodies that lay on it; but the soldiers went over heaps of those bodies, as they ran upon such as fled from them. . . . As for the priests, some of them plucked up from the holy house the spikes that were upon it, with their bases, which were made of lead, and shot them at the Romans instead of darts. . . .

A paved Herodian street at the foot of the Western Wall of the Temple Mount, north of Robinson's Arch; heaps of fallen stones from the wall cover the street (Ancient Jerusalem Revealed. Israel Exploration Society; with permission)

And now the Romans, judging that it was in vain to spare what was round about the holy house, burnt all those places, as also the remains of the cloisters and the gates, two excepted; the one on the east side, and the other on the south; both which, however, they burnt afterward. They also burnt down the treasury chambers. . . . And now the Romans, upon the flight of the seditious into the city, and upon the burning of the holy house itself, and of all the buildings round about it, brought the ensigns to the temple, and set them over against the eastern gate; and there did they offer sacrifices to them, and there did they make Titus imperator, with the greatest acclamations of joy. . . . On the fifth day afterward, the priests that were pined with the famine came down, and when they were brought to Titus by the guards, they begged for their lives; but he replied that the time of pardon was over as to them, and that this very holy house, on whose account only they could justly hope to be preserved, was destroyed; and that it was agreeable to their office that priests should perish with the house itself to which they belonged. So he ordered them put to death. . . .

Now as soon as the army had no more people to slay or to plunder, because there remained none to be the objects of their fury (for they would not have spared any, had there remained any other work to be done), Caesar gave orders that they should now demolish the entire city and temple, but should leave as many of the towers standing as were of the greatest eminency; that is, Phasaelus, and Hippicus, and Mariamne; and so much of the wall as enclosed the city on the west side. This wall was spared, in order to afford a camp for such as were to lie in garrison, as were the towers also spared, in order to demonstrate to posterity what kind of city it was, and how well fortified, which the Roman valour had subdued; but for the rest of the wall, it was so thoroughly laid even with the ground by those that dug it up to the foundation, that there was left nothing to make those that came thither believe it had even been inhabited. This was the end which Jerusalem came to by the madness of those that were for innovations; a city otherwise of great magnificence, and of mighty fame among all mankind. (*BOOK VI, CHAP. IV, 1–2, 5–7; CHAP. V, 1; BOOK VII, CHAP. I, 1.*)

THE THIRD GATE

Jerusalem in Rabbinic Literature

The Damascus Gate at night, July 1968 (Israel Government Press Office; with permission)

Rabbinic literature is a very wide category that encompasses works from the time of the Mishna (200 C.E.) through various midrashic collections compiled in the Middle Ages. Much of this later material, however, either stems from earlier works or is a later adaptation of it. All of it reflects the values of the pharisaic sages and their heirs, the rabbis. It contains interpretations of scriptural verses, saying of the sages, laws and legends concerning Jerusalem. The selection below is but a part of the vast material to be found in rabbinic works but reflects the basic rabbinic concepts connected to Jerusalem.

◈ Jerusalem—the Chosen

Abraham called the place "yireh" as it is said: "And Abraham named that site Adonai-yireh, whence the present saying, 'On the mount of the Lord there is vision' " (Gen. 22:14). Shem called it "shalem" as it is said: "And Melchizedek, king of Shalem" (Gen. 14:18). Said the Holy One, "If I call it 'yireh' as Abraham did, Shem, that righteous man, will complain. If I call it 'shalem' as Shem did, Abraham, that righteous man, will complain. Therefore I will use both names and call it Yirushalayim [Jerusalem]—'yireh-shalem.' " (GEN. RABBA 56:14)

◈

The world is like a human eye. The white is like the ocean which surrounds the earth. The pupil is like the earth. The opening in the pupil is like Jerusalem. The reflection in the opening is like the Temple—may it be built speedily in our days and in the days of all Israel! (DERECH ERETZ ZUTA 9)

◈

The Land of Israel is the center of the world. Jerusalem is the center of the Land of Israel. The Temple is the center of Jerusalem. The heichal [the Temple Hall] is the center of the Temple. The Ark is the center of the heichal. The rock of the foundation is in front of the Ark, and upon it the entire world is founded. (TANHUMA KEDOSHIM 10)

◈

Rabbi Joshua ben Levi interprets the words: Jerusalem built up, a city knit [hubru] together (Pss. 122:3)—a city that makes all Israel one fellowship [haverim]. (YER. HAGIGAH 3:6)

◈

Rabbi Simeon bar Yochai expounded: "He stands and measures the earth; He glances and makes nations tremble" (Hab. 3:6). The Holy One measured all the nations and found none worthy to receive the Torah except Israel. The Holy One measured all the generations and found none worthy to receive the Torah except the generation of the wilderness. The Holy One measured all the nations and found none worthy of having His Presence rest thereon except Mount Moriah. The Holy One measured all cities and found none worthy of having the Holy Temple built therein except Jerusalem. The Holy One measured all the mountains and found none worthy of having the Torah given upon it except Sinai. The Holy One measured all the lands and found none worthy of Israel except the Land of Israel. That is the meaning of the verse: "He stands and measures the earth; He glances and makes nations tremble" (Hab. 3:6). (LEV. RABBA 13:2)

◈

A place which is higher than other places is better than they. The Land of Israel is higher and therefore better than other places [as it is said]: "Let us go up and we shall gain possession of it" (Num. 13:30). . . . The Temple is higher and therefore better than all other temples [as it is said]: ". . . and the many peoples shall go and shall say: Come, let us go up to the mount of the Lord, to the house of the God of Jacob" (Isa. 2:3). (SIFRE DEUT. 37)

❧

There is no beauty like the beauty of Jerusalem. (AVOT DE RABBI NATAN 28)

❧

Praying in Jerusalem is like praying before the Throne of Glory. The gate to heaven is there and it is open so that the Lord may hear. (PIRKE DE RABBI ELIEZER 35)

❧

"May the Lord bless you from Zion; may you share the prosperity of Jerusalem all the days of your life" (Pss. 128:5). This teaches that the Lord blesses them from the same place from which He blesses Israel. How do we know that blessings emanate from Zion? As it is said, "Like the dew of Hermon that falls upon the mountains of Zion. There the Lord ordained blessing, everlasting life" (Pss. 133:3). And it says, "May the Lord bless you from Zion; may you share the prosperity of Jerusalem all the days of your life" (Pss. 128:5)—meaning: May you witness the prosperity of Jerusalem in the future. (NUM. RABBA 8:9)

❧

There was a stone [in the Holy of Holies] from the time of the early prophets called "Shetiyah" . . . because from it the world was founded [hushtat]. . . . The creation of the world began from Zion, as it is said: "A psalm of Asaph. God, the Lord God, spoke and summoned the world from east to west" (Pss. 50:1). And it continues: "From Zion, perfect in beauty" (Pss. 50:2). (YOMA 53B–54B)

❧

On the first day the Lord took snow from under the Throne of Glory, threw it onto the water in the middle of the world, and it became the land, as it is said: "He commands the snow, 'Fall to the ground!' " (Job 37:6). Then He took the foundation stone and hurled it into the place designated for the Temple and founded the world upon it, as it is said: "Who set its cornerstone" (Job 38:6). He called to the land and it stood in its place, so that it would not move here or there as does a ship, as it is said: "God, the Lord God spoke and called the land" (Pss. 50:1). Since the light of Jerusalem and the Land of Israel shone forth, it illuminated the Temple first and from there spread to light the entire world, as it is said: "From Zion, perfect in beauty, God appeared" (Pss. 50:2). (MIDRASH KONEN, BET HAMIDRASH 2)

🔊

"The Lord loves the gates of Zion" (Pss. 87:2). In every city the king has a palace. Which one does he love the most? The palace which is in his own city. Said the Holy One: I love synagogues and houses of study. But what do I love even more than they? The gates of Zion, for that is My own palace. (YALKUT SHIMONI PSS. 836)

🔊

"His foundation on the holy mountains" (Ps.87:1). The foundations of Jerusalem exist because of the merit of two holy mountains: Mount Sinai and Mount Moriah. (YALKUT SHIMONI PSS. 836)

🔊

The Holy One showed Adam an extra measure of love in that He created him from a holy and pure place. From what place did he take [the dust from which He created him]? From the site of the Holy Temple. (PIRKE DE RABBI ELIEZER 12)

🔊

"He [Noah] offered burnt offerings on the altar" (Gen. 8:20). Rabbi Eliezer ben Jacob said: This was on the great altar which is in Jerusalem, for there primal Adam had offered his offering as well. (GEN. RABBA 34:20)

🔊

What is "the coin of Jerusalem"? David and Solomon are on one side and "Jerusalem—the Holy City" is on the other. (BABA KAMMA 97B)

🔊

Why are the cattle of Ginosar not located in Jerusalem? Lest those who come on pilgrimage say, "Had we come to Jerusalem only to eat the cattle of Ginosar it would have been enough!"—thus the pilgrimage would not have been for its own sake.

Similarly . . . why are the hot springs of Tiberias not located in Jerusalem? Lest those who come on pilgrimage say, "Had we come to Jerusalem only to bathe in the hot springs of Tiberias it would have been enough!"—thus the pilgrimage would not have been for its own sake. (PESACHIM 8B)

🔊

Jerusalem is the light of the world, as it is said: "And nations shall walk by your light" (Isa. 60:3). Who is the light of Jerusalem? The Holy One, as it is said: "For the Lord shall be your light everlasting." (Isa. 60:19). (GEN. RABBA 60:19)

◎ Jerusalem—the Unique

There are ten portions of beauty in the world. Nine are in Jerusalem, one in the rest of the world.

There are ten portions of suffering in the world. Nine in Jerusalem, one in the rest of the world.

There are ten portions of wisdom in the world. Nine in Jerusalem, one in the rest of the world.

There are ten portions of godlessness in the world. Nine in Jerusalem, one in the rest of the world.

There are ten portions of Torah in the world. Nine in Jerusalem, one in the rest of the world. *(AVOT DE RABBI NATAN B 48)*

◎

Whoever has not seen Herod's Temple has never seen a beautiful building. Of what did he build it? Rabba said: yellow and white marble. Others say: blue, yellow and white marble. Alternate rows projected out in order to leave room for cement. He intended to cover it with gold but the Rabbis told him not to since it was more beautiful as it was, resembling the waves of the ocean. *(BABA BATRA 4A)*

◎

One who has not seen Jerusalem in her glory has never seen a beautiful city. One who has not seen the Temple when it was standing has never seen a magnificent building. *(SUKKAH 51B)*

◎

"All streams flow into the sea, yet the sea is never full" (Eccl. 1:7). All Israel enters Jerusalem three times each year at the festivals. "Yet the sea is never full"—Jerusalem is never filled up. *(KOHELET RABBA 1)*

◎

Seven things were created before the creation of the world, and they are: The Torah, repentance, the Garden of Eden, Gehenna, the Throne of Glory, the Temple, and the Messiah. . . . the Throne of Glory and the Temple, as it is written: "O Throne of Glory exalted from of old, Our Sacred Shrine!" (Jer. 17:12). *(PESACHIM 54A)*

◎

There were 480 synagogues in Jerusalem, each one with its own school and academy, a school for teaching Scripture, an academy for teaching Mishna. All of them, as well as the Temple, were destroyed by Vespasian. *(Y. MEGILLA 3:1)*

◎

All the trees of Jerusalem were made of cinnamon. When they kindled their wood, their perfume would spread throughout the entire Land of Israel. When the Temple was destroyed, they were hidden away and only a trifle remained. (SHABBAT 63A)

⊛

If one prays in Jerusalem it is as if one were praying before the Throne of Glory, for the very gate of heaven is located there, as it is said: "that is the gateway to heaven" (Gen. 28:17). (MIDRASH PSS. 91:7)

⊛

There were twenty-four plazas in Jerusalem. Each plaza had twenty-four alleys. Each alley had twenty-four streets. Each street had twenty-four courts. Each court had twenty-four inner courts. Each inner court had twenty-four houses. The population of each inner court was double the number of those who left Egypt in the Exodus. (LAM. RABBA 1:2)

⊛

No one was ever crushed in the Temple Court except once on Passover in the days of Hillel when an old man was crushed. They called it the "Passover of the crushed."

King Agrippa once wanted to know how large the population was of Israel, so he told the High Priest to count the Passover sacrifice. He took one kidney from each and there were six hundred thousand pairs, twice the number of those who left Egypt. This did not count those who were unclean or on a journey [and unable to bring an offering to Jerusalem] and no less than ten people registered for each Paschal lamb! They called that the "Passover of the immense throngs." (PESACHIM 64B)

⊛

Because of the fragrance of the incense, brides in Jerusalem did not have to perfume themselves. (YOMA 39B)

⊛

"Fair-crested, joy of all the earth" (Pss. 48:3). . . . Everyone says of her: "Is this the city which is called perfect in beauty, joy of all the earth?" (Lam. 2:15). . . . In what way is she "joy of all the earth"? She makes the entire land rejoice. If a man had transgressed, his heart would trouble him. He would then go up to Jerusalem, bring a sacrifice, and attain atonement; His heart would then rejoice, and he would leave feeling happy. Therefore it is said: "joy of all the earth." (MIDRASH PSS. 48:2)

⊛

No one who lodged in Jerusalem overnight remained guilty of sin. How is that? The morning offering atoned for transgressions committed during the night, while the offering made at dusk atoned for transgressions committed during the day. Thus no one who lodged in Jerusalem overnight remained guilty of sin. (*PESIKTA D'RAV KAHANA 15:7*)

❧

Ten miracles were done for our ancestors in Jerusalem [only eight are listed—ed.]:

No woman ever miscarried because of the smell of the sacrifices;

No man was ever attacked [by demons] in Jerusalem;

No man ever met with an accident in Jerusalem;

No fire ever broke out in Jerusalem;

No buildings ever collapsed in Jerusalem;

No man ever said to another, "I cannot find an oven in Jerusalem in which to roast the passover sacrifices";

No man ever said to another, "I have not found a bed to sleep in in Jerusalem";

No man even said to another, "There is no place for me to lodge in Jerusalem." (*AVOT DE RABBI NATAN 35*)

❧

All good things and blessings which the Holy One will bestow upon Israel in the future will come exclusively from Zion.

Deliverance is from Zion: "O that deliverance of Israel might come from Zion!" (Pss. 14:7).

Might is from Zion: "The Lord will stretch forth from Zion your mighty scepter" (Pss. 110:2).

Blessing is from Zion: "Blessed is the Lord from Zion, He who dwells in Jerusalem. Halleluya" (Pss. 135:21).

The shofar is from Zion: "Blow the shofar in Zion!" (Joel 2:1).

Dew, blessing, and life are from Zion: "Like the dew of Hermon that falls upon the mountains of Zion. There the Lord ordained blessing, everlasting life" (Pss. 133:3).

Torah is from Zion: "For Torah shall come forth from Zion, the world of the Lord from Jerusalem" (Isa. 2:3).

Help and sustenance are from Zion: "May He send you help from the sanctuary, and sustain you from Zion" (Pss. 20:3). (*LEV. RABBA 24:4*)

❧

"There before his eyes was a well in the open" (Gen. 29:2). This refers to Zion. "Three flocks of sheep were lying there beside it" (Gen. 29:2). This refers to three courts, for we have learned: There were three courts there. One at the entrance to the Temple Mount, one at the entrance to the Temple court and one in the Hall of Hewn Stone. (GEN. RABBA 70)

⌘

Just as there were camps in the wilderness, so there was a camp in Jerusalem. From the entrance of Jerusalem to the Temple Mount was the camp of Israel, from the Temple Mount to the Gate of Nicanor was the camp of the Levites, beyond that was the camp of the Divine Presence which corresponded to the place within the curtains in the wilderness.... Said Rabbi Simeon ben Yohai: There was another place, the Court of the Women. There was no penalty [for entering it when impure]. (ZEBAHIM 116B)

⌘

Abba Shaul said: There were two meadows in Jerusalem—the lower and the upper. The lower was sanctified by all of these, but the upper was not sanctified with all these but by the exiles when they returned, without king, urim and tumim. At the lower place, whose sanctity was complete, ordinary people ate offerings of lesser sanctity, and *haverim* ate offerings of lesser sanctity, but not the second tithe, and at the upper, whose sanctity was not complete, ordinary people ate offerings of lesser sanctity but not second tithe, while the *haverim* ate neither. Why did they not sanctify it? Because it was Jerusalem's weak spot from which it was easy to conquer Jerusalem. (TOSEFTA SANH. 3:4)

⌘

Our rabbis taught: During the forty years before the destruction of the Temple the lot ["For the Lord"] never came up in the right hand, nor did the scarlet strap turn white [on Yom Kippur], nor did the westernmost light shine. The doors of the *heichal* [Temple] would open by themselves. Rabban Yohanan ben Zakkai rebuked them saying: "Heichal, heichal, why will you sound your own warning? I know that you will be destroyed, for Zechariah ben Ido has already prophesied about you: 'Throw open your gates, O Lebanon, and let fire consume your cedars!' " (Zech. 11:1).

Rabbi Isaac ben Tabai said: Why is it [the Temple] called Lebanon? Because it whitens [*malbin*] the sins of Israel. Rabbi Zutra ben Tobiah said: Why is it called "forest," as it is written: "Lebanon Forest House" (1 Kings 10:21)? To teach us that just as a forest produces shoots, so does the Temple. As Rabbi Hosea said: When Solomon built the Temple, he planted all kinds of precious golden trees which produced fruit in season. When the wind blew against them, the fruit would fall, as it is said: "May his fruit rustle like Lebanon" (Pss. 72:16). They were a source of income for the priests, but as soon as idolaters entered the Temple, they dried up, as it is said: "And the blossoms of Lebanon wither" (Nahum 1:4). But the Holy One, blessed is He, will restore it to us, as it is said:

"It shall blossom abundantly, it shall also exult and shout. It shall receive the glory of Lebanon, the splendor of Carmel and Sharon" (Isa.35:2). (YOMA 39B)

⁜

When Nicanor went to Alexandria of Egypt to fetch doors [for the gate to the Temple], a storm arose at sea upon his return to drown him. They took one of the doors and threw it into the sea, but the sea would not cease its rage. When they tried to take the other to cast it into the sea, he clung to it and said, "Throw me in with it!" The sea immediately became calm. He was upset about the other door, but when he arrived at Acco harbor, it broke through and came up from under the boat. . . . Therefore, all the gates of the Temple were replaced by golden ones except for the gates of Nicanor, because of the miracles associated with them. Some say: because the bronze of which they were made shone like gold. (YOMA 38A)

⁜

There were five gates to the Temple Mount—the two gates of Hulda on the south, used both for entrance and exit, the gate of Kiponus on the west, used both for entrance and exit, the gate of Taddai on the north, not used [by the public] at all, the eastern gate which had a representation of the palace of Susa over it and through which the High Priest and those who assisted him in the burning of the red heifer would go to the Mount of Olives. (MIDDOTH 1:3)

⁜

There was a place one cubit square on which was a slab of marble. In it was fixed a ring with a chain on which were hung the keys. When closing time came, the priest would raise the slab by the ring and take the keys from the chain. Then the priest would lock up. . . . when he had finished, he would replace the keys on the chain and the slab in its place, lay his garment on it, and sleep there. . . . (MIDDOTH 1:9)

⁜

The Temple Mount was five hundred cubits by five hundred. . . . All who entered the Temple Mount entered by the right and went around that way. They exited by the left. If, however, something had happened, the person would enter and go around to the left. "Why do you go round to the left?" "Because I am a mourner." "May He who dwells in this House comfort you. . . ." (MIDDOTH 2:1–2)

⁜

When the Ark was there, the High Priest could enter and exit by its light. Once it was taken away, he would have to grope in the dark. (Y. YOMA 5:3)

☙ The Destruction of Jerusalem

Because of Kamza and Bar Kamza Jerusalem was destroyed. There was a man who had a friend named Kamza and an enemy named Bar Kamza. He was making a banquet and told his servant, "Go and bring Kamza." He went and brought Bar Kamza. When the host saw him seated there he said to him, "You are always slandering me—what are you doing here? Get out!" [Bar Kamza] said, "Since I am already here, let me stay. I will pay the cost of my food and drink." He said to him, "No." [Bar Kamza] said, "I will pay for the cost of half of the banquet." He said to him, "No." [Bar Kamza] said, "I will pay the cost of the entire banquet." He said to him, "No." He took him by the hand and dragged him out. [Bar Kamza] said, "Since the rabbis were sitting there and did not protest it must mean that they agreed with him. I will go to the government and inform against them." He went and told the Emperor, "The Jews are rebelling against you." He said to him, "How can I be certain of that?" He said to him, "Send them a sacrifice and see if they offer it or not." [The Emperor] sent a fine calf with him, but he made a blemish on its upper lip—some say in the white of the eye—in a place which we [Jews] consider as rendering it unfit, but they [the Romans] do not.

The rabbis were of the opinion that it should be offered in order to maintain good relationships with the government, but Rabbi Zechariah ben Abkulas said, "People will say that blemished animals are being offered on the altar." They thought that they should kill [Bar Kamza] in order to prevent him from informing on them, but Rabbi Zechariah said, "Is one executed for causing a blemish to consecrated animals?!" Said Rabbi Yohanan, "Because of the scruples of Rabbi Zechariah ben Abkulas our Temple was destroyed, our Sanctuary was burned and we were exiled from our land!" . . . We learn from this how serious it is to shame another person, for the Holy One aided Bar Kamza, destroyed His Temple and burnt His Sanctuary. (GITTEN 55B)

☙

Jerusalem was destroyed because they went according to the strict laws of the Torah and did not go beyond the requirements of law. (BABA MEZIA 30B)

☙

Abbaye said: Jerusalem was destroyed only because they profaned the Sabbath there, as it is said: "They have closed their eyes to My sabbaths" (Ezek. 22:26).

Rabbi Abahu said: Jerusalem was destroyed only because they eliminated the recitation of the Shema morning and evening, as it is said: "Ah, those who chase liquor from early in the morning and till late in the evening are inflamed by wine! Who, at their banquets, have lyre and lute, timbrel, flute and wine; but who never give a thought to the plan of the Lord" (Isa. 5:11–12).

Rabbi Hamnuna said: Jerusalem was destroyed only because they neglected the education of children, as it is said: "Pour it on the infant in the street" (Jer. 6:11). Why "pour it" [wrath]? Because "the infant [is] in the street."

Ulla said: Jerusalem was destroyed only because they had no shame before one another, as it is said: "They have acted shamelessly; they have done abhorrent things—yet they do not feel shame" (Jer. 6:15).

Rabbi Isaac said: Jerusalem was destroyed only because the small and the great were considered alike, as it is said: "Layman and priest shall fare alike" (Isa. 24:2), after which it says: "The earth shall be bare, bare" (Isa. 24:3).

Rabbi Hanina said: Jerusalem was destroyed only because they did not rebuke one another, as it is said: "Her leaders were like stags" (Lam. 1:6). Just as one stag puts its head near the tail of the other, so the people of Israel at that time put their heads in the ground and did not rebuke one another.

Rabbi Judah said: Jerusalem was destroyed only because the sages were despised there, as it is said: "They mocked the messengers of God and distained His words and taunted His prophets until the wrath of the Lord against His people grew beyond remedy" (2 Chron. 36:16).

Rava said: Jerusalem was destroyed only because there were no more people of integrity there, as it is said: "Roam the streets of Jerusalem, search its squares, look about and take note: you will not find a man, there is none who acts justly, who seeks integrity—that I should pardon her" (Jer. 5:1).

However Rav Katina said: Even at the time of its downfall, people of integrity did not cease to exist there. (SHABBAT 119B)

☙

Rabbi Yohanan ben Torta said: Why was Shilo destroyed? Because they did not respect the sacred offerings there. Why was the first Temple of Jerusalem destroyed? Because of the idolatry, sexual immorality, and bloodshed that was in Jerusalem. But what of the latter Temple? We know that the people labored in the Torah and were careful to observe tithes. Why were they exiled? Because they loved money and hated one another, thus teaching you that hatred of one's fellow is more weighty before God than idolatry, sexual immorality, and bloodshed. But the last building that will be built in the future—in our lifetimes and in our days!—what is said of it? "In the days to come the mount of the Lord's house shall stand firm above the mountains and tower above the hills; and all the nations shall gaze upon it with joy. And the many peoples shall go and shall say: 'Come, let us go up to the Mount of the Lord, to the House of the God of Jacob; that He may instruct us in His ways, and that we may walk in His paths' " (Isa. 2:3). (TOS. MENAHOT 13:22–23)

☙

Vespasian came and besieged Jerusalem for three years. There were three very wealthy men there, Nakdimon ben Gurion, Ben Kalba Shabua and Ben Zizit Hakeshet. . . . One of them said to them, "I will supply them with wheat and barley." Another said to them, "I will supply wine, oil and salt." The third said to them, "I will supply wood."

The Zealots were then in the city. The rabbis said to them, "Let us go and make peace with [the Romans]," but they would not permit it. Rather they said, "Let us go and make war against them." The rabbis said to them, "It will not succeed." [The Zealots] then went and burnt the stores of wheat and barley so that there was a famine. . . .

Abba Sikra, the son of Rabbi Yohanan ben Zakkai's sister, was the leader of the Zealots in Jerusalem. He sent him a message, "Come to me secretly." When he came, [Rabban Yohanan] said to him, "How long do you intend to continue this way? You will slay everyone through famine!" [Abba Sikra] said, "What can I do? If I say anything they will kill me at once." [Rabban Yohanan] said to him, "Find some way so that at least something can be saved!" He said to him, "Pretend to be ill so that people will come and ask about your health. Put something that smells bad nearby so that everyone will say that you are dead. Then let your disciples and no one else bear your litter so that someone will not notice that you are light, since the living are lighter than the dead." He did so. Rabbi Eleazar took one side and Rabbi Joshua the other. When they reached the door, some [Zealots] wanted to pierce [the body with a spear] but they said, "Do you want [the Romans] to say that they pierced their master?" They wanted to push it. They said to them, "Do you want them to say they pushed their master?" They opened the gate of the city and he got out.

When he arrived [at the Roman camp] he said, "Greetings unto you, O King!" [Vespasian] said to him, "You are doubly condemned to die. Once for calling me king when I am not king and again because if I am king, why did you not come to me before this?" He said to him, "As to what you said about not being a king, you will be king. . . . As to why I did not come sooner, the Zealots would not let me. . . ."

A messenger then came from Rome and said, "Arise! Caesar is dead and the notables of Rome wish to appoint you the leader!" . . . (Vespasian) said, "I am going now. Someone else will be sent here. But you can ask a favor of me and I will grant it." He said to him, "Grant me Yavneh and its sages, [spare] the dynasty of Rabban Gamliel. . . ."
(GITTIN 56B)

❧

When Vespasian came to destroy Jerusalem he said to [its people]: "Fools! Why do you want to destroy this city and burn the Temple? What do I want of you? Only that you send me one bow or one arrow and then I will leave you." They said to him: "As we attacked the two who came before you and slew them, so shall we attack you and slay you!"

When Rabban Yohanan ben Zakkai heard this he sent for the people of Jerusalem and said to them: "My children, why are you destroying this city? Why do you want to burn the Temple? What has he asked of you? Only one bow or one arrow and then he will leave you." They said to him: "Just as we attacked the two who came before him and slew them, so shall we attack him and slay him!"

Vespasian had men stationed within the walls of Jerusalem. Whatever they heard they would write upon an arrow and shoot it over the wall. Thus they reported that Rabban Yohanan ben Zakkai was a friend of the Emperor.

After Rabban Yohanan ben Zakkai had repeated his message for one day, two days, and three days—but they paid no heed—he sent for his disciples, Rabbi Eliezer and Rabbi Joshua. He said to them: "My children, arise and take me out of here. Make a coffin for me and I shall sleep in it."

Rabbi Eliezer held the head end of it and Rabbi Joshua the foot. As the sun was setting they carried it and reached the gates of Jerusalem. The gatekeepers asked them: "Who is this?" They replied: "A dead man. Do you not know that the dead may not remain overnight in Jerusalem?" They said: "If he is dead, take him out." They took him out and carried him until they reached Vespasian. They opened the coffin and he stood before him.

He said: Are you indeed Rabban Yohanan ben Zakkai? Ask what you want me to give you.

He said to him: "All I ask of you is Yavneh, that I may go there, teach my disciples, establish [a place of] prayer and perform there all the commandments."

He said to him: "Go. Do there what you will."

He said to him: "Shall I tell you something more?"

He said to him: "Speak."

He said to him: "You are to be appointed king."

Vespasian asked: "How do you know?"

He said to him: "Our tradition is that the Temple will not be surrendered to a commoner, but only to a king, as it is said: 'The thickets of the forest shall be hacked away with iron, and the Lebanon shall fall by majesty'" (Isa. 10:34).

It is said that no more than a day, two, or three passed before messengers reached him from the city announcing that Caesar was dead and he had been elected to succeed as king.

A catapult was brought to him and set up opposite the walls of Jerusalem. Boards of cedar were brought him which he set into the catapult. With these he struck against the wall until he breached it. The head of a swine was brought to him. He placed it in the catapult and hurled it toward the sacrificial limbs which were on the altar. Then was Jerusalem captured.

Rabban Yohanan ben Zakkai sat waiting, trembling, as Eli had sat and waited, as it is said: "He found Eli sitting on a seat, waiting beside the road—his heart trembling for the Ark of God" (1 Sam. 4:13). When Rabban Yohanan ben Zakkai heard that Jerusalem had been destroyed and the Temple burnt, he rent his garments. His disciples rent their garments, wept, cried aloud, and lamented.

Hebrew inscription from the southwestern corner of the Temple Mount: "to the house of the trumpeting to pr[oclaim]" (Ancient Jerusalem Revealed. *Israel Exploration Society; with permission*)

It says: "Throw open your gates, O Lebanon, and let the fire consume your cedars!" (Zech. 11:1). This refers to the high priests who were in the Temple, who took their keys in their hands and threw them toward heaven and said to the Holy One: "Since we have not been loyal guardians of Your treasure, doing the work of the King and eating from the King's table, here are your keys, O Master of the Universe, which you entrusted to us."

Abraham, Isaac, and Jacob and the twelve tribes wept, cried aloud, and lamented. (AVOT DE RABBI NATAN 4)

❧

"Jeremiah remained in the prison compound until the day Jerusalem was captured" (Jer. 38:28)—at the time when Nebuchadnezzar was gathering his armies to attack Jerusalem. When he [Nebuchadnezzar] reached Riblah he tarried there because he was afraid lest what happened to Sennacherib would happen to him. He then summoned Nebuzaradan, made him head of all his armies and told him: "Go and conquer Jerusalem." Nebuzaradan went and besieged Jerusalem from the ninth year of Zedekiah's reign until the eleventh year, but they were not able to conquer it because God's decree had not yet been finalized. But then the time came for Zion and Jerusalem to be destroyed—such times are set for all human beings, there is a time for the destruction of all living things. On the seventeenth of Tammuz five punishments occurred: the Tablets were shattered, the Tamid offering ceased, the city [of Jerusalem] was breached, Apostomos [identity uncertain—ed.] burnt the Torah, and he set up an idol in the Temple. But the Temple was burnt on the ninth of Ab.

"The famine had become acute in the city" (Jer. 52:6). The daughters of Zion would walk together in the market-place, staring at one another. One would say to the other,

"Has a woman like you ever walked the streets before like a whore?" And the other would reply, "What do I have to hide from you? The plague of famine is hard to bear. I can no longer endure it." They would then support one another and walk around the city searching for food, for something to put into their mouths, but they found nothing. They clutched the pillars and fell dead upon them at every corner. Their infants, who still suckled milk from their mothers, would come crawling on their hands and feet. Each would recognize his mother and would climb upon [the body] and take the breast and put it into his mouth, hoping to draw some milk. But there was none and, driven into a frenzy, he would die upon his mother's bosom. Thus was fulfilled the verse: "Their life runs out in their mothers' bosoms" (Lam. 2:12).

God then said to Jeremiah, "Rise, go to Anathoth and buy the field from your uncle Hanamel." Jeremiah thought, "Perhaps God means to let the inhabitants continue to live here, for He has told me to go and buy the field."

As soon as Jeremiah left Jerusalem, the angel came down from heaven, pressed his feet against the walls of Jerusalem, and breached them, proclaiming, "Let the enemy come and enter the house whose owner is no longer within—plunder and destroy it! Let the enemy enter the vinyard from which the guard has departed and cut down the vines!—Do not boast that you have conquered [Jerusalem]. You have conquered a conquered city, you have slain a slain people."

The enemy came and set up a platform for themselves on the Temple Mount. They went up on the platform, which was centrally located, in the place where King Solomon had sat and taken council with the elders. There—in the very spot where the Temple had been planned, the enemy sat and took council as to how to burn the Temple. Before they could complete their plan, they lifted their eyes and beheld four angels descending carrying four flaming torches, which they placed at the four corners of the Temple, setting it on fire.

When the High Priest saw that the Temple was burning, he took the keys and threw them up to heaven. Opening his mouth he cried out, "Here are the keys to Your house! I was a faithless guardian!" He tried to flee, but the enemy captured him and slew him near the altar, the very place where he had offered the Tamid sacrifice. His daughter ran out screaming, "Woe is me! Father—the delight of my eyes!" They captured her and slew her so that her blood mingled with that of her father.

When the priests and Levites saw that the Temple was burning they took their harps and trumpets and leapt into the flames and were consumed. When the maidens who wove the curtains saw that the Temple was burning, they leapt into the flames and were consumed—so that the enemy would not violate them.

When Zedekiah saw what was happening, he attempted to flee through the tunnel leading to Jericho which served as a water main. He was exausted and his sons were walking before him when Nebuzaradan spied him. He seized him and his ten sons. Nebuzaradan dispatched them to Nebuchadnezzar, who asked, "Tell me, Zedekiah, why did you rebel against me? By what law shall I judge you? If it be by the law of your God, you are doomed to death for having sworn falsely by His name. If by the laws of the kingdom, you are also doomed to death for having broken your oath to the king." Zedekiah answered him, "Slay me first so that I do not see the blood of my sons." And his sons beseeched him, "Slay us first so that we do not see the blood of our father spilled upon the earth."

Thus did he do, slaying them first and then gouging out Zedekiah's eyes, putting him into a cage, and carrying him captive to Babylon. Zedekiah cried out, "Come and see— all you people—that Jeremiah prophesied unto me, telling me: 'You will go to Babylon and in Babylon will you die, but Babylon will your eyes not behold.' But I would not heed him, and here I am in Babylon, but my eyes behold nothing!"

The prophet Jeremiah left Anathoth to come to Jerusalem. He lifted his eyes and saw smoke rising from the Temple. He thought, "Perhaps Israel has repented and is once more offering sacrifices, for behold the smoke of the incense is rising." But when he stood upon the wall he saw the Temple heap upon heap of stones and the walls of Jerusalem destroyed. He began to cry out, "You enticed me, O Lord, and I was enticed; You overpowered me and You prevailed" (Jer. 20:7). He continued on his way, crying out, "What road have those sinners taken? What road have the exiles taken? I shall go into exile with them." As he went, he saw the road covered with blood and the earth soaked with the blood of the slain on all sides. He bent down to the ground and saw the footprints of children and infants going into captivity. He threw himself on the ground and kissed the footprints. When he caught up with the exiles he hugged and kissed them and they cried upon each other. He said to them, "My brothers and my people—so much has happened to you because you refused to heed the words of my prophecy." When they came to the Euphrates River, Nebuzaradan said to him, "If you would like to go with me to Babylon, come. . . ." (Jer. 40:4). Jeremiah thought a moment and said, "If I go into exile with them, there will be no one to comfort those who remain here," so he left them. When the exiles lifted their eyes and saw that Jeremiah had left them they wept aloud bitterly and cried, "Jeremiah—our father—you are abandoning us!" Jeremiah responded, "I call heaven and earth to witness that had you cried thus even once while still in Zion you would not have been exiled!" Jeremiah went along weeping, saying, "Alas for you, most precious of cities!"

Jeremiah said: While I was going back up to Jerusalem I lifted my eyes and saw a woman sitting on the top of the mountain dressed in black, her hair disheveled, crying and pleading, "Who will comfort me?" And I cried and pleaded, "Who will comfort me?" I approached and spoke to her, saying, "If you are a woman, speak to me and if you are a spirit, depart from me!" She replied, "Do you not know me? I am she who had seven sons. Their father went away to a city far away by the sea. A messenger came and said to me, 'Your husband has died in a city by the sea.' As I was going to lament him, another messenger came and said to me, 'Your house has collapsed upon your seven sons and killed them.' I do not know for whom to weep—for whom to dishevel my hair!" I said to her, "You are no better than mother Zion, who has become a pasture for beasts of the field." She replied, "I am mother Zion. I am she who had seven sons, for thus it is written: 'She who bore seven is forlorn' " (Jer. 15:9). Jeremiah said to her,

"Your suffering is like that of Job, who lost his sons and daughters. So have your sons and daughters been taken from you. Job lost his silver and gold. So have you lost your silver and gold. Job was cast upon the dungheap, and you have been turned into a dungheap. But just as God turned and comforted Job, so shall He comfort you in the future. He doubled Job's sons and daughters and in the future He will double your sons and daughters. He doubled Job's silver and gold and in the future He will do the same for you. He lifted Job from the dungheap and of you it is written: 'Arise, shake off the dust, Sit [on your throne], Jerusalem!' (Isa. 52:2). [Says the Lord:] Human beings built you. Human beings destroyed you. But in the future I shall rebuild you! Thus it is written: 'The Lord rebuilds Jerusalem; He gathers in the exiles of Israel' (Pss. 147:2). Amen. May the Holy One speedily—in our days—fulfill that which is written of us: 'And the ransomed of the Lord shall return, and come with shouting to Zion, crowned with joy everlasting. They shall attain joy and gladness, while sorrow and sighing flee' " (Isa. 35:10). (PESIKTA RABBATI 26:6)

❧

Vespasian sent Titus who said, "Where are their gods, the rock in whom they sought refuge?" (Deut. 32:37) This wicked Titus blasphemed against Heaven. What did he do? He took a prostitute and brought her into the Holy of Holies, unrolled a Scroll of the Torah, and sinned upon it. He took his sword and cut the curtain. A miracle occurred and it shed blood. He thought that he had slain Him! . . . He also took the curtain, shaped it into a basket, brought all the vessels of the Temple and put them into it, and put them into a ship in order to parade them in triumph in his city. (GITTIN 56B)

❧

When the Temple was destroyed for the second time, large numbers in Israel became ascetics, binding themselves to neither eat meat nor drink wine. Rabbi Joshua spoke to them and said: "My sons, why do you not eat meat nor drink wine?" They replied: "Shall we eat flesh which used to be brought as an offering on the altar now that the altar no longer exists? Shall we drink wine which used to be poured as a libation on the altar but is no longer?" He said to them: "If that is so, we should not eat bread because the meal offerings have ceased." They said: "True. We can manage with fruit." He said: "We should not eat fruit either since there is no longer an offering of first fruits." They said: "Then we can manage with other fruits [that were not brought]." He said: "But we should not drink water either because there is no longer the ceremony of pouring water." To this they could find no answer, so he said to them: "My sons, come and listen to me. Not to mourn at all is impossible because the disaster has occurred. To mourn overmuch is also impossible. The sages have therefore ordained that a man may stucco his house, but he should leave a little bare. A man may prepare a full banquet, but he should leave out an item or two. A woman may put on all her ornaments, but leave off one or two . . . for it says: 'If I forget you, O Jerusalem, let my right hand wither; let my tongue stick to my palate if I cease to think of you, if I do not keep Jerusalem in memory even at my happiest hour' " (Pss. 137:5–6). What is meant by "my happiest hour"? Rabbi Isaac said: This is symbolized by putting ashes on the head of a bridegroom. (*BABA BATRA 60B*)

❧

Rabbi Jose said: It once happened that I was walking along and entered one of the ruins of Jerusalem in order to pray. Elijah—of blessed memory—came and guarded me at the entrance and waited until I finished my prayer. When I finished he said to me, "Peace unto you, my master." I said to him, "Peace unto you, my master and my teacher." He said to me, "My son, why did you enter this ruin?" I said to him, "In order to pray." He said to me, "You should have prayed along the road." I said to him, "I was afraid lest passers-by stop me." He said to me, "You should have prayed a short version. . . . My son, what sound did you hear in this ruin?" I said to him, "I heard a *Bat Kol* [a heavenly voice] like the keening of a dove, and it said: 'Woe to the children because of whose sins I have destroyed My House, burnt My Temple, and exiled them among the nations!' " He said to me, "By your life and your head! It is not only now but every day—three times—that it speaks so. Not only that, but whenever Israel enters synagogues and houses of study and says; 'May His great Name be blessed!' the Holy One, Blessed is He, shakes His head and says, 'Happy is the King who is praised so in His house! Desolate is the Father who has exiled His children and desolate the children who have been exiled from their Father's table!' " (*BERACHOT 3A*)

Model of the Second Temple, Jerusalem, at Holyland Hotel, 1967 (Central Zionist Archives; with permission)

∾ The Western Wall

"There He stands behind our wall" (Songs 2:9)—behind the Western Wall of the Temple. Why? Because the Holy One swore that it would never be destroyed. (*SONGS RABBA 2:22*)

∾

"The Lord is in His holy place" (Pss. 11:4). As long as the Holy Temple existed, God's Presence dwelt therein. Once our sins caused it to be destroyed, God's Presence removed itself to heaven, as it is said: "His throne is in heaven" (ibid). Said Rabbi Eleazar ben Pedat: God's Presence did not depart from there—destroyed or not!—as it is said: "The Lord *is* in His holy place." Even though His throne is in heaven, His Presence is in the Holy Temple, as it is said: "My eyes and My heart shall forever be there" (1 Kings 9:3). And thus it says: "He answers me from His holy mountain" (Pss. 3:5). Even though it is only a ruined mountain, it retains its sanctity.

Rabbi Eleazar ben Pedat says: Consider what Cyrus said: "Let him go up to Jerusalem that is in Judah and build the house of the Lord God of Israel, the God that is in Jerusalem" (Ezra 1:3). Even though it is destroyed, God Himself has not departed from there. . . .

Said Rabbi Aha: The Presence of God will never depart from the Western Wall, as it is said: "There He stands behind our wall" (Songs 2:9). (*MIDRASH PSS. 11:3*)

∾

"There He stands behind our wall" (Songs 2:9)—this refers to the Western Wall of the Holy Temple which will never be destroyed. Why? Because the Presence of God is in the west. (*NUM. RABBA 11:2*)

Heavenly Jerusalem

"Said Rabbi Simeon ben Yohai: The Temple on high is only eighteen *mil* above the Temple below. How do we know? It says "and that is the gateway to heaven" (Gen. 28:17). The numerical value of the word *v'zeh* ["and that is"] is eighteen.

Another interpretation: The Holy One showed Jacob the Temple when it was standing and when it had been destroyed and yet again when it was rebuilt. "He said: How awesome is this place" (Gen. 28:17). This refers to the Temple when it was standing, as in the verse "You are awesome, O God, in Your holy places" (Pss. 68:36); "and that is" refers to it when destroyed, as in the verse "Because of that our hearts are sick—because of Mount Zion, which lies desolate" (Lam. 5:17–18); "This is none other than the house of God and that is the gateway to heaven" refers to it when rebuilt and beautified in the future, as in the verse "For He made the bars of your gates strong" (Pss. 147:13). (GEN. RABBA 69:17)

Said the Holy One, "I will not enter heavenly Jerusalem until I enter earthy Jerusalem." Is there a "heavenly Jerusalem"? Yes, as it is said: "Jerusalem built up, a city knit together [*hubra*]" (Pss. 122:3). Rabbi Joshua ben Levi said, "It means a city which makes all Israel into one fellowship [*haverim*]." (MIDRASH PSS. 122:4; TAANIT 5A)

One should direct one's heart in prayer toward the Holy of Holies. Rabbi Hiyya said: Toward the heavenly Holy of Holies. Rabbi Simeon ben Halafta said: Toward the earthly Holy of Holies. Rabbi Pinhas said: There is no disagreement here. The earthly Holy of Holies is directly opposite the heavenly Holy of Holies. This is the meaning of the phrase: "The place You made Your abode" [*machon leshivtecha*] (Exod. 15:17)—"directed toward [*mechaven*] Your abode." (YER. BER. 4:5)

"The place You made Your abode, O Lord, the sanctuary, O Lord, which Your hands established" (Exod. 15:17). Jerusalem is directly above, opposite earthly Jerusalem. It was because of the great love [God] has for earthly Jerusalem that He created another in heaven, as it is said: "See, I have engraved you on the palms of My hands, your walls are ever before Me" (Isa. 49:16). Why, then, was it destroyed? Because: "Swiftly your children are coming; those who ravaged and ruined you shall leave you" (Isa. 49:17). Because of that it was destroyed. Thus David said: "Jerusalem built up, a city knit together [*yahdav*] (Pss. 122:3)—that is, a city which God [*yah*] built. The Jerusalem constructed in heaven is joined together as one with the one that is is on earth. God has

Arrival of the Messiah in Jerusalem and Return of the Jews; woodcut from an Italian Passover Haggada; Venice, early 1600s

sworn that His Presence will not enter heavenly Jerusalem until earthly Jerusalem is rebuilt. How do we know that this is so? It is written: "The Holy One is in your midst; I will not enter" (Hosea 11:9). And it says: "What therefore do I gain here?—declares the Lord—for My people has been carried off for nothing" (Isa. 52:5). What is there for Me in Jerusalem once My people has been taken from there? I would enter it for no purpose. (*TANHUMA PEKUDEI 1*)

❧

Elijah said, "I see a great and beautiful city which descends from heaven fully built, as it is said: 'Jerusalem built up, a city knit together' (Pss. 122:3). Built up and refined, its people sitting within it . . . and I see houses and gates of pearl and doorposts of precious jewels. The treasures of the Temple are spread out at the entrance, among them Torah and peace, as it is said: 'And all your children shall be learned of the Lord and great shall be the peace of your children' " (Isa. 54:13). (*NISTAROT ELIYAHU*, BET HAMIDRASH 3, p. 67f.)

∞ Jerusalem—in the Future

Once Rabban Gamliel, Rabbi Eleazar ben Azaria, Rabbi Joshua, and Rabbi Akiba were going up to Jerusalem. When they came to Mount Scopus they rent their garments. When they came to the Temple Mount they saw a fox going out of the Holy of Holies. They began to weep, except for Rabbi Akiba, who laughed. They said to him, "Why are you laughing?" He said to them, "Why are you weeping?" They said to him, "The place of which it is written: 'any outsider who encroaches shall be put to death' (Num. 1:51)—now foxes roam in it! Should we not weep?" He said to them, "That is exactly why I am laughing. It is written: 'I shall call reliable witnesses, the priest Uriah and Zechariah' (Isa. 8:2). What is the connection between these two? Uriah lived at the time of the First Temple, Zechariah, at the time of the Second Temple. Scripture is making Zechariah's prophecy dependent upon that of Uriah. Uriah wrote: 'Zion shall be plowed as a field, and Jerusalem shall become heaps of ruins, and the Temple Mount a shrine in the woods' (Jer. 26:18, 20). Zechariah wrote: 'There shall yet be old men and women in the squares of Jerusalem' (Zech. 8:4). Before the first prophecy came true, I was afraid that the second would not be realized. Now that the first has come true, I am certain that the second will come to pass." Thus did they say to him, "Akiba, you have comforted us, Akiba you have comforted us." (MAKKOT 24B; SIFRE DEUTERONOMY 43)

∞

In the future the Holy One will turn the ninth of Ab into a time of rejoicing, as it is said: "Thus said the Lord of Hosts: The fast of the fourth month, the fast of the fifth month, the fast of the seventh month, and the fast of the tenth month shall become occasions for joy and gladness, happy festivals for the House of Israel" (Zech. 8:19). He Himself will rebuild Jerusalem and gather the exiles of Israel within it, as it is said: "The Lord rebuilds Jerusalem; He gathers in the exiles of Israel" (Pss. 147:2). Rabbi Yohanan says: Whoever mourns for Jerusalem will merit seeing it at its time of rejoicing, as it is said: "Rejoice for Jerusalem and be glad for her, all you who love her! Join in her jubilation, all you who mourned over her" (Isa. 66:10). But whoever did not mourn for Jerusalem will not see it at its time of rejoicing. (YALKUT SHIMONI LAM. 998)

∞

"Daughters of Jerusalem" (Songs 1:5). Said Rabbi Yohanan: In the future Jerusalem will become a metropolis for all the nations and will draw people unto herself as a stream to do her honor. This [is the meaning of "daughters"] as we see in the verses: "Ashdod, its daughters [i.e., dependencies] and its villages—Gaza, its daughters and its villages (Josh. 15:47). (SONGS RABBA 1:5)

"I will make . . . your gates of precious stones" (Isa. 54:12). There will be one great gate in Jerusalem and two wickets made of one great stone. In the future the Holy One will bring jewels and pearls hollowed out ten cubits by twenty and make them the gates of Jerusalem. (MIDRASH PSS. 87:2)

Jerusalem will be redeemed only through justice as it is said: "Zion will be redeemed through justice and her repentant ones through righteousness (Isa. 1:27)." (SHABBAT 139A)

In the future the Holy One will enlarge Jerusalem so that it will occupy the space a horse could cover running from morning until midday. (PESACHIM 50A)

Anyone who mourns for Jerusalem will merit witnessing her joy. Anyone who does not mourn for Jerusalem will not witness her joy. (TAANIT 30B)

In the future the Holy One will bring the mountains of Sinai, Tabor, and Carmel together and build the Temple upon their peak. This is the meaning of the verse: "In the days to come, the Mount of the Lord's House shall stand firm above the mountains" (Isa. 2:2). . . . Furthermore, the Temple will sing aloud and the mountains will answer the song. . . . In the future Jerusalem will become a beacon to the nations of the world and they will walk in her light, as it is said: "And nations shall walk by your light" (Isa. 60:3). (PESIKTA DE RAV KAHANA 21:4)

Great is peace, for the Holy One announces the redemption of Jerusalem only with peace, as it is said: "How welcome on the mountain are the footsteps of the herald announcing peace . . . telling Zion, 'Your God is King!' " (Isa. 52:7). (DEUT. RABBA 5:15)

In the future Jerusalem will expand as far as Damascus, as it is said: "and in Damascus shall be His resting-place" (Zech. 9:1). "Resting-place" always refers to Jerusalem, as it is said: "This is My resting-place forever" (Pss. 132:14). (SIFRE DEUT. 1)

Jerusalem will not be rebuilt until all the exiles have been brought back. If someone says to you that all the exiles have been brought back but Jerusalem has not been rebuilt, do not believe him. Why? For it is written: "The Lord rebuilds Jerusalem" (Pss. 147:2) and then: "He gathers in the exiles of Israel" (ibid). Israel said to the Holy One, "Master of the universe, was not Jerusalem rebuilt once only to be destroyed again?" He said to them, "Because of your sins was Jerusalem destroyed and you were exiled from it, but in the time-to-come I will build it and never destroy it again, as it is said: 'For the Lord has built Zion; He has appeared in all His glory'" (Pss. 102:17). (TANHUMA NOAH 11)

❧

In the future Jerusalem will be raised up until it reaches the Throne of Glory, as it says: "The place is too crowded for me; make room for me to settle" (Isa. 49:20). Yet you do not yet know the full praise of Jerusalem until you see what is written: "And I Myself— declares the Lord—will be a wall of fire all around it, and I will be a glory inside it" (Zech. 2:9). That indicates the praise of Jerusalem! (PESIKTA DE RAV KAHANA 20:7)

❧

And thus you find that in the world-to-come the Holy One will expand Jerusalem, as it is said: "the structure became wider from story to story" (Ezek. 41:7)—until it will reach the heavens. . . . Once it reaches the heavens, it will say, "My place is too small." What will the Holy One do? He will bring clouds and raise it from one heaven to the next. Said Rabbi Eliezer: Eventually it will reach the Heavenly Throne itself! (TANH. TZAV 12)

❧

How many gardens will there be in the rebuilt Jerusalem? Eleven hundred and eighty-four. How many towers? Fourteen hundred and eighty-five. How many mansions? Fourteen hundred and ninety-six. How many fountains? Six hundred and seventy-six. Where will the waters of the fountains come from? From nine hundred aqueducts. . . . How many pools will there be in rebuilt Jerusalem? Thirteen hundred and sixty-nine. How many gates will there be? One hundred and forty-four—twelve for each tribe. (MIDRASH PSS. 48:4)

❧

Indeed, it shall be said of Zion, "Every man was born there" (Pss. 87:5). One who desires [to see Zion] is the same as one who was born there. [Both are children of Zion.] (KETUBOT 75A)

❧

Says the Holy One: In the time-to-come when Zion is rebuilt I shall be a wall unto her, as it is said: "And I Myself—declares the Lord—will be a wall of fire around it, and I will be a glory inside it" (Zech. 2:9). (*EXODUS RABBA 40*)

❧

Rabban Simeon ben Gamliel says: All nations and kingdoms will be gathered unto Jerusalem in the future, as it is said: "All nations shall assemble there, in the name of the Lord, in Jerusalem" (Jer. 3:17). (*AVOT DE RABBI NATAN A 35*)

❧

"Blessed shall you be in the city" (Deut. 28:3). This refers to Jerusalem, which is called "the city," as it is said: "Is this the city that was called perfect in beauty?" (Lam. 2:15). "And blessed shall you be in the field" (Deut. 28:3). This refers to Zion, as it is said: "Zion shall be plowed as a field" (Jer. 26:18). And when will the Holy One bring this blessing upon Israel? When Jerusalem will be rebuilt and the exiles restored to her midst, as it is said: "Like the dew of Hermon that falls upon the mountains of Zion. There the Lord ordained the blessing, everlasting life" (Pss. 133:3). May this happen speedily in our days! Amen. (*TANHUMAH TAVO 4*)

❧

Caesaria (the Roman provincial capital—ed.) and Jerusalem—if a person says to you, "They are both destroyed," do not believe it. "They are both inhabited": do not believe it. "Caesaria has been destroyed and Jerusalem inhabited," or "Jerusalem has been destroyed and Caesaria inhabited": believe it, as it is said: "I shall be filled, now that it is laid in ruins" (Ezek. 26:2). If one is filled, the other is destroyed. (*MEG. 6B*)

❧

"Let my tongue stick to my palate . . . if I do not keep Jerusalem in memory even at my happiest hour" (Pss. 137:6). In the future the Holy One will return all of her happiness to Jerusalem, as it is said: "And the ransomed of the Lord shall return, and come with shouting to Zion, crowned with everlasting happiness" (Isa. 35:10). Whoever mourns for Jerusalem in this world will rejoice with her in the future, as it is said: "Rejoice with Jerusalem and be glad for her, all you who love her! Join in her jubilation, all you who mourned over her" (Isa. 66:10). It was said in the name of Abaye: Rejoicing will come on the ninth of Ab, for mourning was declared for that day, and in the future the Holy One will turn it into a holiday, as it is said: "I will turn their mourning to joy, I will comfort them and cheer them in their grief" (Jer. 31:13). (*PESIKTA RABBATI 28*)

❧

"But I have installed My king on Zion, My holy mountain" (Pss. 2:6). They ask the King Messiah: "Where do you wish to dwell?" He answers: "Do you really need to ask? 'On Zion, My holy mountain' " (Pss. 2:6). (*MIDRASH SHMUEL 19*)

☙

Jerusalem is the light of the world, as it is said: "And nations shall walk by your light" (Isa. 60:3). And who is the light of Jerusalem? The Holy One Blessed is He, as it is said: "For the Lord shall be your light everlasting" (Isa. 60:19). (*YALKUT SHIMONI ISA. 501*)

☙

"When a fire is started and spreads to the thorns, so that stacked, standing, or growing grain is consumed, he who started the fire must make restitution" (Exod. 22:5). Said the Holy One, Blessed is He: I must make restitution for the fire which I started. I kindled a fire in Zion, as it is said: "The Lord . . . kindled a fire in Zion which consumed its foundations" (Lam. 4:11). In the future I shall build her through fire, as it is said: "And I Myself—declares the Lord—will be a wall of fire all around it, and I will be a glory inside it" (Zech. 2:9). (*BABA KAMA 60B*)

☙

Said the Holy One to Israel: By your lives, I burnt it and I shall rebuild it, as it is said: "I will build you firmly again, O Maiden Israel!" (Jer. 31:3). (*PESIKTA RABATI 31*)

☙

"Let the mother go" (Deut. 22:7). This refers to Jerusalem, which is called the mother of Israel. "And take only the young" (Deut. 22:7) This refers to Israel. When they sinned, the Holy One let her go, as it is said: "And your mother was let go because of your crimes" (Isa. 50:1). And it says: "Let them go from My presence and send them forth" (Jer. 15:1). Jeremiah said: "The Lord vented all His fury, poured out His blazing wrath; He kindled a fire in Zion which consumed its foundations" (Lam. 4:11). Why? Because Israel sinned. . . . Said the Holy One: Because of sins I destroyed My Sanctuary and exiled Israel. In the world-to-come I shall rebuild Jerusalem and bring the exiled back to her midst, as it is said: "The Lord rebuilds Jerusalem; He gathers in the exiles of Israel" (Pss. 147:2). (*YALKUT MECHIRI PSS. 147*)

ॐ Laws Concerning Jerusalem

"The Lord rebuilds Jerusalem" (Pss. 147:2). Whoever does not mention a good and spacious land, the covenant, and Torah [in the Blessing after Meals], and the kingship of David in the blessing "Who rebuilds Jerusalem," has not fulfilled his obligation. . . . One begins with the words, "For Jerusalem Your city," and concludes with "Who rebuilds Jerusalem" because of this verse: "The Lord rebuilds Jerusalem" (Pss. 147:2). (YALKUT MECHIRI, PSS. 147)

ॐ

Additions may not be made to the city [of Jerusalem] or to the courts of the Temple except by a king, prophet, urim and tummim (Exod. 28:30), a Sanhedrin of seventy-one members, two loaves of thanksgiving, song, and the court walking after them accompanied by the two loaves of thanksgiving, and all Israel following behind them. (SHEBUOT 14A)

ॐ

A man may compel all [his household] to go up [with him] to the Land of Israel, but none may be forced to leave it. They may be compelled to go up to Jerusalem, but none may be forced to leave it. . . . Our rabbis taught: If [a husband] wishes to go up [to the Land or to Jerusalem] and his wife refuses, she may be pressed to do so, but if she does not she may be divorced without [being paid what is due from] her ketubah. If she wishes to go up and he does not, he may be pressed to do so and if he does not, he must divorce her and pay her ketubah. (KETUBOT 110B)

ॐ

One who sees the cities of Judah in their ruined state recites the verse, "Your holy cities have become a desert: Zion has become a desert, Jerusalem a desolation" (Isa. 64:9) and tears his garment. One who sees Jerusalem in its ruined state recites the verse, "Our Holy Temple, our pride, where our fathers praised You, has been consumed by fire: all that was dear to us in ruined" (Isa. 64:10) and tears his garment.

As soon as he reaches Mount Scopus he tears his garment; he tears its separately for the Temple and separately for Jerusalem. (MOED KATAN 26A)

ॐ

Our rabbis taught: One tears one's garment . . . [when seeing] the Holy Temple or Jerusalem. One tears first for the Temple and then enlarges it for Jerusalem. . . .

[Seeing] Jerusalem in its destruction one says: "Our holy Temple, our pride, where our fathers praised You, has been consumed by fire: and all that was dear to us is ruined" (Isa. 64:10).

As soon as one reaches Scopus, one tears the garment, and he tears it separately for the Holy Temple and separately for Jerusalem. (MOAD KATAN 26A-B)

ᔐ

When a man plasters his house, he should leave a small space unfinished in remembrance of Jerusalem. When a woman adorns herself with jewels, she should leave something off in remembrance of Jerusalem, as it is said: "If I forget you, O Jerusalem, let my right hand forget its cunning" (Pss. 137:5). (MIDRASH PSS. 137:6)

ᔐ

Outside of the Land of Israel those who pray should direct their hearts toward the Land of Israel, as it is said: "and pray in the direction of their land" (2 Chron. 6:38).

In the Land of Israel those who pray should direct their hearts toward Jerusalem, as it is said: "and they pray to You in the direction of the city You have chosen" (2 Chron. 6:34).

In Jerusalem those who pray should direct their hearts toward the Holy Temple, as it is said: "if he comes to pray toward this House" (2 Chron. 6:32).

In the Holy Temple those who pray should direct their hearts toward the Holy of Holies, as it is said: "the supplications which Your servant and Your people offer toward this place" (1 Kings 8:30).

Those in the north face the south, those in the south face the north, those in the east face the west and those in the west face the east so that all Israel prays toward one place. (TOSEFTA BERACHOT 3:16)

ᔐ

Ten things were said of Jerusalem:

Jerusalem does not become unclean through leprosy.

Jerusalem may not be declared a condemned city.

Beams and balconies and sockets may not project over public thoroughfares so that they may not become susceptible to corpse uncleanness;

the dead may not remain there overnight;

the bones of the dead may not pass through it;

graves are not made there except for those of David's house and the prophetess Huldah, which were there since the days of the early prophets. . . .

plants are not planted there nor are gardens or orchards cultivated except for those rose gardens, which were there since the days of the early prophets;

geese and chickens may not be raised there, and there is no need to say that pigs may not be kept there;

garbage dumps may not be kept there because of uncleanness;

the trial of a rebellious son may not be held there; . . .

houses may not be sold there except for the part from the ground up;

a house may not be sold there for more than twelve months;

one may not charge rent for lodging there;

the hides of the sacrificial animals are not sold there. (AVOT DE RABBI NATAN A 35)

✆

One prays constantly for Jerusalem. In the Blessing after Meals: "Builder of Jerusalem." In the Amida: "God of David and Builder of Jerusalem." In the blessings of the Shema: "Who spreads His tabernacle of peace over us, over all Israel and over Jerusalem." (Y. BERACHOT 4:5)

✑ Jerusalem in the Liturgy

Because of its holiness and because of the location of the Temple in its midst, Jerusalem has been a central feature of Jewish prayer. These prayers stem from the early period of rabbinic literature, but were not put into the exact form in which we have them today until the geonic period (eighth to eleventh centuries C.E.).

Hashkivenu. The evening prayer for God's protection concludes with a blessing calling for peace over Jerusalem.

> Blessed are You, O Lord, who spreads His tabernacle of peace over us, over all of the people Israel and over Jerusalem.

Yotzer Or. The first blessing recited in the morning before the Shema includes a plea for Zion's restoration.

> O let a new light shine over Zion and may we all be privileged speedily to bask in its light!

Amida. Recited at each of the three daily services, this prayer features a paragraph asking for the rebuilding of Jerusalem and one in which God is depicted as returning His Presence to the Holy City, the end of the process of redemption.

> Return in mercy unto Jerusalem Your city and dwell therein as You have promised. Rebuild it soon—in our own days—an everlasting rebuilding, And restore the throne of David within its midst. Blessed are You, O Lord, who rebuilds Jerusalem.

> Accept, O Lord our God, your people Israel and their prayers. Restore the service to Your sanctuary and receive there with love their offerings and prayers. May the service of Your people Israel always be acceptable to you. O let our eyes witness Your return to Zion in mercy. Blessed are You, O Lord, who restores His Presence to Zion.

Haftarah Blessings. The extensive blessings recited on Sabbath and Holidays, when a portion from the prophets—the Haftarah—is recited, includes a prayer for Zion's revival.

> Have mercy upon Zion, for it is the center of our life. Save the one who has been brought low. Blessed are You, O Lord, who causes Zion to rejoice in her children.

Musaf Amida for Festivals. Because this prayer concentrates on the Temple services, which were so important on the Festivals, the three times a year when Jews were commanded to come to Jerusalem and offer at the Temple, this prayer contains an elaborate discussion of the loss of the Temple and a plea for its rebuilding.

> Because of our sins we were exiled from our land and cannot make the pilgrimage and appear and bow before You; because of the destruction which has overtaken Your sanctuary, we cannot fulfil our obligations in Your chosen house, that great and holy house which is called by Your name.
>
> May it be Your will, O Lord our God and God of our ancestors, merciful King, to return and have abundant mercy upon us and upon Your sanctuary. Appear and be exalted over us and before all living. Gather our scattered ones from among the nations, and bring in our dispersed from the ends of the earth. Bring them to Zion Your city with joyous song and to Jerusalem the seat of Your sanctuary with everlasting happiness. . . . Our God and God of our ancestors, merciful King, have mercy upon us and seek our good and our welfare. Return unto us in Your abundant mercy for the sake of our ancestors who performed Your will. Rebuild Your house as it was before, establish Your sanctuary upon its foundations. Let us behold its rebuilding, let us rejoice in its restoration. Let priests return to their service and Levites to their songs and melodies and let Israel return to its habitations. There we shall make pilgrimage, appear and bow before You three times, at the Festivals, as is written in Your Torah . . .

Musaf of Rosh Hodesh. The following is recited as part of the Amida of the additional service at the beginning of the New Month.

> Bring us in joy to Zion Your city and with everlasting happiness to Your sanctuary.

Amida of Tisha B'Av. The service on the anniversary of the destruction of the Temple is devoted to the theme of Jerusalem, its destruction and rebuilding. The Book of Lamentations is read, as well as specially composed dirges. In the prayer itself, the following has been traditionally recited:

> Comfort, O Lord our God, the mourners of Zion and the mourners of
> Jerusalem, the city which is in mourning, destroyed, despoiled, and desolate—
> mourning—for her children
> destroyed—all her dwellings
> despoiled—of her glory
> desolate—of inhabitants.
> She sits with uncovered head, like a barren woman who has not given birth.
> Legions have swallowed her,
> Idolaters have inherited her.
> They have put Your people Israel to the sword.
> They have cruelly killed those faithful to the Most High.
> Therefore Zion weeps bitterly,
> Jerusalem raises her voice:

My heart, my heart goes out for the slain.
My bowels, my bowels mourn for the slain.

Have Mercy. The following version of the prayer for God's mercy over Jerusalem is found in Yer. Berachot 4:3:

> Have mercy, O Lord our God, upon us and upon Your people Israel,
> Show Your great mercy and Your faithfulness to the city which is in mourn-
> ing, destroyed, made waste, desolate,
> given into the hands of the cruel,
> inherited by legions
> profaned by idolaters—
> although You gave a portion to Israel Your people
> and an inheritance to the seed of Jeshurun—
> For with fire did You destroy it
> And with fire will You rebuild it in the future,
> As it is said: "And I Myself—declares the Lord—will be a wall of fire all
> around it, and I will be a glory inside it" (Zech. 2:9).

Blessing after Meals. In the blessings recited after each meal, one of the important paragraphs repeats the theme of the rebuilding and restoration of Jerusalem as the seat of God's kingdom.

> Have mercy, O Lord our God, upon Israel Your people, upon Your city
> Jerusalem, upon the dwelling place of Your glory, Zion, upon the kingship of
> the house of David, Your anointed one, and upon the great and holy House
> which is called by Your Name. . . . Rebuild Jerusalem, the holy city, speedily
> in our days. Blessed are You, O Lord, who rebuilds Jerusalem in mercy. Amen.

It is also customary to precede the Blessing after Meals with Psalm 126 ("When the Lord restores the fortunes of Zion") on the Sabbath, festivals, and joyous occasions.

Sheva Berachot—The wedding blessings. As part of the wedding ceremony and at meals recited afterward, one of the seven special blessings includes this mention of Zion.

> May the barren one rejoice and be happy as her children are gathered within
> her in joy. Blessed are You, O Lord, who causes Zion to rejoice in her children.

It is also customary to break a glass at the wedding and recall the destruction of Jerusalem, reciting the verses from Psalm 137:

If I forget you, O Jerusalem,

    let my right hand wither;

let my tongue stick to my palate

if I cease to think of you,

if I do not keep Jerusalem in memory

even at my happiest hour.

THE FOURTH GATE

Jerusalem in the Literature of the Geonic Period

Jaffa Gate to the Old City, late nineteenth century (Photograph by La Maison Bonfils). The Museum of Photography at Tel-Hai Industrial Park; with permission

The period from the end of the sixth century C.E. *until the twelfth century is commonly termed the "geonic period" because of the Geonim, who headed the great academies of Talmudic learning that flourished in Babylonia. The Geonim themselves created a literature that was different from previous Jewish writings. Whereas the writers of the apocalyptic books had disguised themselves as ancient historical figures, and whereas the rabbis has abstained from writing, so that all their traditions were transmitted orally and only later written down, the Geonim did not hesitate to write long letters, responsa, and complete philosophical books. For the first time, the Geonim also issued prayerbooks containing their versions of the liturgy. During this time, however, other forms of literature continued as well—liturgical poetry, mystical writings, and historical accounts of events of the day.*

꩜ Redemption

Saadia Gaon

> *Saadia ben Joseph (882–942) was the head of the Sura academy. The following is taken from his great philosophical work,* The Book of Beliefs and Opinions.

Any Israelite, again, who will remain in the desert or who will have no one of the nations to bring him to Jerusalem, will be brought so speedily by our Lord as though a cloud had lifted him up and carried him, as it is stated by Scripture: *Who are these that fly as a cloud, and as the doves to their cotes?* (Isa. 60:8). Or it would seem as though the winds had borne him, as it is said by Scripture: *I will say to the north-wind: Give "up," and to the south-wind: "Keep not back, bring my sons from far," etc.* (Isa. 43:6).

When, then, those [of the nations of the world] who are alive unite with the living among the Jewish believers, as I have described, *the resurrection of the dead* will take place. . . . Then, too, will our Lord, magnified and exalted be He, restore His sanctuary, as has been described for us: *When the Lord hath built up Zion, When He hath appeared in His glory* (Pss. 102:17).

The structure [of the city] and the Temple will be of the form explained by Ezekiel: *In the five and twentieth year of our captivity, etc.* (Ezek. 40:1). They will be studded with jewels and precious stones, as Isaiah said: *And I will make thy pinnacles of rubies, and thy gates of carbuncles* (Isa. 54:12). The entire land will be inhabited, as it is said in Scripture: *And the parched land shall become a pool, and the thirsty ground springs of water* (Isa. 35:7).

Then the light of [God's] *Presence* will appear shining upon the Temple with such brilliance that all lights will become faint or dim in comparison with it. . . . So brilliant will that light be that anyone who does not know the road to the Temple will be able to travel by its brightness, for it will extend from heaven to earth, as it has been said: *And nations shall walk at thy light, and kings at the brightness of thy rising* (Isa. 60:3).

☙ Jerusalem Rebuilt
The Book of Zerubabel

> *One of many mystical, apocalyptic books composed during this period of time, the Book of Zerubabel contains a vision of the restoration of Jerusalem.*

After that Menachem son of Amiel and all Israel—near and far—will come, and Nehemiah son of Hushiel, and all the end with him, and Elijah the Prophet, and they will go up to Jerusalem. In the month of Ab, when they mourned Nehemiah, the ruins of Jerusalem will be inhabited and there will be great rejoicing for Israel. They will offer sacrifices before the Lord and He will accept them, and the offering of Israel will be acceptable to the Lord as it was at the first and in ancient days, and the Lord will smell the sweet savor of His people Israel and rejoice and be glad over Israel. And the Lord will cause the House built above to descend to the earth, and the cloud of incense which is in the Temple of the Lord will ascend to heaven. The Messiah of the Lord followed by all Israel will go and stand before the gates of Jerusalem, opposite the Mount of Olives, and the Holy God will stand upon the top of the Mount, while His fear will encompass heaven, the heavens of heavens and the nethermost earth, the waters and their fountains, the hills and their foundations, all flesh and all souls—for the Lord will be revealed in the sight of all. The exiles of Jerusalem will ascend the Mount of Olives and will behold Zion and Jerusalem and will rejoice. Zion will say: Who has borne me all of these? Where are they from? Nehemiah will ascend to Jerusalem and say unto her: Behold your sons who were borne unto you and who were exiled from you! Rejoice greatly, daughter of Zion, break forth in song, daughter of Jerusalem! "Enlarge the site of your tent, extend the size of your dwelling" (Isa. 54:2).

Metatron showed me rebuilt Jerusalem, which had been expanded in length and width, and he showed me the walls of Jerusalem, walls of fire surrounding her—"from the wilderness to the Lebanon and from the River—the Euphrates—to the Western Sea" (Deut. 11:24). And He showed me the Temple, build upon the top of five mountains, and he said to me: These are the mountains which the Lord has chosen to bear His Temple. And I asked: which are they? And he answered me: Lebanon, Moriah, Tabor, Carmel and Hermon.

◑ Heavenly Jerusalem
Midreshei Geulah

Building upon the concept of the "heavenly Jerusalem," this mystic text describes an encounter between Moses and the Messiah where this heavenly building and its implications are discussed.

Moses asked the Messiah son of David: The Holy One told me that He will build a Temple on earth, the Temple for Israel but I see that He builds a Temple in heaven by His own hand!

The Messiah said to Moses: Moses! Your father Jacob saw the House that will be built on earth and he also saw the House which the Holy One will build by His own hand in heaven, and he understood completely that the House which the Holy One will build in heaven by His own hand out of precious stones and pearls and the splendour of His Presence—that is the House which will endure for Israel for ever and ever until the end of all generations. That is what Jacob said on the night when he slept on a stone and saw Jerusalem built up on the earth and Jerusalem built up in heaven. . . . And when Jacob saw one Jerusalem on earth and one in heaven he said, "This is none other than the House of God!" (Gen. 28:17).—This is not the House that will endure for my children through all the generations but rather the House of God which He builds with His own hands. And if you say: The Holy One will build Himself a Temple in heaven with His own hands, so will He build it on earth with His own hands, as it is said: "The sanctuary, O Lord, which Your hands established" (Exod. 15:17).

When Moses our teacher—peace be upon him!—heard these things from the Messiah son of David he rejoiced greatly, turned again toward the Holy One and said to Him: Master of the universe! When will this Jerusalem which has been built descend to earth? The Holy One said: I have not revealed the time to anyone, neither the first nor the last ones, and shall I tell it to you? He said to Him: Master of the universe! Give me some hint! The Holy One said to him: I shall scatter Israel throughout the gates of the earth and disperse them to the four corners of the world among all the nations and the verse shall be fulfilled which says: "Even if your outcasts are at the ends of the world, from there the Lord your God will gather you, from there He will fetch you" (Deut. 30:4). And yet again I will gather those who have gone into exile with Yohanan ben Kareach to Pathros and those who will be in the land of Shinar and in Hamath and Elam and Kush—as it is said: "In that day, My Lord will apply His hand again to redeeming the other part of His people from Assyria—as also from Egypt, Pathros, Nubia, Elam, Shinar, Hamath, and the coastlands" (Isa. 11:11). Moses then descended from heaven contented.

☙ Prayer for Jerusalem

Saadia Gaon

Have mercy, O Lord our God, upon Israel Your people

Upon Jerusalem, Your city

Upon Zion, the dwelling place of Your Glory

And upon the destroyed, mournful, and desolate city

Which is ruled by strangers

And delivered into the hands of tyrants.

Foreign legions have swallowed her and idolaters have inherited her,

For You destroyed her by fire

And through fire will she be rebuilt in the future,

As it is written: "And I Myself—declares the Lord—will be a wall of fire all around it, and I will be a glory inside it" (Zech. 2:9).

Blessed are You, O Lord, builder of Jerusalem.

May it be Your will, O Lord our God,

To regard the impoverishment of Your people Israel

Scattered through all the lands,

And the ruins of Jerusalem which has become a desolation,

And Your Temple abandoned as the wilderness.

Let Your jealousy for Your holy name,

Desecrated among the nations, be roused.

Gather the remnant of Your flock

From all the places where they have been scattered.

Return Israel to its habitation

And let Your palace be properly inhabited,

For the sake of Your people and Your inheritance,

Which has been diminished,

Let them be as a mast on the mountain,

As a flag upon the heights.

For the sake of Jerusalem Your holy city

Deprived of all its glory,

Our Holy and wondrous Temple, which has become a burnt ember

And all our precious places, which have become a ruin.

◉ The Jews Return to Jerusalem

This letter of unknown date from the Adat HaRabbanim in Jerusalem, which was found in the Cairo Geniza, describes the return of Jews to Jerusalem under the calif 'Umar I (Omar) in the seventh century and their participation in the cleaning of the Temple Mount upon which the El Aksa Mosque and Dome of the Rock were to be built.

This was the doing of our God, who granted us favor before the kingdom of Ishmael, which has now gained control of the Holy Land from Edom. When they came to Jerusalem they brought with them Israelites who could show them the site of the Temple and who then dwelt with them until this day. And they made an agreement with them that they would honor the Temple and not desecrate it and would pray at its gates, and they would not prevent this.

All the Muslims in the city and surrounding came, together with a group of Jews. Then they were ordered to sweep the site of the Temple and to clean it. Omar was in charge of their work. Whenever they uncovered another layer, he would ask the Elders of the Jews if this was the stone known as the Foundation Stone. One of the Sages explained the various sections of the place until it was uncovered. Then he ordered that the wall of the sanctuary be built and a dome be erected over the stone and overlaid with gold. Afterward the Jews sent messages to all the parts of the Land of Israel to inform them of the way in which Omar had assisted them. And they inquired of them, "How many people will be coming to Jerusalem?" They gathered before Omar and said to him, "How many of the Community of Jews will the Emir of the Believers command to come to this city?" Omar replied, "What will your enemies say? Speak to them and then I will bring an end to the controversy between you." He then summoned the Patriarch and his friends and said to them, "Behold, these Jews have taken over all.... How many of them do you say shall come?" The Patriarch said, "Let the number be fifty households, including women and children." The Jews replied, "Let us be less than two hundred households." The controversy raged between them until Omar decreed that seventy households should come. They agreed to that. After that he asked, "Where do you wish to live within the city?" They replied, "In the southern sector of the city, which is the market of the Jews." Their request was to enable them to be near the site of the Temple and its gates, as well as to the water of Shiloah, which could be used for immersion. This was granted them by the Emir of the Believers. So seventy households including women and children moved from Tiberias and established settlements in buildings whose foundations had stood many generations.

◌ No Jerusalem

(A liturgical poem used in Seder Avodah of Yom Kippur)

No fire and no guilt offering,
   No garments and no oil,
No lots and no coals of fire
   No court and no fine incense,
No Temple and no sprinkling,
   No confession and no fat offering,
No immersion and no purification,
   No Jerusalem and no forest of Lebanon,
No basin and no foundation,
   No Levonah and no shewbread,
No altar and no meal offering,
   No pleasant fragrance and no libation,
No flour offering and no spices,
   No wood and no burnt offering,
No curtain and no sin offering,
   No Zion and no frontlet of gold,
No incense offering and no sacrifice,
   No blending of spice and no fragrant odor,
No gifts and no peace-offerings,
   No thank-offerings and no daily offering—
For through our sins and the sins of our ancestors, all of this has been taken from us.

☙ Burial Kaddish Prayer for Jerusalem

Exalted and sanctified be His great Name in the world which He is to create anew in the future, when He will revive the dead and bring them to life everlasting. He will re-build the city of Jerusalem and restore the Temple in its midst, uproot idolatry from the Land and restore the worship of Heaven to its site.

THE FIFTH GATE

Jerusalem in Writings of the
Middle Ages

Temple of Solomon, Liber Chronicorum, *Nurenberg, 1493 (Collection of
the National and University Library, Jerusalem; with permission)*

ॐ Travelers' Accounts of Jerusalem

During the Middle Ages Jews were dispersed throughout the world, and many of them undertook the difficult and sometimes dangerous trip to see the remnants of Jerusalem. They left behind them letters and diaries that describe the condition of Jerusalem during those years.

JACOB HACOHEN

Rabbi Jacob ben Rabbi Nethaniel HaCohen visited Jerusalem sometime before its conquest by Saladin in 1187.

In Jerusalem are the Tower of David and the Temple and the Sanctuary, and the Western Wall (but its upper stones are new), and King Solomon's quarries, and the Gates of Mercy, and the well in which the priests washed, and the Monument of Absalom, and below Mount Olivet, opposite the tower, is a tower upon a tower and it is (?) cubits high, and no road passes it, and the waters of Siloam are over against Mount Zion and Jerusalem. Between Zion and Jerusalem there is nothing but one wall. These things are known and none knows more. I also saw the Valley of Jehoshaphat into which they throw stones, and every day at least one hundred die and their bodies are brought from Benjamin's Gate down between the monument and the waters of Siloam, a great descent, until they come to Mount Olivet. Three big cisterns are there, and I asked how it is that these cisterns are not full, and they answered that the waters run away and it is not known where the water goes. Then said I, Jacob, to the Rabbis, "This is what our lord the prophet Isaiah said, 'His fire is in Zion and his furnace in Jerusalem'" (Isa. 30:9).

RABBI BENJAMIN OF TUDELA

The most famous of Jewish travelers, Benjamin traveled for many years, beginning around 1160 and returning to Spain in 1172/73. His journeys took him throughout the Mediterranean world and included an extensive trip through the Land of Israel, which was then under the control of the Crusaders. He recounted his adventures in his Book of Travels, first published in 1543.

From thence it is three parsangs to Jerusalem, a small city strongly fortified with three walls. It is full of people whom the Mohammedans call Jacobites, Armenians, Greeks, Georgians, Franks, and indeed people of all tongues. The dyeing house is rented by the year, and exclusive privilege of dyeing is purchased from the king by the Jews of

Ayyubid tower (or gate) beneath the inner side of the southern wall of the Old City, uncovered in the Jewish Quarter (Ancient Jerusalem Revealed. Israel Exploration Society; with permission)

Jerusalem, two hundred of whom dwell in one corner of the city, under the Tower of David. The lower portion of the wall of the Tower of David, to the extent of about ten cubits, is part of the ancient foundation constructed by our ancestors; the remaining part was added by the Mohammedans. The city contains no building stronger than the tower of David. There are at Jerusalem two buildings, from one of which—the hospital—there issue forth four hundred knights, and therein all the sick who come hither are lodged and cared for in life and in death. The other building is called the Temple of Solomon, being the palace originally built by King Solomon. Three hundred knights are quartered there, and issue therefrom every day for military exercise, besides those knights who come from the land of the Franks and other parts of Christendom, having taken a vow upon themselves to serve there a year or two until their vow is fulfilled. In Jerusalem is a large church called the Sepulchre, and here is the sepulchre of that man, unto which the Christians make pilgrimages.

Jerusalem has four gates, called the gates of Abraham, David, Zion, and Gushpat, which is called the gate of Jehoshaphat, facing our ancient Temple, now called Templum Domini. Upon the site of the sanctuary Omar ben al-Khatab erected an edifice with a large and magnificent cupola, into which the Gentiles do not bring any image or effigy, but they merely come there to pray. In front of this place is the Western Wall, which is one of the walls of the Holy of Holies. This is called the Gate of Mercy, and thither come all the Jews to pray before the wall of the court of the Temple. At Jerusalem you also see the stables erected by Solomon, which formed part of his palace, forming a very substantial structure, composed of large stones, and the like of it is not to be seen anywhere in the world. There is also visible to this day the pool used by the priests before offering their sacrifices, and the Jews coming thither write their names upon the wall. The gate of Jehoshaphat leads to the valley of Jehoshaphat, which is the gathering place of nations. Here is the pillar called Absalom's hand and the sepulchre of King Uzziah.

In the neighborhood is also a great spring called the waters of Siloam, connected with the brook of Kidron. Over this spring is a large structure dating from the times of our ancestors. Very little water is found at Jerusalem; the people for the most part drink rain water, which they collect in cisterns in their houses. . . .

In front of Jerusalem is Mount Zion, on which there is no building except a place of worship belonging to the Christians. Facing Jerusalem for a distance of three miles are the cemeteries belonging to the Israelites, who in the days of old buried their dead in caves, and upon each sepulchre is a dated inscription, but the Christians destroy the sepulchres, employing the stones thereof in building their houses. These sepulchres reach as far as Zelzah in the territory of Benjamin. Around Jerusalem are high mountains.

On Mount Zion are the sepulchres of the House of David, and the sepulchres of the kings that ruled after him. The exact place cannot be identified, inasmuch as fifteen years ago a wall of the church of Mount Zion fell in. The Patriarch commanded the overseer to take the stones of the old walls and restore therewith the church. He did so, and hired workmen at fixed wages; and there were twenty men who brought the stones from the base of the wall of Zion. Among these men there were two who were sworn friends. On a certain day the one entertained the other; after their meal they returned to their work, when the overseer said to them, "Why have you tarried to-day?" They answered, "Why need you complain? When our fellow workmen go to their meal we will do our work." When the dinner-time arrived, and the other workmen had gone to their meal, they examined the stones, and raised a certain stone which formed the entrance to a cave. Thereupon one said to the other, "Let us go in and see if any money is to be found there." They entered the cave, and reached a large chamber resting upon pillars of marble overlaid with silver and gold. In front was a table of gold and a sceptre and crown. This was the sepulchre of King David. On the left thereof in like fashion was the sepulchre of King Solomon; then followed the sepulchres of all the kings of Judah that were buried there. Closed coffers were also there, the contents of which no man knows. The two men essayed to enter the chamber, when a fierce wind came forth from the entrance of the cave and smote them, and they fell to the ground like dead men, and there they lay until evening. And there came forth a wind like a man's voice, crying out: "Arise and go forth from this place!" So the men rushed forth in terror, and they came unto the Patriarch, and related these things to him. Thereupon the Patriarch sent for Rabbi Abraham el Constantini, the pious recluse, who was one of the mourners of Jerusalem, and to him he related all these things according to the report of the two men who had come forth. Then Rabbi Abraham replied, "These are the sepulchres of the House of David; they belong to the kings of Judah, and on the morrow let me enter, I and you and these men, and find out what is there." And on the morrow they sent for the two men, and found each of them lying on his bed in terror, and the men said: "We will not enter there, for the Lord doth not desire to show it to any man." Then the Patriarch gave orders that the place should be closed up and hidden from the sight of man unto this day.

RABBI SAMUEL BEN SAMSON

> *In the thirteenth century many Jews from England and France came to live in the Land of Israel. One of them, Samuel ben Samson, emigrated from France in 1210. In a letter to the Diaspora, he describes his arrival in Jerusalem together with other emigrants, including the well-known scholar Jonathan ben David ha-Kohen of Lunel.*

We arrived at Jerusalem by the western end of the city, rending our garments on beholding it, as it has been ordained we should do. It was a moment of tenderest emotion, and we wept bitterly, [Rabbi Jonathan] the great priest of Lunel and I.

We entered by the [western] gate . . . as far as the Tower of David, whence it is customary to proceed for prostration before the approach to the Temple. We fell on our faces before the Shechem Gate, beyond which is the road which leads to the fount of Etham, the bathing place of the priests.

The gate opposite is in the western wall. At the base of this wall there is to be observed a kind of arch placed at the base of the Temple. It is by a subterranean passage that the priests reach the fount of Etam, the spot where the baths were.

From there we went up to Mount Olivet, where in olden times the red heifer was burnt. We said our prayers there twice with a minyan and climbed the mountain. On the Sabbath day we recited the Afternoon Prayer on the spot where the uncircumcised had time and again set up a sanctuary with idols, whose presence the place would not endure, causing them to fall down again as fast as they were set up. It was one of the ten stations visited by the divine Majesty when He came [to earth] from His dwelling-place. Only the foundations remain now in existence, but the place where the Ark stood is still to be seen.

RABBI MOSHE BEN NAHMAN

Also known as the Ramban and Nahmanides, Moshe ben Nahman (1194–1270) was one of the greatest scholars of Spain. Born in Gerona, he functioned in Catalonia until going to the Land of Israel in 1267. In Jerusalem, he organized the community and founded a synagogue and a yeshiva. From 1268 until his death he served as the rabbi of Acre. When he arrived in Jerusalem in Elul 1267, he wrote a letter to his son describing the situation there.

LETTER TO HIS SON

I write you this missive in Jerusalem, the Holy City. All praise and thanksgiving to the Rock of my salvation, for I have been privileged to arrive in peace on the ninth day of the month of Elul. There I stayed in peace until the day after Yom Kippur, when I set out to go to Hebron, the city in which our Fathers are entombed, so that I could bow down before them and arrange for my own resting place in that holy city. What shall I tell you about the Land? How terrible is its abandonment and its desolation. The sum of it is that the holier the place, the worse the destruction. Jerusalem is more desolate than the rest of the Land, Judah more than the Galilee. Yet for all its destruction, it is wonderful. It has nearly two thousand inhabitants, about three hundred Christians who escaped from the Sultan. There are no Israelites among them, for when the Tatar hordes invaded, they fled from there and many were slain by the sword. There are only two dyers who purchase dyes from the government, unto whom a minyan gathers for prayers in their house on the Sabbath. I encouraged them and we found an abandoned building with marble pillars and a lovely arch which we converted into a synagogue, for the city is wide open, and anyone who wishes to take possession of an abandoned building can do so. People have contributed to the refurbishing of the building, and we have already sent to the city of Shechem for Torah scrolls that had been sent there for safekeeping from Jerusalem when the Tatar hordes invaded. And now we have a synagogue in which we can pray. For there are many who come to Jerusalem, men and women from Damascus, Tzova [Aleppo] and other places in order to see the Temple and to weep over it. Who ever is privileged to see it in its destruction will be privileged to see it rebuilt and repaired when the Divine Presence returns unto it. You, my son, your brothers and all your father's household will be privileged to behold the welfare of Jerusalem and the comfort of Zion.

COMMENTARY TO THE TORAH

A mournful sight I have perceived in thee, Jerusalem. Only one Jew is here, a dyer, persecuted, oppressed, and despised. At his house gather great and small when they can get a minyan. They are wretched folk, without occupation and trade, consisting of a few pilgrims and beggars, though the fruit of the land is still magnificent and the harvests rich. Indeed it is still a blessed country, flowing with milk and honey. . . .

Oh! I am a man who has seen affliction. I am banished from my table, removed far away from friend and kinsman, and too long is the distance for me to meet them again. . . . I left my family. I forsook my house. And there with my sons and daughters, and with the sweet and dear children whom I have brought up on my knees, I left also my soul. My heart and my eyes will dwell with them forever. . . . But the loss of all this and of every other glory my eyes saw is compensated by having now the joy of being a day in thy courts, O Jerusalem, visiting the ruins of the Temple, and crying over the desolate sanctuary; where I am permitted to caress thy stones, to fondle thy dust, and to weep over thy ruins. I wept bitterly, but I found joy in my tears. I tore my garments, but I felt relieved by it.

Rabbi Eshtori haParhi

Eshtori (Isaac ben Moses) haParhi was born in Provence in 1280. After the expulsion of the Jews from France he went to Spain, then traveled to the Land of Israel. He settled in Beth Shean and wrote a book describing the land on the basis of his travels. This book, Kaftor vaFerah, was completed in 1322 and was the first real geography of Israel. It also includes the following prayer to be recited at the Western Wall.

PRAYER AT THE WALL

O Unique Lord, God of this House, Light of the world! This humble person cries out, pours out his prayer and voices his bitterness, crying and lamenting, stretching forth his hands and palms toward You, O God, whose countenance is turned toward this place. He awaits Your justice, longs for Your salvation, standing in the public places where the archers of the enemy abound and the stranger not of Your people Israel rules over Your House, while "none of the house being there inside" (Gen. 39:11).

In Your faithful trustworthiness, O my God, rebuild Your house as it was afore. O You who rescues, attend to the treasured people, who are in exile because of wrath, and to Your holy city, to the splendid and renowned palace; bring them there in mercy and faithfulness. Offerings will be brought upon Your altar when You return its fame and glory.

Isaac Chelo

Isaac ben Joseph ibn Chelo (or Hilo) lived in the fourteenth century and provides the following account of his visit in Jerusalem in 1334.

Alas, by reason of our sins, where the sacred building (the Temple) once stood, its place is taken today by a profane temple, built by the King of the Ishmaelites when he conquered Palestine and Jerusalem from the uncircumcised. The history of that event was in this wise:

The king, who had made a vow to build up again the ruins of the sacred edifice, if God put the holy city into his power, demanded of the Jews that they should make known those ruins to him. For the uncircumcised, in their hate against the people of God, had heaped rubbish and filth over the spot, so that no one knew exactly where the ruins stood. Now there was an old man then living who said: "If the King will take an oath to preserve the western wall, I will discover to him the place where the ruins of the holy temple are." So the king straightway placed his hand on the thigh of the old man and swore by oath to do what he demanded. When the old man had shown him the ruins of the temple under a mound of defilements, the King had the ruins cleared and cleansed, taking part in the cleansing himself, until they were all fair and clean. After that he had them all set up again, with the exception of the western wall, and made of them a very beautiful temple, which he consecrated to his God.

It is this western wall which stands before the temple of Omar ibn al Khattab, and which is called the Gate of Mercy. The Jews resort thither to say their prayers, as Rabbi Benjamin has already related. Today, this wall is one of the seven wonders of the Holy City, of which the names are: the Tower of David, Solomon's Palace, the tomb of Huldah the prophetess, the Sepulchres of the Kings, the Palace of Queen Helena, the Gate of Mercy, and the Western Wall.

The first of these is the Tower of David mentioned above, near the gate of that name. It is of very ancient and very solid construction, and in the oldern times, the Jews used to dwell about it. Today there are no habitations in the vicinity but, instead, so many fortifications, as to make this ancient stronghold quite impregnable in our time.

The second is an ancient building called Solomon's Palace. In former days, when the uncircumcised were in possession, this building was appointed to receive the sick of the holy city; today a market of considerable importance is held there.

The third is the tomb of the prophetess Huldah. . . . as was narrated by the great author in the following words: "They allowed no sepulchre in Jerusalem except the tombs of the House of David and that of Huldah, which have been there from the days of the earliest prophets." [Avot de Rabbi Natan 35A]

The tomb of Huldah the prophetess, on the summit of the Mount of Olives, is very beautifully built. But the sepulchres of the House of David which were on Mount Zion are no longer known today either to Jews or Mussulmans; for they are not the Tombs of the Kings about which we are now going to speak.

These latter sepulchres are the fourth of the wonders of the Holy City. They are, as we have already said, near the cave of Ben Sirah. They are of ancient and massive construction, in form a masterpiece of sculpture. All the strangers who come to visit the Holy City say they have never seen anything so beautiful.

The fifth of the curiosities to be seen is the Palace of Queen Helena, who came to Jerusalem with King Monbaz and was adopted into the Jewish religion there. This palace is a fine building inhabited today by the Cadi and his councillors.

Pool of Silwan storing the waters of the Gihon Spring, December 1978 (Israel Government Press Office; with permission)

The sixth is the Gate of Mercy, near the Temple. Formerly there were two gates, the one for wedding parties, the other for mourners, as we are told in the Chapters of Rabbi Eliezer the Great, the German Kabbalist, blessed by his memory! These two gates have been buried in the earth for the fulfilment of the Scriptures.

Finally, the last remarkable thing in the Holy City is the Western Wall, of which we spoke above.

The Jewish community in Jerusalem, God be gracious to her! is quite numerous. It is composed of fathers of families from all parts of the world, principally from France. The leading men of the community, as well as the principal rabbis, come from the latter kingdom—among others Rabbi Chaim and Rabbi Joseph. They live there in happiness and tranquility, each according to his condition and fortune, for the royal authority is just and great. May God re-establish her and raise her to the highest prosperity!

Among the different members of the holy congregation at Jerusalem are many who are engaged in handicrafts such as dyers, tailors, shoemakers, etc. Others carry on a rich commerce in all sorts of things, and have fine shops. Some are devoted to science, as medicine, astronomy, and mathematics. But the greater number of their learned men are working day and night at the study of the Holy Law and of the true wisdom, which is the Kabbalah. These are maintained out of the coffers of the community, because the study of the law is their only calling. There are also at Jerusalem excellent calligraphists and the copies are sought for by strangers who carry then away to their own countries.

I have seen a Pentateuch written with so much art that several peoples at once wanted to acquire it, and it was only for an excessively high price that the Chief of the Synagogues of Babylon carried it off with him to Bagdad.

ELIJAH OF FERRARA

An Italian scholar, Elijah went in 1434 to live in Jerusalem, where he became a dayyan (judge).

LETTER TO HIS SONS

5195—July 1435

I myself fell ill and came nigh to death's door. But thanks be to God, the Physician who exacts no reward, He sent His angel to me and gave me strength to come on here to Jerusalem, the holy city, where I arrived on the 41st of the Sephirah, in the year 5194. My weakness was still, however, extreme, either because I had not yet entirely recovered from my sickness, or by reason of my afflictions and much grieving [the death of two sons on the journey—ed.]. The days of my mourning were not yet over, and my sorrow still lay heavy upon me, when the notables of the community came to visit me and besought me to expound to them, in the synagogue, the Chapters of Maimonides, according to their custom, and from that time they imposed upon me the charge to expound publicly to them three times a day the Ethics of the Fathers in the synagogue, Halakah with Tosafoth in the Beth ha-Midrash and again Halakah with Rashi's commentary in the synagogue towards evening. In addition to all this, I am charged with the duties of a religious adviser in this city, and of giving responses upon questions of law from Misr [Cairo], Alexandria, Damascus, and other remote cities. After all this, you will hardly be able to believe it, but, with the help of the Almighty, I have found strength for all. For all this labour and toil, however, I receive but a small reward, yet one which has enabled me so far to live in plenty, because provisions are plentiful and abundant and cheaper to buy (God be thanked!) than in any other place where I lived in the West. . . .

There is a great plague ravaging these countries, in Egypt, in Damascus, and in Jerusalem. Close on ninety victims have perished here, and five hundred at Damascus; but now (praised be the Physician without reward!) the mortality has ceased.

That you may know how fathers of families earn their living here, some engage in business and sell in shops; others work as carpenters and chemists. They have no adept knowledge of the art of preparing drugs and other matters pertaining to pharmacy, they simply buy them and sell them again. I need hardly say that they know nothing of medicine, but are for the most part ignoramuses. Many of them carry on the work of goldsmiths or shoe-makers; some deal in silks, the men doing the buying and selling, the women the actual work.

The Jews ply their trades side by side with the Ishmaelites and no jealousy between them results such as I have remarked in other places.

MESHULLAM BEN R. MENAHEM

An Italian Jew, Meshullam visited the Holy Land in the 1480s and provided us with this account of the holy places and of his adventures.

On Wednesday, the 29th July, we reached the Holy City of Jerusalem, and when I saw its ruins I rent my garments a hand breadth, and in the bitterness of my heart recited the appropriate prayer which I had in a small book.

Now Jerusalem has no walls except a little on one side where I entered, and although through our sins it is all in ruins there are ten thousand Moslem householders and about two hundred and fifty Jewish householders. The Temple, may it be restored speadily in our days, is still surrounded by a wall. On the east side are the Gates of Mercy, made of brass and embedded in the ground. The gates are closed, and on the sides of the gates are Moslem graves. Opposite this is the site of the Temple of King Solomon and a Moslem building upon it. The hugh stones in this building are a wondrous matter, and it is difficult to believe how the strength of man could have moved them into their present position. Near the sanctuary is a great vaulted building with pillars surrounding the large pavement which covers the Temple area. The circumference of the Temple seems about half a mile. On the western side of the pavement there is a place about three fingers high which is said to be the Eben Shethiah, and there is a great cupola beautifully gilded, about twenty or perhaps thirty cubits square. It is very high, and the Ishmaelites have covered it with lead, and they say that this is doubtless the Holy of Holies. On the border of the Holy of Holies there is a place about two and a half cubits high, and at its four corners there are stones to get up to it. Here there is a well of running water and near it the cupola is built. . . . On the southern side, inside the temple area, there is a large and beautiful house also covered with lead called Solomon's College, and in the middle of the temple area there are about ten olive trees; and now by the King's command they are building inside a place for him when he wishes to go up to Jerusalem. The walls round the temple area where it was broken down and burnt have been built up by the Ishmaelites, and it is now completely surrounded, although very bare. The walls are not as high as they originally were because of our transgressions, and the Moslems who dwell in their houses opposite the walls overlook them. The temple area has twelve gates, of which five are closed; two are the Gates of Mercy, in one of which bridegrooms enter, and in the others mourners. They are of iron closed and embedded about two cubits in the ground and project about four cubits above the ground, and the other three gates are built in the wall, for they were built by the Moslems and their character is evident; and before all these gates you will find wide and goodly roads vaulted with houses on either side, in which pilgrims once dwelt, but now through our iniquities the Moslems make in them shops for all kinds of merchandise. . . .

On the southern side is Mount Zion, that is the city of David, and above it, near to David's tomb, there is a church of the Franciscans. The place of David's burial is a house which has a great iron door, and the Moslems take care of the key and honour the place and pray there. Going down from there on the slope of the hill is the valley of the son of Hinnom, which goes down to the valley of Jehoshaphat; and on the west is Millo, which is a plain near the city where people go out to walk, especially the Jews. On this road, if you go to the west about two miles, a little distance from the road bed to the right on the way to Jerusalem you find a cave with a door of hewn stone by which you enter. It is all covered up and has many caves, cave upon cave, very beautiful, those of the seventy Sanhedrin, and I prayed in that place. . . .

The buildings of Jerusalem are very fine and the stones are larger than in the buildings of the other places that I have seen. . . . I was ill in Jerusalem from the day I arrived until I left to go to Damascus, and I was near death's door, but by the mercy of God an Ashkenazi called R. Jacob Kolvarani, he and his wife and his mother-in-law, gave me food after our custom. . . . It is not to be wondered at that foreigners who go there get ill; the wonder is that they do not all die. This is caused by the troublesome journey and the great heat one has to endure on the way. In Jerusalem there are draughts every day, summer and winter, different winds from the four corners of the earth such as I have never seen. . . . The notable Jews . . . go every year with the congregation behind them to Mount Zion on the ninth of Ab to mourn and weep, and thence they descend to the valley of Jehoshaphat and go upon Mount Olivet, whence they see the whole of the Temple area and mourn for the destruction of the Temple. There are still olives on Mount Olivet, and the Moslems call the whole surroundings of Jerusalem and Mount Zion, El Kuds, that is, the holy land. May it be the will of our Father in heaven that it may be rebuilt speedily in our days. Amen.

OBADIAH DA BERTINORO

This famous Italian rabbi was born ca. 1450 and died sometime before 1516. In 1485 he left Italy and traveled; in 1488 he reached the Land of Israel, where he served as rabbi. He was buried on the Mount of Olives. His letters from Jerusalem describe the situation when he arrived.

About three-quarters of a mile from Jerusalem, at a place where the mountain is ascended by steps, we beheld the famous city of our delight, and here we rent our garments, as was our duty. A little further on, the sanctuary, the desolate house of our splendour, became visible, and at the sight of it we again made rents in our garments. We came as far as the gates of Jerusalem, and on the 13th of Nissan, 5248, at noon, our feet stood within the gates of the city. . . . Jerusalem is for the most part desolate and in ruins. I need not repeat that it is not surrounded by walls. Its inhabitants, I am told, number about four thousand families. As for Jews, about seventy families of the poorest class have remained; there is scarcely a family that is not in want of the commonest necessaries; one who has bread for a year is called rich. Among the Jewish population there are many aged, forsaken widows from Germany, Spain, Portugal, and other countries, so that there are seven women to one man. . . .

The Jews are not persecuted by the Arabs in these parts. I have travelled through the country in its length and breadth, and none of them has put an obstacle in my way. They are very kind to strangers. . . .

The Synagogue here is built on columns; it is long, narrow, and dark, the light entering only by the door. There is a fountain in the middle of it. In the court of the Synagogue, quite close to it, stands a mosque. The court of the Synagogue is very large and contains many houses, all of them buildings devoted by the Ashkenazim to charitable purposes and inhabited by Ashkenazi widows. There were formerly many courts in the Jewish streets belonging to these buildings, but the Elders sold them, so that not a single one remained. They could not, however, sell the buildings of the Ashkenazim, and no other poor had a right to them. The Jews' street and the houses are very large; some of them dwell also on Zion. At one time they had more houses, but these are now heaps of rubbish and cannot be rebuilt, for the law of the land is that a Jew may not rebuild his ruined house without permission, and the permission often costs more than the whole house is worth. The houses of Jerusalem are of stone, none of wood or plaster. . . .

Jerusalem, notwithstanding its destruction, still contains four very beautiful, long bazaars, such as I have never before seen, at the foot of Zion. They have all dome-shaped roofs, and contain wares of every kind. They are divided into different departments, the merchant bazaar, the spice bazaar, the vegetable market, and one in which cooked food and bread are sold. When I came to Jerusalem there was a dreadful famine in the land. . . . Many Jews died of hunger; they had been seen a day or two before asking for bread, which nobody could give them, and the next day they were found dead in their houses. Many live on grass, going out like stags to look for pasture. At present there is only one German Rabbi here, who was educated in Jerusalem. I have never seen his equal for humility and the fear of God; he weaves night and day when he is not occupied with his studies, and for six months he tasted no bread between Sabbath and Sabbath, his food consisting of raw turnips and the remains of St. John's bread, which is very plentiful here, after the sugar has been taken out of it. . . .

Now, the wheat-harvest being over, the famine is at an end, and there is once more plenty, praise be to God. Here, in Jerusalem, I have seen several kinds of fruit which are not to be found in our country. There is one tree with long leaves, which grows higher than a man's stature, and bears fruit only once; it then withers, and from its roots there rises another similar one which again bears fruit the next year, and the same thing is continually repeated. The grapes are larger than in our country. . . . All the necessaries of life, such as meat, wine, olives, and sesame-oil, can be very cheap. The soil is excellent; but it is not possible to gain a living by any branch of industry, unless it be that of a shoe-maker, weaver, or goldsmith. . . .

Persons of various nationalities are always to be found in Jerusalem from Christian countries, and from Babylonia and Abyssinia. The Arabs come frequently to offer up prayers at the temple, for they hold it in great veneration. . . . No Jew may enter the enclosure of the temple. Although sometimes the Arabs are anxious to admit carpenters and goldsmiths to perform work there, nobody will go in, for we have all been defiled [by touching bodies of the dead]. I do not know whether the Arabs enter the Holy of Holies or not. I also made enquiries relative to the Eben Shethiah where the Ark of the Covenant was placed, and am told that it is under a high and beautiful dome built by the Arabs in the court of the Temple. It is enclosed in this building, and no one may enter. There is great wealth in the enclosure of the temple. We hear that the monarchs build chambers there inlaid with gold, and the king now reigning is said to have erected a building, more splendid than any ever before built, adorned with gold and precious stones.

The temple enclosure has still twelve gates. Those which are called the gates of mercy are of iron, and are two in number; they look towards the east of the temple and are always closed. They only reach half-way above the ground; the other half is sunk in the earth. It is said that the Arabs often tried to raise them up but were not able to do so.

The western wall, part of which is still standing, is composed of large, thick stones, such as I have never before seen in an old building, either in Rome or in any other country. At the north-east corner is a tower of very large stones. I entered it and found a vast edifice supported by massive and lofty pillars; there are so many pillars that it wearied me to go to the end of the building. Everything is filled with earth which has been thrown there from the ruins of the temple. The temple-building stands on these columns, and in each of them is a hole through which a cord may be drawn. It is said that the bulls and rams for sacrifice were bound here. Throughout the whole region of Jerusalem, in fields as well as vineyards, there are large caves connected with one another.

The Mount of Olives is lofty and barren; scarcely an olive tree is to be found on it. From the top, Sodom and Gomorrah may be seen in the distance; they now form a salt sea. . . . On the Mount of Olives are the graves of the Prophet Haggai and Huldah the Prophetess and more than ten caves, one leading out of the other. The sepulchre of the seventy Elders, which lies about two thousand cubits from Jerusalem, is splendid, especially that of Simon the Just. . . .

At the foot of the slope of the temple mountain are Jewish graves; the new ones are at the foot of the Mount of Olives, and the valley runs between the grave-yards. Not

Mount of Olives, with monuments in the Valley of Yehoshaphat in the front, Yad Avshalom at the left, 1856 (Photograph by Francis Frith. The Museum of Photography at Tel-Hai Industrial Park; with permission)

far from here are the monuments of Absalom and of the Prophet Zachariah; at the latter place, prayers are offered up on fast days; and on the 9th of Ab lamentations are repeated.

I have taken a house here close to the Synagogue. The upper chamber of my dwelling is even in the wall of the Synagogue. In the court where my house is there are five inhabitants, all of them women. There is only one blind man living here, and his wife attends on me. . . . Most of those who come to Jerusalem from foreign countries fall ill, owing to climatic changes and the sudden variations of the wind, now cold, now warm. All possible winds blow in Jerusalem. It is said that every wind before going where it listeth, comes to Jerusalem to prostrate itself before the Lord, Blessed be He that knoweth truth. . . .

⟫

Finished in haste in Jerusalem, the Holy City. May it soon be rebuilt in our days.   On the 8th Elul, 5248.

AN UNKNOWN WRITER, 1495

On Friday, the 18th of Marheshvan, I saw from afar the deserted and waste city and the ruins of the mountain of Zion, the dwelling-place of lions and jackals; my heart burst into tears. I sat down and, weeping, I made the two prescribed cuts in my garment; I turned to the square of the Temple and prayed that the Lord might lead the captives of Israel into their land soon in order that we may see the dwelling-place of God. Amen.

After having entered the city, I called upon the famous, esteemed and learned R. Obadiah. I poured out my heart to him and told him that I had forsaken my family in my birthplace in order to hide under his wings and to continue my studies with him. He looked like an old, compassionate man, and said to me: "I shall take care of thee, and shall treat thee as my own son." . . . This man is held in great esteem here; nobody dares to do anything without having consulted him. . . .

When I arrived here, I was unable to find a lodging, as the place was so crowded. I was therefore content to rent a room for one month until I could find a definite lodging. I very much wished to live with the scholar Abraham of Messina, may the Lord bless him and his posterity, with the esteemed Moses of Burgo and another cultured and kind-hearted young Sephardi, all of whom stayed in one court and studied day and night. When I revealed this wish to the learned Obadiah, he tried at once with the greatest eagerness to satisfy my desire. He negotiated with the landlady of the court and convinced her that it would be an advantage to me, for the sake of my studies, if I could live together with those persons. And the woman was good enough to let me stay in her house. . . .

In Jerusalem there are about two hundred Jewish families, who abstain from every sin and fulfil the commandments of the Lord with great zeal. All people without distinction, old and young, gather together in the evenings for prayers. There are two God-fearing readers here who read with great devotion and pronounce every syllable distinctly. The whole community is eager to listen twice daily to the sermons of the eighty-year-old Rabbi Zachariah Sephardi, the Lord bless him and his posterity. . . . The highly learned Rabbi Obadiah delivers sermons only two or three times a year, at Passover, Pentecost and Taberbacles and sometimes also on the penitential days. Only the other day his pleasant voice could be heard as he spoke words of the living God. All people, young and adults, were present, and all were so quiet that no breath could be heard. I shall not dare to utter his praises, for from such an humble and ignorant man as I, it would be by no means an honour for him.

Many remain after the prayer and the sermon in the Synagogue in order to devote themselves to the study of Mishnah and Talmud for three hours. Afterwards they visit the sick and distribute alms according to their means. People here are very benevolent although they are poor themselves and live on alms; may the Lord have mercy upon us and fill our granaries and bless our undertakings.

Here in Jerusalem it is very difficult to earn a living. Even artisans, like workers in gold, smiths, weavers or tailors, get hardly enough for their daily needs. . . . On the other hand all is very cheap here, and I think that a man can live here a year for ten ducats. . . .

The houses of Jerusalem are built with blocks of stone, and they have not several flats like those in your country; they are also built without timber. . . . There are five or six rooms in every home, all made of bricks. No fountains with spring-water are to be found here, but there is a cistern in every house into which water pours when it rains. . . . Near the synagogue, in the middle of the city, there is an empty space where the whole community gathers for another prayer in front of the Temple ruins, which are visible from that place.

RABBI ISAIAH HURWITZ

A noted kabbalist born in Prague ca. 1565, Rabbi Hurwitz (or Horowitz) moved to the Land of Israel in 1621 and served as rabbi in Jerusalem. In 1625 he was imprisoned by the pasha and ransomed. He died in Tiberias in 1630. From Jerusalem he wrote many letters to his children.

In Damascus two distinguished men from Safed came to me. They welcomed me and approached me with requests on behalf of the community to settle in Safed and become their head. I answered them that I had to go on to Safed, and that we could take counsel there. My intention was, however, to proceed to Jerusalem. On the same day, when I was just before the gates of the city of Damascus, a special envoy from Jerusalem came to me, one of the leaders and nobles of the city, Rabbi N. of the community of Frankfort, a brother of the Rabbi Henlis of Prague. He brought a long letter from the inhabitants of Jerusalem with an offer according to which they appointed me as Ab Beth Din [head of the Rabbinical Court] and head of the Academy until the coming of the Messiah, and they gave full power to Rabbi N. to grant me a salary according to my wish. He was not allowed to withdraw his hand from mine until I had agreed to accept that offer. For they were much afraid of the people of Safed. I praised the Lord and thanked Him that He had found me worthy to spread the Torah in Israel and Jerusalem, and influence men to serve God in truth and sincerity. . . . I answered the Rabbi that I did not wish to accept a salary from them, as they were so overburdened with obligations, because of our many sins. I told him that they should grant me only a good and comfortable lodging. This is a great thing, because there is a considerable shortage of apartments in Jerusalem, because the community of the Ashkenazim in Jerusalem is twice as big as that of Safed and increases in numbers every day. There are also many remarkable scholars of the Torah in the community of the Ashkenazim at Jerusalem. . . .

Although Jerusalem lies in ruins now, it is still the glory of the whole earth. There is peace and safety, good food and delicious wine, all much cheaper than in Safed. The community is situated in a special district of the city. This is not so in Safed, where the Jews live in an open space. That is why many robberies occur there. The Sephardim also increase very much in Jerusalem, even in the hundreds, and they build big houses there. We consider all this as a sign of deliverance, may it come speedily. Within a short time, you will hear, with the help of the Lord, that the community of the Ashkenazim is great indeed and venerable. For I know that many will come there who are desirous of joining me. May the Lord grant me life and health. I shall develop a wonderful activity for the study of Torah which so far has been without a right guidance. . . .

My beloved children, tell everybody who intends to go to the Holy Land to settle in Jerusalem. Let nobody assume that I give this advice because I shall settle there. Far be this from me! But I give this advice in all sincerity because all good is there, and nothing is lacking. The city is enclosed and surrounded by a wall. It is as big as Lwow, but the most important point is that it is particularly holy and the gate of heaven. I have firm confidence that the Lord will let much knowledge of Torah spread through me, so that the word may be fulfilled that out of Zion shall go forth the Torah (Isa. 2:3). . . .

May it be the will of the Lord that all of you be granted to come to Jerusalem in order to live there in peace, and also the whole house of Israel, that we may see the Holy City rebuilt, and may the Temple be erected soon!

Moses ben Israel Naphtali Porges Praeger

Moses Praeger of Prague wrote Ways of Zion, *from which this excerpt is taken, in 1650 as a guide to those who would travel to the Land of Israel. He describes the routes to the land and the life of Jerusalem at the time.*

Listen, all you men and you women as well,
to what Moses Praeger the scribe has to tell.
This book did I with God's aid indite
through many a day and night.
May His Name be our guide,
and let whoever would do the right
read this book with careful eye,
whether by day or by night.
That no harm may him befall
and he secure himself against all
when he forsakes his land for good and all.
For I did see what me befell
because I did not consider well
the things that I ought to have left behind,
and so lost money and peace of mind.
To Jerusalem many a thing I brought
that there I might full well have bought.
While what in Prague I rushed to sell,
I might have used there full well.
This I saw and a great deal more,
which for all men was in store
who wished to go to Jerusalem.
It never occurred to them
how they would live once they were there.
So it came about they were not aware
that in Jerusalem they would cry and swear.
Why do we wish to take this turn?
We would so gladly home return.
Therefore I thought in mine heart
that none ought to come to loss and smart.
Let each one bethink him in his heart,
from food and from drink he can never part.
As for money and worldly worth,
Jerusalem has great dearth

though she stands at the very center of the earth.

Nor let anybody think

that commerce can him profit bring,

since Ladino, Arabic and Turkish

he has to know before everything.

Best the Jerusalem community to lend,

for now they pay at twelve per cent.

After let each man follow his bent.

But he who can make large buttons of silk

may laugh full well with all of his ilk.

He makes a good living on what he can sell

and God grant other folk do as well. . . .

The only bedding to take along is that which is to be used on the way. Feathers can be obtained cheaply at Jerusalem from the German community. You can never bring along a sufficient quantity of sheets, shirts, veils, tablecloths, handkerchiefs, and all other kinds of linen, for in Jerusalem these things are expensive and not very good. Each person should also take along a pair of good shoes as well as woolen winter stockings, for such clothing is not very good in Jerusalem. Apart from this, winter is cold in Jerusalem, even though it does not freeze. Men's clothing should not be brought along in quantity, for they are not expensive here. In Ofen let each man buy something to wrap around his head after the fashion of the Turks, and if the cloth is quite white you should sew a few colored threads into it, but none of green. It is very dangerous to wear anything of green. Sometimes the borders of the prayer shawl are also green, and this must be changed in advance. Green, the color of the Prophet, is forbidden to Jews in the whole of Turkey and Jerusalem.

In Jerusalem many copper vessels are used and they are very expensive here. Let every man bring along his copper kneading basin, for bread is baked at home and the laundry is also washed there. One should bring copper pots, large and small, which have a tin lining inside. Also an iron tripod on which the pots are placed for cooking, likewise a pan for seething fish and a copper kettle for drawing water out of the cistern in each house. Also a basin which is taken along to the baths. The baths, thank God, are very good and heathful. Do not take much silver and gold along, even if you are rich, for that only attracts attention. But it is good to bring iron padlocks in order to lock up your rooms and boxes.

Books are not expensive in Jerusalem, so you should not burden yourself with them on account of the expense of transportation. Let each person take with him only a thick prayer book, a Pentateuch with commentaries, a Penitential Prayer Book, the Mishnah, Rabbi Mordecai Jaffe's Levush, a Shomrim la-Boker, a Festival Prayer Book according to the Prague usage, a Midrash, En Yaakov, the Shulhan Arukh, and the Yalkut. The women-folk take with them a Teutsch Humash, Festival Prayer Book, and Tehinnah; also other Teutsch books.

The prayer books should be small, for there is no lectern in the synagogues and the books must be held in the hand. A good housewife will also take Spanish sewing needles with her, also pins large and small, such as are needed and used at home.

All kinds of spices are to be found and very cheap; but muscat blossoms are rarely seen. Most foodstuffs are sold in Jerusalem by weight, and naturally other things as well. There is no beef, but now and again there is buffalo meat, which does not taste so good. Geese, ducks, chickens, and doves are found in plenty and cheap. There are two kinds of oil; one called Siridj is very cheap, better than goosefat or butter, and is made of seed. The other oil is sweet oil, cheaper than Siridj but not so good and also not good for burning. Young radishes, all kinds of onions, and parsley root, are all very cheap and can be had all the year round. Large citrons for preserving, oranges, and lemons, appear in the market all the winter. Sometimes oranges go eight for a kreutzer, and sometimes even more cheaply. They are used to make lemonade, and folk keep the juice fresh in glasses by adding a little olive oil on top. Mushrooms or German chanterelles are very cheap. In winter there is fresh fish, both large and small, but different kinds from those to be found abroad. The fish are caught in the sea and brought here in a day and a half. That is why there is no fresh fish in summer; for it can go bad on the way.

For a large living room an annual rent of eight lion thalers is paid; for a smaller, five or six. Folk who dwell in the Synagogue Court, where the Loeb synagogue and the two Houses of Study are, live cramped and often lack water. But on the other hand they can go to the synagogue very early in the morning every day. For the synagogue is locked in the evening as soon as the Evening Prayer is over, and not opened again until the break of day. To go through the streets at night is dangerous. Anyone who does not dwell in the Synagogue Court has ample room and also more water at home. The water is good and healthful. He who so desires can drink it with liquorice at twenty kreutzer the rotl. There are some who drink it with lemonade. The water is only rain water and not well water. Every house has a large, very well whitewashed cistern under the ground, and up above there is a little hole, where the water runs in and is drawn up. In years when there is little water it must be bought from Turks, who bring it into the house in leather sacks.

Let each provide him well, I say,
ere from his home he goes away,
and then no grief he'll need to know,
as at first I strove to show.
And young folk, do not venture here,
you'll only growl and roar, I fear.

The bridegroom his dowry will have to give,
else in Jerusalem he never can live.
Whether he be rich or poor,
he must seek his own kind,
and whether he knows nothing or a great deal,
he'll find only many thistles and thorns.
Therefore let young folks stay in their own land
and the old folk come with money in hand.
A young man will find no sustenance here
though he dwell in Jerusalem a full hundred year.
And since he will have to leave the City,
to come here at all would be a great pity.
So let them not lose their youthful years,
and come to suffer pain and tears.
If a man is rich then let him be sure
to bring here enough for a three years' store.
For sometimes a long time is spent
till things from his own land are sent.

And know this every man always,
though the Land of Israel is waste these days
and in ruins by reason of our sins,
yet in every mood it is always good,
as our great Master the learned Ramban
showed in the letter to his son.

✺ Jerusalem in Mystical Literature

During the Middle Ages, Jewish mystical speculation, which had its origins in early rabbinic times, flourished. The most famous mystical work of the period was the Zohar (The Book of Splendor), which purports to be the work of the Tanna Rabbi Simeon bar Yohai. Scholarly investigation has proved conclusively, however, that it is the composition of the Spanish kabbalist Moses ben Shem Tov de Leon, who died in 1305.

ZION AND JERUSALEM

Rabbi Judah began by quoting, "The Lord thundered in the heavens, and the Most High gave forth His voice; hailstones and coals of fire" (Pss. 18:14). Come and see. When the Holy One, blessed by He, created the world, He prepared for it seven pillars upon which it was to stand, and these pillars all rest upon one single pillar, and they have already explained it, for it is written, "Wisdom has built her house; she has hewn out her seven pillars" (Prov. 9:1), and they all stand at one level, called "the righteous, foundation [*yesod*] of the world" (Prov. 10:25). When the world was created, it was created from the single point of the world, and the center of all. And what is it? Zion, as it is written, "A Psalm of Asaph. God, God, the Lord has spoken, and called the earth, from the rising of the sun to its setting" (Pss. 50:1). From which place? From Zion, as it is written, "Out of Zion, the perfection of beauty, has God shined forth" (Pss. 50:2), from the place that is the limit of the perfection of complete faith, as it should be. Zion is the strength and the point of the whole world, and from that place the whole world was made and completed, and from it the whole world is nourished.

Come and see. "The Lord thundered in the heavens, and the Most High gave forth His voice. . . ." Since it says, "The Lord thundered in the heavens," what need has it to say "and the Most High gave forth His voice"? But here we have a mystery of faith. When I say that Zion is the perfection and beauty of the world, and the world is nourished by it, there are really two levels, namely, Zion and Jerusalem. One is Judgment and one is Mercy, and both are one, Judgment on one side, Mercy on the other. (ZOHAR I, 186A)

THE DESTRUCTION OF THE TEMPLE

Rabbi Hezekiah began by quoting: "The burden concerning the valley of vision. What ails you now, that you have gone up entirely to the roofs?" (Isa. 22:1). Come and see. They have interpreted this to mean that, when the Temple was destroyed, all the priests went up to the roofs of the Temple, with their keys in their hands, and said "Up until now we have been Your treasurers. From this point on, take what is Yours." But come and see: "the valley of vision" is the *Shekhinah* [the Presence of God.—ed.], who was in the Temple. All the world's inhabitants would suck the milk of prophecy from her. Even though the prophets all prophesied from another place, they would actually suck their vision from her, and so she is called "the valley of vision." "Vision"—they have already explained that it is the vision of all the supernal colors. "What ails your now, that you have gone up entirely to the roofs?" When the Temple was destroyed the *Shekhinah* came and went up to all those places where she used to dwell at first, and she would weep for her home and for Israel, who had gone into exile, and for all the righteous and the pious ones who used to be there and had perished. How do we know this? Because it is written "Thus says the Lord: A voice is heard in Ramah, lamentation and bitter weeping, Rachel weeping for her children" (Jer. 31:15). And it has already been explained that at that time the Holy One, blessed be He, questioned the *Shekhinah*, and said to her, "What ails you now, that you have gone up entirely to the roofs?" What is the point of "entirely"? Is not "you have gone up" sufficient? What does "entirely" mean? It is meant to include all the hosts, and all the other chariots, all of whom lamented the destruction of the Temple with her. And so we have "What ails you now?" And she said to Him: My children are in exile, and the Temple is burnt, and so why should I remain here? And yet You have said, "You that are full of uproar, a tumultuous city, a joyous town, your slain are not slain with the sword, nor dead in battle" (Isa. 22:2). "Therefore I said: Look away from me, I will weep bitterly. . . ." (Isa. 22:4). They have already explained that the Holy One, blessed be He, said to her "Thus says the Lord: Refrain your voice from weeping, and your eyes from tears. . ." (Jer. 31:16).

Now come and see. From the day that the Temple was destroyed there has not been a single day without curses. When the Temple was still standing, Israel would perform their rites, and bring offerings and sacrifices. And the *Shekhinah* rested upon them in the Temple, like a mother hovering over her children, and all faces were resplendent with light, so that there was blessing both above and below. And there was not a single day without blessings and joys, and Israel dwelt securely in the land, and the whole world was nourished because of them. Now that the Temple is destroyed, and the *Shekhinah* is with them in exile, there is not a single day without curses, and the world is cursed, and there is no joy to be found, above or below. But in time to come the Holy One, blessed be He, will raise the Assembly of Israel from the dust, as it has been said, "I will bring them to My holy mountain, and make them rejoice in My house of prayer. . . ." (Isa. 56:7); and it is written, "They shall come with weeping, and with supplications will I lead them" (Jer. 31:9). As it was at the beginning, where it is written, "She weeps greviously in the night, and her tears are on her cheeks" (Lam. 1:2), so subsequently they shall return in tears, as it is written, "They shall come with weeping. . . ." (ZOHAR I, 202B–203A)

THE FOUNDATION STONE

[Rabbi Judah] began by quoting: "Beautiful in elevation, the joy of the whole earth, Mount Zion, the uttermost parts of the north, the city of a great king" (Pss. 48:3). Come and see. When the Holy One, blessed be He, created the world, He threw down a precious stone from beneath the throne of His glory, and it sank into the deeps, and another in the realms above. And there was another edge, a supernal one, a single point, which is in the middle of the world, and the world expanded from there, to the right and to the left, and upon all sides, and it is sustained by this central point. This stone is called *shetiyah* [foundation], because from it the world was founded [*ashtil*] on all sides. Moreover *shetiyah* [may be read] *shat yah* ["the Lord placed"]. The Holy One, blessed be He, placed it so that it might be the foundation of the world, and the foundation of all.

The earth expanded in three circles around this point. In the first expansion around this point there existed all the clarity and purity of the world, and it was situated above, over the whole earth, around this point. The second expansion around the first expansion did not have the clarity and purity of the first, but it was fine and clear, with

The Foundation Stone within the Dome of the Rock, 1898 (Central Zionist Archives; with permission)

the greatest clarity that dust can have. The third expansion was darkness and the coarsest type of dust. And around this were the waters of the oceanic sea, which encompass the whole world. Consequently, this point stands in the center, and all the circles of the world's expansion go around it.

The first expansion is the Temple, with all the palaces and courts, the whole array, and Jerusalem, the entire city within the wall. The second expansion is the land of Israel, which is hallowed in sanctity. The third expansion are the other lands, the abode of the other peoples. And the oceanic sea encompasses all. And they have already taught that this mystery is [contained in] the colors in the eye that surround the central point of the eye, which mirrors the whole eye, like the central point, which we have mentioned, that mirrors all. There the Holy of Holies stands, the ark and the ark-covering, which mirror all. Therefore this point mirrors the whole world. And so it is written, "Beautiful in elevation, the joy of the whole earth, Mount Zion. . . ." "Beautiful"—beautiful is this mirror and a joy to all. "Elevation"—the elevation of the tree that is the beauty of all. (ZOHAR II, 222A–222B)

DOVE IN THE ROCK

"My dove that art in the clefts of the rock, in the coverts of the steep place" (Songs 2:14). "My dove" refers to the Community of Israel; "the clefts of the rock" refers to Jerusalem, which is firm and eminent like a rock; "the coverts of the steep place" refers to the place which is called "holy of holies," the heart of the world. It is called "coverts" because there the *Shekhinah* is concealed like a woman who converses only with her husband and never goes out. (ZOHAR, LECH LECHA)

THE TEMPLE ABOVE

Rabbi Jose thereupon began to speak on the words: "The song of songs which is Solomon's" (Songs 1:1). Said he: "This song King Solomon poured forth when the Temple was erected and all worlds, above and below, had reached their perfect consummation. And although concerning the exact time of its singing there is some difference of opinion among the members of the Fellowship, we may be certain that it was not sung until that time of absolute completion, when the Moon—the *Shekhinah*—came to her fulness and was revealed in the full perfection of her radiance, and when the Temple had been erected in the likeness of the Temple that is above. The Holy One, blessed be He, then experienced such joy as He had not known since the creation of the world. . . ." (ZOHAR, TERUMAH)

FOR HER SAKE

Now, when the Holy One created the world, He divided it into two parts: one part that should be habitable and the other a desert, the former on one side and the latter at the other. Then He redivided the habitable part in such a manner that it formed a circle, the centre of which is the Holy Land. The centre of the Holy Land is Jerusalem, and, again, the centre of Jerusalem is the Holy of Holies. . . . The domain of the mystery of the Faith is that very central point of the Holy Land which is in the Holy of Holies, the place where the *Shekhinah* dwelt, and even though She dwells there no longer, and the Holy of Holies exists no more, yet for Her sake the whole world is still supplied with food, and nourishment and satisfaction ever stream forth, emanating from thence to all the inhabited regions of the world. (ZOHAR, TERUMAH)

A SUPERNAL CITY

Thus said Rabbi Simeon: "The Holy One prepared for Himself a holy Palace, a supernal Palace, a holy City, a supernal City, which is called "Jerusalem, the holy City." He who wishes to see the King, must enter through this holy City and thence take his way to the King. (ZOHAR, BESHALAH)

TWO KINGS

[Said] Rabbi Abba: "It is written: 'All this did Araunah the king give to the king' (2 Sam. 24:23). Now, even if we allow that Araunah was a king, yet seeing that David conquered Jerusalem and made it his own, as it says, 'David took the stronghold of Zion,' why did he need to buy the spot from Araunah with money? A simple explanation would be that although David was the ruler of Jerusalem, that spot was the heritage of Araunah, and so it could only be taken from him by his consent; in the same way as Ahab, although king and ruler in Israel, in order to acquire the vineyard of Naboth the Jesreelite, had first to obtain the latter's consent. But a deeper explanation is that Araunah indeed was king and ruler of that spot, and when the time came for it to pass out of his possession, this could only be effected at the cost of much blood and slaughter to Israel. Subsequently, when the Destroying Angel in the execution of his work of slaughter reached that spot he could not prevail there, and his strength was exhausted. It was, indeed, the spot where Isaac was bound on the altar that Abraham built; and so, when the Holy One looked at that place He was filled with compassion, as we read: 'and as he was about to destroy, the Lord beheld, and He repented Him of the evil' (1 Chron. 21:15), meaning that He beheld there the binding of Isaac, and so had compassion on them, and straightway said to the Destroying angel: 'It is enough. . . .' The words 'It is enough' have the same import as the similar words in the passage: 'Ye have dwelt long enough in this mountain' (Deut. 1:6), as much as to say: This place has been long enough in thy possession; thou hast had it for many years, now return it to its rightful owner. And for all that it could only be taken from him at a great sacrifice of life and money." (ZOHAR, VAYAQHEL)

ॐ Customs Relating to Jerusalem

Rabbi Joseph Karo

In his authoritative code of Jewish Law, the Shulhan Aruch, *Rabbi Joseph Karo (1488–1575), who moved to Sefad from Turkey in 1563, recorded the following laws regarding remembering Jerusalem.*

A bridegroom puts ashes on his head where *tefillin* are worn in order to remember Jerusalem. There are places where the custom is to break a glass at the time of the wedding ceremony or to place a black cloth or other sign of mourning on the head of the groom. (*Shulhan Aruch, Orah Haim 560*)

Maimonides

Moshe ben Maimon—Maimonides—was the greatest philosopher and legalist of the Middle Ages. Born in Cordova in 1135, he died either in Egypt or in the Land of Israel in 1204. In his legal code Mishneh Torah *he recounts customs concerning mourning for the Temple.*

When the Temple was destroyed, the sages decreed that one should not build buildings that are plastered and cemented as kingly buildings are. Rather one plasters and whitewashes but leaves a space one *ama* square opposite the entrance unwhitewashed. However, if one acquired a place already plastered and cemented, one is not required to remove the finish from the walls. They also decreed that if one makes a banquet, one should leave something out and leave a place vacant with no setting. When a woman makes silver or gold jewelry such as are currently in use, she should leave something out so that it will not be a perfect set. When a groom takes a bride, he should take some ash and put it on his forehead where the tefillin is placed. All of this is done in order to remember Jerusalem, as it is said, "If I forget you, O Jerusalem..." (Pss. 137:5). They also decreed that instruments should not be played and songs not sung.... Then they decreed that grooms should not wear crowns on their heads, nor any sort of adornment on the head ... and that brides should not wear crowns of silver or gold. Brides may, however, wear cloth crowns. (*Mishneh Torah, Laws of Fasts 5:12–15*)

Jerusalem in Medieval Poetry

From the sixth through the fifteenth centuries, there was a great flourishing of Hebrew poetry, ranging from the early payytanim—writers of liturgical poetry—of whom we know little, through the highly personal and sophisticated Spanish poets. Jerusalem is a major theme of these poets, both as a cause of mourning for its destruction and as a symbol of hope for the restoration of Israel.

JOY OF THE WHOLE WORLD

Yose ben Yose
(LAND OF ISRAEL; CA. 600)

Through Zion make for yourself an awesome name,

Endow it, as in the past, with a royal throne;

Bring back to life the city which is the joy of the whole world

And establish your throne in the royal city;

As bright as the sun display the glories of the metropolis to the people

And manifest in our time the honor of your reign.

(TRANSLATED BY ZALMAN DIMITROVSKY)

THE LIGHTS OF ZION
(A Fragment)

Yannai
(LAND OF ISRAEL; CA. 640)

The lights of Edom have grown stronger and multiplied

   The lights of Zion have been swallowed up and destroyed.

The lights of Edom have grown mightier and brighter

   The lights of Zion have been quenched and have gone out.

The lights of Edom illuminate every corner

   The lights of Zion have retreated far away.

The lights of Edom brighten everything with their splendor

   The lights of Zion have become darker than pitch.

The lights of Edom are full and perfect

   The lights of Zion have diminished and been snatched away.

The lights of Edom have become more glorious and lovely

   The lights of Zion have been captured and extinguished.

193

The lights of Edom are bright enough to illumine the dead

    The lights of Zion are as forgotten as the dead. . . .

               (TRANSLATED BY REUVEN HAMMER)

I REMEMBER

Amittai ben Shephatiah
(ORIA, SOUTH ITALY; LATE NINTH CENTURY)

I remember, O God, and I am vexed

When I behold the flourishing cities of the world

While the city of God is cast down to the depths of Sheol—

Nevertheless we turn toward Yah, our eyes are toward Yah!

May it be Your will, O He who attends the sound of weeping—

To gather our tears in Your cup

And save us from all cruel decrees

For we look to You alone!

               (TRANSLATED BY REUVEN HAMMER)

MY HEART SEETHES

Shmuel Hanagid
(CORDOVA, SPAIN; 993–1055 OR 1056)

My heart seethes: the halls of our youth are stripped bare;

    Urim and Tummim light the exiles' feet.

  I dwell outside Zion, foul as a corpse,

    shamed as one slain, angel-struck.

Can strayed Israel return, walk God's streets again,

    can the proud meet their day?

What store can we put in tradition's store—

    the loosing of chains,

      the slavers brought down,

        the righteous uplifted, redeemed?

Shall song spill from my lips and my sons'

    from the altar steps;

Shall I yet see the sons of the Living God

    wing to Zion like doves?

As God lives: I shall so!

  —nor say, I serve princes and kings,

    mine splendor and might;

Nor open my ear to the Tempter's voice—

    You loom over men like a god!

What gain yours in your people's return?

    What return in the exiles' redemption?

Far best for my soul that I stand in God's courts

    than rule worlds:

  Ambrosia on unclean soil

    I hold lees.

Lord. send forth your rays,

    raise Zion, raise Zion's dear sons;

Restore our lost youth with your love,

    turn us eagles again.

Glut your lamb, lion-torn, with foe's blood

    that my flame lick your altar,

      thick laden with rams.

        (TRANSLATED BY DAVID SIMHA SEGAL)

BELOVED, HASTEN

Meshullam ben Kolonymous
(LUCCA, NORTH ITALY; TENTH–ELEVENTH CENTURIES)

Beloved, hasten to Thy habitation,

And from Thy covenant although we err,

Remember, pray, Thy tabernacle's station,

And all Thy promised grace upon us confer,

Thy city rearing on its old foundation,

Which I above my chiefest joy prefer.

Beloved, hasten to Thy shrine in Zion,

And though from Thy appointed path we stray,

Yet cast, we pray, no unrelenting eye on

Thy hapless folk upon their thorny way,

Nor let Thy wrath go roaring like a lion,

But shelter them beneath Thy wings for aye.

(TRANSLATED BY ISRAEL ZANGWILL)

HOSHANA
(from the Sukkot liturgy)
Author Unknown

The stone of foundation,

The chosen house,

The threshing-floor of Ornan,

The inner sanctuary,

The Mount of Moriah,

The Mount of appearance,

The abode of Your glory,

The dwelling of David,

The goodliness of Lebanon,

The beautiful landscape, the joy of all the world,

The crown of beauty,

The dwelling place of righteousness,

The place where You dwell,

The peaceful habitation,

The tabernacle of Shalem,

The place where the tribes made pilgrimage,

The precious corner-stone,

Zion the outstanding,

The holy of holies,

The pavement of love,

The Presence of Your glory,

Save—we entreat,

The mound of Talpiot

Save—we entreat.

O Lord—save us we entreat!

(TRANSLATED BY REUVEN HAMMER)

A VOICE PROCLAIMS
(from the Sukkot Liturgy)
Author Unknown

A voice proclaims, proclaiming and declaring—

The herald of salvation comes; the voice of my Beloved, behold He comes—
proclaiming and declaring—

He comes with myriad angels; to stand on the Mount of Olives—
proclaiming and declaring—

He approaches to sound the shofar. Under Him the mount will split—
proclaiming and declaring—

He knocks, He looks, He shines forth. Half the mount moves from the East—
proclaiming and declaring—

He words are fulfilled; He comes with all His holy ones—
proclaiming and declaring—

And unto all the creatures of the world; a heavenly voice sounds throughout—
proclaiming and declaring—

The seed He begot is born; a child from his mother's womb—
proclaiming and declaring—

Who has travailed and given birth? Who has heard the like?
proclaiming and declaring—

The Pure One has done this. Who has seen the like?
proclaiming and declaring—

Salvation and time are one. Shall the earth bring it forth in one day?
proclaiming and declaring—

Mighty above and beneath. Can a nation be born at once?
proclaiming and declaring—

The Radiant One will redeem His people at this time; there shall be light at
evening—
proclaiming and declaring—

Redeemers shall ascend Mount Zion. Zion has labored and given birth—
proclaiming and declaring—

It shall be heard throughout your borders; enlarge your tent!
proclaiming and declaring—

Expand your dwelling place unto Damascus; receive your sons and daughters!
proclaiming and declaring—

Rejoice O rose of Sharon! Those who sleep in Hebron have arisen—
proclaiming and declaring—

Turn to Me and be saved! Today—if you will harken to My voice!
proclaiming and declaring—

A man has sprung up; *tzemach* [shoot] is his name; it is David himself!
proclaiming and declaring—

Arise, those buried in the dust; awake and rejoice, sleepers in the earth—
proclaiming and declaring—

The multitude of the people proclaims him king; His king brings salvation—
proclaiming and declaring—

The wicked shall perish; He is loyal to His Messiah, to David—
proclaiming and declaring—

Grant salvation to the eternal people; to David and his seed forever!
proclaiming and declaring—

A voice proclaims, proclaiming and declaring!

(*TRANSLATED BY REUVEN HAMMER*)

EARTH'S BEAUTY

Judah Halevi
(*SPAIN; CA. 1075–1141*)

Earth's beauty and joy
   and Great King's seat—
For you my soul yearns
   from the ends of the west.

My pity moans, mounts
   when I recall you, East—
Your glory exiled
   and your dwelling waste.

Oh, who might set me
    upon eagles' wings
That I might drench your dust
    with tears?

I seek you, though your king be gone;
    and though I find
For Gilead's balm,
    adder and snake—

Shall I not pity, shall I not
    kiss your stones—
    your earth beyond honey
    sweet upon my lips?

    (TRANSLATED BY DAVID SIMHA SEGAL)

MY HEART'S IN THE EAST
Judah Halevi

My heart's in the east and I languish on the margins
of the west. How taste or savor what I eat?
How fulfil my vows and pledges while Sion
is shackled to Edom and I am fettered to Arabia?
I'd gladly give up all the luxuries of Spain
if only to see the dust and rubble of the Shrine.

    (TRANSLATED BY GABRIEL LEVIN)

THE POET REPLIES TO ONE WHO WOULD DISSUADE HIM FROM REMOVING TO THE LAND OF ISRAEL
Judah Halevi

Your phrases drip myrrh,
    your words flow from the mountain of spice;
Your elegance, grace—and your fathers' before—
    praise weeps to attain.
You greet me with fair, rolling hills of speech—
    deserts where swords lie in wait,
    honey-groves thick with thorns.

What—seek not Jerusalem's peace
    because rife with the blind and the halt?!
Then seek, for the sake of God's House, her peace;
    and for brothers and friends.
If your teaching be true, ascribe sin
    to the faces turned east, to bent knees,
And sin to our fathers who walked the land through
    buying vaults for their dead;
Ascribe folly to Jacob and Joseph—embalmed
    and conveyed to her soil.
Fools our fathers, who moaned for her sake,
    a land pagan and bleak:
Hold the altars they built wasted stone,
    and their offerings vain.

Is it well to bewail Spain's dead
    with the ark and the tablets forlorn?
Cherish headstones, the haunts of the worm,
    shun the source of unending life,
Prefer gilded, tiled synagogue walls
    to the Mountain of God?
East or West, do we have such a hope,
    such a fort
As that filled with gates
    facing God's—
The wide gates of Sinai, Carmel and Beth El,
    of the prophets sent forth by the Lord,
And the thrones of the oil-hallowed kings.
Ours he ordained it, ours and our seeds',
    yes, though peopled with jackals and wolves.
Was it other when given our fathers,
    a tangle of thistles and thorn?
Yet they wandered its length and its breadth
    as through orchards of spice—

Wanderers seeking out graves
   like travelers, inns;
But they traveled the roads of the Lord,
   they learned the true path,
Declaring the dead would there rise from the earth,
   there break dust's chains,
There the flesh sing again,
   souls rest.

My friend: think, look, comprehend;
   turn from nettles and snares.
Be not wooed by the wisdom of Greece,
   all flowers, no fruit—
With their notion that earth was not made,
   no heavens outstretched:
   no beginning, no end.
Look, listen: their sages spew wind,
   bricks laid on the void,
To leave your heart empty and dull
   and your mouth filled with weeds.

Speak: why should I torture through twisted roads,
   and abandon the mother of paths?
        (TRANSLATED BY DAVID SIMHA SEGAL)

SOLOMON'S PAVILIONS
Judah Halevi

Solomon's pavilions, now threadbare and drab among the swart
   goathair tents of Qedar, how you have changed!
"The people who once lodged in our midst left us defenceless,
   a ruin, the holy vessels dispatched into exile
profaned—will you demand splendor of a lily among thistles?"
Repulsed by their neighbors, sought out by their Lord—He will call
   them all by name, and not one will be missing.

He will restore in the end their glory, as in the beginning,
   kindling sevenfold their light in the gloom.

                  (*TRANSLATED BY GABRIEL LEVIN*)

ODE TO SION
Judah Halevi

Will you not ask, Sion, of your captives' well-being,
   they who diligently quest
      after your welfare and are the remnant
   of your flock? From west
to east, north to south, Peace from the near
   and far off, from all sides
      round about you, Greetings,
   from a captive of desire,
who sheds tears like the dew of Hermon and longs
   for them to streak your slopes.
      Weeping of your afflictions
   I am a jackal, dreaming the return
of your fortunes, a lute for your songs.

How I yearn for Bethel and Penuel, for Mahanaim
   and all the saintly meeting
      grounds. The Shechina dwelled
   among you there, and your Maker
flung open your gates to face the gates of heaven.
   The glory of Adonai your only light,
      neither sun, moon or stars
   shone over you. I would pour out
my life on the very site where the spirit
   of Elohim once drenched
      your chosen ones. Royal city,
   throne of the Lord, though
slaves have long dethroned your princes.

If only I could roam the grounds
   where Elohim was revealed

to your seers and heralds.
   Who will give me wings to flee far off,
bearing the shreds of my torn heart
    to your cleft mountains? Falling on my knees,
      I would delight in your stones
    and be stirred to pity
by your dust. I would weep by the tombs
   of my fathers and stand
     bewildered in Hebron
   facing the pick of graves.
Crossing your woods and fields, I would stop

in Gilead to marvel at Mount Abarim—Abarim and Hor,
   where rest the two great beacons
     who guided and gave you light.
   The air of your land quickens
the very life of the soul, the grains
   of your dust are oozing myrrh,
     and your streams
   are honey from the comb.
How I would delight to walk naked and barefoot
   among the rubble
    where your shrines once stood:
   here is the site where your ark was hidden away,
and here is the innermost chamber

where your cherubim once dwelled.
   I will raze my crown of hair,
     and curse Time that defiled
   your crowned ones in a polluted land.
How can I enjoy food and drink
   when I see dogs tearing into your young lions?
    How can daylight soothe
   my eyes while I behold the eagle's mangled body
dangling from the Raven's beak.
   Gently, cup of sorrow, be still,

body and soul are filled with your bitterness.
I drink your wrath remembering Oholah,
and recalling Oholibah drain your dregs.*

Love, grace, the very life of your companions
    are bound fast to you, Sion, paragon
        of beauty: they delight in your well-being,
    and weep forlorn at your desolation and ruin;
they long for you even from the pit
    of captivity; they bow, each in his place,
        toward your gates. The flock
    of your people—exiled, scattered,
from mountain range to hillside—have not forgotten
    your borders; they cling to the edge
        of your cloak and strive
    to climb up into your palm
to grasp its fronds. Were Shinar and Patros

ever equal to you in their greatness, can all
    their empty divination
        compare with your Urim and Tummim?
    Who is equal to your anointed
and prophets, who to your Levites and singers?
    Petty kingdoms will perish,
        but your strength is everlasting,
    your crown endures from one
generation to another. God yearns
    to dwell with you: happy the man
        determined to set
    out and settle on your sovereign
grounds; happy is he who waits
    and lives to behold your lights rising as dawn
        breaks over him, and he sees

---

* See Ezek. 23. The two women represent Samaria and Jerusalem (ed.).

your chosen prospering, and thrills
at your joy, when you regain the vigor of youth.

(TRANSLATED BY GABRIEL LEVIN)

LAMENT FOR ZION
Author Unknown

We approached to ask our mother's well-being,
We stood at her door and wept.
The guards found us, they beat us, they wounded us—
"Away, unclean!" they cried to us.

Again we came, but approached not.
Upon a distant mount we stood.
She who dwells alone came out to greet us,
Gazing from her prison she faced us.

We raised our eyes to see her,
But so wasted was she that we knew her not.
Her shape and form were gone,
Bound in chains and burdened with fetters.

We raised our voice in weeping
For the desecration of Mount Moriah,
For our impoverished mother,
With nothing to sustain her.

Our cries rose in her ears
And she joined in our complaint.
She cried in supplication and lamented:
"Behold I dwell as a widow.

My sons have gone into captivity,
My sanctuary is devastated,
I am left naked and exposed—
For this do I weep."

(TRANSLATED BY REUVEN HAMMER)

SHALOM TO THE CITY SHALEM

Judah Alharizi
(SPAIN; 1170–1235)

Stripped of her fabled beauty;

Oh, Where has it vanished?

Ask those who behold her.

I plead for her dust day by day,

She is the sickness of my soul and its dispair;

When my eyes will behold her radiance once again

Clouds of tears will shroud them no more.

O God—who desired her as His dwelling—

Witness her dispair, annul her captivity;

She laments her Beloved's departure.

Upon His return unto her

He will wipe the tears from her cheeks!

(TRANSLATED BY REUVEN HAMMER)

JERUSALEM: CHAPTER 28 OF THE BOOK OF TAHKEMONI

Judah Alhariz

> *In the Book of Tahkemoni (The Wise One) the hero describes a lengthy series of experiences and adventures. In this chapter he travels from Egypt to Jerusalem.*

Let me recall how time tossed me like a ball until I left Memphis for the Western Wall, thinking, Draw no more water, hew no more wood: I shall bring you up from Egypt's wretchedness, that you might see Jerusalem's good. Then I set my feet for the mountain of the Lord, the city chosen of the Lord, once home of a noble race who sat all men above, who looked upon the King's bright face. Once come unto that holy ground I turned myself round to count turrets and towers, then knelt amid showers of the scorpion's hiss to kiss the dust and loose my moans upon my beloved's stones, crying, Zion, goodly are your tents: I shall not stir hence. Soul, fly for I have seen her face; I shall not leave this place. Then, waxing poetic, I sang:

Thirsting from Spain for Zion's pure light

  I rise from the Depths to Heaven's height.

This is the day the Lord has made:
  Oh faithful city, my chief delight!

So many the pious who yearned for this sight;
  what merit has guided this sinner here?
Near dead in the West, my soul revives:
  my pulse is a fountain, my vision clear.

Babylon, Athens, Tyre, Rome—
  what joy can you offer my flowing eyes?
The clouds flock like doves about my bright feet:
  O Salem, towering Paradise.

Here shone the Presence in sight of all men;
  here Wonder's pupils opened wide.
Sucklings and children sucked both at God's light:
  before they sought vision they prophesied.

She is fair, though stripped of her splendour and good;
  though unjeweled and unbraced, I say she is fair.
But my heart turns ashen, my tears pour forth,
  I strike palm to palm, I pull at my hair.

Where is God's Presence, that vanished sun,
  where is the splendour of yesteryear?
O haste, my belov'd, to the Mountain of Myrrh,
  haste, my beloved, even as the deer.

The daughter of Zion is cast from her halls:
  brazen, she fronted her Maker's will,
haughty, she spurned the bright Love of her youth,
  sought stolen waters and drank her fill.

Then the Lord, filled with jealousy, filled up her cup
  with the waters of bitterness, forcing her drink.
She became, in the midst of her people, a curse;
  her belly did swell and her thigh did shrink.

She prayed Exile's waters would wash off her sin
  but God holds her sinful, though long she roam.

One thousand and forty eight years have sufficed not:

> her Sabbaths unpaid, she is barred yet from home.

Sorrowing, dreaming, her sad eyes are ringed

> with black circles of longing: long has she cried—

Cried at the sight of the stranger ascending

> God's mountain while she, Zion's child, is denied.

But the mercies of God are unending; again

> He shall shower salvation and rescue like rain.

His beloved, though old, shall renew her sweet youth:

> she shall lie in the arms of her Lover again.

Now when my song and prayer were ended I rose from off my bended knees to roam the city, afire with grief and pity. Lifting my eyes I saw the Temple's inner court, there where the heathen came—to wrench the candelabrum out and light a pagan flame. On I walked, feverish and weak, tears sluicing each cheek like streams cascading from a mountain peak. At length I met a citizen, who said, You have a foreign look, young friend: do you come from the Exile's end?

Yes, I answered, and would question you if I may.

—Surely; he answered, say what you would say.

When did Jews return here?

—When the city fell under Arab sway.

But why had the Christians driven us away?

—They claim we shamelessly killed their God, who therefore disowns us: if we sacrifice the abomination of the Egyptians before their eyes, will they not stone us?

By what grace, I continued, did you re-enter His sacred place?

—The Lord, zealous for His Name's sake, had pity on His namesake, saying, It is not right that Esau seize Mount Zion's tents and Jacob be driven thence, lest the envious nations scoff, saying God has driven his first-born off, setting the divorcee's child his first-born above, preferring the son of his beloved wife over hers whom he does not love.

So 4,950 years since the first day's light God roused the Ishmaelite ruler to fight, granting him the spirit of counsel and of might, so that he marched up from Egypt with his minions liege and against Jerusalem laid siege. God gave it him to have and hold, and he told the city's dwellers young and old, Speak unto Jerusalem's heart: let all the sons of Ephraim who dwell apart, yea, all Egypt's and Assyria's remnants: speed like the hart! From every corner, come: build you your home!

So here we be by blessed calm approved—unless we be suddenly removed; for we fear the evil that her befalls, the rapine and the violence within these walls, the churning contention and burning dissension defying comprehension. For the cruel leaders of this community are masters of impunity, each the next man's tumbling block and paid; then how shall we remain? They seek their fellows' hurt, each one: the son, his father; the father, his first-born son. Yet father and son together do not falter to gather kindling for the pagan altar. Within each chest curls a poison snake: nothing is done for Heaven's sake. With shouts and bitterness the streets are rife: each eye is a lance, each tongue, a knife; I call this city *Even ha-Mahlokot*—the Stone of Strife. And leaders aside, there are yet others who pit brothers against brothers. They are rogues and liars: one spreads his net, one draws a mighty bow, a third conspires; a fourth prepared contention's altars for new fires.

Then let us pray until God Almighty heeds, and rids us of these noxious weeds. Let Him fill our lungs with salvation's breath; let Him rid us of this death. (*Translated by David Simha Segal*)

IN THE GATES OF JERUSALEM

Rabbi Moshe ben Nahman
(*Spain; 1194–1270*)

Our feet were standing within your gates, O Jerusalem.

The House of God, the gate of Heaven, Jerusalem rebuilt, bound together, with . . .

The tribes, the tribes of Yah went up there,

the stone of the foundation is there upon which the world was based,

from which the foundations of the world and its borders were made firm,

Mount Moriah is there, from which springs rebirth and renewal,

the beauteous mount where dwells God

on which He built His resting place. . . .

The fruits of the land are wondrous and praiseworthy,

its fruits and produce are abundant

she yet flows with milk and honey for those who dwell upon her.

I liken you, my parent, to a woman giving birth, whose child is dead in her
bosom, but whose aching breasts are filled with milk she gives unto pups to suck. . . .

I am the man who has witnessed affliction,

I was exiled from my table,

I was distanced from neighbor and friend

my journey is prolonged.

I am devoid of brothers,

An inn in the wilderness.

I abandoned my house,

I left my inheritance,

there I relinquished my spirit and my soul,

together with the sons and daughters who were my very existence,

with the children whom I raised and nourished upon my knees,

the very beginning of my way.

They were the beloved and the pleasant,

they were my eyes and my heart through all the days . . .

yet it was easy to abandon all that was precious.

One day in Your courts,

visiting Your destroyed Temple,

beholding Your desolate Shrine

is my contentment.

(TRANSLATED BY REUVEN HAMMER)

AWAKE, AWAKE!
Rabbi Moshe ben Nahman

Awake, awake, put on your sorrow and your widow's clothes, O Jerusalem holy city;
Go out with your hands held to your head:
Go to your God, your Master; for He is your lord, so bow in homage to Him;
and you are His chosen portion, and the heritage of His destiny.
In the beginning your people followed Him
as a spouse from youth, in consummate love,
seeking the way before Him in the wilderness,
where no path existed, no roads.
Fragrant with myrrh and aloes, bring peace- and burnt-offerings,
in the dances they sang to Him of His awesome, magnificent deeds—
to thank, extol, praise and glorify, exalt, adore and elevate
the One who dwells above all blessing and praise,
yet grows pleased with entreaties and prayers,
and bountifully grants atonements, forgiveness and pardons—
who acted with kindness and compassion toward you all the days.
Lift up your hands to Him, and pour out your heart like water:
How long wilt Thou not have compassion on Jerusalem? (Zech.1:12)

Our hope is not destroyed with our bodies;

we are not utterly cut off by death, with our return as dust to the earth as we were:

for His hand is not grown too short to rescue.

The blessing of the doomed reaches Him,

and the afflicted soul will He relieve in full.

For every prayer and supplication must find His presence

and our justice emerge as a light to the nations.

Thus and thus did they [our people] speak, and with Thy name

drew strength, as they clung fast after Thee;

when they groan with the moans of the mortally wounded, they cry out to Thee;

will the yearning of Thy heart and Thy compassion for them be then withheld?

Wilt Thou not turn to them, as the Lord God said?

on such a nation as this, wilt Thou not take pity?

Turn from Thy fierce wrath and relent;

for Zion's sake do not be still, and for Jerusalem's sake do not rest,

as their eyes look to Thee in dependence. . . .

To the Messianic end, then, do not leave us;

in Thy forbearing patience, do not take us away

but hasten for us the things to come,

for to Thee are our faces inclined,

and it is we who know and bear witness

that Thy mercies are without end. . . .

Blessed art Thou, O Lord, who redeemed Israel.

May our eyes see Jerusalem a serene habitation,

and the cities of Judah in their restoration,

as Israel's people return to their dwellings,

the *kohanim* to their Temple service and the Levites to their posts. . . .

Then let the Divinely canopied Temple never be cut down. . . .

(TRANSLATED BY CHARLES WENGROV)

COME, MY BELOVED
(From the Sabbath Eve Liturgy)
Solomon HaLevi Alkabetz
(LAND OF ISRAEL; SAFAD, 1505–1584)

Come, my Beloved, to greet the bride—

Let us welcome the Sabbath.

O sanctuary of the King, royal city—
Arise and depart from your overthrow,
Long enough have you dwelt in the valley of tears—
He will have compassion upon you!

Arouse yourself! Rise from the dust!
Don the glorious garments of My people!
Through the son of Jesse, the Bethlehemite,
My soul's redemption is near.

Arouse yourself! Arouse yourself!
Your light has come! Arise and shine forth!
Arise, arise and proclaim the song—
The glory of God is revealed to you.

You shall no more be ashamed or reviled,
Why are you downcast, why are you disquieted?
In you shall the needy of My people find shelter
The city shall be rebuilt on its mound.

Those who despoiled you shall be despoiled,
Your destroyers shall stay far from you,
Your God will rejoice over you
As a bridegroom rejoices over his bride.

You shall spread out right and left
And sing the praises of the Lord—
Through the man—the son of Peretz—
And we shall be happy and rejoice.

(Translated by Reuven Hammer)

CRY, O ZION
(from the Tisha b'Av Liturgy)
Author Unknown

Cry, O Zion and her cities—
Like a woman in travail—
Like a mourning widow
Lamenting the husband of her youth!

For the desolate Temple,
Destroyed because of the sins of her flock;
For the entry of the enemies of God
Into the sanctum of her Shrine . . .

For the exile of the servants of God
Those who sweetly sang her songs;
For their blood freely shed
Like waters of her streams . . .

For the children of her kings
Her nobles from David's house;
For their beauty now vanished
When her crowns were captured . . .

For God's Glory exiled
When her Temple was destroyed;
For the oppression of the foe
Clothing her in sack-cloth . . .

For Your Name desecrated
By those who beseiged her;
For the cries imploring You—
O listen and heed her pleas!

Cry, O Zion and her cities—
    Like a woman in travail—
    Like a mourning widow
    Lamenting the husband of her youth!

(TRANSLATED BY REUVEN HAMMER)

THE SIXTH GATE

Jerusalem in the Literature of the Turkish and Mandatory Periods

Zion Gate to the Old City, ca. 1898 (Central Zionist Archives; with permission)

The material in this section spans a little over two centuries, a period of time in which Jewish settlement increased in the Land of Israel, at first through the actions of individuals, small groups, and philanthropists and then through the more conscious efforts of the newly formed Zionist movement, which began a political program to create a Jewish State. Jerusalem is seen here both as a holy city and as a real place that requires rebuilding and serves as a center of political activity and cultural renewal, and as a focal point of Jewish–Arab tension.

SEEK YE THE PEACE OF JERUSALEM

Gedaliah of Siemiatycze

> On October 14, 1700, Rabbi Judah the Pious (Hasid) came to the Land of Israel with a
> group of his followers in order to hasten the time of redemption. One of them, Gedaliah
> from the town of Siemiatycze in eastern Poland, wrote a book entitled Seek Ye the
> Peace of Jerusalem *describing their aliya and the condition of Jerusalem when they
> arrived.*

Our master, Rabbi Judah the Pious, arrived together with his followers in Jerusalem on
the New Year's Day of Marheshvan [i.e., Rosh Hodesh—ed.] 5461 [1700]. He at once
acquired a house in the Synagogue Court of the Ashkenazim, rented dwellings for his
faithful ones and distributed money for them to live on. Most of them were sick after
the great exertions of the journey. Conditions on the ship had been bad, and the space
allowed for all of us together was far too small.

❧

In the late summer of the year, shortly before our arrival, a beginning was made at the
building of the new synagogue, and of forty dwellings for the poor. The Turks in
Jerusalem had to be heavily bribed before they permitted the building.

Now there is a law in Jerusalem that while building is going on the pasha has to be
paid five hundred lion thalers a year for three years. But as the synagogue had been built
higher than the old one without the permission of the Sultan, another pasha came and
wished to stop the building. So he also received five hundred lion thalers. Finally a new
pasha came from Constantinople to whom five hundred lion thalers had to be given.
Thus the Jews were compelled to borrow money from the Turks at a high rate of interest.

There are also many Christians dwelling in Jerusalem, almost more than Turks and
Arabs. They also suffer greatly and must also pay taxes. Only the poor, the blind and
the lame are exempt. Nevertheless the Turks demand it from them as well, and nothing much can be done about it, for it is a harsh *galut*. However, on Sabbath and Festivals
the tax collector may not press us. So on those days we walk the street without fear.
But on weekdays, it is different. The official may not enter a house to demand money,
or make his way into the synagogue. Sometimes the officials bribe the chief pasha of
the Holy City, and in return receive permission to conduct their searches even in houses
for two or three days.

But let us return to our great worries, which the synagogue building brought about.
Our debts press like a heavy yoke on our necks. We are continually taken into custody
and before one debtor can be redeemed, another has already been detained. One scarcely
dares to go out in the street, where to cap it all, the tax collectors lie in wait like wolves
and lions to devour us.

It is hard for us Ashkenazim to begin to trade here, for we lack knowledge of the languages. The Sephardic Jews talk Ladino, the Arabs talk Aramaic [sic] and the Turks Turkish. None of them understand German. And what should we deal with? There is indeed much wine in the Land of Israel, but Turks and Arabs drink neither wine nor brandy. If a Jew sells an Arab even a little wine or brandy and the Arab is seen drunk, then the Jew is imprisoned and beaten and has to pay a money fine.

A few Jews have grocery shops here. Some of them take a Turk as a partner in order to protect themselves against unfair treatment. There are also a couple of Jewish spice dealers in the non-Jewish markets. There are Jews here who are called Moghrabians [Moroccans], or "Moriscos" in their own tongue. They have a language of their own, but also understand Aramaic [i.e., Arabic]. They go dressed like the Arabs and it is scarcely possible to distinguish them as the Arabs likewise follow the practice of having the beard uncut. These Moghrabians travel on their asses from place to place with spices and other things and in return bring wheat and barley to Jerusalem. From this they make a meagre living. If they, who know the languages of the country, live in poverty, what shall we poor Ashkenazim do here when we have to pass to and fro among the non- Jews as though we were dumb? If we buy something from the Arab, he shows us the price on his fingers and we have to answer on our fingers; so we become a laughing stock in their sight and cannot make a living.

Jerusalem has two Jewish cemeteries, one from ancient times lying at a distance south of the town, and a new one to the east, on the slopes of the Mount of Olives. No gravestone can be recognized any more in the old cemetery, and there are many caves to be found there. There are no caves in the new graveyard and the graves are dug out after our European fashion. Burial may not take place without the written authorization of the Turkish Kadi [Moslem religious judge], who is paid for this according to the wealth of the dead person. He gives permission for the burial of a poor man immediately and free of charge.

The garments of the Turks are long like those of the Poles, but are multi-coloured. Round the turban they wrap a cloth of cotton or silk. The Sephardim wear a white undergarment, and wear it over a black or coloured coat even on the Sabbath. The Ashkenazim go in gleaming white on the Sabbath, but the Sephardim wear white only on the Sabbath before the Ninth Day of Av. The Christians dress as in the kingdom of Poland. For the Turkish law prescribes that each nation should go in its own costume, in order to make the differences clear to see. There are also differences in footwear. The Jews wear blue and dark blue shoes, the Christians red, and yellow is reserved for the Turks.

The Arabs often wrong the Jew publicly. But if the Arab is a respectable man he will cause no injury to the Jew whom he meets in the street.

We have seen something very evil. There are some new-fangled fools who came to the Land only a short time ago, and who wish to revive the old disease of the year 5426 [1661] [Shabbatai Zevi's messianic movement—ed.]. For these fools declare that the Divine Presence is no longer in exile since then, and that there is therefore no reason to mourn its homelessness any longer.

For who does not know that we also shall return home with the return of the Divine Presence? Yet the Arabs will walk about our Holy Place and we are called the strangers to whom entry is forbidden. Even if it were true that the Divine Presence has forsaken our Exile, that fact does not help us, and our wounds are not yet healed.

Yet it is a rare delight to dwell in the Land of Israel, and "he who walks only four ells in the Land of Israel has a share in the everlasting life."

෨

The Western Wall which remains from the Temple is very long and high. For most of its height it is very ancient, and the stones are very large. Some stones are five or six cubits wide, and the same is true for their height. But I do not know how thick they are; if I could see them at the end of the Wall, I could tell, but a courtyard has been built actually against one end of the Wall and at the other end stands the house of an Ishmaelite judge, whom the Arabs call *dayyan*, which is the translation of judge in the Aramaic they speak. The Ishmaelites call him *kadi* in their language. Since these buildings cover both ends of the Wall, it is impossible to see how thick the Wall is. The Ishmaelites are permitted to enter the site of the Temple but not Jews or other peoples unless, God forbid, they convert to Islam. Because they [the Moslems] say that no other religion is worthy enough to enter this holy site. Although God had originally chosen the Jews, because they sinned He deserted them and chose the Ishmaelites. Thus they talk continually. When we go to the Wall to pray, we are actually standing "behind our wall" (Songs 2:9), close by it. On the eve of the New Moon and on the 9th of Av and other fasts, [the Jews] go there to pray and, although the women weep bitterly, nobody objects. Even though the Ishmaelite judge lives close by and hears the weeping, he does not object or rebuke them at all. Occasionally, a young Arab comes to annoy the Jews, but they give him a small coin (*mahat*) and he goes off. If a dignified Ishmaelite or Arab witnesses such impudence, he severely reprimands the child. The Temple site is far from the streets the Jews live in, and we have to go through markets and other streets to get to the Western Wall. Prayer is generally more desirable by the Wall.

WATER DRAWING FESTIVAL

Rabbi Yehoseph Schwarz

> Born in Bavaria, Yehoseph Schwarz (1804–1865) settled in Jerusalem in 1833, devoting himself to the study of the historical topography of the Land of Israel. The following is a letter he wrote in 1837.

To commemorate the joyous Water Drawing Festival, special celebrations are held in the synagogue during the entire Sukkoth holidays. After evening prayer we hold a festive procession in the synagogue, and each celebrant holds a candle in his hands. During this joyous procession, a musical instrument called a "Temprocu" is played, similar to small drums.

In the recently built "Kehal Zion" synagogue, an exquisitely constructed device has been installed which sprays water up into the air during the festivities. This, together with the other customs of the holiday, is very impressive. On Shemini Atzeret, as well as on the night following (the night of Simhat Torah where you live), all the Torah scrolls are removed from the ark, and we dance in a circle with them.

. . . If someone is married during the week, a beautiful canopy stands in the synagogue on the following Sabbath, and the bridegroom sits under it with his best man. When the bridegroom is called up to read from the Torah, his grooms accompany him when he ascends and descends. When he completes the recitation of the Torah blessing following the reading, the cantor sings the seven verses starting with, "Abraham was old," and continuing until ". . . take a wife unto my son from thence" (Gen. 24:1–7). He reads first the Hebrew, and then the Aramaic translation of each. During this song, the "shamash" circulates with a bottle full of rose water, sprinkling a little into the hand of each of those present. This is carried out with great decorum.

LIFE IN JERUSALEM (1834–1863)

Avraham Yaari

> *In his book* The Goodly Heritage, *Avraham Yaari collected stories about life in early Jerusalem, quoting from diaries and other writings of the time.*

Yehoshua Yellin . . . describes in the following pages Jewish life in Jerusalem during his early years. . . .

When my late father came to Jerusalem [1834—ed.] he found the city neglected and deserted. . . . Most of its houses and courtyards were in ruins, and those that remained whole were small, low and dark. Their tiny windows were covered with grilles to hide the women from the gaze of passers-by. The shops were in a similar case. Only a few were occupied by vendors of the rough, black pottery made in Gaza and Hebron, or by leather-workers and cobblers. . . . There were but few shopkeepers. Houses and shops could be bought for next to nothing; but the Jews did not interest themselves in purchasing them, as they did not see any possibility of gaining a worth-while living from them. They were more concerned with obtaining tenancy rights. . . .

My late father, who was always profoundly attached to the Land of Israel, had always wanted to own some property. But as the houses within the walls were old and cramped, and the air within them was foul owing to the narrow, tortuous and filthy streets, he would have none of them, and decided instead to buy a plot outside the walls for all that there was no vestige of human habitation there—only some Christian monks and merchants had acquired plots outside the wall—and despite the fact that the City gates were closed at nightfall by order of the authorities and remained shut all night. Before sunset a soldier would go out and announce that the gates were about to be closed, and all those without hurried inside. Any who tarried had to spend the night in the open.

David Yellin began to negotiate for a stretch of land some distance from the City wall (it is known today as the Russian Compound, in the heart of the modern city). But the parties differed concerning the width of a path that was to run through the land, and the deal fell through. . . .

Though in less affluent circumstances than before, the elder Yellin did not give up his idea of becoming the owner of a piece of land. He therefore joined forces with Yehoshua's brother-in-law, Shaul, who was of a like mind. The two scraped together some money and were offered a stretch of land at the village of Kolnia, about seven kilometers west of Jerusalem. . . . The village lay alongside the Jaffa–Jerusalem highway, and it had the merit of being the site of a place mentioned in the Bible—Motza, by which name it is now known. So charmed were the prospective purchasers by the beauty of the spot, that they decided to acquire it. Foreign nationals, however, were not permitted to buy land outside the City unless by a special dispensation of the Sultan, and so Yellin and his partner consulted James Finn (the British Consul), who suggested a somewhat involved way of getting round the difficulty. . . .

The Consul was held in great awe by the Pasha and other high Government officials. During the time he held office, he had several Pashas removed by complaining of them to the British Ambassador in Istambul; for at the time Britain wielded more influence there than any other country. Even the great sheikh, Haj Mustapha abu-Ghosh, who held sway over all the villages on the northern side of Jerusalem, kept aloof from us and did not interfere. . . .

The sudden death of David Yellin (in 1863) prevented the execution of the scheme.

A REVELATION AT THE WALL

Israel Meir Sofer

> *This description of the wall was written in 1850.*

The Wall runs the whole length of the [Temple] Mount but, on both sides, the Ishmaelites have built many houses so close to the Wall that it has become the Wall of their houses, in our many sins! Only in the center is a section of thirty cubits open and that is where the Jews stand to pray. There are approximately another ten cubits fenced in with a wall, and Jews are not permitted to go there. The Radbaz [David ibn Avi Zimra, 1479–1573—ed.] was granted a revelation at that spot and, since then, the Jews became accustomed to pray there and weep loudly. So the Ishmaelites fenced it off because it is near to their court where the judges sit, and they claimed that the noise the Jews made disturbed them. The Jews wanted to buy the place to build a study-house there, but the Ishmaelites refused, even for a great sum of money.

SIR MOSES PURCHASES A PIECE OF LAND

Dr. L. Loewe

> *A great traveler and philanthropist, the English nobleman Sir Moses Montefiore (1784–1885) first visited the Land of Israel in 1827. He visited there seven times, attempting to buy portions of it and to establish housing and occupations for the Jewish community. The excerpt is taken from* The Diaries of Sir Moses and Lady Montefiore, *edited by his secretary Dr. Loewe, describing his visits.*

Tuesday, June 11th, [1839]—We rode before breakfast through the valley of Jehosphaphat, then to the tomb of King David. The keeper of the place produced an order from Ibrahim Pasha, which prohibited the entrance of Europeans to the tomb. We addressed a letter to the Governor, informing him that the keeper would not admit us. A short time afterwards the Governor arrived. He approved of the conduct of the keeper, but thought, nevertheless, that the Pasha's order did not refer to a gentleman who, like Sir Moses, was the bearer of letters of introduction from the highest authorities in the land, and, leading the way, he invited us all to follow him to the tomb. It was a spacious vaulted chamber, supported in the center by a column. At the further end we saw a trellised window, on the right of which was an arched folding door. Being led to the spot, we beheld through the lattice the tomb, covered with richly embroidered carpets. In the centre was an Arabic inscription, "This is the tomb of our Lord David," on either side of which were the double triangles known by the name of "the shield of David." On one corner of the tomb hung a rich silk sash and a pistol, the offerings of Ibrahim Pasha. The Governor, addressing Sir Moses and Lady Montefiore, said, "I will now leave you to your religious devotions," and then left the place. We recited several psalms, and went away much gratified with the opportunity which we had had of visiting the sacred spot.

On our return we visited the cave of Jeremiah and the tombs of the Kings. In the evening a number of people came up to pass the night on the Mount of Olives, so as to be ready in the morning to join the procession which had been arranged for our entry into the city. Many of our brethren from Hebron, including the spiritual heads and representatives of their congregations, came to offer us their congratulations, and to accompany us the next day to the Synagogue. In the evening a large number of friends, and students from the colleges, assembled round our tents, to recite the evening prayers in front of the place formerly occupied by Solomon's Temple.

ᏉᏦ

Wednesday, 12th.—We rose before four o'clock. The Governor offered to attend us at daybreak, but Sir Moses said he would let him know when we were ready. At six o'clock Sir Moses sent for the Governor, who came attended by the representatives of the several congregations, a number of soldiers, and many of his officers and servants. They took coffee, pipes, etc., and after sitting down some time we set out at eight o'clock in procession. Sir Moses rode a beautiful white Arabian horse, which the Governor had sent him the day before; Lady Montefiore rode her own. We entered the city by the Gate of the Tribes, and passed through most of the streets, which were crowded with men, women, and children, the Governor having made it a holiday. We proceeded to the Portuguese Synagogue, where the Governor left us. His officers and men remained with us till we again reached the Mount of Olives. The Synagogue was beautifully decorated, and attended by as many of the congregation as space would permit. Special prayers were offered up by the Ecclesiastical Chief, who invoked the blessings of Heaven on the pious pilgrims. At the conclusion of the service we received a hearty welcome to the Holy City from all present.

We then went to the German Synagogue, where a similar service was held, addresses delivered, and prayers offered up for the friends of Zion, after which we proceeded to the Western Wall, and recited there the usual prayers in the presence of a large assembly. . . .

The record of this day in his diary concludes with the following words, expressive of the greatful sentiments which filled his heart: "The Lord God of Israel be praised and thanked for permitting our feet to stand a second time within thy gates, O Jerusalem, may the city soon be rebuilt in our days. Amen." "I believe," he continues, "the whole population was looking at us, and bestowing blessings on us."

❧

[July 1855]—Having surmounted the difficulties and impediments which he had to encounter, Sir Moses eventually succeeded in purchasing a track of land to the west of the Holy City, adjoining the high road from Jerusalem to Hebron, in a most beautiful and salubrious locality, and within a few minutes' walk from the Jaffa and Zion Gates. Here a considerable number of our co-religionists and others at once found employment on the land, and in the building of the boundary wall.

Sir Moses being the first Englishman to whom the Ottoman Government granted the permission to purchase land, I give some particulars connected with the transaction.

Ahhmed Agha Dizdar, who had been Governor of Jerusalem during the reign of Mohhammad Ali, and who since the year 1839 had stood in friendly relations with Sir Moses, was the owner of the land in question. When Sir Moses broached the subject of the purchase to him, his answer was: "You are my friend, my brother, the apple of my eyes, take possession of it at once. This land I hold as an heirloom from my ancestors. I would not sell it to any person for thousands of pounds, but to you I give it with-

Yemin Moshe with Montefiore's windmill during the reconstuction of the area following the 1967 War (Israel Government Press Office; with permission)

out any money: it is yours, take possession of it. I myself, my wife, and children, we all are yours." And this was his reply to Sir Moses day after day, whenever he was asked the price for which he would sell the said property.

Ultimately, after a whole day's most friendly argument, which almost exhausted all my stock of Arabic phraseology (having acted as interpreter between him and Sir Moses), he said to me: "You are my friend, my brother; by my beard, my head, I declare this is the case. Tell Sir Moses to give me a souvenir of one thousand pounds sterling, and we will go at once to the Ckadée."

The moment I informed him of the Agha's price, Sir Moses lost no time, and counted out one thousand English sovereigns, did them up in a roll, and proceeded to the English Consulate, together with the Agha and his friends, where the sale was effected.

On our arrival at the Máhhkámeh (hall of justice) to have the purchase confirmed, we found all the members of the Meglis assembled, and the Judge, or Ckadée, with his secretaries, present.

Questions were put by the Judge, both to the seller and the purchaser. The purchase money was counted, and the contract of sale was read aloud, and witnessed by all present.

The wording of the document is to the effect that, "By permission of the Sublime Porte and the Imperial Throne, may the Lord of Creation preserve them, and in conformity with the letters of that subject from the Grand Vizier to Sir Moses Montefiore (Baronet), the pride of the people of Moses, the man of prudence, etc., the son of Joseph Eliyahu (here also follow a number of complimentary titles), Sir Moses purchases a piece of land for the purpose of establishing thereon a hospital for the poor of the Israelites who reside in Jerusalem, and does with it as he pleases."

"Sir Moses Montefiore, Baronet," the contract continues, "presented himself as the purchaser before the Legislative Council in presence of the members of the Council of Jerusalem, to purchase the land hereinafter described with his own money, not with that which belongeth to another, from the vendor, Sir Ahmed Agha Eldizdar (the support of great men), son of Sid Fadh-ed-din Agha."

The contract then defines the exact limits of the property and the Ckadée attests the correctness of the deed of purchase. Sir Moses returned to his camp, and gave orders to remove his tents to the land which had become his own property, whilst I proceeded to measure it, inscribing the initials of Sir Moses' name in large Hebrew characters on a piece of rock forming the angle of its boundary line upon the road, the right side of which, when coming from the Jaffa Gate, leads to Bet-essefáfa.

ꙮ

August 15th.—In the presence of a numerous concourse of spectators of various religious denominations, Sir Moses and Lady Montefiore had the satisfaction and happiness to lay the foundation-stone of the proposed hospital, in the presence of Mr. and Mrs. Guedalla, Mr. Gershon Kursheedt, one of the executors of Juda Touro, the American philanthropist, and myself.

A NARRATIVE OF A FORTY DAYS' SOJOURN IN THE HOLY LAND
Sir Moses Montefiore

[1879] About three o'clock in the afternoon we left for Bab-el-Wad. Here the state of the road improved a little, but still not so as to prevent a carriage from moving without violent jolts, which made us sometimes feel as though we were on the point of being thrown out of the carriage altogether.

I noticed a great deal of activity in the fields, and frequently met a long string of camels carrying various loads to or from Jerusalem. Now and then I saw the omnibus with a number of people; altogether the road I thought considerably more animated by traffic that it was during my former visits to Jerusalem. As we came near Bab-el-Wad, a hut was pointed out to me which, it was said, was occupied by two of our brethren, being engaged there in the preparation of lime. It was quite in a solitary situation, and the occupants must have found it hard work to get even the necessary provisions to that place. At six o'clock we arrived safely at Bab-el-Wad. When I alighted at this spot in the year 5626 (1866), there was only an insignificant little house built of boards or boughs, and the traveller would only stop here to take a cup of coffee; now we entered a house with a commodious dining- or reception-room, four or five bedrooms, and a convenient terrace to enjoy there, in the cool evening or morning air, the invigorating breeze of the hills. The house was built for the accommodation of travellers, and three enterprising Israelites went into partnership, and took it for three years.

We remained here Friday and Sabbath, and had the happiness to offer up our prayers with a full Community, some of them purposely coming from the Holy City. I was longing to see Jerusalem, and decided, notwithstanding my previous arrangements, to start on Saturday night. We waited for the rising of the moon, and twenty minutes past eleven o'clock started for Jerusalem. Those were exciting moments which presented themselves to my mind, now and then, as we ascended and descended the hills and dales on the road; the moon throwing her long and dark shadow when behind a rock. They recalled to memory how much exposed the traveller was in former years to the attacks of a Bedouin, or some feudal lord. Now, thank God, thanks to the protection of the Turkish government, we do not hear of such outrages on peaceable pilgrims. Just as I concluded these meditations, two Bedouins in full speed dashed along from behind some hidden rock, and directed their course right up to our carriage. "Good heavens," I thought, "we ought not to be too hasty here in bestowing praises on the protection of the police; what in the world will they do with us?" But Dr. Loewe, who was with me in the carriage, suddenly called out as loud as he possibly could, "Shalom Aleykhem, Rabbi B.S.; Shalom Aleykhem, Rabbi L.S.," and turning round to me he said, "These are not Bedouins, though they are dressed exactly like them, and gallop along the hills like the sons of the desert, but they are simply our own Brethren from Jerusalem, who, I have no doubt, came to ascertain the exact time of your intended entry into Jerusalem, to give timely notice to the people to come out to meet you." And so it was. A minute afterwards they pulled up the reins of their fiery chargers, and stood before us. "A happy and blessed week to you, Dr. Loewe," they shouted; "where is Sir Moses? how is he? when will he enter Jerusalem?" As I bent my head forward they reverentially saluted me, and stated to me the object of their coming; but as it was my intention purposely to avoid giving any unnecessary inconvenience to my Jerusalem friends, I declined letting them know the exact hour. They again saluted, galloped off, and soon disappeared. I was told that they had left Jerusalem after Habdalah, and now intended being again in the Holy City early in the morning. If there be many such horsemen in the Holy Land like these two supposed Bedouins, they certainly ought not in justice to be regarded as descendants from sickly parents, as some persons supposed.

About four o'clock in the morning we reached Colonia, almost exhausted from fatigue, but I remained firm in my resolution, and after a short stay of half an hour, without descending from the carriage, proceeding on my journey.

At five o'clock in the morning we were already saluted by friends who had anticipated our approach, and, half an hour afterwards, we halted at the spot whence a full view might be had of the Holy City. There we performed the ceremony of Keriah [tearing one's garment as a sign of mourning—ed.] and pronouncing the customary blessing, surrounded by an increasing number of people from all directions.

As we continued moving toward Jerusalem, I had nothing but to look right and left and see the number of new houses; some of them very large buildings, and the mouths of friends did not rest from telling us, "This is a house belonging to one of us"; "That piece of ground has been bought by N.N., one of our Community"; and as we still further proceeded, there was no necessity any more to inform us of the name of any proprietor, as the whole family of the occupants came out of their houses, and I had the happiness of myself seeing hundred of our brethren, lining the fronts of their dwellings. Presently my attention was directed to the presence of my much-esteemed friend, the Rev. Samuel Salant, a gentleman who had been introduced to me, when in Constantinople, by the late Rev. Moses Rivlin, in the year 5601 (1840), and who has been one of my correspondents on matters connected with the Holy Land for the last thirty-five years. His countenance was radiant with joy when he saw me, and he pronounced the blessing of "Shehekheyanoo" [thanksgiving for having lived to experience a special event—ed.]. I was delighted to find him looking so well, appearing almost as young as when I saw him nine years ago. Proceeding a little farther on the road, a new Synagogue was shown to me, in the place called "Nakhalat Shibeah"; it was surrounded by a number of houses, occupied, I was told, by fifty families. Again, a plot of ground was pointed out to me as belonging to a party intending to build thereon sixty houses. And, when coming near the Upper Gikhon pool, not far from the windmill which I caused to be built on the Estate "Kerem Moshe Ve-Yehoodit," eighteen years ago, my attention was directed to two other windmills recently built, which, I was told, gave a good profit to the Greeks who owned them.

Great was my delight when I considered that but a few years had passed since the time when not one Jewish family was living outside the gate of Jerusalem—not a single house to be seen; and now I beheld almost a new Jerusalem springing up, with buildings, some of them as fine as any in Europe. "Surely," I exclaimed, "we are approaching the time to witness the realization of God's hallowed promises unto Zion! 'I will make thee an eternal excellency, a joy of many generations.'—Is. lx.15."

When my carriage reached the Jaffa gate I was obliged to alight. Neither the streets nor the pavements in Jerusalem, the driver observed, are yet prepared for carriages.

❧

Bucharian Jew in Jerusalem, Date unknown (Central Zionist Archives; with permission)

In the evening I received an invitation from the Building Committee of the little Colony called "Meah Shearim" to lay the foundation stone of a new row of houses. "The Company," they said, "on whose behalf we crave the honour of your presence, numbers now 120 members, under the direction of Mr. Salmon Beharan, assisted by the Treasurer, Mr. Ben Zion Lion, and the Secretary, Mr. Jesaias Ornstein. The object is to build every year not less than ten houses, which, on completion, are to be allotted to ten members. The Company was established but two years ago, and there are already twenty houses built and inhabited.

"There will be a Synagogue, College, and School; likewise a Public Bath in the centre of the square, and a very large cistern for the supply of water."

On my enquiry whether they were the only Building Society in Jerusalem, they replied, "No, there are two others. . . ." So that altogether there will be 235 of our Brethren, in a few years, proprietors of most comfortable houses in a very salubrious locality, outside the city, which they secured unto themselves by their own exertions, by their own money.

Friday (13th August) I proceeded to the Western Wall to offer up the customary prayers. The road leading to that hallowed spot, and the houses in its vicinity, are still in a state of ruin, causing man and horse to stumble over detached fragments of ancient structures, and remind the pilgrim that a great deal of work has yet to be done before the paths of Zion will be even and smooth. When I visited Jerusalem, in the year 1866, I exerted myself very much to have an awning made in front of the Western Wall. I had already made an agreement for the execution of the work, but unexpectedly some obstacle occurred, which could not be surmounted, and the matter dropped. A gentleman recently tried to place there some seats for the accommodation of the numerous visitors arriving daily at that spot, and not succeeding in his endeavours, he asked permission to have at least a number of large square marble stones placed there, and was allowed to do so. But they did not remain long in the place assigned to them; first one stone was removed, then another, until at last all of them disappeared. . . .

The Haham Bashi [Chief Rabbi—ed.] having requested me to receive a special deputation, I appointed the afternoon for an interview, though I felt greatly the fatigue from this morning's exertions, and was obliged to retire to my chamber. About two o'clock p.m., Haham Shalom Moshe Khay Gagin, principal of the Yesheebat Toledoth Yitzhak, and Signor Yitzkhak Kalamaro, the Treasurer of the Synagogue "Bethel," entered. They communicated to me their intentions of securing land for the building of 80 houses, a Synagogue, Beth Hamidrash, and a Public Bath. They had already, they said, decided to purchase for that purpose a plot of ground near the City wall, measuring 26,000 builders' yards, at the price of 900 Napoleons, toward which amount the Gurgistan Congregation was ready to contribute 650 Napoleons; but unfortunately the expenses necessary for the purpose of securing the purchase by a proper contract, proved to be so great that they had to relinquish it.

The deputation made to me certain proposals on that subject, which I promised them to take into consideration.

They also communed with me on matters referring to the Kerem Moshe ve-Yehoodit, and I gave them full instructions how to act, so as to secure the object in view.

To Jerusalem

Ludwig A. Frankl

> *Born in Bohemia, Ludwig August Frankl (1810–1894) was an editor and poet who went to Jerusalem in 1856 and founded the Lemel School, which combined religious and secular learning. He wrote of his experiences there in a book* Nach Jerusalem *(1858–1860), from which the following is taken.*

When it became cooler, I set my steps towards the ruins of the Temple, to the one wall that has survived, the wailing place of the Jews who gather there every Friday evening to pray the evening service and to bewail the Temple that was destroyed.

They have an everlasting *firman* from the authorities allowing them to visit this place, for which privilege they pay a small tax.

Doorway to the School for Sewing at the Schneller Woods, date unknown; labeled as "the second house outside the city walls" (Central Zionist Archives; with permission)

After we passed through many streets, we came into a narrow winding street and from there to the Wall. It is 158 feet long and 60 high, which height is made up of twenty-three stone courses of which the bottom nine are of hewn stones, some of which are between twenty and thirty feet in length and five feet wide. Each of these slabs of stone is rounded and on their faces, which have been smoothed as though with an instrument, there is a shining border of about a finger's depth. Lying there, row on row, thin lines can we seen between them, and so the whole Wall looks like a wall of avenues of which the upper courses are of a later origin. From the shape of some of the hewn stones that jut out of the Wall, modern research has concluded that they are the remains of arches leading from the Temple to Mount Zion.

There can be do doubt that this wall, with its courses of foundation stones under the ground, is a memorial for the Jews from Solomon's time which, as Jossipon put it, will never collapse. Anyone who has seen it can testify that it will not collapse until the very foundations of the earth will be shaken.

From a distance we could already hear the sound of the wailing, a cry of pain which pierced the very heart. In chorus, the appeal rang in our ears, "How long, O Lord!"

Jews were gathered there in their hundreds, some in the dress of the Ishmaelites and others in the style of Poland, and, facing the Wall, they bowed and prostrated themselves. At a great distance from the men, stood the women all totally enveloped in white gowns—white doves, tired from their flying, resting on the ruins. When the cantor reached those parts of the prayers to be said by the congregation, their voices rose among the choir of male voices, and spreading their arms on high, they looked in their wide white gowns for all the world like wings spread upwards to the open gates of heaven. Afterwards, they smote their foreheads against the hewn stones of the Temple's wall. Then, when the cantor, exhausted and wasted from his efforts, quietly and slowly weeping, turned his head to the wall, then suddenly, in a moment, a deathly silence covered all.

THE WALL IS OURS

Mordecai ben Hillel Ha-Kohen

> *Ha-Kohen came to Jerusalem from Russia in 1889 and described his reaction to seeing the Kotel for the first time.*

I started to organize my stay in the city, but I soon realized that I did not have the strength to withstand my desire—nay! the urgent need—to hurry to the Western Wall. I remember nothing of the way I went; my legs bore me, and I went blindly like an

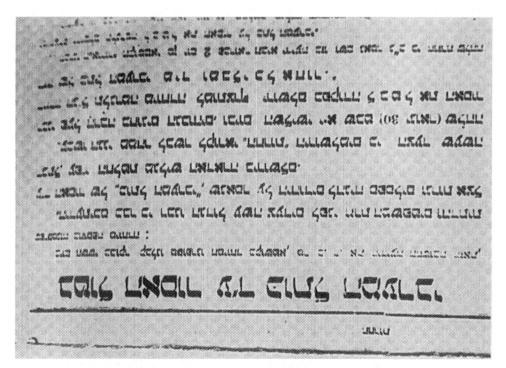

A poster announcing that the ban imposed by the Turkish authorities against Jews bringing benches or candles to the Wall has been lifted owing to the efforts of the rabbis (Central Zionist Archives; with permission)

animal following its herder. My eyes were lifted aloft all the time straining to catch the first glimpse of the Wall. "This is the Western Wall," murmured my guide in a holy whisper; but I would have known anyway. . . . I do not remember how my shoes left my feet, how I fell full length on the ground, how I started kissing the flagstones under me or how I began weeping such copious tears that became torrents. My heart was in turmoil. I did not attempt to control myself or stop the flow of tears which I wept like a small infant without sense or words. The attendant did not approve and interrupted me, handing me a Psalter and showing me the verses which were to be recited at the Wall. Idiot! Did he not realize that at that moment I had no need of any verses, of any prayerbook or of any liturgy!?

I departed the Wall grievously heartbroken. . . . It was not what my eyes saw or the desolation at the Wall that so struck me but rather my inner soul-feeling. For in its appearance there is nothing in this Wall to so disturb the strings of a man's heart and to incite such a storm inside a Jew. There is not even "destruction" there. The stones have been burned with fire, the Wall is not destroyed, the rows of its stones do not cast the shadow of death and, generally, surely the terrible destruction deserved a more fitting memorial than that given by this Wall?! After having said all this, I still must say that what this Wall does is truly awesome; for so great is the holy trepidation that falls on the Jew in this place that for the sake of the Wall and for its sake alone every Jew should make the pilgrimage to Jerusalem. The cities of Judah and the streets of Jerusalem are filled with memorials, by their thousands, dear to every Jew, and with each step he will hear the echoes of pleasant memories and see memorials which silently will tell him what was ours in days long past. But, even if they all did not exist, even if they were all rolled together and stored out of sight, and only the Wall still remained; even then it would be worthwhile for the Jew to take all the trouble in the world to come and see it with his own eyes. There are scholars who cast doubt on the verity of the traditions about this Wall. They have no heart and they lack understanding! They cannot believe that the tradition speaks the truth, that a wall can stand for two thousand years, and that truly there still exists in the world a survival from that "universal house of prayer." A survivor of all the trials and tribulations which have not ceased to visit this wonderful country from the day that Judah was exiled from it and strangers swallowed it. Let the scholars wonder at it as they will—for us it is no wonder! We know that we are a people of legends. Who knows! Perhaps the whole Jewish people is a legend! But in that legend, there bursts forth a spring of life of exalted strength, and that legend can laugh at the facts of real life! Why do I need to know which of the Wall's stones are from the walls of the Temple Mount and which were added to it later? I know that there is no nation and no people in the world which comes to prostrate itself and pour out its heart in front of this Wall; but our brethren come from all the lands of their exile to tell their sins before these holy stones. Only Israel—in all its families—cries there! That is the proof that there we stand behind our Wall. The Wall is ours and let no man dare to touch it!

Eliezer Ben Yehuda at the ceremony of laying the cornerstone for his new home in Talpiot in 1923 (Central Zionist Archives; with permission)

COMING TO JERUSALEM

Eliezer Ben Yehudah

> *Famous for his pioneering work to revive the Hebrew language, Eliezer Ben Yehudah (1858–1922) was born in Lithuania and left Europe for the Land of Israel in 1881.*

After we had eaten lunch in the inn, the owner asked if we wanted to go to Jerusalem that day. If so we would immediately have to reserve places in the coach. In those days the railroad between Jaffa and Jerusalem had not yet been built, and travelers had to go in horse-drawn wagons which left Jaffa daily toward evening in a caravan and arrived in Jerusalem the next morning. The inn keeper secured three places for us, and at sunset we left the city, driving on the main street, which was lined with rows of orange trees on each side. The coach driver was a short, thin Jew, about twenty-five years old named Haim-Yaakov. When we had gone a short way, the driver turned toward us and began to speak to us in French. He told us that soon we would arrive at the agricultural school sponsored by "All Israel is One Fellowship," Mikveh Yisrael. . . . I asked him how he happened to know French. He told me, "I am a student at Mikveh Yisrael." Did he speak Hebrew? Just a little. Nevertheless, I began to speak to him in Hebrew. He replied in halting Hebrew, but with ease. I was exceedingly happy to see that there existed a Hebrew-speaking coachman. Because of that I developed a special feeling for him and thereafter always sought opportunities to hire him whenever I could. Later he would recount with pride how he had brought me to Jerusalem from Jaffa and that we had spoken Hebrew. When the "League of Jewish Coachmen" was organized in Jerusalem and celebrated the Jubilee year of the senior coachman, Haim-Yaakov, I was one of the few non-coachmen to be invited to the festive meal.

The next morning, when the coach stood near the square before Jaffa Gate, two men came up to me and called in Hebrew, "Shalom Aleichem" (Welcome). They had been sent by Reb Yisrael-Dov, the owner of "HaHavatzelet" [a Hebrew periodical—ed.] to greet me and bring me and my wife to our house. . . .

Anyone familiar with Jerusalem today would find it difficult to even imagine the desolation in those days of that square before Jaffa Gate. All the beautiful buildings which you can now see on both sides of the square and above it as you come to "Hamoskovia" [the Russian Compound—ed.] had not yet been built. All that existed was only a few dark, squat, miserable huts on either side, befitting the ruined state of the entire city. As you came to the city there was a long, low, impoverished-looking building on the left containing some dark and dingy stores with low and narrow entrances. As we neared the stores I noticed that in some of them the entrances had been broken down and workers were rebuilding them, raising the entrances, widening them and in general giving the stores a more pleasant appearance. I asked my companions, "Who owns these stores and who is repairing and improving them?" They told me that this was the property of the Armenian Patriarchate which had begun of late to build houses and stores in a European style. I was upset to hear that strangers were building Jerusalem and I sadly voiced my feelings to my wife, but the men sent by Reb Yisrael Dov comforted me by saying: It doesn't matter! They are building for us. When the Redeemer comes— speedily in our days!—all of these buildings will be ours.

These words were uttered with such simplicity and sincerity that there could be no doubting that they believed what they were saying to me completely. And I must say that such belief was held strongly by all the Jewish residents of the Land of Israel at that time. Some years later, when Yemenite Jews began to come to Jerusalem, I heard the same simple, certain convictions from them: They are building and building—everything will be ours when the victorious Messiah comes.

Because of this perfect faith the Jewish inhabitants of the Land of Israel were not bothered by the fact that Jerusalem and the other cities of the Land were being built by strangers. Now that we have been worthy to witness the beginning of redemption, I see that this simple faith of our brothers of the Land of Israel of that generation was not so foolish after all. But at that time, when I has just arrived in the Land of our Fathers, the fact that our mother city was being built by strangers and that the inhabitants were not troubled by it upset me very much, so much so that I could pay attention to nothing else.

It was in that despondent mood that I went through Jaffa Gate into the holy city within the wall—the ruined, desolate city of David King of Israel, cast down to the depths of Sheol. No special feeling was aroused within me. Even the words, "the Citadel of David"—which my companions spoke to me when we passed by the tower to the right of Jaffa Gate—made no particular impression upon me. Had someone told me in advance that my entrance into Jerusalem would be so trivial, so unable to stir my blood or arouse any emotions within me, I would certainly have reprimanded such a person. But I must admit that that is exactly how it was. I was completely apathetic, as if I were walking in the streets of any one of the world's cities. Thus did I go the entire way from Jaffa Gate to the site of the Temple.

AT THE END OF DAYS

Menahem Usishkin

> *Usishkin (1863–1941) was born in Russia and became active in the Bilu movement, which advocated settling the land of Israel, in the 1880s. He was a follower of Ahad HaAm and visited the Land of Israel for the first time in 1891. After many trips and much work for the Zionist movement, he settled in the Land in 1919. For many years he was the head of the Jewish National Fund.*

It happened on Passover eve, 5653 (1893), following the Seder which our group had conducted. A small group of young dreamers sat in the spacious courtyard of the Hotel Kaminitz in Jerusalem. They had come from many different and far-off lands of the dispersion to see with their own eyes the land of their hopes and dreams, to imbibe the scent of the fields of their ancient homeland, to cover the splendour of ancient ruins with tears in order to draw strength for the difficult struggles of the present and to find answers to the questions of the future . . . and, obviously, all of them went to stand before the remnant of our most desirable relic, the Western Wall, where the people would assemble to recite the order of the ritual of the paschal lamb.

One man in the group was particularly notable. He was not tall, but the high, wide forehead of his magnificent head testified that he was an idealogue. It was Asher ben Yeshiyahu Ginzberg, who had then published a few essays using the pen name of Ahad HaAm. Those few essays had already drawn everyone's attention to him and all expected great things of him in the future as a writer and guide. . . .

The place and the occasion created a feeling of elation such as is seldom attained. The place—Jerusalem, the Holy City! That name alone is sufficient to explain the tremors of holiness that filled each of our hearts. "City of the great King" in the past, the city which forged together all of the glories and wonders of the great past of the Hebrew nation, the wondrous shining past of our people! Does not the future await us here? . . . And the occasion—the holy night of the Passover Festival following the Seder, "the night of watching" when Israel emerged from slavery into freedom, the festival which commemorates our creation as a people . . . memories of the great past arise in the our hearts as we sit under the dome of the deep, blue sky resplendent with myriads of twinkling stars.

Our hearts were filled with the desire to penetrate the mist of generations and recapture that time when we were truly free, when the people of Israel would encamp here in full complement, full of strength and power, completely free. Each of us was filled with the belief that with his own eyes he could see not only the past, but the future as well . . . ancient Israel returns to its ancient birthplace . . . every day tens, hundreds of Israel's sons return from the four corners of the earth with one purpose: "to renew our days as of old." . . .

Conversation nearly faded away. We each sensed that human language was too poor to convey what we felt in our innermost hearts; at that exalted moment silence was called for. . . .

Suddenly pointing at Mount Moriah, someone asked, "What will exist there in the end of days when Israel will dwell in its land?"

"A great synagogue," someone else answered. "Many of our synagogues were turned over to strangers. We shall take only that which belongs to us."

"No," replied yet another."We shall turn this place into a sanctuary. But not for prayer and weeping and the like, but a sanctuary dedicated to wisdom and life. Here will be built the high academy for humanities. We have wept and prayed enough. The time has come to study and teach!"

"This question was solved three thousand years ago by the wisest of all men," responded Ahad HaAm quietly but firmly. Turning toward Mount Moriah, he recited in a calm and assured voice the words of Solomon at the time of the dedication of the great Temple which he had built to the God of Israel:

> Oh, hear in Your heavenly abode, and pardon and take action! Render to each man according to his ways as You know his heart to be—for You alone know the hearts of all men. . . . Or if a foreigner who is not of Your people Israel comes from a distant land for the sake of Your name—for they shall hear about Your great name and Your mighty hand and Your outstretched arm—when he comes to pray toward this House, oh, hear in Your heavenly abode and grant all that the foreigner asks You for. Thus all the peoples of the earth will know Your name and revere You, as does Your people Israel (1 Kings 8:39–43).

And the voice of the young author, which had been quiet when he began, grew louder and louder. The words of the king who loved strangers rang out in the silence of the night like the vision of a prophet.

"Yes," concluded Ahad HaAm, "A sanctuary will exist here. Not a synagogue; not a church; not a mosque—'For My house shall be called a house of prayer for all peoples' (Isa. 56:7). 'And all the nations shall gaze on it with joy' " (Isa. 2:2).

Hours thereafter we continued to sit, ponder and consider. We each felt that we had found the beginning of the solution to one of the most complex questions facing humanity. . . .

TRUTH FROM THE LAND OF ISRAEL

Ahad HaAm

> *Asher Hirsch Ginsberg (1856–1927), known best by his pen name Ahad HaAm ("one of the people"), was a great essayist and Zionist leader. His first visit to the Land of Israel took place in 1891, and he wrote his impressions in this famous essay.*

I came to Jerusalem for Passover eve to pour out my thoughts and my anger before the "sticks and stones," the ancient remnants of our most precious places. Obviously my first stop was the Wall. There I found crowds of our brothers, dwellers of Jerusalem, standing and praying in loud voices. Their thin faces, their strange motions and their odd dress seemed to fit the terrible state of the Wall. As I stood and contemplated them and the Wall one thought filled my mind: these stones are witnesses to the destruction of our land; these men—to the destruction of our people. Which destruction is greater? For which should we lament more bitterly? If the land is destroyed but the people remains full of life and strength, a Zerrubabel, Ezra and Nehemiah can arise and the nation will follow them, return and rebuild. But if the people is destroyed, who can restore it and when whence will its help arise? (*21 IYAR 5651*)

A *"Moshav Zekenim" (Home for the Elderly) in Jerusalem, date unknown (Central Zionist Archives; with permission)*

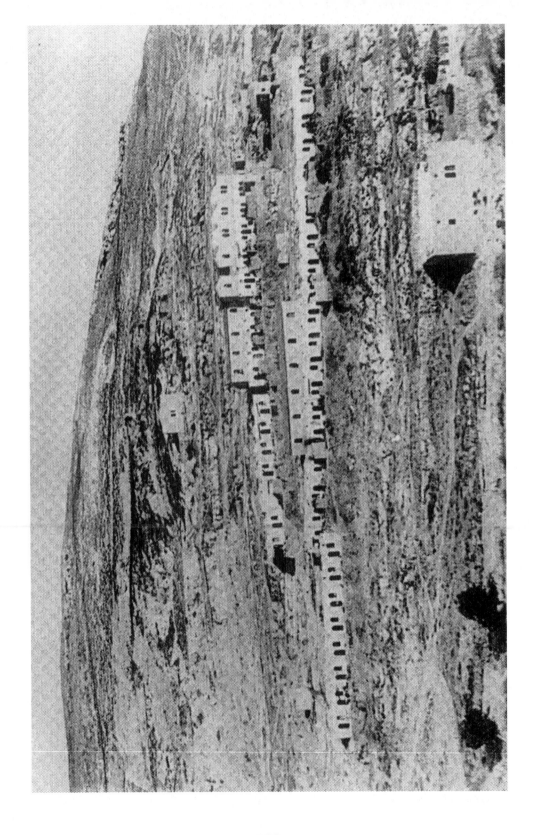

238

MY MEMOIRS

Yosef Yoel Rivlin

> *The Rivlin family settled in the Land of Israel in the early 1800s and participated in the building of settlements outside the walls of the Old City and in the establishment of Jewish life and institutions in Jerusalem. Yosef Yoel Rivlin (1889–1971) was an educator and scholar and wrote these accounts of life in Jerusalem during his youth.*

Every neighborhood had its own synagogue, next to which could be found the "oven"—the only public buildings, even though only a few steps and a narrow path separated one neighborhood from another: Mazkeret Moshe from Mishkanot Yisrael, Mishkanot Yisrael from Even Yisrael. In the more developed neighborhoods, which became the centers for surrounding areas, there was also a Talmud Torah with a few classes for beginners. Strangely enough, Sukkat Shalom, that row of houses which stretched from Mishkanot Yisrael to Even Yisrael, a neighborhood of wealthy old Russians, where most of the homes had two rooms or even two and a half with a balcony enclosed by iron railings, had no synagogue of its own. Those prominent, wealthy men who were known by the city of their origins—I remember "the honorable man from Velkovisk"; Reb Tzvi Mondshein, "the man of Warsaw"—had to pray either in the Mazkeret Moshe synagogue or the Mishkanot Yisrael synagogue.

A narrow path was all that divided Ohel Moshe from Mazkeret Moshe, and the windows of each neighborhood faced those of the other, but only their backs faced each other. The doors and entrances of each neighborhood faced inward, toward the other row of houses within the neighborhood, with a public garden between the two rows. The rectangle of the neighborhood was closed off by short rows of houses in the other directions. That was the plan of all the early neighborhoods.

Ohel Moshe and Mazkeret Moshe were two totally separate worlds, two different entities. In Mazkeret Moshe they spoke Yiddish, pure Lithuanian Yiddish, while Ladino was the language of Ohel Moshe, as spoken by the Jews of Turkey and the Balkans. When the Yemenites came and settled in a group of houses south of Mishkanot Yisrael and east of Mazkeret Moshe, the Hebrew language, in the special accent of Yemenite Jewry, began to compete with the two "official" languages, Yiddish and Ladino.

Only a few Sephardim managed to make their way into the Ashkenazic neighborhood, either to live there or to purchase their own homes. Even fewer Ashkenazim penetrated the Sephardi neighborhood. . . .

← *"The Help of the Needy"—a settlement built at the foot of Mount Zion "with sixty houses to house sixty needy families who will be chosen by a lottery to be held every three years," date unknown (Collection of the National and University Library, Jerusalem; with permission)*

The Misgav Ladach Hospital in the Old City, year unknown (Central Zionist Archives; with permission)

The bath-houses played an important part in my life. I think that when I was a child there were two "steam-baths" in Jerusalem. One was on a wide street, Batrik Street, not far from the path leading to the sepulcher of Jesus. The other, which was fancier, was near the Temple Mount and was called "The Hot Bath of Al-harem." Hasidim and very observant people had nothing to do with it. They said that it was within the borders of the Temple Mount, which was forbidden to Jews so long as there were no "ashes of the red heifer" which could be used for purification. When I was young many people said that some fanatics had proclaimed a "herem" against Moses Montefiore himself because he had entered the courtyard of the Temple Mount. He was probably misled by his secretary, Eliezer Loewe, who cited the lenient ruling of the Ravad that the rule of the holiness of the Sanctuary is not operative at this time, thus leading to a Jerusalem scandal. Father and his friends permitted themselves to go to that bath-house. . . .

Those sweat-baths were among the few pleasures of this world which a Jerusalmite could enjoy at that time. One would enter a large room—directly from the street. In the center was a fountain, in some of which there were little fish or floating lemons, or even flowering plants around it. There were high ledges around the walls, with steps leading up to them on which were padded sofas covered with silk from Damascus. One would sit for a few moments to recover from the walk. Then one of the attendants of the bath-house would come and bring you sheets. You would undress garment after garment and wrap yourself in the sheets—like a thick, wide towel—around your hips and going as far as the knees. You would take off your shirt and he would put a beautiful, colorful silk scarf on your shoulders which covered half your body from the hips upward: he would bring you wooden sandals which were on the steps and then you would pass into an empty inner hallway—it had nothing but a bench in it—which led to the baths themselves. . . .

Early in the morning the day before Yom Kippur we would go to the Western Wall. That was the time when it was most crowded there, for people from all the different groups would assemble there. There were many who prayed the morning service in groups before the Wall, Sephardim, Ashkenazim, Yemenites and Bucharians. At first there was no partition separating men from women at the Wall; the early Sephardim and Perushim did not think of it. But when the number of Hasidim grew and the group of "guardians of modesty" sprang up, they erected one in the northern corner of the Wall on the day before Yom Kippur when there was a large crowd.

RAISE A BANNER TO ZION

Saul Tschernichovsky

> *One of the greatest poets of the period of the revival of Hebrew, Tschernichovsky (1875–1943) settled in the Land of Israel in 1931, living first in Tel Aviv and then in Jerusalem. This poem, however, was written in Odessa in 1897.*

Raise a banner to Zion! Raise a banner to Zion!

Take courage and go up—the dedicated of the people.

Until the last breath our hands will not weaken,

So long as blood flows in our veins.

Young and old—unsheathe the sword.

Who is afraid or faint of heart?

Our wives, our children go to the gate,

We the pioneers go out to battle.

On this day we are brothers in arms.

From Ashdot of Lebanon till the isles of the sea

From the far reaches of the north coming to Damaskas—

For life or death—pride of Jacob—arise!

Raise a banner to Zion and found the kingdom!

It is the temple of Jacob's God

A fortress for the young.

Our hands shall seize the holy task—dagger in hand.

Raise the banner to Zion—heros of Judah!

Ours is a God of strength, my brothers.

We have no fortress, no wall—

We ourselves are the stronghold

Our bodies—the towers of seige

Our hearts—the barricade.

(Translated by Reuven Hammer)

IN PALESTINE

Theodore Herzl

> *Theodore Herzl (1860–1904), the father of modern political Zionism, was born in Budapest and lived in Europe his entire life. He did visit Palestine in 1898 in order to meet with the Kaiser on November 2 in Jerusalem. In his diary, he describes this visit.*

We then took the train in the frightful heat to Jerusalem. It took an hour merely to leave Jaffa station. Sitting in the cramped, crowded, burning-hot compartment was pure torture. While crossing the dismal and desolate countryside I began to develop a fever, and grew more feverish and weaker as we rode further into the Sabbath. For, because of the delay in our departure, and to Wolffsohn's positive despair, we found ourselves traveling on the Sabbath. We arrived at Jerusalem under a full moon. I would have gladly driven the half-hour's distance from the station to our hotel; but the gentlemen made such sour faces that I had to resign myself, down with fever as I was, to walking to the city. I literally tottered along on my cane, while with the other hand I braced myself alternately on Wolffsohn's or Schub's arm.

In spite of my weariness, Jerusalem and its grand moonlit contours made a deep impression on me. The silhouette of the fortress of Zion, the citadel of David—magnificent!

The streets were alive with Jews sauntering in the moonlight.

I felt very sick before going to sleep. I took quinine and vomited after it. Then Schnirer rubbed me with spirits of amphor, and slept that night in my little narrow room. Wolffsohn was quite beside himself; perhaps he had given me up.

In the morning I awoke relieved. But I am still very feeble. It is now evening, and I have not stirred from the house. All I can do is look out of the window and conclude that Jerusalem is magnificently situated. Even in its present decay it is a beautiful city; and, if we get in here, can become one of the finest in the world.

From my hotel window, this afternoon, I saw the Kaiser pass through the triumphal arches—first the Jewish and then the Turkish. He is said to have stopped a little longer at the Jewish.

A 1950 picture of the house in which Herzl stayed in Jerusalem during his visit in 1898 (Central Zionist Archives; with permission)

I was not among those at the Jewish arch, for there are two factions here. One wanted me to deliver a communal address to the Emperor; the other apparently wished to keep me away altogether—me and my Zionism. Since, as I was informed, the Haham Bashi (Chief Rabbi) at Constantinople has proposed to his colleagues here that I be laid under the great ban, I preferred on the whole not to go near these niggling Oriental protesters.

◌

Jerusalem, October 31 [1898]

When I remember thee in days to come, O Jerusalem, it will not be with delight.

The musty deposits of two thousand years of inhumanity, intolerance, and foulness lie in reeking alleys. The one man who has been present here all this while, the lovable dreamer of Nazareth, has done nothing but help increase the hate.

If Jerusalem is ever ours, and if I were still able to do anything about it, I would begin by cleaning it up.

I would clear out everything that is not sacred, set up workers' houses beyond the city, empty and tear down the filthy rat-holes, burn all the non-sacred ruins, and put the bazaars elsewhere. Then, retaining as much of the old architectural style as possible, I would build an airy, comfortable, properly sewered, brand-new city around the Holy Places.

⊘⟩

The Jewish community here is much the same as elsewhere. It now turns out that the man who brought me their supposed invitation had lied. After coming to me, he went to the communal leaders and told them I would very much like to await the Emperor under their triumphal arch. They replied that—all the space was taken.

Among the people who called on me yesterday at the Marx house was the Sephardic Rabbi Meir. He explained that the attitude of the local Chief Rabbis stemmed from their fear of incurring the displeasure of the Turkish government.

Amused, I said: "So as not to cause those worthies any embarrassment I shall also refrain from paying them a visit."

⊘⟩

We have been to the Wailing Wall. Any deep emotion is rendered impossible by the hideous, miserable, scrambling beggary pervading the place. At least such was the case, yesterday evening and this morning, when we were there.

⊘⟩

Yesterday evening we visited the Tower of David. As we went in, I said to my friends, "It would be a neat idea on the Sultan's part if he held me prisoner here."

The views from the crumbling pinnacles seizes the imagination as the city melts away in the evening mists.

Earlier we had walked—rather quickly—through the Via Dolorosa, a route the Jews shun as something maleficent. Seidner, who once lived in Jerusalem, flatly refused to accompany me. I should have considered it cowardice not to go, and despite him went along to the street of the Holy Sepulchre. My friends restrained me from entering the Church itself. It is also forbidden to set foot in the Mosque of Omar and the Temple area, under pain of excommunication by the rabbis—as Sir Moses Montefiore discovered to his cost.

What superstition and fanaticism on every side! Still, I have no fear of any or all of these fanatics.

⊘⟩

We inspected a Jewish hospital today. Misery and squalor. Nevertheless I was obliged, for appearance's sake, to testify in the visitors book to its cleanliness. This is how lies originate.

From the gallery of an ancient synagogue, we enjoyed a view in the morning sunshine of the Temple area, the Mount of Olives and the whole storied landscape.

I am firmly convinced that a splendid New Jerusalem can be build outside the old city walls. The old Jerusalem would still remain Lourdes and Mecca and Yerushalayim. A very lovely beautiful town could arise at its side.

October 31 [1898]

The Kaiser is consecrating the Church of the Redeemer today. While touring the city I avoided his procession. At Mikveh Israel it was good, here it would be bad, to stand in his path.

⟫

In the afternoon we ascended the Mount of Olives.

Thrilling moments. What couldn't be made of this place! A city like Rome—and the Mount of Olives furnishing a panorama like the Giancolo.

I would cordon off the old city with its relics, and keep out all ordinary traffic; only places of worship and philanthropic institutions would be allowed to remain inside the old ramparts. And on the ring of encircling hillsides, which our labor would clothe with greenery, there would gradually rise a glorious New Jerusalem. The élite from every part of the world would travel the road up to the Mount of Olives. Loving care can turn Jerusalem into a jewel. Everything holy enshrined within the old walls, everything new spreading round about it.

We climbed the Russian ("Belvedere") Tower—myself only as far as the first balcony, for I began to feel giddy, but the others to the very top. Incomparable views over the Jordan valley with its precipitous slopes, the Dead Sea, the mountains of Moab, the eternal city of Jerusalem.

A man needs leisure and a tranquil mind to elaborate all of these impressions.

⟫

On our drive back we visited the rock-hewn Tombs of the Kings. They were formerly in the possession of a French Jew, Pereire, who presented them to the French government. So inconceivable it seemed that the Jews themselves should ever own anything.

⟫

November 2 [1898]

. . . Eight minutes past one o'clock. We are already back from the audience. That brief reception will live on forever in Jewish history, and possibly entail world consequences. But how droll were the details of the whole business.

We had finished our sketchy lunch by 11:30. I kept my gentlemen on short rations, so as to have them in good trim.

By noon we were all dressed. Bodenheimer had a grotesque top-hat, and cuffs so big that his shirt-sleeves kept wriggling into view. At the last moment we had to hunt him up another pair. I put on (for the first time) my miserable little Medjidie decoration. . . .

The Tomb of the Kings, date unknown (Central Zionist Archives; with permission)

We drove in the white dust and burning noonday heat to the encampment. A few Jews in the streets looked up as we passed. Pond ducks, when the wild ducks are flying overhead.

The Turkish sentries hesitated to let Schnirer and myself go beyond the railings which enclosed the camp. Then a noncommissioned officer turned up and let us pass.

Once within the enclosure, Count von Kessel, in colonial uniform, met us and directed us to a reception tent. We stood inside for about ten minutes, surveying the little salon with its furniture and richly colored carpets.

Then we were summoned to the Imperial tent. The Kaiser awaited us there, in gray colonial uniform, veiled helmet on his head, brown gloves, and holding—oddly enough—a riding crop in his right hand. I halted a few paces before the entrance and bowed. The Kaiser held out his hand to me very affably as I came in. Somewhat to one side stood Bülow in a dusty, gray lounge-suit, holding my corrected draft in his hand. The four others entered the spacious tent after me. I asked if I might present them; the Kaiser nodded, and I did so. As each name was pronounced he raised his hand to the visor of his helmet.

Then, after exchanging a glance with Bülow, I took the paper and read it aloud, at first in a low and somewhat tremulous voice, but gradually *très à mon aise*. From time to time I glanced up from the paper and looked into the Emperor's eyes, which he kept leveled on me in a steady gaze.

When I had done, he spoke—and said more or less the following: "I thank you for these communications, which have deeply interested me. The matter certainly calls for further study and discussion." Then he expressed some views on the present colonization: "The land needs, above all, water and shade." He made use of several technical terms connected with agriculture and forestry. His personal observations convinced him that the soil was arable. . . .

The Kaiser said: "We have hit the hottest time of the year. That day we met was the worst. We took the temperature at Ramleh: 88 in the shade, 106 in the sun."

Bülow said in dulcet tones: "As His Majesty the Emperor was graciously pleased to observe, water is the main need. Dr. Herzl will know better than I what the Greek poet says: 'Water is the best thing' " (Pindar).

I rejoined: "We can supply the country with it. It will cost millions, but it will produce millions."

"Well, you have plenty of money," the Kaiser exclaimed jovially, and tapped his boot with his riding crop, "more than all of us."

Bülow *abondait dans ce sens:* "Yes, the money which is such a problem for us, you have in abundance."

The Kaiser's procession near Jaffa Road in 1898 (Central Zionist Archives; with permission)

I pointed out what could be done with the water power of the Jordan and drew Seidener, as an engineer, into the discussion. . .

I managed to allude to my idea of restricting the old city to humanitarian institutions, cleaning it up, and building a New Jerusalem which could be viewed from the Mount of Olives as Rome from the Giancolo.

I was not able to bring in Wolffsohn and Bodenheimer, for the Kaiser closed the audience by again giving me his hand. I went out first, casting a quick glance behind me. The Kaiser stood sidewise, facing Bülow and talking to him, and looking as though he wished to give himself a *contenance*.

As we went away Count von Kessel asked, "Already over, the audience?" He was less obliging than at Constantinople and I inferred that our stock had somewhat depreciated.

Upon leaving, I said to Schnirer: "*Il n'a dit ni oui ni non.*"

Again there was some reluctance over letting us pass the barriers. But outside stood the secret-service agent and self-styled Zionist Mendel Kramer, who has followed us ever since Jaffa—by order, I fancy, of the Turkish government—and made them open the way for us.

He said neither yes nor no. Evidently a good deal has been happening behind the scenes. . . .

☙

Jaffa, November 4 [1898]

After the audience, day before yesterday, we drove back to the Marx house. A few persons who had seen us leave and return obtruded themselves in the guise of visitors. It took some trouble to clear out the drawing-room.

At half past three I drove in company with Wolffsohn, Bodenheimer, and the settler Broza to the beautifully situated but still terribly poor colony of Motza, where that sturdy young fellow started four or five years ago to cultivate the then nameless and infertile acres. He has now begun to see and reap the fruits of his stubborn industry. The drive along the picturesque mountain road from Jerusalem to Motza—somewhat reminiscent of the Pyrenees—passed quickly enough while the colonist Broza told about the hardships of the first years. Once, when the vines were just about to sprout, a roe wandered through in the night and ate all the shoots. Thereafter, he camped out with a rifle for three nights and didn't sleep a wink for fear of marauding hyenas, with which the region is infested. Was ever a soil more heroically conquered?

I planted a young cedar on Broza's holding at Motza, down the sheltered slope which faces away from St. Jean (Ain Karim). Wolffsohn planted a young date-palm. Several Arabs helped us, besides Broza and Katz.

We returned to Jerusalem after dusk.

So as not to call attention to our departure, I asked my friends to defer packing until after night-fall. I got up at two in the morning to pack my own things.

A house in Motza, 1903

We took the early train yesterday from Jerusalem to Jaffa. I wanted to get out of the port and the country then and there, and hastened to the harbor. I took a skiff and had the boatmen row me out to a Lloyd steamer which was on the the point of sailing. . . .

AT THE WESTERN WALL

Shneur Dov Har HaZahav

At the Western Wall
In Jerusalem—the holy city—
The tears of Israel are heard on high
Their cries rend the heavens.

"Zion—appear speedily—"
They beseech the Lord,
"Send us the savior,
He we seek daily."

Herzl's remains lying in state in the courtyard of the Jewish Agency building in Jerusalem prior to his burial on Mount Herzl; August 16, 1949 (Photograph by P. Shlezinger. Central Zionist Archives; with permission)

Our God, our Father,
Bring near our salvation.
In You alone do we hope
Bring us to our ancestral land.

In ancient days
Zion was the crown of beauty,
Surpassing in wealth and honor
All the worthless kingdoms.

Like stars surrounding the moon
We appeared in the city of Jerusalem:
Now she sits black and gloomy
And we live as orphans.

Weep, O daughters of Zion, weep.
Weep together, daughters of Jerusalem.

Raise a bitter lamentation with the sound of weeping
How great the fear in my land!

The star of our people has fallen.

Dark is its countenance.

Deposed is the crown of our head
Which was once our greatest glory.

The House has been pounded into fragments.

Our possession has become a mound.

All its vessels have been shattered
All has been despoiled.

(TRANSLATED BY REUVEN HAMMER)

ZION MY PURE ONE

M. Dolitzki

Zion my pure one, Zion my lovely
My heart yearns for you from afar.
May my right hand forget its cunning
If you I forget, O my beauty,
Till my grave is sealed above me.
May my tongue cleave to my palate till I die
If I remember you not, daughter of Zion, my soul.
May my heart dry up if my hot tears flow not for your suffering.
May my house be destroyed, my life be a shame
If the sight of your ruins departs from my eyes.
May my throat rot away, eaten by corruption
If I raise not my voice to sob for your sorrow.
I shall not forget you, Zion, I shall not forget you, my pure one.
As long as I live you are my hope and my longing.
When I die my lips shall murmur in the grave
Of you always, my beautiful one.

(TRANSLATED BY REUVEN HAMMER)

LAND OF DELIGHT

A. S. Hirschberg

In his book Eretz Hemdah, *Hirschberg describes his visit to the wall in 1901.*

On the day after I arrived, I went with one of my young friends to the Western Wall, the place to which every Jew who visits Jerusalem turns first. It was a warm clear day, like one of the days at the beginning of summer in our home country; and here it was the month of Kislev—winter! We came to the vegetable market and from there we passed through narrow, crooked streets, some climbing and some descending, and through alleys, some of which were open and most of which had stone walls on both sides (for the Arabs build their houses inside the courtyards) until we came to a small, narrow alley. One side of this was the Western Wall and the other side was a solid wall of one of the hovels of the Magreb Quarter.

When I arrived, there were only two men standing in front of the wall praying and a few Sephardi beggars asking for alms. Some of the beggars were standing and some were sitting on the ground or on boxes that they had brought with them. The Sephardi beadle came over to me and made a tear in the side of my coat and gave me a little prayerbook from which to recite the special prayer for one's first visit to the Wall. I began to mumble the prayer and suddenly I started to weep as I never had until that day, and I was not able to control myself.

I was in shock. The walk through the squalid streets and filthy alleys, the appearance of the Arabs with their dirty children dressed in rags and barefoot, had depressed me so much that nothing I saw could impress me. When I came to the Wall, I did feel that I was standing in a holy place, but my senses were dulled and my heart laid waste. Then came this prayer touching on all ills man is heir to, replaying all aches in the inner heart and the dam broke! All my private troubles mingled with our nation's misfortune to form a torrent. Here I was standing before the Wall, this silent witness to Israel's glory of ancient times and against it I saw all those places and all those times of suffering and torture throughout the whole world and all history! The inquisitions and the pogroms that have been visited on our pitiful nation passed before my eyes—and these stones do not move. . . . Tears blind me and the letters in the prayerbook dance before my eyes. My nerves jangle and my innermost emotions are totally shaken and sweep over me so that I am almost faint. . . . I turned to escape like a fugitive from this Wall without finishing the prayer I had started, but the beadle held me and gave me a wick to kindle in the small, inferior oil lamp that stood at the end of the Wall. For me it was as though he had given me a memorial candle to kindle for the soul of our people dying there in exile.

For the six months of my stay in Jerusalem it was the Wall that attracted me most because it is the one and only memorial to our ancient greatness that is authenticated both by our tradition and by scholarly research. The Jews of Jerusalem flock there regularly for prayers, particularly for the afternoon and evening services on the eve of the

Sabbath and festivals and for the additional services on those days themselves. Other favorite times are the eve of the Passover festival to read the account of the preparation of the paschal lamb and the night of the fast of the ninth of Av to mourn the destruction of the Temple. They stand before the Wall in groups, and the recitation of the holy prayers never ceases. All kinds of Jews are there. Thin, scrawny, sharp-nosed Yemenites dressed in poor, worn Arab robes recite the prayers in their unique pronunciation. A quorum of rich, fat, elegantly clad Sephardim, in their black coats and tarbooshes on their well-groomed heads, say the prayers solemnly and with great dignity. At their side is a group of Perushim, dressed in a weird mixture of east and west with medieval Polish fur hats on their heads; honoured old men and earnest, pale young men screw up their faces to achieve the concentration fitting for prayer to God. And there are groups of Hasidim, in their kaftans of red, gold or sky-blue silk and velvet, who shake themselves violently until their sidelocks flail, as they respond, 'Holy, holy, holy is the Lord of Hosts' in great ecstasy. And the women! The Ashkenazi women stand a way off and jump little jumps as they respond to every Kedushah prayer they hear. The Sephardi ladies love the Wall with a special love and most of them come to it enveloped in white sheets.

Those who cannot read the texts of the prayers make modest prayerful signs to the Wall. All, when they leave, kiss each stone individually and back away as though they were leaving the royal presence, stretching out their fingers toward it with eyes raised on high.

The square stones of the Wall, arranged one on top of the other, joined together with no sign of cement; these stones which, scratched and cracked though they be, are not consumed in the teeth of time, are a symbol to the people that stands before them in prayer. . . . How can they fail to excite and exalt the heart of every Jew who comes for the first time to the Wall?!

JERUSALEM REBUILT

Boris Schatz

> *Boris Schatz (1867–1932) came to then Palestine from Europe in 1905 after meeting Theodore Herzl. In Jerusalem, he founded the Bezalel School of Art. During World War I the school was closed and Schatz imprisoned. Later, he raised funds in the United States and re-established the school. In his visionary, almost mystic book,* Jerusalem Rebuilt, *he converses with the spirit of the Biblical Bezalel ("my 'teacher' ") about the future of Jerusalem.*

In an instant my "teacher" and I were transported into the clear and pure sky under the blue heavens. Beneath us was a city wondrous in its beauty, spread out over hills and valleys, filled with high towers, domes, roofs clearly spread out, parks, pools and bridges spanning the valleys.

"What is this?" I asked my "teacher."

The frontpiece of Boris Schatz's book Jerusalem Rebuilt, *reading: "A dream while awake—said Rabbi Hoshiah: Jerusalem is to become a light unto the nations of the world and they will walk in its light (Pesikta)" and depicting Professor Schatz in conversation with his "guide," Bezalel*

"Jerusalem—Jerusalem rebuilt."

"Jerusalem rebuilt!" I cried out in wonder. "Let us descend. I will feast my eyes and gladden my heart. I will run in her markets and roam through her streets. I will see everything—how was she built? What was done? How do people live there? Is 'Bezalel' prospering? Does it still exist?"

"Wait. Do not be hasty!" My "teacher" answered with an amused smile. "You are an artist. You should know that one must begin by looking at the over-all figuration. Only then at each section by itself. Only then can one understand the over-all plan properly. This is what we will do: First I will show you Jerusalem, the heart of the Land, from above, from without. Then you shall see the entire Land. After that we will descend to the Land. There we will not fly or ride. Jerusalem must be traversed—length and breadth—by foot. Every place one steps there is holy. Do you see?" With his finger he pointed out a group of buildings in the center of the city. "That is the Temple."

I quickly bent my head, anxious to see the Temple. From the great height where we were hovering I could hardly see anything. I managed to discern the roofs spread out, paved courts. Here and there something that looked like gold glittered, though it might have been water, a blue-green spot of vegetation, the shadow of a tower. But one thing I could clearly discern: this group of buildings far exceeded in splendor all the other buildings of the splendid city and stood in its center. All roads led toward it. Gates in its wall led in every direction. Opposite one of the gates which I recognized as the Golden Gate a bridge spanned the distance over the Valley of Jehoshaphat to the Mount of Olives.

"My teacher and master, do they offer sacrifices in the Temple?"

"They do not now seek forgiveness from sin as did the ancients. Not with sacrifices, not with the shedding of blood of innocent animals will transgression be atoned, but with repentance for evil deeds will sin be atoned."

"What will they do in the Temple? What is found in it?"

"The soul of the People of Israel is forged in the Temple! Every Jew will go there in order to enhance his spirit, to learn to understand the soul of the People. There will be found everything which Jews have created over thousands of years, sharing their creations for the benefit of all humankind. It is a storehouse of the wisdom and art of Israel. There will the spirit of the Lord which God has placed within us dwell."

On the west, opposite Jaffa Gate, upon a mountain near the lower pool I recognized the lovely dome of the Mosque of Omar.

"The Mosque of Omar—which used to stand on the Temple Mount—has been moved to this lovely mountain as a sign of gratitude to the Arabs, our good neighbors, who carefully preserved our holy places."

"And that is the Tower of David?"

"As you have said. But it has been reinforced and improved. Now the musical conservatory and a concert hall are found therein."

A wind blows through David's harp and it comes to life.

Little by little I began to discern one place from another. I recognized the Mount of Olives, the monument to Absalom, I was shocked that the monuments over the graves had disappeared. Instead grass, gardens, domes and towers covered every mountain.

"The mount of Olives has ceased to be the mount of the dead," said the "teacher." "Now it is the mount of the living. Do you see? Here, exactly opposite the Temple, on the road of the Golden Gate, rises a building of surpassing beauty. That is the "Temple of Peace." It belongs to the "League of Peace of All Nations." We donated that building to them as a sign of gratitude for their help in our returning to our land and becoming an independent nation. And that round building nearby is the the seat of the Sanhedrin. Spreading upward on the Mount of Olives are many houses, beautiful palaces, parks, pavilions and towers. Our people can pride itself on all of them. That is "Yavneh," the seat of our glorious university. All the faculties are there, the libraries and the observatory—that's the tall tower with the dome"—he pointed with his finger—"the zoo and botanical garden, all kinds of laboratories for scientists and a gigantic dormitory for the thousands of students who study at 'Yavneh.'"

The aeroplane flew over the aqueduct leading toward Jericho and a new sight was revealed to my eyes. A large park, covered with myriad colors, various flowers and clear lakes. Upon the grass were scattered hundreds of white roofs. The "teacher" said to me, "This is the health center. People are cured of all sorts of diseases here. This is where research is done to eliminate all illness from the world."

"And what is that long building . . . what are those many towers covered with shining roofs surrounding the building?"

"That is the source of light for Jerusalem. On those towers are mirrors which concentrate the rays of the sun. The tremendous amount of energy which is gathered there is converted into electric current. Do you see those great pools of water in which the sky is reflected, as well as our aeroplane? Those are the reservoirs of Jerusalem. They supply water for all the parks, factories and other needs. Water for drinking is brought through pipes from the Pools of Solomon and fountains which surround Jerusalem."

"Where do they get enough water to fill those giant pools?"

"The rain fills them. In Jerusalem the amount of rain which falls is not less than that of frigid Russia. Rain comes down suddenly, and only in the short winter days. The rain water streams down the valleys into the Dead Sea and formerly carried away the earth from the rocks. Now the engineers have managed to save part of that rain water. Therefore Jerusalem does not lack water or shade."

"And what about malaria? Does it still waste the inhabitants of the city?" I asked, remembering how we had suffered because of the water from the rains and the wells.

"Jerusalem has the most wonderful climate. Healthier than that of any other city. She rests high on the hills, covered by sunshine, pleasant breezes constantly blowing. Her plentiful foliage eases the passage from day to night. She never had swamps. The malaria was caused by the wells which everyone had in his yard . . . now everything is done collectively and all is good as well as cheap. . . . Look at these trees growing here. This is where they built 'Children's Paradise.' "

"What is the 'Children's Paradise?' " I asked. . . .

"This is where all the children aged 3–4 to 12–13 are gathered, paid for by the People. This is where they live, grow and learn. They are all together in equal conditions, uniform clothing, with the same method of study. From here they are sent to various trade schools. There too they study for free, each one specializing in what suits him according to his natural tendencies and talents. . . ."

"My teacher and master! How can it be right to take children from their parents! To deprive fathers of the joy of fatherhood—of seeing their children grow up, develop and learn to be adults! To deprive people of the love of children and the divine delight of hugging and kissing them, of feeling their soft and warm bodies full of love and trust for you!"

"Don't be so quick to make accusations, my son. . . . When you see below how it works you will rejoice and only bewail the fact that your own children were born a hundred years too early and had to suffer from 'the love of parents.' " . . .

"What are those glass terraces on the mountain?"

"Those are the dining rooms for all of Jerusalem. Women have stopped cooking in their own homes for their families as they did in your days. The work is done by experts. They cook in large quantities using new methods. Women have ceased being married to the pot. . . . Food is cheaper, healthier and tastier. Women have been liberated from the kitchen and from its ways which only dull the mind. . . ."

"What is this, a monastery for priests?"

"No, that is 'Neve Shaananim,' the artists colony. The 'sons of Bezalel' live and create here. The artist, as a man of the spirit, needs tranquillity, distance from the world of action, separation from worldly things. His soul needs a special atmosphere. Artists must be together. Musicians, poets and all other creators live in Neve Shaananim . . ."

"My master and teacher. I believe with all my heart in the revival of our people. I believe that 'Bezalel' will be its holy temple. . . . Let dreams of light enlighten the darkness of the present!"

Something moved in the dark . . . glimmering in my eyes. I felt a soft and gently hand caress my hair with love, like a warm, gentle breeze. A delicious warmth spread through my heart, enlightened my eyes and caused my head to feel light and dizzy, as if I had been cast upon a soft, rocking bed. . . .

"Come"—as through my sleep I heard the dear voice of my "teacher."

The Bezalel Academy depicted in an early postcard (Central Zionist Archives; with permission)

A Visit to Jerusalem in 1907

Chaim Weizmann

> *Chaim Weizmann (1874–1952) was born in Motol in Russia, lived in England, and became a world-famous scientist. As a young man he became a Zionist and eventually president of the Zionist Organization and then the first President of the State of Israel. His life and his visits to Jerusalem are described in his book* Trial and Error.

My most unhappy experience during the three-weeks tour of the country . . . was Jerusalem. I went up from Jaffa, not without misgivings. Jaffa already had the small beginnings of a new life, and the promise of a new society; Jerusalem was the city of the *Challukkah*, a city living on charity, on begging letters, on collections. Here the reality turned out as bad as the anticipation. From the Jewish point of view it was a miserable ghetto, derelict and without dignity. All the grand places belonged to others. There were innumerable churches, of every sect and nationality. We had not a decent building of our own. All the world had a foothold in Jerusalem—except the Jews. The hotel to which we were directed was a dilapidated and verminous ruin, with nondescript people pouring in and out all day long, and all of them engaged apparently in wasting their own and each other's time. It depressed me beyond words, and I left the city before nightfall. I remained prejudiced against the city for many years, and even now I still feel ill at ease in it, preferring Rehovoth to the capital.

But I was struck, as everyone must be, by the glorious surroundings of Jerusalem; and I thought then that there was only one place where, in time to come, we might erect some building worthy of the Jewish community; there was one hill still uncrowned by monastery or Church—the Scopus, on which stood then only the small villa of Lady Grey Hill, and on which now stands the Hebrew University.

The Western Wall

A. M. Lunz

> *A. M. Lunz (1854–1918) published many books about the Land of Israel and Jerusalem. In an essay about the Wall, he discusses practices associated with it as well as its legal status.*

CUSTOMS AND SUPERSTITIONS PAST AND PRESENT

In the fifth century it was the custom for pious women to clean the alley in front of the Western Wall, and the Ishmaelites did not protest. It is a pity that pious women today do not follow that important custom.

There are those who kiss the stones of the Wall and some (particularly Sephardic Rabbis) take off their shoes when they approach the Wall.

The Wall in 1917 with Austrian soldiers and Jews in attendance (Central Zionist Archives; with permission)

Forty years ago the custom was to light olive oil lamps every Shabbat eve. That custom continued about thirty-two years until the summer of 5673 (1913), when the local authorities prohibited it.

Many of those who go up to the Holy City have been accustomed to writing their names in ink or paint on the stones of the Wall as a memorial or a lucky charm, but that custom should be stopped since it desecrates the beauty and glory of the stones.

Some Jerusalem residents are accustomed to hammering a nail between the stones when they are about to leave the Land for overseas. There are small cracks between the stones and people superstitiously believe that doing this will assure their returning in peace to their homes. It has reached the point where some of these cracks are now full of nails. This custom has no basis at all.

Recently it has become the custom for people to write their names and requests on pieces of paper which they place in the cracks between the stones. The Rabbis and rabbinical courts of various groups should strictly forbid this superstitious custom and proclaim in all the synagogues the severity of the prohibition, for this is a serious sin against the holiness of that place. They should also instruct the Shamash to light a lamp and enlighten all those who come to pray concerning this matter.

OUR RIGHTS TO THE WALL

No community leader has ever possessed a license or proclamation from the ruler permitting us to pray in this place. This is not surprising, since we have never needed it. The Muslims have never looked askance at those who pray, and particularly those who pray to the God of Heaven, the one and unique God in whom they too believe. Therefore they did not prevent us from praying in this place whenever we wished. In the letters and books written by inhabitants of Jerusalem we find that they always went to pray there, even at midnight. . . .

Therefore we have the following basis for our rights:

1. The historic documentation that no one can dispute that this Wall is a remnant of the wall that surrounded the House of our God.

2. Ancient precedent (which has great weight in the law of the land) that for the entire period of some four hundred years and more our ancestors prayed in this place with no protest or no attempt to stop them, neither from the government nor from the inhabitants of that quarter.

In this current century as well, when there has been a great increase in the numbers of our brothers who have come up and settled in the Holy City, and the alley in front of the Wall is filled with men, women and children so that there is no space left, which certainly disturbed those who live at either end of it, nevertheless the inhabitants of these areas did not complain about it to the government, because they knew that this ancient precedent existed permitting the Jews to pray in this place.

How the Glorious Day of Deliverance Came to Jerusalem
Hemda Ben Yehuda

> *Hemda Ben Yehuda (1873–1951), came to Jerusalem in 1892 to become the second wife of Eliezer Ben Yehuda. She was a writer and editor who, in addition to aiding her husband, wrote several books and articles. Oddly enough, the following article which she wrote appeared in a book issued by Christian fundamentalists in America discussing the future of the city of Jerusalem.*

Gaza was taken by the English and recovered by the Turks, remaining in their hands seven months. In June, 1917, General Allenby captured Beersheba and then Gaza. Ludd surrendered, Ramleh fell; on November 16, Jaffa was captured. Victorious English troops then marched upon Jerusalem.

For three years the Holy City had suffered privations and sorrows. It was as if the plague had raged within the walls. Most of the houses were closed because the inhabitants were dead, or deported, exiled or in prison. Deserted were the streets. One dreaded to be seen outdoors for fear of falling victim to the rage of the Turks.

People hid themselves in cellars and subterranean passages, where life continued underground by the light of olive oil lamps.

The musicians composed music, the poets composed verses, the professors meditated upon the pupils whom they hoped to receive in the coming hour of deliverance.

The women kept house underground; but there was little food to prepare. They had forgotten the appearance of a loaf of bread. The babies died for lack of milk.

Even in these hiding places, one heard the roar of Turkish cannon, which was directed against the "Nebi Samuel" (the Tomb of Samuel), where the English had fortified themselves. One passionate desire filled the hearts of Jews and Christians alike as they waited for the hour of deliverance. Their confidence in the victorious strength of the English failed not. The devout souls were uplifted in ardent prayer. Pious vows were pronounced. They prayed that the Lord God would deliver them by a miracle, and show His hand as in former days.

But now it seemed as if the Arm of the Lord was turned against the Jews and deliverance seemed far off. Their fervent prayers were rudely interrupted by the intrusion of Turkish soldiers. The gendarmerie entered and penetrated down to the cellars and arrested the defenceless Hebrews. They tore the husbands from the arms of their wives, and separated the children from their parents. They beat their prisoners and loaded them with chains and drove them outdoors into the mud and rain. The storm lashed the helpless prisoners as they were driven forth without coats and without bread. The soldiers goaded them forward like cattle to the assembly places where those who were to be deported were gathered together. The wives and the young women threw themselves upon the necks of their husbands and fathers and brothers, insisting that they should share the horrors of this terrible forced journey. The victims were taken away in the direction of Jericho.

𝕯

Then the vials of wrath were poured upon the American Jews also. They were arrested on the streets and in the houses and beaten and dragged away and forced to march on foot, exposed to mud and rain, all the way to Damascus. Those who were sick were carried on litters. One American discovered concealed in a cellar was sent laden with chains to Damascus.

In the meanwhile the Turkish cannon was destroying the Tomb of Samuel, and the English were making a movement whose object was to encircle Jerusalem. The Turks and Germans commanded that the city should be defended and they sent for reinforcements from Damascus. The garrison was not sufficiently strong in numbers or in morale to sustain the attack without aid. When the reinforcements failed to arrive, the Turks perceived that they would be obliged to evacuate.

In great haste, they arrested everyone whom they caught on the streets, including the Dutch consul and a distinguished Austrian physician, a member of the Board of Health.

Djemal Pasha had already left for Damascus. Soon after, an edict was issued commanding the deportation of all the Christian and all the Jewish inhabitants of Jerusalem.

The governor did the favor to the Dutch consul and two other distinguished prisoners to allow them a respite of three days in which to prepare for their journey. The Turkish authorities were themselves embarrassed as to the means of executing this last great act of deportation, which included the great mass of the population of Jerusalem. It was expected that the Germans would be of assistance in enforcing the edict, but the Germans were occupied in saving themselves. After the flights, the exiles, the deportations, executions and imprisonments, it was estimated that over thirty thousand Jews and Christians still remained in the city.

In vain the Jews implored Zaki Bey to save them. He replied that nothing could save them! They must prepare for the deportation. Then a bitter suspicion entered the hearts of the Jews. They suspected that even their friend, Zaki Bey himself, was an accomplice of the Turks. It was observed that all of the families with whom Zaki Bey was chiefly associated were the special objects of persecution. The Jews surmised that he had abused their confidence and betrayed them.

In these terrible days in Jerusalem, Jews and Christians fasted and prayed. Their common sorrow and desolation drew them nearer to one another. They sought concealment in the darkest cellars and deepest subterranean passages. Jews and Christians found refuge together.

It was in this darkness and dread that the Jews awaited the coming of their great festival of light and gladness, Hannucca, the Feast of Deliverance in former days, and now approaching as the day of destruction! The women, weeping, prepared the oil for the sacred lights, and even the men wept, saying that this would be the last time they should keep the feast in Jerusalem! They strained their ears to hear the horses' hoofs and the tread of the soldiers coming to arrest them and drive them forth. The women pressed their children to their breasts crying: "They are coming to take us!—the persecutors, the assassins!"

Then, suddenly, other women came rushing from outside down into the depths, crying:

"Hosanna! Hosanna! The English!—the English have arrived!"

Weeping and shouting for joy, Jews and Christians, trembling and stumbling over one another, emerged and rushed forth from the caverns and holes and underground passages.

With loud cries, with outstretched hands, they blessed the company of their deliverers, who advanced in a glory of light, for all Jerusalem was illuminated by the crimson light of the setting sun!

With the victors, entered Justice and Peace, into the city so long ruled by Terror and Pain.

Pious Jews uttered thanksgivings to the Lord God of Hosts who had wrought deliverance in this great historic day, in the very hour of the beginning of "Hannucca," the Feast of the Miracle of Lights.

On the previous day the Turkish troops had evacuated, driving before them numbers of unfortunate prisoners, the last victims of their rule of force. For the last time on leaving, the hated Turkish soldiers had entered the houses to rob and spoil, to carry off everything they could lay hands on.

On the next day after the beginning of Hannucca, the troop of English conquerors entered and shared their own bread with the famished populace, and offered the support of their hands to the feeble and the aged. On the following day, when the great English army entered the city, the women threw themselves on the necks of the soldiers, calling for the benediction of heaven upon them. Young women kissed the hems of their garments, and children threw flowers on their path. It was the time of the early flowers in Palestine—the first flowers which announce the resurrection of Nature after the burning heat of summer is past.

How simple and modest was the entry of General Allenby into the Holy City!

He came with the members of his staff, marching on foot, and passed between the ranks of soldiers who lined the streets on either side and presented arms.

How solemn and imposing was the reception of the hero by the heads of three great religions—the Jewish Rabbis, the Mufti and sheiks, and the Christian priests!

How impressive, and with what relief to waiting hearts, was the proclamation that all the shrines and sacred places of the three religions should be equally respected. These are the words of the proclamation:

> Lest any of you be alarmed by reason of your experiences at the hands of the enemy who has retired, I hereby inform you that it is my desire that every person should pursue his lawful business without fear of interruption. Furthermore, since your city is regarded with affection by the adherents of three of the great religions of mankind, and its soil has been consecrated by the prayers and pilgrimages of multitudes of devout people of these three religions for many centuries, therefore I make it known to you that every sacred building, monument, holy spot, shrine, traditional site, endowment, pious bequest or customary place of prayer of whatsoever form of the three religions will be maintained according to the existing customs and beliefs of those to whose faith they are sacred. . . .

Then life revived in the city which had been ravaged by death. The new rulers distributed medicine and hospital supplies for the recovery of the sick. The soldiers shared their rations with the famished population. As soon as possible, food was procured from Egypt. Seed was given to the peasants and army horses and mules were bestowed to plow the neglected fields.

General Allenby entering Jerusalem on foot near the Jaffa Gate (Central Zionist Archives; with permission)

MEMOIRS

Yitzhak Shiryon

On the ninth of December, early in the morning, the Mayor of Jerusalem, Hassin Efendi El Husseni, accompanied by the members of the city council and several notables of Jerusalem, went out of the city to the place where the advance force of the British Army was encamped, a white flag in his hand, and delivered the keys to the city of Jerusalem to the commander of the British Army. That same day, which was the eve of Hannuka, the British forces entered the gates of Jerusalem as victors.

At first only a small number of cavalry entered and occupied the offices of the post and the telegraph. Stationing guards there, the rest returned to the army camp, which was some distance from the city. That very afternoon the British Army began to stream into Jerusalem from all sides of the city.

The first light of Hannuka illuminated all sectors of the city like a mighty torch. The rejoicing of the inhabitants knew no bounds. Many men who had hidden in cellars and attics for fear of induction into the army and of informers, now appeared with radiant faces and expressed their thanksgiving to the Lord for redeeming them and saving their lives. All the inhabitants of Jerusalem went out to meet the victorious army with happiness and joy hopeful that deliverance would come to them, for just a little while before they had been informed indirectly of the Balfour Declaration and the call by the British for our people to come here and build a national home.

Nevertheless the material situation in Jerusalem remained difficult at first. The Turkish and German armies had taken with them whatever produce and flour remained when they retreated to other cities and villages. There were, of course, certain quantities of wheat, flour, sugar and coffee, which some merchants had hidden away, but when the British entered, these were sold for high prices. Some poor Jews baked bread and cakes which they sold to the British soldiers, who, after spending so much time in the desert and subsisting on dry rations alone, would buy the bread and cakes at exorbitant prices, prices which the local population could not possibly afford. Even though the military government forbade the selling of bread to soldiers, it continued for some little time. On the other hand, the soldiers would give their dry rations to the poor of the city for nothing.

THE THIRD TEMPLE

Menahem Usishkin

> *This paragraph is taken from a speech Usishkin made to a group of pilgrims in Jerusalem in 5688 (1927).*

The tears we shed over these stones of the Western Wall during the past hundreds of years and until recently were tears of mourning for the great past of our people and for its many graves scattered throughout the world. The tears we shall shed on these stones from now on shall be tears of joy and hope for the shining future of our people in our renewed Land. Until now the stones of the Western Wall were the last remaining remnant of the Second Temple. From now on these stones shall be the first stones of the Third Temple.

THE RENAISSANCE OF THE JEWISH SOUL

Chaim Weizmann

> *The following is taken from the address given by Weizmann when the foundation stone for the Hebrew University was laid on Mount Scopus, July 24, 1918.*

The cornerstone ceremony of the Hebrew University, July 24, 1918, with Chaim Weizmann in front of the canopy (Collection of the National and University Library, Jerusalem; with permission)

We have to-day laid the foundation stone of the first Jewish university, which is to be erected on this hill, overlooking the city of Jerusalem. Many of us will have had our thoughts cast back to the great historic scenes associated with Jerusalem, scenes that have become a part of the heritage of mankind. It is not too fanciful to picture the souls of those who have made our history here with us to-day, inspiring us, urging us onward, to greater and ever greater tasks. . . .

What is the significance of a Hebrew University? What are going to be its functions? Whence will it draw its students? What language will it speak? It seems at first para-doxical that in a land with so sparse a population, in a land where everything still re-mains to be done, in a land crying for such simple things as ploughs, roads and har-bours, we should begin by creating a centre of spiritual and intellectual development. But it is no paradox for those who know the soul of the Jew. It is true that great social and political problems still face us and demand their solution from us. We Jews know that when the mind is given fullest play, when we have a centre for the development of Jewish consciousness, then coincidentally we shall attain the fulfilment of our ma-terial needs. In the darkest ages of our existence we found protection and shelter within the walls of our schools and colleges, and in the devoted study of Jewish science the tormented Jew found relief and consolation . . . amid all the sordid squalor of the Ghetto there stood schools of learning, where numbers of young Jews sat at the feet of our rabbis and teachers. . . .

A Hebrew University? I do not suppose that there is any one here who can conceive of a university in Jerusalem being other than a Hebrew one. The claim that the University should be a Hebrew one rests on the values the Jews have transmitted to the world from this land. Here in the presence of adherents of the three great religions of the world, which amid many diversities built their faith upon the Lord who made himself known unto Moses, before this world which has founded itself on Jewish law, paid reverence to Jewish seers, has acknowledged the great mental and spiritual values the Jewish people have given it, the question is answered. . . . By a strange error people have regarded Hebrew as one of the dead languages, but for thousands of my people Hebrew is and always has been the sacred tongue, and in the streets of Tel Aviv, on the farms of Hulda and Ben Shemen, it has already become the mother-tongue. Here in Palestine, amid a babel of languages, Hebrew stands out as the one language in which every Jew communicates with every other Jew. . . .

Our university, formed by Jewish learning and Jewish energy, will mould itself into an integral part of our national structure which is in the process of erection. It will have a centripetal force, attracting all that is noblest in Jewry throughout the world; a unifying centre for our scattered elements. There will go forth, too, inspiration and strength, that shall revivify the powers now latent in our scattered communities. Here the wandering soul of Israel shall reach its haven, its strength no longer consumed in restless and vain wanderings. Israel shall at last remain at peace with itself and with the world. There is a Talmudic legend which tells of the Jewish soul deprived of its body, hovering between heaven and earth. Such is our soul to-day; to-morrow it shall come to rest, in this our sanctuary. That is our faith.

POGROM IN JERUSALEM

Chaim Weizmann

March 1920

We arrived [in Jerusalem] to find Herbert Samuel already in Palestine. Allenby and Bols (the latter was then Military Governor of Palestine) had invited him in as adviser to the administration. Everyone was relieved to have Samuel there, for General Allenby's premonition had been only too sound: we all felt that things were not going well, that there was tension in the country. There was a great deal of open agitation in Arab circles, and there was no evidence that local administrators were making any effort to avert trouble; on the contrary, there were members of the official hierarchy who were encouraging the troublemakers. I am not alarmist by nature, and I was inclined at first to be sceptical about the reports. But they persisted, and some of our young people who were close to Arab circles were convinced that "the day" was set for Passover, which that year coincided with both Easter and *Nebi-Musa*—an Arab festival on which the inhabitants of the neighboring villages assemble in Jerusalem to march in procession to the reputed grave of the Prophet Moses on a near-by hill. Galilee, too, was in ferment owing to its nearness to Syria, whence Feisal was being edged out, and where friction between the English and the French was growing daily. Lawless bands prowled and raided on our northern hills, and as is usual in such cases banditry took on an aspect of patriotism. A month before my arrival Joseph Trumbeldor, one of the earliest and greatest of the *chalutz* leaders, had gone up with some companions to the defense of Tel Hai, an infant colony near the Syrian border; and there he and five companions, two of them women, were killed by marauders. The tragedy had plunged the whole *Yishuv* into mourning.

As Passover approached the tension grew more marked, and by that time some of the more friendly of the British officals—for instance Meinertzhagen (now the Palestine administration's political officer)—were apprehensive. Before leaving Jerusalem to spend Passover with my mother, I called on General Allenby, who was then in the city. I found him with General Bols and Herbert Samuel at Government House, still located in the old German hospice on the Mount of Olives. My representations regarding impending trouble made little impression on them. Bols said: "There *can* be no trouble; the town is stiff with troops!" I replied that I had some experience with the atmosphere which precedes pogroms; I knew also that troops usually proved useless at the last moment, because the whole paroxysm was liable to be over before they could be rushed to the field of action. There would be half an hour or an hour of murder and looting and by the time the troops got there everything would be in order and there would be nothing for them to do but pick up the pieces. However, I could see that I was wasting my breath. I was advised not to worry, and go home to my family for the Passover as arranged. I could feel assured that everything would go off quietly in Jerusalem.

Against my better judgment I went home, though what I could have done after this if I had stayed on in Jerusalem it is difficult to say. Passover in Haifa came and went; and the next morning there was no disturbing news from Jerusalem—no news at all, in fact. I felt uneasy. I tried to telephone, but could get no connection, which naturally increased my anxiety. So I decided—greatly to my mother's disappointment—to go up to Jerusalem and to take Benjy with me. The journey was uneventful as far as Nablus, but there I found a police escort. The Governor of Nablus, who supplied it, dropped a vague hint or two, and I became more and more convinced that "something" really had happened.

Jerusalem, when we got there, looked deserted. A curfew had been imposed, and there was little movement in the streets except for the police and military patrols. We made straight for Dr. Eder's flat in the center of the city, and found him deeply disturbed. The story he had to tell was one that has since become all to familiar: Arabs assembling at the Mosque of Omar, listening to speeches of violent incitement, forming a procession fired with fanatic zeal, marching through the streets attacking any Jews they happened to meet. In spite of all the rumors which preceded the attack, the Jews seem to have been caught completely unawares, and practically no resistance was offered. When one small group of young men, under Captain Jabotinsky, had come out to defend their quarter, they had been promptly arrested. The troops had, of course, arrived when all was over, and quiet now reigned in the city. The situation was "well in hand."

In the trials which followed before a military court, Jabotinsky received the savage sentence of fifteen years' hard labor. He was later amnestied (by Herbert Samuel when he became High Commissioner), but rejected the amnesty with scorn, because it included Aref el Aref, the main instigator of the pogrom, Amin el Husseini (the notorious Grand Mufti of later years) and one or two others of the same type. He insisted on making his appeal, and the sentence was in due course quashed. . . .

All of us felt that this pogrom might have been averted had proper steps been taken in time to check the agitation, had the attitude of the administration been different. The bitterness and incitement had been allowed to grow until they found their natural expression in riot and murder. . . . It might seem, to a dispassionate British observer, that we were making too much of this pogrom. (Only six Jews were killed, though there were many serious injuries.) But it is almost impossible to convey to the outside world the sense of horror and bewilderment which it aroused in our people, both in Palestine and outside. Pogroms in Russia had excited horror and pity, but little surprise; they were "seasonal disturbances," more or less to be expected round about Easter and Passover festivals. That such a thing could happen in Palestine, two years after the Balfour Declaration, under British rule ("the town is stiff with troops!") was incomprehensible to the Jews, and dreadful beyond belief. For those whose facile optimism had led them to believe that all political problems were safely out of the way, and that all we had to do was get on with the "practical" work, this was—or should have been—the writing on the wall.

MY LIFE

Golda Meir

> *Prime Minister of Israel, Golda Meir (1898–1978) was born in Kiev and raised in Milwaukee. She and her husband settled in Palestine in 1921, after which she rose rapidly in the political and governing bodies of the Jewish settlement.*

Strangely enough, when I look back to that time, I realize that I wasn't really aware of any but my most immediate surroundings, even though Jerusalem was the seat of the mandatory government then, the place from which the British High Commissioners—Sir Herbert Samuel, who was replaced in 1925 by Lord Plumer—governed the country. As it has always been through history, Jerusalem was a fascinating city. In part it was then, as it still is, a mosaic of shrines and holy places; in part it was the headquarters of a colonial administration. But above all it was the living symbol of the continuity of Jewish history and the tie that bound, and binds, the Jewish people to the land. Its population was unlike that of any other place in Palestine. Even our neighborhood was exotic, located on the "frontier" of Mea Shearim, the section of Jerusalem that is inhabited till today by ultra-orthodox Jews whose bearing, dress and religious practices have been carried over, almost intact, from sixteenth-century Eastern Europe and who thought that Jews like Morris and myself were only a step away from being pagan. But somehow the city's landmarks and landscapes, the colorful procession of people of all faiths and races who walked Jerusalem's streets even on the most ordinary days, didn't make much of an impression on me. I was too tired, too dispirited and too concerned with myself and my family to look about me as I should have.

One evening, however, I went to the Western Wall—not for the first time. Morris and I had gone there a week or two after our arrival in Palestine. I had grown up in a Jewish home, a good traditional Jewish home, but I wasn't at all pious myself, and the truth is that I went to the Wall without much emotion, just as something that I knew I ought to do. Then, all of a sudden, at the end of those narrow, winding alleys in the Old City, I saw it. The Wall itself looked much smaller than it does today, after all the excavations. But for the first time I saw the Jews, men and women, praying and weeping before it and putting *kvitlach*—their scribbled petitions to the Almighty—into its crannies. So this was what was left of a past glory, I thought, all that has remained of Solomon's Temple. But at least it was still there. And in those orthodox Jews with their *kvitlach*, I saw a nation's refusal to accept that only these stones were left to it and an expression of confidence in what was to come in the future. I left the Wall changed in feeling—uplifted is perhaps the word.

In 1971, some fifty years later, I was awarded the Freedom of Jerusalem—probably the greatest tribute ever paid me—and at that ceremony I told of yet another memorable visit I had made to the Wall, this time in 1967, after the Six Day War. For nineteen years, from 1948 to 1967, we were banned by the Arabs from going to the Old City or praying at the Wall. But on the third day of the Six Day War—Wednesday, 7 June—all Israel was electrified by the news that our soldiers had liberated the Old City and that it was open to us again. I had to fly to the United States three days later, but I couldn't bring myself to leave Israel without going to the Wall again. So that Friday morning—although civilians were not yet allowed to enter the Old City because shooting was still going on there—I received permission to go to the Wall, despite the fact that I wasn't in the government then but just an ordinary citizen, like any other.

I went to the Wall together with some soldiers. There in front of it stood a plain wooden table with some sub-machine guns on it. Uniformed paratroopers wrapped in prayer shawls clung so tightly to the Wall that it seemed impossible to separate them from it. They and the Wall were one. Only a few hours earlier they had fought furiously for the liberation of Jerusalem and had seen their comrades fall for its sake. Now, standing before the Wall, they wrapped themselves in prayer shawls and wept, and I, too, took a sheet of paper, wrote the word "*shalom*" on it and pushed it into a cranny of the Wall, as I had seen the Jews do so long ago. As I stood there, one of the soldiers (I doubt that he knew who I was) suddenly put his arms around me, laid his head on my shoulder and we cried together. I suppose he needed the release and the comfort of an old woman's warmth, and for me it was one of the most moving moments of my life.

FOUNDATIONS

Chaim Weizmann

In 1923 Professor Patrick Geddes was invited to Jerusalem to assist in the replanning of the city. We asked him to undertake the design and layout of the university buildings, and after a study of the site he prepared some magnificent sketches which delighted us all. Unfortunately none of them has been actually carried out, though the general plan has been followed, and for myself I still hope before I die to see the great assembly hall which Geddis designed rising on the slopes of Scopus.

Grey Hill House was rebuilt completely, to house the two institutes of microbiology and biochemistry, the first under Professor Saul Adler, formerly of Leeds, the second under Professor Fodor, who devoted much time to the acquisition of equipment and the adaptation of the building to laboratory use. The American Jewish Physicians Committee supplied much of the money for this beginning, and covered the budget of the two institutes for the first three years. We now felt that we had at least the nucleus of a faculty of sciences.

Most popular of the faculties was, of course, the Institute of Jewish Studies, which was endowed by Sol Rosenbloom of Pittsburgh. Baron Edmond de Rothschild, Felix Warburg and other friends took a personal interest in this branch of the University, and, indeed, there was a stage when I felt there was some danger in the enthusiasm which it aroused. There were too many who thought of the institute romantically in terms of a great center of Hebrew learning and literature; it was placed under the patronage of the Chief Rabbis of London and Paris, and its council included Dr. Magnes. It ran the risk of becoming a theological seminary, like those of London, Breslau or Philadelphia, instead of the school of "literae humaniores" of a free university. Happily the danger was averted when the council of the Institute of Jewish Studies was merged into the general structure of the University. . . .

In addition to the institutes already described, we had, in Jerusalem, the great Rothschild Hospital, which we felt might well be used for research, and later on for teaching. We also had a Jewish Agricultural Experimental Station, with quite a number of research workers, and this might make the beginning of an agricultural faculty.

Altogether, we thought all the foregoing a fair start. . . . What seemed important was to make a start with the materials in hand, and to put them to the best possible use. To this we applied our minds in 1923 and the following years, to such purpose that by the spring of 1925 we could look at "our University" and feel there really was enough of it to justify a formal "opening ceremony." Of course at that early stage no students had been accepted, but a body of research workers was gradually assembling and the various institutes were taking shape. After much discussion and heart-searching, therefore, we sent out invitations for an opening ceremony to be conducted by Lord Balfour on April 1, 1925. I need not say how much his instant and enthusiastic acceptance of the invitation meant to us.

I therefore found myself, in the middle of March 1925, setting forth with my wife and our son Benjy, to join the Esperia in Genoa. . . . The Balfours went on to Cairo, to stay with Lord Allenby, who came with them a couple of days later to Kantara and accompanied us up to Jerusalem.

The situation in Palestine was at the time somewhat tense, but the security officers assured us that, apart from a fairly peacable demonstration in the form of a strike, and the closing of a few Arab shops in Jerusalem, Haifa and Jaffa, nothing untoward was happening. Which was just as well, as our guests were beginning to arrive in considerable numbers: representatives of universities and learned societies from all over the world, not to mention a great influx of tourists. It was not easy to find rooms for all these people in Jerusalem, for hotel accommodation was still scarce, and not of the best. Still, our reception committee did its work well, and I was not aware that any complaints were made. Every resident who had an appropriate house had placed it at the committee's disposal, and one way or another we managed to see to it that our guests enjoyed reasonable comfort.

The Balfour party and the Allenbys stayed of course at Government House. Kisch, Eder and I lived through some days of rather severe tension, with the responsibility of so many distinguished people on our hands under rather difficult conditions. There was, for instance, only one road from the city to the University on Mount Scopus, and that a narrow one, with little room for cars to turn. Control of traffic was a rather alarming problem, for the number of cars traveling to and fro was a record for Jerusalem at that time. Another purely physical difficulty was the actual site chosen for the opening ceremony. There was as yet no hall which could accommodate anything approaching the number of our guests and visitors—we expected some twelve thousand to fourteen thousand people. The only place, therefore, where we could stage the ceremony was the natural amphitheater facing a deep wadi on the northeast slope of Scopus. Round this amphitheater we arranged tiers of seats, following the natural rock formation. Everything was rather rough and ready, but the setting had such natural beauty that no art could have improved on it.

The snag was that, to face the audience in this amphitheater, the platform had to be on a bridge over the wadi itself. The gorge was deep, sheer and rocky; the bridge was an improvised wooden affair which inspired—in me at least—little confidence. I was told that it had been repeatedly tested, but my blood ran cold at the thought that something might give way at the crucial moment. . . . The builders, however, were convinced that the platform could safely bear two hundred or two hundred and fifty people. However, two hundred of our sturdiest young *chalutzim* volunteered to dance an energetic *hora* on the contraption. Nothing happened—except a great deal of noise—and I felt a little easier. Minute inspection of the platform failed to reveal any damage.

One final problem remained: the guarding of the tested platform during the night before the opening. Again our young *chalutzim* (members of the Haganah this time) came to the rescue: they established a sort of one-night camp in the wadi, and conducted frequent inspections, the last only a few minutes before the guests began to arrive.

Though the accommodation might be simple, even primitive, the surroundings—the austere magnificence of the landscape which opens out before one from this part of Scopus—more than made up for it. I doubt if anyone who made the pilgrimage to Mount Scopus that day, and the arrivals began before dawn, regretted the nonexistence of the Central Hall. Apart from our foreign visitors, people came from all over the country, people of every class and age and type. Only the three or four front rows of the amphitheater were reserved; the rest were open to the public, and needless to say were thronged hours before the ceremony began, I noted with some pride the discipline and good humor shown by the crowds.

Half an hour or so before the opening time the speakers and other platform guests assembled in the Grey Hill House to don their academic robes; then they passed, a colorful little procession, through the University grove on to the platform. The party from Government House approached direct, from the opposite side. Lord Balfour's appearance set off a tremendous ovation, which was hushed into complete stillness as he took his place on the platform.

The ceremony itself is a matter of historic record, and I need not describe it here. Many of the speakers were deeply moved. One or two of them were, as was only to be expected, rather long winded. I remember thinking at the time that Bialik (of all people!) was rather straining people's patience: he spoke in Hebrew, which to many of those present was a strange tongue. Moreover, I knew that at sunset the air would cool rapidly, and I was afraid that Lord Balfour (who was a man of seventy-seven) and some of the others might suffer, since all were bareheaded and without overcoats. However, we did finish before sundown; the crowds dispersed in orderly fashion; the guests departed to rest before the dinner party arranged for the evening; and the various committees responsible for the arrangements heaved a sign of relief that everything had gone off without a noticeable hitch.

Dedication ceremony of the Hebrew University Campus on Mount Scopus being addressed by the Earl of Balfour (Collection of the National and University Library, Jerusalem; with permission)

A JERUSALEM DIARY

Simon Greenberg

> *Simon Greenberg (1901–1993) was Vice Chancellor of the Jewish Theological Seminary. A committed Zionist, he attended the Hebrew University and graduated in its first class. In his diary, he described his life in Jerusalem at that time.*

Thursday, January 15, 1925

I am surpassingly happy, this evening reaching a state approaching unbounding ecstasy. [Judah] Magnes, [Max] Margolis, Is[adore Hoffman] and I walked from the University through the fields back to town. Darkness had already enveloped the city, but not completely. The last rays of the sun reddened the borders of the clouds on the horizon and brightened those higher in the heavens. They appeared like vast mountains of richly colored glass, rising directly behind the city. To this expanse of physical territory before us, was added the wide scope and unbounded hopes which filled all our hearts for the future of the University and of our work here. Time and again Magnes kept asking us as students and Margolis as a lecturer, "Did you ever anywhere else in the world, feel the significance of the subject matter as much as you do here, when it is delivered in Hebrew, before an audience that understands?" "Did you ever think that the form in which a subject is delivered, should influence the content, so profoundly?"

. And the student body, how they sit and drink in every word spoken by the professor. What a thirst there was here for some word of the Lord, for knowledge of a higher and profounder type.

And what joy it is for me to be here, and feel part of it all. Such days can never be repeated again, at least not in my life.

SOUND THE SHOFAR!

Moshe Segal

> *The following is an excerpt from* The Diary of Moshe Segal *in which he describes the situation of Jews in regard to the Western Wall in 1929.*

. . . Some time ago I had decided to pray on Yom Kippur at the remnant of our ancient Temple, the Western Wall. This is the Wall that our enemies and those who manipulate them have started to desecrate in recent years, in order to abuse our deepest feelings; abuse which signifies the beginning of an attempt to deprive us of our rights in our land. In the month of Av, 1929, we all swore an oath at this Wall to guard and protect it, and so it is the duty of us all, of every Jewish boy, to visit it whenever possible and to participate in the traditional prayers there, particularly on our people's most holy day. I went up to Jerusalem. Because of the difficulties of the journey from the Galilee, I said the evening prayers in the Hebron Yeshivah, which I love because of its wonderful atmosphere. . . . The following morning I went to pray at the Western Wall.

Notwithstanding the fast, very many people visit the Wall on this day and a great number stay there the whole day to pray, without leaving it at all. This year, the British policemen guarded the place properly; they accompanied the Mugrabis [Arabs] whenever they crossed the area, necessarily or otherwise, with trays laden with steaming cups of coffee and various sweetmeats, to aggravate the thirst of the fasting Jews. The cantor, a very old man, led all the day's prayers. . . . When he came to the prayer, "Close the mouths of our adversaries and accusers! Rid us of pestilence, the sword, captivity and destruction! Raise up the glory of Israel, Your people!" he put special meaning into his mighty voice which stirred the worshipers greatly. The sun began to set. The *Ne'ilah* prayer, in which our fate is sealed until next Yom Kippur, is full of warmth and emotion and exalted ethical meaning and stretches out its hand to welcome penitents. You forget all the intrigues and conspiracies around the Wall. There is only one feeling: the eyes of all Jews, wherever they are, are turned towards these stones; all Jewish hearts are praying this sublime prayer together with you, and you are confessing, "The Lord is God!" and in honour of His majesty the shofar is sounded every year. And then, suddenly you remember: sounding the shofar is forbidden! . . . Who forbade it? The evil government under whose auspices innocent blood is shed. Do we have to accept the yoke of this government? And with all the emotion in your heart you want to grasp the shofar and sound it with all your strength to acknowledge that the Lord of Israel is God and there is none other. . . . the innermost thought of your heart drives you to action. . . .

A hand, by force of its orders, arrested me. . . . Darkness in the hearts of the surprised worshipers; a darkness which spread in the hearts of all our brethren in their exiles. How long will gentiles defile our holy sanctuary?

TO S. Z. SCHOCKEN AFTER THE 1929 RIOTS

S. Y. Agnon

> Shmuel Yosef Agnon (1888–1970) was the greatest of modern Hebrew writers. Born in Galicia, he came to the Land of Israel in 1907. From 1924 on he settled permanently in Jerusalem, the setting of many of his stories. In 1966 he was awarded the Nobel Prize for Literature. Agnon had an extensive correspondance with his friend and patron, the famous publisher Shneur Zalman Schocken. In this letter he describes his experiences during the 1929 riots in the Jerusalem neighborhood of Talpiot, where he lived.

On Friday morning the Talpiot Neighborhood Secretary came to me and asked if I would go out to guard the neighborhood, because all the guards were exhausted. I stared at him in astonishment. The whole thing seemed to me like a kind of joke, and I found it hard to give up even one hour of my work time. When I left my room I saw some Arabs walking armed in the streets and one of them shook his sword at Jerusalem. But still I did not see any cause for fear. I expected that the Arabs and the Jews in the Old City would come to blows, but I was not really afraid. In the afternoon things took a different turn. Everyone who had a shop in the town came home, one complaining that he had been forced to close his shop and another saying that Arab dignitaries had come to plead with him to persuade the Jewish shopkeepers not to close their shops. In the meantime the people of Talpiot were forming little groups. People who did not know each other began to speak with one voice. Suddenly there was a rumour that a band of Arabs had attacked the Women Workers' Farm which is next to Talpiot and destroyed it. The Arabs had also attacked the Workers' Brigade, just a fifteen-minute walk from Talpiot and wounded one of the workers (he died of his wounds). Among the people of Talpiot were many optimists who said the Arabs would never come to Talpiot; after all, many of them earned their living there. There were also some who boasted that they had pistols and in the event of an attack they could defend Talpiot. All this time we were asking the Governor for help, and in the end an armoured car came with three or four English soldiers and an Arab policeman and a Jewish policeman. On the face of the Englishman I saw a hidden sneer at the Jews crowding together and in his voice there was a kind of bravado. As if to say, you don't have to be afraid as long as I am here. In the meantime the sun set and I went into the synagogue. I said to myself: Today there will surely not be many worshippers and this place must not be without prayer. When I came there I found only four old men who clung to the hem of my coat and wanted me to tell them what would happen. I stood and prayed by myself and made haste to leave the synagogue and go home to say grace. When I had finished my meal I went to my neighbour's house where the defence guards were gathered. When I saw that they did not need me I went home and brought them something hot to drink and then I went back again and sat in my doorway with two or three neighbours and we spoke about the events of the day. Close to eleven o'clock some people came and said, leave your houses and go to Gordon's. The maid and I set out (for my wife and children, may they live long, were then at Dr. Brin's in Bat Galim). We had to go to the home of Gordon, the director of the Anglo-Palestine Company, for all the people of our street were gathering there. I went to Gordon's house. There were about forty people there, men, women and children. They had locked all the doors and placed armed guards at the gates. I sat in the room for about an hour and went out to stand with the guards. Finally, when nothing was heard from the Arabs some of our people decided that we could go home. I went back home and got undressed and lay down on my bed, but sleep did not come to me. I kept going out to hear if there was anything new. Suddenly two or three neighbours knocked on the door and said, Come out! I was vexed at all this muddle and replied, what do you want of me? Once again we went to Gordon's. I felt no fear but a great languor such as I had never felt before. I kept thinking how good it would be to be asleep in my own bed. Close to sunrise I decided to go home. I woke our maid too and said: Get up, you silly girl and go to sleep in your own bed. You can sleep until noon. She went and I too was about to go but I was delayed on the way by a man who told me different things. Suddenly a foul, mouldy smell reached my nose. I looked and saw that a man was sitting on a stone and one of his feet was shod in a half-torn felt shoe and the other was tied up in a rag. I asked, what does it mean? And they told me that he was from the *Haganah* and had not taken off his shoes or socks for five days and five nights and now his feet were swollen. At that moment I no longer felt the smell at all, as if there was no smell. When I was standing there we heard shots that shook the air. We ran into Gordon's house. All the time I kept on thinking that our maid was also alone in the house and wondering if she was safe. I spoke to X and to Y but they did not listen and those who did answer me out of respect said that nothing would happen to her. I imagined how the girl would hide and how she would save herself. I said, at a time like this she will put her curiosity aside and sit quietly in a corner. And thanks to this I held out for about half an hour. Before our maid went home three young girls went to Dr. Klausner's house (one was their maid and two others went along with her). She went to tidy the house before the Klausners woke up (they were sleeping in a neighbour's house). Suddenly we heard a dreadful cry: Help! Save me! I'm dying! We peeped out and saw a young girl bleeding. Immediately two of our men crawled out: Mr. Saltzman, the owner of the electric shop in Talpiot, and a Yemenite called Sha'altiel, and they brought back two young girls covered in blood. Klausner's maid was badly wounded in the arm and kept on screaming: I'm a poor girl, I have to work for my living, if I have no arm how can I work? I shall die of hunger, Oh mother, mother. In the meantime the third girl was still in Dr. Klausner's house and our own maid was in my house. I stood there helplessly without knowing what to do; they would not let me go out and there was no one to fetch her. The armed men stood guard and the cowards stood and trembled in every limb at the sound of the firing. Suddenly there was a lot of smoke. The Workers' Brigade house was on fire. One shot followed the other and Gordon's house shook beneath the feet of terrified men and women and the children cried without stopping. I who was not armed took first one baby and then another to calm them, but how could I calm others when I myself was full of fear for the fate of the young girl in my house? Between one shot and the next X and Y came up to me and said: you should be grateful that your wife and children aren't here. But I as usual was not sensible of my good fortune but only of my great sorrow, for possibly at that very moment that same young girl was, God forbid, being killed in my house. At last I found two people who had come in an automobile from the city and I said to them: Come with me to save a Jewish soul, and my voice made such an impression on them that they went and brought her to Gordon's house, and two others joined them and brought the third girl from Klausner's house too. The young girl who worked as a maid in our house was called Haya. And when the young men brought her I cried aloud: Haya! And they said it's not Haya, for they had brought the young girl from Klausner's house. At long last the two young men came with Haya and I saw that it really was Haya. At that moment my heart was eased and from then on I did not feel our terrible and dangerous situation. Even when a bullet passed over the heart of our neighbor Mrs. Kornberg while she was nursing her son I felt nothing. All the time I was full of the feeling that this young girl had been saved and her fate would now be the same as my fate and the fate of all the other people there with me. Then someone came and told us that a young man from Talpiot had been badly wounded. In the meantime the Arabs stopped shooting and my neighbor, the architect Kornberg, went to see his house and came back and said that it was on fire. I sat with him on the ground, because of the bullets which might be fired into the house, and my heart was empty of pity. All that time I saw before my eyes the Klausners' little maid with her hurt dead arm and I thought what was all a man's property worth in comparison to that dead arm? In the meantime silence fell on Talpiot. But the silence was worse than the shooting. After the silence had lasted for a while we began to breathe again. Then I said: I'll go to my house and see what's happening there. I went and my maid went with me. I filled two small bags, one bag with my manuscripts about which I shall tell you another time. The girl wanted to take silverware and I scolded her. All the time I had the Klausners' maid before my eyes. After a few minutes we returned to Gordon's. In the meantime the rest of the residents of Talpiot had gathered there, ready to depart for the city. Professor Klausner and his wife came. Professor Klausner said with great pathos that if only they had given his wife a bed he would have remained in Talpiot, and told us about his state and feelings. He also complained bitterly about how his wife was not well and how they had not allowed the doctor to go to her (the doctor was with us to take care of the wounded). It was a heartrending sight when Kornberg took his two children and his wife took the baby and they set out from Talpiot leaving nothing behind them but a plot with a charred house. These poor people who had worked all their lives from five in the morning to late at night left without complaining about their situation.

Toward evening the Oxford people came. I gave them something to eat and they treated us with respect and sympathy. One of them showed me a big knife made by a fine craftsman which he had removed from the hands of an Arab. Not knowing English

The smashed door of a home in Talpiot damaged during the riots of 1929 (Central Zionist Archives; with permission)

I let others speak to them while I myself stood and served them. After eating and drinking they announced that we had to leave Gordon's because they wanted to fortify themselves in the house. They said the women must leave for the city and only those men able to defend themselves could remain. We went to a neighboring house and lay down on the floor. It passed through my mind: the owner of this house has already managed to hide his carpets away. It was more comfortable at Gordon's. In the meantime they phoned the Governor and City Council to send us help and also put out all the candles so that we would not, God forbid, be a target for the Arab bullets. There were some residents of Talpiot who demanded categorically that we all leave Talpiot and stop exposing ourselves to danger. As against these there were some who said that they would not leave for the sake of the honour of the neighborhood. I, who all these years had not had a good opinion of Talpiot, suddenly felt an attachment to the place and I too said that I would not leave, and thus we lay (those of us who were unarmed) on the floor while those who were armed stood by the windows. At nine o'clock a volley of loud shots was fired. I was lying there when suddenly I was called to the telephone. My wife was phoning from Haifa. I could not understand what she was asking and she could not hear what I was saying. Suddenly we were cut off. To me it seemed that my wife had fainted and I started thinking about her more and more all the time. I imagined her in a critically dangerous situation. Thus we lay, about twenty people in a closed room, with a young man armed with a revolver at every window. At nine o'clock loud shots were fired one after the other. Suddenly a sweet voice said: When I count to three, fire. And someone said: Close your eyes. I closed my eyes and heard one, two, three— and suddenly I saw flames and I was almost blinded. I thought what a good thing that my wife is not here, that my children are not here, and suddenly another thought came into my head: what was happening to them there in Bat Galim?

There were shots coming from both sides of the house. Between the shots I heard a voice in Arabic saying *hawaja*, which means Sir. Were the Arabs so close to the house? The shots grew louder. I touched my ears, trying to see if my hearing had been damaged. Suddenly the alarming thought came to me that we were alone in Talpiot with no one to defend us, for there was no response to the Arab shots from the English. Had the English deceived us?

For four hours we were without any defence and our only arms were the little pistols and one broken gun. All the events of the day passed before my eyes. I thought about the wounded girl from Klausner's house and remembered that I had made a vow to give her a pound, and I thought, God grant me the chance, that I will be able to keep the vow. And then I thought about how I had the biggest archive in the world on the history of *Eretz Yisrael* and how much labour I had invested in arranging it and now it would all be lost. Perhaps I should have said to the Oxfordians: I am ready to give you one-tenth of the whole archive for Oxford if only you will save it. But as long as the archives belonged to me I had no right to place it above anything else at a time when the whole community was in great danger. But why should I dwell on such matters when the firing was getting louder and louder?

Interior of a home in Talpiot damaged during the riots of 1929 (Central Zionist Archives; with permission)

At three o'clock the residents of Talpiot agreed to leave the quarter. A big convoy came from the city to take us. Once twenty and twice twenty men. I wanted to take the two bags of manuscripts that I had brought with me and I could not find them. In all the commotion they had been lost and I could not on any account remember where they were. And I was forbidden to light a candle here, lest we betray our refuge to our enemies. In the meantime the people were being urged to get onto the bus. And I thought that I would have to leave my manuscripts behind and rely on the grace of God, for it was impossible that all these suffering people should stand and wait for me. In the meantime the Neighbourhood Secretary came and lit a candle and found my manuscripts.

We left the house and boarded the bus. One soldier stood and counted us twice and then another soldier came and counted us again. The bus started off. There were two or three shots. The soldiers among us hid their heads.

One man buried his head between my knees and by so doing he forced me to sit up very straight. I thought that he had succeeded in finding a good hiding place for himself and perhaps because of this hiding place he would be saved from all the bullets and they would hit me, God forbid. I don't remember if it was out of pity for the man or in an act of thoughtlessness that I spread my hands on my knees too, so that if a bullet came it would on no account enter that man's head. Thus we drove very fast until we reached the Russian Compound, where the army was stationed. There they took us off the bus and the bus went back to Talpiot to take the rest of the people who had remained behind. Then they brought us to the City Council building. The Council building was full of refugees from all around Jerusalem, some mute with fear, some crying with misery for themselves and for their brothers, and some sitting and drinking tea. I went to B.A., the head of the *Haganah*. He lay on the balustrade and asked me for news of Talpiot. I told him about the boy from Talpiot who had been badly wounded and he replied that he had buried him. An hour ago he had returned from the Mount of Olives, where he had buried all who had been killed in Jerusalem. Many people who knew me asked me if I had saved my manuscripts. I answered: I have saved them, but the archive is still in my house, the archive on the history of *Eretz Yisrael*. They started telephoning all the "top people" to tell them to send a convoy and save the unique archive. One was not at home and a second found some excuse and a third was busy with some other matter. Suddenly Broza [Makleff] arrived from Motza weeping bitterly. I left the Council building with my two bags in my hand and slippers on my feet and I did not know where to turn. One moment I thought I must have a cup of tea, and the next I thought first I must put my manuscripts away in a vault for safekeeping. Why hadn't I had a cup of tea at the City Council? Since Saturday night I had had nothing hot to eat or drink. All around me I saw hundreds of eyes looking at me with astonishment and tears, for in the meantime they had heard about all what had passed in Talpiot. Someone came to ask me to go with him to Rabbi Kook, for the rabbi had inquired after my health. But I did not go to the rabbi. I knew that he had other worries. At last I found an acquaintance who took upon himself the responsibility for my manuscripts and I gave them to him for safekeeping. And another acquaintance, a shopkeeper, found me and took me by the hand and led me to his house and gave me water to wash my hands and face and also a cup of tea, and he also opened his shop despite the danger and sold me a pair of shoes. I recovered my spirits a little and set off to find out what was happening in Talpiot. But some old men from Talpiot dogged me every step and would not let me be. They said that they wanted to stay with me. I knew that I should give them comfort and that it was not right to abandon them in the streets of Jerusalem, but their own inquisitiveness saved me from them, for upon finding some acquaintances of theirs they stopped to talk to them and thus I was rid of them and went on my way.

Where to? It was impossible to take a single step. Here I was held up by people asking questions, there by the sounds of the weeping of the plundered, and there by my new shoes. In the meantime the sun rose and I who had left my house dressed in woolen clothes was sweating like a wax candle in the light of the sun. Suddenly I saw one of the drivers of Talpiot driving a car. I climbed in next to him and heard that he was going to X in Talpiot to collect some things from his house. I said that I would go with them. I went with him to ask a soldier to accompany us. In the meantime, other people came and took our car. While I was standing there I saw Mr. Krishevsky, who used to be the Deputy Commissioner of Jerusalem. I approached him and told him about my archives and two or three people who were standing next to him laughed bitterly at the man who came at a time of such trouble to talk about some old books. But Krishevsky said that such an archive was as precious as human lives. He told me to wait twenty minutes for him and then we would see what to do. He went off and I stood there and different soldiers kept coming and chasing me away from my place, there was hardly a square foot of the Russian Compound from which I was not banished. In the meantime I met the milkman from Mekor Baruch and he lamented his four cows which he had left behind there. At last Krishevsky came, bringing with him two other Jewish soldiers, and we went to Talpiot. Krishevsky spoke to the soldiers on guard. They fired a few shots to find out if there were any Arabs there. There were no shots from the Arab side. Nevertheless they ordered us to be very careful and to wait another ten minutes and then to crawl slowly to the house. At last I reached the house. The doors were open and inside everything was in ruins. I did not know what to do first. The archives were scattered all over the house and on the balustrade and in the yard, what should I take first and what last, and Krishevsky telling me all the time to hurry, we only had permission to stay for ten minutes and we had already wasted as much outside. I removed some manuscripts which I had left behind on Saturday from my writing desk and then I took a manuscript of *Yalkut Teman* which is the only one of its kind in the world, and also a manuscript commentary on the *Sayings of the Fathers* written four hundred years ago by a pupil of Rabbi Asher, of blessed memory, and a manuscript of the *Saragossa Scroll*, and I also took some manuscripts from the archive. And Mr. K did the same, taking whatever he found, and we returned to the city. On the way we met some Arabs; from their faces we could see they had come to loot. [Someone] asked if we should kill them. Krishevsky said No! We all knew that if it had been the other way around they would have done the opposite. At last I returned to the city with a handful of manuscripts and the clear knowledge of what had been done in my house and the houses of my neighbours. Afterwards I went to send a telegram to my wife telling her that we were alive.

Afterwards we met an acquaintance who was staying in a hotel and he drew me unwillingly into his room and offered me his bed. I thought that I would fall asleep at once, after all I had not slept for two days and two nights, but thinking is one thing and doing is another. So I got up and sent my acquaintance with a telegram to you, my esteemed friend, *Manuscripta und Leben gerettet* [Manuscripts and life safe] and he told me afterwards that he had corrected the telegram and added the word "*nur*" [only]. I suppose that he meant well.

From then on nothing of importance happened to me. Except that for three days I remained without any word from my wife and children and to make things worse, on that same day (that is, Sunday) whenever people asked me, where are the wife and children? I would sometimes reply in Talpiot, when I should have replied in Bat Galim. And the eyes of all those who heard my answer filled with tears. When I saw their tears I was afraid and asked: "Why, is there still danger?" and people turned away from me weeping. Before evening I sat down to rest and everyone who passed me shook their heads and pointed at me. Indeed, those hours were very hard. . . .

Torn and desecrated books in a home in Talpiot following the riots of 1929 (Central Zionist Archives; with permission)

The terrible impression made by the upheaval in my house cannot be described in words. Three thousands books (many of which I inherited from my late father-in-law) overturned and scattered and torn, and among them an ancient illuminated *Haggadah* with its big shining letters crying out from the page: And we shall cry out to the Lord, God of our fathers, and He shall see our affliction.

Much more have I to tell you, my noble friend, and God grant that I live to tell you these things in a time of gladness and rejoicing. And now I have no more words. May the Lord give strength to His people and may He bless His people with peace.

JERUSALEM, GOD'S VEILED BRIDE

Else Lasker-Schüler

> *The German-Jewish poet Else Lasker-Schüler (1869–1945) first visited Palestine in 1934 and settled in Jerusalem in 1938.*

. . . Hanging everywhere: a shred of Jerusalem. Often where one doesn't expect to find it—between the wrinkled, sad, tired worker's hands of a mother, or the back of a wasteland rock. Everywhere, if you pay attention, a small stone rolling passes you, the ante-diluvial pyramid of Jerusalem; you indeed stumble over its edge.

Palestine is the land of the Godbook, Jerusalem—God's veiled bride. I came from the desert, travelled to a sacred wedding, invited for the festival always surrounding Jerusalem. There's always a wedding under heaven's canopy. God loves Jerusalem. He's locked it in His heart, chosen this eternal city of cities. Each guest entering this city changes his clothes for holy ones. This pious change obliges him to behave solemnly and nicely so as not to scare the intent mood of the chosen lofty city. I must say I've never heard a loud word or a shrill tone in Jerusalem, not in its streets, not in its houses and palaces. That's why you can hear God breathing. Overcome by His nearness, you start to tremble. You have to get used to God. It's a good thing to purify yourself so as to get better and better. The soul, gripped by deep fright, begins burning. Sometimes I'd like to hide from God. Not everyone who journeys to Palestine understands his task. Palestine obliges!!! To convalesce, especially in a spiritual sense of that word, Jerusalem, Palestine's capital, is the right place, the soul's healing bath. Because the city blesses anyone longing for it, the pious city comforts anyone wanting to be comforted. Jerusalem is the observatory of the life beyond, the pre-heaven of heaven. The First Temple was built in this heavenly creation.

There's not much green and colour growing in the mountains round Jerusalem; March and the month of April very diligently stitch the carpet of land with indescribable flowers and grasses. The wanderer meets, from time to time, on heights, small poppies, red-sunk-in-themselves-faded ancestors of the opening poppies of Europe. I could never pluck an Ur-flower like that and certainly not out of exuberance. But I plucked the just-opened red flowers of Golgotha to give some happiness to pious Christians on the River Spree, two of my best friends. I'd imagined Golgotha completely different. Also I once in a dream stood on the lonely hill with playmates, watching out the night so as to make up for what my invincible tiredness couldn't do. Three hillocks quarrelled until recently about their authenticity. On the crumbling road beneath the lonely little mountain where I now stand, digging Jews laying out a new quarter found a gate who had died, "the city gate" at the foot of the graveyard hill of the Eternal City. The gate who until then had been sleeping, after embalment was buried again in the earth. Golgotha all covered with poppies isn't higher than a weeping willow, and I'd fretted how I could ever climb "the Rock." The old criss-cross alleys of Jaffa Road did enough to give new tasks every day to my heart. Now I stood relaxed, very moved on the hill of grief, thinking about unsolved events, and looking down into the valley. Dominicans walk silently along the garden-paths because the evening is bright, the heavens haven't economised with their light. I promised the holy men not to miss the way to Emmaus. They gave me some more religious attentions for my way and I thanked them. A long cactus hedge and stones, everywhere stones fallen from the hearts of arriving Jews. That's the legend of Palestine. I passed gigantic claws of antediluvian rock monsters, Stoneichthyosaurs indeed, looking for the road the dignified Jew had climbed with his disciples. Down in the petrified jaws of the pre-world gorge, suddenly it tears itself up to the heights of the

Holy City. The raised dust of a white caravan almost blew my little car into the abyss. Two or three dark-skinned children sit on the back of a patient animal, and, very leisurely on a donkey galloping behind, in white robes, a woman. "Shalom!" we called to each other, and my eyes, very pleased, follow this peaceful jaunt. Now I find myself again in the middle of Jerusalem, and the beautiful quiet did me good. You have to live in Palestine or to live there for some time not to question any more the truth of our blessed books. Staying in the Holy Land, particularly in Jerusalem, strengthens belief in God, in the "Resting Godhood." On its cheek rests Jerusalem.

THE LOVE OF JERUSALEM

HaRav Avraham Yitzhak HaCohen Kuk

> *HaRav Kuk (Kook) (1865–1935) was the first Ashkenazi Chief Rabbi of the Land of Israel, a post to which he was elected in 1921. A confirmed Zionist, he had emigrated to the Land of Israel from Eastern Europe in 1904.*

From the heights of the holy mountains, from the depths of the soul of Israel, springs the resurrection of the nation. The force of life which streams within our people and arouses us to life after the death-sleep of hard and bitter exile is the life of the entire soul of Israel, the soul of the entire nation. Not just a part of it, not merely certain of its abilities, but the entire spirit of life it all its might, in all its hues and glory. The seal which encaps this eternal spirit is stamped on the wholeness of the city of God, "Jerusalem built up, a city knit together" (Pss. 122:3); the Spirit which lives forever, the higher eternal knowledge, found its resting place on Mount Zion which it loved—Selah. And Israel is cognizant of this in the depth of its living soul. It knows that it must prepare to be a people. It knows that the Land needs the people. It knows that the people need both the material and spiritual factors, a life of work and action, farmers, vintners, plowmen. builders, masons, scribes and artisans of all sorts; it wishes to activate all of these talents from its rich and vital spirit. But most of all it knows that it possesses an exalted soul, that it is the people of the eternal God, the people of wonders, the source of belief, the source of the eternal life of the spirit; the light of God and the soul of He Who Lives Forever animate it. This soul of the living God which gives life and substance to the world, enlightens and enlivens, infuses eternal life into every spirit and soul, purifies and sanctifies the universe, continually expands and elevates it from all disgrace . . . the Presence of the Living God dwells in Israel, in its national, historic, familial and personal qualities, and in Zion does He desire to dwell. From Jerusalem God's Presence will never move. When we come to speak of Jerusalem, all worldly poetry fades, all the culture derived from the nations becomes as silent as stone. Here the Lord alone leads us. Here the great one of Israel stands in all His glory and might. Israel's eternal pride has not been humbled by the repeated destructions, the waves of sorrows which have risen above its head. On the contrary, they have added to its status and strength, eternal pride and glorious maturity.

Like the sound of a great shofar, its echo sounding through the assembled mountains, calling together throughout all the scattered communities of Israel to which they have been exiled: *Build Jerusalem*! Improve it, beautify it, create within it an everlasting memorial. Individuals and communities, young and old, "Walk around Zion, circle it; count its towers, take note of its ramparts; go through its citadels, that you may recount it to a future age. God—He is our God forever; He will lead us evermore" (Pss. 48:13–15). The voice cries out for the building of Jerusalem, and the myriad of holy emotions stream forth toward it from the depths of our soul when we respond: We have come to the city of God to be built. . . . The holiness and the strength which fill our hearts from all that is contained in the name the city of the Lord will be a mighty shield for us against all troubles.

❧

From the ruins of Jerusalem a voice cries out, "A heavenly voice which mourns like a dove and says, 'Woe is Me—for I have destroyed My house, burned My Temple and exiled My children among the nations of the world.'" The voice cries out again, the heavenly voice mourns like a dove, "Woe to the father who exiles his son, woe to the children who are exiled from their father's table." This heavenly voice which mourns in the sad voice of a dove for thousands of years, penetrates throughout the generations, speaking to the hearts and the souls of the living and the dead who have gone to their eternal rest and are bound in the bond of life, "the dead in their darkness await the day when the light of Your dawning will break through."

And the mourning voice of the dove penetrates into the depths of our hearts: Jerusalem the holy city, the sanctuary of the great King, the eternal seat of the kingdom of priests and the holy nations, Jerusalem, the city of God—selah—when she is destroyed and despised and desolate the heavens cry out bitterly and the heavenly angels weep bitterly. That heavenly voice which mourns like a dove and says, "Woe is Me—for I have destroyed My house," cries in our ears like a suffering invalid, but its sound grows stronger and our ears attend to that terrible, strong, awesome voice, the voice of an entire camp, the voice of God when He speaks, the howl of a lion-cub the roar of a lion—the Lord shall roar like a lion: "He makes His voice heard from His holy dwelling; He roars aloud over His [earthly] abode" (Jer. 25:30). Our souls tremble and shake as we stand and listen to the voice of the mourning dove from the ruins of Jerusalem, which grows more and more bitter until it becomes loud as the roaring of lions, as the voice of a great shofar, as the sound of terrible thunder, streaming and exploding: if that voice of the mourning dove ascends to our ears from the ruins of Jerusalem, saying: "Woe is Me—for I have destroyed . . ." how much greater is the voice like that of an invalid that we hear from the buildings of Jerusalem which strangers have established and which are for us double destructions! "A cry is heard in Ramah—

wailing, bitter weeping—Rachel weeping for her children. She refuses to be comforted for her children, who are not" (Jer. 31:15)—for her children, the best of her children, "are not" to be found among among the builders, among those who comfort the mourning of the dove who says, "Woe is Me—for I have destroyed. . . ."

The time has come. The events of these days call to us with a great sound: Israel—build the holy city, remember, eternal people, holy people and guardian of of the faith, remember your oath made at the waters of Babylon: "If I forget you, O Jerusalem, let my right hand wither; let my tongue stick to my palate if I cease to think of you, if I do not keep Jerusalem in memory even at my happiest hour" (Pss. 137:5–6). And if you have kept the easiest part of the oath, for your tongue does not stick to your palate—for Jerusalem is always on your tongue and always will be—it is now your right hand which is needed so that it will be outstretched and ready to act with force and vigor, an upraised, mighty, right hand, the first part of that eternal oath—the mourning voice of that dove from the ruins of Jerusalem vigorously demands that it be fulfilled: Hear O Israel, from the rising of the sun until its setting, from all the lands where you have been scattered, turn your face toward the Lord when it is the time of His favor, at each moment of His favor, when holy longings are aroused in the depths of our hearts to-

Crowds on Jaffa Road during the funeral of HaRav Kuk in 1935 (Central Zionist Archives; with permission)

ward Jerusalem, the holy city, "our holy and glorious city which our ancestors praised"—hear the voice of the cooing dove from the ruins of Jerusalem and the roaring of the lion which calls out from the buildings of strangers who laugh at our indolence and our laziness at this time of possibilities, when God's hand is stretched out for good—the time to begin to work and build for ourselves the city of our glory, to raise her from her desolation, to adorn her gloriously with wondrous buildings, with glorious institutions, with the splendor of holiness.

The time has come for us to recognize the voice of the Lord in all of the events which have occurred, in all the inclinations of our hearts, in all the movements of life, small and big, the voice of the Lord in strength calling to us from the ruins of Jerusalem and its desolation: Arise, My children, build the soul, raise the destroyed holy city, remember God from afar and raise Jerusalem upon your hearts!

THE SEVENTH GATE

Jerusalem in Modern Nonfiction

The Lions' Gate, ca. 1989 (Central Zionist Archives; with permission)

In the period from the establishment of the State of Israel until today, writing about Jerusalem has proliferated as never before. This reflects both the conditions of modern life in general and the special place that Jerusalem has played and continues to play in the historical events surrounding the founding of Israel. This section and the two that follow it are all devoted to this period of some fifty years. This section contains material from diaries and other personal accounts and reflections about Jerusalem written by those who participated in the great events of our time.

JERUSALEM, THE ETERNAL CAPITAL

David Ben-Gurion

> *The first Prime Minister of Israel, David Ben-Gurion (1886–1973) was born in Plonsk*
> *(Russian Poland) and settled in the Land of Israel in 1906. His vigorous leadership led*
> *to his election as Chairman of the Jewish Agency in 1935 and eventually to his becoming*
> *Prime Minister.*

The Six Day War and the phenomenal victory of the Israel Defense Forces, unprecedented in our history and also perhaps in the history of other nations, has stirred the Jewish people, not alone in Israel, but throughout the world, more than any other event in our generation, more even than the establishment of the State and the War of Independence.

This quick, decisive victory of the Israel Defense Forces was won on all the three fronts on which we were obliged to face the enemy—the whole of the Sinai Peninsula, the West Bank of the Jordan, the Syrian Heights. But the blaze of joy and pride was kindled by the liberation of the Old City of Jerusalem, "the city in which David dwelt," David, King of Israel, conqueror of Jerusalem, the man who, three thousand years ago, created it the eternal capital of Israel.

None of the credit for the six great days can be taken from the Israel Defense Forces; but their victory is the culmination of that won by the men who fought for independence. On Wednesday the 27th of Iyyar, 5727, June 6, 1967, the Old City and its environs were liberated, and yet the struggle for Jerusalem did not begin during the unforgettable Six Days. On April 6, 1948, just over nineteen years earlier, when the Executive Committee of the Zionist Organization met in Tel Aviv, the Chairman of the Executive [Ben-Gurion—ed.] delivered a report on the four months of fighting that had begun just following the decision of the UN Assembly to establish a Jewish state in part of the country, a small area not containing Jerusalem, which the UN decision intended to be an international city under UN rule. Speaking of the fate of Jerusalem, the Chairman of the Executive said:

> It is superfluous to explain to the Executive of the Zionist Organization what
> value Jerusalem has in the history of the Jewish people, of this land, and of
> the world. The value of Jerusalem cannot be measured, weighed, and counted.
> For if a land has a soul, then Jerusalem is the soul of the land of Israel. The
> fight for Jerusalem is decisive, and not alone from a military point of view.
> Jerusalem demands and deserves that we stand by her. That vow we took by
> the waters of Babylon obligates us today as it did then. Otherwise we shall
> not deserve to be called the Jewish People—our enemies know that the fall
> of Jewish Jerusalem would be a mortal blow to the whole Jewish people.

On Passover eve, 5708, three weeks before independence was proclaimed, the Chairmen of the Zionist Organization broadcast to the nation from Jerusalem and, turning to the inhabitants of Jerusalem, he said:

> The whole weight, the heavy blows of the war, have fallen on you, Jerusalem, for you are the battle's center of gravity. Do not lose heart, you have stood fast in fearful suffering—the entire Jewish People stands with you; and the best of our youth, the defenders and the convoy drivers, have risked and will continue to risk their lives for your sake. A chain of enemy positions to your West and North is being destroyed and taken by our fighters. We shall not forget you, O Jerusalem, our right hand shall not be forgotten.

And then, while the War of Independence was still going on, the Prime Minister, on the 23rd Ellul 5708, September 27, 1948, said in the temporary Council of State:

> In the case of a military decision, it is not impossible that we shall be able to take the road to the Negev, Eilat, and the Dead Sea, and secure the Negev in our hands, and also to widen the corridor to Jerusalem on the north and south, to free the remainder of New Jerusalem (Sheikh Jarah and the University and Hadassah Hospital area), and to capture the Old City, to take all central and western Galilee, and to widen the borders of the state in several other directions.

Most of these hopes had been realized by the end of the War of Independence, on the 7th of January, 1949, but the Old City of Jerusalem remained in the hands of the Arab Legion, its Jewish inhabitants were taken captive, and Jewish synagogues in the Old City were destroyed. The provisions of the cease-fire agreement with Jordan, signed on April 3, 1949, granting every Jew access to the holy places in the Old City and to the cultural institutions of Mount Scopus, as well as to the Mount of Olives, were violated by the Jordanian Government, and until the Six Day War Jews were not allowed into Old Jerusalem or into the holy places, and the city of Jerusalem was split into two—the New City, under control of the Government of Israel, and the Old City, under control of the Government of Jordan.

Twice in our history, fateful wars caused the destruction of Jerusalem and the Jewish State, once in the days of the First Temple and again in the days of the Second Temple. We do not have a full, detailed description of the war of Judah and Jerusalem in the days of the First Temple; but we know in detail about the war of the Jews against the Romans, the desperate defense of Jerusalem waged for years by our zealots, and its destruction by Titus. The Romans did not open their war with the capture of Jerusalem; on the contrary, they left Jerusalem for the last. To begin with, they fought for Galilee and Judea. Only later, after they had conquered almost the entire country, did they besiege Jerusalem, for it is impossible to hold Jerusalem unless one holds the entire country.

During the War of Independence, the entire country, from Dan to Beersheba, was in flames, and our enemies penetrated into the interior of the country, in the North,

East, and South. The Haganah, and its successor, the Israel Defence Forces, were obliged to fight for every point and settlement in the country, all being under attack by enemies that ranged everywhere within the borders of the young State of Israel. New Jerusalem was rescued only when our forces had routed and expelled the enemy from the whole territory that had been assigned to the State of Israel by the UN. Even more was won. But Old Jerusalem remained in the hands of our enemies.

All the roads in the country, including the roads that led to Jerusalem, were then in the hands of the enemy, and the Haganah and Israel Defense Forces had to defend all the isolated settlements and to battle for ways of communication.

Anyone familiar with the New Jerusalem of today cannot imagine Jerusalem during the war preceding the establishment of the State, the War of Independence. New Jerusalem was a patchwork of Jewish quarters scattered among Arab quarters. "Islands" of Jews and Arabs were interspersed. In Old Jerusalem there was one isolated Jewish quarter unfortunately placed in a sector the great majority of whose inhabitants were non-Jewish. To the Arabs, Jerusalem was open from four directions, from Ramallah, Hebron, Jericho, and Latrun. Our way was open in one direction only, to Latrun, and that too was cut off from time to time. Under a rain of fire and death, food was brought hundreds of kilometers from the farming settlements of the Galilee and the Emek to Jewish Jerusalem—one of the marvelous epics in the Haganah's fight for Jerusalem. The Israeli drivers and the Palmach and Hish escorts, who daily brought the farm produce of the Upper and Lower Galilee, Jezral Valley, and Jordan Valley, to the Jews of Jerusalem, wrote one of the splendid chapters in our present-day book of valor.

About a year after the War of Independence, the UN Assembly again went into session to deliberate on the fate of Jerusalem. The Prime Minister found it necessary, on the 14th of Kislev, 5710, December 5, 1949, to make the following announcement in the first Knesset:

> Our membership in the UN obligates us to respond from here, from the podium of the first Knesset of Israel, to all the nations gathered in the UN Assembly and all those in the world who cherish peace and justice, and repeat what has been in the heart of the People of Israel from the time it became one nation under the scepter of King David, three thousand years ago, concerning Jerusalem, its holy city, and its attitude towards the shrines of all the faiths.
>
> In proclaiming the renewed State of Israel, on the 14th of May, 1948, we affirmed and obligated ourselves before history and before the world, that the State of Israel shall guarantee freedom of religion, conscience, language, education, and culture; shall guard the holy places of all the religions, and shall be faithful to the principles of the United Nations. In accord with this, our delegation has announced in the UN that the State of Israel obligates itself to honor all existing rights relating to the holy places and the religious structures in Jerusalem, and promises freedom of worship and free access without any discrimination to all the holy places and religious structures under its jurisdiction.

A convoy of trucks bringing food to Jerusalem on Joseph ben Matityahu Street in 1948 (Central Zionist Archives; with permission)

At the same time, we feel it our duty to proclaim that Jerusalem is an organic, inseparable part of the State of Israel, as it is an inseparable part of the history of Israel, the faith of Israel, and our people's soul. Jerusalem is also the heart of the State of Israel.

We cannot conceive that the UN will uproot Jerusalem from the State of Israel or infringe on the jurisdiction of Israel over Israel's eternal capital.

Had we not succeeded in resisting the aggressors who rebelled against the UN, Jewish Jerusalem would have been wiped from the face of the earth, the Jewish settlement would have been destroyed, and the State of Israel would not have been established. Since the UN has not succeeded in implementing its decisions, the November resolution on Jerusalem is, in our opinion, null and void.

In the meanwhile, however, the UN Assembly had again resolved that Jerusalem should be a separate, international entity. Eight days after his first announcement on Jerusalem, the Prime Minister, on December 13, 1949, announced in the Knesset:

> One week ago, in the name of the Government I made an announcement to the Knesset on Jerusalem. Our announcement remains in force and there has not been and cannot be any change in our stand. As you know, the UN Assembly has in the meanwhile resolved by a large majority to place Jerusalem under international rule as a separate entity. *This resolution cannot in any way be implemented.* The State of Israel has had and shall have one capital alone—eternal Jerusalem. So it was three thousand years ago; so shall it be, we have faith, to the end of days.

The Knesset and most of the Government offices moved at once to Jerusalem, New Jerusalem, for Old Jerusalem had been conquered by the Arab Legion, its Jewish settlement destroyed, and its gates closed before every Jew, contrary to the cease-fire agreement.

The Six Day War was conducted almost entirely within enemy borders, and not only Old Jerusalem and its environs, but also the Gaza Strip, the West Bank, the Syrian Heights, and the whole Sinai Peninsula were conquered by the Israel Defense Forces. Jerusalem with all its environs, complete and united, will be the capital of Israel, while the holy places will be guarded with the most meticulous care.

The task of the saviors of Jewish independence of nineteen years ago has been completed, and the capital of Israel three thousand years ago, the city taken and wholly freed by the heroes, the living and the dead, of the Six Day War, will remain the capital of Israel forever.

August 14, 1967

Jerusalem Is Called Liberty

Walter Lever

> *Walter Lever, who taught English literature at Manchester University in England, was invited by the Hebrew University to teach a course there in the Spring of 1947. Thus he and his wife Anita lived through the days of the birth of the State in Jerusalem.*

Jerusalem did not sweep me into transports of enthusiasm as had the heady experiences of my first day on the Carmel. The dry, thin air was temperate and sobering; the buildings looked solid and unpretentious. Nothing was mean or repulsive; yet I experienced an obscure sense of disappointment. I cannot say what I expected to see. Subconsciously

I had formed two mental pictures, contradictory yet co-existent: a romantic back-drop of eastern towers and minarets, derived, I suppose, from memories of the stained-glass window in the synagogue; and a brand new, utopian set-up of model dwellings and spacious parks, inspired by the carefully-selected photographs of propaganda brochures. Instead, there were the pines and clean stone fronts of King George Avenue; the Gaumontesque cinema of Zion Square, with the Cafés Europe and Vienna and one stately eucalyptus tree; the steep narrow thoroughfare of Ben Yehudah street where I was staying, with its tasteful shop windows and numerous bookstalls. I walked up to Meah Shearim and found the teeming courtyards of an old ghetto: I paid visits in Rehaviah, which had the atmosphere of a cultured middle-class suburb is some western city, save for its Judean stone, its carob trees and cypresses. What I saw I liked; there was an undertone of dignity and tradition which gathered to itself all the diverse aspects of the city. Jerusalem, I said to myself, was a middle-eastern Oxford, with touches of exotic colouring in the strange robes and oriental faces that mixed with the predominantly European crowds. But even while I said it, I knew that this could not be all. There must be something more; some unperceived relation between the actual city before my eyes and the inchoate visions of my dreams.

At moments I almost found it. I would catch a glimpse of the ancient weathered walls of the Old City while walking toward the Jewish Agency building with its bleak

The neighborhood of Rehavia during the pre-State period, date unknown (Central Zionist Archives; with permission)

modernity. Or occasionally there would be a quiet courtyard with the light glistening on the stones; or a sudden, ecstatic flush of sunset on roofs and balconies. There was some enigma in the clear, bright eyes of a knot of boys coming from school, and in the timeless gaze of an old bearded Jew in his round felt hat and kaftan. Something, something; it ached to be resolved, but I had not the answer.

Physically I was shut in by all kinds of barriers. The mandatory government had cut the city up into "zones" and prohibited areas. Barbed wire fences, dragons' teeth fortification and great screens shut off the view in every direction. A hundred yards on from Zion Square was the "central zone" round the post office and the main shopping streets. Half of Rehaviah was requisitioned and forbidden to all civilians without a special pass. The broad open vistas of southern Jerusalem were available only to the soldiers and police. As for the Old City which I so much wanted to visit, I was warned on the first night under no circumstances to go except in a conducted party, since no police protection could be counted on in case of trouble.

From the hour of my arrival I could sense the political tension in the city. When I took the bus for the first time, it was stopped suddenly by steel-helmeted soldiers who pushed their way between the seats with their loaded sten-guns at the ready, and curtly demanded to see each passenger's identity card. On another occasion it took their fancy to order us all out of the bus, line us up in the street, and paw our clothes for illicit weapons. A shot or explosion in any outlying quarter set the sirens wailing as if an air-raid was in progress, and all traffic throughout the city had to stop in its tracks for anything between twenty minutes and two hours, until the all-clear sounded. I do not remember that these elephant-and-flea tactics resulted in a single terrorist being caught during my stay, and suspect that their real purpose was an assault upon mass psychology, an attempt to overawe the populace by a constant exhibition of armed force. . . .

"Town" for the Jerusalem Jew consisted in those days of the triangle formed by Jaffa Road, Ben Yehudah Street and King George Avenue, reaching past the municipal gardens to the Jewish Agency Building and the approach to Rehaviah. Beyond stretched the British zones and the Arab quarters. The whole distance could be walked, at a sauntering pace, in less than twenty minutes. Within these bounds, urban life was necessarily simple, and had an agreeable quality of intimacy. Few people had a surplus of spending money, and amusements were mainly self-created. One visited friends at their homes, attended an occasional concert of chamber music or a lecture, walked out to the open country around Beth Hakerem or Bait Vegan on a Sabbath morning. The young generation's notion of a good time consisted principally of an evening stroll under the pines of King George Avenue refreshed by coffee and ices at Café Allenby or Marcus, with friends round the table and acquaintances to hail from the open windows. Girls wore neat, gaily embroidered blouses and eschewed the more elaborate kinds of make-up; the boys were sufficiently dressed for any occasion in shorts and open-necked white shirts— or, for a touch of dandyism, in Russian-style linen tunics with high, embroidered collars. In the mild air, with older people sitting at their balconies and the street lamps making a golden glow, Jerusalem seemed like the home of one large family.

The British compound—"Bevingrad"—on Princess Mary Street prior to the proclamation of the State in 1948 (Central Zionist Archives; with permission)

A small town, indeed, with its less than a hundred thousand inhabitants. Yet the mentality of Jewish Jerusalem was not narrow. Most of the professional, administrative and academic talent of the country was centered here. . . . Jerusalem had, in fact, an intellectual society, interested in books and music and ideas, quite out of proportion to its size. Moreover, the sense of belonging to a great city permeated every section of the populace and affected each ordinary person. It rested on more durable supports than the presence of the mandatory government and various Zionist institutions. The petty craftsman and the stone mason, the market man and porter, judged Jerusalem by a different set of values. To define their attitude requires the use of grandiloquent phrases for a habit of thought almost as natural as breathing. Handed down from father to son was an unquestioning acceptance of Jerusalem as the one real and eternal city, the centre of existence, the theme of all the history they knew or cared for. This belief was perhaps the one force uniting the incredibly varied communities; Germans and Bukharans, Yemenites and Poles, all shared the same pride in their city. It did not materialize, as with the gentiles, in a reverence for holy places, still less in anything resembling the Londoner's or New Yorker's delight in monuments and public buildings. The stalls of the market, the narrow, crowded courtyards and unpaved alleys were, for each community, the visible manifestations of Jerusalem's sanctity. Yet the grandeur and holiness of the city were not without worthy tokens. They appeared eternally in the roseate, glowing rock from which it was hewn; in the clarity of the sunlight which irradiated the stones so that they glistened like marble; in the pure rarefied air wafted from the surrounding hills, and the nearness and brilliance of the multitudinous stars.

❧

The news of what happened on the Scopus road that afternoon was announced on the evening radio and appeared in the press the next morning. I relate the story as it was told me by S., an American neighbour holding a position in one of the university offices, when I visited him the following day. At 4:15 in the afternoon . . . two buses packed with students, lecturers and staff workers left the university for the city. "Near Sheikh Jarrah," said my neighbour, "the first bus slowed down to go round the bend. I was sitting at the front, near the driver. Suddenly I saw the glass of the windscreen splinter. It's odd, but I don't recollect hearing shots fired. The driver must have braked in time, for the bus came to a halt. I didn't know anyone was hit till I saw the driver's head sink slowly down on the wheel. It was a queer movement, just as if he'd nodded off to sleep. I remember staring at him, then realizing in a flash that in a few seconds the next bus would catch up, not able to pass, and we'd all be trapped on the road. Shots were already coming through the side windows: I got up and began tugging at the driver to see if I could budge him from his seat. He was a stout, heavily built man and a dead-weight now that he was unconscious. I tugged away like hell until I had got him out and set myself in his place, then I put my foot down on the accelerator and thank God, we started to move. The bullets came in over my head and behind me I could now hear the moans of those who had been wounded. There was a girl with a splinter of glass in her eye, who kept screaming that she was blind. I've never driven a bus before in my life, but I stuck it out, keeping my foot on the accelerator and sounding the horn like a madman all the way, while people shouted directions and tried to guide me. The journey seemed as if it would never end, but at long last we were back in the city. I drove across to the Hadassah City Clinic and there we stopped and took in the wounded for treatment."

That was the last time that lectures were held on Mount Scopus. For some weeks the university was closed and the buses ceased to run.

❧

May 14th, 1948

Or day one, year one of the apocalypse . . . There's no world left except this city, cut off in space, ringed round with enemies. There's no month of May, no year 1948: only day and night, with chances changing every hour and tomorrow as arbitrary as the particles of the quantum theory. . . .

The new era began early this morning. There was a ring at the door just as I was waking up. B. from our *emdah* [position—ed.] stood on the step telling me that I was to go at once to Bait Vegan and report for duty. . . .

At the road-block outside Bait Vegan, which marks our front line on this sector, they gave me a pickaxe and directed me toward the wadi below the quarry. It reaches all round the southern outskirts as far as the Bethlehem road. I climbed down the rough slope. It was a morning of matchless beauty; the hills radiant; every wild flower between the rocks gemlike and unearthly. Over to the left was the long white skyline of Jerusalem. A terrific battle was raging there. I could hear the ceaseless rattle of automatic gunfire and the perpetual crash of bombs. The din mounted in an infernal crescendo; it seemed that the city could stand no more; that at any moment it would break into fragments.

Down in the wadi the air was hot and still. Stripped to the waist, a number of men were hacking out a deep trench to serve as a tank trap . . . I fell into line with them and copied their stroke. . . . We worked on steadily. . . . An argument started up between Shelomo, a chubby, lively boy of twenty from our quarter, and a man from Bait Vegan, lean and grave, with a fair beard and the black skullcap of the orthodox. He remarked quietly, as he laid his pickaxe down:

"Now we shall see the miracle in our day, when God stretches out His arm to save His people."

Shelomo, who had become an atheist in his last school year, retorted:

"If anyone saves them, it'll be us of the Haganah."

The man stared at him with blue, scornful eyes.

"Perhaps you have not read in the Torah how the Red Sea was divided, and the people passed between?"

"Natural causes," grinned Shelomo provocatively. "It is also written in the book of Amos that God brought up other peoples from bondage: the Philistines from Caphtor and the Syrians from Kir. What if He now helps the Arabs, or even the British?"

"You will see the answer with your own eyes," said the other man calmly. And he began to quote, also from Amos, how the Lord would regather His people, and raise up the fallen tabernacle of David.

In the midst of this battle of texts, came someone running down the hill-slope, waving his arms wildly and yelling:

"Cheers! Cheers! The Police Headquarters—and the Central Post Office—and Barclay's Bank—with all Rehaviah and Talbieh—in our hands, boys! Long live Hebrew Jerusalem!"

He had come from town with dispatches, and breathlessly told us the news. The great central zone of "Bevingrad" was occupied by the Haganah at the very moment the British were departing. They penetrated it from the side approach and nullified all the elaborate fortifications. From there they stormed down Princess Mary Avenue, past the Arab road-blocks, and on as far as Allenby Square, a hundred yards from the Old City. At the same time Zone B in Rehaviah and Talbieh was peacefully occupied, and the fighters fanned out down Mamillah Road and to the bottom of King George Avenue. Everywhere the Arabs were in flight; it could only be a matter of hours before the Old City fell.

I came home toward evening. . . . I threw myself back in a chair and tried to get the news on the radio. But the electric current was too feeble, so I got up again and went across to the house of S. our neighbours. Their radio was just audible and we caught the Haganah broadcast from Tel Aviv. Ben Gurion's speech to the Provisional Council was being relayed, proclaiming the independent "State of Israel." . . . On tiptoe Mrs. S. crept over, handing us each a little glass of *rishon* wine. Fainter still, we heard the strains of Hatikvah: now our national anthem. Rather solemnly we stood up, raised our glasses and drank to the future of Israel. Before the anthem was played to an end, the current failed completely, and the radio went dead.

THE FAITHFUL CITY

Dov Joseph

> *Dov Joseph (1899–1980) came to Jerusalem from Canada in 1921 after serving in Palestine in the Jewish Legion. In April 1948 he became military govenor of Jerusalem and later served in the Knesset.*

Disorders in the Old City began with an Arab demonstration on December 1, accompanied by the stoning of Jewish homes and firing at Jewish buses. The next day three Jews were shot through a break in the concrete wall separating the Arab and Jewish quarters. On December 8 two Jews were stabbed to death and an attempt was made to break into a synagogue, and three days later Arabs set fire to a Jewish house and tried to mob the quarter. Sniping by now had become regular. Shops were forced to close, schools did not open, sanitary services stopped functioning. The Arab attacks were designed to drive the Jews out of the Old City and physically to destroy the Jewish quarter.

After one night of violence and terror, the Armenian and Christian communities, which had lived in friendship with the Jews, broke off contact with them. This cut the Jews off from their chief intermediaries with the Arab venders of vegetables. Food could now reach them only by convoy through Arab districts. The British supplied guards for the evacuation of Arabs from their homes in the New City. Those Jews who left said they did so because their livelihood was outside the Old City and they did not wish to eat the bread of charity.

The technique of the Arab attacks on the Jewish quarter, in fact the technique of fighting in the Old City in general, had not changed much since the days of the Romans. The revolver and the submachine gun replaced the bow and arrow, and the mortar the ballista. The struggle remained one of fighting from house to house, from window to window and from roof to roof. Each battle, of the hundreds fought by day and by night during the six months the siege of the Old City lasted, was identical in principle and resembled the battles which had taken place throughout the centuries in such Eastern cities.

The Hagana command now made its preparations for the defense of the quarter. It was divided into two main sections; one comprised all the part eastward of the Street of the Jews and the other all the area sloping upward to the west of it.

The enemy consisted of members of Arab gangs. They took control of the Armenian quarter and used their mosques for military purposes. Later they were helped by the Arab Legion, which seized positions on Mount Zion and sniped over Zion Gate. British secret-service men could be seen moving about among the Arabs. Ten British policemen were stationed permanently in an Arab mill just opposite our Kahana position.

In general the Armenians remained neutral. They did, however, provide a number of spies for the Arabs. They walked about the Jewish quarter photographing our positions. The Assyrians, who lived mostly in the Armenian quarter, maintained strict neutrality.

The immediate Hagana problem was to increase its force inside the Old City from eighteen to at least 120 men. By private arrangement with a few British guards, two buses and three taxis entered the Jewish quarter on December 10 and their passengers quickly scattered to their positions. This was the only substantial reinforcement that was to arrive. The occasional bribing of another British guard or the introduction of personnel disguised as teachers or religious functionaries added only a handful more. The total number of armed defenders never exceeded 150 and eventually, by the attrition of war, fell far below that figure. The Arabs, of course, entered the Old City at their will without being searched.

Hagana arms were mainly revolvers, Sten guns and hand grenades. There were one two-inch mortar with very few shells, one Lewis machine gun, about a dozen rifles, some explosives, wireless equipment and medical supplies. The Hadassah Medical Organization maintained a medical unit inside the quarter throughout the siege.

Some ammunition had been hidden in the Old City in advance. One of the chief caches, which included ten tommy guns, was a "slick" held by the Etzel, who obstinately refused to reveal its whereabouts to the defenders. This dissident organization at first refused to take orders from the Hagana commanders. They could not be utilized rationally. They often left positions that we thought were standing firm, without informing us beforehand. We were thus exposed unnecessarily to the danger of enemy infiltration. The conduct of all the members of the dissident organizations in the Old City highlighted the profound difference which exists between the organization of acts of terrorism and the steady, trained action required to defend or carry out the planned operations of a nation at war. . . .

We never solved the problem of supplying the Old City. At the end of December the Arabs set up roadblocks, manned by armed men, to stop all Jewish traffic into the

Jewish quarter. The British authorities were responsible for these roadblocks, since their police stood by as the Arabs enforced their control of entry. It took the most agonizing negotiations to arrange for a British convoy to escort our trucks past these roadblocks. This was no military matter, but a straightforward political act: the British wanted the Jews out of the Old City and were prepared, if necessary, to starve them into leaving.

The distance the convoys had to travel was only a few hundred yards, and an operation would normally take from twenty to thirty minutes. The trucks, already loaded, were inspected by British police and Army. Three armored cars and a strong escort would convoy them to the Zion Gate, which was the gate the Arabs insisted be used for such convoys. The police inspector would unlock the gate from the inside and send a patrol to remove the bars the Arabs had set up outside. Then the trucks would back to the gate one by one and be unloaded very rapidly by some forty Jewish porters, who carried the goods another 150 yards to some of the houses where they were stored.

In the first five days of January, not an ounce of food entered the Old City. There was an acute shortage of kerosene for cooking and no milk whatsoever for the children. An official of the Jewish Agency who was inside the Old City reported that while the inhabitants of the Jewish quarter were not starving, they were completely isolated and contact had to be re-established. Jewish dead in the Old City had been unburied for five days. On the fifth of the month the matter was twice raised with the authorities. The government was asked to see that convoys went through at all costs, or they would have to be sent through under Jewish armed escort. The regular answer received from the British was that the matter was "delicate."

It was while these negotiations were going on that the Etzel decided to plant a bomb at the Arab National Guard outpost at the Jaffa Gate entrance to the Old City, which was blocking food convoys to the Jewish quarter. It killed fourteen Arabs and wounded forty others. While retreating, three of the Jews were shot dead by police and soldiers. This happened on January 7, which was the day the British had finally promised that a convoy would go through. Naturally, it did not pass that day. Negotiations continued without result. Finally our spokesman announced, "If you hear a loud explosion from the direction of the Old City, you can take it that we have blown a hole in the wall." It would have been no mean undertaking to make a hole in the Old City wall, which was some four yards thick at the top and about ten yards thick at ground level. But the announcement, made without histrionics, in cold, level terms, had its effect. The British promised to see to it that convoys passed through.

❧

We had two objectives inside Jerusalem which we wanted desperately, for old and tangled reasons: the recapture of the Old City, the citadel of our Biblical dreams and the symbol of so many ancient forces which had helped to make us a nation, and the capture of Sheikh Jarrah, the vital link which would re-establish contact for us with the

Hebrew University and the Hadassah Hospital on Mount Scopus, two great symbols of the reborn strength of the Jewish people. We failed in both. This was because we chose deliberately to concentrate what strength we had on another objective: the clearing of a safe road from new Jerusalem to the sea. In this we succeeded. A hundred years from now historians may say that our choice, which assured the inclusion of Jerusalem in the State of Israel, was a major turning point in the history of the Middle East. . . . At the Jerusalem end of the road, it was imperative that we take the villages of Malha and Ein Karem. The first was captured on July 13 by a youth unit of Hagana troops; it was one of the points from which the Arab Legion had bombarded Jerusalem and it closed the ring we were drawing tight around Ein Karem. This large village fell four days later. Most of the Arab Legion and the Egyptian troops which held it managed to escape before the end; the rest had no choice but to surrender. This same operation won for us the heights now known as Mount Herzl, where the national military cemetery of Israel is located and where my younger daughter, killed in action in the Negev, is buried.

☙

The Old City had not been demilitarized, and we had made as careful preparations to capture it as our supply and manpower position permitted. But the first week of the renewed fighting had seen our forces concentrated on widening the corridor to the sea, and although our demolition squads broke through the Jaffa Gate twice and blew up snipers' buildings, it was not until Friday, July 16, that we could mount an attack on the scale necessary to have any chance against the new defenses organized by the Arab Legion. Even this was hurried; that same afternoon I had received instructions from Tel Aviv that we were to cease fire at 5:45 the next morning if the Arabs agreed to accept a new demand by the United Nations for a truce inside Jerusalem three days before the second truce became operative throughout the country.

So we had roughly five and a half hours. Shaltiel decided to make the try anyway, even though he was not completely ready and the time was too short. In this he was obviously right. We attacked at two points. Our troops broke into the Old City at the New Gate and established a bridgehead within the walls. We tried unsuccessfully to breach the wall near the Zion Gate with an unusually large charge of explosives, and our attacking unit had to withdraw. But this was as far as we could go in Operation *Kedem*, or Antiquity, which was the last Jewish attempt to recapture the Old City.

An unavoidable hitch had delayed the preliminary softening-up bombardment in this operation, which was a combined one, Hagana forces co-operating with Irgun Zvai Leumi and Lehi units. The enemy was expecting the attack and had concentrated large forces. The Arabs opened a violent bombardment along the whole length of the walls, since they did not know precisely where our attack would develop. At 3 A.M. New Gate was blown open by explosives, and our forces advanced 150 yards and seized ten buildings, which they held in expectation of a second wave of attack. This reinforcement did not materialize due to some failure in planning. Finally, at 5:45 A.M., the general order was given to all our troops to cease fire and break off the action, and those in the Old City were ordered to withdraw. One of the accidents which had delayed the commencement of the action and so conditioned the subsequent withdrawal was that an Arab shell scored a lucky hit on an ammunition vehicle which was in one of the rear bases of the Etzel detachment. Thousands of bullets were destroyed and two men were killed. The other incident was at the New Gate. There the Arabs had built a roadblock of wood and shavings. This was ignited by a shell, and it took twenty minutes before the blaze could be extinguished and our men could move forward. These were irrevocable, precious moments and it is on such flickers of fortune's eyelash that one can say the fate of the Old City was determined.

THE SIEGE OF JERUSALEM

Pauline Rose

> *Pauline Rose was invited to come to Jerusalem in 1945 by her sister. She made a trip in March 1946 and returned to England in June. She came again in Feburary of 1948, settled there, eventually on Mount Zion, and wrote two books recounting her experiences during the War of Independence and then the Six Day War.*

THE HOLY CITY

At midday, in blazing heat and dazzling sunshine, I arrived in Jerusalem—the Holy City.

My sister was waiting at the station to meet me, and I was welcomed by her friends. That same afternoon I was taken for a drive to Mount Scopus, and from that height I looked down upon Jerusalem.

The Old City walls encircled a small area from which rising towers, minarets, domes and spires were the visible signs of the invisible forces concentrated there. Outside the Old City the new one had grown, built of the same rough stone—a warm, rose-tinted yellow. New towers, domes and minarets outside the walls united the character of the old with the new.

I stayed at the King David Hotel and the first few days were filled with visits to all the places of interest which had emerged from the new creative life in the city—the Hadassah Hospital, the University, the Municipal Buildings, the children's home, the private houses. I saw also the many improvements and developments in the general amenities of life.

But besides all this outward expression and visible form, resulting from the creative activity which had returned to the land, I was most strongly impressed by the overwhelming spiritual forces at work in the unseen spheres.

Jerusalem, the centre, the focal point of all spiritual streams, seemed to have above its head a crystal globe divided into many fragments; each fragment suspended above one of the divers churches, synagogues and mosques, imbuing them with a power which flowed out into the world and returned again to its starting point—Jerusalem.

✑

There was a tense atmosphere of hostility in the city. Barbed wire protected the buildings occupied by the Mandatory Power. Armed British soldiers, armoured cars, and other warlike precautionary measures were apparent on all sides.

On June the 29th, 1946, at an hour between midnight and dawn, I was awakened by loud voices and the sound of motor cars and much activity in the streets. I was living in Rehavia, very near to the Jewish Agency Building.

Voices from loudspeakers, making important announcements, travelled through all the streets. Most of the noise and activity came from the direction of the Jewish Agency Building.

After a period of restrained curiosity I went downstairs and found R's husband sitting beside his radio.

"The Jewish Agency Building has been occupied by the British, and the leaders have been arrested," he said, in answer to my look of enquiry. "It is forbidden to go outside the door of one's home."

As I sat at breakfast with the family that morning, there was an atmosphere of depression and anxiety. During the many years they had lived in Jerusalem they had experienced so many disturbances. Their lives had been in danger so many times. What next?

THE OLD CITY

A Sabbath morning! The Old City is in flames! Smoke is rising from the burning synagogues within its walls!

Driven out of their burning homes, after months of attack, hunger and thirst, those brave Jewish people: men, women and children—a mere handful in comparison with the numbers of the enemy—have been forced to surrender. For many months they had defended their homes, their synagogue, their lives. With little ammunition, cut off from all supplies of arms and food, from all communication with their brethren outside the walls, their power to hold out so long cannot be explained in terms of this world.

✑

My friend Malla, the Rabbi's daughter, came in, looking very pale and distressed. She shook my hand.

"The women and children are being escorted out of the Old City to-day," she said. "Come with me to help in receiving them."

It was only ten minutes walk to Kiryath Shmuel, the suburb where many beautiful houses had been abandoned by the Arabs after battles during the previous weeks. In

The Stambuli Synagogue in the Old City after the liberation in 1967 (David Harris; with permission)

these empty houses the refugees were being lodged. Crowded together, sitting on the floor, all earthly possessions tied in a bundle beside them, were old men and women; rabbis who had spent their lives in the now smouldering synagogues of the Old City; women who knew nothing of the world beyond the homes in which they had served their husbands and families. Their primitive lives, lived in the tradition of centuries, were expressed in their faces.

They were now uprooted from their world, unable to grasp the meaning of the calamity that had befallen them. Some wept in despair; others were resigned—praying silently whilst a few shouted hysterically in anger and bitterness. Then there were the younger women, and the sad faces of children with fear in their eyes and thin half-starved bodies. Young mothers held babies in their arms. Signs of suffering were on all faces. In the streets more were arriving—old men and women. The young men were held prisoners by the Arabs.

It was a very hot day. The refugees carried their tins, begging for a drink. There was no water.

An old woman saw Malla and fell at her feet weeping. She had been a neighbour of theirs in the Old City. Words were difficult between them.

"Everything has gone," the woman muttered between her sobs. "At first they came into our houses and shot at us. Then, as they set fire to our homes, we retreated. We hid for days in cellars and kept alive with a little food we had stored. When they came to burn the last houses, we had to surrender."

"And our home?" asked Malla, her last hope dying. For a moment the old woman could not answer. Then she cried: "I saw it burning with my own eyes."

I remembered again the portrait of Malla's sister, who had died in Poland—her mother's most precious possession; the old Rabbi's *Tenach* which he valued above all things, and which even the Nazis had permitted him to take with him. I remembered the different things that had been collected together to make that home in the Old City. What the Nazis had permitted them to take out of their Polish home the Arabs had destroyed in their home in Jerusalem!

I looked at Malla. She was very pale and very brave.

"They can destroy our possessions and burn our houses," she said. "But we will build new ones. They cannot take our land from us. We are in Israel."

There were shouts and people were running to the end of the dusty road—the water-cart had arrived! Each one received a small ration of water. Later the bread arrived and was cut into measured chunks. There was nothing else that day. The next day there was hot soup, a little margarine, and some black olives.

Smoke was still rising from the burning synagogues and homes in the Old City. The flames had done their work.

🆚

14th May, 1948

With the obvious signs of the infant state in the womb of Israel nearing its time of delivery, a hostile world intrigued to bring about a pre-natal destruction, or at least to cripple the life that would not be destroyed.

The Jewish right to freedom in the land of Israel could not be denied, but it would be restricted freedom in a partitioned land; a divided state, where the neighbour state could be used as a mask for the hostile world.

With the acceptance of partition, the labour pains commenced. The Jewish State was about to be born! The painful travail of the past six months was in the final stage preceding birth.

It was the last day of the British Mandate. British military forces were evacuating their security zone in Jerusalem. All the Government officials were ready to leave. The High Commissioner bade farewell to Jerusalem over the radio.

The Sabbath eve! The shooting died down. All through the night the imminent event cast an awed silence over the city. Jerusalem waited breathlessly.

🆚

15th May, 1948

The pre-natal pains are over! Amidst bloodshed, suffering and anguish, in an atmosphere of hostility, the Jewish State is born. It is named: "The State of Israel" and is destined to withstand all its enemies. It is born a partitioned land, not yet receiving the full blood-stream from its throbbing heart—Jerusalem!

The frustrated world is compelled to accept the partitioned State—the body. But Jerusalem—the heart, the soul—is the seat of the battle.

On this momentous day of birth—the Sabbath day—I write from the city of Jerusalem, the Jewish city, the Holy City. The palpitating heartbeats, throbbing with life's destiny, can be felt in all people, in all places, at all times.

In the morning the hushed silence continued, charged with suppressed excitement, fearful expectancy, anxiety-veiled joy. The streets are emptier than usual. Small groups of people gather anxiously and curiously at corners near the entrance to "Bevingrad," the evacuated British security zone. Later the Jewish flag is hoisted on the "Generale Building," which had housed the British police. Only an occasional shot is heard in the distance.

The silence is tense; the people wait for the proclamation of birth. No newspapers! No electricity! No radio broadcast! Undercurrents of suppressed joy and fear flow through the city in alternate waves.

What is happening to the new-born life? Will it be allowed to take breath? Will the world accept it? Are the enemies' fingers round its throat intending to strangle it?

The heartbeats are loud and fast in the Jewish city of Jerusalem.

Before long the silence is broken; the awe of birth is over. The guns, silenced momentarily by the powers turning the page of destiny, open fire and volleys of shots are poured into the throbbing heart of Israel's city.

Moslems, aided by "Christians," are attacking the Jews from Mount Zion. . . .

☙

18th May, 1948

It is two days since the birth of the State of Israel. An aftermath of pain, anguish, fear and bloodshed; of courage, sacrifice and faith; of chained freedom and obscured joy.

The enemy surrounds us—is on our doorstep! Terrible battles are in progress. All sections of the Jewish city are being shelled. Heavy explosions continually rend the air, leaving behind a trail of destruction, death, pain and shattered nerves. Helpless men, women and children are being injured and killed. Shops are closed, streets are cleared. Jerusalem is a desolate city: no food, no water supply, no lighting, no news broadcasts. All able men and women are called up for full-time service. The enemy is pushing at the door. . . .

Jerusalem is like a city under sentence of death, bearing within it the certainty of life. The heart of Israel cannot be destroyed. Death in the Holy City can only mean resurrection—new life.

☙

20th May, 1948

A deathly pallor still rests on the face of Jerusalem. From midnight to dawn the cannons roared, shells exploded, machine guns rattled, and every other type of gun added

Rockets firing over Mount Zion in June of 1948 (photograph by Werner Braun; with permission)

to the infernal noise which penetrated every house in the city. The sleepless, helpless inhabitants listened in tense silence and darkness to the battle of life and death.

With the first rays of dawn, the birds made a brave effort to counteract the nerve-racking sounds of continuous battle. The light of day brought with it the relief of abated shooting and shelling, followed by a period of comparative quiet.

I went out to get some news. The *Palestine Post*—for the first time in its history—could not be printed. We received a few stenciled pages. News passed from mouth to mouth.

"Mount Zion is in Jewish hands!"

"Our flag flies on the Tower of David!"

"The Haganah have joined up with the defenders within the Old City!"

Fifteen hundred Jews had held their positions for many days against thirty thousand Arabs within the walls of the Old City! Last night a handful of Jews penetrated the massive ramparts surrounding the city, and brought relief to the brave defenders within.

News items continued to be passed on.

"Reinforcements of troops, guns and tanks are pouring in for the Arab Legion."

"Amongst the captured Arab prisoners are British officers. . . ."

As I write bullets and shells whiz past overhead, exploding at all distances, near and far. Women and children strained with fear, anxiety, lack of food and water, and many sleepless terrifying night, seek safe places of shelter.

Darkness is now awaiting the departure of the sun. It is symbolic that Jerusalem is at this time without light. In the utter darkness of this life and death struggle, the light of prayer is making a trail in the heart of mankind. There is much prayer opening the way to God in this tormented city. It will need more prayer and dependence upon the God of Israel, before the State of Israel can come into its full inheritance.

The struggle for the new life continues, the shadows are darkening. What has this night is store for us?

GOING INTO CAPTIVITY

Aharon Liron

> *Aharon Liron fought in the War of Independence and was one of the defenders of the Old City of Jerusalem. Afterwards, he felt it a duty to tell the entire story of the seige of the Old City and the battles surrounding it in a comprehensive book in Hebrew titled* The Old City of Jerusalem in Siege and Battle.

More than once history records that the leaders and commanders of Jerusalem met in fateful sessions to debate the future of their city. Thus King Zedekiah and his ministers convened in the days of the First Temple. Thus too the leaders of the revolt in Second Temple times met, and thus did the leaders of the Jews and the Arabs meet in the days of the Crusades. And now so too did the commanders, heads of the community and the representative of the military (Mr. Ben-Shemesh) convene for the distressing, fateful and historic meeting that Friday. May 28, 1948, at 13:00 hours in one of the rooms of Batei Mahse.

Mr. Mordechai Weingarten and Commander Shaul Tawil gave a report of their mission:

> We proposed a cease-fire so that the wounded could be evacuated and the dead removed from the Quarter, but Abdullah Bek al-Tel refused to accept this proposal. He contended that in a previous incident (in the Katamon neighborhood) the Jews had taken advantage of the lull in fighting to reorganize and afterwards conquered the entire area of Katamon. "Therefore," he contended, "this is war. I have casualties and you have casualties. I do not evacuate mine, and you do not evacuate yours." He proposed instead that we surrender according to the terms he proposed, and the delegates accepted his idea.

At the conclusion of the meeting an open, individual vote was taken. Everyone there was asked if he was for or against surrender. One after the other, they all voted for surrender, with the exception of Issar, who abstained.

Mr. Weingarten and Commander Tawil left in order to formulate the final terms. The leaders of the Legion wanted Moshe Rusnak to personally sign the document of surrender, and in the end he went out and joined the talks in which the document was being formulated. According to the recollection of those who participated in formulating it the document went as follows:

> Since the Jews requested a cease-fire, the representative of His Majesty Abdullah, Abdullah Bek al-Tel, presented the following terms, which the Jews have accepted, and these are they:
>
> 1. All armaments, weapons and military equipment will be surrendered.
>
> 2. All males capable of carrying arms will be taken into captivity. It has been verbally agreed that the captives will be taken to Amman under the supervision of the United Nations commander for Jerusalem, Dr. Pablo de Azcarate.
>
> 3. All inhabitants, women and children, wounded and fighters, will be evacuated from the Jewish Quarter and taken outside the Old City under the supervision of the representative of the United Nations. Inhabitants who so wish may remain in the Quarter under the protection of the Legion and will enjoy the same rights as all other inhabitants of the Old City.
>
> 4. The signatory to this agreement on behalf of King Abdullah is responsible, in his name and in the name of his fellow officers and commanders, for the well-being of all the inhabitants taken captive and all the wounded until they arrive at their destination.
>
> 5. The conquest of the Jewish Quarter by the armies of the Arab Legion is complete.

"At approximately 14:00 hours, in the headquarters of Abdullah Bek El-Tel, I signed two copies of this document—one in Arabic and one in English," relates the military commander of the Quarter, Moshe Rusnak. "Abdullah Bek al-Tel and Dr. Azcarate also signed. Azcarate was the representative of the United Nations. I had several run-ins with him. Tel had agreed to several of my additional demands, such as the presence of a representative of the Red Cross, and I took it upon myself to invite him to come from the city, but solely because of Azcarate no representative of the Red Cross was actually present. Mr. Weingarten also wanted to sign the document. Abdullah Tel said that the signature of the commander of the Haganah was sufficient for him. Weingarten insisted and Abdullah Tel agreed. Tel took one copy and gave me the other. We returned with Abdullah Tel to the Jewish Quarter in order to execute the agreement. Since I wanted our organizations to receive the copy I had—so that they could demand that the agreement be carried out properly and could retain the historic document—I turned it over to Mr. Weingarten, while we were returning to the Quarter. I assumed that he would not be a captive, but the document did not reach its intended destination."

The first few moments after we received the news of the decision to surrender, we did not know how to react.

"You are going to Jerusalem," we said to the women enviously.

They were sad. They looked at us encouraging but with pity, "And you are journey-ing to Rabbat-Ammon."

The group at Batei Mahse grew larger. The inhabitants came out of their hiding places and filled the square and the courtyards, talking with one another about the terms of surrender.

Those stationed at the various posts came running to ask what their instructions were. At first the commanders themselves did not know what should be done.

When the initial confusion had passed, runners were sent to all the posts with Motke Pincas' message: "All arms are to be collected and put into the yard at Batei Mahse. Lose yourselves among the inhabitants."

When the messenger came to the position at Batei Mahse he found the guys dis-cussing whose turn it was to clean the weapons. . . .

A few of them amused themselves with target practice. For the first time they wanted a taste of not having to conserve ammunition. . . .

Many of us washed our feet for the first time in two weeks. Those who had spare clothes, changed their garments.

Judith Jaran came into the hospital in a panic: "What's to be done? Some Arabs rec-ognized me. They are pointing at me and whispering."

We calmed her down and found a solution: we cut her hair, put her in a nurse's uni-form and she went to tend the wounded.

We were surprised by the first Arab officer who entered the hospital accompanied by two sergeants. His manner was restrained and his look was pleasant. He sat down to drink some coffee and said, "Those are the fortunes of war."

Mother saw Haim and approached him, her head bowed. Haim lifted up her face with his finger upon her chin. "Mother, I want you to laugh," he said. She smiled a mo-ment, then tears welled up in her eyes and she began to sob.

"Don't worry," Haim comforted her. "You have other sons. Tell Yosef to take revenge upon them as much as possible. . . . I hope those outside will continue the fight."

Many of the troops who had been sent as reinforcements, mainly the older ones and the heads of families, removed their garments in the room where I was, and put on civil-ian clothes, especially Hassidic garments. Some went to various families in order to leave with them as family members. One succeeded.

When I left that room I suddenly met Albert, the only British soldier to have joined us on the thirteenth of May.

"What will happen to you?" I asked him.

"I spoke with the British commander of the Arab Legion," he replied, "and requested to be taken captive with you. We will go together."

At exactly 17:00 hours, when Legionnaires were already walking around the nearby rooms, the last message concerning the surrender was broadcast by wireless to Jerusalem: "We have surrendered according to the terms of evacuation. Tell Mount Zion to be pre-pared to receive us. Tell the hospital to prepare places. It is not clear if they intend to take captives. They are liable to take the fighters. In the meantime, it is probable that the place will be evacuated." After the departure, the office was destroyed, to the distress of Yael, the teacher, who had sat there for weeks on end, night and day, red-eyed, and Uri Golani, who had been in charge of the technical areas.

Afterwards, all the papers belonging to the Haganah and to Etzel were destroyed.

In the late afternoon hours the orders were given: "Everyone is to assemble in the yard of Batei Mahse. The wounded are to go into the hospital immediately."

A group of Legionnaires entered the Quarter in order to carry out the surrender agreement.

Abdullah Bek al-Tel, the military commander of Arab Jerusalem on behalf of the Legion, personally directed the action, in the presence of Moshe Rusnak, the commander of the Haganah in the Jewish Quarter. He looked over the group and then called out, "All the soldiers are to be separated out."

To the consternation of the entire group, the first to come forth was Reb Moshe Yitzhak, an elderly man of seventy-eight, bent over, leaning on his cane, who stepped forward very slowly. An old man like that—and a resident yet! Among the residents, especially the Ashkenazic ones, we had seen many who were not particularly positive toward us.

What he did made such a strong impression that the young men who had thought to try to sneak into Jerusalem as residents stepped forward from the group—almost all of them—some thirty-five. Motke Pincas lined them up. When the Arab commander saw the number of fighters who had stood up to his entire army he was terribly ashamed: "That is all the soldiers?" he asked. "Thirty-five men killed more than two hundred of our soldiers? Had I known that before, I would have sent in my men armed with batons."

And here he was going to have to display his captives all along the route—in the villages of Jerusalem, in Jericho, in Shuna, in A-Salt, in Amman, in Zarka and in Mifrak. What is he going to display? Thirty-five men? He will become a laughing stock. No indeed! The victory must make a strong impression in the Arab world. He commanded his troops to take every man they could see. The old, the sick, youngsters, children were all taken. When Moshe Rusnak protested, Abdullah Tel replied that he would sort them properly later.

The men were lined up and proceeded under guard.

Before the evacuation of the residents to the area outside the wall, we were asked to send someone out to the Jewish forces on Mount Zion to make contact with them. Commander Nissan Zeldas, who was appointed for that task, was summoned to Abdullah Tel and assured him that he would return. He went out with Hava Kirshenbaum, carrying a white flag. They left through Zion Gate and contacted the members of the Palmach. The next morning Nissan and Hava Kirshenbaum returned, as promised, in order to maintain the honor of the Jewish soldier.

A group of Legionnaires entered the hospital with orders to take out anyone who appeared healthy. They took any wounded man who could walk around and sent them to the group of residents who were still gathered in the yard. We sat crowded on both sides of the wide porch on piles of mattresses. Inside the wounded lay on beds or on the ground.

The row of buildings opposite hid the yard and all that happened there from our view. From afar arose a loud sound of voices which gradually became quieter until it disappeared in the distance. A strange quiet reigned. Our ears were accustomed to constant noise—to the sound of shooting, to echoes of explosions, to the explosion of shells, and now all sound disappeared and it was as if our ears were deprived of something. We seemed to continue to hear those sounds. The noise of shooting and the explosion of bullets still echoed in our ears.

Fighters from the Legionnaires and other armed groups passed between the rows of mattresses. The Arab fighters who knew the people who lived here, approached, shook hands and joked with one another. Conversations were started. The Arabs expressed their surprise, even disbelief, at the small quantity of our weapons and the small number of our soldiers.

Our people answered sharply: "It's not such a big thing to conquer a small area like ours when you have so much ammunition and so many soldiers. If we had had your arms, you wouldn't be here now."

Everything was murky. The red color of the roof opposite us was dim and mixed little by little with the yellow-rose wall. Everything was dull and gray. The windows became dark stains and the shadows of the columns and their arches stood out on the facade of the building opposite.

A red light which illuminated the wall of the next building drew my attention.

"They have lit a bonfire in the yard," someone said as if talking to himself.

Our guards sat down on chairs, leaned their rifles against the wall and looked around indolently. There was a slight breeze. Talk was frozen, only silence emerged from the depth of our hearts, memories, pictures, experiences and feelings; we were disturbed, full of questions, wanting answers, wanting to understand why and how this had ended thus. It was a time of soul searching.

An experience full of hope and pain is coming to an end. Difficulties, gratefulness, shame and glory. Yes, glory. Many of us will remember with thanks the doctors, the nurses, the medics, the women and the girls who cooked, washed and performed all kinds of services. Last but not least—the children. The doctors who tended at least four hundred cases, operated well into the night by the light of kerosene lamps, and only at dawn managed to get some sleep on the operating room floor; those who washed garments for the hospital during all the days of fighting; those who cooked, supplying three meals a day and hot drinks twenty-four hours a day! Sixteen-year-old Sarah who obtained all the needed supplies for the kitchen; the baker who managed to make pitta for us even when it was dangerous; the children, from eight to sixteen, who brought food and ammunition to the various positions and conveyed orders and information, even in the most dangerous times—tremendous work done with courage and heroism such as one sees only occasionally even among soldiers. Children—messengers—wounded and even killed. Glory to all of them!

A street in the Jewish Quarter of the Old City, ca. 1944 (Central Zionist Archives; with permission)

JERUSALEM EMBATTLED

Harry Levin

> The Levines, Harry and Anita, had come to Jerusalem from England and recorded their experiences during the seige of the city.

May 29

There is a motionless haze over the Old City, like a ghastly jelly. Only the nearer sky-line is smudged with smoke and shimmering with heat. All the colours have disappeared; the habitual blue, pink, green, are all grey now. A great silence and solitude enwrap it. Out of the haze a single smoke spiral has pushed its way upward, very tall and slender and elegant. I picture the crackling flames below it, the stones turning black.

Hard to think of the Old City without a single Jew. When last was there such a time? Nearly eight hundred years ago Maimonides found Jews there. The old underground Synagogue of Yohanan ben Zakkai is reputed to have been standing nearly two thousand years ago; now, like the neighbouring Hurva, it is a shambles. Jews were in the Old City when the Seljuks conquered it, and in the days of the Crusades, and when the Turks took it over. Allenby found them when he conquered it from the Turks. But today not one is left.

I watched the refugees arrive at the once elegant Park Lane Hotel in Katamon; from there they will be distributed among the Katamon houses. Some of them have not seen the sun for weeks, hardly ventured out of their Old City cellars even into the darkness of the night. Only the children seemed to be living in the present. They streamed in by the hundreds, older ones holding younger brothers and sisters by the hand. They sat there in the sunshine, some in speechless misery, others just solemn and quiet, absorbing the relative freedom from terror, their eyes taking in this strange new world of modern houses. Most of the adults were not even sad, just stupefied and exhausted. Their yellow, bloodless faces and lean hands moved in slow motion. But some were utterly broken.

There was one man whose face keeps floating though my consciousness. I spoke to a girl who was trying to help him. She was a social worker who knew him well. A devout, simple man, unworldly, who barely made a living out of his little shop. He used to speak about the Old City with a depth of feeling that moved her. To live there was not for him, as for some other natives, a birthright taken for granted, nor, as for others, a mark of superior lineage. Old Jerusalem was something whose shadows he felt it a privilege to touch. Until the siege of the Jewish Quarter, he prayed daily at the Wailing Wall. When his father's *Yahrzeit* (death anniversary) came around he was resolved at least to recite the Kaddish at the Wall. Through the Jewish and Arab lines he found a way of contacting an Arab friend who smuggled him through the Arab quarter and watched over him while he prayed at the Wall. For the first time in weeks, the social worker saw him again during the evacuation this morning. His cheeks were wet. His feet dragged along the ground; he stumbled. suddenly gone very aged and frail. I watched him now sitting in a corner at the Park Lane Hotel: an empty shell of a man whose soul had died within him. Only stiff, shrunken limbs were left and eyes that saw nothing.

Esther C. is dead, wounded on Thursday by a shell that crashed into her *emda* (position). She died very early this morning, while evacuation was under way. It was her second injury. A week ago she was wounded in the hip, but left the bed to join in the last desperate defence. "That's where they need me most," I remember the last words she said to me, "in the Old City. . . ."

The Legion behaved well. After the surrender yesterday they formed a cordon round the remnant of the Jewish Quarter. When the frenzied rabble got out of hand, howling for the Jews to be handed to them, the Legion fired to keep them at bay. Finally, when the fires the mob started threatened the hospital, Legionnaires forced a way out for the patients into the Armenian Quarter. There were only two orderlies, and no stretchers. All but the most gravely injured had to stumble on their feet, one helping the other. When the Jewish relief party arrived at dawn with the Red Cross to remove them to the new city, the seventy patients were lying on the paving stones of an Armenian courtyard. Behind the wall of the Armenian Quarter, a few hundred yards away, the Jewish hospital had gone up in flames.

THE FIRST YOM HAATZMAUT

Yona Cohen

> Born in Jerusalem in 1920, Yona Cohen worked as a journalist on HaTzofe and wrote many books on Jerusalem and Israeli life. This excerpt is taken from Jerusalem Under Siege, which was written during the events of the founding of the State and immediately thereafter.

5 Iyyar 5705; May 4, 1949

The first independence festival in Jerusalem. The rejoicing cannot be described. For some reason, it feels as if many years have passed since "the British left us alone."

There was true joy for each and every Jerusalemite. Each one gave this Independence festival an individual flavor. One person decorated his balcony with flowers, hangings and pictures of the early dreamers and fighters for the establishment of Israel. The wall of the Poel Mizrachi restaurant on Strauss Street was decorated with pictures of the struggle for independence. Others put up signs on their balconies with such slogans as "We were born for freedom," "As the days of suffering and the years of our oppression, so is our rejoicing," "Jerusalem—a city of strength unto us," and so forth.

At the Orion cinema they had a free showing all day long of the "Carmel" newsreel showing scenes from the building of the young state. The agency for the newspaper *Maariv* showed slides on the wall on Ben-Yehuda Street about the nation and the state. In synagogues special prayers were recited in memory of the fallen in the war of liberation.

In the middle of the day all Jerusalem gathered to watch the festive IDF parade. No one stayed home. All the sidewalks on the streets in the center of town and the balconies were crowded with people. Some who had been invited to be guests of honor in Tel Aviv preferred to stay in their own city, Jerusalem, in which they had suffered and could now enjoy some relief.

In the Valley of the Cross, in the field which was once used as the Jerusalem airstrip, where, during the siege, the "Primusim" had helped more than a bit to strengthen the hands of the defenders and the residents, the army held a review. The hills surrounding it were full of people. To the sound of the police band, the army marched through the streets: Ramban, Usishkin, Keren Kayemet, King David, Strauss, Meah

An early Independence Day celebration in Jerusalem, date unknown (Central Zionist Archives; with permission)

Shearim and Turim. Next to the Histadrut building the reviewing stand was erected upon which sat the Chief of Staff, Yaakov Dori, the commander of the army for Jerusalem, Segan Aluf Moshe Dayan, the commander of the front, Tvi Ayyalon, Aluf David Shaltiel, and the former military commander of Jerusalem, Dov Joseph.

The parade lasted about an hour and was saluted by all those commanders. A group of motorcycle troops were at the front, followed by mounted troops carrying the flag, open cars in which stood the commanders of the Sixth Division and the region. After them, one following the other, came the Moriah division and the other groups, the communications corp, which by rather primitive means had managed to keep in touch with isolated groups and settlements far away from the Jerusalem area and save them from the feeling of isolation. The mine sweepers, flame throwers, veterans of the Hagana—and at their head the flag of Jerusalem. The people's guard, the youth brigades whose honored role in repulsing the enemy is well known to all. The women's corps—Chen—the medical service and the Red Star of David. Donkeys and their owners which had carried stretchers and the wounded. Armored trucks and half-tracks. Artillery, light and heavy, jeeps and cannons which the Jerusalemites cheered mightily. The engineering corp and heavy trucks. The transportation corp and mobile units for repairing trucks. Fire-fighters; and in a special car, wounded soldiers. At the rear came people from settlements near Jerusalem in their cars which were decorated with greenery and banners with the words: We willed it—and it is no longer a dream.

In the late afternoon the army held a variegated athletics demonstration at the Y.M.C.A. field. In the evening many guests arrived, foreign consuls, heads of various institutions and cities were received by the regional head, Dr. A. Bergman (Biran). The police band played and guests spent many pleasant hours in this aura of celebration.

At night huge crowds gathered at the Valley of the Cross where massive bonfires were lit and the regional commander, Levi Yitchak (Levicha) greeted the celebrants in Jerusalem. A ballet troupe performed, and the "Voice of Jerusalem Symphony" played. The "Tzizbatron" group entertained the audience with skits about army life. The Gadna did a sports demonstration. The celebration concluded with folk-dancing with the Harel troupe, girls from Chen, and so forth.

In a modest but appropriate ceremony, a scroll was placed in the foundation of the memorial for the defenders of Jerusalem in Nordau Circle in Romema. Among the signatories were the Chief Rabbis Herzog and Uziel, members of the city council, the board of the Jewish Agency, the commanders of the IDF and others.

This is what was written in the scroll:

> ... One thousand, eight hundred seventy-nine years after the conquest of Jerusalem by the enemy, the year one of the beginning of her redemption and her liberation by the State of Israel, we lay this cornerstone in the entrance to the city as a memorial to the holy and pure, the defenders of Jerusalem, her fighters and guardians, her redeemers and liberators who sacrificed their lives for her sake during the time of siege and who did not live to see her joy.
>
> This stone is a witness to the gallantry of those who hurled their lives into her defence and stood in the breach when Ishmael and Edom rose against us to seize Jerusalem from Israel; to the heroes of the underground secret war

The Independence Day celebration, May 4, 1949, at Mar Salaba ground (photograph by Freund. Central Zionist Archives; with permission)

who were not recognized as soldiers and not permitted to wear uniforms and wave flags—they did not live as soldiers, but died like them.

This stone is a witness to those who died defending Jerusalem in the years 5680–5681 (1920), to those of her defenders who were a wall around her for three years and fell in the years 5696–5699 (1935–1939), to those of her fighters who fell in the War of Liberation and Redemption in the years 5708–5709 (1947–1948).

This stone is a witness that Jerusalem has not been and will not be separated from the body of the State of Israel and from the heart of the people of Israel; for her sake we have been slain, we her sons and daughters, residents of the Land and of the Diaspora who came to her aid and opened a road to her when the enemy placed her under siege.

Through their blood have we reached this day upon which we dedicate the cornerstone of this memorial, for Jerusalem is part of Israel in the sight of the sun, Israel and the nations.

This stone is a witness and this monument is a witness to those things which have not yet been accomplished and which it is our duty to do; it is a witness to those heroes who fell in a battle which was hopeless, the few against the many, devoid of armament against heavy arms, when they defended the Old City and the settlements cut off in the hills of Judea and Jerusalem, and in their deaths they commanded us to complete the task of liberating the holy city, the city of David, the heart of Israel and of liberating all the settlements of Israel in the Land of Israel which fell into enemy hands.

Thus ends these chapters of this diary. The story of the battle for the life of Jerusalem, her liberty, unity, greatness and glory continues and will continue until God establishes her forever as the joy of the entire world, the city of the great King.

A GENERATION'S DREAM IS REALIZED

Uzi Narkiss

> *General Uzi Narkiss, born in Jerusalem, served in the army for twenty-seven years and was the commanding officer of Central Command during the Six Day War; he was responsible for the battle that liberated the Old City.*

At 9:00 came Motta's [Motta Gur—ed.] message that Augusta Victoria had been captured and everyone at Binyanei Ha'ooma was seized with its impact. The time has come. We were upon the walls.

"Shall we move?" I murmured impatiently.

We moved.

The forward H.Q. group—two half-tracks and two jeeps—were waiting and in we climbed, with Didi Menussi and Raffi Amie, a Kol Israel man, whom Didi had graciously invited for "the experience of your life." We drove toward the Mandelbaum Gate, still

The Mandelbaum Gate passage between new and old Jerusalem, 1968 (Central Zionist Archives; with permission)

blocked because of the mines, and therefore switched direction to the P.Ag.I. houses, taking the paratroops' assault axis to the police school. I wanted to get to the Rockefeller Museum to see Motta, since I'd had no contact with him after he announced the occupation of Augusta Victoria. We passed the East Jerusalem Y.M.C.A., whose smashed windows and besmirched walls gave bleak evidence of battle. The American Consulate on the right was also battle-scarred; a destroyed gas station stood next to the temporary memorial erected by the paratroopers to their fallen comrades. We sped by, passing an undamaged mosque and the bullet-riddled buildings in an alley, called "the Alley of Death" by paratroopers, for the fallen who had attempted to rescue their comrades.

Suddenly the [city] wall rose before us, and the battlements of Nablus Gate. The Gate was not yet ours; Legionnaires guarded the parapet and we turned back to Salah e-Din Street, where broken windows, burned automobiles, and derelict electric wires spoke of war. Opposite the Rivoli Hotel was a damaged Egged bus and several paratroopers. I asked what they were doing.

"Wounded evacuation point," one replied.

"Are there wounded?"

"Two, not seriously."

"And what's ahead?"

"Don't know. Shooting."

Another group of paratroopers halted our advance, warning about shooting at the end of the road, where Salah e-Din Street meets Herod's Gate and the Old City walls. We could travel on it no farther and turned around, Haim Bar-Lev taking the wheel. Back on Nablus Road, we encountered all the terrible and pathetic remnants of war: death and destruction and chaos. Nothing stirred.

"I think they've all run away," I said to Bar-Lev.

The next day proved me wrong. The residents of East Jerusalem had simply hidden in their cellars, to emerge when the shooting stopped.

By 09:45 we were on Mount Scopus, gazing at the town below, which seemed idle and empty. All at once I saw smoke rising inside the Old City, behind the walls, and contacted Arik. "Are the paratroopers shelling the Old City?" When he said that they were, I ordered him to stop immediately, and at the same moment, I heard the paratroop G-Branch officer commanding his mortar units to stop shooting.

"We're going in," he cried.

"Where are you?" I called.

"At the Lions' Gate," and before the last word had been uttered we were back in our vehicles, racing down the mountain, our hearts as loud as the motors. We were going into the Old City!

Nineteen years earlier we had broken through the Zion Gate and entered the Jewish Quarter, only to leave it again in despair and bitter disappointment.

"Let us not go in if it's just to go out another time," I breathed.

"We shall never leave again," said Haim Bar-Lev.

Our convoy was on the slope of the hill below Rockefeller, where the road branches towards Gethsemane. From the corner position on the wall opposite, shots were still coming, and beneath, on the traffic island, was a silent Sherman tank and the sunshade of the policeman who was not on duty to use it.

The intermittent shots of the snipers could be heard from the walls. I threw a smoke-grenade, under cover of which we crossed to the abandoned tank, which had been hit the night before during the "Battle on the Bridge."

Snipers fired on a column of paratroopers, who marched on without changing pace, like men fatiqued to the point of trance. One fell, and then another, but forward tramped the rest.

Next to the damaged tank, completely exposed, a paratrooper with a bazooka stood, legs apart, fighting a private duel with the snipers on the walls. He silenced the corner position.

We went back to the cars, abandoning the slow-moving half-tracks, and sped off in the jeeps. Ahead, on the road from the valley to the Lions' Gate, was a column of paratroopers, led by General Rabbi Shlomo Goren, Chief Army Chaplain, a *sefer Torah* under his arm, a shofar in his left hand, his beard bristling like the point of a spear, and his face bathed in perspiration. He was panting.

"Rabbi," I called out, "come aboard. We're going to the same place."

"No," he replied, "to the Temple Mount one goes on foot."

"Then we'll meet there." The jeep sprang forward. On the move I contacted Motta to find out where he was.

"The Temple Mount is ours!"

I couldn't believe it.

"I repeat," said Motta. "The Temple Mount is ours. I'm standing near the Mosque el-Omar right now. The Western Wall is a minute away."

Now was the time for the jeep to sprout wings, but at the moment it lacked not just wings but one of its wheels. Bang, and the jeep veered so sharply that only with all my strength could I stop it before it tumbled off the road. The tire was in shreds. We had no time or inclination to change. We crowded into the second jeep, leaving Yoel Herzl with the radio, thus cutting ourselves off from contact and the possibility of finding out what was going on. But, more important, we drove up the narrow road toward Lions' Gate. On the square in front of it an Arab bus was steadily burning. Electric cables were down. Legionnaires' bodies lay all around; a section of the gate had been torn from its hinges; the second section was flung open, and the arch above the Gate had been hit, so that its loose masonry threatened the heads of passers-by. But the carved lions were undamaged.

We drove through, along the road to the Gate of the Tribes and the Temple Mount, and down the Via Dolorosa to the second arch. It was blocked by the lead tank of the paratroopers. We climbed over it and continued on foot.

Yoel, behind us, picked off a sniper shooting at us from one of the houses. Except for that, the Via Dolorosa was cool and silent, the windows shuttered, the streets empty. Had our men been through here, I wondered. Beyond the second arch lay King Feisal Street, a brief, narrow, covered, tunnel-like lane, closed at the far end by a wide gate with a small wicket where pedestrians entered. This, too, was closed, but the bolt was not locked. We stepped through, and the breath caught in our throats.

We beheld the huge paved courtyard, crowned, against the blue sky of June 7th, 1967 (the 28th of the month of Iyar in the year 5727), by the golden cupola of the Dome of the Rock, gleaming, glistening, taking its gold from the sun.

A spectacle of legend.

We ran toward Motta Gur, standing on the Mount, where the flag of Israel flew. We were joined first by Moshe Stempel, Motta's deputy, and then by Rabbi Goren. We embraced and the Rabbi prostrated himself and genuflected toward the Holy of Holies. In a resonant voice he recited the ancient Prayer to Battle (Deut. 20:3–4):

> Hear, O Israel, ye approach this day into battle against your enemies; let not your hearts faint, fear not, and do not tremble, neither be ye terrified because of them; for the Lord your God is he that goeth with you, to fight for you against your enemies, to save you!

Hastily, I visited the Mosque and was delighted to find no damage, except to a glass door from the brief battle in the courtyard. There had apparently been resistance from inside. As the cleaning up continued, I told Motta once again to make sure that no holy places or shrines were touched.

We made our excited way through the streets to the Mugrabis' Gate, along a dim alley, turned right down a slight of steps, impatiently faced another right turn—and there it was. The Western Wall. I quivered with memory. Tall and awesome and glorious, with the same ferns creeping between the great stones, some of them inscribed.

Silently I bowed my head. In the narrow space were paratroopers, begrimed, fatigued, overburdened with weapons. And they wept. They were not "wailing at the Western Wall," not lamenting in the fashion familiar during the Wall's millennia of being. These were tears of joy, of love, of passion, of an undreamed first reunion with the ancient monument to devotion and to prayer. They clung to its stones, kissed them, these rough, battle-weary paratroopers, their lips framing the *Shema*. Returned, it seemed to the Temple. . . .

But more exalted, prouder than all of them, was Rabbi Goren. Wrapped in a *Tallit* (prayer shawl), blowing the ram's horn, and roaring like a lion: "Blessed be the Lord God, Comforter of Zion and Builder of Jerusalem, Amen!" Suddenly he saw me, embraced me, and planted a ringing kiss on my cheek, a signal to everyone to hug and kiss and join hands. The Rabbi, like one who had waited all his life for this moment, intoned the *Kaddish*, the *El moleh Rahamim* (O God, full of mercy . . .), in memory of those who had fallen in the name of the Lord to liberate the Temple, the Temple Mount and Jerusalem the City of the Lord: "May they find their peace in Heaven . . . and let us say Amen."

The restrained weeping became sobs, full-throated, an uncurbed emotional outburst. Sorrow, fervor, happiness and pain combined to produce this mass of grieving and joyous men, their cheeks wet, their voices unsteady. Again the *shofar* was blown: *tekiya* (a short, but unbroken sound), followed by the *shevarim* (a short but tremolo sound). And Rabbi Goren intoned, like a herald: "This year, at this hour, in Jerusalem!" (*le-shana hazot, be-sha'a hazot, beYerushalayim.*)

Until that moment I had thought I was immune to anything. Even the stones responded. "We shall stand at attention and salute! Attention!" I shouted. "And sing *Hatikva*," came the choked voice of Haim Bar-Lev. We started to sing. To our voices were added those of the paratroopers, hoarse and indistinct. Sobbing and singing, it was as though, through the *Hatikva*, we could unburden our hearts of their fullness and our spirits of their emotion.

We spent ten minutes in front of the Western Wall and at 10:55 were on our way back to the basement of Binyanei Ha'ooma. There was plenty of work to be done. The Old City had not yet been cleared of snipers, and the West Bank had not yet been taken.

Meanwhile, we learned, the Jerusalem Brigade had at the last minute made an improvised entry into the Old City through the Dung Gate. Amos, the G-Branch officer, having heard the 55th Brigade's announcement that Augusta Victoria had been taken, realized that the paratroops would immediately break into the Old City and determined that Zahal's Jerusalem Brigade, which for nineteen years had defended the divided city, must participate in that historic entry. Two companies of the battalion which took Abu-Tor were assembled at Mount Zion and moved along the Walls to the Silwan stream to enter through the Dung Gate. They reached the Temple Mount shortly after 10 A.M. and from there turned westwards. . . .

At Binyanei Ha'ooma an Order-of-the-Day was born:

> We are standing on your threshold, Jerusalem. Today we entered your gates. Jerusalem, city of David and Solomon, is in our hands.
>
> This morning, in the shadow of the Western Wall, we sang *Hatikva*, we mourned our dead, fallen in the battle for the city.
>
> Troops of the Command, brave fighters, devoted warriors, this day and your valor shall be in our hearts forever.
>
> —Major General Uzi Narkiss

REDEEMING THE VOW

Rabbi Shlomo Goren

> *Shlomo Goren (1917–1994) was born in Poland and came to the Land of Israel with his family in 1925. After studying at Hebron Yeshiva, he joined the Hagana in 1936 and became a chaplain during the War of Independence. He later served as Chief Ashkenazi Rabbi of Israel.*

Soldiers of Israel, beloved of your people, crowned with valor and victory!

God be with you, valiant warriors!

I am speaking to you from the Western Wall, remnant of our Holy Temple.

"Comfort, oh comfort My people, says your God" (Isa. 40:1).

This is the day for which we have hoped, let us be glad and rejoice in His salvation.

The dream of all the generations has been fulfilled before our eyes. The City of God, the Temple site, the Temple Mount, and the Western Wall—symbol of the Jewish People's Messianic Redemption—have been delivered this day by you, heroes of the Israel Defense Forces.

This day you have redeemed the vow of the generations: "If I forget you, O Jerusalem, let my right hand wither" (Pss. 137:5). We did not forget you, Jerusalem, our Holy City, home of our glory. And it is Your right hand, the right hand of God, that has wrought this historic deliverance.

Whose is the heart that will not exult at hearing those tidings of redemption? Henceforth the gates of Zion and of Old Jerusalem, and the paths to the Western Wall, are open for the prayers of their children, their builders and their liberators in the Land of Israel, and to the Jews of the Dispersion who may now come there to pray.

The Divine Presence, which has never forsaken the Western Wall, is now marching in the van of the legions of Israel in a pillar of fire to illuminate our path to victory, and is emblazoning us with clouds of glory before the Jewish people of the entire world. Happy are we that we have been privileged to earn this, the most exalted hour in the history of our people.

Rabbi Shlomo Goren, then Chief Chaplain of the Army, blowing the shofar at the Wall, June 1967 (Israel Government Press Office; with permission)

To the nations of the world we declare: we shall respectfully protect the holy places of all faiths, and their doors shall be open to all.

Beloved soldiers, dear sons of your people! To you has befallen the greatest privilege of Jewish history. There is now being fulfilled the prayer of the ages and the vision of the prophets: "For You, O God, didst destroy her in fire, and You will surely build her up again in fire, as it is written: 'And I Myself—declares the Lord—will be a wall of fire all around it, and I will be a glory inside it' (Zech. 2:9). Blessed are You, O Lord, consoler of Zion and builder of Jerusalem."

And to Zion and to the remnant of our Temple we say: Your children have returned to their borders, our feet now stand within your gates, Jerusalem: city bounded together once more with New Jerusalem; city that is "perfect of beauty and joy of the whole earth," capital city of the eternal State of Israel.

In the name of the entire community of Jewry in Israel and in the diaspora, and with joy sublime, I herewith pronounce the blessing: "Blessed are You, O Lord our God, King of the Universe, who has kept us alive and sustained us and brought us to this day."

Next year in rebuilt Jerusalem!

June 7, 1967

WINDOW ON MOUNT ZION

Pauline Rose

Wednesday, June 7, 1967

As the first rays of light uncovered the darkness of that terrible night, the shooting died down and there was much movement in Garden Square. It was suddenly filled with soldiers and trucks, and by the time the sun had risen a little above the horizon the shooting had almost stopped.

We went outside for the first time. I looked at our house—it was still standing intact. I rushed upstairs. Everything was covered with a thick layer of dust and dirt which had fallen from the ceiling with every explosion, but I could not see any damage, not even a broken window. I was astonished. Then I went into our bedroom and saw holes in the wall. Six bullets had left as many holes in the wall above the wardrobe; they had pierced the window, making six holes in the curtains. No other damage.

"But where could that loud explosion have been?" I was thinking, when Brother Daniel came to tell us that a shell had exploded in the house belonging to the Church next to the Gallery.

In addition to this, the Church dome had suffered, and a few more holes had appeared in the walls of the military post. We could not see any other damage on the whole of Mount Zion. Where had all the bullets and shells landed during those two days and nights of constant battle? It really was a miracle. Mount Zion seemed to have been specially protected. I remembered the Commander's words: "It was as though someone else was commanding. . . ."

Yona and I talked to the fifty or so soldiers who filled the Square. They were very tired, but the time had not yet come for them to rest. We made them strong Turkish coffee, and never was coffee more appreciated or of greater help. They had not had a hot drink for almost thirty hours—hours of harrowing experiences, and difficulty, still lay ahead of them in the Old City.

There was an atmosphere of excitement among them all. Something portentous was going to happen. Then the Commander of the unit said to me: "We are now going into the Old City through this border on Mount Zion to meet up with our boys who are entering the City through other gates. But we have no flag with us, and we *must* have a flag." He looked at me questioningly. "Can you help us? There is no time to lose."

"Come with me," I answered, and rushed upstairs. I took a sheet out of the linen cupboard and remembered that I had a new tube of blue watercolour paint.

We spread the white sheet on the kitchen table and excitedly, with the watercolour running, painted on the Star of David. My heart beat very fast as we attached and then rolled up the flag on a stick from the garden and gave it to the Commander.

We watched the jeeps and half-tracks, filled with soldiers, descending the hill and crossing the border into the Old City. We wondered what would happen to those boys and our hurriedly improvised flag. Many thoughts passed through my mind. The flag of the State of Israel was going from this house into the Old City. Would it be the flag of victory hoisted on the walls of Jerusalem when the City was liberated?

The shooting started again. There was hard fighting in the streets and blood flowed in the narrow alleyways of the Old City. A high price was being paid in human lives and suffering in order to break down the walls of hatred and division.

There are moments on the road of destiny which inspire fanciful thoughts, perhaps even prophetic thoughts. I looked into the future, the promised future, when the State of Israel would become the Kingdom of Israel, the Kingdom of Peace, the Kingdom of God on earth with the Messiah ruling on the throne of David, and bringing peace to all the world.

The flag of the State of Israel had been made on Mount Zion at this hour of destiny. Could it be that the flag of the Kingdom of Israel would also be made here? It would be hoisted high on Mount Zion for all the world to see, a time of great rejoicing when "the Lord of hosts shall reign in Mount Zion and in Jerusalem—gloriously."

Later in the morning there was a silence, a strange silence, broken only by occasional shots from snipers and the frenzied voice of a demented man crying loudly in the Old City. The silence became so impelling it seemed to enter into the soul; I felt that I was holding my breath on the brink of eternity. Then the sound of a trumpet could be heard, that long blast of the ram's horn—the shofar—shattering the silence. The battle for Jerusalem was over. Rabbi Goren, the army chaplain, was blowing the shofar at the Wailing Wall, the wall of the Temple, and we could hear him singing the prayers.

At that moment all Israel was pouring out its heart in prayers. For the first time for nearly two thousand years, independent Jews were again in the City of David, at the Temple Wall, freed of its enemies. I remembered the time when Jews had stood praying at that Wall and had been stabbed in the back as they prayed.

Everybody wept for joy that morning. Even soldiers who were never in any way religious were stirred to the depths of their being and acknowledged the miracle from God. Who could have believed that only two days after fighting began we would be in the Old City again? God had shown His power in Israel for all the world to see.

During the next few hours hundreds of soldiers were sent up to Mount Zion. For two days it became a military camp. Units were sent from here to different places and were continually being replaced. It was a military camp in action. Cooks were preparing the food, and men were lying and resting on every available space on the ground.

In the afternoon Yona was allowed to go to Paulita, and it was possible for Albert and Raymond to return to Mount Zion. I ran to meet the car bringing them up the hill, our own car—completely undamaged. . . . Albert and Raymond told of their experiences and narrow escapes during the shelling of the city, but most of the time they had been safe in shelters.

Albert was quiet with emotion, "Imagine the flag of Israel on the walls of the Old City of Jerusalem after nearly two thousand years!"

"I noticed that the flag flying on David's Tower did not appear to be the usual printed flag. It looked more like a home-made one!" Raymond remarked.

My heart beat a little faster as he spoke and then I told them the story of the flag made so hurriedly on the kitchen table at Ha-Ohel—the flag destined to mark another milestone in Jewish history. How many other flags had been hoisted there since it was first a city of the Jews! How much suffering and persecution the Jews had endured under those flags since the time of King David's reign!

When we came back to the house and saw the mess that had to be cleared up, we thought at first that we would have to sleep in the Gallery. Yet with a special effort we were able to eat together in our own kitchen once more, and sleep in our own beds. It was almost impossible to grasp the fact that only two days had passed and the battle for Jerusalem was over.

However, the war had not yet ended and we listened intently to the news coming over the radio. We heard that Jericho was in our hands, and later, Hebron and Bethlehem, Ramallah and all the surrounding towns and villages. We were quite dazed. It seemed so incredible.

During the night we heard the soldiers singing as they sat around their camp fires. But intermittent shots from hidden snipers in the Old City continued. We were all exhausted, more from emotion than anything else, when we fell asleep in our own beds. . . .

THE SEVENTH DAY

After the Six Day War a remarkable book was compiled by Kibbutz members, consisting of conversations with soldiers who expressed their feelings concerning the overwhelming events in which they had participated. The Hebrew name of the volume was Siach Lohamim—"Soldiers' Talk." *The following excerpts were taken from the English version of that book.*

LIKE A PSALM OF PRAISE

A LETTER BY ELIEZER

I was lucky that I served with the paratroop brigade that liberated Jerusalem. I believe that the hand of God was in my participation in the battle for the liberation of and reunion of Jerusalem. I see in it the hand of God, for ever since I reached maturity, and especially since I joined the army thirteen years ago, I've had a constant desire to take part in a war for the liberation of Jerusalem. On the other hand, this contradicted my social and political belief in the need for a dialogue with the Arabs as a basis for peace. But my yearnings to fight for the liberation of Jerusalem were above and beyond my political ideas.

Fears, natural in the face of possible death, were replaced by a great pride. I felt jubilant, here I was about to fight—and perhaps to die—for Jerusalem. Do you know the significance of Jerusalem for a religious man who prays three times a day: "And return speedily to Jerusalem, Thy city, in mercy, and dwell within it as Thou hast spoken"? . . . The Western Wall was never an archaeological site as far as I was concerned, not even a "holy place" as it's officially called. My education, my prayers and my longings transform Jerusalem in its entirety into an organic part of my very being, of my whole life. . . .

I felt as if I had been granted the great privilege of acting as an agent of God, of Jewish history. Because of all the great tension and turmoil of the war, I didn't at first have the time to think about the experiences and feelings of the other soldiers. But the atmosphere was full of a sense of greatness and holiness. We were in the Rockefeller Museum, just before we took the Temple Mount, and I asked a fellow soldier, a man born in Kibbutz Sha'ar Ha'amakim, what he thought of it all. He answered me with a verse from the Bible: "I was glad when they said unto me, let us go unto the house of the Lord. Our feet shall stand within Thy gates, O Jerusalem. Jerusalem is builded as a city that is compact together." He smiled as he spoke, perhaps because it's not "fitting" for a member of HaShomer Hatzair [an extremely left-wing, secular group—ed.] to talk this way. But I saw his eyes, and I knew that that was how he really felt.

When we broke into the Old City and I went up to the Temple Mount and later to the Western Wall, I looked searchingly at the officers and the other soldiers. I saw their tears, their wordless prayers, and I knew they felt as I did: a deep feeling for the Temple Mount where the Temple once stood, and love for the Wall on whose stones so many generations have wept. I understood that it wasn't only I and my religious friends who sensed its greatness and sanctity; the others felt it too, no less deeply and strongly. It was easier for me to define my feelings, because I had my *tefillin* in my pack (perhaps King Solomon wore ones just like these when he built the Temple) and in my pocket there was the book of psalms written by David, the King of Jerusalem.

As I stood weeping by the Wall, there wept with me my father, my grandfather and my great-grandfather, all of them born in a Land of Israel where they needed Abdulla's permission to pray at the Wall. As I caressed its stones, I felt the warmth of those Jewish hearts which had warmed them with a warmth that will for ever endure.

I saw my friends, kibbutz-educated toward an attitude of scorn for traditional religious values, now overwhelmed by a feeling of holiness, and as elated and moved as I was. Then I saw the proof of what I had previously assumed, that there is in all of us, religious and non-religious alike, in the entire Jewish people, an intense quality of Jewishness that is neither destroyed by education nor blurred by foreign ideologies and values. The morning after the battle I said my morning prayers on the Temple Mount, and as the sun rose over liberated Jerusalem I lingered over the verse, "And may a new light dawn over Zion and may we speedily merit its radiance."

TONIGHT WE'RE MAKING HISTORY: A DISCUSSION

MICHA: I'm not a very emotional person about this sort of business. But I do remember how this whole question of Jerusalem gripped us. We certainly saw it as something special. I can truly say that I remember thinking that we were about to do something of real importance, of historical significance. That's how we put it to one another, "Tonight we're going into the Old City and it's . . ."

DANI: "Tonight we're making history. . . ."

MICHA: Yes. Without question. Apart from the fact that the whole war was something of historic significance, Jerusalem was extra special. . . . Look, I don't want to destroy any legends, but it wasn't as earth-shaking as it looked from the evening papers that day. It's true that some people were very moved; that for some of them it was something special. Lots of boys who hadn't had much to do with Judaism and weren't at all religious said that this war had made them feel that the Jewish people is something special. They appreciated the meaning of the verse: "Thou hast chosen us." I heard a lot of people say that. But I also heard lots of them say that it didn't mean anything to them. To them it was merely the climax of a specific assignment, without any Jewish significance. Historical significance, yes; but not something specifically Jewish.

I remember that one of the things I thought about later on, something that really affected me, was the business of Giora, our company commander. He was killed right next to me, near the Wall. One evening, we'd had a big 'do' in the amphitheatre on Mount Scopus. We sang "Jerusalem of Iron," and there were some professional artists. It was all very impressive, the moment itself, the background, the place and all that—and that was when I thought about Giora. Why wasn't he here with us? It's what one generally thinks at these moments. I really was very moved then. But in the middle of the fighting—when it happened, I remember that my only thought was that now I had to carry on and continue to advance, without saying a word to any of the men. Just not tell any of them—only tell them when it's all over. Some of them were completely broken up by the news.

DANI: If you were to ask me what day the Old City was taken on, I wouldn't be able to tell you. We'd crossed the border without a single radio, so we didn't hear about it immediately. But when we did find out, there was a truly spontaneous reaction. Most of the men began dancing around, jumping on and off the vehicles, under them, hugging one another. It was like being in exile and suddenly hearing that Jerusalem was ours. I had very mixed feelings about it. On the one hand, it didn't mean anything to me; on the other hand, it showed we'd given them a beating. I knew that one was supposed to feel pleased about it. But I wasn't specially happy about taking Port Tawafik. I wasn't even specially happy that Jerusalem had been taken in this fantastic way. I didn't feel particularly excited. . . . They asked me, "Is it true about the Wall?" And I said, "Okay, so what? We've taken Port Tawafik too!" I'll tell you something: holy or not, it left me cold.

MICHA: Morning prayers at the Wall were very awe-inspiring. All the time I kept thinking that the Wall symbolized the Jewish people's yearning for unity, its deep roots in the country; that we represented a whole people, a whole history. It meant a lot to me. I can't say that I felt any deep spiritual link with the stones themselves. It isn't like that. People don't realize that Judaism doesn't attach any sanctity to places as such. For example, the Bible says about Moses' burial place, "And no one knew where he was buried." For the same reason, there's nothing holy about the Wall. But for us, the Wall's really— what I saw before me was the realization of our people's unity, of their longing, of the whole Jewish people. Not that particular place, but what it means to the whole Jewish people. . . .

THE LIONS' GATE

> *The following selections are taken from another book compiled after the Six Day War,* The Lion's Gate *(Hebrew), edited by Yisrael Harel, consisting of reminiscences by members of the Parachute Brigade who conquered the Wall.*

FEAR AND TREMBLING

MOSHE AMIRAV

It is with a smile that I remember how we looked for the Wall. We ran there, a group of panting soldiers, lost on the plaza of the Temple Mount, searching for a giant stone wall. We did not stop to look at the Mosque of Omar even though this was the first time we had seen it close up. Forward! Forward! Hurriedly, we pushed our way through the Magreb Gate and suddenly we stopped, thunderstruck. There it was before our eyes! Gray and massive, silent and restrained. The Western Wall! I remember that I had such a feeling only once before in my life; it had been when I was a child when my father brought me near to the Holy Ark in the synagogue. I, a little infant, had been afraid that something would come out of the Ark, something big and terrible from another world. . . .

Slowly, slowly I began to approach the Wall in fear and trembling like a pious cantor going to the lectern to lead the prayers. I approached it as the messenger of my father and my grandfather, of my great-grandfather and of all generations in all the exiles who had never merited seeing it and so they had sent me to represent them.

Paratroopers at the Wall immediately after its liberation in June 1967 (Israel Government Press Office; with permission)

Somebody recited the festive blessing: "Blessed are You, O Lord our God, King of the universe who has kept me alive, and maintained us and brought us to this time," but I could not answer "Amen." I put my hand on the stone and the tears that started to flow were not my tears—they were the tears of all Israel, tears of hope and prayer, tears of hasidic tunes, tears of Jewish dances, tears which scorched and burned the heavy gray stone.

KISSING HISTORY

ABRAHAM DUVDEVANI

Narrow alleys, filthy passageways, garbage at the entrance of shuttered shops, the stench of dead legionnaires—but we paid no attention. Our eyes were fixed on the golden dome which could be seen from a distance. There, more or less, it had to be! We marched faster to keep up with the beating of our hearts; we were almost running. We met a soldier from one of the forward units and asked him the way and hurried on. We went through a gate and down some steps. I looked to the right and stopped dead. There was the Wall in all its grandeur and glory! I had never seen it before but it was an old friend, impossible to mistake. Then I thought that I should not be there because the Wall belongs in the world of dreams and legends and I am real. Reality and legend, dream and deed, all unite here. I went down and approached the Wall and stretched out my hand toward the huge, hewn stones. But my hand was afraid to touch and of itself returned to me. I closed my eyes, took a small, hesitant step forward, and brought my lips to the Wall. The touch of my lips opened the gates of my emotions and the tears burst forth. A Jewish soldier in the State of Israel is kissing history with his lips.

Past, present and future in one kiss. There will be no more destruction and the Wall will never again be deserted. It was taken with young Jewish blood and the worth of that blood is eternity. The body is coupled to the rows of stones, the face is pushed into the spaces between them and the hands try to reach its heart. A soldier near me mumbles in disbelief, "We are at the Wall, at the Wall. . . ."

AT THE WESTERN WALL

Elie Wiesel

> *Nobel Prize winning author Elie Wiesel was born in Romania in 1928 and was imprisoned in various concentration camps. After the war he lived first in Paris and then in New York. His feelings about the events of the Six Day Way led to the writing of his novel Beggar in Jerusalem. The following is a personal account he wrote of his visit to Jerusalem at the end of that war.*

They tell me this is the Wall.

No, I don't believe it. I am not able—I am afraid to believe it. Deep down, of course, I realize that they are right, that indeed it is the very Wall—which Jew cannot recognize it instantly! Yet I cannot believe that it is I—I who now stands before it, gazing as if in a dream, breathlessly confronting it as though it were a living being, ominipotent, all knowing, master of the secrets of the universe . . . above time, a being that bears me to a strange and distant world, where each stone has its own will, fate and memory. . . . I cannot believe that it is I who has conceived such stormy fantasies, that it is I who now trembles like a wisp of the wind!

Crowds coming from the Wall soon after the end of the Six Day War in 1967; note the tractors and bulldozers used to clear the plaza area (Central Zionist Archives; with permission)

I feel a weird sensation. . . . This is the first time that I am here, yet I feel that I was at this very spot before. I have already seen these Jews, have heard their prayers. Every shape seems familiar, every sound as though it has arisen from the depths of my own past. But there is a difference. Before there were no young men and women milling about in uniforms. . . . What are they doing here? And why are they crying? I do not know. They themselves neither know nor say. They see nothing—except the Wall before them. But it is theirs, for it is they who bore it on their shoulders year after year and generation after generation. And their tears—their tears are the Wall's.

Indeed, the coverage of this war should be handled not only by newspaper columnists and military experts but by poets and kabbalists as well—for what has happened cannot be described in neat, logical terms.

Even if we knew every last detail of the war, we would still not understand what happened; even if all the military and political secrets were suddenly disclosed, we could not measure the great mystery in which we are encloaked as if by the command of the Almighty Himself.

There are those who speak of *Hasgacha Elyona*, Divine Providence and of the merit of our forefathers which protected us. And there are the rationalists who are willing to consider just the possibility of miracles. But there is no officer I've met who has not agreed that there are aspects to what has happened that dry intellect alone will never grasp.

Even the "freethinkers" interpret the experience as organically a religious one—it has compelled each Jew to confront his people, his past and his God.

To borrow the language of the rabbis: the enemy prophesied, but didn't understand his own prophecy. It was total, for he was defeated not only by the soldiers and officers of an army—he was defeated by the totality of Jewish history itself! Two thousand years of suffering, longing and hope were mobilized for the battle, just as the millions of martyrs of the holocaust were enlisted to the ranks. Like the biblical pillars of fire they came and shielded their spiritual heirs. What enemy could ever conquer them?

The words and phrases our enemy used caused the memory of the holocaust to defeat him. He did not realize that there are words which are forbidden to be uttered, not in our generation, not in regard to the Jewish people. . . . He didn't realize that a person can bring destruction on himself not only in one moment, as our rabbis of old tell us, but with one word!

He was too quick, too fast to threaten the destruction of Israel, and this was a monumental blunder.

True, the world community was not moved very much by his threats, but the Jewish nation throughout the globe shuddered and rose like one alongside the Jewish State, which for two weeks lay under heavy siege. A few words by Nasser was enough to make the situation a fight for survival of the whole Jewish people.

This time the soldiers of Israel felt they were not alone. Behind them were organized hundreds of wealthy and dedicated communities.

University students flooded embassies to enlist for the fight; the Hassidim of Williamsburg declared days of fasts and prayer; youngsters from assimilated homes organized fund raising drives and joined in protests; millionaires cast aside their businesses and took off for Jerusalem; community leaders went sleepless night after night because of the great efforts and profound anxiety. Never was the Jewish people so united, never so moved and anxious, never so ready and prepared to offer and sacrifice everything it had, its "might, heart and soul."

I know oldsters who withdrew their last savings from the bank and donated them to Israel; I know young students who cast away their studies and tests and joined in the fight; I know men who had stood "outside the Jewish camp," who had drifted from their people but now returned to it: more than one apostate took upon himself the yoke of Judaism anew because he now wanted to identify with his people. The miracle which took place among our people throughout their vast dispersion was as great as the miracle within the land itself.

Thus, it is only justice that mystics and poets have a hand in writing the history of our deeds. . . .

I try to understand, to believe—I succeed a bit . . . but the truth is, I still don't understand. The more the professional experts try to explain—the less I understand. It all seems like an ancient legend; as though we had all gone far, far back to the past. Perhaps that's why I have an almost palpable feeling of victory—we have conquered time itself! And my generation is not privileged to boast many such victories.

However, let's not fool ourselves. The world already envies our victory. Already we can hear the strident voices. . . . Israel is being extreme with its "hard" stance, some declare. Israel should show special patience, forgiveness and magnanimity towards her enemies, suggest others. There will be pressures, attempts to squeeze out of us this or that compromise. Even our "friends" are not likely to forgive that we were victorious—that it was such an impolite, swift victory, so complete, so magnificent. It is understandable. We have suddenly stripped them of the chance to pity us or even help us.

No, the war is continuing and will continue a long, long time. Except that now it will be fought with words. Let Israel's spokesmen, who must deal with the diplomats, ministers and heads of state, make certain not to surrender to the fine rules of "logic." The events that took place have finally freed Israel from the paralyzing chains of "logic." Let the world know: two plus two equals two thousand years when the subject is the Wall and its stones. Even the Almighty cannot allow what has happened to become as though it had not happened.

CITY OF DREAMS

Rinna Samuel

> *An author and editor living in Rehovot, Rinna Samuel wrote this piece expressing her feelings immediately after the reunification of Jerusalem.*

Somehow, in the years since 1948, we adjusted to the loss of Jerusalem's heart; we craned, and stood on tiptoe, and peered through various cracks in the huge and hideous cement barriers that divided the City; and looked at the walled town and thought our own thoughts.

For pious Jews, the wound was always fresh, but they mourned the symbolic city, not so much the real lovely, dusty, stone one. The rest of us accommodated ourselves, never quite free of bereavement and never reconciled to what seemed the certainty of permanent division.

The New City slowly evolved into a capital; the government offices and ministries moved there, one by one; what had once been primarily a group of western suburbs of the historic Jerusalem became, in the course of time, a genuine city.

New Jerusalem has always had its landmarks and its points of interest. It has always had a population more exotic and more colorful than almost any city in the world. When development eastward, after the War of Liberation, became impossible, new Jerusalem developed to the west.

The Tower of David in the Jordanian-held Old City, viewed from the Israeli side through barbed wire, date unknown (Central Zionist Archives; with permission)

It grew slowly and with difficulty. Industry was reluctant to move there; the pace of life in Jerusalem has always been, compared to Tel Aviv, slow and tranquil. Israelis talked of Jewish Jerusalem as provincial; a dreary university town; a civil servants' hideaway.

Tourists tended to do Jerusalem rapidly. Often, her rare quality escaped them as they rushed from the stunning Israel Museum to the monumental Yad Vashem where Israel pays homage to the victims of the holocaust; from the terrace of the King David Hotel, where pink and mauve and pale blue shadows fall tantalizingly across the view of the forbidden walls, on to the Knesset, Israel's parliament, and up to the new campus of the Hebrew University and the great complex of the Hadassah Medical Center.

But somehow new Jerusalem, for all her vividness and other-worldliness, could never compensate for the loss of the City of David. . . .

Layer upon layer, the various civilizations that had once dominated Jerusalem became an integral part of her; the Romans, the Byzantines, the Arabs, all contributed to the sum total. But Jerusalem's greatest glory was when she was in Jewish hands; when David reigned, and Solomon, and during the Maccabean and the Herodian periods. Then, her influence radiated outward, and she acquired new and lasting dimensions.

Glance at the Mosaic of Jerusalem's history, trace the steadfastness of Jewish desire for the city, of which David sang: "Beautiful in elevation and the joy of the whole earth," and effortlessly you connect all that has gone before with all that is happening now.

The first announcement came a second after the bulletin about the capture of Sharm el Sheik. *Kol Yisrael*, Israel's broadcasting service, is not, in general, given to doing things with much flair. But the Israel Defence Forces are. It was oddly touching that in the very heat of battle—on June 6, one day after the war had started—the army spokesman had taken time out to think how he would tell the people of Israel the great news. He did it most effectively. A terse statement about the Straits of Tiran being in Israel's hands was followed by a short pause. And then, said the spokesman, he had one other short announcement. The Israel Defense Forces had surrounded the Old City and broken through. "Jerusalem is ours."

It is hard to remember exactly how we felt. Ecstatic, I think, is the most accurate word—and faintly disbelieving. Almost simultaneously, people began to learn the human price paid in Jerusalem for Jerusalem, and the edge was taken off the first wild, splendid happiness.

But not for long. In fact, when I think back to those six amazing days, what typifies them most was the bombardment of our emotions. There was, literally, no time to respond totally to anything. The triumphs came so hard on the heels of our great apprehension before the war, and they followed each other with such rapidity, that nothing registered in an absolute way for citizens at home, glued to their radios.

But the news about Jerusalem was different. It dominated the whole remarkable week; its implications were available instantly to all of us. Lacking television, there was much we missed. But we heard it all: the young soldiers weeping with fatigue, relief, and the burden of their historic victory, their bearded faces resting against the warm old stones of the Western Wall; the short, unheroic, immensely moving little speeches that Dayan and Rabin made at the Wall, and repeatedly through the noise of war and the sound of crowds of soldiers, we heard the shrill possessive elation of the shofar.

Within a day, without official notice, without anyone having started it, all Israel began to travel to Jerusalem. The first weekend, only VIPs entered the Old City. It became a status symbol to have danced at the Wall with the God-intoxicated Hassidim who were there with the soldiers, before anyone else. But after the first Saturday, everyone began to go. Israel's total population is some two and a half million; it is a breathtaking statistic that by mid-July almost the entire population of the Jewish State has already been inside the Old City.

Long caravans of buses toiled incessantly up and down the mountain road carved in the Judean hills like happy elephants; in between darted private cars, trucks, and taxis. People, forgetting the heat and the dust and still possible perils such as mines and snipers, took parents and babies and sandwiches and set off on a pilgrimage, disguised as sightseeing, but, in fact, a holy ascent.

And because Jerusalem, City of Peace, is what she is, the quality of the meeting between those who had been denied the city for so long, and those who had lived in it
for all the missing years, acquired a uniqueness of its own.

Emotions made themselves felt in an unexpected way. Everywhere in the Old City,
along the Via Dolorosa, and outside the Holy Sepulcher, everywhere the Arabs set up
stands and sold whatever they had to sell. And everywhere, the Israelis bought.

No one, entering Jerusalem during the first few days of her liberation, could have
guessed that war had only ended two, or three, or four days ago. Nor that these Arabs,
bedecked with their flowing *keffiyahs* or crimson fezzes like upturned flower pots, hawk-
ing their wares in pidgin English and a few incorrect Hebrew words, had, so very recently, been utterly committed to the slaughter of the Jews.

Instead of a city broken and lamenting its defeat, Old Jerusalem became a carnival
town. Here and there, in an Arab café, eyes were averted from an inquisitive Israeli

*Crowds coming from the
Wall soon after the conclusion of
the 1967 War (Central Zionist
Archives; with permission)*

gaze; now and then, a smile was not returned. But in the main, overwhelmingly, hands reached out to grasp hands. No one said anything—but the unspoken message of peace was given and received, though the medium tended to be the sale of cheap pencils from Red China, plums and straw mats, and other trivial and essentially worthless commodities.

In and out, the masses of Israelis wove their way through the intricate mazes of the Old City. Most of them formed organized groups, identifiable by a frenzied leader, shepherding his unruly flock with a flag raised in the air so that he could be located in the press of people. From one church to another, along the outside of the Old City walls, into the Citadel and David's Tower, on to the Western Wall—there was no end to the dense procession, no end to the need of the Jews to imprint themselves upon the city again.

Nowhere was the stand of the conqueror apparent; nowhere was more than petty advantage taken of the vanquished Arabs; in no way whatsoever did the mass of bargain-hunting pilgrims threaten or boast. It was their Jerusalem, they had come back to it after nearly twenty years, and in their enormous happiness, they were able to include the Arabs, too.

It took a day longer, the end of the first week of the city's deliverance, but the Arabs, understanding at last that the city was really one and they too shared it, ventured out to New Jerusalem. At first, they went in groups of four and five; tentatively, inconspicuously. Then, they went the way the Jews had come to the Old City, filled with curiosity that could not be contained. We saw them everywhere, pointing out buildings they remembered from twenty years ago, marveling over new structures, puzzled by alterations.

They had dressed up for their first visit to the New City; many of the men wore the typical "ice cream" suit in some pale pastel color; their wives, mostly, were heavily veiled. Then, they moved about more freely, as the fact of the government's unification became clearer to them. If they were citizens of a united Jerusalem, then, except for the curfew which kept them home at night, they could move around anywhere—and they did. They began to visit old friends in Rehavia and Talpiot. All week, well-dressed, middle-aged Arabs knocked on Jewish doors, shook hands with colleagues and one-time cronies and reminisced. All week, the strange Alice-Through-the-Looking-Glass confrontation went on, in a hundred different ways. . . .

War already seems startlingly remote here; although the hospital wards are still filled with wounded soldiers, many of them hurt in the brutal hand-to-hand fighting that went on in the Old City itself; although hundreds of Jerusalemites were maimed and killed in the three-day shelling of the city from its eastern side; although only yesterday, Jordanian prisoners filled the high school yard in Rehavia and the tennis courts of the university. But it is as though war never was; as though the force of the city herself had annealed the deep injuries done to her; as though an inward magnet had drawn her people together.

STRANGE CITY

Amos Oz

> *One of Israel's best-known writers and peace activists, Amos Oz was born in Jerusalem in 1939. Although from the age of fourteen he made his home in Kibbutz Hulda, he often chooses Jerusalem as a setting for his fiction. This piece, however, is a reflection about the city that appeared in* The Seventh Day. *It stands in contrast to the reaction voiced by Rinna Samuel writing at the same time.*

I was born in Jerusalem and lived there throughout my childhood; when I was nine I lived through the days when Jerusalem was besieged and shelled. It was then that I first saw a dead man: a shell fired from the Arab Legion's gun batteries on Nebi Samuel hit a pious Jew and tore his stomach apart. I saw him lying in the street. He was a small man whose chin sprouted a meagre beard. His face, as he lay there dead, was white and amazed. It was July 1948. For many days afterwards I hated that man because he kept appearing in my dreams and frightening me. I knew that Jerusalem was surrounded by forces whose only desire was the city's death and mine, too.

Later I moved away from Jerusalem. I still loved her with a stubborn love as one might love a woman who holds aloof. Sometimes on my free days I would go to Jerusalem to pay court to her. Her alleyways knew me well though they affected not to.

I loved Jerusalem because she was journey's end, a city one arrived at but could never pass beyond; and also because she was never really a true part of the State of Israel; with the exception of a few roads Jerusalem has always held herself aloof, as if she had consciously chosen to turn her back on all the flat white commercial cities: Tel Aviv, Holon, Herzlia and Nethanya.

Jerusalem was different. She was the absolute negation of towns made up of cube-like blocks of flats, all painted white. She was different from the flat stretches of citrus groves, the gardens surrounded by hedges, the red roofs and irrigation pipes shining in the sun. Even the blue of her summer skies was different. Not for her the dusty white heavens of the coastal plain and the Sharon valley. An enclosed city. Wintry. Even in the summer it was always a wintry city. Rusty iron railings. Grey stone, sometimes imperceptibly shading into pale blue, sometimes into a reddish hue. Tumbledown fences. Rocky hillsides. Walled courtyards, closed in as if in anger.

And its citizens: a silent people, bitter as if for ever overcoming some inner fear. Observant Jews. Ashkenazi Jews in their fur *streimels* and old Sephardim in their striped robes. Soft-stepping scholars wandering through the streets, as if at a loss. Dreamy-eyed girls. Blind beggars, dumb or cursing. Madmen abroad with the divine spark in their eyes.

For twenty years Jerusalem turned her stubborn back on the stream of modern life. A slow-moving town in a country of feverish activity. An old, neglected mountainous suburb whose few flat stretches, crammed with buildings, burst at the seams with overflowing energy. The sad capital city of an exultant state. And the stranglehold. There were mutilated streets descending to blocked alleys. Barricades of concrete and rusty barbed wire. A city which is all border. A city not of gold but of tin sheeting, bent and full of holes. A city surrounded at night by the sound of foreign bells, foreign odours, distant views. A ring of hostile villages surrounded the city on three sides: Sha'afat, Wadi Jos, Issawia, Silwan, Azaria, Tsur Bachr, Bet Tsafafa. It seemed as if they had only to clench their hand and Jerusalem would be crushed within their fist. On a winter night you could sense the evil intent that flowed from them toward the city.

There was fear too in Jerusalem. An inner fear that must never be expressed in words, never called by name. It grew, solidified and crystallized in the twisting alleyways and the desolate lanes.

The city fathers, the heads of government, the housing estates, the newly planted trees, the traffic lights, all tried to tempt Jerusalem into a union with the State of Israel; and she, with the exception of some few streets, refused that union. Twenty years. Jerusalem continued to preserve a faded, obstinate Mandatory character. She remained sad.

Not within the State of Israel, but alongside it; Jerusalem as opposed to Israel.

I loved this town, because I was born there and because people who stand aloof tend to love towns which hold aloof.

This was a love which was received without mercy: Jerusalem was often the background for nightmares and dreams of terror. I no longer live in Jerusalem, but in my dreams I am hers and she does not relinquish her hold on me. I would see us both surrounded by enemies. The enemy in my dreams came not only from east, north and south, but completely surrounded us. I saw Jerusalem falling into the hands of her enemies. Destroyed, pillaged and burned, as in the stories of my childhood, as in the Bible, as in the tales of the destruction of the Temple. And I too, with no way of escape, with no place to hide, was trapped in the Jerusalem of my dreams.

Many were the stories I was told as a child of Jerusalem under siege. Jewish children always died in these stories. They died heroically, or were slaughtered, but the stories always ended with the town burning and the children dying. Sennacherib, Titus, the Crusaders. Riots, terrorists. Military rule. The High Commissioner, searches, curfew. Abdullah, the desert king. The guns of the Arab Legion. The convoy to Mount Scopus. The convoy to the Etzion bloc. An incited rabble. Inflamed mobs. Blood-thirsty ruffians. Brutal armed irregulars. All forever aimed at me. I always belonged to the minority, to the besieged, to those whose fate was sealed, who lived a life hovering on the brink of disaster.

So this time too, the city will be attacked. We shall die there like that little pious Jew who lay in the street, his face pale and amazed, as if he had suffered some grave insult. And more.

After the siege was lifted, a border was drawn though the heart of the city. All my childhood was passed in dead-end alleyways, facing streets one was forbidden to enter. The scar of destruction, no-man's-land, mine fields, wasteland, ruined, blackened buildings. Twisted, despairing iron girders rising starkly out of her ruined houses. And ever opposite: the other Jerusalem. The city surrounding my city. Foreign sounds and smells emanated from it, pale lights flickered there by night, and the cry of the muezzin at dawn. Atlantis. The lost continent. A city which was forever the focus of one's most insubstantial visions. I had blurred memories dating from my earliest childhood, the memory of colourful alleyways in the Old City, the narrow arched street leading to the Wall, Mandatory Arab policemen, street-vendors' stalls, tamarind, a riot of colour, an ever-present sense of lurking danger.

From over there, from beyond the border, an angry threat has been directed at me throughout most of my life. I remember wandering down the streets of Musrara at dusk, to the edge of no-man's-land. A glimpse of Schneller Woods from afar. Forbidden views seen from the observation point at Abu Tor. The shattered square of Notre Dame. The towers of Bethlehem opposite the woods of Ramat Rachel. Desert hillsides falling away from the suburb of Talpiyot. The Dead Sea glittering in the distance like a mirage. Rocky valleys at dawn.

On Sunday, 11 June 1967, I went to see the Jerusalem that lay beyond the border. I came to places which with dreams and the years had become petrified symbols within my heart, and lo and behold—people lived there—houses, shops, stalls, signposts.

And I was thunderstruck, as if my whole inner world had collapsed. The dreams were a deception. The world of terrible tales became a mockery. The perpetual threat was nothing but a cruel, twisted joke. Everything was burst asunder. Laid wide open. My Jerusalem, beloved and feared, was dead.

Now the town was different. Long-forgotten, neglected corners had come to life again. Bulldozers pushed new roads through heaps of rubble which I had imagined would be there for all eternity. Districts which had been utterly forgotten were filled with fever-ish activity. Hosts of pious Jews, soldiers in battledress, amazed tourists, smartly dressed women from Tel Aviv and Haifa, all streamed eastward. The tide flowed strongly to Jerusalem. The rest of the country poured into the open city. Everything within her or-bit took an air of festivity. And I along with it.

These things cannot be expressed in words. Again I say that I loved Jerusalem in its entirety, but what does it mean? It is like a love affair, a contradictory, tortuous force: she is mine and yet strange to me, conquered but hostile, devoted yet inaccessible.

I could disregard all this. The skies are the same skies and the Jerusalem stone is the same throughout. Sheikh Jarrah is almost like Katamon.

But the city is inhabited. People live within her streets, and they are strangers. I do not understand their language; they are there—in their homes—and I am the stranger who comes from without. Courteous people, courteous to the point of offense, as if they have reached the very peak of happiness in having merited the honour of selling me postcards or Jordanian stamps. Welcome, we are brothers, it is just for you alone that we have waited all these years, just so that we could embrace you. And their eyes hate me, wish me dead. The accursed stranger. It grieves me, but I cannot order my words in a rational way.

I was in East Jerusalem three days after the conquest of the city. I arrived there straight from El Arish, in Sinai, wearing uniform and carrying a sub-machine gun. I was not born to sound the trumpet or liberate lands from foreign yokes. The lament of an enslaved people finds an echo in my ears, but I am deaf to the lament of "enslaved territory."

In my childhood dreams it was the Arabs who wore uniforms and carried machine-guns. Arabs who came to my street in Jerusalem to kill me. Twenty-two years ago, a slogan painted in red appeared on a courtyard wall not far from our house: "Judah fell in blood and fire; by blood and fire will Judah rise again." One of the underground had written these words at night in burning red. I don't know how to write about blood and fire. If ever I write anything about this war, it will be about pus, sweat and vomit and not about blood and fire. With all my soul, I desired to feel in Jerusalem as a man who has dispossesed his enemies and returned to the patrimony of his ancestors. The Bible came to life for me: the Prophets, the Kings, Temple Mount, Absolom's Pillar, the Mount of Olives. The Jerusalem of Abraham Mapu and Agnon. I wanted to be part of it all, I wanted to belong.

Were it not for the people. I saw enmity and rebelliousness, sycophany, amazement, fear, insult and trickery. I passed through the streets of East Jerusalem like a man breaking into some forbidden place. Depression filled my soul.

City of my birth. City of my dreams. City of my ancestors' and my peoples' yearnings. And I was condemned to walk through its streets armed with a sub-machine gun like one of the characters from my childhood nightmares. To be a stranger in a very strange city.

JERUSALEM OF MY CHILDHOOD

Muki Tzur

> *Born in Jerusalem, Muki Tzur is a member of Kibbutz Ein Gev. A prominent writer and educator, he served as the Secretary of the United Kibbutz Movement.*

The nocturne of Jerusalem which accompanied my childhood sounds again in my ears in these post-war days. Again I hear the whistle of the wind blown through the thousands of pine needles. Again I see the grey stone, the cramped alleyways which sought not breadth but only height, the narrow strip of sky high above, the heavy iron balconies, the bridges, the water tanks, the laundry blowing pennant-like in the backyards.

The days of the siege which filled my childhood come back again to me. Father helping us to fill sacks of earth to barricade the window-sill. Running off to school to see the Palmach soldiers; the sound of their evening sing-songs before they went out on duty. The onions which all the children planted in the gardens in an attempt to stave off the hunger of the siege. The refugees from the Old City who fled to the stone Arab houses of Katamon.

I remember a time when I cried: the tears I shed over the fall of the Etzion bloc. I couldn't grasp how it could possibly have been taken by the Arabs. "But they're heroes," I wept in despair. So my father explained that knowing how to face defeat was part of the process of war. Many are the faces that flash before me now: the soft-drink vendor and his shiny steel barrel, the old lady who would bring a basket of strawberries or figs to the corner of the road and weigh them up with stone weights.

Yes, these days have brought back many a picture of the city, of the far-off days of explosions and tears and happiness, homesickness and many dormant question-marks. Sometime I still hear my father's voice, in other words, but with the same tone, "In a war, my child, you have to know how to be victorious."

JERUSALEM—A CHARISMATIC CITY

Abraham Joshua Heschel

> *One of the great spiritual leaders of American Jewry, Abraham Joshua Heschel (1907–1972) came to America in 1940. He wrote numerous volumes on Jewish life and philosophy and taught at the Jewish Theological Seminary. Immediately after the Six Day War he visited Israel and wrote his impressions in the book from which this excerpt is taken,* Israel: An Echo of Eternity.

July, 1967. . . . I have discovered a new land. Israel is not the same as before. There is great astonishment in the souls. It is as if the prophets had risen from their graves. Their words ring in a new way. Jerusalem is everywhere; she hovers over the whole country. There is a new radiance, a new awe.

The great quality of a miracle is not in its being an unexpected, unbelievable event in which the presence of the holy bursts forth, but in its happening to human beings who are profoundly astonished at such an outburst.

My astonishment is mixed with anxiety. Am I worthy? Am I able to appreciate the marvel?

I did not enter on my own the city of Jerusalem. Streams of endless craving, clinging, dreaming, flowing day and night, midnights, years, decades, centuries, millennia, streams of tears, pledging, waiting—from all over the world, from all corners of the earth—carried us of this generation to the Wall. My ancestors could only dream of you—to my people in Auschwitz you were more remote than the moon, and I can touch your stones! Am I worthy? How shall I ever repay for these moments?

The martyrs of all ages are sitting at the gates of heaven, having refused to enter the world to come lest they forget Israel's pledge given in and for this world:

"If I forget you, O Jerusalem, let my right hand wither . . ." (Pss. 137:5).

They would rather be without heaven than forget the glory of Jerusalem. From time to time their souls would leave the gates of heaven to go on a pilgrimage to the souls of the Jewish people, reminding them that God himself is in exile, that He will not enter heavenly Jerusalem until His people Israel will enter Jerusalem here (Zohar, I,1b).

Jerusalem! I always try to see the inner force that emanates from you, enveloping and transcending all weariness and travail. I try to use my eyes, and there is a cloud. Is Jerusalem higher than the road I walk on? Does she hover in the air above me? No, in Jerusalem past is present, and heaven is almost here. For an instant I am near to Hillel, who is close by. All of our history is within reach.

Jerusalem, you only see her when you hear. She has been an ear when no one else heard, an ear open to prophets' denunciations, to prophets' consolations, to the lamentation of ages, to the hopes of countless sages and saints; an ear to prayers flowing from distant places. And she is more than an ear. Jerusalem is a *witness*, an echo of eternity. Stand still and listen. We know Isaiah's voice from hearsay, yet these stones heard him when he said concerning Judah and Jerusalem (2:2–4):

It shall come to pass in the latter days . . .

For out of Zion shall go forth Torah,

and the word of the Lord from Jerusalem. . . .

He shall judge between the nations,

and shall decide for many peoples; . . .

Nations shall not lift up sword against nation,

neither shall they learn war any more.

Jerusalem was stopped in the middle of her speech. She is a voice interrupted. Let Jerusalem speak again to our people, to all people.

The words have gone out of here and have entered the pages of holy books. And yet Jerusalem has not given herself away. There is so much more in store. Jerusalem is never at the end of the road. She is the city where waiting for God was born, where anticipation of everlasting peace came into being. Jerusalem is waiting for the prologue of redemption, for new beginning.

What is the secret of Jerusalem? Her past is a prelude. Her power is in reviving. Having silence is prediction, the walls are in suspense. It may happen any moment: a shoot may come forth out of the stock of Jesse, a twig may grow forth out of his roots. . . .

This is a city never indifferent to the sky. The evenings often feel like Kol Nidre nights. Unheard music, transfiguring thoughts. Prayers are vibrant. The Sabbath finds it hard to go away.

Here Isaiah (6:3) is heard:

Holy, holy, holy is the Lord of hosts:

the whole earth is full of His glory.

View of the city of Jerusalem and the Temple Mount in 1937 (Central Zionist Archives; with permission)

No words more magnificent have ever been uttered. Here was the Holy of Holies.

Jerusalem has the look of a place that is looked at . . .

"the eyes of the Lord your God are always upon it, from the beginning of the year to the end of the year" (Deut. 11:12). Psalms inhabit the hills, the air is hallelujah. Hidden harps. Dormant songs.

☙

Jerusalem is "the city where I have chosen to put my name," "the city of our God which God established for ever"; the city of prophecy.

On the holy mount stands the city he founded:

The Lord loves the gates of Zion . . .

more than all the dwelling places of Jacob.

Glorious things are spoken of you,

O city of God . . .

And of Zion it shall be said,

"This one and that one were born in her";

for the Most High himself will establish her. . . .

Singers and dancers alike say,

"All my springs are in you."

(Pss. 87:1–7)

God has chosen Jerusalem and endowed her with the mystery of His presence; prophets, kings, sages, priests made her a place where God's calling was heard and accepted. Here lived the people who listened and preserved events in words—the scribes, the copyists.

There are moments in history which are unique, moments which have tied the heart of our people to Jerusalem forever.

These moments and the city of Jerusalem were destined to radiate the light of the spirit throughout the world. For the light of the spirit is not a thing of space, imprisoned in a particular place. Yet for the spirit of Jerusalem to be everywhere, Jerusalem must first be somewhere.

It was almost cruel. No image, no likeness, no icon of God! No man can see God and live. God, why not be considerate and show us Thy face? Thy justice is hidden, who should not Thy face be revealed?

Jerusalem is comfort, intimation of an answer.

History is not blind. The world is an eye, and Jerusalem corresponds to the pupil of the eye (Derekh Erets Zuta, chap. 9). . . .

THE WIDOW IS A BRIDE AGAIN

Jerusalem is not divine, her life depends on our presence. Alone she is desolate and silent; with Israel she is a witness, a proclamation. Alone she is a widow, with Israel she is a bride.

Where is God to be found?

God is no less here than there. It is the sacred moment in which His presence is disclosed. We meet God in time rather than in space, in moments of faith rather than in a piece of space. The history of Jerusalem is endowed with the power to inspire such moments, to invoke in us the ability to be present to His presence.

I did not enter the city of David to visit graves or to gaze at shrines. I entered in order to share cravings welled up here, to commune with those who proclaimed and with those who preserved the words we now read in the Book of Books; with those who declared as well as with those who persevered in teaching us trust.

Here was no waste of history. Here you discover the immortality of words, the eternity of moments. Wherever I walk in Jerusalem I am near a world in a state of trance, near a stillness that shelters eternity. . . .

Zion is not a symbol but a home, and the land is not an allegory but a possession, a commitment of destiny. How can anyone expect us to betray our pledge: "If I forget you, O Jerusalem, let my right hand wither" (Pss. 137:5)? . . .

Jerusalem is called the mother of Israel (Pss. 147:4) and she is also used as a synonym for Israel.

"We have never left Jerusalem, we have never abandoned the city of David." For thy servants hold her stones dear and have pity on her dust" (Pss. 102:15).

Jerusalem, the mother of Israel, we enter your walls as children who have always honored you; we have never been estranged from you. Your weight has been weighed in tears shed by our people for nearly two thousand years. Laughter was suppressed when we thought of your being in ruins. You are not a shrine, a place of pilgrimage to which to come and then depart. "Wherever I go, I go to Jerusalem," said Rabbi Nachman.

Jerusalem, all our hearts are like harps, responsive when your name is mentioned.

Jerusalem, our hearts went out to you whenever we prayed, whenever we pondered the destiny of the world. For so many ages we have been love-sick. "My beloved is mine, and I am his," Jerusalem whispered. We waited through unbearably long frustration and derision.

In our own days the miracle has occurred. Jerusalem has proclaimed loudly: "My beloved is mine, and I am his!"

What happened on June 7, 1967? God's compassion has prevailed. So many devastations. Thousands of communities wiped out. Synagogues burned, people asphyxiated. No tombstones, no graves, all monuments meaningless.

In its solitude the Wall was forced into the role of an unreachable tombstone for the nameless dead. Suddenly the Wall, tired of tears and lamentations, became homesick for song. "O come, let us sing to the Lord, let us chant in joy to the rock of our salvation!" (Pss. 95:1). It will be called the Rejoicing Wall.

Break forth together into singing,
  you waste places of Jerusalem;
for the Lord has comforted His people
  He has redeemed Jerusalem.
The Lord has bared His holy arm
  before the eyes of all nations;
and all the ends of the earth shall see
  the salvation of our God.

(ISA. 52:9–10)

We have arrived at a beginning; the night often looked interminable. Amalek was Führer, and Haman prevailed.

For centuries we would tear our garments whenever we came into sight of your ruins. In 1945 our souls were ruins, and our garments were tatters. There was nothing to tear. In Auschwitz and Dachau, in Bergen-Belsen and Treblinka, they prayed at the end of Atonement Day, "Next year in Jerusalem." The next day they were asphyxiated in

View of the newly created plaza in front of the Wall in 1967 (Central Zionist Archives; with permission)

gas chambers. Those of us who were not asphyxiated continued to cling to Thee. "Though he slay me, yet I will trust in him" (Job 13:15). We come to you, Jerusalem, to build your ruins, to mend our souls and to seek comfort for God and men.

We, a people of orphans, have entered the walls to greet the widow, Jerusalem, and the widow is a bride again. She has taken hold of us, and we find ourselves again at the feet of the prophets. We are the harp, and David is playing.

Spiritually I am a native of Jerusalem. I have prayed here all my life. My hopes have their home in these hills.

You will not understand what Jerusalem means in terms of generalizations or comparative history.

Jerusalem, we were forced to leave when driven out by conquerors, but we never abandoned, never relinquished you. Our parting was a pain to which we would never reconcile ourselves. . . .

THE WALL

The Wall . . . At first I am stunned. Then I see: a Wall of frozen tears, a cloud of sighs.

Palimpsests, hiding books, secret names. The stones are seals.

The Wall . . . The old mother crying for all of us. Stubborn, loving, waiting for redemption. The ground on which I stand is Amen. My words become echoes. All of our history is waiting here.

No comeliness to be acclaimed, no beauty to be relished. But a heart and an ear. Its very being is compassion. You stand still and hear: stones of sorrow, acquaintance with grief. We all hide our faces from agony, shun the afflicted. The Wall is compassion, its face is open only to those smitten with grief.

So tough, so strong, so tenacious. How she survived the contempt of ages! For centuries while garbage was heaped in her front to cover her face, she remained impervious to desecration, mighty, of mysterious majesty in the midst of scorn.

So many different rulers held sway over the city, so many cataclysmic changes, so many upheavals, so many eruptions of passion came to pass—the Wall kept a silent watch. ". . . A thousand years in thy sight are but as yesterday when it is past, or as a watch in the night" (Pss. 90:4).

"Behold, I made him a witness to the peoples" (Isa. 55:4). These stones have a heart, a heart for all men. The Wall has a soul that radiates a presence.

When Jerusalem was destroyed, we were driven out and like sheep have gone astray; we have turned every one to his own way. The Wall alone stayed on.

What is the Wall? The unceasing marvel. Expectation. The Wall will not perish. The redeemer will come.

Silence. I hug the stones; I pray. O, Rock of Israel, make our faith strong and Your words luminous in our hearts and minds. No image. Pour holiness into our moments.

The Wall is silent? For an instant I am her tongue. Then I hear: I am a man of unclean lips. . . . O God, cleanse my lips, make me worthy to be her tongue. . . .

Suddenly ancient anticipations are resurrected in me. Centuries went and came. Then a moment arrived and stood still, facing me.

Once you have lived a moment at the Wall, you never go away.

THE CHALLENGE

The mystery that is Jerusalem, the challenge that is Jerusalem! How to unite the human and the holy? How to echo the divine in the shape of words, in the form of deeds?

Now that we are at home in the city of David, what is required of us? What message does this new chapter in Jewish history hold in store?

How shall we live in Jerusalem? She is a queen demanding high standards, What does she expect of us, living in an age of spiritual obtuseness, near exhaustion? What sort of light should glow in Zion? What words, what thoughts, what vision should come out of Zion?

The challenge is staggering. Let us pray that we may not fail. Let us prepare the minds and the hearts for the vision of Isaiah concerning Judaism and Jerusalem.

. . . For out of Zion shall go forth the law,
    and the word of the Lord from Jerusalem.
He shall judge between the nations,
    and shall decide for many peoples;
and they shall beat their swords into plowshares,
    and their spears into pruning hooks;

nation shall not lift up sword against nation,

    neither shall they learn war any more.

(ISA. 2:3–4)

We must beware lest the place of David becomes a commonplace.

One is terribly apprehensive. How do you live in the city of God? How do you match the infinitely holy with justice and compassion, with song and prayer? How do you live in a sanctuary day and night? . . . What should come out of Zion? Renunciation of lies, compassion, disgust with violence, help to overcome the infirmity of the spirit.

Jerusalem is more than a place in space or a memorial to glories of the past. Jerusalem is a prelude, anticipation of days to come.

> At that time Jerusalem shall be called the throne of the Lord, and all nations shall gather to it, to the presence of the Lord in Jerusalem, and they shall no more stubbornly follow their own evil heart (Jer. 3:17).

How to prepare the city for such destiny? How to qualify for such calling?

It is one of the great marvels of history that Jerusalem is sacred not only to the Jews but also to Christians and to Moslems all over the world. . . . Who will fan and force the fire of truth to spread across the world, insisting that we are all one, that mankind is not an animal species but a fellowship of care, a covenant of brotherhood?

None shall fear, none shall hurt.

There is cursing in the world, scheming, and very little praying. Let Jerusalem inspire praying: an end to rage, an end to violence.

Let Jerusalem be a seat of mercy for all men. Wherever a sigh is uttered, it will evoke active compassion in Jerusalem.

Let there be no waste of history. This must be instilled in those who might be walking in the streets of Jerusalem like God's butlers in the sacred palace. Here no one is more than a guest.

Jerusalem must not be lost to pride or to vanity.

All of Jerusalem is a gate, but the key is lost in the darkness of God's silence. Let us light all the lights, let us call all the names, to find the key. . . .

NEXT YEAR IN JERUSALEM!

Anatoly Shcharansky

> *Anatoly Shcharansky, one of the most famous of all Jewish refuseniks, spoke movingly of Jerusalem when he was sentenced by a Soviet court after being accused of treason in 1977.*

Five years ago, I submitted my application for exit to Israel. Now I am further than ever from my dream. It would seem to be cause for regret. But it is absolutely otherwise. I am happy. I am happy that I lived honestly, in peace with my conscience. I never compromised my soul, even under the threat of death.

I am happy that I helped people. I am proud that I knew and worked with such honest, brave and courageous people as Sakharov, Orlov, Ginsburg, who are carrying on the traditions of Russian intelligentsia. I am fortunate to have been witness to the process of the liberation of Russia's Jews.

I hope that the absurd accusation against me and the entire Jewish emigration movement will not hinder the liberation of my people. My near ones and friends know how I wanted to exchange activity in the emigration movement for a life with my wife, Avital, in Israel.

For more than two thousand years the Jewish people, my people, have been dispersed. But wherever they are, wherever Jews are found, every year they have repeated, "Next year in Jerusalem." Now, when I am further than ever from my people, from Avital, facing many arduous years of imprisonment, I say, turning to my people, my Avital: Next year in Jerusalem.

THE EIGHTH GATE

Jerusalem in Modern Fiction

View of the Jewish Quarter of the Old City, probably ca. 1937 (Central Zionist Archives; with permission)

Jerusalem is the setting of so many modern works of fiction that the most that this anthology can do is present a small sample of the novels and short stories that feature Jerusalem as their background. The selections that appear here are for the most part selections from longer works and were chosen not so much for the stories they tell as for the descriptions of Jerusalem and life in Jerusalem at various periods of time which they convey.

CITY OF MANY DAYS

Shulamith Hareven

CACHEZ-VOUS, CACHEZ-VOUS!
GARDEZ-VOUS, GARDEZ-VOUS!

A game of hide-and-seek in the alley. Colorful voices slip like busy birds through the window bars of the houses, bearing news of summer on the large stones. A boy plays; a man walks; a woman does the wash. No need to prove anything. Growing up in Jerusalem is an identity all one's own.

❧

The school: named after its philanthropic founder, a German nobleman; a luxuriant ca-per plant, its flowers wedding-white, blooming spectacularly on its high wall.

❧

She grew and grew as though soaring toward some limitless height. She became bossy. Neither family, school, nor street claimed her allegiance anymore. She couldn't wait to be independent of them all. Meanwhile, she took to pitying at random, in sudden awak-enings that came and went, frightening her as they did. On Jaffa Road a shop had been opened for orthopedic shoes with a manikin in the window: its dark hair neatly combed, its face agonizingly contorted, it sat there holding its aching foot while a hidden ma-chine swung its head back and forth with an expression of eternal pain. Sara could never pass by the window without getting tears in her eyes. It wasn't the suffering itself that overwhelmed her, it was the fact that it never stopped. Day and night, while the rest of the world ate, slept, enjoyed itself, and went about its business, the poor manikin sat suf-fering in the window, on and on. Even when it was dark out. Even when nobody saw it, and the last bus, cart, donkey, and man had ceased moving down Jaffa Road, it kept shaking its head from the pain, unable to utter a sound because the mechanic who gave it its twisted, rather English face, its neatly combed hair and very red mouth, hadn't given it the power to cry. Somehow, for Sara, this was the height of indecency. She was sure that if only the manikin could whimper, someone in the shop would remember to shut off the machine that propelled it, at least for the night, so that it might get a little rest.

❧

Meanwhile, she remained in her tower. She read a lot. A closed garden.
   I am a rose of Jerusalem and my halo is dust, a lily of the Valley of the Cross strewn with garbage, a queen in weary Zion reeking of cabbage breathing the breath of stones.
   All words are dirty, impossible. Only the stone before dawn is clean and clear. Absolute.

Who didn't try to civilize them. Once their class was visited by a delegation of religious old ladies from England, most of them hobbling on canes because of the gout, who came to see how they studied the Scriptures. They were in the middle of Ezekiel that day, and the blushing teacher quickly skipped the chapter of the two whoring sisters, Oholah and Oholibah, so as not to embarrass the ladies. There were visits from American philanthropists, too, who came to see them doing exercises in the small yard, their baggy sweatshirts making them look like the inmates of an institution for pregnant orphans. One bitter winter day, when heavy gusts of wind trod visibly in the pale lemon-and-black light through the thistly field nearby, a guest of honor arrived from the Foundation of French Culture, or perhaps it was of French Friendship. A short man with ugly, glittering eyes, he wore an immaculate suit and spoke French with a carefully cultivated voice that was perhaps the one attractive thing about him. He stood before them with the look of a man who has eavesdropped on life and not liked what he has heard. Their principal, rubbing his hands, introduced him as Monsieur Gaston. In a French like rattling peas, the Culture Director, or perhaps it was the Friendship Director, proceeded to deliver a speech about the greatness of the Encyclopédistes, whom he, Monsieur Gaston, would now tell them about in Jerusalem. *Grandeur. Gloire.* The light of human reason. Enlightenment. The kerosene heater was on the blink that day and they were all nearly poisoned by the smoke. The girls sat looking gloomily at the fists of rain hammering on the melancholy windowpane, until a dark hail began to fall and drown out the speaker entirely. Monsieur Gaston whipped out a giant umbrella and disappeared like an evil dwarf.

Even their French teacher, fat old Monsieur Schnur of the Francofied Schnur family, disapproved of the lecturer. Perhaps Monsieur Gaston of Paris had slighted old Schnur, the patient torchbearer of the Encyclopédistes in the Holy City, but a few lessons afterward he declaimed to them in a sarcastic simper:

"In Paris, the city of light, the center of the great French culture, of which I, Monsieur Schnur, am about to tell you in Jerusalem, there is a museum. The name of the museum is le Louvre. And in the museum of le Louvre in the city of light stands a statue. The statue is nude. Do any of you know why this statue is nude? The statue is nude because the sculptor who made it was poor and had no money to buy it any clothes."

All the old man's chins trembled with laughter. The girls liked him. He had deserted the Friendship Director and gone over to them.

They were being civilized with penmanship, embroidery, and prayer. No longer did they pray for the health of Sultan Abd-el-Hamid, but they still thanked the Lord for their souls every morning. In music class they sang:

In valley deep and mountainside
God His bounty doth provide.

They were quizzed in science too.

"Amarillo, how does light travel from place to place?"

The dormitory of the Alliance School in Jerusalem in 1908 (Central Zionist Archives; with permission)

"On the waves of ether."

"Saporta, what is the smallest part of matter which is indivisible?"

"The atom."

"Laniado, why does water go up a siphon?"

"Because it's scared of the vacuum."

The city kept growing on them. The British built a thousand and one wonders: the YMCA, its tower resembling a tall erection, its interior decorated with Persian carpets, inlaid Damascus tables, Hellenistic mosaics, and English hunting scenes. They built the massive post office to look like one of Queen Victoria's railway stations, done up inside in strange, imported green marble. Dirt paths and wagon trails turned into paved roads, by the sides of which cypresses stood straight as sentries, drawing back from the dust of the horses. The Jews and the Arabs went on building as they always had, with flesh-colored Jerusalem stone and red roof tiles from Motsa. They draped grapevines on trellises, sat in courtyards under fig trees, and cured olives in soldered tin cans. The more educated among them went to browse in the British libraries. When Sara grew older, she began to borrow books from the YMCA. Once she went there on His Majesty's birthday and found it closed. The doorman, a black Sudanese dressed in a shiny white robe, a shiny red fez, and sneakers on his sockless feet, didn't open the heavy, European-wood door for her as usual. Instead he jigged up and down with joyous abandon:

"No mees, no mees, no libarry, no libarry, beeg day for you, beeg day for me, long leev de Keeng."

The air in the neighborhood: vibrant, familiar, smelling of stone that is lived in, used. She fell asleep at night to the high voices of the cistern cleaners returning from work, cradled by the sharp metallic bang of the shutter bolts, which Grandfather Amarillo always inspected shutter by shutter in case of thieves. Then came the cranking of the pulley-chain of the grandfather clock, which he set every evening. Cats rustling and yowling among the wild olive shoots. The kitchen clock chiming slowly. It was half a tone lower and then seconds faster than the other: soon the grandfather clock would chime too. A long, starry, oboelike breeze.

Early in the morning she was brought back to the light by the braying of Mahmousm Shabu's donkey, and the gurgly clink of the bottles of red wine from Mr. Hamkes's store that blistered in the sacks on his back. A pinkering light in the stone. A window yawning open. *I thank Thee my God, King everlasting, Who restoreth to me my soul*, all washed and shiny. Followed by the litany of the vegetable man from Bet Sahur who arrived every morning with dawn: *Yallah*, orranges! *Yallah*, frresh orranges! Tomat, tomat, tomat! The muezzin from the mosque. the church bells and the goat bells. White parachutes of shivering sheep cluster cold on the fog-snagged hill. Back to work come the cistern cleaners in their clothes that stink to high heaven so that the waters of Jerusalem might be clean.

The sounds of a small city. As small as a man's palm.

◈

The arched transoms of the Amarillos' windows are made of stained glass, so that at any given hour of the day the light plays somewhere on the floor tiles of the house in red, green, blue, violet, or an ochrous lion-yellow like the hills of the Judaean wilderness at dusk. Only one side of the house never gets any sun, not only because of its northern exposure, but because it faces out on a high, blind wall of Sa'ada's whorehouse. Sa'ada's girls wear heavy makeup and have red purses that swing at their sides. She has procurers working for her too, sallow, stupid young men whose job it is to shout, "Hello, George, hello, George" at every passing man. Once, when Zaki Amarillo was still a proper husband and father, a sudden gust of wind blew some sheets that were drying on the Amarillo's roof into Sa'ada's courtyard. It happened to be a day when Bukas was off. The family debated who could be sent to fetch them. Not Gracia, who mustn't be seen in the courtyard; not Zaki either, because there might be gossip; Elder Amarillo was certainly out of the question; while Sara, when she volunteered out of pure curiosity, got a spanking for her pains.

"Couldn't you get along without them?" Zaki asked Gracia.

But Gracia refused.

"The plain ones, I don't care about, but the *broderie anglaise* ones, I got them from my grandmother."

The whole family went below and called, "Sa'ada. Sa'ada," in a chorus. Sa'ada didn't hear them, but the whole neighborhood did and laughed. So did Sa'ada's young panderers, who stood there shouting in high falsetto: "Sa'ada. Sa'ada. Where are you, *ya* Sa'ada?"

In the end Tia Victoria came to the rescue. "Why the hell should I care," she said.

She went over to Sa'ada's, a cigarette in the corner of her mouth, and came out a while later with the pile of sheets in her arms.

"Bravo, Victoria!" the curiosity-seekers congratulated her.

"What's the matter with you?" answered Victoria with a look of disdain. "She's all right, that Sa'ada. She would have brought the sheets over herself in another minute if she didn't feel so embarrassed."

✌

The city still squats on its haunches . . . a ripple of red roofs draped with a shimmering halo of heat like a clean muslin net that softens its colors and lines. Jerusalem is a veiled lady on a still, torrid day, feminine, forlorn, softly dreaming, self-absorbed, sucking time sweetly like an old sugar candy, her sons gathered under the many folds of her robe, picking rockrose and herbs. Other days she is a man, fierce, dry, and ancient, smelling of thyme and wild goat, his head covered with a sack against the wind, bare feet viny-veined, brusque-voiced and ornery, sniffing the slippery scent of sin in abandoned alleys, the odor of prophecy in public squares. The city lives without mirrors, each of its dwellers the key to an ancient, ironlike place, lattice-faced, wall-chested, sandaled feet skipping lightly over crooked, anonymous cobblestones, through openings, endless doors. Always an unsolved remainder, footprints belonging to no one, improbable clues, a taste of permanent mystery. A veiny, living tension from street to street, house to house. Each solemn girl in a courtyard is more girl than anywhere else, each baby wrapped in a shawl the only baby on earth, each single person the leaven of life. The city tenses its muscles under your feet. Put your hand on a wall and you feel the stone pulse. The very light percolates through it with each breath of the desert heat. Every house is itself. Alive. Alive.

✌

The Barzels stroll slowly through the twilight. Slowly, because Bimbi still has pains and a cough in his chest, and Hulda is pregnant. The child is large; Hulda smiles whenever it kicks her moonlike body, now taut as a drum. She calls it Goliath. They are out for their evening walk, like good Jerusalemites. It is almost autumn and the nights are getting cold. The young trees of Rehavia are growing up. New buildings are going up all around.

"Every true native of Jerusalem," says Professor Barzel, "is always hungry for the absolute. Even if he reaches it, he goes on pining for it. That's what Jerusalem is about"

"The problem is," says Hulda sadly, "that everyone has his own absolute. Look at the sky, Bibmi, how the blue behind those scaffolds is so much deeper than the blue in front of them."

He stops to rest for a minute: "They're building too much. It's changing the whole character of the city. Jerusalem shouldn't be so crowded or so square-angled. And those water tanks are an error."

"When I was a girl in Bet Hakerem, there was once an old stonemason working down the street. One day Amatsia asked to be shown how to lay stones. There's nothing to it, the old man said. Just lay the stone however it wants to be laid."

A spasm of pain comes and goes as he smiles.

"Hulda, what will become of us? You'll have an old wreck for a husband."

"I'll have a Bimbi for a husband and a Goliath for a child."

In order to help pass the time, Professor Barzel conducts a study of the names of Jerusalem's neighborhoods, about which he writes to a friend in Germany:

The question of nomenclature is most interesting. Some neighborhoods here have names like prayers for succor and strength that never seem to come. As the present is always bad, the Jews have learned to live in a future that is always sure to be better. Romema, "Uplifted." Ruhama, "The Pitied One." Ezrat Yisra'el, "The Aid of Israel." Ge'ula, "Redemption." Talpiot, "Great Heights." Yemin Moshe, "The Right Hand of Moses"—perhaps this last refers to Sir Moses Montefiore who built it, and perhaps to Moses the Prophet, who held both hands aloft while the Israelites prevailed. Some live in Mekor Hayyim, "Life's Source," while others dream of Sha'arei Hesed, "Mercy's Gates"; still others who never planted a seed in their lives named their quarter Me'ah She'arim, "The Hundredfold Crop." And there are more modest, more secular names too: Nahalat Ahim, "The Brothers' Estate," Nahalat Shiv'a, "The Place of the Seven," Yegia Kappayim, "The Laborer's Lot," Kerem Avraham, "Abraham's Vineyard," Bayit ve-Gan, "House-and-Garden."

The Arabs, on the other hand, are more concerned with illustrious figures from their past. They have a quarter named after Sheikh Jarrah, a healer in Salladin's camp; they have an Omariyyah after Omar the Great, and Talbiyyah after Taleb. Ahmed Abu-Tor, a warrior of Salladin's who used to ride on an ox, gave his name to the neighborhood of Abu-Tor, "The Master of the Ox." The name Abu Dis derives from a forgotten Greek monk, Batabudission. The houses by the Saint-Simon Monastery were once called in Greek *kata monis*, "by the monastery," and the name Katamon has stuck to this day. A section of the city that was covered with sharp pebbles, *sarrar* in Arabic, became known as Musrara, Pebbletown. And imagine, among the filth and caved-in ruins of an Arab slum, coming across the glorious street name of Gottfried de Bouillion! Thus we live, my friend, caught between a forgotten Crusader past and a yearned-for biblical future, with nothing to hold onto but the present, this damnably difficult here and now.

❧

A light-and-shade-struck city of light-and-shade-struck people. A narrow, arched passageway, gravid-shaped, wide enough for a small donkey; the soft light behind it incandescing not on the man but on the red flap of his clothes, his dark patch of a head barely brushing the moss growing out of the wall. A burro slowly climbs the narrow steps. Around the corner the aquamarine mosaic of the Dome of the Rock, a sudden treasure to look at, a prismatic jewel in a setting of stone.

☙

A city you long for the more you are in it; in which you are most yourself and most miss yourself; in which whatever you find, you will want again from afar. A dichotomous city in which everything is its own looking glass, forever mirroring, always the same sky reflecting domed rock cut from sky, always the same broad evening light casting back in reverse the red roofs of the houses. People draw near and recede as in mirrors. A few last gilded roofs. Still the spires of the minarets. Evening comes with an avalanche of longing, and you walk slowly through Zion Square as the first lights go on and buy a coal-hot order of stemmed *hamleh m'lan* from the scarfaced Sudanese vendor, eating it as though there will never be food in the world and no you, only this one perfect hunger that must be shared with a friend because everything is in it, this entire evening, and that is more than one person can bear.

☙

A city on the desert's edge, its populace holding on with bare nails, high-strung, quarrelsome, haggling, wrangling, cupidous. The weaver weaves and hawks his wares; he sells his wares; the buyer buys. None turn to look at the desert from which their forefathers had come, scaling the heights from below to conquer this place.

And yet on certain nights, when a dry sirocco wind that has assembled its forces on the Plain of the Jordan, that has marshaled them again on the Mount of Qarantal, that has gathered reinforcements in the ascent of the Edomites, bursts through the streets of the city like the footfalls of an invisible invader, the desert overruns Jerusalem again. There is a groan, a stillness, a wound. And then silence once more. The broken tablets of the Law. Until morning.

☙

On the subject of reincarnation, Elias was sure that he had lived in Jerusalem in Herod's time and had been trampled to death there by a horse-drawn chariot in a narrow alley. In his nightmares he saw the horse bearing wildly down on him and the frightened eyes of the charioteer, he felt the wall against him, sudden and hard, and knew he could back off no farther. The dream kept recurring.

He felt at home, so he said, in the Herodian remnants of Jerusalem, in the ruined towers of Phasael and Antonia with their margined, finely dressed stones. A toga would have befit his tall frame. His sad, knowledgeable mouth could have spoken all the tongues of that complicated city without tripping. Greek sounded well on Elias. Not the Greek of Madame Savvidopoulos, but the blunt, wise, stinging Greek of those times.

No city lives closer to the almost invisible ghosts of past lives than Jerusalem; no city is better at blind, secret love. Hermetic, ironic, a sink of cold tempests, the city stands upright on the mountain against the cold night, most strong and most vulnerable, something in it never falling asleep. All placed outside of it are like a somehow undeserved vacation. Or is there any place at all outside of Jerusalem?

❧

Sara stepped out of the building on Mount Scopus in which she taught, a silent presence, the whole city spread at her feet, and looked at the soft fleecy light out over the mountains, over the houses drowning in radiance, as if once this city, long, long ago, soon after Creation, had burst from some great rock, its truth flown molten and shiny over the hills. She could feel the moment to the quick. Now this is me, she told herself, now this is me, here on this hill, with this feeling of great peace that will never last, or standing in the street, people know me, I have three sons and so little time. Now this is me in this moment of hers. Tomorrow I'll be gone and the street will be gone, or another street and another time. And always, forever, this fleecy pile of light, that rock tumbled halfway down the hill to a lonely stop, a terraced alley, a dripping

The Hebrew University Campus on Mount Scopus, ca. 1928 (Central Zionist Archives; with permission)

cypress tree, a caper plant in a wall. A place to walk slowly. A place to touch the sky: now it is close. To breathe in mountain and light. Now.

(Translated by Hillel Halkin with the author)

Tehila: The Praise of Jerusalem

S. Y. Agnon

At the eve of new moon I walked to the Western Wall, as we in Jerusalem are accustomed to do, praying at the Western Wall at the rising of each moon.

Already most of the winter had passed, and spring blossoms had begin to appear. Up above, the heavens were pure, and the earth had put off her grief. The sun smiled in the sky; the City shone in its light. And we too rejoiced, despite the troubles that beset us; for these troubles were many and evil, and before we had reckoned with one, yet another came in its wake.

From Jaffa Gate as far as the Western Wall, men and women from all the communities of Jerusalem moved in a steady stream, together with those newcomers whom The Place [God—ed.] had restored to their place, albeit their place had not yet been found. But in the open space before the Wall, at the booth of the Mandatory Police, sat the police of the Mandate whose function was to see that no one guarded the worshippers save only they. Those who had come to pray were herded together and driven to seek shelter close up against the stones of the Wall, some weeping and some as if dazed. And still we say, How Long, O Lord? How long?—For we have trodden the lowest stair of degredation, yet you tarry to redeem us.

I found a place for myself at the Wall, standing at times amongst the bewildered bystanders. I was amazed at the people of the world: as if it were not sufficient that they oppressed us in all lands, yet they must also oppress us in our home. As I stood there I was driven from my place by one of the police who carried a baton. This man was in a great rage, on account of some ailing old woman who had brought a stool with her to the Wall. The policeman took a flying kick, throwing the woman to the ground, and confiscated the stool: for she had infringed the law enacted by the legislators, which forbade worshippers to bring seats to the wall. And those who had come to pray saw this, yet held their peace: for how can right dispute against might? Then came forward that same old woman whom I knew, and looked the policeman straight in the eye. And the policeman averted his glance, and returned the stool to its owner.

I went up to her and said, "Your eyes have more effect than all the pledges of England. For England, which gave us the Balfour Declaration, sends her officer to annul it; while you only looked upon that wicked one, and frustrated his evil intent."

She replied, "Do not speak of him so, for he is a good gentile, who saw that I was grieved and gave back her stool to that poor woman. . . . But have you said your afternoon prayer? I ask because, if you are free, I can put in your way the *mitzvah* of visiting the sick. The *rabbanit* is now really and truly ill. If you wish, come with me and I shall take you by a short route." I joined her and we went together.

From alley to alley, from courtyard to courtyard, we made our way down, and at each step she took she would pause to give a piece of candy to a child, or a coin to a beggar, or to ask the health of a man's wife or, if it were a woman, the health of her husband. . . .

". . . how is it that we keep walking and walking, yet we have still not come to the house of the *rabbanit?*"

She said, "You still have in mind those courtyards we used to take for a short cut. But now that most of the Old City has been settled by the Arabs, we must go by a roundabout way."

We approached one of these courtyards. She said, "Do you see this courtyard? Forty families of Israel once lived here, and here were two synagogues, and here in the daytime and nighttime there were study and prayer. But they left this place, and Arabs came and occupied it."

We approached a tumble-down house. She said, "Do you see this house? Here was a great academy where the scholars of the Torah lived and studied. But they left this house, and Arabs came and occupied it."

We came to the asses' stalls. She said, "Do you see these stalls? Here stood a soup-kitchen, and the virtuous poor would enter hungry and go forth satisfied. But they abandoned this place, and Arabs came and occupied it. Houses from which prayer and charity and study of Torah never ceased, now belong to the Arabs and their asses. . . . My son, we have reached the courtyard of the *rabbanit's* house. Go in, and I shall follow you later. This unhappy woman, because of the seeming good she has known abroad, does not see the true good at home."

"What is the true good?" I asked.

She laughed. saying, "My son, you should not need to ask. Have you not read the verse, 'Happy the man thou choosest to dwell in thy courtyards?' For these same courtyards are the royal courts of the Holy One, the courts of our God, in the midst of Jerusalem. When men say 'Jerusalem,' their way is to add the words, 'Holy City.' But when *I* say 'Jerusalem,' I add nothing more, since the holiness is contained in the name; yes, in the very name itself. . . . Go up. my son, and do not trip on the stairs. Many a time have I said to the keeper of the community funds that these stairs are in need of repair; and what answer did he give me? That this building is old and due to be demolished, therefore it is not worth while spending a penny on its upkeep. So the houses of Israel fall into disuse until they are abandoned, and the sons of Ishmael enter and take possession. Houses that were built with the tears of their fathers—and now they abandon them. But again I have become a chatterer, and hasten my end."

Tilli entered the room. She was carrying a bowl of soup, and seeing me she said:

"Ah, you are still here! But stay, my friend, stay. It is a great *mitzvah* to visit the sick. *Rabbanit*, how much better you look! Truly, salvation comes in the wink of an eye; for the Name is healing you every minute. I have brought a little soup to moisten your lips, now, my dear, raise your head and I shall prop up your pillow. There, my dear, that's better. My son, I am sorry that you do not live in the City, for then you would see for yourself how the *rabbanit*'s health is improving day by day."

"And do I not live in Jerusalem?" I said. "Surely Nachalat Shivah is Jerusalem?"

"It is indeed," answered Tilli. "God forbid that it should be otherwise. Rather may the day come when Jerusalem extends as far as Damascus, and in every direction. But the eye that has seen all Jerusalem enclosed within her walls cannot accustom itself to viewing what is built beyond the walls as the City itself. It is true that all the Land of Israel is holy and, I need hardly say, the surroundings of Jerusalem: yet the holiness that is within the walls of the City surpasses all else. My son, there is nothing I have said which you do not know better than I. Why then have I said it? Only that I might speak the praise of Jerusalem."

I could read in the eyes of the *rabbanit* a certain resentment, because Tilli was speaking to me rather than to her. So I took my leave and went away.

Various preoccupations kept me for a while from going to the Old City; and after that came the nuisance of the tourists. How well we know these tourists, who descend upon us and upon the land, all because the Place has made a little space for us here! They come now to see what has happened; and having come, they regard us as if we were created soley to serve them. Yet one good thing may be said for the tourists: in showing them "the sights," we see them ourselves. Once or twice, having brought them to the City to show them the Western Wall, I met Tilli there. It seemed to me that a change had come over her. Although she had always walked without support, I noticed that she now leaned on a stick. Because of the visitors, I was unable to linger. For they had come to spy out the whole land, not to spend time upon an old woman not even mentioned in their itineraries.

When the tourists had left Jerusalem, I felt restless in myself. After trying without success to resume work, I bestirred myself and walked to the City, where I visited of my own accord all the places I had shown to the visitors. How can I describe what I saw? He who in His goodness daily renews the works of creation, perpetually renews His own City. New houses may not have been built, nor new trees planted; yet Jerusalem herself is ever new. I cannot explain the secret of her infinite variety. We must wait, all of us for those great sages who will one day enlighten us.

I came upon a man of learning, and he drew me to his house, where he set before me all his recent findings. We sat together in deep contentment, while I asked my questions, and he replied; or spoke of problems, which he resolved; or mentioned cloudy matters, which he made clear. How good it is, how satisfying, to sit at the feet of one of the learned men of Jerusalem, and to learn the Law from his lips! His home is simple, his furnishings austere, yet his wisdom ranges far, like the great hill ranges of

Jerusalem which are seen from the windows. Bare are the hills of Jerusalem; no temples or palaces crown them. Since the time of our exile, nation after nation has come and laid them waste. But the hills spread their glory like banners to the sky; they are resplendent in everchanging hues; and not least in glory is the Mount of Olives, which bears no forest of trees, but a forest of tombs of the righteous, who in life and in death gave their thoughts to the Land.

(TRANSLATED BY WALTER LEVER)

THE DEBT OF BLOOD

Elisha Porat

In the army, I was lying and reading in my tent. It was the rare soldier who succeeded in reading a book in the army in those days: newspapers and light magazines were as much as most people could manage. My favorite poet at that time was Avraham Ben Yitzhak. In the one slim volume containing all his poems I found a hidden treasure of beauty. I would shut myself off from abrasive surroundings and contemplate his poems. Between one poem and the next, I would look wonderingly about me and soar on the wings of my thoughts far from the army camp which so oppressed my spirits. Once I was reading "The hills joined together around my town" when a soldier pushed past my bed. He stopped and bent down to see what I was reading that so absorbed my attention. When he saw the book his eyes widened. His eyes softened and he sat down on my bed. We introduced ourselves. Something stronger than we were drew us to each other, and we became friends. True, bosom friends. He had the body of a farmer and the soul of a poet.

From our posts in Jerusalem we would phone each other on the urban line, like a pair of lovers.

"Listen, I want to read you something, something great," he would tempt me.

"I'm listening, I'm listening."

And over the telephone on the local line, he would read me wonderful pages from Yizhar's *Tziklag Days* until the switchboard operator would interrupt us with typical military narrow-mindedness: "What's all this then—official business?"

"Yes," my friend would yell, "very important business." I pressed the receiver to my ear. I couldn't get enough of S. Yizhar's beautiful words. Nobody had ever read Yizhar to me like this before. Later, years later, when I read the book myself something strange happened to me. The eyes skimming the printed pages were mine, but the voice which I heard reading the words in my ears was his. I laid the book down and closed my eyes tightly. The autumn wind of Jerusalem blew through the leaves on the fig-trees and the flowers on the caper bushes shone like little torches. On our nocturnal walks he would show me the distant stars, the silhouettes of towers, and all the hills encircling Jerusalem.

"Even on the darkest night," he would boast, "I can identify every dome, every valley, every mountain range."

It was as if he had been born in Jerusalem, as if he had never seen another town in his life. I would remind him of the beginning of our friendship. Of the hills joined together around our town. And he would smile wordlessly. We would spend our leaves together, wandering about the town. Walking and talking. It was clear to him that we had some special destiny to fulfill. He was sure that he had something important to say, and that people would have to listen to him. He loved the Land of Israel with a burning passion. He would laugh at the various experts who knew the country by its flora and fauna, its geological formations, its history.

"With me, it's in my blood," he laughed. "You can put me down anywhere in the country and I'll know where I am by sticking out my tongue and sniffing the air."

Once we were walking in an orthodox quarter on a Friday evening. The façades of the houses were already steeped in a Sabbath peace, but on the back verandahs, facing the border, men sat playing cards with an absorption that looked as if it would last all night long. The sight of these men sitting in their undershirts and playing cards made him furious.

"Is that what we came to this country for?"

"Is that what we joined the army for?"

"Is that worth paying the price for?"

That night something cracked in him. He told me things about himself which he had never dared to speak of before. He was very agitated, and his voice shook strangely. He told me about a letter he had written to his girl. About the words he had written her in reply to certain fears she had confessed to him.

"The debt of blood, you understand? The debt of blood, that's what I believe in!"

He seized my hand, my shirt, he came very close to me.

"Don't you see, it's impossible to live in this country without some hugh debt. A terrible debt we have to pay so that we can go on living here." How strange his voice sounded in that orthodox quarter in Jerusalem on the Sabbath Eve. If I had compared him then to some prophet it would have been ridiculous. But his words tore something apart in my soul. From that night on I saw him differently. You could even say that I was a little jealous of him. I thought that he had outstripped the rest of us in some mysterious way. That perhaps he had already begun to grasp things which were deeper, truer, that were perhaps the beginnings of a dimension which I too was seeking then. And seeking with all my soul. I probed his words to find something which would make sense of the things we had done, some justification—you might also say, some opening to a new, different faith.

"And you," he asked me, "do you feel that you owe a debt?"

"Perhaps," I said, "I don't know."

And afterwards I had a bad feeling, as if I had missed an opportunity which might never return to me again. I could never speak about my private beliefs to anyone else. It seemed to me like something crude, revolting, almost indecent. As if we had come as close as possible to each other without risking collision. And then continued moving apart. Each one on his own course, moving inevitably, endlessly further away. Years

A monument to the soldiers of the Israel Defence Forces who fell in the 1967 War; photograph taken in 1968 (Central Zionist Archives; with permission)

later, in an army camp we had conquered from the Arab Legion, east of Nablus, I remembered him again. In the newspapers coming out after the week of war, the names of the fallen began to appear. I read his name slowly, stammering, joining the syllables together one by one as if I was beginning to read my first words all over again. I was sorry then that I had ever learnt to read. In that orthodox quarter of Jerusalem under those same balconies, he had fallen. For a moment I seemed to hear his voice at my side, to feel his trembling hand clutching my shirt.

"Is that what we came to this country for? Is that worth paying the price for?"

In the hills which had joined together around this town, something had been orphaned. And I seemed to grow a few years older at once. Sometimes, although I know it's cheating, I continue my conversation with him. From the point at which I had been afraid of exposing myself then.

"Yes," I answer him from the distance of the years. "Yes, I feel that I owe a debt."

"The debt of blood we spoke of then?"

"Any debt you like," I shout at him from my groaning heart.

Happy are they who sow and do not reap, happy are they who set forth and do not return.

In the first year after the war, when I was approaching the middle of my life, I learnt to read Hebrew on tombstones. I learnt fast. Within the space of a few days I could read the names, the dates. After a week or two I could draw a map of gravestones. And after a month I had already covered the whole country in monuments to the fallen. At first I would read the names aloud, in a slightly hesitant voice, syllable by syllable. Afterwards I pronounced them silently, only my lips moving. And today I already know how to read them to myself, in my head, or as some say: in my heart. I myself don't know.

(TRANSLATED BY DALIA BILU)

IN THE HEART OF THE SEAS

S. Y. *Agnon*

> *The story is excerpted from Agnon's novel set in the early nineteenth century telling of the pilgrimage of a group of Jews to the Land of Israel.*

When the morning star arose, they said their prayers, and ate the morning meal, and then got on their asses and journeyed until they reached a certain spot called Motza, from which in ancient times willow boughs were brought to the altar, as we learn: "There is a place below Jerusalem called Motza, to which people go down to gather willow boughs which they afterwards set up beside the altar." And willows are still to be found there.

There they made a resting place and stopped over. All these ways are desolate because of robbers, and even the Ishmaelites themselves dare not pass on these ways unless they go out in a caravan together. But his Name, be blessed, took pity on our comrades, so that no mishap occurred to them on the road except that their sacks fell from the backs of the asses once or twice. There are chains of high and lofty mountains all along the way, with all manner of clouds covering them, clouds of blue and purple, clouds radiant and gently bright, with the radiance of the jewels and blossoms of the Garden of Eden.

Every hour a new light made its appearance, and none of the lights resembles one another; and goodly odors there were on every side, issuing from all manner of fragrant plants. And castles, and palaces whose beauty was once the glory of the country now stand desolate, and there is no settled place, nothing but the black tents of Kedar dispersed and forsaken among the mountains, and goats trailing down the mountainsides, sustaining themselves on the thorns and thistles and brambles and briars mentioned in the Scriptures; and half-naked men sit there, wearing nothing but a shirt and girdle and a black kerchief bound by a woolen rope on their heads. And fine springs and streams of water run down into the valleys from the mountains, and they taste like the springs in the Garden of Eden. Our comrades drank of those waters, and in those waters washed their hands before the prayer, and rinsed their eyes because of their tears over the destruction of the Land, and hallowed their hands in honor of the Holy City.

This they did for three days, until the Sabbath eve arrived, and the Holy City, the joy of the whole world, appeared before them in the distance. At once they descended from their asses and rent their garments, weeping bitterly, and proceeded on foot until they reached the gates of Jerusalem. They kissed the stones of her walls and rent their garments a second time in memory of the Temple. May it be His will that it shall be rebuilt speedily and in our own days. Amen.

Within a very short while their arrival became known throughout the city. All Jerusalem came forth to meet them, both the pious and the devoted scholars; and they wished them peace, greatly rejoicing in them and offering them every manner of honor, and saying to them, Happy you are to have come hither without considering your bodies and your wealth, but thinking only of your souls; so that you have been found worthy to stand in the Temple of the King who is King over all kings, the Holy One, blessed be He.

ॐ

In brief, they were welcomed by the Holy Congregation of Jerusalem with every manner of honor and respect, and the people of the city showed their affection by taking our comrades to their homes, and fetching them food and drink, and preparing them beds with pillows and cushions. They refreshed themselves and rested their weary bones until noon, when they went to the bath to purify themselves in honor of the Sabbath and in honor of the city. And the bath of Jerusalem is the most praiseworthy of baths, because it has inner and outer rooms. In the outer rooms people take off their clothes, in the inner they are naked. And there is a room in which attendants rub down the bathers after they have finished their baths. And they have an oven there under the ground, which is stoked with animal droppings and manure. All the rooms are hot, some hot and some hotter; there are reservoirs of water and a perennial pool of fresh water, which is neither hot nor cold, but lukewarm. The bather pays two pennies to the bathing master and one to the attendant and receives a sheet for modesty's sake.

Well, they went down and dipped themselves in the ritual bath. Then they went up and sweated and afterwards proceeded to the room where the attendant rubbed them down and poured cold water over them. They went and dipped once again, came up and dried themselves, put on white garments, and came out like new-born creatures. And when they came out they gave the attendant a penny, and he wished them good health. Back they went to their homes, put on Sabbath garments, and proceeded to the Western Wall.

Now the Western Wall is all we have left of our beloved Temple since ancient times. It has been left by the Holy One, blessed be He, by reason of His great pity for us, and is twelve times as tall as a man, corresponding to the Twelve Tribes, in order that each

The Wall in the late nineteenth century (Photograph by La Maison Bonfils. The Museum of Photography at Tel-Hai Industrial Park; with permission)

man in Israel should devote his heart and will to prayer in accordance with his height and his tribe. It is built of great stones, each stone being five ells by six, and their like is not to be found in any building in the world; and they stand without pitch or mortar or lime between them, in spite of which they are as firmly united as if they were one stone, like the Assembly of Israel which has not even the slightest sovereign power to hold it together, yet is nonetheless, one unit throughout the world. Facing the Wall on both sides are courtyards belonging to Arabs, who dwell there with their beasts and do not disturb Israel in their prayers.

Our men of good heart kneeled, and prostrated themselves, and kneeled, and took off their shoes, and washed their hands, and walked with bowed head until they reached the Wall, and weeping kissed each and every stone. Then they opened their prayer books and recited the Song of Songs with great passion and devotion, their souls being roused more and more with every verse. Rabbi Moshe rested his head against the Wall and remembered that he was standing at a spot from which the Divine Presence itself had never moved. He began reciting the Song of Songs with awesome fervor and with the very chant with which his brother, Rabbi Gershon, may he rest in peace, had departed from the world. But here Rabbi Moshe managed to complete the entire verse, the joy of the Land of Israel entered into him, together with a fresh vitality.

Having come to the synagogue, they prayed sweetly with full hearts. Who shall describe the great virtue of prayer in the Land of Israel, and all the more in Jerusalem, where once the Temple rose of which it is written, "Mine eyes and My heart shall be there perpetually." Rabbi Shelomo went up twice to recite the priestly blessing, since in Jerusalem the priests raise their hands in blessing every day and not merely at festivals as is the practice throughout by far the greater part of the Exile; and on days when the Additional Prayer is said, they raise their hands in blessing both at the Morning and Additional Prayers. And Rabbi Shmuel Yosef, the son of Rabbi Shalom Mordekhai ha-Levi, poured water on the hands of the priests from a silver ewer which Rabbi Moshe had brought from the home of his grandfather, Rabbi Avigdor. Rabbi Shmuel Yosef used to fulfil with fervor every injunction which came his way and all the more so those which served as a commemoration of the Temple. While pouring the water, his hands trembled so for joy that the ewer beat against the basin and it gave forth a sound like the musical instruments of the Levites of old. The Priests went up to their platform, turned their faces to the people, parted their bent fingers on which the blessings are engraved, raised their hands on high, blessed the congregation in a voice like the voice of the wings of the cherubim in the Garden of Eden, and prolonged the blessings until the congregation had said the Thanksgiving, which they then closed with Amen. Great was the joy of Rabbi Shelomo, and great indeed the love with which he chanted his blessing when he first had the merit of going up to the priest's stage, to recite the blessing in Jerusalem, the Holy City. The blessings fairly tripped over themselves in their haste.

After the Sabbath our comrades hired themselves a dwelling near the Western Wall, the windows of which directly faced the site of the Temple; and so they found themselves in the presence of the Divine Presence. The women purchase themselves garments of white wool and the choicest food and drink of the Land, and of its fruits. They cooked and baked and conducted their households with wisdom. They lacked for nothing, even having goat's milk for the Feast of Weeks.

Our comrades resided before the Lord in the Land of Life, in Jerusalem, devoting themselves to Torah and prayer and good deeds and the practice of charity, and to love and to fear and to humility. And on the eve of the New Moon and the other days on which the Prayers of Supplication are said, they would go out to the Holy Places and pray for themselves and their brethren in exile.

All hours are not the same. It is widely known that every righteous man who comes up from outside the Land to the Land of Israel must begin by falling from his original level. For the air of the Land of Israel is holy and a reduction is necessary to precede Being. But His Name, be blessed, came to their aid and gave them the strength to accept submissively all that befell them, until they were worthy to receive a fresh intelligence, the intelligence of the Land of Israel. Day after day they were tried and tested, by insults and by curses, by loss of money and injury to their persons. For Jerusalem is not as the places that are outside the Land, since never has a man gone to sleep in Jerusalem bearing unrequited sins. For day after day the Holy One, blessed be he, settles that day's accounts, in order that the spiritual debts of Jerusalem might not increase and multiply. Like a judge of flesh and blood, who considers and reconsiders the cases of those brought before him that they might be found innocent; so the Holy One, blessed be He, turns, as one might say, his eyes on Jerusalem and chastises its inhabitants that they might be cleansed of every iniquity.

ᕲ

And so our redeemed brethren dwelled together within the Holy Congregation of the Holy City, joyously fulfilling the commandment to dwell in the Land of Israel; until their end came and they passed away, returning their souls unto Him to whom all souls belong, and leaving their bodies to the bosom of their mother; for they were found worthy to be buried in the soil of the Holy Land on the Mount of Olives at Jerusalem, facing the Temple of the Lord, at the feet of the Holy One, blessed be he; until the time comes for them to awaken to everlasting life, on the day of which it is written: "And His feet shall stand in that day upon the mount of Olives."

(TRANSLATED BY I. M. LASK)

JERUSALEM PLAYS HIDE AND SEEK

Ariella Deem

> *This section of the novella takes place in Jerusalem in 1888.*

Why were the eyes of the children of Hacham Nehunia's wife always so infected? Weak and bleary and watery? She, whose eyes were like black silk curtains, their black—the world; their white—the ocean that encircles it. Like the pools in Heshbon bathed in milk.

But her children?

Yosef would stand over them silently, washing their eyes, dressing them, bandaging them. Their father had already told his neighbors in the synagogue: "Yosef's heart is a locked garden. *A garden locked, a fountain sealed.* But his hands—his hands are the hands of Asaf."

And the word spread, and people in the village were saying, "His hands are the hands of Asaf."

And the hands were the hands of Asaf the Healer.

And the toddlers who crawled on the ground, at the doorstep, and in the courtyard minded Yosef and heeded his silence.

They obeyed him when he asked them to open their mouths wide, so that he could see their small tongues and squeeze some lemon drops on them to relieve their sore throats. They obeyed him, those tiny ones who writhed in pain in the evenings, as the worms in their intestines began to torment them. They stood silently every evening, those pitiful little ones, and drank his bitter elixirs.

One spring day the line of suffering children was very long, and their ills were many. Yosef spent most of the noon hours with them in the yard. Finally he asked:

"Is this the last of the lads?"

"There is still the youngest," she said. "He has a toothache."

She spoke to Yosef as she always did.

And his soul failed him when she spoke.

But he stood there, rubbing salve on the baby's gums with warm oil—those sore, decaying gums. Oh, you miserable ones! Vinegar out of wine! Look at your mother's teeth. *All of them bear twins, not one among them is bereaved.* Like a flock of shorn ewes. *Like a flock of ewes that have come up*—and he suddenly stopped. Frozen.

Flee, my beloved. Make haste, Yosef. Turn, be like a gazelle, or a young stag upon the Mount of Olives. And run down the slopes to the village of Siloam, to the abandoned shack. Run. To the spot where Nahal Kidron meets the Valley of Hinom leading to Ein Rogel, by the lepers' hospital.

And, indeed, Yosef headed that way.

He hastened his steps. And suddenly, as if from within the strange afternoon light, a bewildering sight unfolded before his eyes.

It was several months since they had begun erecting a church over there, near the Garden of Gethsemane. It was said that the Muscovites were building their house of worship there.

They had been working on it for many months; they had reached the roof line. The domes, however, were still missing—*We have a little sister and she has no breasts.*

And Yosef wondered: *What should be done for her on the day when she is spoken for? If she were a wall, they surely would build upon her a battlement of silver.*

Suddenly she ripened. Overnight. Ripened, she towered in all her arched loveliness. Those strange, protruding curves. And admiring herself she said: *I am like a wall and my breasts are towers.*

Yosef started to run.

He ran and ran, his feet hardly touching the ground. It was as though he were growing taller, rising, soaring.

Suddenly he stopped in his tracks. There was a rustling among the thorn bushes. A scream froze in his throat like a lump of clay: On the ground glistened a slithery black snake.

Only this shrewdest of all creatures, the most accursed, did not crawl upon his belly, but raised himself to half his size.

Legend has it that a Sanhedrin of seventy-one executed the decree against the ancient serpent. He was silenced when his hands and feet were chopped off, and he suffered greatly. His agonized cries went from one end of the world to the other, but his voice could not be heard. And if indeed that one was the first snake, he would get up in no time, and Sammael, Prince of Demons, would come and mount him, for he had chosen him of all creatures to be his friend and accomplice. It must have been that snake, for his bearing was upright!

No, Yosef, no. They are only a pair of snakes. Look, they are joined together in their mating dance.

Yosef stood there, transfixed, his hands gripping, clutching the leather belt around his waist, he couldn't move. His flesh tightened, and his eyes fastened on the snake as if it were a lodestone.

In the meantime, the couple had disengaged themselves and slipped away, he to the right, she to the left, for the whole earth was theirs to roam.

They turned and slithered off.

A heavy weariness settled into Yosef's knees, and he crouched down, panting.

A strange plant was growing there.

Its broad, fleshy leaves were shiny and lay flat on the ground. And in between them there were three stems carrying three bluish-purple blossoms. He had not seen the likes of them before.

He bent over the plant and touched it with his fingertips. The bluish petals felt soft and warm and fuzzy. What could they be?

What could they be?!

Then he saw a fruit ripening among them. A berry-like fruit, juicy and red. Strange of form. He had not seen the likes of it before.

What could it be?!

What?

Rav said: Mandrake. Rabbi Levi said: A violet. Rabbi Yonatan said: A peony. And the violets are essentially short plants with fragrant flowers.

The mandrake root is said to be dangerous. It has a cord that extends from its center into the ground and is shaped like a human, and if you take a string and tie one end of the string around an animal's neck and the other end to the mandrake root, and if the animal wrenches it out of the ground, it dies instantly.

What did Reuben do? Reuben tied his donkey to the mandrake root and walked to the fields. On returning, he found the mandrake torn out of the ground and the donkey lying dead. *And Reuben brought the mandrakes to his mother, Leah. Then Rachel said to Leah, "Give me, I pray, some of your son's mandrakes." But she said to her, "Is it a small matter that you have taken away my husband? Would you take away my son's mandrakes too!"*

Oh, do *give me, I pray, give me some of your son's mandrakes . . . that he may lie with you tonight for your son's mandrakes.* Yosef stretched his hand toward the flower, and his heart thrilled within him. He began to stroke the strange flower slowly; it was as soft as down. He brushed his hand over the round fruit, caressed it.

No, *you must come in to me; for I have hired you with my son's mandrakes, I have hired you,* hired-you, you-ooh you-ooh—His hand passed between the curve of the leaves, stroking, and suddenly it plucked the flower and squeezed the fruit. A pungent odor rose from the milky substance that squirted stickily between his fingers.

Yosef lay on the ground and buried his head in the leaves. He lay there crying.

Cry, Yosef; weep, innocent lad. Cry on the mountains: *Cry over the purity of your soul, over all the tender flowers of youth.*

> (Alexandria, Scene V)
> *Enter Cleopatra*
> CLEO.: Charmian!
> CHAR.: Madam?
> CLEO.: Ha, ha!
>   Give me to drink mandragora.
> CHAR.: Why, madam?
> CLEO.: That I might sleep out this great gap of time. . .
> *Exit Cleopatra*
> *Exit Cleopatra, but enter Iago*
> IAGO.: Look where he comes! Not poppy, not mandragora,
>   Nor all the drowsy syrups of the world
>   Shall ever medicine thee to that sweet sleep
>   Which thou ow'dst yesterday.

Rise then, Yosef, rise and go down to the Valley of Kidron, to your beloved Ein Rogel. To the tree of the prophet Isaiah. Remember the tale? When Isaiah the prophet fled from King Menasseh, who wanted to kill him, he ran until he reached the carob tree. And the carob opened itself wide and swallowed the prophet. And Menasseh, King of Judah, had woodworkers saw the carob tree, and the blood was dripping. . . . But Isaiah did not cry out, neither did he weep as he was being sawed.

And a mulberry tree is standing there today.

And right beside it, a pile of stones. And when Yosef reached the mound, he found Hiram Alistair lying unconscious there. He revived him and helped him to his feet, and he walked him in the direction of the village of Siloam. He guided him into one of the caves in the rocky slopes of the hills overlooking the Valley of Kidron. Inside the cave he put him on a bed of dried grass sewn into a striped sheet of many colors, and he nursed him there for three nights and four days.

And on the fourth day, Hiram Alistair got up and left. For a while he could be seen wandering about the Khan courtyard of the railway station, and then he disappeared. He was never seen again or heard from in Jerusalem. . . .

And during those days, Um Ibrahim fell ill.

From a distance still, before he even entered the gate, Yosef could hear the women's voices dissolving into wails—measured, rhythmical wails, for they were trained in lamentation. And at the threshold they crowded around him, each pushing herself in front of the other, to be the first to tell him that, according to the symptoms, Um Ibraham lay dying. They had already put a pinch of salt in the palm of her hand and waited. And the salt remained dry. Allah have mercy.

Woe—wail.

Yosef walked in gently. He approached the bed, bent over her, and peered into the pupils of her opened eyes. But, indeed, he could not see his reflection in them.

Surely the bitterness of death had passed.

The bitterness of death?

He placed his hand over her forehead very slowly. Her eyes closed, as if confirming the source of pain. Yosef pulled out of his pocket a glass flagon. He pulled it out very carefully, for it contained a most choice cure.

He had worked on it for many days. First he put some leaves from the elder tree inside the container and sealed its mouth with dough. He made sure the leaves did not touch the glass but hung loosely in there. Then he left the container in the sun for two days. Next he removed the old leaves, replaced them with fresh ones, and repeated this action several times until the flagon was filled with a liquid that had been extracted from the elder leaves. This clear liquid was good for severe pain.

Yosef pulled the delicate flask out of his pocket and sprinkled the liquid on her forehead and temples, massaging them with his wise, calm hands.

The hours passed, and he kept on wetting and gently massaging her forehead and temples, as well as her forearms.

It was already past noon when she suddenly opened her eyes and a spark of recognition was kindled in them. She began mumbling, moving her lips, trying to tell him something. Yosef leaned close to her face and seemed to hear her whisper in his ear:

"This one, is this one from Hezekiah the king?"

And he thought he glimpsed a trace of a smile in her eyes. A last flicker of triumphant light.

Strange, as if a tinge of envy had stolen into Yosef's heart. The cunning one! She's got the upper hand. She was now learning a secret she would never reveal. A secret he would never be able to read about. Not in any of the books.

Wickedly, she was about to take it with her.

The day passed, and on the mountains the hour descended when it was impossible to distinguish blue and white, one dog from another—they all seemed like wolves. Would Yosef stay over at the monastery?

He would.

Someone lit a candle in the corner of the room. Yosef sat across from it, his legs folded under him. When it burned out, he lit another and contemplated it.

*Who supplies the candles for the light? And those who will supply the candles for the light
. . . the Holy One, blessed be He, will reward them. . . .*

It is said of Rabbi Meir that his name was not Meir—he who shines—but Nehorai—
he who enlightens. So why was he called Rabbi Meir? Why? Yosef tried hard to remember but could not, because a song the Ashkenazi children used to sing around the
bonfire in Jerusalem possessed his mind:

Cheers, Rabbi Meir, cheers!

Precious oil,

Oil of joy

You have given to your peers. . . .

No, no. That's wrong. That was not the way it went. His name was not Rabbi Meir.
What was it?

How strange. There he comes. Rabbi Meir himself, riding his horse on the Sabbath
in the marketplace.

Was it Rabbi Meir who had ridden his horse on the Sabbath? The fact is that it was
his teacher, Elisha ben Abuyya, who had done so. But the one riding now is none other
than Rabbi Meir. And he is coming closer to Yosef, and there is a mocking smile in his
kind eyes, mixed with triumphant light. And he invited Yosef to ride on his shoulders.

And Yosef is already perched up there.

And it is told of Rabbi Samuel son of Rabbi Nachmani that when he was still a boy
he was seated on his grandfather's shoulders going up from his own town to Kefar Hanan
via Beth-Shean. And it was there he heard Rabbi Shimon ben Elazar lecture on the
commentary according to Rabbi Meir: *And God saw everything He had made, and behold,
it was very good.* In the book of Rabbi Meir it is written; "It is very good [*tov me'od*]—
and death is good [*tov mavet*]."

Here, death is good.

(TRANSLATED BY NELLY SEGAL)

FATHER'S NOTEBOOK

Chaim Brandwein

> The story is set in the Jerusalem prior to and during the War of Independence.

ONE

It was a spring morning. A genial sun slipped over the mountains and shone on the
scattered rocks along the tops of the hills. A silken, golden-pink, honey-colored glow
settled on the red tiles of the rooftops and on the sheet-iron rain gutters to which they

sloped. Vistas of olive trees burned in the light as though enveloped by flame. Hidden corners and chinks in old walls that had retired into themselves for the night now reemerged and bared themselves to the dawn. The birds too felt the sunshine and the warmth of the day: fluttering about and hopping down from the treetops to the window sills, they sent their first whistles and chirps trilling into the silence.

Just then the first rays of sunlight struck against the back of a long row of houses. They fell upon the stone arches over the windows and embroidered the heavy curtains in patterns of red, gold and brown. Pushing into still-slumbering rooms, they rubbed against the bindings of books yellow with age, smiled to fluted silver candlesticks, and impishly glittered on the bronze crowns of old bedposts.

The good folk of the Quarter-of-the-Walls awoke from their sleep. They washed their hands as the morning ritual prescribes and gave thanks to the Lord of All Things for having restored the souls to their lifeless bodies.

Morning had come to the Quarter-of-the-Walls. Doors grated as they scraped against stone floors. Sandals pattered hurriedly back and forth. Yawns. The gush of flowing water. The smell of steaming coffee and of freshly poured milk. Morning had come.

All this while Meir remained in bed, his eyes half-open and his senses half-awake, dimly absorbing the sounds, stillnesses and shadows of the dawn which spread themselves out on the walls on his room and frisked in the bright blue light. For a long time now he had been permitting himself the luxury of lying still in bed to greet the new day, his left arm dangling down to the floor and conducting the electric chill of the smooth stone tiles through its fingers. Suddenly he felt depressed. His eyes opened wide and the empty space before them filled with the dreary old objects he knew so well. He tried to shut his eyes again but this time they would not stay closed. The dreary objects filled the room once more.

A dismal sadness came over him. Meir ran a hand across his forehead and surrendered himself to his thoughts. "What's past is past. It's dead and over with. All our yesterdays are dead. Father is dead. And you can't live off the dead. It can't be done. The dead are buried and underground. Here lies so-and-so. . . . Period.

"Father liked to pass his days sitting in the easy chair in the yard. He'd shut his eyes and bask in the sun. And mother would sit across from him and try to pry his eyes open with her own. So that he'd see things as they really were. As other people saw them and did them. She was wasting her time.

"But maybe"—Meir grabbed a lock of his abundantly thick hair and turned over on his side—"maybe those who can drown their dreams are the lucky ones. All they have to do is sit back in their easy chairs and forget."

This last reflection was never finished, for suddenly Meir was overcome by a great tiredness. The wrinkles vanished from his brow. His eyelids drooped once more.

When his eyes were open Meir was a handsome boy. He was handsome when he shut them too, but in a different, more distant way. Then his unruly curls fell loose, casting flickering shadows over his arched brow, and the upward turn of his pointed chin revealed a neck that looked much longer than it really was. The prominent, outcurved lips would part as though in a smile and the sunken cheeks and cheekbones would seem more angular and elongated than when he was awake. "When Meir is sleeping," his mother Devorah liked to say, "he looks as though he were listening to music."

Meanwhile the clamor of the day grew louder. The multicolored rays of the sun reposed submissively on the floor of the room, the curtains on the windows flapped in the morning breeze, and a smell of starched sheets pervaded the air.

When Meir awoke a second time the sun was already high overhead. Behind the long row of windows the fields lay ablaze in the fierce Jerusalem sun. On the hillsides the shadeless olive trees suffered the transparent sky in silence, while the rocks clung to the terraced earth as though seeking shelter.

Nearby lay the Valley of the Cross, denuded by the light down to its last, small, yellowish clump of thorns. The bright air hung heavily over the fields and stripped each blade of grass of its cover. Midway in the valley, standing out from the fields and trees, the spire of the Monastery of the Cross lifted its pinnacle toward the sky.

Meir rose from his bed, raised one edge of the curtain on the window, and peered outside at the brilliant landscape of brown terraced earth and stony hills. "How bare and brutal it is," he mused. "A murderer of dreams."

He stretched out his arms and returned them to his sides, then tore himself away from the window and faced back into the room.

"As long as father was sitting in his easy chair in the sun and seeing things with his eyes closed," he went on whispering to himself, "everything was different from the way it is now. The day that he died all kinds of things that I never even knew existed died with him. It was as though he had made it impossible for anyone around him to breathe freely. All day long he'd be as sunk in himself as a well. Now he's gone, and the house has lost its bitterness, and with it whatever real character it ever had."

Suddenly, as though he had just become aware of the lateness of the hour and recalled that he had urgent affairs to attend to, Meir began to dress with exceptional haste. Pulling on his socks and buttoning his shirt, he continued to ponder how things had once been that weren't any more, and how even what had remained was no longer the way it used to be.

By the time he was dressed and ready to step out, he was absolutely certain that this time he was leaving his mother's house without the intention of returning. This time he was leaving for good.

TWO

For three long years, from the time his father had passed on to the world of rest, Meir had struggled with both himself and his mother over whether or not to move away from the house and from the Quarter-of-the-Walls. More than once he had told himself:

"Every hour that I go on living in this funeral home is an hour that's lost forever. I'm not accomplishing a thing here. I've got to move out. If I don't my whole life will be wasted. I'll always be alone and apart, I'll never amount to a thing."

And still he didn't move.

He would pace back and forth through the empty rooms, which were cluttered with furniture and old things, unable to bear the thought of leaving his mother in them all alone by herself. Days passed, then months. Meir thought and thought about leaving home but he did nothing about it. Great plans for the future, as well as everyday affairs, distracted him from carrying out his wish. The plans met with disappointment, the affairs came and went, but the desire to move remained as persistent as ever.

"As long as I'm buried here inside the walls of the quarter I'll never do anything worthwhile. I've got to pack a suitcase and walk through the door. I've got to shut my eyes and leave and not look back. If I don't . . ."

But he stayed right where he was.

At times, when he felt particularly burdened and helpless, he would set out from home and wander from coffeehouse to coffeehouse all over Jerusalem, talking passionately with whomever he met and on whatever subject chanced to arise, tearing down all the great plans he had labored to create over so many days and nights. Pale and worn out he would return to his mother and unburden himself before her:

"Don't you see, here I just can't seem to make anything matter. I feel completely alone and apart. Maybe if I were somewhere else, in Tel Aviv perhaps, things would be different. Maybe."

His mother would look at him with brimming eyes, showing him all the wrinkles in her face, and would tell him of the great love his father had borne for him, of how handsome he had been as a child, and of how she had been the envy of her friends and neighbors each time she had taken him out for a stroll.

"You're a fine-looking boy, Meir, and clever too, God bless you and watch over you. But you're still young. You're not even twenty years old yet. What's all this moaning and moping about like an old woman? You're still young, Meir. Someday you'll find out that it's possible to acquire anything in this world, friends, wisdom, a good wife, anything—except for a mother's heart."

Meir would listen to his mother's remonstrances and would let her have her way. Shutting the door of the small study behind him, he would burrow for hours in the possessions and manuscripts that his father had left behind, weighing and turning and leafing through them until his head began to ache.

Whenever he looked up he would see his father's face suspended before him in midair. It was just as he remembered it, the face of a man who had withdrawn from the world and surrounded himself with a circle of silence.

But sometimes, late at night, his father would appear to Meir with a different face, one that was preserved in his memory from the earliest days of childhood. Those were the days when Meir's father would come home from his office at the hospital beaming and smiling, would grab Meir in his arms and toss him in the air, and would catch him with twinkle-eyed laughter as he came down. They were the days when he would take Meir's small hand in his own and lead him through the streets of the quarter, telling him in a melodic voice about the men who lived in olden times and about all kinds of animals and birds. In fact, they were the best days that Meir had ever known. Simply to think of himself walking down the street with his head coming up to his father's waist made him feel good even now. Those days were gone forever, and his father with them, but the memory of their taste and abundant warmth lived on in his blood and bones.

Meir needed only to shake himself to awake from these visions. The door of the study would reappear before his eyes and he would turn his attention once more to the notebooks and paper that his father had left behind.

Meir would browse through the writings which he father had set down on paper at times when the sun no longer brought warmth to his bones. Then the words and letters would beat against his eyes until he could no longer make out a thing: old debts owed to his father and debts which his father owed, inscriptions from the tombstones on the Mount of Olives, fragments of the history of the first Jews of Jerusalem, of how they had first ventured beyond the confines of the Old City and built the Quarter-of-the-Walls outside of its walls.

"What was Father looking for, what did he expect to find in all this? He copied every debt that he ever paid over and over. Dates of death and inscriptions from all over the Mount of Olives. What was it that made him choke back his laughter and wrap himself in silence?"

Sitting behind the closed door of the study reminded Meir of the many nights that his father used to spend locked up in the same room, filling page after page of paper with figures and letters. The figures made him think of his father's deathbed. All the while he lay there dying he never ceased to murmur numbers under his breath. "Zalman Lewinger—eighty-two pounds. Reb Ephraim Solomon—two-hundred pounds. . . ."

His mother Devorah once said:

"Your father was willing to do absolutely anything to make himself seem good-hearted. And really, he had a heart of gold. He was happiest when he had someone to pity. It was because he felt so much pity that he got himself into so much trouble."

"But what does that have to do with his papers?"

"It has a great deal to do with them. He became so involved in the favors he was always doing for others that in the end they became his whole life."

"But what made him copy all those inscriptions from the tombstones on the Mount of Olives?"

"That was something he started to do after the death of your Aunt Rachel."

THREE

On the first anniversary of his father's death Meir and his mother, accompanied by friends and relations, set out to visit the grave on the Mount of Olives. Meir looked stolidly at the tomb and at his mother's tear-filled eyes. Everything seemed terribly far away, as though it were not real at all but a fanciful figment of his imagination. He was surprised at himself: all year long he had grieved for his father and for the utterly de-

The view of the Temple Mount from the Mount of Olives, with the stones of the cemetery in the foreground, 1934 (Central Zionist Archives from the bequest of Max Walters; with permission)

pleted house, but now that the body was actually lying in the ground at his feet and his mother stood beside him with her eyes full of tears, it all seemed terribly remote. He jammed his hand into the pocket of his pants, pinched himself on the thigh, and thought:

"All this year I kept nosing like a dog through my father's old things trying to discover what it was that ailed him, why he stopped laughing while still in his prime, and why he spent his last minutes on earth murmuring about old debts that he'd paid long ago. And now I look at this grave and it could just as well be an empty hole full of sticks and stones. All the time I was feeling sorry for him none of it was real. It wasn't for him I was feeling sorry because he wouldn't ever walk again from his cramped little study to his easy chair in the yard, but for myself, because a long time before he departed from the world he had already departed from me. And it's not for him that I'm mourning now, but for myself again, because my father is gone and I never got to know him."

The company stood around the grave while Meir recited the mourner's prayer. They looked at one another and then at the tomb, said "amen" in the proper places, and began to trudge slowly homeward.

Before Meir and his mother had taken more than a few steps they were accosted by Yaakov-Yosef, the dead man's brother:

"Devorah, if you'll wait for me a minute I'd like to take a look at Rachel's grave."

Turning to Meir, he added:

"You come too. Come along. She loved you with all her heart."

"I'll go with you," said Devorah.

Meir and his mother turned to follow Uncle Yaakov-Yosef. They strode among the rows of tombstones, their eyes on their hearts and their hearts in the graves that flitted past. They walked in silence as far as the fence of the Sefardic cemetery, passed it, and continued onward still without saying a word. At last they came to a second fence which marked the burial place of victims of unnatural deaths: here lay suicides who had taken their own lives, and Jewish patriots martyred by the British.

Yaakov-Yosef went over to a tombstone of veined Jerusalem stone, bent to read the inscription, and rested his head upon it. Meir looked at the chiseled writing and read with his lips:

"Rachel. The twenty-fourth of Tishrei, 5691."

As they descended the hill Yaakov-Yosef said to Devorah:

"It was on that night that he stopped laughing. He buried himself in the history of the first Jews to return to Jerusalem and shut himself off from the world."

That same evening Devorah told Meir:

"Rachel, Yaakov-Yosef's first wife, was the only daughter of Professor Ben-Zion the Sefardi. She was very beautiful. She had a face like an angel, was silent as a dove, clever and modest in her ways, and a truly pious woman. She was blessed with grace and charm and nobility. Only one thing was denied her—fruit of the womb. How badly she wanted a child! No one but the Lord above can ever know how dearly she loved children.

"And you, Meir, she loved with all her heart. She used to spend entire days here in this house dandling you on her knees, feeding you with her own hands and lullabying you to sleep. She loved you with all her heart. When you were two years old she began taking you home with her for a day or two days or even a week at a time."

Devorah hesitated and stared at Meir, who was sitting across from her. She frowned and looked to one side, then turned her head and looked to the other, as though she were standing at a crossroads and trying to make up her mind which way to go. Laying her hand over her heart, she continued in a whisper:

"One evening she came to see us. I can see it now before my eyes as though it had all just happened yesterday. She was paler than a corpse and kept stumbling over her words. She looked straight at your father and said: 'Yaakov-Yosef left for Damascus this morning. He went there to see an old manuscript which Father asked him to look at. . . . A German gynecologist has just arrived in Haifa. They say he's a great expert, that he can work miracles.'

"I can remember to this day how your father sat there glued to his seat. I looked at him and trembled. His face had turned white and he had the expression of a blind man."

Devorah placed one hand on top of the other. She took a deep breath and went on in a weary, broken voice:

"The next day your father and Rachel left for Haifa. They returned seven days later. That night Rachel killed herself. Your father wouldn't talk. He shut himself up with his papers and stopped smiling."

"But why . . . ?" Meir's voice echoed in the sudden silence.

"Why? I don't know. From that day on he never mentioned her name again."

Devorah fell contemplatively silent. After a moment's pause she went on with her story in a completely changed voice:

"The night they returned from Haifa, Rachel wanted to take you home to sleep with her. You began to howl and cry. You wouldn't even let her come near you. In the end she went home by herself. In the middle of the night she went up on the roof and threw herself down into the courtyard."

After the night on which his mother told him about Rachel and her death Meir never again brought up the subject of leaving home. He busied himself with various projects, made and abandoned plan after plan, and told himself over and over: "As long as I'm stuck in this funeral home I'll always be alone and apart and I'll never amount to a thing."

Two years went by. Meir did one thing and another, spent long hours in the coffee-houses of Jerusalem, and other long hours in the little study. Now and then he would pick up his father's papers and read his way through the inscriptions from old tomb-stones and the accounts of the first Jewish settlers to return to Jerusalem. By day and by night the thought of leaving his mother's house continued to stir within him and beat upon his heart.

But still he stayed where he was.

Until that Jerusalem morning when, with the sun shining in his window, Meir finally had it out with himself and moved to Tel Aviv.

FOUR

During his first days in Tel Aviv, Meir thought often of Jerusalem, of the Quarter-of-the-Walls, and of his mother's house. "That city of many quarters and winding lanes isn't far from here at all," he would muse to himself. "For a few small coins you can buy a bus ticket and be there in an hour. And yet all the same there's a great distance between here and there. There in the mountains everything is surrounded by bare rocks and shadow-breathing canyons that whisper to themselves at night, and these become part of the people who live there so that they go about slouching and dragging their legs. But here on the seacoast the streets are straight and run parallel. People know how to get things done and they keep a sharp eye on their business."

In time, however, Meir ceased to think about the distance between the two cities and became a citizen of Tel Aviv in every respect. Had any of his old acquaintances chanced to meet him in those days they would hardly have recognized him as the same boy who used to spend long nights sitting by himself in his father's study. He had become thoroughly at home, like a true native: he ran his words together when he spoke, drank quantities of fruit juice, and shouted and waved hello to many people at once.

When ever the memory of his last morning in his mother's house would appear before his eyes, Meir would immerse himself in a flood of activity until the unwelcome visions were driven away. Only in his dreams, which were not subject to what he wanted or did not want to see, did he return again and again to his mother's yard in the Quarter-of-the-Walls and see his father walking weakly back and forth, searching for something in the pockets of his pants. His mother he never saw. But dreams such as these were no cause for concern: Meir knew his father could not really be walking in the yard, that his unworn pants were still hanging in the closet, and that if anyone was walking in the yard at all it was his mother, who was still alive and well.

So Meir spent many days and nights in the city on the coast until the streets began to thunder with the noise of weapons and guns. Different times had arrived, times that bore no resemblance either to those that Meir had spent in the Quarter-of-the-Walls or to those that had followed. Darkness descended everywhere: people shrunk into themselves and blackened their houses in fear of the Angels of Destruction. Walls collapsed, and children and grown-ups were maimed and killed. Trenches were dug around the cities and rooftops were turned into outposts. Sandbags . . . Rifle butts . . . Ironclad vehicles . . . Prayers said in hiding . . . If only the horror would pass.

But the horror did not pass.

Jerusalem, city of the mountains, city whose streets had always hummed with the sounds of prayer and the joyous cries of children, went into mourning. In the arched windows the lights were extinguished. One no longer bought a ticket on the bus and went where one pleased. Few went anywhere at all, those who did spent a long time preparing to go, and not all who did go ever got to where they were going.

At about this time Meir found himself in a column of armoured cars, coated with iron on the outside and with thick gloom within, which was making its way along the twisting road that ascends to Jerusalem. The light where he sat was murky and dense, but he could still make out the rise and fall of the road, the angry rocks and the grieving red-loamed hills, the scanty trees and the bluish horizon that dipped to meet the mountain tops.

When the roar of the engines subsided a group of young men clad in woolen caps, their clothing wrinkled and their eyes marked with strain, emerged from the iron chambers and stood aimlessly about. Meir jumped down and joined them. One of the group removed his woolen cap, waved it in the air, and said:

"I will tell you, this whole street looks just like the Wailing Wall minus the big stones and the fur hats of the Hasidim."

Another blinked his eyes and remarked:

"The whole town of Jerusalem looks just like the Wailing Wall all the time."

Meir stood thinking. Most of the group were natives of Jerusalem themselves and the houses in which they grew up were not far from where they were standing now. They were trying to talk about everything at once and so they were really saying nothing.

The men remained standing in place, chatting about one thing and another, until they were told to move on. They shouldered their packs, flexed the muscles on their backs, and began to walk. Meir followed them. Before long they came to a place that was called the "assembly point." Formerly it had been a house like any other, but now overnight it had been robbed of its warmth, and the familiar sounds of quarrels and laughter were no longer to be heard in it. Below the naked walls lay a floor covered with mattresses. Crowded bookcases stared sadly from the corners. A discarded white tablecloth. A pot full of flowers and windows barricaded with sandbags.

Each of the men took a mattress and stretched out on it. Meir did the same. They lay quietly on their backs until they grew accustomed to where they were. Then their tongues loosened a bit and they began to whisper and talk.

So they united into a single band facing one common danger, each with a body of his own that could feel the cold floor through the mattress on which it lay. But by the time this had happened, their shadows intermingling on the floor and their voices blending together, an order had already come from above sending them on their final destination.

FIVE

And so Meir returned to Jerusalem. It did not even occur to him to try to visit his mother, for the fighting raged everywhere, and one came home to the place of one's birth without really coming home. Not everyone who did come home, in fact, found a home to come to. Some found nothing but a pile of stones and dirt. Houses were emptied wholesale of their tenants and entire families flocked to the cellars to live.

Meir followed the group he was with automatically, as a blind man follows his cane. He laughed when they laughed, when they walked he walked after them, and when they stretched out on their bedding, he stretched out on his. All that he saw he saw exactly as they did, as though he were seeing it through their eyes.

Together with the others Meir reached a hilltop to the west of Jerusalem. Here they were ordered to dig in and hold. When Meir finally left the hilltop, however, he left by himself, and it was by himself that he crawled as far as he could toward his mother's house. Only when he got there he did not find his mother whom he had left alive. He found his father who was dead.

When they had arrived on the hilltop each of the men took the place he was told to, laid his rifle and grenades by his side, and lapsed into thought. A starry Jerusalem night hung overhead. All around them the canyons were silent, the dusky horizons spread deep and wide, and the heavens caressed the boulders on the hills. Everything felt of peace and contentment. And then, suddenly, everything went berserk.

For three days and three nights the men held on to the hill. Bullets whistled, shells burst with a shriek. Explosions and trajectories of fire punctured the stillness and the darkness. And still the men held on.

Strips of white cloth, flashing blades, inhuman screams, rent the air. And still the men held on.

The seige of Jerusalem in 1948 (Central Zionist Archives; with permission)

Lips narrowed to a crack from the sun and from thirst. Torrents of blood collected in puddles. And still the men held on.

One by one hearts ceased to beat. Bodies turned blue with open eyes. And still the men held on.

On the fourth night silence descended once more on the hill.

In the morning the sun shone brightly on the mountains. Meir opened his eyes and saw the light upon the hills and his comrades lying quietly in their own blood.

An animal cry burst from his lips. His fists pounded against the sides of his head. He began to crawl. Meir crawled over fields and hills, through puddles of water, swamps, rocks and brambles. Meir kept crawling. He crawled until the darkness beat against his eyes, and then he stopped.

When Meir awoke in the hospital, time was standing quietly around him and a white sheet glistened beneath his body. The same animal cry broke from his throat again and his fists crashed down upon his head.

Some time later, when Meir entered the courtyard of his home in the Quarter-of-the-Walls, he was greeted by a vision of his father seated in his easy chair and basking in the sunlight. Meir felt pinpricks in his wounded thigh; he looked at the door of the house and saw that it was shut. Then he knew that his mother was not in the yard and would not be in the house.

When he opened the door he was not surprised by what he saw inside. Somewhere, it seemed, he had seen it all before. He saw peelings of plaster, fragments of stone, rubble and dust, heaps of smashed glass and splinters of wood. Windows with broken panes hung crookedly from their sashes as though trying not to fall. A three-legged table stood upright in its place. The fourth leg lay on the ground together with a solitary candlestick, loose pages torn from books, and the butt-end of an old candle.

In the space between the two windows there was a round black hole,

Slowly and blankly Meir approached it. He stood across from it and stared and knew again what he had known before he opened the door, that his mother was no longer walking in the yard and was no longer walking anywhere at all. He stood and stared until he heard a whisper in his father's voice call, "Meirke." But when he turned to face it there was no one there. Abandoning the place where he stood, he entered the little room where for so many days and nights, pen in hand, his father had sat by himself. Boxes of tobacco were scattered over the desk, each with its own shape and form: there were oblong boxes made of silver and round ones made of tin, and there was one box made of olive wood with a Tower of David stamped on its lid. It suddenly came back to Meir how his mother used to sit on her bed and pull boxes of snuff out of the pockets of his father's pants. Angry but silent, his father would pace back and forth from wall to wall.

"What is beyond me," his mother would begin, "is why a man like you, who won't even make the effort to put on phylacteries every morning and pray like a proper Jew, should go to so much trouble to cultivate a habit like this, stuffing tobacco up your nostrils like a filthy beggar."

"All right. You win. I'll never buy any more again."

"To listen to you talk you'd think it was the first time you'd ever told me that!"

"All right. You don't win. I'll keep buying it. And as for phylacteries—what matters is the newness of the dawn, not the straps that you put on your arm. . . . God in heaven, what wouldn't I do for a little bit of dawn!"

"What is it you want from God in heaven?" his mother would say, turning her back and addressing the ceiling. "God in heaven! What do you want from Him?"

The memory of this scene between his parents made Meir recall a dream he had had in the hospital. In it he had seen his father sitting in his study and writing in a small blue notebook. And now he remembered too that he father really did have a notebook like the one he had dreamed of.

Meir ransacked the house, rummaging through everything, until he found what he was looking for among his mother's possessions. He took a chair and placed it by the hole in the wall, then sat down and began to read.

Meir swallowed the words with his eyes, page after page. All that his father had to say about himself in the notebook, he read: about the pair of phylacteries he had received from the father of his father, about the bliss of first owning them, about how he had taken them off one day for the last time, and about how afterward his brow had felt feverish and bare. And he read too his father's thoughts about the first settlers in Jerusalem, about how they had left their native lands and voyaged to the holy city because the phylacteries of their fathers were no longer enough. They wanted phylacteries of their own that would be totally new, they were seeking for a dawn of which their fathers had never heard.

So Meir sat opposite the hole in the wall through which the shell had fallen that killed his mother and read in his father's notebook. He read until he came to the place where he finally found his father.

"The morning of the twenty-fifth of Tishrei, 5691," Meir read. "Today they buried Rachel, of whose dust I am unworthy to speak. Rachel the Matriarch died in childbirth, but Rachel the daughter of Ben-Zion died because she had no children. For children mothers live and for children mothers die.

"The best years of Jacob's life were the seven that he worked for Rachel whom he loved. But what would have happened, I wonder, if at the very moment that Jacob discovered he had been falsely married to Leah he had opened the door and found the real Rachel lying dead upon the threshold? How would he ever have lived with the memory of those seven good years then?

"And Rachel died. . . . And Jacob set up a pillar upon her grave. . . . The same is the pillar of Rachel's grave until this day. . . .

"It was the greatness of the old Jews of Jerusalem," Meir read, "that they had the strength within themselves to follow their dawn. But my own legs were weary. They could not carry me to a dawn of my own. Now all I have left are my weary legs. Free from phylacteries, free from dawn. 'And Rachel died.' "

A JOURNEY THROUGH THE LAND OF ISRAEL

Pinchas Sadeh

MOUNT ZION

After many years I ascended Mount Zion again. The old dirt track was overgrown with weeds, and I took the stairs instead. Various signs greeted me, some with verses from the Bible, others announcing institutions and shops. A guard stopped me at the entrance to King David's tomb and lent me a skullcap. Four men were reciting psalms by the catafalque. Tourists of both sexes circulated through the dark interior beneath massive Gothic vaults. I climbed the minaret outside. A wind was blowing. Across from me, its tombstones gleaming whitely, was the Mount of Olives, and beyond it the mountains of Moab, screened by blue haze. When I looked at the nearby church steeple I saw that the holes from the shells that had hit it during the 1948 war, when I was first here, were still visible. Doves of peace were roosting in them now.

I climbed back down. I had time on my hands, and so I lingered for a while in the crypt beneath the vaults. Next to me sat a man behind a small table, selling certificates in testimony that the bearers thereof had trod in this holy place.

There was nothing to make me feel that this was really David's grave—nor had there been anything back then, during the war. At the time, it was true, I hadn't known that the tradition was a late one, originating apparently with the medieval traveler Benjamin of Tudela. The biblical City of David, in a corner of which the king no doubt lies, was hundreds of meters northeast of here. The Christian tradition that the Last Supper took place on this site, where the Church of the Dormition now stands, is undoubtedly much older, for the writings of Saint Epiphanus and, after him, of Saint Cyril date it back to as far as the third century. Then, though, I knew nothing about this either. No one had told me about it, nor had I encountered it in any book.

Throughout those days and nights, however, I had sensed something primeval, dark, about the place.

The wall of the Old City had loomed grayly before me by day, blackly at night. An Arab sniper lurked behind its apertures. No one dared set foot in the narrow lane between the church and the wall. It was enchanted ground. Whoever infringed on it paid with his life.

I used to stare at the wall from our firing positions in the church as though bewitched. Only a few dozen paces lay between me and it, yet they led through the gates of death.

Haganah soldiers on King David Street, 1948 (Central Zionist Archives; with permission)

Sometimes, at night, I would sit by one of the windows in the church and send long bursts of fire from my machine gun at the wall, like a jackal howling at the moon. Invisible in the darkness, the mouths of the wall lit up in return each time the hidden machine gun opposite me flashed quickly back. The sound of my own gun, though deafening, was like a musical drumroll, and I liked the smell of the burned powder.

I saw no newspapers, had no radio, read nothing, heard nothing. I knew nothing about the conduct of the war, about where it was being fought or who was winning or losing it. Nor did I waste my time thinking about it. It had simply fallen on me from out of the blue, and I accepted it for what it was.

Forgotten fragments, like scenes from a dream, came back to me now.

When the fighting began, before I was sent to Mount Zion, I spent a few days in an Arab neighborhood of Jerusalem called Musrara, in a rear position near the broadcasting station. There had been a piano in one of the studios there, and I used to shut myself up in the dark, soundproofed room and hammer away on it, though I knew nothing about music at all.

All the houses of Musrara had been abandoned, as though in a dream. In some of them, food was still left on the tables, yet you couldn't find a living soul in them. From time to time Jews would come, soldiers or civilians, to loot what rugs, furniture, or radios were left. What they wanted any of it for was beyond me. The world was totally spiritual then, totally religious: all its conventions and givens had melted away, shells whistled through the air like flying angels of death, and one could have really died at any minute. Yet even I made off with something, a small reproduction of Van Gogh's *Sunflowers* that I found on somebody's wall. It cheered me to have it, because Van Gogh and Gauguin were my two favorite painters in those days. I can still remember that yellow.

Afterward, in Abu Tor, a neighborhood separated from Mount Zion by hell on earth, I found an abandoned house with a room that was empty except for an armchair and a large mirror. I used to sit for hours in the depths of the chair, opposite the mirror, writing poems on a pad of stationery that bore the letterhead of an Arab commercial firm.

I liked best climbing onto the roof of that house in Abu Tor, a neighborhood named after a comrade-in-arms of Saladin, and throwing hand grenades from it at the Arab position down the street. It didn't accomplish much, but I had a weakness for the sudden flash, and for the thud of the explosion that followed.

Later, on Mount Zion in the Church of the Dormition, from which the Virgin Mary supposedly ascended in her sleep to heaven, I used to sit for long periods in the forsaken cells of the monks. Thus I managed to live in a variety of times at once, among them my own and the Middle Ages.

Now and then I would descend into town. The connecting passageway was a low, narrow tunnel that had been dug to the Jewish neighborhood of Yemin Moshe. You had to traverse it doubled over, like a worm burrowing through the earth. Once in the city, I went to see two girls I knew, Hava and Ada. Sometimes, walking along a deserted street, it would occur to me that I was living to see the fulfillment of Nietzsche's words that man's destiny in life was to be a warrior and woman's to be his paramour. The thought amused me, since—with a helmet shaped like a chopping bowl on my head and army pants a size too big for me that kept threatening to fall off—I looked like anything but a prophetic vision of the Übermensch. In general, though, those walks were a strange hallucination of empty city blocks, bloodstained sidewalks, suddenly shrieking shells, thirst, and a smell of sperm and sweat.

Those days were distant. Now I stood on the mount by the Old City wall, opposite Zion Gate, but neither mount, wall, nor gate was what it had been. Those days belonged to such another world and such another time that I could almost have believed that the war I took part in had been fought in crusader times, or back in the age of Joshua.

ME'A SH'ARIM

The streets are narrow here. They wind among the columns of the houses like the spaces between the lines on a page of the Talmud.

Small, crooked alleyways, like letters of Rashi script.

Me'a She'arim, Bet Yisra'el, Batei Ungarn, Sha'arei Hesed.

How many nocturnal hours I spent wandering through these alleys during the years I lived in the area. Deathly silent hours of the night, when you could hear a pin drop. When the only sound was the echo of my footsteps on the cobblestones.

In the houses, behind latticed windows, Jews were covered by slumber as the fallen Israelites in the desert were covered by sand.

Sometimes I would pass a house of study. Through the window, by the light of a feeble, yellowish electric bulb, I would see two or three young students bent over their books, rocking softly back and forth while they chanted the ancient Aramaic words of the Gemara in a melancholy murmur: *Thus say the rabbis . . . wherefore Rabbi Levi bar Hama differs with Rabbi Hanina . . . on the one hand, this one says . . . and on the other hand, this one . . .* the torts and case laws of the Talmud . . . the world of Rava and Abayei, of Rav Ashi and Rabbi Abahu. . . .

Sometimes I would stop to read one of the placards affixed to the walls. Proclamations, prohibitions, excommunications. "In the name of our rabbis and officers of the Law, may they live in peace, amen . . . Be it hereby made known . . . For as when the time of the Messiah grows nigh, heresy and apostasy stalk the streets . . . And whereas on account of our innumerable sins the wicked thrive and prosper . . . Wherefore the Holy One Blessed Be He bestows on them success that we may be brought into temptation and withstand it . . . May the Compassionate One have mercy on us and save us . . . For Thou alone, O Lord our God, shall rule over us . . . And may it be granted us to see the coming of the Redeemer. . . ."

Today I have come here on a workaday afternoon. Women are shopping in the market. Men are about their business. My eye is caught by a large notice on the wall. "Help!!!" it says. Its contents are trivial, but I know that all such cries here are essentially addressed to God.

Nearby stands a pretty boy with a proud, wise look on his face. A little scholar of the Law.

To tell the truth, I could never identify with these people (for if I could, I would have come to live with them as an observant Jew) who live by the rule of the Torah and its codes. To be religious, in my terms, means to understand that life is a parable of which God is the meaning—that is, to live life as a struggle to make contact with the divine. Somewhere else I have written about the instructive historical fact that the official codification of the Bible in the days of Ezra the Scribe was accompanied by the cessation of prophecy—in other words, by the drying up of the previously renewable source of human contact with God.

And yet still I feel close to them, these people who live as though in a fortress under siege, surrounded by a secular world they disdain and by a "culture" that revolts them. Their life is without compromise, without concessions. It is a waiting for the Messiah.

When I was called to the army in the War of Independence, it grieved me to think that I might have to die defending the Hebrew University, or the bourgeoisie of Rehavia, or the offices of the press. These and many other things meant nothing to me then and mean nothing to me now, nor do I hesitate to say so. But the Torah is something else. I have no difficulty understanding that whoever believes in it must be ready to die for it. One must never refuse to be a martyr for God. There can be no other significance to life beside worshipping Him. The rest is simply a question of how one understands this worship—that is, of how one understands God.

Worshipping God, as the phrase suggests, has nothing to do with pleasure or cultural frills. It is work, hard work, like paving a road, or farming land, or building a house. In general, I don't believe that the purpose of life in this world is to snatch a little pleasure here or there. If it were, we might as well have been born bedbugs. In whatever we live and do—in our happiness, our suffering, our love, our hate, our passions, our thoughts—we must live and do it not just for itself, but as a parable, as a question, as a war. As work. As worship.

What is man? Man is a question. God is the answer. If the answer were available here, in this life, the question would be unnecessary. The painful tension between the two gives life its energy.

(TRANSLATED BY HILLEL HALKIN)

THE NINTH GATE

Jerusalem in Modern Poetry

The synagogue of Judah Chassid in the Old City, August 1937 (Central Zionist Archives; with permission)

The subject of Jerusalem is important in modern Jewish poetry writen in Hebrew and other languages even if it is no longer as dominant as it was in medieval times. The aspect of holiness remains, but one also hears about Jerusalem as a city of history, of beauty, of memory, of love, of everyday life, and even as a subject of humor. The poetry here has been arranged neither by chronological order nor by author, but in a way as to lead from one theme to another by connection or by contrast.

FROM JERUSALEM: A FIRST POEM
Gabriel Preil

Under these historic skies
I am older than Abraham and his stars,
and I am the young father of the children
playing among pink trees.

On Alharizi Street, on a violet afternoon,
such an hour of grace
gazes out of an arched frame
as sometimes whispered to the prophet
weary of fires,
who dreamed of a village
cool among the stars.

(TRANSLATED BY ROBERT FRIEND)

THE FIRST DAY
Marcia Falk

High wind and a blackbird
push the sky across
the pale Judean hills.
The windows shake. She pulls
herself out of the blankets,
a flash strikes the eastern walls
of houses. It is morning,
the city a cup full
of light, a bright
flask of wind
to rise to.

IN THE JERUSALEM HILLS
Leah Goldberg

I lay like a stone between these ridges,
In grass orange and blighted and summer-burnt,

The Judean hills near Jerusalem, ca. 1935 (Central Zionist Archives; with permission)

Inert and silent.
Pale skies touch rock.
From where came the yellow-winged butterfly here?
Stone among stones—I know not
How ancient my life
Or who will yet come
With foot shoving me
And I will roll downhill.
Perhaps this is beauty frozen forever.
Perhaps this is
Eternity moving slow.
Perhaps this is
The Dream of death
And the one love.

I lay like a stone between these ridges,
in thorn and thistle,
Across from the road flowing townward.
Come wind blessing all
To caress pine-tops
And mute stones.

(TRANSLATED BY AURA HAMMER)

HEAVENLY JERUSALEM, JERUSALEM OF THE EARTH
Leah Goldberg

1

Divide your bread in two,
Heavenly Jerusalem, Jerusalem of the Earth,
jewels of thorn on your slopes
and your sun among the thistles.
A hundred deaths rather than your mercy!
Divide your bread in two,
one half for the birds of the sky:
the other,
for heavy feet to trample
at the crossroads.

2

People are walking in the counterfeit city
whose heavens passed like shadows,
and no one trembles.
Sloping lanes conceal
the greatness of her past.

The children of the poor
sing with indifferent voices:
"David, King of Israel, lives and is."

3

Over my house
one late swallow.

All the other swallows
have already returned to the north.

Over my head
towards evening,
in a city
weary of wanderings,
in a city of wanderers,
small, trembling wings
trace circles of despair.

A sky of Hebron glass.
The first lamp of night.
Swallow with no nest.
Arrested flight.

What now?

(TRANSLATED BY ROBERT FRIEND)

AT YOUR FEET, JERUSALEM
Uri Zvi Greenberg

Kings cast wreaths at your feet and fall upon their faces
    And they are then wonderful servants to you and your God.
Rome too sends its marble, crystal and gold
    To build within you a summit sanctuary for fame and glory.
And we, we your barefoot sons and daughters
    Who come to you beggared from the ends of the world,
We are, as we here are, children
    Of Sovereignty: of the cactus growing by itself, of the waves of the cliffs.
We who leave Jewish community
    In the world, put our coat of many colors, like a snail, into the bag.
Father scolded, mother wept, and the white bed was orphaned.
To you we have brought blood and fingers, love and muscles:
        unburdened
    Shoulders to carry the Hebrew globe with its open sores.
All our dreams and our ambitions we gave up
    That we might be poor laborers in the wasteland.

Where in the world can you find its like? Ask, you who were burned by Titus!

Where do they love rusty sovereignty with eternal love?

Where is the wailing of jackals heard with great compassion?

Where do they fever in red song, where do they shrivel and grow silent,

And cool flaming foreheads and kiss the cliffs?

The heatwind here slowly burns away our dear youth

Whose ashes are scattered daily over the crevices like gold

And we ask no compensation for our destruction.

And with our precious bodies we cover the swamps.

As our hands drive into them the eucalyptus trees.

We who provide a feast for the worms of Canaan,

We are prepared with faithful bodies, fevering

To be the warm bridge for the sovereignty that comes

Over the abyss of blood.

Should a sword be sharpened in Canaan against you—

We would make for you a witness-pile of bodies like an outer wall.

And someone who denies the glory in pain and in your disaster

Struggles from cliff to cliff here, cursing and reviling—

Yes, you will forgive him, and allow him to abuse:

To pass from cliff to cliff because his spleen has risen up.

It is impossible to snap the head off the body with one's hands

And throw it like a pot on one of the angry rocks.

But the hiss of this serpent is also the shadow of a melody!

And the soles of his feet danced a Hora here,

Crying, "God will build the desolation," in the light of the stars

And until he goes to Jaffa, to the office of the émigrés,

And puts his muddy coat, like a lizard, into the bag—

Yet many days

Will he stand and quarry your rocks—at your feet—

And he will eat his bread in a sweat—the shew bread—

Bitterly will he smoke a cigarette with his blood in his eyes.

Perhaps he will also dance another Hora

With his dragging feet—one last time—

And shout "God will build" in the light of the great stars!

(TRANSLATED BY RUTH FINER MINTZ)

JERUSALEM

David Rokeah

Your stones I shall polish into a mirror
For in them is my yearning,
Pines' loftiness and their hearts' resin.

In dawns' topazes
I shall store
The reflection of your day
Rising early on the city wall
Like a stream of light
On a slope of flint
In a bronze mortar sheath.

Your stones I shall polish until my dreams course in you
Like a flow smashing your rocks—
Your yearning, wanderer.

(TRANSLATED BY RUTH FINER MINTZ)

Street of the Prophets, date unknown (Central Zionist Archives; with permission)

ON NEVI' IM STREET (THE STREET OF THE PROPHETS)
Yehoash Biber

Shadows of large trees

lash the surface of Nevi'im Street.

As on a shaky ladder I will go down to Damascus Gate.

To the voice of the wind's howl, the street will move beneath me,

and many a time drop from under my feet,

shake me about,

hang me

above a vast abyss.

I will cover my face and listen

to God's voice

roaring in Zion.

(TRANSLATED BY AURA HAMMER)

LONGING (I)
Ruth Finer Mintz

In the translucent light of Jerusalem

I go at four o'clock to greet,

The Prophet Isaiah.

And he greets me as I greet him

with silence.

I stand looking toward his sanctuary

shaped like a clay jar, keeping his scroll

guarding his peace, thousands of years:

from the desecrations of man

and from the desiccation of time.

Now it rests here, in time out of time,

in Jerusalem, a fragment of eternity.

Its letters are black on white, clear

as at their recording. Parchment

preserved in dried earth. Earth

from which Adam was first created.

Earth to which Adam returns, crumbling.

Thus a scroll is like a man, fragile crumbling

yet preserving for thousands of years

words, ideas, beliefs.

One, Three. Seven.

Love, The Presence. Peace.

Here their shadow falls upon me in the shade of a tree.

Now their light overwhelms me, transfiguring

limestone to pointing fingers of ivory upon parchment.

And the light rests where all revelation must rest,

in words, till the heart of stone turns flesh.

This Valley, these hills are unbelievable

Therefore, they exist in the age of unbelief.

To deny the law of gravity which is downfall.

To contradict the law of optics.

Even as I know that all that was lost

has been returned to us, from the cave of our disaster:

The longing possess me utterly, yet escapes

my suppliant fingers, my outstretched hands.

For it rests, half underground, in the sanctuary

of wrought stone, above the olive valley.

And in the translucent light of Jerusalem

The Olive Valley burns with green Grace.

The expanse of God flickers before my eyes.

ON BEN PELEH: JERUSALEM
Shin Shalom

I knocked on your gates, O Jerusalem,

At midnight, at your Western Wall.

Eyes stared at me from the Temple Mount.

Were they God's or an Arab's eyes?

I climbed dead stairs. Upon the wall
Footsteps are swallowed in the path of the moon.
Who is it paces at my heels atremble?
Orphaned here the Shekhina mourns.

I listened in silence to the stillness
Of your alleys and the pits of your caves.
At times my hand was sadly knocking
Upon the stones that cover the graves.

Eternal dead, you rest from toil and labour.
Silent tombstones, alas, you reply:
Whose was the hand that was just knocking?
Whose is the footstep? Who and what am I?

For you, O Jerusalem, have reawakened
My longing which does not fade.
The world about sees only with the eye,
But you perceive the sorrow of the heart.

I will grace your walls in trembling,
With my tears I will moisten your stones.
With every sunset aflame in your Western sky
I offer my life entire, a sacrifice of yearning.

In the dimness of your sanctuaries still remain
Bright sages who shoulder the burden of the world.
And those redeeming with their blood your captives
Are in shadow, their voice is not heard.

There are still dreaming youths in your coverts,
And in their eyes is the redeemers' glow.
In your cellars they weep for your affliction
By the candle's swaying, flickering light. . . .

Autumn in Jerusalem, drizzle and wind.
Desolation covers all horizons.
Up to my ankles in water I wade,
I cannot continue yet must go on.

Dampness, wet wall. Through the streets
A jackal flees. I see its maddened gaze.
I come to a door and open it,
My weary eyelids can scarcely move. . . .

Morning. Against my window the olive leaves
Still are dim. Patches of cloud float by.
With a bag of hewer's tools in my hands,
Quietly I go out of the house.

O Jerusalem, on my way I meet
Your sons who rise up early for prayer.
My house of prayer is a heap of your stones,
My sledge hammer beats at word after word.

I am faithful here to my work. I know:
The eyes of eternity silently watch.
The best of my days I labour and toil
On the slightest hollow, the angled line.

O Zion, may my stones, wrought in love,
Be for your glory. They alone
Are the one remembrance that I leave
For all of my burned-out flames.

My desire is pure, but these hands are flesh,
They are no dull and common tool.
Your stones are stained, O Jerusalem,
With the sap of my flesh, the gush of my blood.

Your sun is bright, but these eyes are weak,
And the heart grows sorely faint.
Thus your stones, O Jerusalem, are covered
With my streaming sweat, my torrents of tears.

Yihyeh, my teacher from Yemen, bears
On his forehead a scar from Ishmael's sword.
Threescore years before, the slaughter began,
Still is Israel not redeemed.

For threescore years he has pounded the rock.
His children were born, they married and died.

Threescore years he waits, Selah, for Him.
Still the Messiah has not passed by. . . .

Fair is our portion. Opposite on the mountain,
Rises Zion's wall, David's tower looms high.
Like a marvellous tapestry woven,
Moab's hills, Valley of Vision, Prophecy.

In an hour when the world is emerald, ruby clear,
And pure is the heavenly expanse,
Yihyeh rises, claps his hands: "Glorious
Is the radiance of the world. Let us dance."

"Let us dance, my brother. Rejoice we are worthy
To strike our hammer on holy rock.
Thousands of years have we sat and wept,
Now let us lift up our feet and dance!"

"Dance, my brother, for we have come up
From trouble's mire, from the valley of weeping.
Seeking the tears of joy in our eyes,
Our Heavenly Father will clap His hands."

Two Jews dance in Jerusalem.
One from the East, the other from the West.
On each other's shoulder they join their hands,
To each other they lift their eyes high.

With them dance rocks, olive trees, sky,
Zion's walls, Jordan, Moab's hills.
Two Jews dance in Jerusalem
From high noon till a star gleams forth.
(*Translated by Victor E. Reichert and Moses Zalesky*)

Holy Grandmothers in Jerusalem
Esther Raab

Holy grandmothers in Jerusalem,
May your virtue protect me.
The smell of blossoms and blooming orchards
I suckled with my mother's milk.

Feet soft as hands, fumbling

In the torrid sand,

And tousled eucalypti

Laden with bees and hornets

Whispered a lullaby to me.

Seven times shall I steep myself

Into the Mediterranean

To prepare for King David, my beloved,

And I shall go up to him, with glorious dignity,

To the mountains of Jerusalem;

I shall sit with Deborah under the date-tree,

Have coffee with her and talk

About war and defence.

Holy grandmothers in Jerusalem,

May your virtue protect me.

I can feel the smell of your garments,

The aroma of Sabbath-candles and naphthaline.

(*Translated by Abraham Birman*)

Inhabitants of Meah Shearim, date unknown (Central Zionist Archives; with permission)

RELIGIOUS QUARTER
A. C. Jacobs

Grandfather, to-day I walked in Mea Shearim
And it was a little like it must have been
In Vilna seventy years ago.

               Small boys
Walked between their dangling curls
With already the strange sensuality of talmud
Scholars. Merchants, in fur coats, relaxed
In the slow pace of their closed, coinless
Sabbath; matrons went with their love blown
Away into a nagging over-all welfare
And young girls were concealing their sex
In a terrible kind of shapelessness.

                     And all this
Under the hot sky of Jerusalem.

It was a little, grandfather, of the sea
Of the past, out of which you sailed
To leave me in the north,

                  whose speech
I take to tame, oh, centuries of such
Isolated quarters striving in my blood.

PASSOVER IN JERUSALEM
Avigdor HaMeiri

Passionate angels serenaded today in Jerusalem—
Thousands of springs were concentrated in me today
And from its grave every dead skeleton breathes sun.
—Welcome fragrances, the crop-God's messengers,
I wait today, I wait this time
For the redeemer, the seducer—for whoever comes, If only he comes:
Today is Passover and faith has no bounds.

Thousands of past kisses resound today in Jerusalem,
And the world begins to weep in God's choking provender

And from my ancestors' graves wells the song of blood.

—Jerusalem, Jerusalem, city of the arid and the prayer.

Today will you spread for me the warm nuptial couch,

For the kiss of the husband of your youth, bridegroom of blood,

Mourner of blood,

From under your heart, the King Messiah to bear?

(TRANSLATED BY RUTH FINER MINTZ)

BUILDING PARTNER
Elisha Porat

I also want to be a partner

in the building of Jerusalem. With you

sing hymns to her with a great voice

in the assemblage of her mutes;

with you encompass her wall

in a glory-march among her lame celebrants.

I have the right to be a partner, after all

I spilled the fury of my youth on her:

fights with zealots and night patrols

in the shadow of fences, sniping from her lattices.

Wait, don't finish without me, I've

bought rough sandals and white linen

to flourish with you on her towers,

before I smash myself on the squares

and am pounded by her stones like you

powdered fine

coveting the dust of her saints.

(TRANSLATED BY RIVA RUBIN)

TO MY CITY JERUSALEM, 1967
Amir Gilboa

I knew in the dream the dream wouldn't fly like a dream.

I knew in the dream that in me myriads are dreaming the dream.

I woke. Midnight. Who turns the dark of night into the light of day?

The sun stands still in the window in the dream as on that day in Gibeon I recall.

Look, here comes the night that is day and not night

and the endless day comes in the midst of the night. And it will never darken.

And morning light glows. I wake. Look, here before me, Jerusalem.

And I see it. I see it with myriads of eyes.

Was there ever anything like this—

a dream dreamed at the same time

by myriads where they dream.

(*Translated by Shirley Kaufman and Shlomit Rimmon*)

HOMAGE TO JERUSALEM; JERUSALEM 1967
Yehuda Amichai

This year I travelled far

to view the quiet of my city.

Rocking soothes a baby, a distance soothes a city.

I lived in my longing. I played a game

of four severe squares of Yehuda Halevi:

my heart, my self, the East, the West.

I heard bells ringing in time's religions,

but the howl I heard within

is still from my Judean Desert.

Now that I'm back, I cry again.

At night the stars come up like bubbles from the drowned.

Each morning I cry the scream of a newborn baby

From the blind chaos of homes and all this great light.

❧

Light against the Tower of David, light

on the Church of Maria, light on the Fathers

asleep in their double-graves, light on your face

from within, light on the transparent honey

cakes, light on the clock face, and time

is lighted passing between your thighs
when you take off your dress.

Lighted the round cheeks of my childhood,
lighted the stones that wished to be
lighted, with those that wished to
sleep in the darkness of squares.
Lighted the spiders of railings, and
cobwebs of churches and acrobats of
spiral stairs. But of all these, most
is lighted, the true and terrible X-ray
in letters of white bones and lightning:
Mene   Mene   Tekel   Upharsin.

In vain you'll look for barbed wire fences,
You know such things
don't disappear. Another city, perhaps,
is now cut in two: two lovers
separated; other flesh tormented
by these thorns, refusing to be stone.

In vain you'll look. You lift your eyes unto the hills.
Perhaps there? Not these hills, accidents of geology,
but The Hills. You ask
without raising the voice, without question mark,
to do your part in asking questions
gone now. But a great tiredness wants you with all your heart and gets you. Like death.

Jerusalem, the only place in the world
where even the dead have a right to vote.

It's not time that takes me from my childhood,
but this city and everything in it. Now
to have to learn Arabic, to reach Jericho

from both sides of time; and length of walls
added to heights of towers and domes
vast without limit. All these
widen my life and force me
to migrate anew from the smell
of rivers and forest.

My life's stretched out; thinning like cloth,
transparent. You can see through me.

☙

The city plays hide-and-seek between names
Jerusalem, El-Kuds, Shalem, Jer, Yeru,
whispering: Y'vus, Y'vus, Y'vus, in darkness.
Weeping with longing: Aelia Capitolina, Aelia, Aelia.
She comes to all who call her
at night, alone. But we know
who comes to whom.

☙

Jerusalem stone is the only stone
that hurts. It has a network of nerves.
From time to time Jerusalem gathers
to mass protest like the tower of Babel.
But with big clubs God—The Police beats
her back: houses razed, walls torn down,
and then once more the city disperses, midst jabbering
prayers complaint and random cries from churches
and synagogues and minaret shout from mosques.
each one to his place.

☙

I and Jerusalem like blindman and cripple.
She sees for me
until the Dead Sea, until the end of days.

And I hoist her on my shoulders
and walk blind in my darkness beneath.

                        ⟑

On this clear autumn day
I build Jerusalem anew.
Foundation scrolls
fly in the air, birds, thoughts.

God is angry with me
because I force him, always,
to create the world from Beginning:
Chaos, Light, Second Day, to
Man and back again.

                        ⟑

In the morning the shadow of the Old City falls
on the New. In the afternoon, the reverse.
Nobody profits. The muezzin's prayer
is wasted on the new houses. The ringing
of bells rolls like a ball, and rebounds. Seraphic
praise from synagogues will fade like grey smoke.

At the end of summer I breath this air,
the parched and aching. A silence
like many shut books is thought:
many closed books, most of whose pages are
stuck like eyelids in the morning.

                        ⟑

I go up David's Tower
a little above the most exalted prayer,
halfway to heaven. Some
of the ancients succeeded: Muhammad, Jesus
and others. But didn't find rest in heaven,
they entered a higher excitement. But

the applause for them hasn't let up
below.

◌

Jerusalem is built on vaulted foundations
of a held-back shout. Without a reason
for the shout, the foundations would give, the city would totter;
if the shout is shouted, Jerusalem would explode skyward.

◌

Poets come with evening into the Old City
and leave it loaded with images
and metaphors and little maxims
and twilight similes between vaults and rims.
Darkening fruits and
wrought-iron filigree of the heart.

I lifted my hand to my forehead
to wipe the sweat
and brought up Else Lasker-Schüler
by chance. Light and small as she was in her life,
how much more so in her death. But her poems!

◌

Jerusalem, port city on the shores of eternity.
The Holy Mount is a hugh ship, a luxurious pleasure
liner. From the portholes of her Western Wall happy
saints look out, travellers. Chasidim on the dock wave
goodbye, shout hurrah till we meet again. She's
always arriving, always sailing. And the gates and the docks
and the policemen and the flags and the high masts of churches
and mosques and the smokestacks of synagogues and the boats
of praise and waves of mountains. The sound of the ram's horn is heard: still
another sailed. Day of Atonement sailors in white uniforms
climb among ladders and ropes of seasoned prayers.

And the trade and the gates and the gold domes:
Jerusalem is the Venice of God.

(TRANSLATED BY HAROLD SCHIMMEL)

LESSON IN GEOLOGY
Elisha Porat

"The anomaly of Jerusalem is not simple to perceive.

At a glance, transparent: mountain platform and chalkstone,

an elevated Holy Site."

He tapped with his stonemason's hammer,

chipping crimson flakes off a stone taken from a wall.

"The flawless Red stone of Jerusalem testifies

that there in the subterranean depth of the city,

all is broken burst and smashed.

Like a gigantic inverted funnel—

a cistern for Jewish blood pumping,

draining into it from all worlds."

I remember his lesson as if it was yesterday:

the city afloat, the street suddenly swaying,

the veins of rust and dim and deep beneath me,

the rustle and seethe of a primeval river.

(TRANSLATED BY RIVA RUBIN)

JERUSALEM, 1968
David Rokeah

I

You want to know the number of gates

in Jerusalem. I count seven gates open

to you, four barred to me,

a golden gate for the lingering Messiah.

II

In deciphering letters

that burn on a cold stone

Jewish Quarter and New Synagogue; from Palestine in 1860 *(Glasgow: 1860) (Photograph by John Cramb. Collection of Mr. William P. Wolfe, Montreal; with permission)*

you will explore the language of darkness
and the language of shadows. Motionless
in prayer, like a hunchbacked olivetree,
you will search for keys
lost by God in the wadi of Kidron.

    III

Formed out of stony earth
of solitude fencing this town
where the sorrow of the defeated
is a yashmak veiling the faces of women
where candles of life never set
I am digging in time built
into walls beneath walls.

      (TRANSLATED BY ALAN BROWNJOHN)

JERUSALEM
Else Lasker-Sch ler

God formed out of his spine: Palestine
Out of one single bone: Jerusalem.

I wander as through mausoleums—
Our holy city turned to stone.
Stones lie along the bed of her dead waters
Instead of the water-silk at play: flowing and ebbing.

Transfixed by earth's cold stare,
The wanderer founders in the starry chill of her nights.
There is a fear I cannot overcome.

Were you to come . . .
Wrapped in a snow-bright Alpen-coat
And take the twilight of my day—
My arm would encircle you, framing a holy image.

As once, when I suffered in the dark of my heart—
There were both your eyes: blue clouds.
They took me from my melancholy.

Were you to come—
To this ancestral land—
You would reproach me like a little child:
Jerusalem, arise and live again!

We are greeted by
Living banners of the One God,
Greening hands, sowing the breath of life.
(TRANSLATED BY AUDRU DURCHSLAG AND JEANETTE LITMAN-DEMEESTERE)

AUTUMN IN JERUSALEM
Oded Peled

And I heard thee wandering the Hebrew Land / southward and eastward your gaze
turns:

A n d   t h e   r a i s i n   o f   t h e   w o r l d   i s   s t i l l
i n t a c t

lo, a thin white in the tropic of the eye will accompany thee in the streets of Yerushalem*/

come I will show thee summer blaze like a handful of consciousness blinded by tweaks of light / come out to the balcony facing eastward and southward:

Ramat Rachel and a nearby Arab village (Zur Baher?) a sketch

on the forehead of light forehead of light, border of the Judaean desert Dead Sea

stain like distant azure—here, at dawn, ye shall wake to the winged flutter of

sparrow scurrying in the high boughs of the window,

his Strength and Song is the Lord:

> lift up your heads oh ye heavens and your eye a frontlet of wisdom, above your chiefest joy she will rise, her days are yet to come—

for he whose lips are seraph will shed genuine light and an exile in his heart will return to God's Land:

(TRANSLATED BY AURA HAMMER)

A VIEW OF JERUSALEM
To Tamara
T. Carmi

1

Soft light, green
of treetops—one green,
the fir; another,
the pine. A blue nest in the middle
for the morning bells—one bell
for the fir; another
for the pine.
That is what the eyes see,
that is what the ears hear
in the northern window. There is nothing,
nothing like Jerusalem,
in which this distance says
something obscure, muted
and explicit.

---

*Yerushalem: the ancient Cannanite name of Jerusalem.

The birds see the sound,
my wife sees the birds,
and I cannot lie to her.
There is nothing.

2

Child, child, little flower,
can I already play with you at words?
If I say to you that mine is ours,
that the button opens and none can close,
that the flower closes and none can open—
                              come here beside me.
Even when the sun is shining,
walk in the middle of the street.
When the street-lamp is before us,
put your shadow in mine.
When the street-lamp is behind us,
your hand in mine.
                    Always be visible,
within range of eye and voice,
and I will teach you games of hide-and-seek.

3

Naked. Bone, stone, sky.
Sirens drain our blood,
air foams in the wake of their sound.
Open wide. Dust—blind—and ashes.
Windowpanes make room for eyes,
eyes for the sound of sirens.
That is all a man is, now.
                    Take off your clothes.
I have to touch you.
Now.

4

Everyone speaks in song:
thinks one thing,
and says another;
says one thing, and thinks.

A winter landscape filled with clocks.
A man puts on his smile like a coat.
Don't look at the lining.

The mine is a name.
The raid is a door.
The trap is a part.
There is no thing
that does not compel its opposite.

A grammar of fears.
The rules—extremely sudden,
and it's hard to talk.

One thing is clear:
everyone plays.
And another thing:
you are no exception.

5

Now. Tomorrow will surely come,
in my window.
And the walls without a window?
The windows covered with stone?

My wife sees the birds
hidden,
her eyes wide open.
I see my wife:
in the noon of night,
a silver dome at her right hand;
in the dark of day,
at her left a dome of gold.

Sirens in the eyes
and stones from a wall.
(Flash of entangled horns.
A nail glittering in the Roman sun.)
A stone rises
like a small cloud—

           child, child,

little hand,
can I already say to you Jerusalem,
soft light, tomorrow, another green.
(AFTER THE MAHANEH YEHUDAH EXPLOSION, 1969)

        (TRANSLATED BY STEPHEN MITCHELL)

CITY OF WOUND
Haim Guri

I have another city of my own blood containing too much wine
and too much tar.
City of large stones and torn iron.
Half of her in rock;

Crowds looking at a building on Ben Yehuda Street demolished by a car bomb February 22, 1948
(Central Zionist Archives; with permission)

Half of her flying, gliding, to Kings' Heaven above her,

Pleasant light till the night.

City of hills, I'm a stranger to her, falling toward ravine,

She faints there

Shattering.

She leaps up

Higher and higher in the loneliness of her towers,

In love with the sky.

City of yearning, another city

built of strangled cries.

I have a city of wound.

(*TRANSLATED BY AURA HAMMER*)

I STOOD IN JERUSALEM
Zelda

I stood

in Jerusalem

which hung by a cloud,

stood in a graveyard

with people crying,

a twisted tree.

Blurred hills,

a tower.

You are not,

said death

to us,

nor are you,

he said to me.

I stood

in Jerusalem

that was framed in sun

and smiling like a bride,

stood in a field

near thin green grass.

Why were you afraid of me yesterday in the rain?
said death,
I am your older, your silent
brother.

(*TRANSLATED BY ZVI JAGENDORF*)

HOUSE DOG
Uri Zvi Greenberg

Never have I raised a veil across my face before the abyss.
Nor covered my eyes from encountered fear:
Only once here I tried covering my eyes with my own hands:
Not to see the abyss of Jerusalem opening—
And I saw through the hand, shut-eyed, much fearing:
The third fire in hiding—
Now my eyes are open, lashes singed from the fire.

(*TRANSLATED BY AURA HAMMER*)

JERUSALEM
Moshe HaNa-ami

On the road to Bethlehem I live.
And in Emek-Refaim my friend
Bakes small cakes, scatters sugar
In the German colony. Amazing

How the old to the new is joined
Like sewage pipes on an old wall
In this Jerusalem, as if on canvas
A painter added, here flower, here tree—

And here me with detective novel,
And there old woman, and here railroad tracks,
And church, and Ethiopian priest.

And one man who for his messiah waits.
And a hand which on wall writes:
Holy place, pissing not allowed.

(*TRANSLATED BY AURA HAMMER*)

JERUSALEM POEMS III
Ruth Finer Mintz

At dawn,
Jerusalem is a doe.
Her golden eyes reflect the morning.
Her fauns, rays of light,
skitter across the hills.

At noon,
Jerusalem is the stag
that has escaped the hunters.
His golden antlers uphold the sun.

Late afternoon,
Jerusalem is a lion.
Her mane illumines the towers and domes.

But at night
Jerusalem is a lioness guarding
the remnant of her young.

All night her footfall echoes on Mount Zion.
All night her eyes gleam into the valley.
All night her breath is in the trees.

Weaving anew the flowering hillsides.
Weaving, weaving anew the blue tent of morning
from which shall come, like a bridegroom,
the day called, Peace.

SUDDENLY THE SUN LETS THE PEAKS GO AND LEAPS
Benzion ben Shalom

Suddenly the sun lets the peaks go and leaps
Down to the deeps.
Orphan is day. From out a silvern sky
Settle a spate of yearnings soundlessly
To wander through
This city turning rose-and-blue.

The Temple Mount, late nineteenth century (Photograph by La Maison Bonfils. The Museum of Photography at Tel-Hai Industrial Park; with permission)

Faint is the noise of men.

The pace of cars is dull and dim,

But longings all around raise voices once again.

Jerusalem, move slow, at gentle pace.

For yearning then to yearning now will croon

And mysteries will silently embrace.

Messiah-longings rustle everywhere,

And every street is a sanctuary for prayer.

Now my own childhood pure, and far away

So many a long long day,

Draws near to me

In secrecy.

It strokes my hair
And whispers consolations in my ear.

(TRANSLATED BY I. M. LASK)

THE WARM STONE ON THE HILL OF JERUSALEM
Ayin Tur-Malka

To attach our cheeks to the warm stone on the hill of Jerusalem:
this stone softer than softness.
That within her rigidity waves of voices
which rise in the ear's imagination.
That within her hardness abysses pull.
To rest the head on her like resting it
on water.
Within her sun-heat and rain combine.
A settling of dense delight.

And when our father Jacob the loving
crowned by the retribution of love
(which warmly reaches to the root of pain)
rested his head on the stone
and the stone mellowed the headrest of his spirit
carried on to heights—

(TRANSLATED BY AURA HAMMER)

JERUSALEM' S WALLS
Israel Efrat

From late afternoon on,
are lit the stones of Jerusalem's walls.

From the King's street, through Mount Zion,
and in the semi-circle to Katamon westward—
like tall torches Jerusalem's walls.

Like priests' foreheads as they push back their tallit
after lifting their palms,
like a tune silent-silent burning.

From gaping light like a great recollection,

to saffron and gold, to crimson-torment-deep-

each hour and the color of its flame—

until buds of fire float in a lake of air.

Look, look

all the roads reach for Jerusalem,

and she herself?

For what does she burn so forcefully?

Toward what is she road?

Until night comes from behind, from Temple Mount,

lingers a while,

and in a dark veil hushes the city walls.

(TRANSLATED BY AURA HAMMER)

ABU-TOR

David Rokeah

Since evening

the hill hasn't moved. The stones that absorbed

tales of a thousand and one nights

continue to dream. My memories

are outdated. The shadow of my love

between the stones like a wire.

(TRANSLATED BY AURA HAMMER)

EVENING IN JERUSALEM

Yehuda Karni

The evening here does not approach in stealth,

   With feline bounds;

Night is no velvet of luxurious wealth

   To wrap you around.

The evening never oozes from the soul

   Until the last small drop is gone,

Nor does Night's curtain slowly fall

   Between the bright and dun.

The evening seizes, fetters,
   Hands on to the night;
The latter clutches, batters,
   Kills and buries tight.

(TRANSLATED BY ABRAHAM BIRMAN)

SIEGE

David Rokeah

The evening in Jerusalem is late to
Forget the warm words of the summer captive
Within the mountain clefts.
Smoky from burned-off weeds, time
Invests the body. The body images that
Enfold their jealousy in shadow, are
Invested by the battlements that circle as
A school of gulls laying siege to
The entrance of a port.
Night after night I go with the wind that
Blows from the sea to the wind that comes from
The caves which honeycomb the groundwork of
The wall.

Night after night your voice that questions the end-tellers
Fears the wind that speaks out from the earth
The magic letters on the cloister wall
Beyond the battlements.

          (TRANSLATED BY D. SARAPH)

JERUSALEM MOON

Gabriel Preil

The moon has risen above the festive city.
It is not now a silver vessel on an azure sea,
nor any other metaphor that drops
from rhetoric's tired trees.

In the great city
of sleeping kings,
I rise with the moon,
the single slice of bread
to feed my hunger—
an explication, perhaps,
of the festivity.

No longer am I caught on the horn of renunciation.
A violet morning prophesies: It is never too late.

(TRANSLATED BY ROBERT FRIEND)

I DON' T KNOW IF MOUNT ZION
Abba Kovner

1

I don't know if Mount Zion would recognize itself
in the fluorescent light at midnight
when all that remains of Jerusalem

Mount Zion, the Dormition Abbey, and the walls of the Old City, ca. 1912 (Central Zionist Archives; with permission)

is her beauty wakeful
in the milky light spreading over her limbs
still wings raising it above the desert which sank away
so slowly above the stars
this eerie seashell floating from the midst of night
a transparent giant
so much sky sweeping over it
I don't know if Mount Zion looks
into my heart which holds its breath now behind a latticed window
out of torment and delight and for whom it's meant
in the heart of night.

2

These olive trees
which never bowed with the hidden knowledge
and the grooved wrinkles that this whole blue fan
over the Gehenna road
I don't know if Mount Zion sees the things
that changed our image
beyond recognition. The hands that touched it daily
like a mother touching her son's forehead fell
elusively into the slumber
of the Dead Sea
Does it hear the cry
from the Marketplace of Gates or the thrust of my prayer from the shade—
What good are friends who watch from the balcony
while our heart wrestles on the stage
and what use are we poets if we
don't know how to speak
—Does Mount Zion really exist or
is its light like our love beaming from a source
rising every
night

(TRANSLATED BY WARREN BARGAD AND STANLEY F. CHYET)

MORIAH

Levi Ben Amitai

My days have marched unto
The fragrant mount.
My feet have stood upon
The mount eternal joy.

I close my eyes and see
The whiteness of the stone
The skies of Moriah.

What can man add to
The glory of these things?
All I have are words
So poor and few.

I say unto my soul:
It is enough, enough.
(TRANSLATED REUVEN HAMMER)

YOUR BLISS AND CALM

Yehuda Karni

Pour out in me, Jerusalem, your bliss and calm.
Beneath yon skies I roam,
Where days strew rays across their palm
And stars enhance their jet nocturnal dome.

Or pin me to your folk, the chosen stem,
And I shall blindly trail behind their orbit.
Behold, your sapphired crown has caught my gem—
Your ever-studded splendour will absorb it.

Or bid me do your wish wherever needed,
Observe your pure demands in gate and cave.
Yea, though by prouder priests I am preceded
I shall but serve you better as your slave.

(TRANSLATED BY ABRAHAM BIRMAN)

CITY OF DAVID
Zerubavel Gilad

By daylight she is a village
Wrapped in the smell of smoke
And dung.
But in the dark, as her lights blossom
With a young girl's laughter,
I am reborn at her feet
And like my father's father's father
When young,
I hear on her streets at midnight
The melody of
David's harp.

       (TRANSLATED BY AURA HAMMER)

JERUSALEM
Yaakov Fichman

Jerusalem! Cry of the hungry heart, oblivion's
garden beyond the hills when refugees fled the storm—
Silence you are, submission and rebellion.
Because of you, heart shudders, the griefs swarm.

By green of your earth I swear and by your sunlight.
I inherit the desolation that remains.

I stand like a tree in stone, by you held spellbound—
soul woven with soul, my root in your dry veins.

I love what survives in you as in cold lava,
the rejoicing sound of ancient days,
echoing still from your white rocks of silence.

But with your holiness is now my strife,
and I have come to small rocks into clods.
Dead spendour rests on furrows of new life.

       (TRANSLATED BY ROBERT FRIEND)

PENALTY KICK
Ronny Someck

You'll never walk alone Beitar Yerushalaim.
In the Mahane Yehuda market they sew your Shabbat dress,
and a ragball heart rolls
between a pound of tomatoes
and an olive tin.
In these streets they brewed history over a paraffin stove.
Jesus was a bench player and Josephus Flavius
an acquisition for Italy's national team.
Close your eyes Beitar Yerushalaim
time is a penalty kick of both kicker and kicked.

(TRANSLATED BY AURA HAMMER)

TO JERUSALEM YES
Gabriel Preil

I left that city for a little while,
its homey and its exotic raiment,
the undiminished wisdom of the olive,
the youthful arrogance of the cypress,
not knowing whether someone there
would one day read my name
upon a tombstone.

But in a cafeteria here,
as in more innocent days,
poems are written still that defy the last incursion
and they are like the weathers that keep on returning.

The hot, brown wind in the hills,
the cool drizzle turning blue upon the slopes
extend competing invitations,
and my reply is Yes.

(TRANSLATED BY ROBERT FRIEND)

OLD AGE
Elisha Porat

I who was a ram in Jerusalem
A young man of lean muscles in Jerusalem
Skipping and lusting on the stairs of Jerusalem,
Now calculate every step every stride
Up toward the love-dens that have forsaken me.
I slide clumsy on the slope
Rolling down with Jerusalem stones,
Clutching like a desperate survivor the memory of my youth:
A forgotten lesson from the classroom
About a cruel and precise law
Of the sloping plane.

(TRANSLATED BY AURA HAMMER)

LEAVING JERUSALEM
Marcia Falk

I've worn through the soles of my shoes—
my feet so tough they no longer feel the ground
where cyclamen split rocks, recklessly.

I've put on a lizard's skin,
the Salt Sea slides down my neck
like oil in the sun.

Now I'm heading west,
my suitcase stuffed with chunks of halvah,
sacks of chickpeas and almonds.

Tomorrow I'll beat my clothes
like the Bedouin women at the streams,
but the viscous scents will cling

like musk to the skin
where the body claims its home.

JERUSALEM: LADDERS OF LOVE
Gabriel Preil

I've returned to New York. For months
I am struck by the Jerusalem moon.
The stones of Jerusalem tell me wine,
testing the hues of my love.

So will it be if I too
reach the very white years.
The dreams that will walk in me then
will thunder like lions in their thirst.

Meanwhile mother Jerusalem
sends me regards
more peaceful than flocks
to a tower-burdened son.

(TRANSLATED BY GABRIEL LEVIN)

RETIREMENT
Elisha Porat

Poets do not retire
On reaching their time to be silent,
Praising the beauty of Jerusalem
They are pushed slowly eastward
Thrust aside forgotten to the desert.
And there, suddenly in absolute secrecy
Drop mutely from the cliff,
And the bone of their poetry, drying
Bleaching and gathering dust
Descends to the cave opening.
Sinks slowly, gathered
In the dust cloud of the scrolls.

(TRANSLATED BY AURA HAMMER)

Montefiore Quarter, date unknown (Central Zionist Archives; with permission)

FROM THE STREETS OF JERUSALEM
Abba Kovner

When did the flocks pass from the streets of Jerusalem?
We went out into her street and there were
no flocks in Zion Square Jerusalem.

When was the wolves' howl silenced in the nights of Jerusalem?
In that winter we awoke
for the desert had retreated from the bounds of Jerusalem.

When did the camel caravans cease in the avenues of Jerusalem?
Yesterday an old man died
he had yet seen camels make their way through the dust of Jerusalem.

And do mad dogs yet wander through the alleys of Jerusalem?
I saw a blocked up well in Yemin Moshe and
there is a new moon, why should
wild dogs be missing within Jerusalem.

And how does a man die in Jerusalem. In turn

each man is bequeathed one day

his own death. Even if flock by flock

they still fall on the altars of Jerusalem.

And when is there none so beautiful as Jerusalem—always

when I hear two Jerusalemites

saying to each other: Let us go home

and make ourselves a light.

(TRANSLATED BY AURA HAMMER)

TOURISTS

Yehuda Amichai

Visits of condolence is all we get from them.

They squat at the Holocaust Memorial,

They put on grave faces at the Wailing Wall

And they laugh behind heavy curtains

In their hotels.

They have their pictures taken

Together with our famous dead

At Rachel's Tomb and Herzl's Tomb

and on the top of Ammunition Hill.

They weep over our sweet boys

And lust over our tough girls

And hang up their underwear

To dry quickly

In cool, blue bathrooms.

Once I sat on the steps by a gate at David's Tower, I placed my two heavy baskets at my side. A group of tourists was standing around their guide and I became their target marker.

"You see that man with the baskets? Just right of his headthere's an arch from the Roman period. Just right of his head." "But he's moving, he's moving!"

I said to myself: redemption will come only if their guide tells them, "You see that arch from the Roman period? It's not important: but next to it, left and down a bit, there sits a man who's bought fruit and vegetables for his family."

(TRANSLATED BY GLENDA ABRAMSON AND TODOR PARFITT)

THE TENTH GATE

Jerusalem in Jewish Folklore

Zion Gate, May 1968 (Israel Government Press Office; with permission)

JERUSALEM OF GOLD

Shalom M. Paul

Professor Shalom M. Paul has served as chairman of the Department of Bible of the Hebrew University and is the author of many important books of biblical scholarship.

On the coast of Syria is an ancient port called Ugarit, which flourished between the fifteenth and thirteenth centuries B.C.E. Beginning in 1929, texts were discovered there which are especially important for understanding the poetic and linguistic background of the Bible. One of these texts contains an inventory* of the Queen of Ugarit's personal possessions, including a piece of jewelry, identified in the Sumerian language as "a city of gold." The expression is undocumented in all Mesopotamian and Ugaritic literature. Its identity was an enigma. Now, however, with the aid of rabbinic texts, written more than fifteen hundred years after Ugarit vanished in about 1200 B.C.E., the meaning of this intriguing object can finally be deciphered, for rabbinic texts also refer to a *city of gold*.

The rabbinic sources establish that:

- A *city of gold* is a piece of jewelry worn by women:

  "All women's ornaments are susceptible of being unclean, for example, a *city of gold* . . ." (Mishnah, Kelim 11:8).

  "A woman may not go out [on the Sabbath . . . wearing] a *city of gold*" (Mishnah, Shabbat 6:1).

- It is an expensive piece of jewelry worn by upper class women:

  Rabbi Elazar said, "Whose practice is it to go out [wearing] a *city of gold*? A woman of rank" (Talmud Shabbat 59b).

This expensive piece of jewelry figures in a famous case of female jealousy: "Rabbi Akiba made a *city of gold* for his wife. The wife of Rabban Gamliel [the Patriarch] saw her and became jealous. Rabban Gamliel's wife came and reported Rabbi Akiba's gift to her husband. He said, 'Have you done for me what she did for him? Rabbi Akiba's wife sold the very braids on her head and gave [the money] to him so that he might be able to study Torah' " (Talmud Yerushalmi, Shabbat 6:1, 7d; cf. Talmud Yerushalmi Sotah 9:16, 24c).

A rabbinic source which describes the tremendous wealth which Rabbi Akiba amassed in his later years states that before he "departed from the world he owned tables of silver and gold and mounted his bed on ladders of gold. His wife used to go about in golden sandals and [wearing] a *city of gold* [of which Rabban Gamliel's wife was so jealous]" (S. Schechter, *Abot de Rabbi Nathan*, pp. 29–30).

*J. Nougayrol, *Le Palais Royal d'Ugarit*, Vol. III (Paris, 1955), No. 16.146–161, pp.182–186.

A more specific description of this *city of gold* is obtained from a variant source of the report describing Rabbi Akiba's latterday wealth which states: "They say that [Rabbi Akiba] did not die before he slept on beds of gold and until he made a *crown of gold* for his wife" (Schechter, *Abot de Rabbi Nathan*, Version B, Ch.12. p.30). In this passage the expression, *a city of gold*, is replaced by its equivalent, a *crown of gold*.

This identification of *city of gold* as a *crown of gold* is further substantiated by another passage from the Talmud: When the question is raised, "What is meant by the *crowns of brides?*" The answer is given, "a *city of gold*" (Talmud Sotah 49b).

This *city of gold* or *crown of gold* had another name in Talmudic sources: "What is meant by a *city of gold*: Rabban b. Bar Hannah answered in Rabbi Yohanan's name, 'A *Jerusalem of gold* such as Rabbi Akiba made for his wife'" (Talmud Shabbat 59a–59b). This gift of a *city of gold* or *Jerusalem of gold* which Rabbi Akiba gave to his wife Rachel was in fulfillment of a promise which he had made to her when still a very poor man: "If I could only afford it, I would attire you with a *Jerusalem of gold*" (Talmud Nedarim 50a). Thus the *city of gold* is also referred to as a *Jerusalem of gold*.

Both iconographic and epigraphic evidence enable us to identify the design of this golden crown. In antiquity cities were often depicted surrounded by walls with protecting towers. Turreted and battlemented wall crowns are known throughout the ancient Near East. They appear in the thirteenth century at Yazilikaya, a great rock sanctuary about two miles from Boghazkoy (in modern Turkey), capital of the Hittite empire in Asia Minor. On the face of the cliff at Yazilikaya there is a bas-relief carving depicting a tribute scene of the gods and goddesses of the Hittite kingdom; the females deities are wearing turreted crowns. . . .[*]

Epigraphic evidence provides final corroboration that the *city of gold* was in fact a turreted crown. The Jerusalem Talmud (Shabbat 6:1, 7d) reports that the rabbis of Caesarea referred to the crown by a unique Greek expression. In the course of time this Greek expression became corrupted and thus, unintelligible. Recently Professor Saul Lieberman[**] reconstructed the original reading of the phrase, which turned out to be a

---

[*]K. Bittel, *Die Feldsbilder von Yazlikaya* (Bamberg, 1934), pl. 12; K. Bittel, R. Naumann, and H. Otto, *Yazilikaya: Architektur, Feldsbilder, Inschriften und Kleinfunden*, pp. 116–118, fig. 46; E. Akurgal, *Späthethitische Bildkunst* (Ankara, 1949), pp. 10–12, and *The Art of the Hittites* (New York, 1962), pp. 11–12, fig. 19 and pls. 76–77. For other examples see E. Porada, *The Art of Ancient Iran* (New York, 1965), pp. 66–67, fig. 42, and p. 234, n. 46; A. Parrot, *The Arts of Assyria* (New York, 1961), p. 118, fig. 133; H. Frankfort, *Art and Architecture of the Ancient Orient* (London, 1954), pl. 114; E. R. Goodenough, *Jewish Symbols in the Greco-Roman Period* (New York, 1953–68), Vol. II, figs. 58, 160. See O. Seyffert, *Dictionary of Classical Antiquities*, revised and edited by H. Nettleship and J. E. Sandys (New York, 1959), p. 164, 586b.

For such a crown on coins, see L. Kadman, *The Coins of Caesarea Maritime* (Jerusalem, 1957), Vol. II, 3, 126, 127, 189, 218.

[**]S. Lieberman, originally in a personal communication. See now his *Tosefta Ki-Fshutah. Part VIII, Order Nashim* (New York, 1973), p. 179.

Scene from the rock sanctuary at Yazilikaya showing battlemented crown worn by female deities (after Akurgal)

"turret of gold," an exact description of the crown. Thus while some rabbinic sources refer to the crown by its traditional name (*city of gold* or *Jerusalem of gold*) the rabbis of Caesaria described its distinct features, a diadem surrounded by turrets. . . .

This distinctive crown, commonly called a *city of gold*, was naturally identified by Jews as *their* city *par excellence*, that is, Jerusalem, hence to them this crown was also known as *Jerusalem of gold*.

KING DAVID'S TOMB IN JERUSALEM

Folk Tale

Eighty years ago, in a Polish yeshiva, there were two pupils who were aroused with a longing for redemption. Both of them eagerly desired to ascend to Eretz Yisrael, the Land of the Fathers. They especially wished to see King David's tomb. Day and night they dreamed about it, and at last they began to think how to turn their dream into reality. They did not have money, so they decided to ascend on foot. As they decided, so they did. They set off taking only sticks and knapsacks. On the way they met with many obstacles, but with the help of God they overcame them all and arrived at last at the

The synagogue of Elijah the Prophet restored following the Six Day War, (Photograph by David Harris; with permission)

holy city of Jerusalem. They trembled and were happy in their hearts to be at the holy place and to arrive safe and sound at their destination. Still overcome with joy, they found themselves suddenly just opposite the walls of Mount Zion. They did not know, however, exactly where King David's tomb was or which road led there. While they were wondering, Elijah the Prophet, of blessed memory, appeared before them and showed them the way.

"Now my sons, when you reach the tomb and when you enter and go down the steps, keep to the bottom of the tomb. Your eyes will be blinded by all the visions of desire that you see there, silver, gold, and diamonds. Woe if you should lose your senses! You must look for the jug of water at King David's head. Pour water from the jug onto King David's hands as he stretches them toward you. Pour water three times over each hand, and then the King will rise up and we shall be redeemed. For King David is not dead; he lives and exists. He is dreaming, and he will arise when we are worthy of it. By your virtue and the merit of your longing and love, he will arise and redeem. Amen, that this may come to pass."

As Elijah the Prophet finished these words, he disappeared. The young men then ascended Mount Zion, guarded by Elijah, the Prophet. They went down into the depth of King David's tomb. Just as Elijah the Prophet had said, so it was. King David stretched out his hands to them, and there was a jug of water at his head. But because of our many sins, the riches around blinded the young men's eyes, and they forgot to pour water onto the hands outstretched toward them. In anguish the hands fell back and immediately the King's image disappeared.

The young men were startled when they realized that through them the redemption had been delayed again and the *galuth* would go on longer. They both wept from bitter anguish because the mitzvah of redemption had been in their hands and they had let it slip through their fingers.

May it come to pass that silver and gold will no longer dazzle our eyes. And when the right hour comes again, let it not be delayed. Amen and Amen.

(RECORDED BY NEHAMA ZION FROM MIRIAM TSCHERNOBILSKI BORN IN POLAND.)

(TRANSLATED BY GENE BAHARAV)

THE CLASSIC TALES

Ellen Frankel

ASMODEUS AND THE SHAMIR

After Solomon had been king for many years, God commanded him to build a Temple in Jerusalem.

"My House must be built without tools of iron," said God, "for out of iron, nations make swords, shields, and spears to wage war. It was because of his own bloody hands that I did not permit your father David to build Me a Temple."

"But how can I cut stone without iron tools?" asked Solomon.

"With the Shamir!" answered God.

"And where can I find the Shamir?" asked Solomon.

But the heavenly voice was silent.

So Solomon summoned his chief minister Benaiah ben Yehodaya and said to him, "At twilight on the Sixth Day of Creation God created the Shamir, a miraculous little creature that can cut through any substance on earth but lead. I need the Shamir to build God's Temple, but I do not know where it is. The only one who knows is Asmodeus, King of the Demons."

"But surely he won't tell you!" said Benaiah.

"Then I must capture him and make him tell!" said Solomon.

"And how do you propose to do that?"

"Asmodeus lives on a very high mountain," answered the king. "Each morning before he leaves to do his day's mischief, he places a giant stone over his drinking well so that no one else can drink from it while he is gone. Each night when he comes back, he checks to see that no one has drunk from his well, then drinks his fill and falls asleep."

Then Solomon lowered his voice so that no demon might overhear and warn Asmodeus about the king's plans.

"I want you to go to Asmodeus's mountaintop and bring with you a strong chain, a drill, a bundle of wool, a skin of wine, and my magic gold ring with the Secret Name of God engraved upon it.

"After Asmodeus leaves in the morning, drill a hole at the bottom of the well and drain out all the water. Then plug up the hole with half of the wool. Drill a second hole near the top of the well, below the stone lid, and fill the well with wine. Then plug up that hole, too, and wait for Asmodeus to return home."

Benaiah did exactly as the king had commanded. Taking with him a chain, drill, wool, wine, and the king's magic ring, he traveled for many days until he reached Asmodeus's mountaintop on the other side of the wilderness of Palmyra. Then he crouched behind a boulder waiting for the Demon King to depart. As soon as he was gone, Benaiah drained the water from the well and refilled it with wine. Then he crouched behind the boulder to await Asmodeus's return.

Just as the sun was setting, Benaiah heard the giant's horny chicken-feet scrambling up the mountain. Just as Solomon had said, the first thing Asmodeus did was to check the great stone on top of his well. Satisfied that no one had tampered with it, the giant removed the stone. Then he reached down one hairy hand and scooped up a lakeful of water. How surprised he was to taste wine! Laughing, he reached down for more. Within moments, he had drained the entire well. Suddenly he fell to the ground like a stone, shaking the mountaintop so that Banaiah had to hang on to the boulder to keep from falling off.

When Benaiah was sure that Asmodeus was fast asleep, he crept out from his hiding place and tied the heavy chain around Asmodeus's thick, hairy neck. When the demon awoke hours later, he tried to escape, bellowing like a mad bear. Then Benaiah showed him Solomon's magic ring.

"It's no use trying to escape, Asmodeus," he told the giant demon. "God is mightier than you."

Benaiah brought Asmodeus to Solomon's palace, where the king sat upon his throne, waiting for him.

"Tell me, Asmodeus," commanded Solomon. "Where is the Shamir?"

Asmodeus grumbled, "I know but I will never tell you!"

Then Solomon held up his magic ring and glared at the demon. "In the name of God, I command you to tell me!"

Asmodeus lowered his hairy head and snorted, "God gave the Shamir to the Hoopoe. She has hidden it in a secret place."

"And where is the Hoopoe's nest?"

"Far, far away, on a mountain on the other side of the sea. But she will never part with it!" Asmodeus warned Solomon. "She has promised God to guard it with her life." He laughed so loudly that the cedar rafters of the ceiling rattled like dry bones.

Then Solomon imprisoned Asmodeus in his deepest dungeon and sent Banaiah to bring back the Shamir. This time he gave his minister a piece of glass, a lead box, and enough food for a long journey.

Benaiah traveled for many days, across the sea, through forests and deserts, until he came to the Hoopoe's nest. He hid himself and waited until the Hoopoe flew away to find food for her babies. Then he put the piece of glass over her nest.

When the mother bird came back with a worm in her mouth, she discovered a strange, invisible wall separating her from her babies. She could see them but not touch them.

Off she flew and soon came back with a small creature in her beak. She dropped it on the glass, which shattered instantly. At that moment, Benaiah jumped out from behind the rock, shouting and wildly waving his arms. The Hoopoe was so surprised that she flew away. Benaiah quickly scooped up the Shamir in the lead box and raced down the mountain. He hardly stopped to eat or sleep until he reached Jerusalem.

When the Hoopoe realized what had happened, she was so desolate that she jumped off the mountain and drowned herself in the sea.

Solomon immediately set to work building a beautiful Temple for God in Jerusalem. The tiny Shamir cut all the stones to make the floors and walls.

At last it was done. The great Temple, covered with gold inside and out, shone like the sun itself. But when Solomon commanded Benaiah to bring him the Shamir, it had disappeared! All the king's servants searched high and low but it was nowhere to be found.

To this day no one has ever seen the Shamir again.

ALEXANDER ENTERS JERUSALEM

Alexander led a great army out of Macedonia and conquered every land in his way. Mighty Egypt fell before him. So did Edom and Gaza and Tyre. Then he prepared to take Jerusalem.

The night before he marched on the city, he had a dream: An angel dressed in white linen appeared before him brandishing a fiery sword. The angel lifted the sword above the king's head and prepared to strike him.

"Wait, my lord!" Alexander cried. "Why do you wish to kill me? I am your slave!" And he bowed low to the ground.

"The angel replied, "It is I who have brought you all your victories. God has sent me to subdue all the peoples in your path. But now you have set your heart on doing evil to God's people and God's holy city. So you must die!"

"I will turn around then, and return home."

"No!" said the angel. "You will enter Jerusalem as you have planned. But when you meet a man who bears my image and dress, bow before him and do whatever he asks of you. If you do not, that day will be your last."

When the king awoke from his dream, he was furious. Was he not Alexander the Great, conqueror of the world? He would bow before no man!

But when he approached the gates of Jerusalem and saw the high priest Hananiah walking toward him, dressed all in white and wearing a flashing diadem upon his head, Alexander leapt off his charger and prostrated himself on the ground before him.

His generals were astounded. "What are you doing, Alexander?" they cried. "This behavior is not befitting the ruler of the world!"

Then he told them his dream, and they fell silent.

Alexander then said to Hananiah, "Blessed be the God of Israel who has such love for you and your people! To acknowledge your God's great power, I shall give much gold to your craftsmen to erect a statue of me so that you may set it in your Holy of Holies as a memorial."

"We cannot accept your gift, your majesty," said the priest.

Alexander's face darkened. "And why not?"

"God forbids us to bow to any graven image. But let me suggest another memorial that will be far better than the one you propose."

"And what is that?"

"Give your gold to the priests to sustain them and the poor among our people. In return, every male child born to our priests this year in the whole of Judah shall be given the name Alexander. In this way your memory shall never depart from our midst."

Hananiah's words pleased Alexander, and he did as the high priest requested. Alexander then made a covenant of peace with the people of Judah and gave them many gifts.

And then he departed to conquer the remainder of the world.

THE PASHA'S LANCE

Once when the Pasha of Jerusalem visited the Tomb of David, his lance slipped out of his hand and fell through a grate into the tomb. Immediately the Pasha ordered one of his servants lowered into the tomb to retrieve it. For this was no ordinary lance, but one encrusted with precious jewels and crowned with gold.

Minutes later, they pulled the lifeless body of the servant out of the tomb. Then the Pasha ordered another servant lowered into the tomb, but the same thing happened. So it was with the third and fourth servants.

"Your majesty!" cried one of his chief ministers. "If you do not stop, we shall all soon be dead!"

"I will not leave this spot until I have my lance back!" declared the Pasha.

"Then send a messenger to the *Hakham* of the Jews," advised the minister. "Tell him that he must send a Jew to retrieve the lance or all the Jews of the city will die. Surely one of them will succeed in retrieving your lance, for this people has a special place in David's heart."

When the *Hakham* received the Pasha's message, he burst into tears and tore his clothes. How could he ask one of his own people to set foot in such a holy place? He would surely be condemning that man to death. He pleaded with the Pasha's messenger to give him three more days to reply, then summoned all the Jews of the city to the synagogue. For three days, the Jews of Jerusalem prayed and fasted. Many went to the Tomb of Rachel to beg that she intercede for them in heaven.

On the morning of the fourth day, the *Hakham* said to the people, "Who among you will go down to the tombs of the kings?"

No one came forward.

"Then we must draw lots," said the *Hakham*.

The lot fell upon the *shammash*, a poor, simple man.

The Tomb of David on Mount Zion in 1900 (Central Zionist Archives; with permission)

"I am the servant of the God of Israel!" he declared, and he prepared his soul for death. Saying farewell to his family and friends, he climbed Mount Zion, where the Pasha and his men eagerly awaited him. In the synagogue, the Jews continued to pray, hoping that a miracle might save the synagogue attendant from heaven's wrath.

Carefully the Pasha's men lowered the *shammash* into the tomb and waited. Moments passed, but no sound came from below. Just as the Pasha was about to order the rope raised up, a thin voice cried out from the tomb, "Pull me out!"

Quickly they pulled on the rope. The first thing that emerged was the gold point of the Pasha's lance, then the shaft, sparkling with precious jewels in the bright sun. Finally the pale face of the *shammash* rose out of the tomb. He held the lance out to the Pasha, whose face betrayed the greatest astonishment and awe.

All of the Pasha's men fell on their faces and cried, "Blessed be the God of Israel!"

From that day on the Pasha held the Jews in his domain in the greatest esteem.

As for the Jews themselves, they rejoiced greatly in their good fortune and heaven's grace. But the joy was greatest in the house of the simple *shammash*, who received many gifts from the community and from the Pasha himself for his brave deed. Many wished to know what had happened to him in the tomb, but his lips remained sealed.

Only the *Hakham* ever heard his story: As he had stood trembling in the gloom, an old man, dressed in gleaming white robes, had appeared before him and silently handed him the lance.

SEVEN HUNDRED YEARS OF SANCTITY

Meir Ben Dov

> *Meir Ben Dov is one of Israel's leading archaeologists; he has served as Deputy-Director of the excavations at the Western Wall.*

During the Six Day War the forces of the Israeli Army stormed into the Old City through the Lions' Gate, going from there to the court of the Temple Mount and one of the most beautiful buildings of the ancient world, the Dome of the Rock. The radio announced, "The Temple Mount is in our hands." The magnificent Muslim structure from the seventh century was erected near the site of the Second Temple, the most holy and honored of all Jewish structures.

When the first storm of emotions had passed, the group of paratroopers—the first conquerors—made their way to the Western Wall, where they unfurled the flag of Israel. From their point of view, their task was accomplished. They had reached the spot which was the most holy and most symbolic of all sites in the eyes of the Jewish people. Throughout the generations both Jewish leaders and the masses had become accustomed to separating themselves from the Temple Mount and clinging to that bit of an outer support wall—the Western Wall.

The motivation of masters of Jewish law in past generations was the assumption that if something cannot be attained, but will only arouse riots and a storm of useless emotions, it is better to turn it into a heavenly possession, something abstract, that one can aspire to, while leaving the actual right to possess it to the Messiah.

This assumption was well fortified by laws which subsequent generations erected. Obviously the masters of Jewish law did not accept the Messianic-nationalistic ideas which guide such groups as the Temple Mount Faithful.

Although it would appear that sanctity was first ascribed to the Western Wall on the day of the destruction of the Temple, the 9th of Av in the year 70 C.E., in actuality the status of sanctity was granted the Wall only five hundred years ago or possibly in the thirteenth century, some seven hundred years ago, but certainly not prior to that.

From the point of view of architecture, the Temple stood on the top of a mountain with slopes on all sides. In order to create a large plaza which would permit the populace to enter and observe both the structure and the rituals performed outside of it, the planners were forced to build walls on the slopes which would support the plaza. This was done when King Solomon built the first Temple, and the builders of the second Temple did the same thing. At the time of Herod, the numbers who came on pilgrimage reached new highs. Therefore it was necessary to double the size of the plaza of the Temple Mount from 70 dunam (70,000 square meters) to 145 dunam (145,000 square meters)—a gigantic plaza unknown in any other sanctuary in the ancient world. Four retaining walls were built around it. They are the walls of the Temple mount—the eastern, the southern, the western and the northern.

The longest wall outside the plaza of the sanctuary—certainly not part of the walls of the sanctuary itself—is the Western Wall, which is 485 meters long. In its southern half there are extant the remnants of four gates. Two gates are in the lower part of the wall and two in the upper part. The remnants of arches and platforms which led to them are known as "Robinson's Arch" and "Wilson's Arch" after the men who first revealed them. The gates are also known by the names of those who discovered them, "Barkley's Gate" and "Warren's Gate." The southern most gate is the Mograbi Gate. Part of its lintel can be seen at the right side of the women's prayer space and consists of a stone which weighs more than 100 tons.

In the midst of the great space thus created the Temple itself was erected. The Ark of the Covenant stood near its western wall. In the Second Temple the Holy of Holies was completely empty, except for the "rock of the foundation," which was thought to be the rock on which the world was founded.

Obviously at the time of the Second Temple no sanctity was ascribed to the supporting walls of the Temple Mount, including the Western Wall. Along that wall ran a street lined by shops on both sides. The shops on the eastern side were part of the wall and reached a height of 3.5 meters.

On the 9th of Av in the year 70 the Temple Mount was conquered and the Temple destroyed. On the 8th of Elul, a month later, the Upper City—in our days the Jewish Quarter, the Armenian Quarter and Mount Zion—was conquered. The area of homes was plundered, destroyed and burned, and all the inhabitants were exiled from the city. The Roman imperium decreed that Jews were not to be permitted to live in Jerusalem or to visit there. The destroyed city served only as a camp for the Roman legion which remained there as a stationary force. After the Bar Kokhba revolt (135 C.E.) the Emperor Hadrian decreed that the city was to be rebuilt and renamed Aelia Capitolina in honor of the Emperor Aelius Hadrianus and the Capitoline Hill in Rome upon which stood the Temple of Jupiter.

The decree forbidding the entrance of Jews to Jerusalem remained in force during the hundreds of years of the Byzantine Empire which followed Rome, until the Persian conquest in 614 and, later, the Arab conquest in 638. On rare occasions Jews managed to enter the city or to visit the area of the Temple Mount, but always at the risk of their lives.

During those more than five hundred years, if a Jew wanted to contemplate the holy places, he would climb up to the Mount of Olives and gaze upon the ruins of the Temple Mount and the Sanctuary. The wall which could be seen was the eastern wall, which became the most honored and sacred part of the Temple Mount.

When Jews were permitted to settle in the city, they held their prayers at the southern wall which, in the days of the Second Temple, had been the entrance, with two gates leading into and out of the Temple area. Nor was the eastern wall neglected. Now they could cling to its actual stones.

Until the crusaders came and destroyed the Jewish community of Jerusalem (1099 C.E.) we have reports of Jews worshipping at the bottom of the Temple Mount, but only at the eastern or southern walls. The western wall is never mentioned.

It would seem that the tradition of praying at the foot of the western wall began with the renewal of the Jewish settlement in Mameluke Jerusalem. This took place in 1267 when Nachmanidies came to the city. Nachmanidies began to repair the Jewish quarter, including the synagogue, the area which is still known as the Jewish Quarter of the Old City. Unfortunately we do not have exact information. In the middle of the eleventh century, the size of the area of Jerusalem was reduced and the southern wall of the city was built following the line of the later wall of Suleiman's, that is from El Aqsa mosque to the heights of Mount Zion. This excluded most of the southern wall, especially Hulda Gate, from being within the city.

Going to pray at those sacred sites became very dangerous for Jews. In their search for an alternate place of worship, it appears that they found a part of the remaining western wall with gigantic stones from Herod's construction. They began to pour out their prayer at that section of wall.

We know that organized prayer at the Western Wall began in the days of the Ottoman Sultan Suleiman the Magnificent, who built the walls of Jerusalem in the first half of the sixteenth century, i.e. 450 years ago. Suleiman wanted to draw Jews exiled from Spain and Portugal who were scattered throughout Europe and North Africa to his kingdom. Amongst the enticements this sultan offered was an orderly place for prayer at the Western Wall.

When Jews began to pray at the Western Wall, whether at the time of Nachmanides at the end of the thirteenth century or in the days of Sultan Suleiman in the first half of the sixteenth century, it was necessary to make the place precious to Jews. This was accomplished mainly by connecting it to the tradition of holiness which in our sources was attached to "the Wall." Never mind that the tradition was not really attached to the support wall of the Temple Mount; they managed to transfer it to that wall.

In the first years of the common era, it seems that the western wall of the Temple building itself still existed. Thus it is reported in one source: "It was decreed from heaven than it should never be destroyed. Why? Because the Divine Presence is in the west." To this was joined the legend which says that when the Romans conquered the Temple Mount, Titus gave the work of destruction to four commanders of the legion, one wall to each of them. They all began destroying the walls except for the commander Pengar, an Arabian count, in whose section was the western wall. When Titus asked him why he had not carried out his orders, he contended in his defence that he wished to leave a vestige standing so that people would see and marvel at Titus' destructive force and at the size of the Temple he had destroyed (Lam. Rabbah 1:30). Our sources tend to ascribe the fact that this wall was not destroyed to the personal intervention of Heaven, since the Divine Presence was found in the western wall of the Temple.

In those days, when those tales were told, the western wall of the Sanctuary still stood in place. When they began to pray at the western retaining wall of the Temple Mount, the prayer-site of our time, they transferred the legend to the western retaining wall of the Temple Mount. In the course of time, that stretch of wall where prayers were held became the holiest place for the Jewish people, even though the tradition of its holiness was born only seven hundred years ago.

A seven hundred-year-old tradition is not to be sneezed at. The prayers, the emotions and the memories of those years contributed to the holiness of the Western Wall—a holiness which drew hardened fighters from the site of the Sanctuary itself to the Wall.

JERUSALEM RECIPES
Danby Meital

JERUSALEM KUGEL (SAVORY)

SERVES 20

> *Traditionally served on the Sabbath at Kiddush following morning services, it is also served on holidays and festive occasions such as Brit Milah (circumcision).*

1 large package (19 ounces; 500 grams) fine egg noodles

$\frac{1}{2}$ cup oil, plus 1 tablespoon for pan

6 tablespoons sugar

3 eggs, beaten gently

1–2 teaspoons black pepper

3 teaspoons salt (or to taste)

Cook the noodles in boiling salted water as directed on package. Drain and pour into mixing bowl. Do not rinse. Meanwhile, boil the oil and sugar in a frying pan, stirring constantly until the sugar caramelizes. Pour the mixture over the hot noodles, stirring quickly, to coat the noodles. Add the eggs, salt, and black pepper.

Taste and add additional salt and pepper as needed. Oriental families prefer food spicy.

Cooking options:

1. Preheat oblong baking pan with tall sides, greased with 1 tablespoon of oil. Pour the noodle mixture into the pan and bake uncovered for 1 hour at 375°F.

2. (for Shabbat) Following the same procedure as above, use a round pan with tall sides, put it on a low flame on the stove for 15 minutes, and leave overnight on a heating tray (*Shabbos plata*).

Serve with spicy pickles.

TABBOULEH SALAD

(PARSLEY AND MINT WITH CRACKED WHEAT BURGUL)
SERVES 6 TO 8.

1 cup cracked wheat (burgul or bulgar)

Boiling water to cover

$\frac{1}{2}$ cup finely chopped mint leaves

$\frac{1}{2}$ cup finely chopped parsley

1 cup finely chopped onions or scallions

1 cup diced tomatoes, plus diced tomatoes for garnish

$\frac{3}{4}$ cup olive oil

1 cup lemon juice

Salt and pepper to taste

Place the cracked wheat in a mixing bowl and add boiling water, barely covering the wheat. Let stand for 30 minutes or until all the liquid is absorbed. The wheat should become tender, yet still be somewhat firm to the bite. If the wheat is too dry, add a little more boiling water. If excessive water has been added, drain, press, and let cool completely. Meanwhile, cut the remaining vegetables by hand or all together with a quick spin in the food processor. Mix together all the ingredients. Season to taste. Garnish with additional chopped tomatoes when serving.

ROASTED CHICKEN IN POMEGRANATE SAUCE

SERVES 4.

1 roasting chicken cut up

1 lemon sliced in half

1 large onion sliced in rounds

1 cup pomegranate juice, strained (save the seeds)

1 cup concentrated frozen orange juice

$\frac{1}{2}$ cup honey

2 teaspoons granulated garlic

$\frac{1}{2}$ teaspoon black pepper

1 teaspoon cinammon

1 tablespoon chopped parsley

1 tablespoon chopped dill (optional)

5 diced scallions

Sweet paprika

Place the onion slices on the bottom of the roasting pan. Rinse the chicken pieces and rub with lemon. Set aside in the roasting pan, skin side down, on top of the onions. Mix the remaining ingredients (except the paprika) and pour over the chicken. Cover tightly (aluminum foil is recommended). Roast for 30 minutes in preheated over (350° F., 200° C.). Uncover, turn the chicken pieces, sprinkle with sweet paprika, baste with pan juices, return to the oven, and roast for another 30 minutes uncovered until brown and crispy. Sprinkle pomegranate seeds over the chicken pieces and serve with potatoes or rice. Best prepared in the fall (September to November) when pomegranates ripen on the trees.

THE ELEVENTH GATE

Archaeology of the Old City

Jerusalem from the air, photographed by a German pilot in 1917 or 1918 (Central Zionist Archives; with permission)

WALKING THE OLD CITY: A JERUSALEM TOUR

Herbert Alexander

> *Herbert Alexander, formerly professor of psychology, is now a guide and lecturer in Jerusalem.*

There is a saying: "When the world was created, ten measures of sorrow came down to earth. Nine fell on Jerusalem and one on the rest of the earth." No city has known more conflict and suffering. Though conquered by foreign invaders some thirty-seven times in her more than four-thousand-year history, she remains the symbol of man's noblest visions of peace. The proverb continues that nine-tenths of the world's beauty and holiness also rained upon the city, bringing into existence a place full of vibrant tensions: between darkness and light, spirit and substance, war and peace. Those tensions, for all their modern guises—souvenirs for sale amid the shrines, soldiers patrolling the holy streets—still confound and fascinate.

This walk is tailored to fit into two days, but you could rush through it in one—or, better, savor it in seven.

Montefiore's Windmill, across from Liberty Bell Park, and the Mishkenot Sha'ananim building below it were the first built outside the Old City walls, in 1860. The Yemin Moshe neighborhood was the beginning of modern Jerusalem. From its observation platform, the Old City spreads out before you. To the left is Jaffa Gate, with banners flying from the Tower of David. The Old City walls, built by the Turks only 450 years ago, are in fact the newest city walls. They sit on the remains of Crusader walls from 1100, which sit on Byzantine remains from 550 and follow almost exactly the Roman walls from 135, which replaced the walls the Romans destroyed in 70.

The valley before you, Gai Ben Hinnom—*gehenom*, Hebrew for hell—has been by turns the site of pagan idol worship, Canaanite child sacrifice, a leper colony, and tombs. "Yes, though I walk through the valley of the shadow of death"—this is it. As the border between Jordanian-occupied Jerusalem and Israel from 1948 to 1967, this valley also bears some of the deepest scars of the long Arab–Israeli conflict. Arab Legion troups occupied the Old City walls, firing sporadically into the Yemin Moshe neighborhood, which became a boarded-up slum. The destruction in Jerusalem during these years saw 90 percent of the Jewish Quarter reduced to rubble. Beyond is the Judaean Desert.

Nineteenth-century *Yemin Moshe* is the "new" Jerusalem. Restored after the Six Day War, it is now a charming neighborhood of high-priced homes where noted artists have studios.

Descending Yemin Moshe Street, at the bottom of Yemin Moshe, bear right and cross the bridge to the foot of Mount Zion. A path to the left takes you up the hill to the southwest corner of the wall, with spectacular views of the New City along the way.

The tour of the Old City could begin at Zion Gate, but we recommend the more spectacular Ramparts Walk from (1) *Jaffa Gate*. Follow the path to the Citadel, turn right before entering Jaffa Gate, then walk over the wall and around the Armenian Quarter to (2) Zion Gate. From the top of Zion Gate, the Jewish Quarter, the Temple Mount with the gold Dome of the Rock, and the lead-domed Al Aksa Mosque come into view. Beyond the Old City you can see the Hebrew University on Mount Scopus, the *Mount of Olives* with the churches at *Gethsemane*, and the ancient *Jewish Cemeteries*; and, to the southeast, the Judaean Desert stretching to Jordan.

Descend at Zion Gate and step outside. The pockmarks are damage from the fighting in 1948. This became the border after the evacuation of the Jewish Quarter. On re-entering, turn right, follow the street to and across the parking lot, and turn left to the (3) *Four Sephardic Synagogues*, all largely destroyed between 1948 and 1967 and reconstructed after the Six Day War. Built in the early 1600s, the Yohanan Ben-Zakkai is the largest and one of the most beautiful in Jerusalem. Two-thirds of this three-story synagogue was built below street level, so as not to challenge Muslim architectural domination of the landscape. Continue along the street to the reconstructed arch of the (4) *Hurva Synagogue*. Built in the late 1850s, this was the largest in Jerusalem in 1948 and was intact at the time the Jewish Quarter surrendered to Jordan. It stands today as a memorial to the destruction of 1948.

(5) *The Cardo* (below street level), the main business avenue of Roman, Byzantine, and Crusader Jerusalem, was discovered in excavations in the Jewish Quarter in the 1970s. The northern part of the street, built by the Romans in about 135, starts at *Damascus Gate* and runs between the Muslim and Christian quarters to David Street. A small portion at Damascus Gate has been excavated. The Byzantines extended the street through the Jewish Quarter in 550, and the Crusaders rebuilt part as a closed shopping mall in the 1100s. In the days of the Byzantine Cardo, columns supported a covered sidewalk on both sides, and arched shops lined the street—some can still be seen. Note that only half the width of the street is exposed.

Continue north. The pointed Gothic arches indicate the covered Crusader Cardo, occupied by modern shops. Prices on the Cardo tend to be fixed, but it never hurts to say, "It's nice, but I didn't want to spend that much," and see what happens.

Midway along the Cardo is the (6) *Cardo Culinaria Restaurant*, a first-century kosher Roman restaurant. The furnishings and decor are based on excavations in the Jewish Quarter, the menu on a Latin cookbook of the period.

Just above the Cardo, at 34 Habad Street, (7) *Archeological Seminars* offers in-depth walking tours in the Old City. To the south on Habad Street, search in (8) *Sachs Gallery* and the *Cardo Center* for ancient coins and antiquities.

Go back down again to the Cardo and turn right past the Culinaria. Go up four or five steps to street level. To the left, just before the Muslim Quarter, is (9) *Tamar*, a shop barely big enough for two. The owner works mostly in silver. Back down the street near the Hurva, (10) *Baruch Hadaya* has very elegant modern pieces.

Halfway between Hadaya and Tamar, a side street takes you to the (11) *Broad Wall*.

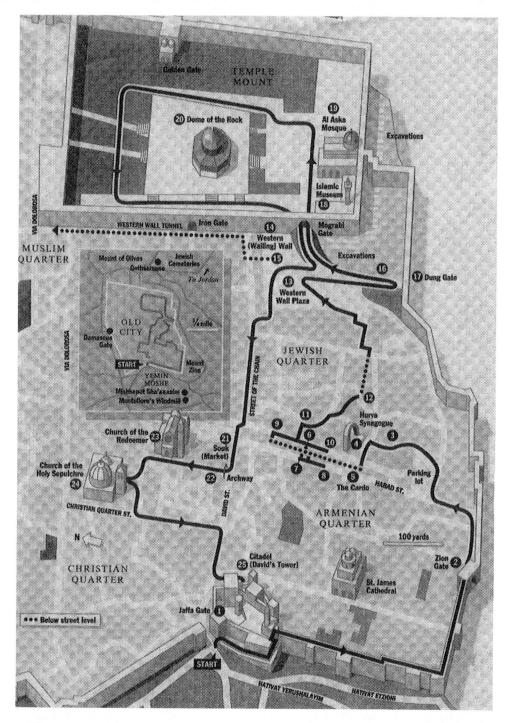

Walking tour map, courtesy of Condé Nast Traveler. Copyright © 1993 by The Condé Nast Publications, Inc.

Built by King Hezekiah before the Assyrian siege of Jerusalem in 701 B.C.E., this was the northern border of the city twenty-seven hundred years ago. Under a nearby school stands the gate through which the Babylonians captured the city in 586 B.C.E., ending the First Temple period.

Return to the Hurva area and cross to the (12) *Wohl Archaeological Museum (Herodian Quarter)*. Beneath Yeshivat HaKotel are the remains of six mansions that belonged to wealthy priests in Herodian times. The structures were burned by the Romans in 70 C.E., but mosaics, frescoes, furniture, and ritual baths survived.

You come out down the hill on your way to the (13) *Western Wall Plaza*. The Temple Mount ahead of you is crowned by the gold Dome of the Rock, built in 691 after the first Arab Conquest. Muslim tradition says that Mohammed ascended from this spot to heaven on his Night Journey. The Dome sits on or near the site of the Sanctuary of the great Second Temple, destroyed by the Romans in 70. It had, in turn, replaced the First Temple of Solomon, which had stood for about 350 years before its ruin by the Babylonians in 586 B.C.E. For Jews this is the holiest place on earth; for Muslims, the site of the third holiest mosque, Al Aksa; for Christians, the site of major events in the life of Jesus. So if you come here on a Friday afternoon, you will hear the call of the muezzin from the mirarets, the peal of bells from the Church of the Holy Sepulchre, and the singing of Jews greeting the Sabbath Bride.

For the last thousand years, the Jews' most sacred place of prayer has been the Kotel of (14) *Western Wall*, of the Temple Mount. It was long believed to be the only remains of the Temple and closest to the site of the Holy of Holies, though both of these claims have been disputed by recent scholarship. Still, this is the place where a Jew has the greatest sense of standing with the generations whose most fervent prayer has been "Next Year in Jerusalem." On Friday evening, song and dance greet the Sabbath. For festivals, tens of thousands of people fill the plaza in front for prayers. At noon on Friday, the Holy Day for Muslims, thousands flock to the Al Aksa Mosque. At three, the Franciscans walk in procession along the Via Dolorosa to the Holy Sepulchre.

Two recent excavations reveal the extent and magnificence of the Temple Mount. North of the plaza the (15) *Western Wall Tunnel* was dug under the Muslim Quarter to the northwest corner of the Temple Mount. Inside is a replica of the Second Temple, Herodian masonry, and much more. Walk to the huge (16) *South Wall Excavation*, where you can see Crusader, Umayyad, Byzantine, and Second Temple Jewish remains, and to the southeast the original steps and pilgrim gates to the Temple Mount.

Had enough for the day? The No. 38 bus just outside (17) *Dung Gate* will take you close to our starting point in about three stops. But if you want to continue, a ramp to the right of the Western Wall leads to *Mograbi Gate*, which is the visitors' entrance for the (18) *Islamic Museum*, (19) *Al Aksa Mosque*, and the (20) *Dome of the Rock*, all of which are open to non-Muslims some hours of every day, except Friday and Holy Days. Strolling around the Temple Mount is free, but buy tickets for the Muslim buildings at one of the kiosks. And dress modestly—in other words, don't wear shorts—to visit this place of great sanctity.*

Follow the path around the Temple Mount and back to the Western Wall Plaza and take the stairs to the Street of the Chain. Turn left and continue up the hill toward Jaffa Gate. When you crossing the Cardo, the street becomes David Street. You are now in a medieval (21) *Arab souk* with shops selling spices, clothing, brass and copper, jewelry, and souvenirs. Bargaining is absolutely expected. Your opening offers should be about half the asking price; where you end up depends upon how much you want the thing. There are tremendous bargains on things you don't want.

At Muristan Street, turn right through the arch into the (22) *Christian Quarter*. The Lutheran (23) *Church of the Redeemer* at the end of the street, the Protestant church nearest the Holy Sepulchre, was built in the 1890s on Crusader ruins. Turn left to the (24) *Church of the Holy Sepulchre*. For sixteen hundred years this has been the focus of Christian pilgrimage to Jerusalem. Constantine built the original Byzantine church in about 333 at the site of the Crucifixion and Tomb of Jesus. The church was damaged many times; its destruction by the Muslim caliph Al-Hakim in the eleventh century inspired the Crusades.

Today's Crusader structure was built in the twelfth century on the site of the much larger Byzantine original. Property rights today are divided among Roman Catholics, Greek Orthodox, Armenians, Syrians, Copts, and Ethiopians, but the keys have been kept by a Muslim family since the days of Saladin.

Inside the church are what are traditionally regarded as the last stations of the Via Dolorosa. A balcony to the right of the entrance encloses what some believe to be the hill of Golgotha, where Jesus was crucified. Directly ahead is the Stone of Unction, where his body was prepared for burial. To the left we come to the reconstructed Byzantine Rotunda and the Anastasis, or Chapel of the Resurrection, with the Tomb under the great dome. The rotunda and dome inspired the Dome of the Rock in 691, which reflects the same interior architectural plan.

In the crypt below the church is an ancient stone quarry, now the Chapel of Saint Helena, named for Constantine's mother, who in 326 claimed she found the True Cross there. The quarry dates from the time of Herod. It is thought that some of the stones of the Western Wall match those in this quarry.

---

*There are different opinions concerning the halakhic permissability of entering the Temple Mount area. The Chief Rabbinate of Israel has posted signs warning that it is forbidden to do so. Some Orthodox authorities, such as Rabbi Shlomo Goren, were of the opinion that at least part of the area was not included in the prohibition. The Law Committee of the Rabbinical Assembly of Israel (Masorti-Conservative) has issued an opinion stating that it is permissible to enter the Temple Mount, but not the Dome of the Rock or the raised platform surrounding it. A minority opinion stated that the entire area is permissible except the place where the Holy of Holies was situated (i.e., the central area within the Dome of the Rock) and that in all cases proper dress and an attitude of reverence are required. It was suggested that Psalm 15 be recited before ascending to the Mount.—ed.

It's a typical Jerusalem story. Muslims have the keys to the church where Helena found the Cross in an abandoned quarry that Jews are said to have used to cut stones for the Second Temple.

On leaving the Church of the Holy Sepulchre, turn right; walk to Christian Quarter Street and make a left, then walk to David Street, turn right, and walk to the (25) *Citadel* at Jaffa Gate. This ancient structure, which has archeological remains going back two thousand years in some places, houses the Tower of David Museum of the History of Jerusalem. A walk though a series of chambers takes you through the entire history of Jerusalem, with models, audiovisual displays, and film clips. Don't miss the twenty-minute animated film.

The 360-degree view from the top of the Tower is spectacular. In the late afternoon light, the city takes on a pink and then a golden glow as flecks of mica in stone reflect the setting sun.

Many believe there is a heavenly Jerusalem just above the earthly one of tension and conflict. It is a city of perfection, with streets of gold and buildings of sapphire and pearl, where everyone lives in perfect harmony with his neighbor and his God. A thin gold chain hangs down from this Celestial City, just over the gold dome on the Temple Mount, waiting for the Messiah to pull it down and make the two one. From the top of the Tower, as the sun sets and turns the stones of the city to gold, you may catch a glimpse of it.

TWENTY-FIVE YEARS OF EXCAVATIONS IN JERUSALEM, 1967–1992

ACHIEVEMENTS AND EVALUATION

Hillel Geva

> *Hillel Geva, an archeologist working with the Israel Exploration Society, assisted the late Prof. Nahman Avigod in his work in Jerusalem.*

The reunification of Jerusalem in 1967 sparked a dramatic surge of archaeological activity in the ancient city. Widespread investigation of the ancient remains was initiated on a scale which overshadowed all such previous work. Excavations were conducted throughout the entire extent of ancient Jerusalem, including places within the Old City walls where the spade of the archaeologist had never broken ground. Building and structural remains, and the artifacts that have come to light in the course of the last twenty-five years of intensive archaeological research in Jerusalem, now make it possible to re-evaluate and summarize some of the key questions concerning the topography and architectural features of the city during various periods of its history. As a result, much of our understanding of the city's past has been revolutionized.

One cannot summarize the decades of archaeological research in Jerusalem without mentioning the enormous and often insoluble difficulties—some of them specific to

Jerusalem—that have always been inherent in archaeological excavations there. Most of the urban area of ancient Jerusalem today lies within the walls of the densely built Old City and the adjacent neighborhoods. This severely limits the possibilities for excavating large areas, which is the only way to obtain a comprehensive overview of the city's topography. Religious sensitivity and political factors also hinder archaeological research in key parts of the city. Jerusalem has been inhabited continuously and intensively for thousands of years. On the slopes upon which the city was built, and in the surrounding valleys, archaeological deposits consisting of layers of occupation and accumulated debris were later covered by large, deep dumps. Buildings constructed upon steep hillsides collapsed and suffered erosion, leaving only foundations in some places. With each subsequent rebuilding, foundations had to be sunk more deeply through the previous occupational levels to achieve the necessary stability. Earlier structures were dismantled and their building stone reutilized. Sometimes, as a result of official building activities in the city, such as the construction of the Temple Mount in the days of Herod, all previously existing structures along its outer sides were razed to make room for the new foundations. In view of the difficulties and limitations on the investigation of Jerusalem's past, the overwhelming achievements of archaeological activity, and particularly the excavations of the last twenty-five years, are the more remarkable.

THE BRONZE AGE

The excavations by Y. Shiloh in Area E on the eastern slope of the City of David in 1978–1985 revealed significant remains of the earlier settlement of the city, indicating a limited occupational presence in the Chalcolithic period—as early as the fourth millennium B.C.E. During the third millennium B.C.E., in the Early Bronze Age, the first structures were erected on the bedrock of the steep eastern slope of the hill above the Gihon Spring. In the course of these excavations, a long segment of the city wall of the beginning of the second millennium B.C.E. was uncovered. This was part of a southern extension of fortifications first found by Kenyon in the 1960s. A succession of remains of Middle and Late Bronze Age settlements discovered in Kenyon's, and mainly in Shiloh's, excavations presents firm evidence for occupational continuity in the City of David in its early days.

THE FIRST TEMPLE PERIOD

So far no evidence has been encountered at the City of David for its conquest by members of the tribe of Judah or, at a later date, by King David, as described in the biblical narrative. These recorded events of the earliest history of Jerusalem still remain without satisfactory explanation from an archaeological point of view and perhaps manifest the need for re-evaluating the correlation of the historical and archaeological data.

Shiloh's work in Area G provided new evidence that the stepped stone structure at the top of the northeastern slope of the City of David, previously excavated by Macalister and Duncan, and later by Kenyon, dates to the tenth century B.C.E. Shiloh assigned these remains to King David's Fortress of Zion mentioned in the Bible. Recent analysis of finds from this area for final publication has led J. M. Cahill and D. Tarler, members of the Shiloh expedition, to propose the possibility that the stepped stone structure was constructed in the days of the Canaanites-Jebusites (thirteenth–eleventh centuries B.C.E.) before David's conquest of the city.

Warren's Shaft, the ancient water supply system of the City of David, was uncovered and cleared in the framework of Shiloh's excavations. However, there still is no conclusive dating for its construction.

In the eastern part of the Ophel, south of the Temple Mount, B. Mazar and E. Mazar uncovered a complex of monumental buildings attesting to royal construction activities during the ninth–eighth centuries B.C.E. This complex consists of several contiguous construction units which together formed a massive fortification system—the eastern defense wall of the city—during the First Temple period. Among these buildings are a tower and remains of an adjacent structure which the excavators identified as a four-chambered gatehouse—the biblical Water Gate.

Discoveries by N. Avigad in the Jewish Quarter have finally resolved the long-standing debate concerning the date of Jerusalem's westward expansion over the Western Hill of the ancient city. The many structures and artifacts he found on bedrock throughout the Western Hill, particularly the remains of the Broad Wall, indicate that settlement on the hill began as early as the eighth century B.C.E. At the end of that century, King Hezekiah fortified the Western Hill by encompassing it with a strong wall. Additional sections of fortifications excavated by Avigad north of the Broad Wall probably indicate a second phase of fortification-building activity toward the end of the First Temple period—to strengthen the northern side of the city, which lacks deep natural barriers. These remains of fortifications exposed on the Western Hill confirm Josephus's account that the First Wall of Jerusalem dates originally to the time of David and Solomon (the First Temple period). It is also clear now that portions of the early city wall of the end of the First Temple period were later incorporated into the reconstruction of the First Wall erected around the Western Hill by the Hasmoneans in the late second century B.C.E. As a a result of numerous excavations and studies conducted along the western sections of the First Wall above the Hinnom Valley, there is growing evidence pointing to the existence of fortified segments dating to the end of the First Temple period on this side of the city. To my mind, it conclusively confirms the view held by most scholars that the late First Temple period city wall encompassed the entire Western Hill up to the present Jaffa Gate, and continued southward above the Hinnom Valley around Mount Zion, and down toward the southern tip of the City of David. A minority opinion visualizes a smaller city on the Western Hill.

Shiloh's excavations brought up evidence for the existence of a sparse extramural residential neighborhood in the eighth century B.C.E., located outside the eastern wall of the City of David and contemporary with the early stage of the settlement of the Western Hill. An unfortified squatters' neighborhood north of the Western Hill (in the present-day Christian and Muslim Quarters) began to develop during this period. A

Corner of an Israelite tower (right) and a Hasmonean tower abbutting it (left) as uncovered in the Jewish Quarter (Ancient Jerusalem Revealed. Israel Exploration Society; *with permission)*

contemporary workshop building, discovered by M. Broshi outside the western wall of the city, should also be seen in the context of such extramural construction. It would seem that the impetus for construction of residential areas outside the walls of Jerusalem at the late First Temple period ceased with the Syrian siege by Sennacherib in 701 B.C.E. and the resulting deterioration of security. Unfortified quarters were probably abandoned at that time, their residents preferring to live within the walled city.

The First Temple period cemeteries around Jerusalem have also been thoroughly investigated in the past twenty-five years. Over a hundred First Temple period tombs are known to us from surveys and excavations around the city, although, regrettably, only a few were found with their contents intact.

In 1968–1970 D. Ussishkin surveyed and documented tens of burial caves in Silwan Village on the eastern slope of the Kidron Valley opposite the City of David. We now have a comprehensive picture of this sumptuous cemetery, which served Jerusalem's upper classes during the First Temple period (ninth–seventh centuries B.C.E.).

Several groups of burial caves dating to the end of the First Temple period (eighth–sixth centuries B.C.E.) were excavated on the slopes of the Hinnom Valley by M. Broshi, A. Kloner and D. Davis, by G. Barkay, and by R. Reich. Their location provides further evidence for the city's westward expansion at the end of the First Temple period. Among the many artifacts discovered by Barkay in the Ketef Hinnom cemetery are two small, rolled silver plaques bearing the biblical priestly benediction from Numbers 6:24–26.

A few rock-cut tombs of the end of the First Temple period were reinvestigated and published by G. Barkay, A. Kloner and A. Mazar. Two such tombs in the grounds of the Saint Etienne Monastery are the largest and most luxurious of that period known to date in Jerusalem—or elsewhere in the Land of Israel. Their unexpected location is indicitive of the northward expansion of Jerusalem's unfortified residential areas at the end of the First Temple period. Although it is difficult to establish whether they can be identified as the royal tombs mentioned by Josephus to have been situated in this vicinity, they probably give an idea of the monumental sepulchers in which the kings of Judah and high-ranking officials were buried.

Avigad's excavations on the Western Hill, B. Mazar and E. Mazar's excavations at the Ophel, and Shiloh's work in the City of David provide archaeological evidence that sheds light on the biblical account of the destruction and burning of the city by the Babylonians in 587/6 B.C.E. The most important testimony for this event comes from Area G in the City of David, where fragmentary remains of several burnt buildings containing assemblages of vessels characteristic of the period were discovered. In one of the rooms, which once contained an archive of documents, were more that fifty clay bullae that had been fired in the conflagration. This important epigraphic find provided a long list of Hebrew names, two of which have been identified with biblical personages active in Jerusalem on the eve of its destruction by the Babylonians: Gemariah son of Shaphan and Azariah son of Hilqiah.

Unique artifacts relating to the Temple and to the political administration in Jerusalem at the time of the First Temple have been published recently. The most important is a small ivory pomegranate bearing the Hebrew inscription: "sacred donation for the priests [in] the house of Yahweh." It apparently belonged to a group of objects utilized in the Jewish Temple in Jerusalem, of which no architectural remains are yet known. Also of great interest are two identical bullae depicting two figures, a king and a high personage facing each other. Beneath them is the Hebrew inscription: "governor of the city." These impressions were most probably made by the seal of an official under one of the last kings of the Judean monarchy.

THE SECOND TEMPLE PERIOD

Finds from recent excavations of the City of David have provided new information on the extent and urban features of Jerusalem during the Persian and early Hellenistic periods, before the renewed expansion of the city toward the Western Hill. For the first time, an occupational level of the Persian period was uncovered—by Shiloh at the City of David—in a clear stratigraphic context. Kenyon's and Shiloh's excavations also provide important evidence that the remains of fortifications on the crest of the eastern slope of the City of David were originally constructed during the Second Temple period, and possibly even as early as the time of Nehemiah (mid-fifth century B.C.E.)—but not in the Bronze Age (the Canaanite period) or the Iron Age as had been thought previously. This shows that at the beginning of the Second Temple period the earlier line of fortification of the City of David, at the lower part of the eastern slope above the Gihon Spring, was abandoned in favor of one better placed, along the crest of the hill.

In all, the information gleaned from the new excavations clearly indicates that settlement in Jerusalem after the destruction of the First Temple and until the Hasmonean period (sixth–second centuries B.C.E.) was once again confined only to the traditional boundaries of the City of David, the Ophel, and the Temple Mount.

Remains of Hasmonean construction uncovered in the Jewish Quarter (Ancient Jerusalem Revealed. *Israel Exploration Society; with permission)*

The exact location of the Seleucid Akra fortress, known from historical sources to have been erected in Jerusalem during the second century B.C.E., is still enigmatic after a hundred and fifty years of archaeological research in the city. The absence of any supportive finds on the Western Hill no longer justifies looking for it at the western side of the city, as had been suggested by some scholars. Several locations proposed more recently for the Akra focus upon controversial archaeological remains in the southeastern part of the Herodian Temple Mount precinct or on the Ophel. So far, such proposals remain inconclusive. The information we do have may lead us to reconsider one of the other hypotheses: that the Seleucid Akra was one in a series of citadels erected from the time of the Ptolemies (and perhaps even earlier, during the First Temple period or the return from Babylonian exile) until the construction of the Antonia fortress by Herod on the dominating hill next to the northwestern corner of the Temple Mount.

All the excavations on the Western Hill attest to a resumption of permanent settlement there during the second century B.C.E. This process apparently reflected a change in the status of Jerusalem during the middle of that century, when it became the capital of the merging Hasmonean kingdom. Toward the end of the Hasmonean period, in the mid-first century B.C.E. and particularly from the time of Herod, large, elaborate, lavish dwellings were built in the wealthy suburb on the Western Hill known as the Upper City. At the beginning of Hasmonean rule (the second half of the second century B.C.E.) the First Wall was rebuilt around the Western Hill along the line of the circumvallation at the end of the First Temple period. The excavations along the line of the First Wall in the north, west and south exposed long sections of the wall and several of its towers. Evidence was found for the incorporation into the Hasmonean First Wall of older sections of fortifications of the late First Temple period.

In the Tower of David Citadel, R. Sivan and G. Solar brought to light impressive testimony of the siege of Jerusalem by the Seleucid King Antiochus VII Sidetes in 134–132 B.C.E., which left hundreds of ballista stones and arrowheads at the foot of the wall.

Only traces of the foundations attributed to Herod the Great's palace that stood at the northwestern corner of the Upper City were uncovered in excavations by K.M. Kenyon and A.D. Tushingham, by R. Amiram and A. Eitan, and by M. Broshi and D. Bahat in the area of the present-day Tower of David Citadel and the Armenian Garden south of it. This extensive palace is believed to have occupied most of the area of the present Armenian Quarter up to the Old City wall in the south.

Avigad's excavations in the Jewish Quarter revealed remains of large, sumptuous private dwellings in Jerusalem's Upper City from the days of Herod the Great (the second half of the first century B.C.E.) until the destruction of the city in 70 C.E. Of these, the most impressive is a palatial Herodian mansion that included several dozen rooms arranged around a central courtyard. The dwellings built in the Upper City at that time had some particularly splendidly decorated rooms with colored mosaic pavements, and fine-quality plastered, frescoed and stuccoed walls. In the houses, Jewish ritual baths (*miqva'ot*) were found cut into the bedrock.

One of the most outstanding finds in the Jewish Quarter excavations is a graffito of the Menorah on two plaster fragments. This has come to be considered the most detailed, authentic early depiction of the Menorah that stood in the Temple in Jerusalem during the Second Temple period.

B. Mazar's excavations at the Ophel exposed the massive foundations of the southern wall and the southern corners of the Herodian Temple Mount platform. These discoveries followed up and complemented the thorough investigation along the outer walls of the Temple Mount started by Warren a century earlier. Abutting the walls of the Temple Mount, remains of impressive Herodian public works now uncovered to their full extent include wide, paved streets, flights of stairs, and plazas used by those who came to the Temple.

Robinson's Arch was found to be part of a series of vaults that supported a staircase giving access from the level of the main street in the Tyropoeon Valley to a gate once located high at the southwestern corner of the Temple Mount.

The Western Wall of the Temple Mount was exposed along its entire length, north of the present prayer plaza, by means of a tunnel excavated with considerable difficulty beneath the buildings of the Old City under the supervision of M. Ben-Dov and later by D. Bahat. The dating of Wilson's Arch remains uncertain. Some scholars consider it to be the original arch—part of the bridge built during the Second Temple period over the Tyropoeon Valley; others prefer an Early Arab period dating and consider that it was built over the remains of the original arch. In the Wall north of Wilson's Arch, a gigantic stone weighing over 300 tons (!) was discovered. Further north, the façade of Warren's Gate, as it was rebuilt in the Early Arab period, was entirely exposed. At the northern end of the Western Wall, the builders of the Herodian Temple Mount had to cut into the living rock of the hill in order to continue building the Wall in a straight line. The pavement of the street hugging the Wall here remained unfinished for some reason. Still further north, a rock-cut aqueduct, apparently of the Hasmonean period, that had been reported by Warren, was rediscovered and investigated anew. It seems to support the increasingly prevalent view that Herod's Antonia fortress was confined only to the rock outcrop between the Temple Mount and the Convent of the Sisters of Zion to the north.

The location and date of the Second Wall still remain unresolved problems in the topography of Second Temple period Jerusalem. Avigad's discovery at the northwestern side of the present Jewish Quarter of the remains of a fortification system in the line of the First Wall, which he identified as the Ginat Gate complex, is perhaps indirect evidence that the Second Wall indeed passed north of there, along a course largely corresponding to that proposed by Kenyon.

The long-standing controversy among scholars concerning the precise line of the Third Wall of Jerusalem, constructed at the northern side of the city during the reign of Agrippa I in the first century C.E., now seems to be near resolution. The accumulating evidence conclusively confirms Sukenik and Meyer's identification of the fortifications remains north of the Damascus Gate as the Third Wall, and clearly shows that the Third Wall did not follow the course of the present north wall of the Old City.

Surprisingly, a number of excavations along the conjectured eastern and western line of the Third Wall have not yielded any results. A possible explanation of this may be inferred from the excavations along the northern line of the Third Wall, which seems to have been extensively robbed of its stones, mainly for the building of Aelia Capitolina, leaving only fragments of its foundations. It may be, therefore, that those eastern and western sections of the Third Wall that were closest to Aelia Capitolina were dismantled to the last stone without leaving a trace. A hypothetical reconstruction of the line of the eastern and western portions of the Third Wall would perhaps have it running slightly inside the present wall of the Old City.

A. Mazar's new archaeological survey and study, in the late 1960s, of the remains of ancient aqueducts that supplied water to Jerusalem brought to light new information on their exact course and the engineering details of their construction. Segments of the Lower Aqueduct were recently uncovered south and west of the city limits. Particularly impressive is the long tunnel piercing the Armon Hanaziv ridge (the Hill of Evil Counsel).

The extensive cemeteries which surrounded Jerusalem during the Second Temple period have been the subject of intensive excavations and research in the years after 1967. Tens of new tombs excavated primarily north of the city, in the area of Mount Scopus and the new Giv'at Hamivtar and French Hill neighborhoods, have raised the known number of Second Temple period burial caves in Jerusalem cemeteries to over 830. Notable among recently discovered tombs is the burial cave of the Nazirite family excavated by N. Avigad, and a burial cave uncovered by V. Tzaferis in which an inscription was found mentioning one "Mattathiah son of Juda[h]," identified by some scholars with Mattathias Antigonus, the last king of the Hasmonean dynasty. Another tomb, excavated by Tzaferis, contained an ossuary bearing the inscription: "Simon the Temple builder" and the bones of a man executed by crucifixion. South of the city, Z. Greenhut recently excavated a tomb containing an ossuary inscribed "Joseph son of Caiapha"—perhaps related to the family of the Jerusalem high priest Caiaphas mentioned in the New Testament in connection with the crucifixion of Jesus.

For the first time we have vivid, concrete evidence for the violent conquest of Jerusalem by Roman Legions in 70 C.E. and the intensive destruction of its buildings. Deep accumulations of stones from walls and buildings of the Temple Mount were encountered in B. Mazar's excavations next to the southern and western walls. These substantial remains, which included ornamented architectural fragments, covered destroyed buildings and streets alongside the Temple Mount. Next to the southwestern corner of the Temple Mount, a fragmentary Hebrew inscription incised in stone was found, reading: "to the house of the trumpeting to pr(oclaim)." This stone was originally embedded in the masonry high at the top of the corner here. Avigad's excavations in the Jewish Quarter uncovered evidence of the total destruction of the luxurious structures of the Upper City. The destruction wrought by the Roman conquest is particularly evident in the Burnt House found buried under a thin layer of charred remains and collapse. A stone weight inscribed "[belonging] to bar [son of] Kathros"—the name of a well-known priestly family of Jerusalem during the Second Temple period—was found in this building.

THE ROMAN PERIOD

(SECOND–THIRD CENTURIES C.E.)

Recent excavations have shed new light on the construction activities of the Roman Tenth Legion, which, after 70 C.E., built its camp on the Western Hill of Jerusalem over the ruins of the Upper City of the Second Temple period. A small unit of the Tenth Legion occupied several scattered buildings on the Western Hill, of which many fragmentary remains came to light mainly in the vicinity of the Tower of David Citadel.

The northern gate of Aelia Capitolina with its tripartite arched entrance flanked by two towers, located under the present Damascus Gate, was entirely exposed by M. Magen. The gateway is built mainly of large ashlars taken from destroyed Second Temple period buildings. Magen's work confirmed that this monumental gateway, modelled on Roman triumphal arches and preserved to an impressive height, was originally constructed at the time of the foundation of the Roman colony Aelia Capitolina by Hadrian at the beginning of the second century C.E. The excavation results seem to indicate that Aelia Capitolina was an unfortified city, with the possible exception of the three massive Herodian towers and the western section of the First Wall, which, as Josephus tells us, were left in place to protect the camp of the Tenth Legion stationed in the city after 70 C.E.

Information concerning various public and religious buildings in the northern, civilian, portion of Roman Aelia Capitolina is still very fragmentary. We are mainly familiar with Roman street pavements and plazas. Inside the Damascus Gate, M. Magen uncovered part of a massive Roman pavement which is firmly identified with the open plaza depicted on the Madaba mosaic map. The pavement in the basement of the Convent of the Sisters of Zion, northwest of the Temple Mount, venerated as the Lithostrotos in Christian tradition (the courtyard of the Antonia fortress) can now be dated more confidently to the Roman period. Apparently, it was part of the eastern forum of Roman Aelia Capitolina, where a tripartite triumphal arch stood—of which the central, highest archway is the Ecce Homo arch in the Via Dolorosa.

Structural remains attributed to the Roman period were discovered from the 1960s on in a survey and in excavations of limited extent conducted by V. Corbo and others during the restoration of the Church of the Holy Sepulcher. The most impressive of these Roman remains are the walls attributed to the raised platform (*temenos*) constructed here by Hadrian in the second century C.E. next to the forum. Other walls may have been part of the foundation of the Roman temple, and possibly also of a basilica that stood here.

The remains of several buildings of the Roman period uncovered by B. Mazar's excavations south of the Temple Mount and next to its southwestern corner are of great interest because of their locations and functions in connection with the activities of the Roman Tenth Legion.

THE BYZANTINE PERIOD

Several architecturally uniform sections of the Byzantine city wall and its towers are known today from both past and recent excavations. These seem to indicate that the Byzantine city wall stretched along the line of the Damascus Gate in the north, the Jaffa Gate in the west, around Mount Zion in the south, and along the eastern side of the City of David and the Ophel in the east. It was probably erected originally as one concentrated construction project at the beginning of the fourth century C.E., and several of its sections were reconstructed during the late Byzantine and the Early Arab periods.

Important, unique discoveries by Avigad in the Jewish Quarter gave a new perspective on the development and urban character of the Byzantine Zion Quarter. Remains of the southern portion of the main north–south street of Jerusalem—the Cardo with its two colonnades as depicted in the Madaba mosaic map—were discovered, thus extending the northern part of the Cardo, which dates to the period of the foundation of Roman Aelia Capitolina in the second century C.E. The archaeological evidence shows this southern portion of the Cardo to have been constructed in the mid-sixth century C.E., during the reign of Justinian, to connect in a straight line the Church of the Holy Sepulchre with the new Nea Church.

At the southern end of the Cardo, in the southern part of today's Jewish Quarter, several sections of foundation walls of the Nea Church complex, also built by Justinian in the mid-sixth century C.E., were uncovered and identified by Avigad, thus enabling us to appreciate its huge dimensions and massive construction. The estimated length of the church proper is 115 meters (!) The southern part of the church complex was supported by the vaults of an immense underground cistern. An inscription in plaster on one of its walls commemorates the emperor Justinian and this monumental project.

The Kenyon-Tushingham excavations in the Armenian Garden, Broshi's excavations on Mount Zion, and Y. Margovsky and Ben-Dov's excavations on the eastern slope of Mount Zion all revealed many additional remains of streets and private, public and religious buildings that densely covered the Zion Quarter during the Byzantine period.

B. Mazar's excavations at the Ophel uncovered remains of a residential quarter established there already at the beginning of the Byzantine period. The structures are more-or-less uniform in plan. They include many rooms arranged around central courtyards, many of them paved with mosaics. Their well-preserved remains give us a clear picture of the domestic architecture in Jerusalem at that time. Later in the Byzantine period, this neighborhood became more crowded with additional construction. In one of the structures near the southwest corner of the Temple Mount unexpected evidence

attests a brief period of Jewish settlement there at the end of the Byzantine period, perhaps following the Persian conquest of the city in 614 C.E. The finds demonstrate that
some of the Byzantine buildings continued to be used alongside the palaces constructed
south and west of the Temple Mount at the beginning of the Early Arab period.

The picture which has emerged from excavations north and west of the Old City,
regarding the extensive Byzantine construction beyond the city walls, is both important
and innovative. North of the Old City several Byzantine-period structures serving religious functions were previously known. The most famous of these are the Armenian
and the Orpheus floor mosaics. Near these Ben-Arieh and Nezer uncovered the remains
of a large building which they identified as a Byzantine monastery. Additional monastic buildings were discovered nearby by Tzaferis and others. These include a large number of rooms, burial chapels with a mosaic pavement, and many tombs. Remains of another monastery which belonged to the Armenian community in Byzantine Jerusalem
were uncovered by D. Amit and S. Wolff. The excavated finds illustrate the development, during the latter part of the Byzantine period (fifth, and mainly sixth, centuries
C.E.), of an unwalled urban quarter of Christian religious character, north of the city
wall. At the same time, remains of commercial complexes with workshops were excavated by A. M. Maeir and R. Reich just beyond the present-day Jaffa Gate—outside the
western Byzantine city gate.

THE EARLY ARAB PERIOD

Finds of the period following the Muslim conquest attest to the efforts of the new
rulers in changing the city's Byzantine-Christian character. The most important discoveries dating to the Early Arab period are the remains of two large palaces and several other royal buildings uncovered in the course of B. Mazar's excavations at the Ophel
and near the southwestern corner of the Temple Mount. These impressive palaces—
part of a royal administrative center—were constructed next to the walls of the Temple
Mount during the rule of the Umayyad caliphs toward the end of the seventh and beginning of the eighth century C.E. They are contemporaneous with the foundations of
the earliest mosques on the Temple Mount and incorporate also restorations of parts of
the destroyed walls and gates of the Temple Mount. The palaces follow a nearly identical plan with a central courtyard surrounded by porticos and rooms. Building materials taken from collapsed and destroyed walls of the Second Temple period Temple
Mount, as well as columns and various architectural components from destroyed
Byzantine churches, were utilized in their construction. The palaces were in use for only
a short time. They were severely damaged by the earthquake that shook Jerusalem in
747 (or 749) C.E. and were subsequently abandoned. Various structures were erected
upon their ruins during the Fatimid period.

In the context of royal building activity in Jerusalem at the beginning of the Early
Arab period, a new fortress was erected in the area of the present Tower of David Citadel
south of the Jaffa Gate. Apparently at the same time, several sections along the line of

the Byzantine city wall, which continued to protect the city during the Early Arab period, were restored.

The decline of Jerusalem as a Christian city began with the inception of Abbasid rule in the mid-eighth century C.E. and continued through the ninth century. During this period the city gradually became Muslim, both architecturally and demographically.

Avigad's excavations along the southern wall of the Old City uncovered a section of fortifications—the earliest city wall found along this line—with a gateway protected by a pair of inner towers dated to the end of the Early Arab period (tenth–eleventh century C.E.). This indicates that the southern city wall was not shortened before this period to the line of the present-day southern wall of the Old City, leaving Mount Zion, the City of David and the southern issue of the Tyropoen Valley outside of the walled area of the city.

THE MEDIEVAL PERIOD

New information is now available about the fortifications of Jerusalem in the Medieval period. Digs conducted by Ben-Dov, Avigad and Broshi along the southern and western lines of the present Old City wall and at its foundations, from the Tower of David Citadel in the west and as far as the Dung Gate in the south, uncovered long sections of an earlier city wall with towers and gates. The foundations of the new wall were laid during the Ayyubid period (or perhaps previously, under the Crusaders) over the line of the even earlier wall of the tenth–eleventh centuries C.E. Inscriptions uncovered on Mount Zion by Broshi also clearly indicate fortification-building activity there at the beginning of the thirteenth century C.E. But as we know from literary sources, this construction was purposely dismantled shortly afterwards by the Muslim rulers. At the northwestern corner of the Old City wall, D. Bahat and M. Ben-Ari uncovered remains of the façade of the Medieval Qal'at Julad (Goliath's Tower) and the moat which protected it from the outside. During the Crusader period the Damascus Gate was refurbished by the addition of an outer fortified gateway, the remains of which were excavated by Kenyon and Hennessy.

The digs conducted in the Tower of David Citadel have exposed only fragmentary remains of the foundations of the Medieval fortress. It seems that the present Ottoman Citadel, which dates originally to the Mamluk period, had the same proportions and plan as the one constructed there by the Crusaders.

Within the Old City, several underground Mamluk building complexes, west of Wilson's Arch were cleared and re-examined. These consist of a series of vaulted subterranean rooms along a central vaulted passageway which served also as substructures of the houses above. In the Jewish Quarter, A. Ovadiah cleared the ruins of a Crusader monastery comprising a church and other buildings on two levels. Along the course of the Byzantine Cardo Avigad uncovered a two-stories vaulted Crusader bazaar with buildings added at some indeterminate time. A public building, probably of monastic character, its central room having a roof supported by four heavy, round stone pillars was

Remains of a columned room of the Crusader period uncovered in the southern part of the Jewish Quarter (Ancient Jerusalem Revealed. Israel Exploration Society; with permission)

also found by Avigad in the southern part of the Jewish Quarter. In the Armenian Garden, Bahat and Broshi uncovered a few remains of the royal Crusader palace.

For the first time, the archaeological investigation of Jerusalem is accompanied by wide-ranging restoration and preservation projects comprising excavated remains of all periods. It is now possible to visit many sites that illustrate and bring to life much of ancient Jerusalem, and to follow and understand the urban and architectural history of the city—from its beginnings, thousands of years ago, through the Ottoman period.

THE TWELFTH GATE

Jerusalem in Children's Literature

Yemin Moshe in 1910 as seen from the Sultan's Pool (Central Zionist Archives; with permission)

THE TWO BROTHERS

A LEGEND

Chaya M. Burstein

Many years ago, on a beautiful hill in the land of Canaan, there lived two brothers. Both were farmers; both tilled the soil. One lived with his wife and children on one side of the hill; the other lived alone in a little hut on the other side of the hill.

One summer God showered His goodness upon the land and upon that hill. When the brothers had sown their seeds, God sent down rain to make the seeds sprout. The warm sun looked down and made them grow. When the time for gathering of the harvest came, the reapers found a bountiful crop. The sheaves were piled high in the fields on both sides of the hill.

Both brothers came to the fields in the evening to thank God for his mercy.

On the east side of the hill stood the married brother, looking at his sheaves. "How good is God," thought he. "Why does He bless me with as much as my brother has? I have a wife already and children, but my brother has neither wife nor children. How many years will he have to toil before he can live as I do, with a loving family? I do not need all these crops. He needs all he can get. When my brother is asleep tonight, I shall carry some of my sheaves to his fields. He will never notice what I have done."

While the married brother thought thus to himself on the east side of the hill, the unmarried brother stood musing in his fields on the west side of the hill.

He said to himself, "God be praised for His kindness! But I wish He had done less for me and more for my brother. I have need of little, but my brother has a wife and many children to share his goods with him. At midnight, when all are asleep, I shall place some of my sheaves on my brother's field. He will never know that he has more or that I have less."

Thus both brothers waited, each happy in the thoughts that had come to him. Toward midnight each loaded his shoulders high with sheaves and turned toward the top of the hill. The married brother went west, the other one east. And it was midnight when on the summit the brothers met and embraced.

When God saw the meeting of the brothers and the love each had for the other, He chose that place to be the site of the Holy Temple.

TWO DOVES

Levin Kipnis

Two doves

Flew to Jerusalem.

—What did they eat?

Flakes of light.

—What did they drink?

Water of might.

—Where did they dwell?

On the heights of the Wall.

—What did they dream?

Israel lives all!

Two doves

Return from Jerusalem.

—What do they tell?

Gru gru gru!

There is a Wall

Where the folk of Israel throng

To praise with joyous song

And come next year

The city will be strong!

(*Translated by Reuven Hammer*)

A Private War Diary

Galila Ron-Feder-Amit

Sunday, June 1, 1948

I am writing these words in the Anglican Hospital in Jerusalem. I am lying on an iron bed with my head slightly raised. A curly headed nurse brought me a piece of wood and fixed me up so that I could write, half-sitting and half-lying down.

Mother brought me this notebook. After many hesitations I decided to tell her where she could find it. Until I explained it to her she had no idea that I was keeping a diary.

I have been here two weeks already. My room is more like a hall than a room. It is a long hall, very large, filled with iron beds like mine. An injured person lies in each bed; bed after bed, each with its own injured person.

Once this hospital was filled with English doctors and English nurses. Now, they are all Jews. The only thing that remains the way it was is the name of the place—the Anglican Hospital.

How did I get here?

I got here in terrible condition, and even now my condition is not so great. None of the doctors can tell me with any certainly exactly when I will leave here—and in what condition.

The difference between when I arrived and now is that then I thought I was dying and now I know that I am not. I am alive.

But I have terrible pains. My entire left leg is in a cast and I cannot get up or sit up or walk.

This is how it happened: One day after the proclamation of the State of Israel, shells started to explode in all kinds of places in Jerusalem. We would hear their whistling sounds from far away—and when we heard that we knew we had to find shelter quickly.

I was in a very bad mood after the State was declared and I seldom left my house. I walked around the room, going from wall to wall, like a man in prison, until even mother told me that it was about time I went outside and got a little fresh air.

I went outside just to get some air. I hoped that I would meet Ilana, but I didn't. Suddenly I saw two men running toward the grocery store which belonged to Haim, the father of Yigal who belonged to the Etzel underground. I stopped them near the entrance to our house and asked them where they were going.

One of them said that there was a rumor going around that you could now get chocolate bars in the groceries in Jerusalem.

The very thought that there was chocolate in Haim's store was exciting. It had been months since I had eaten any chocolate. I quickly ran out of our yard and followed them.

I did not have my family's ration book with me, but Haim knew me well. If he really had any chocolate, he would mark down that he had given it to Oded Levin, and later, when mother would bring him the booklet, he would take the coupon for chocolate.

Because of the siege and the severe shortage of food, the Jerusalem command had allocated specific amounts of food to each family. Anyone who received the amount coming to him had to give the appropriate coupon from the family ration book.

I started to run, thinking about the chocolate. I thought of nothing but the chocolate. I thought how happy my brothers and sisters would be if I brought them a real

An armored car in beseiged Jerusalem, 1948 (Central Zionist Archives; with permission)

chocolate bar. I was so worked up about it that I felt like someone who has drunk too much. I could taste chocolate on my tongue and its sweetness warmed my insides. It warmed me so much that when I heard the shriek of the shell, I just kept on running as if its approach had nothing at all to do with me.

And then I heard this enormous explosion.

At first I was certain that I was lying on the ground because I had thrown myself down to hide from the shell. I was so convinced of this that—in the most natural way— when I thought the danger had passed and the shell had exploded somewhere else I wanted to get up.

But when I tried to get up, I suddenly felt a strange warmth spreading over me. It was a feeling I had never experienced before. It was as if I was wrapped in a warm blanket from within.

I am wrapped up and warm. I am so warm . . . so warm that I am wet from all the warmth. The wetness starts at my legs, the left leg—the bottom part of the leg. Then I lifted my head and saw that my leg was in a pool of blood.

Immediately I lay down again. At first I couldn't believe what I had seen. I thought: this can't be, its my imagination. Why should my leg be in a pool of blood? I just fell down to hide from the shell which exploded. Where would the blood have come from?

I sat up again. I tried to move my leg out of the pool, but it didn't move. O God! My leg isn't moving! It stayed there in the pool of blood and didn't move even though I tried to move it! I'm moving my leg and my leg isn't moving! It's shattered!

I sat up a third time. I looked around to the right and the left, but there was no one in sight. Everybody had hurried to find shelter from the exploding shell, and I was alone, lying on the ground.

Very cautiously I turned to lie on my right side. I put my hand on my wounded leg as if it weren't my leg at all, as if it were a board or some piece of stone. I lifted it up and put it on my good leg.

My clothes were soaked with blood, my trousers were torn. I was so busy putting my left leg on my right that I didn't even stop to think if I was in pain or not. The street was still empty.

I lay on my side and started to crawl slowly toward Haim's store. I remembered the training exercises in crawling we had taken with Joel. We had crawled on our bellies. Joel knew two kinds of crawling: one he called "sixty-sixty crawling," that was done on the knees, the other was "Indian crawling," which was done with the aid of hands and heels.

The kind of crawling I was doing now I had never learned. It was my own invention. It was the only kind of crawling I could manage with one leg shattered so that I was worried that parts of it—God forbid—

That thought—that I was liable to reach Haim's store without the leg—gave me extra strength. I crawled a little further. One more meter—two—

I was wet and weak. I was so weak, weaker than I had ever been. Nevertheless I continued crawling.

Now I could see the path leading to the store opposite where I was. I began to hear people's voices. I pulled myself onto the path and then stopped.

I took a deep breath. I wanted to scream. Oh did I want to scream! I opened my mouth and tried to cry "Help!" but my voice couldn't be heard. I called "help" in my mind but I was the only one who heard the sound which did not emerge. In total despair, I broke out in tears. I lay there on the path leading to Haim's store and did not have the strength to raise my head and drag myself to the entrance to the store. I didn't even have the strength to cry anymore. Tears came out, but the crying stopped and I knew that here, on this path, my brief life was coming to an end. . . .

I heard a woman scream, "Haim! There's a boy here who's been hurt!"

"Somebody call an ambulance!" I heard a man's voice say.

"Boy!" someone said to me, "What's your name?"

"Raise his leg a little. . . ." I think that someone touched me. "Let's wrap him in a sheet. . . ."

"Boy," that person said again, "What's your name?"

"Oh . . ." I tried to speak.

"We'll take you to the hospital, don't worry," the woman said to calm me down.

"Let him alone!" I think it was Haim speaking. "I know him. It's Levin's boy."

The voices surrounded me, touched me. They came from above and from all sides. They covered me, they stroked my hair. The voices also lifted me up. They put me on something. The put me into something. The voices were mixed with the smell of medicine.

The voices were like angels in a story. The hovered above me. They were like wings. They became a song. They were like the song which Ilana wrote for me after I gave her the boat I carved out of wood.

Later a nurse dressed in white spoke to me.

"Don't be frightened," she said, wiping my sweating brow. "We're only cutting off your trousers." Then she immediately added, "and taking you to the operating room." She disappeared.

I remember that they gave me a shot. I remember that I saw nothing but the ceiling. I remember that I woke up in a cast which covered my entire leg and I asked the nurse where I was.

She answered, "In the Anglican hospital," and added no further details.

❧

Friday June 6, 1948

Today is a special day for me. Actually it's special not only for me but for all of us. It is special for all of us because the road to Jerusalem has really been opened at last. It is special for me because at last I have been taken outside and was able to sit in the sun for an hour and to breath pure air—with no smell of medicine in it!

Let me begin with the opening of the road to Jerusalem. In the afternoon one of the doctors came into our room, got up on a chair, and with great pomp informed us that a convoy had arrived in Jerusalem via the "Burma Road."

You should have seen all the patients. Suddenly they stopped groaning and clapped their hands with great enthusiasm, after which they began to sing.

It was a very strange song session. No one said "One-two-three," or "Come—let's sing!" The song just broke out all at once, a hoarse song of the wounded, a song of people with amputated legs, a song of fighters encased in casts.

And I could not be different. I joined them, even though I didn't know some of the songs. I pretended to be singing.

They sang for a good half-hour until their voices faded away. I turned to the fellow lying next to me—I know now that his name is Dubik—he had been seriously wounded in Operation Kilshon. Operation Kilshon took place on May 14, just a few hours before the British evacuated the Land of Israel. The purpose was to seize several strategic areas of Jerusalem such as the German Colony and the Allenby Barracks and the Arab neighborhood of Sheich Jerach. He had been brought to the hospital several days before me.

"What did he mean when he said that the convey came via the 'Burma Road?' " I asked him.

"That's a new road which our soldiers carved out of the hills of Jerusalem," he explained. "There used to be a very narrow path there. After the Arabs began attacking the convoys coming up on the road, they started to prepare that road. You didn't think they would leave us to the mercy of the Arabs, did you?"

I shrugged my shoulders.

"No," I said.

"Well—the guys decided to widen that narrow path, and now the work is finished. From now on it will be possible to reach Jerusalem on the 'Burma Road' without worrying about being attacked. The next stage, as far as I know, will be to lay a water pipe along the road and then we'll have a secure supply of water for the city as well and not die of thirst through the summer."

"The 'Burma Road,' " I muttered. "Isn't that a strange name?"

"Strange maybe, but there's a reason," Dubik replied. "During the Second World War Burma was besieged and cut off. A special road was paved in order to break through the siege. The siege of Jerusalem has also been broken. You can bet that this time it has been broken for good!" He put his head back on the pillow and closed his eyes.

I also lay back and closed my eyes like him. I thought about Haim's grocery store and how next week all kinds of supplies would arrive there from the coast to fill the empty shelves. I thought about my brother and about Rinaleh who would finally get a little chocolate. I thought about the water pipe.

Those last weeks before I was hurt Mother would use the same water for cooking, washing dishes and doing the wash. Every drop was precious. The summer had come,

Workers creating the "Burma Road" passage to Jerusalem to break the seige in 1948 (photograph by A. Hirshbein. Central Zionist Archives with permission)

the rains had stopped, the cisterns were almost completely empty, the water pipe to Jerusalem had been blown up and now water was given out from containers. Instead of washing as we usually had done, Mother would wet a washcloth and clean us up in some symbolic way.

ᔕ

Tuesday July 22, 1948

I've come home!

I still can't walk without crutches, but the doctors said my bones are mostly mended and soon they'll be able to take off the cast and give me a smaller one that will come only below the knee. With that kind of a cast I'll be able to walk. If everything is alright, they'll take that off too in a few months.

The battles, which started up again after a lull, went on for ten days, and then there was another lull.

When he came to take me home from the hospital, Father told me that there will probably be a cease fire soon and that the war is really over.

Yigal, who came with me to the entrance to the hospital in his wheelchair, disagrees with Father. He says that as long as the Old City of Jerusalem is not liberated, there will be no agreements. It's not possible that Jerusalem will be divided, with one part belonging to Jordan and one part to Israel. Who can live like that—with a border going right through the city.

Father explained that there were some people in the United Nations who think that Jerusalem has to be an international city because it is holy to all faiths.

I asked, "How will an international city be run?" Father had no answer. I think that deep in his heart he believes what Yigal said, but for some reason won't say it.

Father ordered a taxi since I couldn't possible walk home. That was the first time in my life I was ever in a taxi. I had often seen people riding in taxis, and for some reason I had thought that only rich people rode in them.

I spread out on the back seat and felt not only rich but heroic as well. I leaned against the window and looked out, but hardly recognized my city.

I don't know exactly what had changed. Maybe nothing had changed. Maybe I had changed, and therefore it seemed to me that everything had changed. Maybe it had really changed, that city I knew so well when the British ruled it, and I was not used to driving through the streets after the British left and the State of Israel had been created.

At home, everyone waited to greet me.

K'TONTON GOES UP TO JERUSALEM

Sadie Rose Weilerstein

K'tonton was in Israel. He had just arrived and was standing outside the airport. "Abraham may have once stood on this very spot," K'tonton thought. "Or King David, or Rabbi Akiba."

K'tonton wanted to see the whole country. He looked for a car to take him around. Then he saw the perfect one. It was a very old car. The fender, bent and battered, almost reached the ground, so that K'tonton could reach it and hoist himself up. The dents in the metal gave him a foothold. The upholstery inside had torn places for his fingers to dig into. Up the back of the red seat, K'tonton climbed. At the top, quite close to the window, was a perfect hole.

"I can hide in here and get a good view at the same time," K'tonton thought, as he fitted himself inside.

Mind you, K'tonton didn't need to hide. Every Jew is welcome in the State of Israel. But it seemed easier to K'tonton to hide than to explain how he had come to Israel.

The driver came up, threw a number of packages into the trunk of the car, then got in. The engine coughed and chugged. The car was on its way. Only K'tonton and the driver were inside. The rest of the tourists had chosen the shiny cars ahead.

Zoom, rattle, bang! The car sped down the road, then lurched around a corner. They were climbing into the hills, in and out along a corkscrew road. A signpost caught K'tonton's eye.

K'tonton's heart leaped.

Illustration by Marilyn Hirsh from The Best of K'tonton *(Jewish Publication Society; with permission)*

"We're going to Jerusalem," it sang, "to Jerusalem, where the Holy Temple stood. It's like it says in the Psalms:

I rejoiced when they said to me,

'Let us go up to the House of the Lord.'

Only I'm not *saying* it, I'm *doing* it!"

The song in K'tonton's heart rose up and up. He couldn't hold it back. It burst from his lips, thin, and sweet, and clear.

The driver heard it and turned. There on top of the rear seat, his feet fitted snugly in a hole in the upholstery, stood a tiny, thumb-sized boy.

"Shalom!" said the driver, looking interested but not surprised. He was used to seeing all kinds of Jews in Israel—blond Jews, black Jews, giant Jews from the Caucasus, brown lean Yemenite Jews with side curls, cave-dwelling Jews. This was a thumb-sized Jew.

"Shalom!" he said again. "Why do you sit there by yourself?" He grinned down at K'tonton. "The front seat upholstery also has good holes."

Without slowing down, he stretched out an arm to make a bridge for K'tonton to cross over.

From the top of the front seat, K'tonton looked up into the man's face. It was a pleasant face, browned by the sun and weather, with a nice big nose and blue eyes with wrinkles under them. "For the smiles to run down," K'tonton thought. The man's shirt was open at the neck. A beret was tipped back from his forehead.

"And where do you come from?" he asked, one eye on K'tonton, the other on the road, which at that moment was making a hairpin turn.

"I'm going up to Jerusalem," K'tonton said. He knew that this wasn't an answer to the question, but at the moment where he was going seemed more important than where he had come from.

The hills grew steeper and more barren. Stones and boulders covered them. Suddenly K'tonton pointed excitedly. Men with pickaxes were splitting huge rocks.

"The stones! Are they iron?" K'tonton asked.

"Iron?"

K'tonton answered with a Bible verse:

"A land whose stones are iron and out of whose hills you may dig brass."

"I see you know your Bible," said the driver. "That makes you half an Israeli already. The stones you are talking about are down in the Negev near King Solomon's mines."

"Do you mean King Solomon who built the Holy Temple?" K'tonton's voice was filled with awe.

"The very one! They're digging copper out of those old mines right now."

He was going to tell about the discovery of the ancient mines, but K'tonton's eyes were again on the hills. The dead, gray stones were gone. Grapevines rose in terraces. Pine trees covered the hill tops. Barns and neat red-roofed houses hid among green orchards.

"Trees!" K'tonton said in wonder. "Hills covered with trees! Maybe those are the ones the coins from my blue-and-white box paid for. Maybe my tree that was planted when I was born is up there?"

He climbed out of the hole and leaned out of the window to get a better view.

A pull at his shirt brought him back.

"Easy there!" said the driver. "You're not trying to leave me, are you?" I thought you wanted to go up to Jerusalem."

His blue eyes looked into K'tonton's dark eyes that were shining like stars.

"What did you say your name was?" he asked.

"I didn't say," K'tonton answered. "It's Isaac Samuel ben Baruch Reuben, for short K'tonton." Then in the same breath, "Are those Jewish National Fund trees? Are there any almond trees up there? Do you think there might be one my age, because. . . ."

The man's eyes were laughing. "So your name is K'tonton. You ask so many questions. I thought your name was Question Mark."

He pointed to a grove of olive trees ahead. Through the silvery tops rose the towers of Jerusalem. The car turned a corner.

"We're here, K'tonton," the driver said. "Where do you want to get off?"

They were on a noisy crowded street. People hurried in and out of stores, stood in long lines on the corners. Buses and taxis honked.

Suddenly Jerusalem seemed to K'tonton very big and strange, very far from home.

"I'll get off at . . . at . . ." he hesitated.

"Because," the driver went on, "if you haven't any special place to go to, you could come home with me." He brought the car to a stop. "My wife would enjoy a guest for Passover. You are so good at asking questions, you could ask the *Mah nishtanah*." He meant the Four Questions the youngest child of the family asks on Passover Eve.

"Don't you have a son to ask?" K'tonton's eyes were filled with sympathy.

"Oh, I have a son all right, a fine, smart child," the driver assured him. "But he can't manage the *Mah nishtanah* by himself. He's only a year and a half old."

"My father has one son, too." K'tonton said gravely. "Me. I don't know who will ask *him* the *Mah nishtanah* this year."

Suddenly a tear slid down K'tonton's cheek and caught in a corner of his mouth. He sucked it in quickly.

That night K'tonton wrote to his parents. He wrote about his flight and everything that had happened to him since he arrived in the Holy Land. Their answer came before Passover. "We are glad you have found friends in Israel," the letter said. "You may stay until we save enough money for tickets. Then we will come and join you."

THE THIRTEENTH GATE

Jerusalem Day Services

Jerusalem from the north, from Palestine in 1860 *(Glasgow: 1860).
(Photograph by John Cramb. Collection of Mr. William P. Wolfe, Montreal;
with permission)*

The Hebrew date of the liberation of Jerusalem, 28 Iyyar, has been declared a holiday by various rabbinic bodies and is celebrated in synagogues throughout the world. Jewish communities often have Jerusalem Day celebrations at a suitable occasion on or near that date.

The Order of Service for Jerusalem Day

Israeli Chief Rabbinate

Evening Service (*Ma'ariv*): after the Amida recite:

> May He who wrought miracles for our ancestors and for us and redeemed us from slavery to freedom, speedily redeem us completely and gather our exiles from the four corners of the earth. All Israel is one fellowship, and let us say, Amen.

This is followed by the recitation of the complete Hallel without a blessing.

✲

Morning Service (*Shaharit*): After the Amida recite the complete Hallel without a blessing; recite Psalm 107.

A Suggested Order of Readings for a Celebration of Jerusalem Day

Reuven Hammer

1. O sanctuary of the King, royal city—
   Arise and depart from your overthrow,
   Long enough have you dwelt in the valley of tears—
   He will have compassion upon you!

   Arouse yourself! Rise from the dust!
   Don the glorious garments of My people!
   Through the son of Jesse, the Bethlehemite,
   My soul's redemption is near.

   Arouse yourself! Arouse yourself!
   Your light has come! Arise and shine forth!
   Arise, arise and proclaim the song—
   The glory of God is revealed to you.

   You shall no more be ashamed or reviled,
   Why are you downcast, why are you disquieted?
   In you shall the needy of My people find shelter
   The city shall be rebuilt on its mound.

Those who despoiled you shall be despoiled,

Your destroyers shall stay far from you,

Your God will rejoice over you

As a bridegroom rejoices over his bride.

You shall spread out right and left

And sing the praises of the Lord—

Through the man—the son of Peretz—

And we shall be happy and rejoice.

(FROM LECHA DODI)

2. Psalm 122

3. Reading from Biblical texts:

Comfort, oh comfort My people,

Says your God.

Speak tenderly to Jerusalem,

And declare to her

That her term of service is over.

Ascend a lofty mountain,

O herald of joy to Zion;

Raise your voice with power,

O herald of joy to Jerusalem—

Raise it, have no fear;

Announce to the cities of Judah:

Behold your God!

For the sake of Zion I will not be silent,

For the sake of Jerusalem I will not be still,

Till her victory emerge respendent

And her triumph like a flaming torch.

Truly the Lord has comforted Zion,

Comforted all her ruins;

He has made her wilderness like Eden,

Her desert like the Garden of the Lord.

Gladness and joy shall abide there,

Thanksgiving and the sound of music.

Awake, awake, O Zion!
Clothe yourself in splendor;
Put on your robes of majestry,
Jerusalem, holy city!

Judah shall be inhabited forever,
And Jerusalem throughout the ages.

The ransomed of the Lord shall return,
And come with shouting to Zion,
Crowned with joy everlasting.
They shall attain joy and gladness,
While sorrow and sighing flee.

Instruction shall come forth from Zion
The word of the Lord from Jerusalem.

All who are inscribed for life in Jerusalem
Shall be called holy.

When you gaze upon Zion, our city of assembly,
Your eyes shall behold Jerusalem
As a secure homestead,
A tent not to be transported,
Whose pegs shall never be pulled up,
And none of whose ropes shall break.

Rejoice with Jerusalem and be glad for her,
All you who love her!
Join in her jubilation,
All you who mourned over her—

Walk around Zion,
circle it;
count its towers,
take note of its ramparts;
go through its citadels,
that you may recount it to a future age.

May the Lord bless you from Zion;

may you share the prosperity of Jerusalem

all the days of your life,

and live to see your children's children.

May all be well with Israel!

(SOURCES: *ISA. 40:1–2; ISA. 40:9; ISA. 62:1; ISA. 51:3; ISA. 52:1; JOEL 4:20; ISA. 35:10; MICAH 4:3; ISA. 4:3; ISA. 33:20; ISA. 66:10; PSS. 48:12–13; PSS. 128:5–6*)

4. Readings from medieval poetry. See pages 193–213.

5. Readings from diaries of the Six Day War. See pages 323–337.

6. Jerusalem of Gold. See page 447, 507.

7. Reading from Abraham J. Heschel. See page 349.

8. Reading from Elie Wiesel. See page 337.

9. Readings from rabbinic statements:

There is no beauty like the beauty of Jerusalem.

Ten measures of beauty descended into the world.
Jerusalem took nine.

Praying in Jerusalem is like praying before the Throne of Glory.

Jerusalem will be redeemed only through justice.

Says the Holy One: In the time-to-come when Zion is rebuilt I shall be a wall unto her.

In the future the Holy One will return all of her happiness to Jerusalem.

In the future Jerusalem will become the metropolis of the entire world.

In the future Jerusalem will become a lamp for the nations and they shall walk by her light.

(SOURCES: *AVOT DE RABBI NATAN 28; KID. 49B; PIRKE DE RABBI ELIEZER 35; SHABBAT 139A; EXOD. RABBA 40; PESIKTA RABBATI 28; EXOD. I RABBA 23:10; YALKUT SHIMONI ISA. 499*)

10. Jerusalem songs. See pages 505–516.

11. Selections from modern poetry. See pages 401–444.

12. If I Forget You (Pss. 137). See page 72.

13. *Shir HaMaalot* (Pss. 126). See page 73.

14. *Hatikva.*

THE FOURTEENTH GATE

Jerusalem in Song

Women reciting special prayers of lamentation at the Wall in 1935 (Central Zionist Archives; with permission)

Y'rushalayim Shel Zahav

N. Shemer
© by the authors
Used by permission of CHAPPEL and Co.

A - vir ha - rim tsa - lul ka - ya - yin v' - ré - ach o - ra -
nim ni - sa b' - ru - ach ha - ar - ba - yim im kol pa - a - mo -
nim uv - tar - dé - mat i - lan va - e - ven sh'vu - ya ba - cha - lo - ma ha -
ir a - sher ba - dad yo - she - vet u - v' - li - ba cho - ma Y' - ru - sha -
la - yim shel za - hav v' - shel n' - cho - shet v' - shel or ha - lo l' - chol shi -
ra - yich a - ni ki nor Y' - ru - sha - nor
ra - yich a - ni___ ki - nor___ ki - nor

L'man'an Tsiyon

Music: S. Rockoff
Lyrics: Isaiah
© by the authors

Uri Tsiyon

Music: M. Wilensky
Lyrics: Isaiah
© by the authors

Hakotel

Music: D. Seltzer
Lyrics: J. Gamzu
© by the authors

Am - da na-a-ra mul ha - ko-tel___ s'fa - ta - yim kér - va v'-san -

tér am - ra li t'ki-ot ha-sho-far cha-za-kot hén a - val ha-sh'ti-ka od yo-

tér am - ra li Tsi-yon har ha - ba-yit___ shat - ka li ha-g'mul v'-ha-

z'chut u - ma she-za-har al mits - cha bén ar-ba-yim ha - ya ar-ga-man shel mal-

chut ha - ko - tel___ e - zov v'-a - tse - vet___ ha -

ko - tel___ o - fe-ret va - dam___ yésh a - na - shim im lév shel

e - ven___ yésh a - va - nim im lév a - dam___

Od Yishama

Music: S. Carlebach
Lyrics: Wedding Liturgy
© by the authors

Od___ yi - sha - ma___ b' - a - ré___ Y' - hu -
da___ u - v' - chu - tsot u - v' - chu - tsot Y' - ru - sha -
la - yim___ kol___ sa - son v' - kol sim -
cha___ kol___ cha - tan v' - kol ka - la___ kol___ sa -
son v' - kol sim - cha___ kol___ cha - tan v' - kol ka la___

Ki Mitsiyon

Music: N. Shachar
Lyrics: Liturgy
© by the authors

Allegretto

Ki mi - tsi - yon té - tsé To - ra ud - var Ha - shem mi -
ru - sha - la - yim ki mi - tsi - yon té - tsé To - ra ud - var Ha -
shem mi - ru - sha - la - yim yim Ba - ruch she - na - tan to -
ra l' - a - mo To - ra l' - a - mo Yis - ra - él ba - ruch she - na -
tan To - ra l' - a - mo Yis - ra - él bik - du - sha - to ki mi - tsi -

Sisu Et Y'rushalayim

Music: A. Nof
Lyrics: Isaiah
© by the authors

Si - su et Y' - ru - sha - la - yim gi - lu va___ gi - lu va kol o - ha - ve - ha

kol___ o - ha - ve - ha si - su et Y' - ru - sha - la - yim gi - lu va___

gi - lu va___ kol o - ha - ve - ha o - ha - ve - ha ve - ha al

cho - mo - ta - yich ir Da - vid hif - ka - d' - ti shom - rim

kol ha - yom___ v' - chol ha - lai - la al cho - mo - ta - yich ir Da - vid hif -

ka - d' - ti shom - rim kol ha - yom v' - chol ha - lai - la kol___ ha - lai - la

Y'rushalayim

Music: Folktune
Lyrics: A. Hameiri
© by the authors

Mé - al pis - gat___ har ha - tso - fim esh - ta - cha
ve lach a - pa - yim___ mé - al pis - gat___ har ha - tso -
fim sha - lom lach Y' - ru - sha - la - yim___ mé - a do -
rot cha - lam - ti a - la - yich liz - kot lir - ot b' - or___ pa -
na - yich Y' - ru - sha - la - yim Y' - ru - sha - la - yim ha - i - ri fa - mé-
na - yich liv - néch___ Y' - ta - yich ev - néch___
chor- vo-

Lach Y'rushalayim

Music: E. Rubenstein
Lyrics: A. Etinger
© by the authors

Lach Y' - ru - sha - la - yim___ bén cho - mot ha - ir___

lach Y' - ru - sha - la - yim___ or cha - dash ya - ir___

b' - li - bé - nu b' - li - bé - nu rak shir e - chad ka - yam___

lach Y' - ru - sha - la - yim___ bén yar - dén va - yam___

bén yar - dén va - yam___ bén yar - dén va - yam___

Tsiyon Tamati

Music: D. Seltzer
Lyrics: J. Gamzu
© by the authors

Tsi-yon ta-ma-ti Tsi-yon chem-da-ti lach naf-shi mé-

ra-chok ho-mi - ya tish-kach y'-mi-ni im esh-

ka-chéch ya-fa-ti ad te-tar bor kiv-ri a-lai____ pi-ha

Tsi-yon ta-ma-ti Tsi-yon chem-da-ti lach naf-shi mé-

ra-chok ho-mi - ya tish-kach y'-mi-ni im esh-

ka-chéch ya-fa-ti ad te-tar bor kiv-ri a-lai pi-ha

THE FIFTEENTH GATE

Jerusalem: Toward the Future

An aerial view looking toward the Rockefeller Museum with the Italian Hospital, now the Ministry of Education (front), 1937 (Central Zionist Archives; with permission)

JERUSALEM

Avraham B. Yehoshua

> *Avraham B. Yehoshua, usually called in Hebrew simply "Aleph Bet Yehoshua," is one of Israel's formost novelists and commentators on the social scene. This article was first published in 1981 and reflects his thinking on issues of the future of Jerusalem which have become even more critical than they were then.*

Every month for some years now it has happened in the same way. It is Saturday evening, the close of the Sabbath, at the first shades of twilight (the twilight in the Middle East is very short). We are driving towards the west, on the main road which runs between the thinly wooded mountains. Jerusalem has already disappeared behind us, all at once, between the mountains. The children are silent in the back seat and try to find a place amidst the bags of sweets, cakes and pots of jam which my mother lavished on us at the end of the family visit. In the boot, wrapped in an Arabic newspaper, is some "find"— a little rug, a veil, a blouse bought in the *suq* (bazaar) of the Old City. A weariness and a sense of relief overtake us at the prospect of returning to our home in Haifa. The burnt-out skeletons of military vehicles from the War of Independence on the sides of the road show that we are approaching the end of the mountain area. Here bloody battles were fought then to keep the way open to a besieged Jerusalem. We are at Sha'ar ha-Gai ("The Gates of the Valley"). All at once, the mountains end, and the plain, lit by the last rays of the sun, come into view and spreads out before us, and, immediately, a dampness and a heaviness penetrate the clear air. Something darkens over. This is where Jerusalem ends and where it begins. The rocks become flat and low, the dust loses its coppery tinge and grows greyish brown; the earth becomes richer and heavier.

Where does a city begin and where does it end? Is this merely an administrative question with an administrative answer? In which abandoned street of Levalois or Ivry does one feel that Paris comes to an end? Once the way in and out of a city was through a large gate in the walls. Nowadays, this gate has become a small faded sign between two tired traffic lights, hidden behind a parked car. So how, in our days, does one demarcate a city's boundaries? What starts up the symbolic radar in one's mind which suddenly arouses on approaching a city which one loves, the feeling of "Here I am!"? What causes it? The way people are dressed?

Jerusalem for its part, has no suburbs in the ordinary sense of the word. Around a relatively small centre with octopus-like tentacles, various neighbourhoods spread out, scattered over the hills of the city. From the centre you can, if you wish, take a short trip of ten minutes in any direction you like, and find yourself in a cultivated field, on the wooded slope of a mountain, among the thickets of a deep valley, or in complete desert—yellow, barren and desolate. Drive on for five more minutes and you will find residential areas—houses, pavements, shops. On its western side, however, the radiations of the city extend to this point where the mountains end, and anyone coming up to Jerusalem from the coastal plain will feel, here, the nearness of the city from the sudden change in the air. And here, at this point when Jerusalem is behind us and our car picks up speed on a road straight as a ruler, my wife always addresses me as follows:

"Don't you want to go back and live there?" She asks me. "No," I answer quickly, "not yet. . . . Perhaps in a few years . . . We'll see . . . Not yet . . . To die there, certainly . . . I mean, our last years . . . Even before . . . But, for the time being, no . . . I feel really relieved every time I leave the place." And yet, every time we come to Jerusalem, during the twenty-four hours we spend there, we swoop down upon the city like tourists who are only passing through it; we are astonished more at its beauty, its charm, its singularity, and between one family meal and another, between two loaded visits to friends, we never stop touring the city. On Friday at the approach of the Sabbath, as soon as we arrive, we unpack our case, leave the children and set out for a drive through the quiet streets of the religious quarters in the north of the city and see how the Sabbath comes in there. Then we head East, toward the Arab part of the city, and drive along the southern wall and come to a halt in a narrow road, in a denuded landscape without a blade of grass; we look at the Arab children scrutinizing us darkly, raise our eyes to the two lofty towers marking the eastern boundary of the city (facing the desert) and register the lightning-flash of the golden roof of the Dome of the Rock, and the sense of the hard stoniness of the city, which is built only of stone by municipal decree. Now we focus our attention on the Jewish cemetery, which pours its white marble over the side of the Mount of Olives, the place where, as tradition has it, the resurrection of the dead will begin. We again look upwards and see the luxurious Intercontinental Hotel built by King Hussein, with its arches of reddish stone, and lower our gaze once more onto the broad valley and the dusty, fenced-in areas of archaeological excavations whose successive layers reveal civilization upon civilization. And suddenly we see above us, on the broken line of the wall, an Israeli soldier in his greenish uniform holding a submachine gun, looking as if he were floating in the sky.

Back in our car, we enter the main street of east Jerusalem, where a noisy weekday's activity is drawing to a close. We go into a toyshop or a chemist's to buy something from the mustachioed and polite Arab salesman who speaks to us in English and gives us the feeling that we are shopping in a foreign city. We go back, walking among the black-gowned Arab peasant women, barefoot and erect, carrying high straw baskets unswervingly on their heads, and carve a way through a group of tall Scandinavians with huge knapsacks. Again we get into our car, and within five minutes we are back in the Jewish part of the city, skirt some streets closed to vehicles during the Sabbath, and reach the centre of town, driving carefully on account of some skull-capped American Jewish tourists making their way, with proprietary ease, along the middle of the road to the main synagogue.

And then, when evening comes, we have still not had enough. Late at night, after a visit to friends, we return, making a detour through the official area of Jerusalem, with the stolid government buildings situated on a hill of rocks and the Knesset building lit up with a murky, yellowish light, go quickly back towards the Old City and arrive at the forecourt of the Western Wall. We do not go up to the great stones, but look from a distance at the black-garbed Jews, members of extreme religious sects, who at night take possession of the Kotel (the Wall), pray, weep and sway backwards and forwards with a powerful rhythmic motion. I try to follow their glance, to make some sort of connection with them, but their look passes me by as if I were air, as if I were nothing. They do not recognize me, they do not recognize this state; they are directly linked to eternity—metaphysical beings who fascinate me, whom I hate and who hold an attraction for me. Somebody touches me on the shoulder and I start back with surprise: without speaking, an old toothless Arab holds out to me a paper skull-cap to cover my head. A Holy Place . . .

Next morning, we again feel a physical need to wander around the city. Between two telephone calls, between literary or political discussions, in the relentless Jerusalem sun, with the children or without them, we do not cease for a moment travelling around Jerusalem, and, driven by some indefinite urge, we are again in the narrow and crowded street of the *suq* and hunt around it amidst the colours and aromas, and then go off to Mount Scopus and look at the desert, near and far, the Mountains of Moab and the other side of the Jordan, glimpse the end of the Dead Sea like a streak of blue lightning, and come back and climb an impossibly steep hill to the Russian Church, that looks like a little Kremlin, and return discovering new corners, strange people, other possibilities. In Jerusalem we are eternal tourists.

And yet I was born in this City; I lived here for twenty-seven years. My father, my grandmother and her forebears for five generations were born there and lived there. It is the everlasting and inexhaustible subject of my father's documentary books describing the life of its inhabitants—Jewish and Arab—at the beginning of our century, and giving an account of each house, each quarter, each political and social event which had taken place there in the past. All my best friends and most intimate acquaintances still live there. In a certain sense it will always be my home, but for my children home is the city of Haifa. Jerusalem, for them, is an alien city.

CONFLAGRATION

Thousands of books have been written about Jerusalem, and thousands more are still to be written. It is one of those cities whose physical being is detached from and oppressed by their spiritual and national significance. Jerusalem is one of the most complex cultural, religious, national and human admixtures, and in a period of violent religious renaissance it is a dangerous political explosive which could give rise to an uncontrollable conflagration. It is an inexhaustible source of nostalgia, for pilgrimages steeped in fantasy and romance. It is fixed in the consciousness of millions who have never set foot there and who never will.

Yet, nevertheless, taken all in all, it is only a rather small city, situated at an altitude of nine hundred metres, with quiet residential quarters, whose population consists of officials, university teachers, some tradesmen, and simple people, without any significant middle class. It has a small, dismal commercial centre which has recently been brightened up. But at its heart, inside the not very lofty Turkish stone walls, lies the hard nucleus of *Yerushalayim shel Ma'ala*—the Heavenly Jerusalem.

Within a radius of half a kilometre, there are famous sites. There is the small damp Church of the Holy Sepulchre, which throughout history has seen numerous Christian denominations quarrel for possession of every inch, of every key. From there, via the Via Dolorosa, you reach the gigantic wall of stones which has survived from the Jewish Temple enclosure: a high, isolated wall linked to nothing, a kind of perpetual reminder of a destruction which will never be forgotten and the obstinate promise of something which will never be built—an intermediate situation which is so well suited to Jewish life. Above it, bestriding an immense stone esplanade, are two mosques, the Dome of the Rock and the Mosque of al-Aqsa, Muslim holy places built over the ruins of the Jewish Temple. And again, a short distance away, there is an Orthodox church, next to it an Armenian church, and, between the two, a yeshiva; nearby is a Protestant mission school, next door a Muslim school, and so on. Religion beside religion, religion beneath religion, religion wedged into religion, religion threatening religion. Religion upon the ruins of another religion. Every place has a history of destruction, of attempted change of identity (the Holy Sepulchre was destroyed by the Muslims, the mosques of the Temple Mount were transformed into churches by the Crusaders). Mingled stones, mixed beliefs. In academic gatherings in Europe, in congress halls, amiable professors, cultured theologians, enlightened men of religion can meet quietly and speak of cooperation, brotherhood and common roots. But here, a stone is moved and it's a note from the Security Council, some pipes are repaired and it's an ecumenical question; a wall is knocked down, and it's a national provocation.

In history, there have been cities in which various changes of civilization have taken place; churches have been transplanted by mosques, and vice versa. These, however, were painful historical processes which have come to an end. Here, on the other hand, the struggle is alive and unceasing, and any accommodation that is made is only temporary. A hurried tourist can go quickly from one famous site to another, happy that he is able to "do" so many famous places in a short time, but a thoughtful visitor will feel the weight of an enormous tension. A hard city. . . .

PROPHECIES

"When your ancestors were playing with monkeys in the forests of London and Oxford, our ancestors were listening to the noble moral preachings of the prophets in the streets of Jerusalem!" In these words, the Zionist leaders answered the cold, thin British High Commissioners who governed the country until the middle of the century, in an attempt to convince them of the Jewish people's deep connection with this city.

Indeed, it was here that Jeremiah, Isaiah and Micah walked the streets—extraordinary, wonderful men who came up from Galilee, Samaria or the desert and prophesied, and it was to this city that John the Baptist and Jesus finally made their way. Men burnt by the sun came up to Jerusalem to speak to it. In alleyways similar to those of today but lower (two or three meters lower according to the archaeologists) they moved around and made their prophesies of anger and admonishment, consolation and love.

But do these help us today, or do they merely make things more difficult? Will the wonderful spiritual power poured out over this city help us to find a path towards life, and some human status quo for this mixture of people flowing through the city so that blood will no longer flow there? For blood has always flowed in Jerusalem, and it is still flowing there today. Every house, every corner can tell a story of war and destruction, recent or long distant. Every archaeological stratum which is uncovered reveals the root of a great fire, signs of shattered stones. One part of the city always attacks the other part, besieges, bombards it. A city of struggle . . .

Jerusalem exemplifies in concentrated and almost absurd fashion one of the most burning problems of our time—the achievement of unity within disparity, cooperation with the preservation of one's identity, international brotherhood, but within carefully defined limits—and as long as Jerusalem cannot solve this problem, we will feel the weight of the anguish. My own short biography alone covers three phases in the life of Jerusalem, three dimensions: I am still expecting the fourth one.

Ben Yehuda Street, May 12, 1937, decorated in honor of the coronation of King George VI and Queen Elizabeth (Central Zionist Archives; with permission)

The protective walls near the Jordanian section in divided Jerusalem prior to the 1967 War (Israel Government Press Office; with permission)

There was the Jerusalem of my early childhood, a city united under British rule: foreign domination for all its inhabitants. A city of hypocrisy in which there were polite but wary contacts between Arabs and Jews, who lived as minorities with equal rights but with no sovereignty. A relationship in which intercourse was mingled with enmity, and below the surface, a constant preparation for the approaching hour of combat.

And then, there was the war of 1948, a cruel struggle between the two parts of the city. An attempt of the Arab, eastern part to dominate the Jewish western part—an attempt which failed—followed by an opposite attempt which also failed. There was an armistice. The front line, frozen, became a fixed frontier raised up in the middle of the city, high, concrete walls and barbed-wire fences were erected, windows were sealed and look-out posts went up. Each part of the city became a complete entity in itself, lived its own existence and decided its own character.

Then, after nineteen years, came the third period. A lightning war, a sudden, unexpected unification, this time under Israeli rule. The frontier was demolished and a stream of Jews flocked in to settle in the "conquered" or "liberated" eastern part. Electric cables were connected up, piping systems laid down, and the frontier which had been like a deep scar in the heart of the city was erased, and when I look for traces of it to show my children the places where it zigzagged across the city, such as the remains of a bullet-ridden wall, a destroyed house in the centre of the city or a concrete anti-tank barrier still standing in the city park, they think that I am showing them archaeological discoveries.

The frontier-line, however, whose physical remains I am searching for, is like a sort of hallucination crying out for a new political identity, failing which Jerusalem, like a deadly mine, will explode any agreement that is made.

It is now summer, the holiday season. People would prefer to read human-interest stories and avoid political problems, but there are some cities in the world such as Belfast, Berlin and, of course, Jerusalem, in which the political clouds which brush lightly against other places are settled like a thick fog, penetrating every nook and cranny. I cannot think of my city, my home, without associating it with political concepts. Politics weigh down upon them, and they also weigh down upon me. Here in these streets, within this difficult admixture, a cool head, imagination and courage will be needed in order to find a lasting solution in the near future. The city must remain united from the human point of view, but diversified from the point of view of sovereignty; it must be a single city for all its inhabitants, yet at the same time two capitals for two peoples; it must function as a single whole, yet divided up between its various religions and national entities. Several flags ought to fly here in mutual toleration. The city is too important to its inhabitants, is too much part of them, to be controlled by sterile UN forces consisting of Swedes and Nigerians under an Austrian officer. The solution must be an organic one, coming from within through a process of patience and goodwill.

Its history is against it: a gloomy, pessimistic history. Will the city have the power to oppose that history, and at the same time to preserve it? Jerusalem is held as a kind of threat against itself.

JERUSALEM—TODAY AND TOMORROW

Teddy Kollek

> *Teddy (Theodore) Kollek was born in Vienna and settled in then Palestine in 1934. His career as a public servant began in 1940 with the Jewish Agency and culminated in his serving as Mayor of Jerusalem from 1965 to 1994. He was therefore the first Mayor of united Jerusalem. Of this article he says, "Although this was written in 1980 and, were I to write it today I might change some details, in general it still reflects my views."*

The place of Jerusalem in the process of seeking peace in the Middle East is unique. Its historical, emotional, and international complexities set it apart from other issues that may be solved on the basis of mutually agreed-upon boundaries. The Jerusalem question cannot be decided by drawing a line. The future of Jerusalem cannot be resolved by division.

This does not mean that Jerusalem is an insoluble problem. It means that Jerusalem's people of differing faiths, cultures, and aspirations must find peaceful ways to live together other than by drawing a line in the sand with a stick. It is no solution to rebuild concrete walls and barbed wire through the middle of the city.

The problem of Jerusalem is difficult because age-old and deeply felt emotions are encrusted over the rationality necessary to find solutions. But I am convinced that these solutions can be found by people of goodwill.

To be perfectly candid, what I dread most is that this city—so beautiful, so meaningful, so holy to millions of people—should ever be divided again; that barbed wire fences, mine fields, and concrete barriers should again sever its streets; that armed men should again patrol a frontier through its heart. I fear the redivision of Jerusalem not only as the mayor of the city, as a Jew, and as an Israeli but also as a human being who is deeply sensitive to its history and who cares profoundly about the well-being of its inhabitants.

Jerusalem is, of course, one of the oldest cities. Signs of human habitation have been found dating back at least four thousand years. In the course of these millennia it has been coveted and conquered by a host of people: Canaanites, Jebusites, Israelites, Babylonians, Assyrians, Persians, Romans, Byzantines, Arabs, Seljuks, Crusaders, Mamluks, Ottomans, British, Jordanians, and Israeli. But throughout those thousands of years, Jerusalem has been divided for less than two decades, from 1948 to 1967. It must never again be divided. Once more to cut this living city in two would be as cruel as it is irrational.

Why have all these various peoples sought this city? It has no natural resources; it has no port; it has no material wealth. It has been coveted primarily for spiritual reasons; it was the site of the Temple of the Jews, the site of the Crucifixion of Jesus; and the place from which, according to tradition, Muhammad rose to heaven.

The fact that all three great monotheistic religions find meaning in Jerusalem cannot be a random accident. I think the reason is clear. First of all, Jerusalem is a beautiful place set in the mystical Judean Hills, conducive to meditation and thought and wonder at the meaning of life. And second, for all their tensions and exclusiveness, the three great religions are historically deeply interrelated. Jesus came to Jerusalem because he was a Jew who made the pilgrimage to the City of David and the Temple. Muhammad, whose roots were in Mecca and Medina, still the main Holy Cities of Islam, is said to have visited Jerusalem during his night ride because his ideas and his vision were interrelated with Judaism and Christianity. We must live with the reality of these connections. For centuries men have fought and died because of them. But I am not alone in feeling intensely that men can also live in brotherhood because of them.

These very connections make any division of Jerusalem a senseless exercise. The remaining Western Wall of the Temple enclosure, the Church of the Holy Sepulchre, and the Dome of the Rock are all in the Old City within yards of each other. The Dome of the Rock is actually atop the Temple Mount, the very site of the Temple of the

Jews. . . . The centrality of Jerusalem in Jewish faith and tradition and the intensity of Jewish feeling about Jerusalem are reflected in the two-thousand-year-old prayer repeated throughout the centuries, "Next year in Jerusalem." This symbolizes not only a religious hope but memories of ancient glories under Jewish rule and an unyielding struggle for their revival. All this is expressed for Jews in the word "Jerusalem." The Jewish people cannot give up Jerusalem, nor can they, nor will they ever again, remove their capital from Jerusalem.

But independent of these intense feelings, internationalization will not work for pragmatic reasons. Past experience, whether in Trieste, Danzig, or Shanghai, has shown its unworkability. In the case of Danzig, indeed, it contributed to bringing on a world war.

A city cannot be run by a committee, particularly a city of such complexity and diversity as Jerusalem. Before building a road or a sewage system, the committee members would have to refer back to their foreign offices or to a UN bureaucracy. And who would pay the bills? . . .

When I look at the future of Jerusalem there are two premises with which virtually everyone in Israel agrees: that Jerusalem shall remain undivided and that it shall remain the capital of Israel. Most Jerusalemites of every persuasion would agree that, under whatever political solution, the city should remain accessible to all and the rights of every religion to its Holy Places should be preserved.

These two conditions have now existed for thirteen years, since the city was so unexpectedly unified after the Jordanians attacked Israel in the June 1967 War. And I think that the history of relations in Jerusalem among Jews, Muslims, and Christians during this decade points to the kind of solution we should eventually evolve for Jerusalem.

Tensions do exist in the city and nobody can deny them. But it was a much less happy city when walls and barbed wire divided it; and it was certainly a more violent city than it is today. We have made progress toward a city of tolerant coexistence in which common interests are emerging, and we have established crucial principles that made continuing progress possible. Four of these principles are

- There shall be free access to all the Holy Places regardless of creed or nationality, and they shall be administered by their adherents.

- Everything possible shall be done to ensure unhindered development of the Arab way of life in the Arab sections of the city and to ensure the Muslims and Christians a practical religious, cultural, and commercial governance over their own daily lives.

- Everything possible shall be done to ensure equal governmental, municipal, and social services in all parts of the city.

- Continuing efforts shall be made to increase cultural, social, and economic contacts among the various elements of Jerusalem's population. And, in fact, civic affairs, law enforcement, infrastructure services, urban planning, marketing and supply, and to a great extent, specialized medical services are centrally provided to all Jerusalemites. . . .

For some time now, I have envisioned a future structure in Jerusalem under which the city would be governed through a network of boroughs. Each borough would have a great deal of autonomy over its own municipal services and its lifestyle. It would decide its own needs and priorities. It would be modeled not on the boroughs of New York but on those of London, which have their own budgets and a great deal of independence.

Of course, the borough idea is not a panacea. The Arabs will want the Temple Mount to be in their borough, and no Jew would agree to that. But the proposal does suggest an approach under which many of the aspects of everyday life can be delegated to local authorities and the people of the various neighborhoods can feel some increasing control over their own lives and the decision-making process. . . .

We do not want to make Jerusalem a parochial city but to restore its ancient glory. We have built a handsome Israel Museum, perhaps the major museum of international art and archaeology between the eastern Mediterranean and Tokyo. The Jerusalem Museum of Islamic Art and Culture, opened a few years ago, is one of outstanding excellence. The Jerusalem Theater has given us a home for the performing arts. . . . We have built an embryonic center for writers, artists, and musicians at Mishkenot Sha'ananim.

෨

Jews care intensely about Jerusalem. The Christians have Rome and Canterbury and even Salt Lake City; Muslims have Mecca and Medina. Jerusalem has great meaning for them also. But the Jews have only Jerusalem, and only the Jews have made it their capital. That is why it has so much deeper a meaning for them than for anybody else.

When the city was reunited, all Jews, not only the religious but also the secular, felt the ancient prophecy fulfilled. Jerusalem was our capital even when few were here—for two thousand years. Since the Muslim conquest only the Crusaders and the British ever made it the administrative capital of the country. On the two occasions when the Arabs could have made Jerusalem their capital, they did not. In the Middle Ages they chose Ramleh, near Lydda on the way to Jerusalem, and in 1948 they chose Amman, which they preferred to Jerusalem.

We do not aspire to find solutions to all the problems of the Middle East in Jerusalem. This is a complicated city with conflicting interests, and it is impossible to satisfy the wishes of everybody.

Sometimes people outside the Middle East ask: What is the relevance of what we are doing in Jerusalem in making the city viable, beautiful, and peaceful to the ultimate question of the sovereignty of the city? We can only look at the situation realistically. If, at worst, Muslim and Jewish differences prove irreconcilable, we will have to live in tension for a long time. All the more reason to care for the city as much as we can to ensure its welfare and well-being in spite of the strains and stresses. If, at best, Jews and Arabs find accommodations that are acceptable to the aspirations of all three faiths, no one would argue that what we are doing for Jerusalem today has been irrelevant. . . .

Within an undivided city, everything is possible, all kinds of adjustments can be made, all kinds of accommodations can be considered, all kinds of autonomy can be enjoyed, all kinds of positive relationships can be developed.

These have been my ideas for many years, and now even more so with the new reality created by the peace agreement signed between Israel and Egypt. The new reality exists, but it should be stressed that we are at variance with ideas expressed by Egyptian spokesmen, which also reach us from time to time from Jordan, namely, that Jerusalem come under dual sovereignty. It is emotionally inconceivable to divide any city, certainly not Jerusalem, which was a united city from its inception four thousand years ago until 1948. Nor can this work from a practical point of view. How could one city have two sets of laws, two different courts, different police forces? Within no time there would be frontier barriers, and the walls and the barbed wire would return to where they had been for nineteen years. Anyone who really cares for Jerusalem cannot even fathom this situation, Moreover, more than one hundred thousand Jews now live in areas beyond the former border. On the other hand, Jerusalem has shown in practice that coexistence is possible. In Jerusalem, there already exist many of the aspects of autonomy that the Israeli government has proposed as part of an over-all peace settlement. Thus I believe that the ideas expressed here answer this new reality.

In 1967, when attacked by the Jordanians, the Jews were willing to sacrifice their lives for Jerusalem. They would again. Israel gave up Sinai; some Israelis would give up the Golan and some the West Bank and Gaza. But I do not think you can find any Israelis who are willing to give up Jerusalem. They cannot and will not. This beautiful golden city is the heart and soul of the Jewish people. You cannot live without a heart and soul. If you want one simple word to symbolize all of Jewish history, that word would be "Jerusalem."

JERUSALEM: THE TORN CITY

Meron Benvenisti

> *Meron Benvenisti, who once served as Deputy Mayor of Jerusalem and was in charge of Arab affairs, is one of Israel's most active experts and commentators on the problems of Jerusalem—and one of the most controversial.*

Jerusalem's variegated beauty, atmosphere and attraction are the products of four pairs of co-existing opposites: the arid and the fertile; the holy and the temporal; the East and the West; the Arabs and the Jews.

The dominant element in Jerusalem's natural landscape is the sudden sharp transition from the Mediterranean zone to the arid wilderness. The watershed traverses the city, dividing it into two ecosystems. the green shrubbery of the Mediterranean predominates in the west, having withstood thousands of years of neglect and periodic destruction; while, east of the watershed, the desert predominates, gray-white, together with the bare chalk landscape of the Judean wilderness and its deep canyons, both descending steeply to the Dead Sea. It is this natural variety, its special hues which change with every hour of the day, and the multi-colored assortment of its building stones.

Sanctified by three religions, the city is richly endowed with the holy sites and relics of all the peoples who have fought over Jerusalem because of its sacred character. Sanctity and reverence for God are still a dominant element in the day-to-day life of Jerusalem—more so than in any other city. At the same time, its streets jammed with vehicles, high-rise buildings dotting the landscape, and other urban amenities abounding, Jerusalem is a modern city where hundred of thousands of people live fully secular lives—as in any other city.

But, in Jerusalem, even the secular life is bi-polar. At one extreme, tens of thousands of people maintain an occidental life-style, inhabiting multi-storied buildings or garden suburbs, remote from their neighbors, dressing in the latest fashions, shopping at supermarkets and whiling away their time in cafés, with complaints about the leaders whom they repeatedly re-elect in democratic elections. At the other end, tens of thousands, Jews and Arabs, maintain the traditional oriental way of life, boundlessly loyal to their extended family, obedient to the *paterfamilias* who rules them like a biblical patriarch; people who believe that haste is Satan's invention, who live in single-story houses and feel a mystical bond to the soil.

Jerusalem is also the city of two peoples, and it is loved by each after his own fashion. It is the only city in Israel in which commercial activities do not halt for a single day and whose inhabitants are obliged to converse in two languages; a city in which neither of its two peoples can withdraw into itself; a city which is cosmopolitan and rich in human variety. For the past two generations, the conflict between the two cousin-peoples has been a bloody one. Jerusalem has remained the only city where they live in proximity. And here, more than anywhere else, one can sense the awful tragedy of the conflict between Israeli and Arab.

In some miraculous manner, all these opposites fuse into a single unity. Anyone depriving Jerusalem of these contrasts, anyone upsetting the equilibrium by trying to make any one factor predominant over another, or by trying to prevent the dynamic confrontation of the opposites, would make Jerusalem cease to be herself.

For nineteen years, a hermetically sealed wall separated these opposites, and Jerusalem did indeed cease to be herself. The barbed-wire fences left the East with the desert, the sanctity, the traditional oriental way of life, and all the Arabs; they left the West with its greenery, its secular aspect, its modern occidental life-style, and all the Jews.

Removing the barriers gave the city back its unity of opposites. For the first time in the chronicles of modern Jerusalem, responsibility for maintaining its character was in

A break in the wall leading to the Jewish Quarter of the Old City, 1967 (Central Zionist Archives; with permission)

Israeli hands. This responsibility has never been a light one, but the conditions created after the Six Day War have made it almost unbearable. Political and economic conditions have sharpened the conflicts, engendering pressures which threaten to upset the delicate balance between them. The city's color and character have progressively changed. The decisive question is: will the city find a renewed equilibrium, or will it be overcome by forces which will totally alter its character?

ᗩ

During my search for political solutions, I came to the realization that anyone who wants to play this dangerous game must accept three pre-conditions: first, he must rid himself of all myths; second, he must learn the lessons of the past; and third, he must not set himself up as a judge between the opposing sides.

There is no place which arouses such deep, fanatical feelings as does Jerusalem. the city's atmosphere nurtures an exclusive possessiveness. There is no place where man feels his historical continuity more than in Jerusalem. The feeling that everything has been here since the beginning of time, gives those who live in the eternal city a feeling of modesty and humility. There is no other place where one feels the tragedy of two nations fighting for their homeland more than in Jerusalem. This is the only place in the world today where Jews and Arabs live side by side, and where the struggle is a real, everyday occurrence and not an abstraction. He who decides to judge between the two sides must remember that only in fairy tales is one side all good and the other all bad.

I belong to a nation fighting for its soul, and its soul is Jerusalem. I identify with my nation's longing for Jerusalem. I, too, experienced the transcendental experience of our return to the holiest of our places. At the same time, I am a son of this city and know the meaning of a son's love for it. I cannot, and will not, forget the love, it is as strong as my own, of the Arab residents of Jerusalem for this city.

In the light of this tragic conflict, which has wracked Jerusalem during the past generation, an observer longs for a catharsis, for an end to the damaging myths spread by both sides, and for the transformation of the love that both sides have for this city into a uniting, rather than a dividing, force. Right now, this is only wishful thinking, but perhaps past experiences will help to bring about its realization.

EPILOGUE

David's Tomb on Mount Zion, date unknown (Central Zionist Archives; with permission)

JERUSALEM, HOLY CITY

R. J. Zvi Werblowsky

> *Prof. Werblowsky is Professor of Comparative Religion at the Hebrew University,*
> *Jerusalem, and author of numerous scholarly articles and books.*

One way in which people have experienced and, as it were, crystallized their sense of holiness, was in relation to space. There are holy lands—that is lands which are considered holy by virtue of the bond that binds human groups to the earth on which they live. It is a bond of gratitude and love that often, and at times imperceptibly, turns into veneration. In one of the temples in Benares the object of worship is a map of Mother India. *Bande mataram!* There are holy places as distinct from holy lands, places where the divine became manifest, in one way or another, to the eyes of believing men and women, and which were cherished or revered as concrete, tangible, spatially defined testimonies to the reality of the divine as it had become visible in experiences or traditions of theophanies, revelations, miracles, or the lives of saintly men. There are holy cities as distinct from holy places: cities that acquired their holiness as a result of historical circumstances or events, or cities that are holy because either in theory or in actual fact they were constructed so as to reflect cosmic reality—a kind of micro-cosmic spatial reflection of the cosmos and its underlying divine ground as conceived and spelled out in mythological tradition. There are cities which are holy because they harbor and possess a holy object, or shrine or relic. We can think of Mecca, Benares, Lhasa, Angkor, Roma (Roma Quadrata!) and many others. As a modern example we may instance Tenri (near Nara) in Japan, which is a holy city not only because it is built around the "navel of the earth," the sacred *Skanrodai*, but also because it is constructed according to a divine plan. Hence also the importance which students of religion attach to that branch of their science which is called *geographia sacra*.

The case of Jerusalem is in many ways unique, since this city is a focus of devotion, piety and religious symbolism for three related religions, two of which are universal religions counting hundreds of millions of followers. Nevertheless, it is the third which, for our purpose, is the first—and not merely for chronological reasons. Judaism is a non-universalistic religion which specifically conceives of itself as the religion of a particular (and incidentally rather small) people. But it is this religion which became the "mother" of the attachment of Christianity and Islam to this Holy City. It is this triple attachment which is the cause of the complicated, and often tragic, history of the city. Mecca is of no interest to Hindus, and Buddhists care little for Benares. Jerusalem is charged with profound emotions of piety, devotion, ardent longing, theological symbolism and—alas—fanaticism and desire of domination for three hostile brothers.

The pre-history of the city, fascinating as it is for archaeologists, is not our concern here. A careful reading of the Hebrew Bible record shows that the City played no role during the early period of the settlement of the Israelite tribes in Canaan. The main cultic centers were Beth El, Gilgal, Shiloh and others. The episode of the meeting of Abraham with Melchisedek, the priest-king of Shalem (Gen. 14) probably reflects later, post-Davidic ideology, bent on cementing the association of the Holy City with the ancestor of the nation. Jerusalem entered Jewish history and historico-religious consciousness with its conquest by David, who realised that in order to unite the tribes into a nation he had to establish his capital in "neutral" territory, not associated with any tribe (thus avoiding the suspicion of aspirations of hegemony by the tribe of Judah), but solely with his personal prestige as king and the Lord's Elect. National/political and cultic center, royal residence, and temple of God—in antiquity the two often went together. (Cf. e.g., Amos 7:13 à propos Beth El: "Royal sanctuary.") Jerusalem–Sion–City of David: City of God. Surprising and, indeed, unique is the rapidity with which the ideas of God's Covenant with his Chosen People, with the Promised Land, with the Chosen City and the Temple, and with the Chosen House of David merged into one integrated symbol (see the Book of Isaiah, the Psalms, or Jeremiah 31:34–39; 33:14–26). The name of the city soon acquired a historical, indeed existential significance superimposed on its original geographical meaning. When the prophets bewail the agony, suffering and exile visited upon the people, they never speak of the people of Israel. They say: Jerusalem sheddeth tears, the daughter of Zion crieth. And when they speak of the final redemption and the ingathering of the exiles, they say: rejoice O Jerusalem, exult O daughter of Zion. In the tradition the destroyed and ruined city, now in the hands of "enemies," also served as a symbol of hope and trust in God's eternal promise for a suffering and persecuted and massacred people. It is not surprising that the modern movement of national renaissance did not call itself "Jewish risorgimento" but "Zionism."

Jesus was the teacher and master of a group of Jewish disciples. His career, as the Gospels testify, took place in the Jerusalem-centric framework of contemporary Judaism. Even his attacks on the Temple and its unworthy priests and worshippers, even his prophecies of destruction, were not much different from those of other and earlier prophets (see especially Jeremiah). The consummation of his terrestrial ministry, his passion, burial, resurrection and ascension took place in specific sites in Jerusalem (and it does not matter, for our purposes, whether the places indicated by pious tradition or eager tourist guides are historically "authentic" or not). From the fourth century on, largely through the activities of the Emperor Constantine's mother, Helena, Jerusalem rapidly became a center of pilgrimage not only in the Byzantine empire but for Christendom as a whole. Christ (the word is the Greek translation of the Hebrew term for the Lord's "Anointed") being, by definition, the Messiah Son of David (see Mat. 1), the link between Christianity and the "City of David" was obvious. Center of devotion, piety, pilgrimages—the very name of Jerusalem was capable of provoking (in combination with other factors) powerful movements, and even leading western Christianity to one of its saddest and most unchrisitian adventures: the Crusades. But the role of

Jerusalem in Christian spirituality is far more complicated than that. The universalist element in the message of Jesus necessarily led to a universalisation of the traditional Israelite notions of a "chosen people" and a "chosen land." The holy people was henceforth the Church, that mystical body of which Christ was the head, and the holy land was the whole world to the extent that the life of Christian holiness was lived there. But this omnipresent terrestrial Jerusalem was a mere reflection of the true celestial Jerusalem, "the mother of us all." The latter concept also stems from Judaism, but there it plays only a secondary role whereas in Christianity it became primary. In the world of the medieval poet:

Urbs Sion unica, mansio mystica, condita caelo.

And every terrestial church, reflecting the heavenly Jerusalem, is dedicated (in the Latin rite) with the beautiful hymn:

Urbs Jerusalem beata
Dicta pacis visio
Quae construitur in caelis
Vivis ex lapidibus.

The case of Islam is, from the historian's point of view, the most remarkable. How did Jerusalem gain such importance in a religion that originated, and developed, far away from the city, in the part of the Arabian peninsula known as the Hedjaz? And yet, during the first years of Islam the prescribed direction of prayer (*gibla*) was toward Jerusalem. Even after the Prophet changed the *gibla* in the direction of Mecca, one of the names of the City remained *'ula al-giblatheyn* ("the first of the two giblas"). At the time the Arab peninsula was heavily populated by Jewish and Christian tribes, and the traders reaching Mecca with their caravans must also have contained many Jews and Christians. It is not, therefore, surprising that many biblical influences were absorbed by the Prophet during the crucial period when his message as it were "incubated" and matured. Jerusalem was integrated into the Muslim heritage of belief by being linked to the ministry of the Prophet himself: The references in the Koran (Sura 81:9, 53:1ff. and 17:1) to the Prophet's miraculous nocturnal journey and to his ascension—the *'isra* and the *mi'radj*—were combined into one event and linked to Jerusalem. Another Judeo-Christian heritage was the role ascribed to Jerusalem in Muslim eschatology. In due course Jerusalem became the third holiest city after Mecca and Medinah. But it always remained a purely religious center, and never was a capital—political, administrative or merely provincial. Islam, however, has a political dimension also as a religion (cf. the division of the world into *dar al-Islam* and *dar-al-harb*). It is therefore inconceivable to a Muslim mind that a territory or a city, let alone a holy city, which had for over a thousand years been under Muslim domination, should now be under the rule of infidels. The rise of a new and specifically Palestinian nationalism renders the problem even more acute.

All these elements together make up the unique character of the city which a popular (but incorrect) etymology has traditionally interpreted as "the city of peace" but which, in reality, has more often than not been a city of conflict and violent clashes. Few cities in the world, not to speak of "holy" cities, have seen so many wars, conquests, and blood flowing in its streets than this "city of peace." Perhaps the popular etymology reflects not so much a reality as a hope or even challenge to the three religions concerned: will they ever succeed in transforming this place of hated, violence, competition and political intrigue (often masked as "religious") into a center radiating peace? The true mystery of the city may well be in its future rather than its past, a future prepared for it by those who (in the words of the psalmist) "love Jerusalem" and who seek in and through it that Peace of God that passeth all understanding.

The animal market at the Sultan's Pool in 1900 (Central Zionist Archives; with permission)

JERUSALEM THE IRREPLACEABLE

André Neher

> *The late Professor André Neher, born in Alsace, became one of the leading figures of French Jewry after the Second World War. He held the chair of Jewish Studies at Strasbourg and later divided his time between Jerusalem and France.*

The intertwining of Jerusalem and of the irreplaceable has never been felt by human consciousness with as much obstinate strength and poignant evidence as by the very consciousness that discovered it on the banks of the rivers of Babylon and which, ever since, without respite, pause or parenthesis, has sensed it, sung it, cried out for it throughout the course of history—Jewish consciousness,

Indeed, Christian consciousness very rapidly found another Jerusalem in Rome and in the heavens; Moslem consciousness too, from the time it came into being, built one in Mecca and Medina; finally, agnostic consciousness erected still others in Paris, New York and Peking.

Only the Jews, long before there were any Christians, Moslems or believers in a third testament, *would have no other* and have, ever since, with fierce steadfastness, persisted in their refusal to replace Jerusalem, though it be only ruins and dust, by another Jerusalem, though it be heavenly or like Paradise.

We will have no other, cried the Jews, during the nights of bitter weeping and in the first light of dawn; we will have no other, said the Jews, gritting their teeth or with the ghost of a bitter smile, every time that, on the road of their long Exile, they were offered in exchange a final and peaceful stopping place within a Jerusalem other than that which, lying there, on its rock, seemed quite dead and could only present them with the stones of an aging Wall, the access to which, moreover, would soon be denied them.

I will have no other because, indeed, the Exile has never been to me a fortuitous march without a compass. Never, in the worst of my flights, have I been a wanderer without landmarks. Every step had a meaning; never have I been the Wandering Jew. I have always been the Pilgrim of Jerusalem. Every wandering was oriented towards it. Never have I felt settled anywhere: my prayers, my offerings, my yearnings, and often my steps made me the everlasting Lover of Zion. Every martyrdom was a sacrifice, because the endless dreams of my people brought the humblest, but also the most sorrowful of my ashes to the Mount of Olives.

Thus, Exile itself was a road, the road returning to Jerusalem. And now that this road has brought me back to Jerusalem; now that its name is Israel and that there it exists, built up, lined with tears, laughter, trees and human-beings as manifold as the millions of irreplaceables—who, while they lived and when they died, had no other name upon their lips but Jerusalem; now that Jerusalem is not anymore the *symbol* of the irreplaceable but stands for its *reality*; now, do you believe that I, a Jew, would love another, have another, accept another one?

View of the Temple Mount and the horizon of new Jerusalem from Mount Zion, July 1981 (Israel Government Press Office; with permission)

Pʀᴀʏ ꜰᴏʀ ᴛʜᴇ Wᴇʟʟ-Bᴇɪɴɢ ᴏꜰ Jᴇʀᴜꜱᴀʟᴇᴍ

S. Y. Agnon

> *The Nobel Prize–winning author, S. Y. Agnon, expressed the meaning of Jerusalem to him in this rather sarcastic reply to a letter asking him to answer certain questions about his attitude toward the city.*

It would have been better, Madam, had you not sent me your queries, and now that you have, it would have been better had I not been pressured to answer them. I am a man preoccupied with my own queries, to which I have as yet found no answer. However—for the honor of Jerusalem I will do what I can to attempt to answer your queries. That which God puts in my mouth, I shall speak.

You ask: what does Jerusalem symbolize for me? You ask me? Ask rather the sages of all generations throughout the ages from the time of the first prophets until our own day what Jerusalem is and what they have said. What does a man like myself have to add and of what importance is it if I reinforce their words? For it is from their words that I live and I guide my thoughts by theirs. If only I were worthy to behold Jerusalem in my peak hours as they beheld her in their most trivial ones. Jerusalem never departed from their hearts during their entire life times. They needed no "symbols." If you have read my book *A Guest for the Night* you know my opinion of symbols.

That is my answer to your first query: what does Jerusalem symbolize for me.

Now that we have disposed of one query, perhaps we can dispose of the second one. You ask: why did I choose Jerusalem as my dwelling place?

I must candidly admit that such a query never occurred to me in all my days. I live in Jerusalem because I was privileged to be among those that God chose to permit to live in His city which is called by His name. Perhaps it would be better to say: God was merciful to me when He perceived that I had made up my mind to go up to Jerusalem, and from the time that I was so privileged to go up, I paid no attention to all the troubles that have come upon me in Jerusalem, be it the earthquake of 5687 or the riots of 5689 or the noise of vehicles which gives me no peace day or night—not even on the Sabbath or Festivals. It seems as if He agreed to permit me to be gathered into His city.

Now, Madam, I shall attempt to answer your third query which is the most difficult of all. You ask: in what lies the superiority of Jerusalem? Has it not already been stated that "The Lord loves the gates of Zion more than all the dwellings of Jacob. Glorious things are spoken of you, O city of God" (Pss. 87:2–3)? If God—who possesses the entire world—who loves all of the Land of Israel—loves the gates of Zion more than all the dwellings of Jacob—shall not a mortal man—dust and ashes who has nothing but what he can attain all his days and after length of days and years, would that he would be worthy of possessing even one grain of the dust of Jerusalem—shall not such a one love Jerusalem more than all the dwellings of Jacob? To say nothing of all the other places in the world.

And now, Madam, I shall attempt to answer your fourth query: how do I perceive Jerusalem?

All moments and days are not equal. We have the Sabbath and Festivals, and then there is Tisha B'Av. Nor am I the same all moments and days or hours, but would that I could truly perceive Jerusalem for one day, one hour or even one brief moment!

I see that your fourth query really contains another question as well which is itself two-fold: what places in Jerusalem are particularly precious to me and why?

I have nothing to say regarding the first part since all of Jerusalem is precious to me. From the moment that that part of the city which is within the walls was taken from me for the time being, I perceived all of Jerusalem which remains in our hands until the Redeemer shall come as one precious entity. If I may use the language which is unique to Jerusalem, I would say that all of Jerusalem is holy unto me.

As for the second part of the query, i.e. "why?" I know not what to reply. All the answers in the world would not be sufficient.

I assume, Madam, that you are not satisfied with my answers. But I must tell you that I too am not satisfied with my answers, although not for the same reason. You expected to receive answers from me that would be acceptable to the general populace, that is matters which any normal person who speaks the language of normal people would reply, while my answers were quite far from that.

This, Madam, this is the punishment of one who makes inquiry of a man such as myself, who sees nothing problematic in any of these queries. This is the punishment of the man who must answer queries such as these which are not queries to him nor in themselves.

I have finished my words. From now on, I want to return to my own queries to which I seek answers. But I tell you, I am willing to give up all the answers for one day of repentance, so that I shall be worthy to dwell in Jerusalem.

⤷ Afterword

In 1996, Jerusalem will reverberate with the sounds of celebration marking three thousand years since David, the King, made this hilltop town the capital of his Jewish kingdom.

Since its founding, Jerusalem has been the heart of the Jewish people, the focus of its faith and central thread of its historical memory. There is an eternal tie between Jerusalem and the Jewish people, a tie which has no parallel in the history of nations. The Temple was erected in Jerusalem and pilgrimages were made to it; chapters of the Bible were written within its wall and there the prophets prophesied. The eternal symbol of the hopes, dreams and aspirations of the Jewish people, Jerusalem is the source of inspiration to Jewish artists and visionaries the world over.

Today, Jerusalem is also a vibrant, modern and progressive capital with well-preserved historical sites and a rich cultural life. It is a cosmopolitan city, the home of a varied mosaic of different races, peoples, religions and sects, which have lives together for generations. And Jerusalem is an international destination, welcoming millions of visitors from a hundred nations.

Jerusalem is unique in history and unique in the world and the tri-millennium celebrations will be a unique year for Jerusalem. Hundreds of thousands of visitors will relive the splendor of the historic ancient city as it has blended into the landscape of a thriving capital. They will attend a myriad of cultural events, from a monumental sight and sound spectacular, to opera, poetry, concerts, gospel choirs, pageants, banquets, theater, dance, exhibitions and much more. The tri-millennium activities reflect Jerusalem's enormous artistic and spiritual heritage and above all Jerusalem's unique power to inspire artistic, spiritual and intellectual expression.

The essence of Jerusalem's uniqueness flows through the pages of this special anthology which has gathered so many wonderful examples of how this city has inspired Jewish poets, writers, philosophers and scholars—through the ages and throughout the globe. And with this volume, once again, Jerusalem has been the source of creative endeavor and its pages promise that Jerusalem will continue to be an inspiration for the Jewish people for many millennium to come.

Reading through these pages, I am reminded once again what an immense and humbling responsibility it is to hold the office of Mayor of Jerusalem. Jerusalem is so much more than a city—it is the symbol of a nation, the focus of attention both in Israel and the world; a universal spiritual center with room for all religions, peoples and traditions.

Ehud Olmert
Mayor of Jerusalem

ꙮ A Selected Jerusalem Bibliography

The following list of books in English includes both books excerpted in this volume and others that may prove of interest to the reader.

ꙮ

Adler, Elkan Nathan. *Jewish Travelers*. London, 1930.

Adler, Marcus Nathan. *The Itinerary of Benjamin of Tudela*. London, 1907.

Agnon, S.Y., *In The Heart Of The Seas*, New York, 1947

al-Harizi, Judah. *The Book of Tahkemoni*. Translated by David Simha Segal. Oxford, forthcoming.

Alon, Amos. *City of Mirrors*. New York, 1989.

Amichai, Yehuda. *Great Tranquility*. New York, 1983.

———. *The World is a Room*. Trans. by Elinor Grumet. Philadelphia, 1984.

———. *Poems of Jerusalem*. Jerusalem, 1980.

———. *Songs of Jerusalem and Myself*. Translated by H. Schimmel, New York, 1973.

Ancient Jerusalem Revealed. Ed. by Hillel Geva. Jerusalem, 1994.

An Anthology of Modern Hebrew Poetry. Selected by S. Y. Penueli and A. Ukhmani. Jerusalem, 1966.

An Anthology of Modern Hebrew Poetry. Ed. and trans. by Abraham Birman. New York, 1968.

The Apocrypha and Pseudepigrapha of the Old Testament in English. Vol. 1. Ed. by R. H. Charles. Oxford, 1913.

Aristeas to Philocrates. Ed. and trans. by Moses Hadas. New York, 1951.

Avigad, Nahman. *Discovering Jerusalem*. Jerusalem, 1980.

Bellow, Saul. *To Jerusalem and Back*. New York, 1976.

Ben-Arieh, Yehoshua. *Jerusalem in the 19th Century: The Old City*. Jerusalem, 1984.

———. *Jerusalem in the 19th Century: The Emergence of the New City*. Jerusalem, 1986.

Ben-Dov, Meir. *In the Shadow of the Temple*. Jerusalem, 1982.

———. *Jerusalem, Man and Stone*. Tel Aviv, 1990.

Bentwich, Norman, and Bentwich, Helen. *Mandate Memories, 1918–1948*. New York, 1965.

Benvenisti, Meron. *The Torn City*. Jerusalem, 1976.

The Book of Tobit. Trans. by Frank Zimmerman. New York, 1958.

Brandwein, Chaim. *In the Courtyards of Jerusalem*. Trans. by Hillel Halkin. Philadelphia, 1967.

Burstein, Chaya M. *A Kid's Catalogue of Israel*. Philadelphia, 1988.

Carmi, T., and Pagis, Dan. *Selected Poems*. Middlesex, 1976.

Collins, Larry, and Lapierre, Dominique. *O Jerusalem!* London, 1972.

Deem, Ariella. *Jerusalem Plays Hide and Seek*. Trans. by Nelly Segal. Philadelphia, 1987.

The Diaries of Sir Moses and Lady Montefiore. Ed. by Dr. Louis Loewe. Chicago, 1890.

The Diaries of Theodore Herzl. Ed. by Marvin Lowenthal. New York, 1956.

The First Book of Maccabees. Ed. and trans. by Sidney Tedesche. New York, 1950.

Falk, Marcia. *This Year In Jerusalem*. Brockport, NY, 1986.

Folktales of Israel. Ed. by Dov Noy with the assistance of Dan Ben Amos. Chicago, 1963.

Frankel, Ellen. *The Classic Tales: 4,000 Years of Jewish Lore*. Northvale, NJ, 1989.

Gilbert, Martin. *Jerusalem: Rebirth of a City*. Jerusalem, 1985.

Goldberg, Leah. *Selected Poems*. Transl. by Robert Friend. San Francisco, 1976.

Gruber, Ruth. *Israel on the Seventh Day*. New York, 1968.

Har-El, Menashe. *This Is Jerusalem*. Jerusalem, 1977.

Hareven, Shulamith. *City Of Many Days*. Trans. by Hillel Halkin and the author. San Francisco, 1993.

Hazzaz, Haim. *More Sa'id*. New York, 1956.

Hazelton, Leslie. *Jerusalem, Jerusalem*. New York, 1986.

Heilman, Samuel. *A Walker in Jerusalem*. New York, 1986.

Heschel, Abraham Joshua. *Israel: An Echo of Eternity*. New York, 1967.

Holtz, Avraham, ed. *The Holy City: Jews on Jerusalem*. New York, 1971.

The Image of Jerusalem. ADAM International Review. 1968. Ed. by Miron Grindea. Rochester, NY, 1968.

Israel Argosy 8. Ed. by Isaac Halevy-Levin. New York, 1962.

Israeli Poetry. Ed. by Warren Bargad and Stanley F. Chyet. Bloomington, IN, 1986.

The Jerusalem Cathedra 2. Ed. by Lee I. Levine. Jerusalem, 1982.

Jerusalem—City Holy and Eternal. Ed. by B. Dworkin. New York, 1954.

Jerusalem Eternal. Ed. by Azriel Eisenberg. New York, 1971.

Jerusalem: 5,000 Years of History. Les Dossiers D'Archeologie. Paris, 1992.

Jerusalem: Its Redemption and Future. New York, 1918.

Jerusalem: Most Fair of Cities. Ed. by Henia Stein and Franklin Jagodnik. Jerusalem, 1977.

Jerusalem: Problems and Prospects. Ed. by Joel Kramer. New York, 1980.

Jerusalem Revealed: Archaeology in the Holy City, 1968–1974. Jerusalem, 1975.

Jerusalem through the Ages. Jerusalem, 1967.

Joseph, Dov. *The Faithful City*. New York, 1960.

Koestler, Arthur. *Promise and Fulfilment*. London, 1949.

Kolleck, Teddy. *For Jerusalem—A Life*. Jerusalem, 1978.

Kolleck, Teddy, and Pearlman, Moshe. *Jerusalem: A History of Forty Centuries*. New York, 1968.

Kroyanker, David. *Jerusalem Architecture*. Jerusalem, 1994.

Kurzman, Dan. *Genesis 1948*. London, 1970.

Else Lasker-Schüler. *Hebrew Ballads and Other Poems*. Philadelphia, 1980.

Letters of Jews through the Ages. Ed. by F. Kobler Frazn. London, 1952.

Lever, Walter. *Jerusalem Is Called Liberty*. Jerusalem, 1951.

Levin, Harry. *Jerusalem Embattled*. London, 1958.

The Life and Works of Flavius Josephus. Trans. by William Whiston. Philadelphia, no year.

Meir, Golda. *My Life*. London, 1975.

Millgram, Abraham E. *Jerusalem Curiosities*. Philadelphia, 1990.

Mintz, Ruth Finer. *Jerusalem Poems, Love Songs*. Tel Aviv, 1976.

Modern Hebrew Poetry. Ed. and trans. by Ruth Finer Mintz. Berkeley and Los Angeles, 1966.

A Narrative of a 40 Day's Sojourn in the Holy Land. Montefiore, Sir Moses. London, 1875.

Navon, Yitzhak. *The Six Days and the Seven Gates*. Jerusalem, 1978.

Narkiss, Uzi. *The Liberation of Jerusalem*. London, 1983.

New Writing in Israel. Ed. by Ezra Spicehandler. Tel Aviv, 1976.

The Old Testament Pseudepigrapha. Ed. by James H. Charlesworth. New York, 1983, 1985.

Phillips, John. *A Will to Survive*. New York, 1976.

Philo. Vol. V, VII and X. Trans. by F. H. Colson. Cambridge, MA, 1962.

Prawer, Joshua. *The Latin Kingdom of Jerusalem: European Colonialism in the Middle Ages*. London, 1972.

Preil, Gabriel. *Sunset Possibilities and Other Poems*. Trans. by Robert Friend. Philadelphia, 1985.

Rabinovich, Abraham. *The Battle for Jerusalem*. Philadelphia, 1972.

———. *Jerusalem on Earth*. New York, 1988.

Raphael, Chaim. *The Walls of Jerusalem: An Excursion into Jewish History*. New York, 1967.

Retrievements: A Jerusalem Anthology. Ed. by Dennis Silk. Jerusalem, 1977.

Rose, Pauline. *The Seige of Jerusalem*. London, no year.

———. *Window on Mount Zion*. London, 1973.

Saadia Gaon, The Book of Beliefs and Opinions. Trans. by Samuel Rosenblatt. New Haven, CT, 1948.

Samuel, Edwin. *A Lifetime in Jerusalem*. Jerusalem, 1970.

Selected Religious Poems. Trans. by Israel Zangwill.

The Seventh Day. English version by Henry Near. London, 1970.

Shalom, Shin. *On Ben Peleh*. Trans. by Victor E. Reichert and Moses Zalesky. Jerusalem, 1963.

The Story of Jerusalem. Ed. by Dr. Beno Rothenberg. Trans. by M. Kohansky and Ben-Ami Sharfstein. Tel Aviv, 1967.

Tracks to the Promised Land. Ed. by Nahman Ran. Tel Aviv, 1987.

Steckoll, Solomon H. *The Gates of Jerusalem*. Tel Aviv, 1968.

———. *The Temple Mount*. London, 1972.

Uris, Leon and Uris, Jill. *Jerusalem—Song of Songs*. New York, 1981.

Vilnay, Zev. *Legends of Jerusalem*. Philadelphia, 1973.

Weilerstein, Sadie Rose. *The Best of K'tonton*. Philadelphia, 1980.

Weizmann, Chaim. *Trial and Error*. Philadelphia, 1949.

The Western Wall. Ed. by Meir Ben-Dov. Ministry of Defence. Tel Aviv, 1983.

The Western Wall. Ed. by Menahem M. Kasher. New York, 1972.

Wiesel, Elie. *A Beggar in Jerusalem*. Trans. by Lily Edelman and the author. New York, 1970.

Wilhelm, Kurt. *Roads to Zion*. Trans. by I. M. Lask. New York, 1948.

Wilson, Sir Charles W. *Jerusalem—The Holy City*. Jerusalem, no year.

The Wisdom of the Zohar. Fischel Lachover and Isaiah Tishby. Trans. by David Goldstein. Oxford, 1989.

Yaari, Avraham. *The Goodly Heritage*. Jerusalem, 1958.

Zion in Jewish Literature. Ed. by Abraham Halkin. New York, 1961.

The Zohar. Trans. by Harry Sperling and Maurice Simon. London, 1933.

𝒟 Index

Places in Jerusalem appear in boldface, a page number followed by f. indicates an illustration.

﹞ About Reuven Hammer

Reuven Hammer received his ordination and doctorate in theology from the Jewish Theological Seminary. He holds a Ph.D. in Communicative Disorders from Northwestern University. After serving as a chaplain in the U.S. Air Force and a congregational rabbi for 15 years, he and his wife made *aliya* to Israel in 1973 and have lived in Jerusalem ever since. He has taught Jewish studies and special education at various institutions, including the Hebrew University, David Yellin College, and Oranim.

Rabbi Hammer served as dean of the Jewish Theological Seminary of America's Jerusalem Campus and was founding director of the Seminary of Judaic Studies. He has taught and lectured throughout the world and is the author of five books. He is currently at work on a JPS High Holy Day companion, which explains both the holidays and the accompanying Mahzor.

CPSIA information can be obtained
at www.ICGtesting.com
Printed in the USA
LVOW04s2233081017
551670LV00026BA/1677/P